THE WEST

A NEW HISTORY

ANTHONY GRAFTON
DAVID A. BELL

THE WEST

A NEW HISTORY

VOLUME ONE

W. W. Norton & Company

NEW YORK • LONDON

W. W. NORTON & COMPANY has been independent since its founding in 1923, when William Warder Norton and Mary D. Herter Norton first published lectures delivered at the People's Institute, the adult education division of New York City's Cooper Union. The firm soon expanded its program beyond the Institute, publishing books by celebrated academics from America and abroad. By midcentury, the two major pillars of Norton's publishing program—trade books and college texts—were firmly established. In the 1950s, the Norton family transferred control of the company to its employees, and today—with a staff of four hundred and a comparable number of trade, college, and professional titles published each year—W. W. Norton & Company stands as the largest and oldest publishing house owned wholly by its employees.

EDITOR Steve Forman
ASSOCIATE EDITORS Scott Sugarman and Justin Cahill
PROJECT EDITOR Melissa Atkin
EDITORIAL ASSISTANTS Kelly Rafey and Travis Carr
DEVELOPMENTAL EDITORS Alice Vigliani and Harry Haskell
CARTOGRAPHIC EDITOR Charlotte Miller
COPYEDITORS JoAnn Simony and Alice Vigliani
MANAGING EDITOR, COLLEGE Marian Johnson
MANAGING EDITOR, COLLEGE DIGITAL MEDIA Kim Yi
ASSOCIATE DIRECTOR OF PRODUCTION, COLLEGE Benjamin Reynolds
MEDIA EDITOR Laura Wilk
MEDIA PROJECT EDITOR Rachel Mayer
MEDIA ASSOCIATE EDITOR Michelle Smith
MEDIA ASSISTANT EDITOR Chris Hillyer
MARKETING MANAGER, HISTORY Sarah England Bartley
PHOTO EDITOR Stephanie Romeo
PHOTO RESEARCHER Lynn Gadson
DESIGNER Jillian Burr
PERMISSIONS MANAGER Megan Schindel
PERMISSIONS ASSOCIATE Elizabeth Trammell
LAYOUT ARTIST Brad Walrod/Kenoza Type, Inc.
CARTOGRAPHER AND ILLUSTRATOR Mapping Specialists—Fitchburg, WI
MANUFACTURING Transcontinental Interglobe Inc.—Beauceville QC

The Library of Congress has cataloged the one-volume edition as follows:

This edition:
ISBN: 978-0-393-62453-3 (pbk.)

W. W. Norton & Company, Inc., 500 Fifth Avenue, New York, NY 10110
wwnorton.com

W. W. Norton & Company Ltd., Castle House, 75/76 Wells Street, London W1T 3QT

1 2 3 4 5 6 7 8 9

TO OUR STUDENTS

ABOUT THE AUTHORS

ANTHONY GRAFTON is the Henry Putnam University Professor of History at Princeton University. A specialist in the cultural history of early-modern Europe, he is the author of many acclaimed books, including *The Footnote: A Curious History*, and *New Worlds, Ancient Texts: The Power of Tradition and the Shock of Discovery*, which won the Los Angeles Times Book Award in History, and intellectual biographies of Leon Battista Alberti, Girolamo Cardano, and Joseph Scaliger. Among his many honors from universities and cultural institutions around the world, Professor Grafton was awarded the Balzan Prize for History of the Humanities and the Andrew W. Mellon Foundation's Distinguished Achievement Award. At Princeton, where he regularly teaches the survey of Western Civilizations, he was honored with the President's Teaching Award. He is a member of the American Philosophical Society, the British Academy, and has served as president of the American Historical Association.

DAVID A. BELL is the Sidney and Ruth Lapidus Professor in the Era of North Atlantic Revolutions in the History department at Princeton University. His specialty is modern Europe with a focus on political culture in the age of revolutions. Among his recent works, *The First Total War: Napoleon's Europe and the Birth of Warfare As We Know It* was a finalist for the Los Angeles Times Book Award in History. Professor Bell regularly teaches undergraduate surveys of early-modern Europe, the Enlightenment, and the French Revolution. He is a regular contributor to *The Nation* and other general-interest periodicals. Professor Bell's current project is a transnational history of political charisma in the Atlantic revolutions of the late eighteenth and early nineteenth centuries.

CONTENTS IN BRIEF

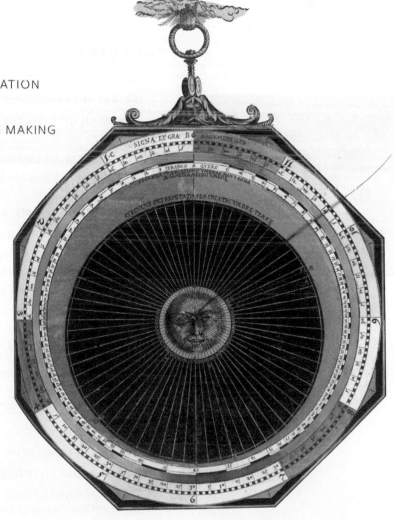

CONTENTS

5. The Roman Empire and the Rise of Christianity, 14–312 CE   147

6. The Late Roman Empire and the Consolidation of the Church, 312–476   181

9.   Consolidation and Crisis: The High Middle Ages, 1200–1400   287

10. Renaissance Europe: A World Transformed, 1400–1500   325

11. Reformations: Protestant and Catholic, 1500–1600   371

MAPS

PRIMARY-SOURCE FEATURES

The story of the West is an epic. This might seem strange to say, because there has never been a single, unified, easily defined place called "the West." Even the Roman Empire at its height did not control all of the territories that have come to form part of the West, and its hegemony lasted only a few centuries. The boundaries of the West have never been fixed or agreed upon. Moreover, whether in imperial Rome or Europe today, these borders have always been porous. People, goods, and ideas have constantly flowed across them in both directions, sometimes peacefully and often violently. What we today call "the West" is in significant measure a product of this unending process of exchange.

Even so, there is something we can call "the West." It is a web of societies, centered in Europe and its extensions, loosely linked by shared and interacting histories. These histories incorporate debts to other societies around the world and the results of conflicts both internal and global.

At their core are ideas and institutions—cultural, political, social, and economic—that have outlasted the individual societies that gave them birth and been developed and transformed to meet new needs. The story of the West is not one of repeated triumph or unbroken progress. It is not a story of a single tradition. But it is a story of epic proportions. It has been a story of hatred and intolerance, but also one of men and women fighting hatred and intolerance, and finding ways to rise above them. It has been a story of people who rejected the earth for heaven, and of people who wanted to build heaven on earth. It has been a story of breathtaking idealism and breathtaking cruelty, of innovation and competition, creation and destruction, new habits of thought, and of centuries-long conversations that we call "traditions."

The story is full of dramatic moments: moments when individuals and movements challenged established authorities and customs, when reformers transformed legal codes

and religious practices, and when revolutionaries over-turned governments. It is a story of individuals of titanic achievement: people who have given their names to ways of thinking and arguing, understanding the universe, and building and maintaining states. It is a story of blinding new insights into what justice really means, and one of blindness to the exploitation and persecution of others.

But it has also been a story of daily life: of men and women whose names we usually do not know who struggled to survive and raise children under the shadows of hunger and illness, war and displacement. It is the story of how daily life remained the same in many ways for thousands of years: of how most people lived close to the soil, trying to scratch out sustenance from it with their own muscle power and that of animals, according to the rhythm of the seasons. But it is also a story of how, starting in the seventeenth and eighteenth centuries, individuals and groups slowly developed new ways of wringing more food from the land—and how, by doing so, they changed the world.

Last, but by no means least, it is a story about how, in the last centuries, virtually everything about daily life changed, often at dizzying speed: factories rose, cities grew to sizes never seen before, gender roles were challenged and transformed, religion lost its commanding place in society, governments became newly pervasive, education

spread, new technologies emerged, new media flourished, and vast new forms of wealth were created. It is a story of how modern nation-states were forged and of how populations migrated into and out of Europe.

The story was not the work of Europeans alone. Indeed, the civilization that took shape in Europe has arguably been more dependent than any other on what it could borrow, beg, or steal from the rest of the world. For much of its history—amid the competing city-states of ancient Greece and the fierce rivalries of the western Middle Ages and Renaissance—the West has been smaller, poorer in resources, more politically divided, and less sophisticated than rival civilizations elsewhere in the world. Only with the capture of the immense resources of the Americas in the early modern period, and the harnessing of fossil fuels during the Industrial Revolution, did the natural resources that Europe possessed make themselves fully felt in the worldwide balance of power. Yet precisely as a result of the West's relative poverty and political fragmentation, Western politicians and thinkers, soldiers and tinkerers were driven constantly to innovate with the resources they had and with the ideas and techniques they borrowed from other cultures. Writing came to the West from the Near East—from the Phoenicians, a Semitic people who lived in Palestine and the Fertile Crescent. So did the idea of setting down in writing massive works that described the adventures of humans and the hierarchies of gods. But the two Greek epics traditionally ascribed to the poet Homer are distinctively different from the great Near Eastern epic *The Song of Gilgamesh*, in the ways that they portray relations between gods and humans and in the voices that they give to their own societies.

Many elements of this story will seem strange to young people who live in the West today. The physical and mental worlds of an ancient Greek soldier, a medieval nun, or an African slave in an early-modern European colony were all enormously distant from those of today's students. Indeed, the scale of change in every area of life in modern times—political, economic, cultural, religious, technological—can easily lead to the conclusion that an unbridgeable gulf separates the more distant past from the present. Can a cohesive story encompass present-day Europeans, the poorest of whom can generally count on living to old age in conditions of relative physical comfort, and their predecessors of whom half did not live beyond adolescence, with the remainder at constant risk of death from infectious disease and possibly starvation, not to mention chronic, debilitating pain? Is it possible to draw connections between the Europeans of today, almost entirely literate and able instantly to summon vast libraries of text, image, and sound on devices they carry in their pockets, and predecessors who learned about the world principally from oral tradition, religious authority, and travel limited by the speed of wind, animals, or their own legs?

We think it is possible. If you live in the West today, and particularly if you are a student, this story is your story. It is not by any means the entirety of your story, but it is a critical part of it, and for two reasons. First, it is the story of how significant parts of your world came into being. The political systems that exist in the West today, nearly all of which claim the mantle of democracy, trace their origins back to the ancient Greek world in which the word "democracy" itself was invented. They are part of a tradition—a long process of evolution, debate, and conflict—in which the meaning of democracy has changed radically to include new conceptions of rights, political representation, civic and social equality, and a separation between the realms of politics and religion. This long process did not take place solely in the West, but it was centered there. It was also shaped by forms of political competition and fragmentation that have been characteristic of the West throughout most of its history and that distinguish the West from many other historical regions of the world.

Similarly, the capitalist system that most of the West lives under today has roots that reach far back: to the trading cities that developed in the ancient world, to patterns of commerce and banking that developed in medieval Europe, and to ideas about the organization of societies and the operations of markets that were formulated during the European Renaissance and Enlightenment. This system depended, from the start, on currents of trade, exploration, and exploitation and conquest that stretched far beyond the West, and it has subsequently developed strongly on a global scale. But at its core this system was centered in the West.

More broadly, the very ways in which we learn to read, think critically, devise arguments, innovate, and express ourselves creatively derive in significant measure from millennia-long conversations that began in the ancient Near East, were carried on throughout the classical Mediterranean world, and thence into other parts of Europe and the world. These conversations were rarely harmonious. Their basic assumptions were challenged, in fundamental ways, by new voices from both within and without. Their subjects and forms changed repeatedly. But as this book will show, important continuities can still be traced within these conversations.

And this is the second reason why the story of the West is your story. The habits and practices of learning, critical thinking, and effective expression that are necessary for citizens of contemporary Western industrial democracies are intimately related to the complex history that produced them.

History does not just help us better understand the world around us; it helps us function more effectively in it. This lesson, and this awareness, are themselves part of the Western story, and they lie at the heart of one of the most important Western traditions: the tradition of higher learning that is today carried on in colleges and universities. Ancient Romans trained for positions within their own society by learning Greek and studying important works of Greek philosophy and literature. During the Renaissance, so-called humanists sought to revive ancient Greek and Roman learning not just for the sake of learning, but in order to train young men as civil servants and diplomats, lawyers, and doctors. These systems of education could function as forms of social discrimination, excluding from desirable careers those who lacked the means to study Latin and Greek—a category that included virtually all women. But learning about Western history and traditions can also serve as a means of social inclusion, drawing diverse student populations into conversation with peers from all corners of their own society, with their own predecessors from centuries past, and with some of the most brilliant and creative minds the world has known.

As historians who have both taught Western history for decades, we recognize that the story of the West is complex and often challenging for introductory students. It ranges across the fields of politics, society, economics, war, religion, philosophy, science, culture, and much else. It is a story marked by discontinuities such as the sharp differences among different regions of the West, and by the many different forms of exchange and contact between the West and other areas of the globe. But precisely because of these complexities, we believe in the importance of integrating the history with strong narrative threads and telling the story in as cogent, engaging, and fluid a manner as possible.

We have therefore chosen to proceed in as close to a strictly chronological manner as possible, presenting subjects like the development of Christianity or the scientific revolution as they unfolded alongside other contemporary events, rather than cordoning them off into separate chapters. We believe it is important for the chronology of events to be clear and visible for beginning students. We wish also to show students the mutual interplay over time of politics and society, ideas, beliefs, and material conditions. These many overlapping layers of history should be understood together, developing over time, rather than as disconnected strands of the story. We have done our best to achieve the right balance in attending to these many dimensions of history. We have also tried to incorporate the best new scholarship in these fields along with the insights of previous generations of scholars.

The book covers as broad a sweep of history as is practical in two volumes designed for a year-long survey course. Volume One, written primarily by Anthony Grafton, begins with a Prologue on prehistory and takes the story from the ancient Near East up through the Reformation. Volume Two, written primarily by David Bell, begins with the Renaissance and continues to the present day. Both volumes range in scope far beyond Europe. Volume One emphasizes the origins of the Western story in the Middle East and gives due attention to the societies around the

Mediterranean basin during antiquity and the Middle Ages, including the rise, expansion, and cultural flourishing of Islam. It also deals with patterns of global exchange and the expansion of European political power that began in the fifteenth century. Volume Two centers its narrative on Europe and its extensions, focusing on the continuing dynamics of disorder and order, cohesion and fragmentation, as they played out in politics, culture, and society over the modern period.

THE WEST comes equipped with a full complement of illustrations (more than 500), newly drawn maps (more than 130), and useful pedagogical features described in the coming pages. But at the core of history is narrative, and we hope that THE WEST demonstrates our belief that clear, engaging prose remains the most effective means of introducing students to history.

Anthony Grafton
David A. Bell

ACKNOWLEDGMENTS

Heartfelt thanks to Steve Forman, our eagle-eyed and ever cheerful editor, and to his colleagues at W.W. Norton, who inspired me, prodded me, and turned sometimes inchoate drafts into a finished book; to my colleagues at Princeton, who have taught me so much about history; and, above all, to the students who have taken History 211. Many of the tales told here were first spun for them, and their lively responses, in class and out, to lectures, readings, and expeditions to the Rare Book Room have given me both pleasure and enlightenment over the years. It is a pleasure to join David Bell in dedicating this book to our students.

Anthony Grafton

Many thanks to all the colleagues at Johns Hopkins and Princeton who helped me over the years with suggestions and comments. I am grateful to the terrific staff at W.W. Norton, and especially our wonderful editor, Steve Forman, for everything they have done to bring this project to fruition. As always, my deepest gratitude to my wife, Donna Farber, and to my children, Elana and Joseph Bell, for their love and support. One of the greatest joys of the profession I am in comes in the moments of one's students' discoveries, watching them see into the past in a new way. It is in memory of these moments, and in gratitude to those who have passed through my classrooms, that I am delighted to join Anthony Grafton in dedicating this book to our students.

David A. Bell

THE WEST is a collective work in many respects, most pleasurably in its reflection of the commitment we share with many of our colleagues to the introductory course and its students. We would like to thank the following scholars for reading and commenting on our draft chapters. We have benefitted enormously from their criticisms and suggestions.

Megan Armstrong, McMaster University
Kenneth Bartlett, University of Toronto
Jean Berger, University of Wisconsin at Fox Valley
Hilary Bernstein, University of California, Santa Barbara
Nick Bomba, Northern Virginia Community College
Curtis V. Bostick, Southern Utah University
Jonathyne Briggs, Indiana University Northwest
Tobias Brinkmann, Pennsylvania State University
Bill Bulman, Lehigh University
Jeremy Caradonna, University of Victoria
Shawn Clybor, Utah State University
Susan Cogan, Utah State University
William Connell, Seton Hall University
Alix Cooper, State University of New York at Stony Brook
Mairi Cowan, University of Toronto at Mississauga
Andrew Daily, University of Memphis
Leah DeVun, Rutgers University
David Dorondo, Western Carolina University

Mary Duarte, Cardinal Stritch University
Bonnie Effros, University of Florida
John Eglin, University of Montana
Kyle Fingerson, University of Wisconsin, Rock County
Christopher Frank, University of Manitoba
Andrew Gallia, University of Minnesota
Phil Haberkern, Boston University
Amanda E. Herbert, Christopher Newport University
Rowena Hernández-Múzquiz, Broward College
Laura Hutchings, University of Utah
Bruce Janacek, North Central College
Erik Johnsen, Portland Community College
Donald Johnson, University of North Carolina at Wilmington
Edward Kolla, Georgetown University in Qatar
Jodie Kreider, Colorado State University
Greta Kroeker, University of Waterloo
Matthew Laubacher, Ashford University
Anne E. Lester, University of Colorado, Boulder
Yan Mann, Arizona State University
Benjamin Marschke, Humboldt State University
Bruce McCord, Aiken Technical College
Jeri McIntosh, University of Tennessee, Knoxville
Murat Menguc, Seton Hall University
John Patrick Montaño, University of Delaware
Rosemary Moore, University of Iowa
Seán Farrell Moran, Oakland University
George Munro, Virginia Commonwealth University
William Myers, University of Alaska, Anchorage
Lawrence Okamura, University of Missouri
Katrina Olds, University of San Francisco
John Powers, Virginia Commonwealth University
Jennifer Purcell, Saint Michael's College
Andrew Reed, Arizona State University
Walter Roberts, University of North Texas
Nicholas L. Rummell, Trident Technical College
Emily Rutherford, Columbia University
Linda B. Scherr, Middlesex County College
Edward Schoolman, University of Nevada, Reno
Colleen Shaughnessy Zeena, Endicott College
Linda Smith, University of Alabama at Birmingham
Ginger Smoak, University of Utah
John Swanson, University of Tennessee at Chattanooga
Emily Sohmer Tai, Queensborough Community College, CUNY
Paul Teverow, Missouri Southern State University
Corinna Treitel, Washington University in St. Louis
Liana Vardi, State University of New York at Buffalo
Corinne Wieben, University of Northern Colorado

PEDAGOGY AND FEATURES

The West offers an array of pedagogical features to guide students through the chapters and enrich their understanding of people and events.

All chapters open with a list of **focus questions** that correspond to the major section headings in the chapter. These questions, which appear also in the relevant running heads at the tops of pages, are meant to keep students alert to the key developments in each section. All chapters also open with a **chronology** of major events and an **immersive narrative vignette** to draw students into the reading. The chapters end with a review page that includes **study questions**, a list of the **key terms** (with page references) that appear in bold in the chapter, and a set of **Core Objectives**—key points that students should take away from the chapter. These Core Objectives are reinforced in the exercises provided in the online Student Site for *The West*. The key terms are all defined in the Glossary located in the Appendix, which also includes the authors' lists of **Further Reading** for each chapter.

Since one of the most important course goals in the introductory survey is to train students in the use of primary sources, each chapter also includes three **primary-source features** intended to introduce students to different types of documents and help build their critical-thinking skills.

The first of these features, **Making Connections**, consists of paired primary documents that connect to each other and the text itself. Brief headnotes and questions focus students on the issues to consider. The **Documenting Everyday Life** feature, comprising a source, a headnote, and questions, helps students understand an aspect of the everyday life of the period. The **Understanding Visual Culture** feature presents an image as a primary source to be examined critically by students.

The West also presents an innovative feature entitled **City Life**, intended to enhance the text's theme of cultural change and give students further work in developing history skills. We have eight of these full-page features in the text, four in Volume I and four in the non-overlap chapters of Volume Two. Each one focuses on a city at a critical moment, from Fifth-Century Athens and Imperial Rome to Renaissance Florence and fin de siècle Vienna. Through source quotations, images, a central map, and short questions that connect to text discussions, the features ask students to reflect on distinctive aspects of life in the cities, whether the ways in which the emperors reshaped the city of Rome or the commercial context of art in Renaissance Florence. The digital resources connected to the City Life features further enhance student history skills.

Understanding Visual Culture

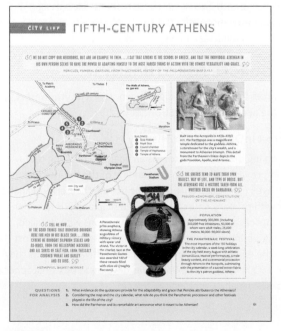

City Life

DIGITAL RESOURCES FOR STUDENTS AND INSTRUCTORS

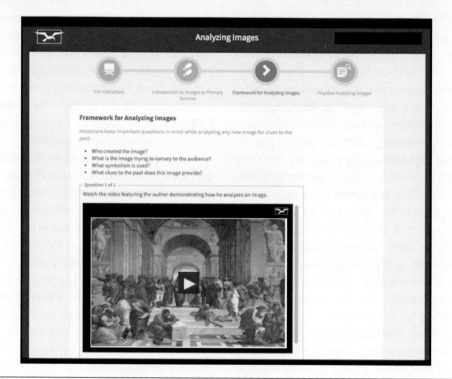

W. W. Norton offers a robust digital package to support teaching and learning with *The West*. These resources are designed to make students more effective textbook readers and to develop their critical thinking and history skills.

RESOURCES FOR STUDENTS

Resources are available at digital.wwnorton.com/thewestv1 with the access card at the front of this text.

Norton InQuizitive for History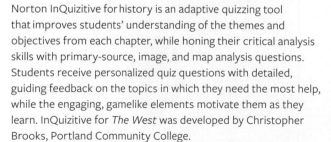

Norton InQuizitive for history is an adaptive quizzing tool that improves students' understanding of the themes and objectives from each chapter, while honing their critical analysis skills with primary-source, image, and map analysis questions. Students receive personalized quiz questions with detailed, guiding feedback on the topics in which they need the most help, while the engaging, gamelike elements motivate them as they learn. InQuizitive for *The West* was developed by Christopher Brooks, Portland Community College.

History Skills Tutorials

The History Skills Tutorials feature three modules—Images, Documents, and Maps—to support students' development of the key skills for the history course. These tutorials feature videos of the authors modeling the analysis process, followed by interactive questions that will challenge students to apply what they have learned.

Student Site

The free and easy-to-use online Student Site offers additional resources for students to use outside of class. Resources include interactive iMaps from each chapter, author videos, and a comprehensive Online Reader featuring more than 300 additional primary-source documents and images.

Ebook

Free and included with new copies of the text, **the Norton Ebook Reader** provides an enhanced reading experience that works on all computers and mobile devices. Features include intuitive highlighting, note-taking, and bookmarking as well as pop-up definitions and enlargeable maps and art. Direct links to InQuizitive also appear in each chapter. Instructors can focus

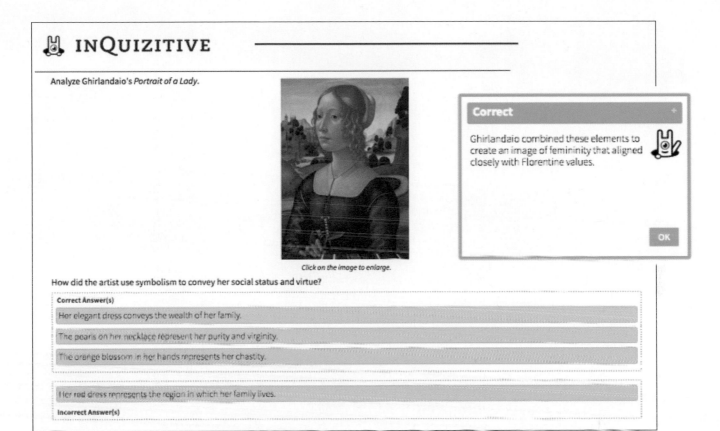

INQUIZITIVE

Analyze Ghirlandaio's *Portrait of a Lady*.

Click on the image to enlarge.

Correct

Ghirlandaio combined these elements to create an image of femininity that aligned closely with Florentine values.

OK

How did the artist use symbolism to convey her social status and virtue?

Correct Answer(s)

Her elegant dress conveys the wealth of her family.

The pearls on her necklace represent her purity and virginity.

The orange blossom in her hands represents her chastity.

Her red dress represents the region in which her family lives.

Incorrect Answer(s)

---

student reading by sharing notes with their classes, including embedded images and video. Reports on student and class-wide access and time on task allow instructors to monitor student reading and engagement.

RESOURCES FOR INSTRUCTORS

All resources are available through www.wwnorton.com/instructors.

NORTON COURSEPACKS

Easily add high-quality digital media to your online, hybrid, or lecture course—all at no cost to students. Norton's Coursepacks work within your existing Learning Management System and are ready to use and easy to customize. The coursepack offers a diverse collection of assignable and assessable resources: **Primary-Source Exercises, Guided Reading Exercises, Review Quizzes, Flashcards, Map Exercises, and all of the resources from the Student Site.** The resources were developed by Matthew Mingus, University of New Mexico, Melanie Bailey, Piedmont Virginia Community College, and Gregory Vitarbo, Meredith College.

Test Bank

The Test Bank was authored by Rosemary Moore, University of Iowa, John Patrick Montano, University of Delaware, and Curt Bostick, Southern Utah University, and contains 2000 multiple-choice, true/false, and essay questions.

Instructor's Manual

The Instructor's Manual contains detailed Chapter Summaries, Chapter Outlines, Suggested Discussion Questions, and Supplemental Web, Visual, and Print Resources. This resource was authored by Craig Pilant, County College of Morris, Joel Anderson, University of Maine, and Mark Ruff, Saint Louis University.

Lecture and Art PowerPoint Slides

The Lecture PowerPoint sets authored by Nicholas Rummell, Trident Technical College, and Matthew Laubacher, Ashford University, combine chapter review, art, and maps.

THE WEST

A NEW HISTORY

Humanity Before History

The early history of human life is a long and complex story. It rests on physical evidence rather than the words of past humans, and has been told by geneticists, climatologists, and archaeologists rather than historians.

It starts in Africa, sometime after 200,000 BCE, when human beings anatomically identical with us—*Homo sapiens*—evolved from primate ancestors. By 130,000 BCE, these humans were migrating out of Africa, north and west into the Near East and Europe. A second wave, sixty or seventy thousand years later, moved eastward along the southern shore of Asia and eventually populated Australia and Micronesia. By 50,000 BCE—possibly long before, though the known archaeological record does not prove this—these humans learned how to make tools—stone blades, for example, in multiple regular shapes—and personal ornaments for men and women. Craft and art, in other words, existed long before humans developed writing.

The blades, scrapers, and brooches that survive from this period reveal a great deal about their makers. *Homo sapiens* was not alone. Earlier forms of human also populated the world—Neanderthal peoples in Europe and the Near East and *Homo erectus* in Africa and Asia. More than a million years ago, these species were using stones that they had shaped to fight one another, butcher animals, and cut wood. As they moved from Africa across the other continents, *Homo sapiens* learned from these older species that different materials, including human and animal bones as well as stones, could be shaped in different ways. They worked out how to strike one stone with another in order

▲ **Cave Painting** The walls of the Chauvet cave at Vallon-Pont-d'Arc, France, preserve a glimpse of early human culture: paintings made by Paleolithic humans around 30,000–28,000 BCE. This scene depicts horses, rhinoceroses, and aurochs (ancestors of modern domestic cattle), and may have served a religious purpose.

to produce a sharp implement for cutting or stabbing, and how to finish that weapon's edge. And they invented ways of teaching these skills to their young. Humans are not genetically programmed to make tools or wear bracelets. But they are programmed, evidently, to develop sets of skills—some of which they borrow from others. By 50,000 BCE or so, in other words, human beings were changing places and learning as they did so. But they were learning slowly. Human culture developed as a glacier moves, very slowly: similar tools are found in deposits separated by thousands of miles and thousands of years.

After 50,000 BCE, in the period known as the Upper Paleolithic, the last period of the Old Stone Age, history began to move more rapidly. Living conditions were hard, especially during the Last Glacial Maximum—the period, lasting approximately from 24,500 to 18,000 BCE, when an ice sheet covered most of northern Europe, forcing most humans to retreat south into Italy, the Iberian Peninsula, and the Balkans. Yet the signs of change were everywhere. Soon after 40,000 BCE, men and women were decorating the walls of caves with paintings of horses, rhinoceroses, and other animals. By 32,000 BCE, they were making and firing human figures out of clay. Some of these images, painted and sculpted, may portray gods or reflect religious visions and practices: evidence that their makers asked questions about the world and devised answers. Soon after 30,000 BCE, they learned how to make and shoot bows and arrows. As the ice retreated, the pace of change picked up. Humans learned to tame and live with animals: herders domesticated reindeer, farmers domesticated dogs, and both were portrayed on the walls and ceilings of caves.

Human ingenuity was already powerful—but not yet powerful enough to overcome the hardships imposed by nature. Sometime around 10,000 BCE two new epochs began. The Neolithic, a period in human history beginning around 10,000 BC and lasting 5000 to 7000 years, marked a transition in human culture. As we will soon see, settled societies took shape and their inhabitants intensively developed techniques for exploiting nature. The beginning of this historical era corresponded roughly with the start of a new geological period, the Holocene, which continues to the present. After thousands of years of violent fluctuations, temperatures stabilized at a new high level, where they have generally remained ever since. Such periods of warmth have been relatively short by the measure of geologic time. They come about, seemingly, every

▲ **Stone Tools** These sharp-edged tools from the Upper Paleolithic may have been used to tip spears, carve bone and horn, or fashion other tools.

hundred thousand years or so. Their effects are dramatic, and not always benign. The opening of the Holocene was accompanied by the extinction of such large mammals as the Mastodon and the Mammoth.

For humans, however, the new climate system offered unique opportunities to apply their skills and ingenuity in new ways. In the first place, agriculture—intensive, systematic cultivation of plants and animals—now became possible. In the Near East—as we will see in more detail in the first chapter—farmers cultivated cereals and raised animals for multiple purposes. Gradually, evolution cooperated with culture. At first, wild grasses were cut and their seeds pounded in mortars. Over time, systematic harvesting favored grasses like wheat and barley, the seeds of which lent themselves to human use. Herbivores—cattle and sheep above all—living in symbiosis with humans spread across the Eurasian land mass. Farming for cereals and dairy products developed with them.

In many cases, techniques passed from one place and people to another. Near Eastern farming techniques moved in all directions, reaching all the way east to India by 5000 BCE and all the way west to Britain by 4000 BCE.

EARLY HUMANITY

PLEISTOCENE EPOCH ca. 2,600,000–10,000 BCE	**PALEOLITHIC PERIOD (CA. 2,500,000–10,000 BCE)**	
	ca. 200,000 BCE	*Homo sapiens* evolve from primate ancestors
	ca. 130,000 BCE	Migration out of Africa
	By ca. 50,000 BCE	Invention of tools
HOLOCENE EPOCH ca. 10,000 BCE–Present	**NEOLITHIC PERIOD (CA. 10,000–4000 BCE)**	
	ca. 10,000 BCE	Invention of agriculture
	By ca. 8000 BCE	Settlement of first towns
	By ca. 4000 BCE	Near Eastern farming techniques reach Britain

In other cases, though, humans showed their ability as independent inventors. The natives of the Americas were nomads when, around 20,000 years ago, they crossed the land bridge that connected Asia with North America. In the Americas, they developed their own systems of cultivation in the fourth millennium BCE, growing maize (corn) and domesticating the llama, neither of which came from Eurasia. Did culture cross continents through colonization, through peaceful contact, or by independent inspiration? All of the above.

By now, inventions were radically changing the texture of human life. Consider the clay pot and the storehouse. By 8000 BCE at the latest, cultivators had begun to settle down in towns like Jericho, in Palestine. They were accumulating large amounts of seed and food, which they had to protect against both the elements and hungry animals. Large clay pots, crude and unadorned, provided a more-or-less airtight and rodent-free form of storage for grain and other edibles. Other inventions followed: the wheel, the cart, and the plow. The culture of sedentary cultivators became more and more complex—and more and more different from that of the nomads who still wandered with their herds, gathering and hunting what they needed rather than winning it from the earth. In settled communities, living standards rose. So did social hierarchies and diseases, like technologies, spread rapidly from one settlement to another.

Stone and clay were highly adaptable, but they had their limits. When points or blades were fashioned thin enough to cut well, they became fragile. Pottery lasted well unless struck by hard objects, but was often thick and clumsy. Neither was well suited for jewelry. Early in the Holocene, individuals learned that hammering could change the shape of metals—especially copper and gold. Later they found that heat could be applied to make metals thinner without depriving them of all their strength. Copper, for instance, abundant and relatively easy to work, could be made stronger when alloyed with tin to form bronze. In

▲ **Neolithic Pottery** This pottery bowl was handmade around 5500–5000 BCE by the Halaf people of what is now Iraq. The pattern is an early example of painting on pottery in the Near East.

time, techniques for smelting and working iron ore in large quantities were developed. The forge, with its anvils and hammers, became a central feature of social life, and a new world of weapons, tools, and ornaments appeared.

Soon the settled people would be writing. That is another story—the story with which this book properly begins. It is, as we will see, rich and dramatic, and involves many changes as well as some continuities. Many of the characteristics that humans had acquired in the early centuries of the Holocene would continue to shape their lives. They moved, endlessly, in search of new places to settle and new resources to exploit. They enslaved others and appropriated their labor. They were inventive, both at devising new tools and decorations and at passing them on to further generations. But they were also receptive: where one people devised its own ways of breaking the earth, five more borrowed them from others.

They recognized no limits to their power. The smoke of their forges and kilns blackened the skies, leaving a trail of dirt that can still be detected in the thick ice cap of the North Pole—though possibly not for very much longer. In some areas—such as Palestine, which was denuded of trees by 6000 BCE—their needs led to disastrous deforestation and other environmental damage. Humans were no longer simply the victims of their natural environments, forced to move as ice sheets covered what had once been habitats they loved and decorated. They were actively changing the environment they lived in—a process that has continued through the Holocene, transforming the face of the world over and over again. The continuity between human life before the invention of writing and after is nowhere clearer than in the endless social and technological innovations that have made possible our exploitation of the earth.

CHRONOLOGY

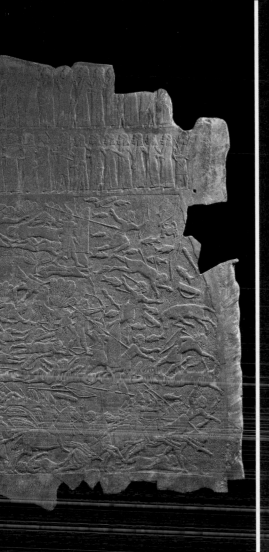

1

Origins

THE NEAR EAST, EGYPT, AND GREECE

12,000–600 BCE

O n a winter day sometime around 700 BCE, a Greek chieftain sat with his family and retainers in the smoky main hall of his house. They had sacrificed an ox; burnt its bones, along with barley and cakes, as an offering to the gods; and roasted the rest for themselves. The men had eaten the meat and drunk large cups of wine diluted with water. Still reclining, as they had while eating, they discussed the things that mattered to them most: prospects for trade and warfare, the family histories of friends and enemies, the chances of marriage among members of their class, and the like. The women, after serving them, had remained, silent but present.

A bard began to recite:

When early dawn appeared, rosy-fingered,
The dear son of Odysseus rose from his bed,
Put on his clothing, hung a sharp sword from his shoulder,
And laced his handsome sandals to his shining feet.
He left his room, his face like a god's.
Immediately he asked the clear-voiced heralds
To call the long-haired Greeks to an assembly.

Reliefs from King Assurbanipal's Palace These large panels relate a vivid narrative of a great Assyrian victory over their long-standing enemies, the Elamites, around 653 BCE. The battle's climax is depicted here, with Assyrian soldiers brutally killing the Elamite leader and preserving his head as a trophy.

- How was the ancient Near East innovative in culture, society, and the uses of power?
- How did Egyptian society remain so stable for so long?
- How did a distinctive religion emerge in a world of great powers?
- How did the Greeks adapt and modify Near Eastern and Egyptian art, culture, and technology?

> The heralds called, and the Achaians quickly assembled.
> When the gathering had come together,
> He came straight into the assembly, a bronze spear in his hand,
> Not alone, for two swift dogs followed him,
> And Athena rained grace upon him.
> When he arrived, the people stared at him,
> As he sat in his father's throne, and the elders yielded to him.

This traditional story is one episode from a long series of tales about an older world in which men and gods mingled freely. In this case, Telemachus, son of the Greek hero Odysseus, has become a man during his father's participation in the long siege of Troy, a city-state on the distant coast of Asia Minor. Idle noblemen have gathered in Odysseus's house to feast and drink. Believing Odysseus must now be dead, they demand that Telemachus's mother marry one of them. Telemachus calls an assembly of the Achaeans—the men of Ithaca, the land his father had ruled. Because Athena, goddess of wisdom and daughter of Zeus, loves Odysseus, she helps his son by giving him a powerful, almost divine presence. The assembly eventually breaks up in disorder, but Telemachus takes the opportunity to outfit a ship and sail away in search of information about his father.

With that action the *Odyssey*—one of two Greek epics ascribed to a poet named Homer—was under way. Other parts of the poem take its characters—and its listeners—across the Aegean Sea, where they visit strange settlements and encounter everything from storms and monsters to a goddess who transforms Odysseus's crew into pigs with her magical potions. Later in this chapter, we will come back to Homer and examine his work, as well as the eighth-century BCE revolution in Greek culture that it belonged to. For now, we will look—as the characters in his stories did—outside the Greek world, to the south and east, where, as the Greeks knew well, societies far older than theirs had built great cities and powerful empires.

THE NEAR EAST TO THE BRONZE AGE CRISIS

It was in the ancient Near East—a vast territory in southwestern Asia that now makes up parts of Iran, Iraq, Syria, Palestine, and the northern region of Egypt—that much of **civilization** as we know it came into being. This immense, open landmass attracted migrants and invaders of many kinds. From the fourth millennium BCE, Semitic peoples—groups that spoke the ancestral languages of modern Arabic and Hebrew—settled here, coming into contact and, often, into conflict. Here plants and animals were **domesticated**, clay was transformed into pottery, wheels were fashioned and used for chariots and carts. Cities were built—and then assembled, sometimes by force, into empires. Here **monotheistic** religions and mathematical sciences both took shape for the first time. Without these diverse inheritances, our own civilization could never have come into being.

This region was defined to the east by the mountains that bound the Iranian plateau, to the west by the Mediterranean Sea and the border of the cultivated area of Egypt, to the north by the Black Sea and the Caucasus Mountains, and to the south by the Arabian Desert. The core area of settlement within it, the so-called Fertile Crescent, stretched from the Persian Gulf in the southeast, through Egypt, to the Levant (an area corresponding to modern Palestine, Syria, and western Jordan) in the northwest. For thousands of years, as late as the Mesolithic Period (20,000–12,000 BCE), individuals and small groups with their herds ranged across the vast plateau and hills, never remaining long in one spot. Groups came from the northwest (Asia Minor and beyond) and the southeast (the area known today as India), some passing through and others remaining to establish footholds.

NEOLITHIC AGRICULTURAL SETTLEMENTS (12,000–4300 BCE)

As early as 12,000 BCE, settlements of a new kind sprang up in the region. Earlier societies had moved, slowly but constantly, in search of grazing land for their herds. Now, in the period known as the Neolithic or New Stone Age, people began settling in one place, mostly in hillside villages: clusters of a few dozen mud houses, each with a few rooms and an open area around it, surrounded by cultivated land. Gradually these groups learned that they could improve both plants and animals by choosing seeds or particular animals and cross-breeding them. They began to grow barley with larger, softer grains and to raise sheep with richer meat and thicker, softer wool.

They also began to make more sophisticated tools and utensils, which enabled them to cultivate the land more intensively and to keep any surplus from what they grew. Seeds and other supplies had traditionally been stored in leather bags, which were vulnerable to moisture. Now the villagers worked out how to turn, fire, and glaze clay vessels. The decorated pottery that this new technology produced enabled them to store seeds and other products for much longer periods. The wheel, also invented around this time, was put to use in plows and carts.

Most of these **agricultural** settlements remained small during this period. They were largely populated by clans of connected families, which likely managed their business by making collective decisions.

IRRIGATION IN MESOPOTAMIA

Between roughly 5900 and 4300 BCE, the new agricultural civilization moved down into the plains. The southern

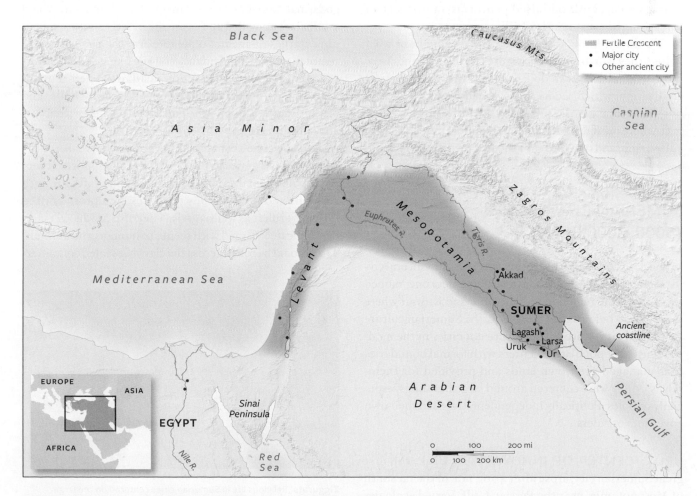

The Ancient Near East, ca. 3000 BCE The innovative Sumerian culture in southern Mesopotamia centered on the major city-states of Ur, Uruk, Lagash, and Larsa. But other cities lined the Tigris and Euphrates Rivers throughout Mesopotamia; and soon after, monarchs ruled a unified Egypt. Throughout the Near East, settlements were built along rivers, where irrigation allowed for agriculture and the support of large populations.

flatlands of southwestern Asia receive little or no rain, but in Mesopotamia—the alluvial plain created by the Tigris and Euphrates Rivers—new possibilities for agriculture existed. Natural flooding occurred each spring, depositing rich sediment along the riverbanks. Irrigation controls were then needed to draw the springtime floodwaters away from the new seedlings and bring water back to the fields after flood season to nourish the crops through the arid summer.

The land, once treated in this way, became astonishingly fertile: in some areas, it returned as much as ten times the amount of grain used to seed it (for comparison, normal land fertilized in a traditional way might return two to four times the amount of seed sown in it). To dig and maintain the necessary irrigation trenches, specialized, stable labor forces developed, and some villages grew much larger than others. Surplus grain was collected and sold, and the profits supported new, larger projects. Shrines arose, built on raised platforms—a first sign of something like an organized religion.

We do not know what these people thought or what beings they worshipped (the figures in their shrines were mostly female). But we do know that this new, peaceful civilization, which seems to have made few or no weapons, had real vigor. It spread to the north in Mesopotamia, where rainfall and wells could support more intensive cultivation, and outward into the Levant and Asia Minor.

SUMERIAN CITY-STATES (5000–3000 BCE)

In the fifth and fourth millennia BCE, this agricultural civilization of Mesopotamia gave way to a new one, named for Sumer—the region in modern Iraq and Kuwait where it came into being. After 5000 BCE, the Sumerian culture developed **city-states**. These were not cities in the modern sense, but population centers with formal boundaries that managed their own lands and provided for themselves. Many were centered around large buildings, especially temples. Politically independent, they had their own governors or rulers.

URUK: CENTER OF INNOVATION Uruk, the first great Sumerian city, arose after 4000 BCE in the far south of Mesopotamia, near the Persian Gulf. Varied ecologies came together there: soil fertilized by floods for farming, steppes for flocks, and marshes where fish and birds could be hunted. The relative abundance of food enabled some

inhabitants to specialize in crafts, which in turn allowed the settlement to develop on a scale never seen before. The walls of Uruk, at their greatest extent, were more than six miles in circumference, and the city probably had 50,000 or more inhabitants. At the beginning of the third millennium BCE, it was the biggest city in the world. Uruk may have established colonies as well: other cities, often on water routes, from the Mediterranean to areas of modern Iran, were built on similar lines and likely engaged in trade with Uruk. Perhaps these cities supplied materials that were in short supply in Uruk, such as timber and stone.

In place of modest shrines, Uruk had temples—vast complexes of buildings set on platforms, known as **ziggurats**, their walls decorated with colored clay cones set in patterns. The temples administered extensive lands of their own, which were cultivated by a large labor force, its members apparently free, whom the temples paid and fed. Their work sustained the priests and the artisans. The gods, male and female, were imagined in human form and seen as strong-willed and capricious. Artists created stunning statues of them. Some, like An, the sky god, were remote; others, like Innana, the warlike goddess of fertility, engaged directly in human affairs. Their temples were like palaces, with bedrooms, assembly halls, and pleasure gardens where the gods were regaled with feasts and concerts.

Uruk became a center of innovation. The wealth of the city's rulers attracted skillful artisans and supported them as they developed sophisticated arts and crafts for both religious and nonreligious purposes. Sculptors crafted images of rulers as well as gods. They also produced cylinders delicately carved with scenes of humans and animals. These could be rolled across the clay that sealed containers

Ziggurats Religious life in Sumerian cities centered on the large temples called ziggurats. They featured stacked terraces accessible by several sets of steps, often with a shrine at the top. This temple of Nanna, built in Ur around 2100 BCE by King Ur-Nammu, was one of the largest.

and storerooms to assert a person's ownership of the contents. New skills developed: the inhabitants experimented with new ways of fabricating uniform bricks for building and laying out plots of land for cultivation. Large households supported staffs of workers—legally free men and women who were paid for their labor, the scanty records suggest, in food and housing. This seems to have been the condition of most of the ordinary men and women who built the temple walls and grew the crops.

URUK AND THE DEVELOPMENT OF WRITING

Most remarkable, Uruk's inhabitants invented writing. For the first time in human history, people could keep formal records, and thus preserve the memory of their political and economic achievements long after the physical traces of them had been obliterated. It all started, in the fourth millennium BCE and perhaps before, with counters—little clay spheres or tokens marked with symbols of possessions to be inventoried. Throughout Mesopotamia, these were assembled in clay envelopes, which were then inscribed with the number of tokens they contained. The earliest symbolic representations were not as consistent as later writing, and they did not yet rest on coherent abstract understandings of, for example, numbers. The same sign could stand for different numbers of different commodities.

By the beginning of the third millennium BCE, these methods developed into the "Uruk system"—writing in the full sense. Both pictures and abstract symbols represented Sumerian words on the same clay spheres, almost 6,000 of which survive. The scribes who made them used their complex system—comprising more than 1,900 characters—for many purposes, from maintaining receipts to managing account books. They compiled lists of the names of animals, tools, and professions into the first dictionaries, probably to train the professional scribes who were the only ones to master this difficult but powerful early form of writing. Scribes made themselves indispensable to temples and other authorities, and were rewarded accordingly, as one noted: "The scribal art is a good lot, one of wealth and plenty."

The Uruk system was complicated and difficult to use because it is hard to draw lines and curves in clay. Over time, the scribes developed a system of writing that used combinations of wedge shapes, called **cuneiform**, which was both more practical and more abstract. The wedge shapes were used to represent individual sounds and, in combination, whole words, rather than to depict objects. The thousands of surviving tablets from Near Eastern cities preserve everything from treaties and other official

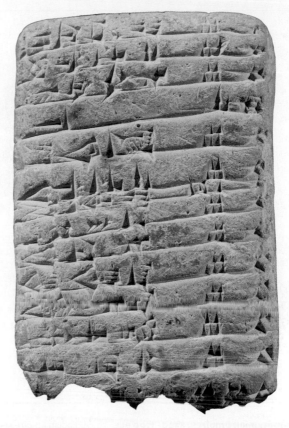

Cuneiform On a clay tablet dating from 2100–2000 BCE, the barley ration allocated to seventeen gardeners was recorded by a scribe using the complex cuneiform writing system.

documents to prayers and epic poems, in Sumerian, Akkadian, and other languages—the work of generations of highly trained scribes, who played central roles in the government of all Near Eastern states.

MESOPOTAMIAN EMPIRES (2300–1700 BCE)

During the third millennium BCE, powerful states formed in the region: Sumer and Akkad, Assyria and the Amorite kingdoms, and Babylon. The earlier city-states of Mesopotamia had competed for resources and clashed when their interests dictated. But Akkad, Assyria, the Amorite kingdoms, and Babylon were different. The rulers of these great empires set out not only to conquer other states but to incorporate them in their own domains, installing their own governors. They amassed precious metals through conquest and tribute, and displayed them lavishly to buttress their claims to power. Above all, they claimed divine status for themselves. Reliefs portrayed emperors wearing

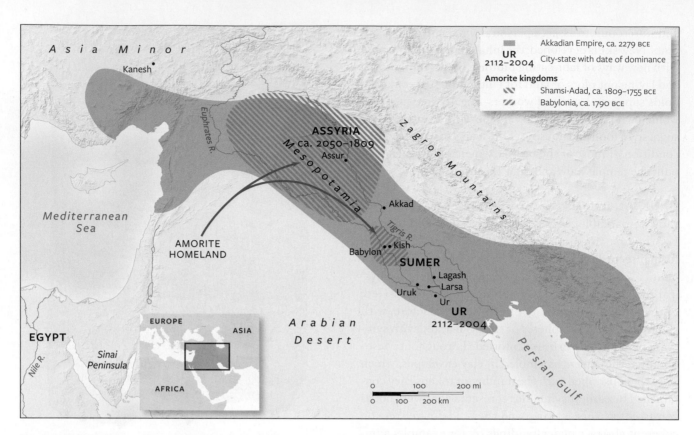

Mesopotamian Empires, 2300–1700 BCE The Akkadian Empire spread from the city of Kish to govern vast territory across Mesopotamia. When the empire collapsed (by 2154 BCE), smaller empires centered on capital cities took shape: Ur in southern Mesopotamia and Assur in Assyria. Some 350 years later, the Amorites came from Syria to establish kingdoms in northern and central Mesopotamia. Economic, political, and military links allowed rulers to control large areas outside their capitals.

the signs of divine status and ascending into the realm of the gods. These states did far more than maintain order and protect cultivation; they were aggressive, fast moving, and unwilling to recognize any limits to their power and authority.

SARGON AND THE AKKADIAN EMPIRE (2334–2112 BCE)

The greatest of the early emperors—Sargon (r. 2334–2279 BCE) of the central Mesopotamian city of Akkad—usurped the throne of the Sumerian city of Kish, and then embarked on a comprehensive program of invasion and conquest. Leading lancers and bowmen who moved far more quickly than the Sumerians with their heavy battle wagons, Sargon defeated them and amassed power across Mesopotamia.

Sargon also seems to have conquered the rulers of Asia Minor and Arabia. He appointed a force of soldiers and administrators, some 5,400 strong, whom he fed every day and on whom he could rely absolutely. His Akkadian Empire ruled Sumeria and maintained diplomatic relations with other lands as far away as the Mediterranean.

He was remembered as a great general who conquered all opponents, destroying one city that opposed him, according to a chronicle, "to the last spot on which a bird could perch." Sargon also replaced Sumerian, the dominant language of the area, with Akkadian, a Semitic language, so far as practical affairs were concerned. (Sumerian continued to be used for religious purposes.) For the first time in known human history, a brilliant military leader had set out, successfully, to build an empire.

UR (2112–2004 BCE)

After Sargon's death in 2279, revolts broke out, and though his sons extended the Akkadian Empire's territory, it collapsed by 2154. For nearly a century, from 2112 to 2004 BCE, the Sumerian city of Ur in the far south of Mesopotamia held dominance. Ur-Nammu, brother of the king of Uruk, made Ur his capital. He claimed to be king "of Sumer and Akkad," and he founded a dynasty, now known as the Third Dynasty of Ur. Like the Sumerian kings, those of Ur claimed divine favor and superhuman abilities: "When I sprang up," a hymn about a later king reads, "muscular as a cheetah, galloping like a thoroughbred ass at full gallop, the favor of the god An brought me joy." The kings of Ur ruled a large state composed of what had formerly been independent cities. Governors, chosen from prominent local families, administered those in the heartland. Others were ruled directly by military garrisons.

The state of Ur was powerful. Each province paid heavy taxes in goods particular to it: grain in one case; wood, reeds, and leather in another. Military provinces were forced to pay tribute in cattle, sheep, and goats. Some of the revenues went to support local governments. More, however, went to the kings, who used their wealth to maintain and extend the canals that irrigated the land. Most labor was legally free, but the state conscripted hundreds of men and women, some to work on the canals year-round, paying them with food and other necessities. The state also maintained substantial armies and a corps of scribes that kept elaborate records of its income, expenses, and diplomatic correspondence.

ASSYRIANS AND AMORITES (2050–1700 BCE)

Yet conditions were not stable. In the middle of the twenty first century BCE, the Assyrians threw off the domination of Ur, whose empire broke up, and established their freedom. Assur, in northern Mesopotamia, became a prosperous merchant city with a distinctive constitution. A council of elders served as a brake on the power of the king of Assur. Even more unusual, every year a citizen was selected by lot to collect the taxes. In much of Mesopotamia, years were named after rulers; in Assur, they were named after this official. The merchants of Assur built family partnerships. Using their own resources, not state support, they spun extensive networks. In the city of Kanesh in central Asia Minor, as far from Assur as Chicago is from New York City, they built their own settlement, where they successfully sold rich fabrics from Mesopotamia. Constant correspondence maintained both trade and family relations across long distances.

For two centuries, the Assyrian kings successfully defended and enlarged their kingdom. But the Amorites, a Semitic pastoral people, came into the land from Syria during the period of Ur's hegemony. Seminomadic, they lived with their flocks of sheep and goats, staying with them in river towns in the summers and moving out into the steppe in the winters. Organized in tribes, the Amorites seemed uncivilized to city dwellers: "He is dressed in sheep's skins; He lives in tents in wind and rain; He doesn't offer sacrifices." Gradually, however, they integrated themselves into southern Mesopotamia, taking up residence in cities as well as in the countryside. In 1809

Standard of Ur This mosaic of shell, limestone, and lapis lazuli buried in a large grave at the Royal Cemetery of Ur around 2550 BCE depicts the soldiers and chariots of Ur.

BCE the Amorite Shamsi-Adad I deposed the native king of Assyria, took his place, and created an empire across northern Mesopotamia.

After the breakup of Sumerian rule in the south, other kingdoms whose rulers bore Amorite names were established throughout Mesopotamia. The Amorites divided large blocks of land devoted to supporting the temples and claimed that they had "freed the inhabitants of cities"—a process that remains mysterious. Larsa and other Amorite kingdoms depended on local tribal leaders to maintain herds and farms and to collect taxes on their behalf. A free-wheeling economy developed in the Amorite cities: individuals bought and sold properties and joined together to invest, for example, in merchant ships that sailed the Tigris and Euphrates Rivers down to the Persian Gulf.

The Amorite kings continued to claim divine status, and in their temples the old gods were worshipped in the traditional way. Slowly—we do not know exactly when or how—the idea grew up that kingship should be transmitted from one semidivine figure to his son, and onward in the direct male line of descent. Dynasties—series of monarchs from the same family—now took shape, and new rulers, especially those whose authority might be shaky, liked to claim that they, too, were descended from an ancient lineage of kings.

In the nineteenth century BCE, an Amorite dynasty

founded the city of Babylon in the center of Mesopotamia. The city rose to great wealth and power, and under Hammurabi in the eighteenth century BCE it became the capital of an empire in its own right. It became, as we will see, one of the principal centers of the distinctive civilization of the ancient Near East, playing a central role in the development of law, religion, and divination.

STATE AND ECONOMY IN THE ANCIENT NEAR EAST

These new states of the ancient Near East mobilized resources on a vast scale. Tens of thousands of tablets record official efforts to build and administer a command economy. They drew together large numbers of workers, not by enslaving them but by requiring them to put in a month or two a year as laborers on state projects such as irrigation systems. Even scribes and other individuals of high status could find themselves forced to provide labor in this way.

Conscripted workers built enormous temples out of durable materials, such as blocks of limestone, which were transported from quarries in the desert to create façades of sufficient strength and dignity. Their lot must have been hard: occasionally individuals or small groups tried to flee rather than work. In addition to conscript labor, slavery was a presence throughout the ancient Near East. Institutions and families held slaves, whose status was clearly lower than that of free people. Official documents assumed that Mesopotamians would not enslave other Mesopotamians, and warned the young against capture by slavers who worked from the mountains to the northeast. Many slaves were captured in war.

New technologies helped the developing states of the region to thrive. The plow adopted at Uruk, which had an automatic feeder to place seeds at proper intervals in the furrows it dug, made the soil of the Fertile Crescent live up to its modern name. The smiths of Mesopotamia became expert at working copper and tin into durable bronze, the material of choice for both weapons and tools. This favorite metal gave its name to the larger historical period in which the societies of the ancient Near East and early Greece took shape. The Bronze Age, as we will see, would last until almost the end of the second millennium BCE. The restless ingenuity of the artisans whom the state employed helped create the splendor of the Mesopotamian states.

These states had more in mind than displaying their wealth and the brilliance of their crafts. They devoted massive resources to supporting military professionals, especially after the rise of the horse-drawn chariot in the sixteenth century BCE. But at the same time, aristocratic families built up vast land holdings, which could escape the control of central authorities. Basic institutions could spin into disorder, as sheer scale and weight pulled them apart. Instability and defeat always threatened. Rulers and diplomats did their best to maintain alliances and respond immediately to threats, but the second duty often canceled the first: "He makes peace with one king"—so a ruler wrote of one of his fellows—"and swears an oath, then he makes peace with another king and swears an oath, then he repudiates the previous king he made peace with, as well as the new king he made peace with." Again and again, assassinations toppled royal dynasties.

NEAR EASTERN RELIGIONS

Mesopotamian cities were sacred as well as political spaces. Near Eastern religions were **polytheistic**—a form of belief and practice that can be hard for many in the West today, used to the exclusive claims of monotheism, to appreciate. Mesopotamian men and women acknowledged multiple gods, whose cults were supported by public rather than individual action. Though more powerful than human beings, these gods were not omnipotent or omniscient: each one carried out particular tasks, and gods and human beings could in some cases conceal their deeds from the divine view. Some gods died, especially those whose function had to do with fertility. Others entered battle on behalf of their supporters—a relief at Lagash shows one god capturing the city's enemies in a net and striking them with a mace. The gods of Mesopotamia were believed to inhabit the statues that represented them in the temples. When a city was defeated and its conquerors carried the statues away as booty, its inhabitants knew that the gods were angry with them and had departed.

As peoples traded goods, migrated, and fought, they began to notice one another's gods and temples, and to compare them—perhaps the first efforts to understand the universe. Polytheism is usually flexible: a common response to an encounter with a new and attractive god was to adopt his or her worship, enlarging one's pantheon. As a strategy this could prove especially helpful to monarchs trying, as so many did, to integrate foreign peoples into their expanding states.

DIVINATION Most Mesopotamian religions centered on **divination**—formal ways of predicting the future, especially that of the ruler and his people. With state power precarious and invasion often threatening, rulers sought ways to gain knowledge of what was to come, and priests did their best to supply this. They imagined the universe as a complex, buzzing web of messages about the future. Nothing was accidental, everything was predetermined, and the gods continually provided signs that revealed the future to those who could interpret them. Every time an animal was sacrificed, the form of its liver told informed interpreters what the kingdom could expect. In practice, interpreters often disagreed about particular signs, and temples competed to offer the most accurate predictions.

FROM ASTROLOGY TO ASTRONOMY Over a period of about a thousand years, from roughly 1800 BCE onward, Mesopotamian priests and scribes developed a sophisticated form of astronomy. From atop their ziggurats, they charted the stars and worked out that the motions of the sun, moon, and planets repeated themselves. In the belief that the motions of the stars also provided information about the future, interpreters at first declared what eclipses and the planetary positions portended for the kingdom as a whole. Eventually they decided that the heavens also determined the fates of individuals. In the fifth century BCE, diviners began compiling collections of individual horoscopes—charts of the positions of the planets at the day and time of a person's birth. The horoscopes that still flourish in newspapers and on the Web are a living remnant of an ancient Near Eastern vision of the universe. So, too, is the astronomy that scientists practice in observatories and teach in universities. The first quantitative science in history was born out of what today looks like superstition.

RULES OF CONDUCT: HAMMURABI'S CODE

It is not only agriculture, pottery, and mathematical science that we have inherited from the ancient Near East. For all the chaos and mutual distrust, the rulers of ancient Mesopotamia created fundamental features of Western political and administrative practice. From Uruk on, scribes developed systems for recording city revenues and expenses in publicly archived documents. Working together, rulers and scribes also recorded formal rules for governing conduct in public and private, with provisions for enforcement and punishment of violators.

Around 1754 BCE Hammurabi, the sixth king of Babylon, set out a code of specific statements about justice, couched in the everyday language of ordinary people. This **Code of Hammurabi** was probably not meant to govern the conduct of courts—contemporary legal documents do not refer to it—but to serve as a record of the ways in which Hammurabi had pursued justice. Some 300 laws and cases were copied on clay tablets and on at least one basalt stele, a tall stone slab. In this monumental form, the code makes a claim to divine sanction. Hammurabi himself appears in a relief sculpture at the top of the stone, wearing a royal headdress and showing reverence to the sun-god, who brings him his rod and ring, the symbols of authority. Modesty was not Hammurabi's vice: in an inscription, he claimed that he had led his people "into green pastures" and prevented them from ever having to worry.

Hammurabi's pronouncements were not meant to

Hammurabi's Code The top of this stele, or stone slab, from the eighteenth century BCE is a portrait of Hammurabi seated on a throne, receiving his rod and ring, the insignia of his power, from the sun-god. The text of the Code is carved in cuneiform at the bottom.

serve as a form of legislation in the modern sense. In normal Babylonian life, professional judges dealt with civil actions, such as lawsuits over property, for a fee, and judges working with a second body of elders presided over serious criminal cases. Verdicts imposing the death penalty—which was given for crimes ranging from burglary and encroaching on the king's highway to incest and adultery—could be appealed to the king, who had an absolute right to bestow pardons. There was not much place for a comprehensive legal code. But the fragments of earlier laws that archaeologists have unearthed make clear that Hammurabi followed Babylonian tradition when he tried to show how actions should be connected with their consequences.

A ruler with a passion for detail, Hammurabi examined relations between husbands and wives, sellers and buyers, masters and slaves. His code incorporated a strictly hierarchical vision of society. Individuals were classified, and penalties assessed, by social standing: "If anyone strikes the body of a man higher in rank than he, he shall receive sixty blows with an ox-whip in public"; "If a freeborn man strikes the body of another freeborn man of equal rank, he shall pay one gold mina"; "If the slave of a freedman strikes the body of a freedman, his ear shall be cut off." Hammurabi's rules made no evident allowances for mitigating circumstances: "If anyone commits a robbery and is caught, he shall be put to death." But by providing procedures for investigation when the truth of a matter was in doubt, they showed a clear concern for justice.

One could, Hammurabi believed, also do harm to others by engaging the help of malevolent supernatural powers. Fortunately, nature itself could be enlisted to determine whether this had occurred. If one man accused another of putting him under a spell, the accused had to dive into the sacred river. If he drowned, his accuser could take his house. But if he survived, "his accuser shall be put to death. He that plunged into the sacred river shall appropriate the house of him that accused." Perjurers should be liable to appropriate punishment, even if it could not be proved that they had deliberately lied: "If a man has borne false witness in a trial, or has not established the statement that he has made, if that case be a capital trial, that man shall be put to death." Proposed penalties for corrupt officials were severe: large fines and expulsion from office.

Hammurabi had every reason to portray himself as a defender of divine justice. How his subjects responded to these enactments, and how far they were put into practical effect, we cannot know, since he himself provides the little bit of evidence that survives. But it seems clear that Hammurabi, in his passion to represent himself as a just ruler and a servant of the gods, began the process of creating what we now know as legal codes.

EVERYDAY LIFE IN THE ANCIENT NEAR EAST

Like the Code of Hammurabi, much of the evidence of the Mesopotamian archives takes the form of official documents, which tell us more about how kings and elites wished others to behave than whether poor people and slaves actually did as they were supposed to. But enough documents survive to enable us to make some contact with the individual men and women who lived and worked in the region's sophisticated urban societies. Many of them are letters written not by the individuals whose voices they preserve, but by professional scribes following instructions or taking dictation.

VOICES Officials write to subordinates as they try to maintain order and justice: "I have written you repeatedly to bring here the criminal and all the robbers, but you have not brought them here nor have you even sent me word. And so fires started by the robbers are (still raging) and ravaging the countryside. . . . I am holding you responsible for the crimes which are committed in the country." Merchants appear, looking for accurate commercial intelligence and working with partners to avoid losses: "When I stayed there, they (two debtors) told me the following: 'No sale can be made on the market.' Today I hear, however, that many sales are being made on the market. Therefore, make them pay the silver."

Women speak, too—for example, a Sumerian who casts herself on the mercy of her lover: "When I saw you recently, I was just as glad to see you as I was when (long ago) I . . . saw (for the first time) the face of my Lady (the goddess Aja). And you too, my brother, were as glad to see me as I to see you. You said: 'I am going to stay for ten days.' . . . But you left suddenly and I was almost insane for three days. . . . I was more pleased with you than I was ever with anybody else." Even a female slave writes to her master to beg for help because the baby she has been carrying is dead: "May it please my master (to do something) lest I die. Come visit me and let me see the face of my master!"

WORK Many of these men and women worked in the palaces, as slaves captured in war or inherited by members of royal families. Every court needed finely woven and embroidered clothes for rulers and courtiers. Groups of women spun wool and wove it into cloth. Men provided the wool that the women worked, and likely carried out other processes, such as dyeing and finishing the cloth. Women also ground grain, baked bread, and prepared cooling drinks in the summer. Others might serve as entertainers or—in at least one documented case—as a doctor.

Outside the palaces, in the cities, the citizens who inhabited mud-brick houses were legally free and maintained impressively active lives as artisans and traders. Women came to marriage with dowries, carefully listed in binding documents that enabled them to reclaim their property if their husbands died or divorced them. Dowries might include household equipment such as beds and chairs, livestock, or wool. In many merchant households, women and men collaborated effectively. Women bought raw materials and oversaw the making of cloth, while their husbands undertook long treks, either in caravans carrying loads of wool and tin or on ships bearing cargoes for exchange as far away as Bahrain. There they traded grain, wool, silver, and resin for tin and copper. Poets celebrated the island city of Bahrain as a paradise where the ferries ran all night and no servant ever dared to empty dirty bathwater into the street.

A FOUNDATIONAL EPIC: GILGAMESH

In Babylon, which fostered the arts, erotic sculpture and poetry flourished. Here an unknown author of the time of Hammurabi composed the oldest epic that we have—the story of Gilgamesh, a king with almost divine powers who travels the universe, refuses to marry a goddess, and kills the Bull of Heaven when she sends it to avenge the slight. After his traveling companion dies, Gilgamesh sets out on another long and dangerous voyage, in the hope of finding the secret of immortality. He fails—but the failure is a great lesson in itself, since his journey gives him knowledge of the human condition in all its tragic limitations.

Like the Code of Hammurabi, the **Epic of Gilgamesh** was a compilation—a new, comprehensive version, written in Akkadian, of shorter tales that had originally circulated in Sumerian. Both reveal the extraordinary extent to which scribal culture flourished in Babylon: though most scribes spent their lives composing contracts and administrative records, others wrote and rewrote hymns, stories, and religious texts. Many of these were lost for thousands of years because of continued political turmoil. As cities were abandoned, the scribes' tablets were left behind, to be rediscovered and deciphered only in the nineteenth and twentieth centuries. They provide further proof—if any is needed—that central elements of Western history have their roots in the earliest history of the ancient Near East.

THE HITTITES AND THE ASSYRIAN EMPIRE (1700–1200 BCE)

The Babylonian Empire of Hammurabi briefly dominated Mesopotamia, but dissolved soon after its creator died in 1750 BCE. Alliances between the rulers of the major Amorite kingdoms shifted endlessly, as they challenged one another for supremacy. A revived Assyria conquered much of the territory that had belonged to Babylon, and though the Amorite dynasty retained control of Babylon for a time, it ruled little more than the city.

New peoples—including some who spoke Indo-European languages, which are directly related to the ancestor language of modern English—entered central Asia Minor. Though it is not clear if the Hittites were originally one of these peoples, they adopted the region's Indo-European language as the official language of their court and administration. Their first kingdom took shape around a capital in Hattusa in the eighteenth century BCE and after. A conglomeration of vassal states, the Hittite Empire shifted borders constantly.

While the Hittites engaged in trade and esteemed their merchants highly, they were known above all as fierce and effective warriors. Their armies were a mixture of infantry, drawn from the free Hittite population with added levies from neighboring states, and charioteers. Three-man teams rode and shot their bows from two-wheeled chariots, which were quick but required great skill to manage. These men became professional soldiers, elaborately trained and bound by oaths to their rulers. They learned to fight at night, and when necessary knew how to attack and conquer walled cities using battering rams. And although the Hittites pioneered the forging of iron, a harder metal that would eventually replace bronze for use in weaponry, they used the results mostly in ceremonies, and continued to make their own weapons from bronze.

In 1595 BCE the Hittites conquered Babylon, which they sacked again in 1531, and their allies the Kassites took over rule of the city. Although urban growth slowed under their rule, the Kassites reconstructed older cities across Babylonia and even built a new capital, Dur-Kurigalzu (Fortress of Kurigalzu), with an enormous central palace and temple, in the far north. After 1500 the Hittite kingdom

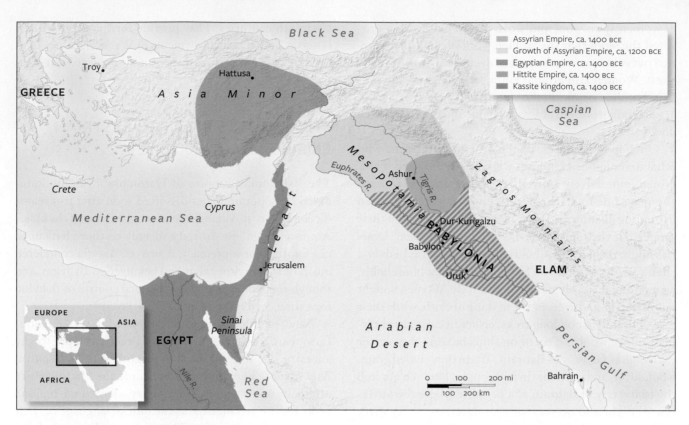

Mesopotamia to the Bronze Age Crisis, ca. 1400–1200 BCE In the latter half of the second millennium BCE, powerful empires covered a wider area of the Near East: from the Egyptian Empire in the west, stretching all the way to the Levant; to the Hittite Empire in Asia Minor, and their allies the Kassites in Babylonia; to the powerful Assyrian Empire, which by 1200 BCE controlled all of Mesopotamia.

entered a phase of weakness, but in the next century it revived and acted as a great empire.

More and more, however, it was the Assyrian Empire that dominated the area. Ashur-uballit I (r. 1365–1330 BCE) began the process of recovery and expansion. The Assyrians, like the Hittites, made effective use of the chariot in warfare. By the thirteenth century BCE, they had repeatedly prevailed over the Hittites and conquered Kassite Babylon. Assyrian rulers built enormous new palaces and temples at their capital of Ashur and created massive new cities on the Tigris and elsewhere. Their royal servants, rewarded with grants of land, became an aristocracy, while free farmers were largely forced into slavery.

THE BRONZE AGE CRISIS (12TH CENTURY BCE)

At the beginning of the twelfth century BCE, the Near East—like other cultures of the time—entered what historians call the Bronze Age Crisis. The causes of the crisis are controversial: though there is evidence of earthquakes and drought, for example, it is not clear that either had dramatic effects. Those who lived through these great transformations, and others who looked back on them in later centuries, point to disruptive movements of populations. Egyptian observers in the first half of the thirteenth century BCE recorded the attacks of "sea peoples" whom no one seemed able to resist. These powerful invaders—including the Philistines and other nations, their place of origin as uncertain as their reasons for migration—fought their way across the Near East, and continued doing so in the twelfth century. Layers of dateable ash show that cities around the region, including the historical city of Troy, fell to the invaders. The Hittite kingdom collapsed. But the Assyrian Empire, the dominant power in its region, survived and flourished. Nebuchadnezzar I of Babylon (r. 1125–1104 BCE) defeated a rival power to the east, the Elamites, only to be defeated by the Assyrians. Thereafter Assyria dominated Babylon for centuries, even as new Semitic peoples entered and settled in what had been Babylonian territory.

LIFE AND DEATH IN EGYPT (3000–332 BCE)

The states of the ancient Near East were not the only great powers and cultures to take shape in the years after 3000 BCE. Egypt was connected to the Near East by the ecology of the Fertile Crescent and by constant contact, which took every form from brutal warfare to delicate diplomacy. Like the Near Eastern states, Egypt was ruled, from the beginning of the third millennium, by monarchs—the kings, later known as pharaohs—who were thought to have the gods' support and themselves to be divine. Like the Assyrians and Babylonians, the Egyptians built vast temples and other ceremonial buildings. Like them, too, they kept elaborate records using a difficult form of writing practiced by specialized scribes. And like the Near Eastern states, Egypt looked back to origins so ancient that no record described them.

UNIFICATION

In other respects, though, Egypt was distinctive—even unique. The king unified two very different worlds: southern or Upper Egypt, where a narrow band of agricultural land stretched along the Nile River, surrounded by immense deserts; and northern or Lower Egypt, where the Nile branched out into its delta and watered a vast territory of fields and marshes. At some point around 3000 BCE, as the Egyptians themselves remembered, the Nile Valley was fully settled. Mass immigration from Upper Egypt brought peoples from the south into the fertile lands of the Delta, in Lower Egypt.

Somehow—we do not know how—kings took advantage of Egypt's unique topography and unified these peoples. Their achievements were celebrated in powerful images: for example, the Narmer palette (ca. 3000 BCE), a rock slab used to hold pigments for painting, is inscribed on one side with an image of King Narmer the Hawk wearing an Upper Egyptian crown and leading an attack. The reverse shows his soldiers marching and enemy leaders being beheaded. Although there is no evidence that Narmer actually conquered Lower Egypt, the powerful imagery of the palette—which must have taken a skilled artisan hundreds of hours to carve and polish—suggests that to Narmer and his followers, he was the aggressive ruler of a unified country. In the lower part of the Delta, large settlements took shape, with warehouses, threshing

Narmer Palette Dating from the thirty-first century BCE, this large ceremonial palette depicts King Narmer of Upper Egypt conquering his enemies, perhaps a representation of the mythical battles that unified Upper and Lower Egypt. Archaeologists have interpreted some symbols on the palette as the earliest form of Egyptian hieroglyphs.

floors, and slaughterhouses large enough to support a massive population. Eventually—it is not known exactly when—Memphis, at the mouth of the Delta, became the capital of a united Egypt.

A DURABLE MONARCHY

The Egyptian monarchy survived, with intervals of disorder, through thirty dynasties that lasted almost 3,000 years. By the time of the Old Kingdom (2649–2150 BCE), the Egyptians were already building the enormous pyramids for which they are still famous. Through the Middle Kingdom (2030–1640 BCE) and the New Kingdom (1550–1070 BCE), the monarchy remained mostly united. Egypt's strong social and cultural unity prevailed even when a foreign people, the Hyksos, conquered the country around 1650 BCE, and when the pharaoh Akhenaten briefly

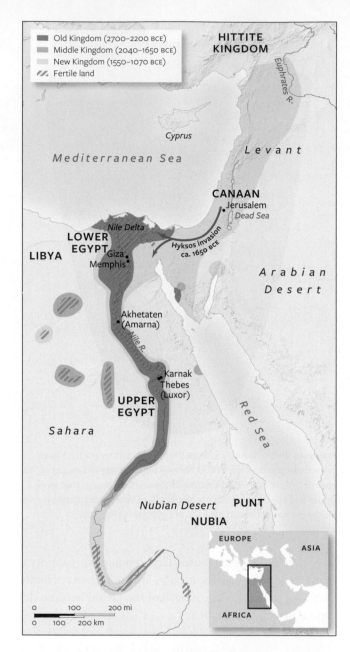

Ancient Egypt, 2700–1070 BCE In Egypt, population was centered in fertile areas along the Nile—in the kingdoms of Lower Egypt near the Nile Delta and in Upper Egypt farther upstream, which were unified in 2700 BCE. The Egyptians then spread north as far as the Euphrates during the Middle Kingdom period and farther up the Nile during the New Kingdom, despite challenges such as the invasion of the Hyksos people in 1650 BCE.

introduced a monotheistic religion in the fourteenth century. During the early Bronze Age Crisis, the Egyptians fought off the Sea Peoples again and again. Rameses III (r. ca. 1186–1155 BCE) conducted three victorious campaigns against them, but at great cost: he was assassinated and his successors proved weak. Attacks by Libyan and other

African peoples, and a revolt by Canaanite peoples whom the Egyptians had conquered, took a further toll. Yet even in the centuries of relative weakness that followed, Egypt continued to challenge the power of Assyria and to maintain its own religious and artistic traditions.

Amid its remarkable longevity, the Egyptian state experienced change. After the collapse of the Old Kingdom, power passed to local governors and priests. One reason that the kings of the subsequent Middle Kingdom built extraordinarily lavish temples and tombs was that they had to convince important local officials to accept them as divinely appointed monarchs and to recognize their prerogatives. But even in Egypt's last period of native rule (664–332 BCE), which was interrupted twice when the Persian Empire (a powerful state that emerged in modern Iran) conquered and occupied it, the Egyptians saw their land as the oldest and grandest of states, favored by the gods. They passionately argued that their traditions had lasted seamlessly over the millennia—and never more passionately than after they had suffered a defeat. In the first millennium BCE, when Egypt was conquered by Assyria in the seventh century and then by Persia in the sixth and fourth, their sculptures of pharaohs made clear that the kingdom had not suffered any substantial change. More even than the ancient Near East, Egypt offered a powerful political and social model: a single land, vast in extent and varied in its terrain, unified under the rule of a single king who enjoyed divine sanction.

THE NILE AND EGYPTIAN POWER

The Egyptian state had to wrest food for its people from an environment that could be both generous and unpredictable. The Nile made agriculture possible in Egypt by annually flooding and fertilizing the land along both banks in the late summer. But the extent of the flooding and how much land was fertilized varied from year to year. As the story of Joseph in the biblical book of Genesis makes clear, Egypt's rulers and inhabitants faced lean as well as fat years, and had to prepare for them. For much of the third millennium, the kings and their officers addressed these problems by centralizing the state and organizing the life of its people. The kings installed their own chosen followers as local administrators, heads of temples, and military commanders, and extended their command down into every sphere of life.

Egypt's officials took action to reinforce the operations of nature. They built canals to move the Nile floodwaters more effectively, and dug basins to retain water in the plains. The laborers who did this work, as slaves or free

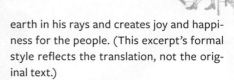

RELIGION AND NATURE

The ancient Mesopotamian and Egyptian civilizations had widely disparate ideas about religion, especially as it pertained to the natural world. In Mesopotamia the Tigris and Euphrates Rivers flooded unpredictably. In some years, flooding damaged crops and cities; in others, the flood was not sufficient and crops could not grow. This irregularity led Mesopotamians to a pervasive feeling that poor floods meant they were being punished by the gods for their misdeeds. Egyptians, on the other hand, saw themselves as blessed by their gods with a predictable and regularly flooding Nile. Egyptians generally believed that their deities wanted to help and protect them by providing what they needed to thrive and prosper. Expressing less anxiety than the Mesopotamians, the Egyptians composed hymns and poems lauding the benevolence of their gods.

Poem of the Righteous Sufferer

Mesopotamian people were constantly trying to determine how best to please their gods to avoid punishment in the form of natural disasters or illnesses. This source, from Mesopotamian wisdom literature (ca. 1700 BCE), illustrates this uncertainty and fear.

I survived to the next year; the appointed time passed.

I turn around, but it is bad, very bad;

My ill luck increases and I cannot find what is right.

I called to my god, but he did not show his face,

I prayed to my goddess, but she did not raise her head.

Even the diviner with his divination could not make a prediction,

And the interpreter of dreams with his libation [offering of wine] could not elucidate my case…

Like one who has not made libations to his god,

Nor invoked his goddess when he ate,

Does not make prostrations nor recognize (the necessity of) bowing down…

Who has even neglected holy days, and ignored festivals,

Who was negligent and did not observe the gods' rites…

And abandoned his goddess by not bringing a flour offering…

What is good for oneself may be offense to one's god,

What in one's own heart seems despicable may be proper to one's god.

Who can know the will of the gods in heaven?

Who can understand the plans of the underworld gods?

He who was alive yesterday is dead today…

Debilitating Disease is let loose upon me;

An Evil Wind has blown (from the) horizon,

Headache has sprung up from the surface of the underworld…

(They all) came on me together,

(They struck) my head, they enveloped my skull…

My symptoms are beyond the exorcist,

And my omens have confused the diviner.

The exorcist could not diagnose the nature of my sickness,

Nor could the diviner set a time limit on my illness.

My god has not come to the rescue nor taken me by the hand;

My goddess has not shown pity on me nor gone by my side.

Hymn of Praise to Ra

In this hymn (ca. 1550 BCE) from the Book of the Dead, an ancient Egyptian funerary text, the sun-god Ra is portrayed as the "god of life" and "king of the gods," who bathes the earth in his rays and creates joy and happiness for the people. (This excerpt's formal style reflects the translation, not the original text.)

Homage to thee, O thou glorious Being, thou who art dowered [with all sovereignty]…. When thou risest in the horizon of heaven, a cry of joy cometh forth to thee from the mouths of all peoples. O thou beautiful Being, thou dost renew thyself in thy season in the form of the Disk within thy mother Hathor; therefore in every place every heart swelleth with joy at thy rising, for ever. The regions of the North and South come to thee with homage, and send forth acclamations at thy rising in the horizon of heaven; thou illuminest the two lands with rays of turquoise light. O Ra…the divine man-child, the heir of eternity, self-begotten and self-born, king of earth, prince of the Tuat [the Other World]…O thou god of life, thou lord of love, all men live when thou shinest, thou art crowned king of the gods…. Those who are in thy following sing unto thee with joy and bow down their foreheads to the earth when they meet thee, thou lord of heaven, thou lord of earth, thou king of Right and Truth, thou lord of eternity, thou prince of everlastingness, thou sovereign of all the gods, thou god of life, thou creator of eternity, thou maker of heaven wherein thou art firmly established! The company of the gods rejoice at thy rising, the earth is glad when it beholdeth thy rays; the people that have been long dead come forth with cries of joy to see thy beauties every day.

QUESTIONS FOR ANALYSIS

1. In "Poem of the Righteous Sufferer," what are some of the actions the writer takes to placate the gods?
2. In "Hymn of Praise to Ra," how is the sun-god Ra portrayed as a life-giver?
3. What are the contrasting religious ideas about the world and the gods evident in these two sources?

Sources: Robert D. Biggs, trans., *The Ancient Near East, Volume II: A New Anthology of Texts and Pictures* (Princeton, NJ: 1975); E. A. Wallace Budge, trans., *The Book of the Dead: The Chapters of Coming Forth by Day* (London: 1898), pp. 10–11.

Nile Agriculture Egyptian agriculture was state-planned and highly organized. In this wall painting from a late-fifteenth-century BCE tomb, surveyors measure a wheat crop to determine whether it can be harvested. A couple offers gifts to the surveyors, and a scribe holding a palette waits to record the measurements.

conscripts, suffered terribly: many skeletons show slipped disks, teeth ground down by stony bread, and poor nutrition. Yet by the beginning of the third millennium, agriculture in the Nile Valley was immensely productive. Its regular, cyclical work fed masses of stonecutters, scribes, potters, and other craftsmen while they labored on the large projects thought appropriate for divine kings, such as the immense tombs on the Giza Plateau.

Great Pyramids Towering over the landscape, the vast pyramids at Giza are a testament to the wealth and power of the Egyptian kings.

THE PYRAMIDS OF GIZA By the middle of the third millennium BCE, it must have seemed as if the king of Egypt ruled the universe. This sense of cosmic power was reflected in the kings' greatest projects: the pyramids of Giza. Egyptian technology, less inventive than that of the Mesopotamians, boasted relatively few machines. Yet the wealth and power of the Egyptian state made it possible to muster the enormous teams of workers that created these immense structures. The sides of these great tombs were aligned precisely on north-south and east-west axes, staking a claim for the relation between the ruler's power and accomplishments and the order of the cosmos itself.

EGYPTIAN WRITING

In Egypt, perhaps thanks to the Sumerian example, symbols that first appeared in art were recast early in the third millennium BCE as the characters of a complex, expressive written language. These symbols played many roles: they represented the sounds of individual characters, stood for whole words and parts of words, and clarified the meanings of ambiguous terms. The Egyptians used these characters—which the Greeks later called **hieroglyphs** ("sacred carvings")—to inscribe the great monuments that they began to construct during this period.

A second form of writing called hieratic—more cursive than the formal hieroglyphs, with characters connected as they were written—was often used to compose the texts of books on **papyrus**. This writing material, made from reeds that grew along the Nile, became the standard not only in Egypt but throughout the ancient Mediterranean world. The oldest surviving surgical text, which describes the sophisticated operations carried out by Egyptian surgeons, was written on papyrus as early as 1600 BCE. Different forms of hieratic writing were used for administrative documents and for literary works.

Although Egypt was a highly sophisticated society, literacy remained confined to limited groups, and literature tended to be their exclusive property. Like the writing of the Mesopotamian scribes, hieroglyphs and hieratic script were difficult to master. They could not even be read without the formal training scribes gained in schools. Even those monarchs who dictated their words for preservation were often illiterate. In the seventh century BCE and after, a much simpler system of writing known as demotic ("popular") script was devised for keeping official records and other practical purposes.

EGYPTIAN RELIGION

Egyptian religion, like that of the Mesopotamian states, was polytheistic and public. Egyptians believed that the falcon-headed Re or Ra, the god of the sun, created all life. With Horus he ruled the world and protected the Egyptian kings. The jackal-headed Anubis presided over the judgment of the dead. Isis, the powerful female deity, was connected with the giving and preservation of life, and she protected women in childbirth. These and other gods were worshipped in the state temples. They were also seen as the protectors of the individual kings, not only in this life but in the next, for Egyptians envisioned their monarchs as enjoying a new life after death in a separate realm.

The pyramids of Giza were dedicated to commemorating dead kings and, even more, to protecting them and the retinues and goods interred with them for use in the world of the gods. The elaborate techniques—as complex as the surgical ones—by which the Egyptians preserved bodies from decay, turning them into mummies, were inspired by this fascination with death. More than in any other society known to history, Egypt's rulers continued, over the millennia, to see life above all as a preparation for death—a second life that would last much longer and, ultimately, matter far more than life on earth.

Hieroglyphs This papyrus, dating from around 1600 BCE, is the world's oldest surviving surgical text. Written in cursive hieratic script, with the main text in black and explanatory notes in red, it details forty-eight kinds of injury and how to treat them.

ROYALTY AND VIRTUE IN THE MIDDLE KINGDOM

From early on, Egyptian kings professed that their absolute duty was to maintain a just order in society and the state—*ma'at* was the term both for justice and for the goddess who represented it. During the Middle Kingdom, when royal authority had to be reestablished, the kings referred increasingly to ideals like *ma'at* to prove that their power was legitimate. Like their predecessors in the Old Kingdom, the Middle Kingdom rulers built great temples and necropolises (cities of the dead) that established their power in the civil and cosmic orders. But they relied more and more on elaborate official rituals and public records to convey a new vision of what royalty and virtue meant.

Some rulers exemplified this vision through their skill and independence. Hatshepsut was the strong-minded queen who took a throne name and ruled Egypt for more than twenty years early in the fifteenth century BCE. She built a massive palace and new temples at Karnak, near Luxor in Upper Egypt. Hatshepsut sent expeditions to Nubia, in what is now southern Egypt and northern Sudan. She traded with the mysterious land of Punt in the Red Sea, and with Cyprus and the Levant. But even this steely woman warrior had to manipulate the symbols of rulership, such as the beard she wore in some official sculptures, to maintain her power. (In other images she appears as a beautiful woman.) After her death, her charms ceased to work. Her monuments were desecrated at the orders of one of her successors, and her name was erased from public inscriptions—a fate that would have horrified any Egyptian ruler.

Kingship and virtue drew closer together with changes in Egyptian visions of the afterlife. In the Old Kingdom, kings and priests imagined that rulers would live on after death, but in their tombs on earth. In the Middle Kingdom, by contrast, rulers and their officials treated the afterlife as taking place in the realm of the gods. And the nature of one's afterlife would depend on the life that he or she had led. Each individual would be judged after death—and, if successful, vindicated against death itself. During this period, the god Osiris became prominent in Egyptian religion as the ruler of the underworld. His myth held that he was murdered by his brother, but then brought back to life by the goddess Isis. This god of regeneration represented the possibility of a spiritual rebirth for the virtuous.

Rulers and officials now had to demonstrate that they had disciplined their lives to the pursuit of virtue. Epitaphs from the Middle Kingdom period reveal this new commitment in the ways that they describe particular careers. Officials boasted that they had provided grain for widows and orphans, given wise advice to those who asked their counsel, and protected the land of Egypt. Yet

virtuous conduct alone was not enough. Motives mattered, too. Even great men and women must demonstrate, as their actions were weighed against ma'at in the cosmic scales, that they had been wholly dedicated to the pursuit of good ends. As one official carefully explained:

> My heart it was that urged me
> To do [my duty] in accordance with its instructions.
> It is for me an excellent testimony,
> Its instructions have I not violated,
> For I feared to trespass against its directions
> And therefore have I thrived mightily.

RELIGIOUS CHANGE IN THE NEW KINGDOM

In the first centuries of Egyptian history, only the ruler could aspire to union with the gods after death. During the Middle Kingdom (2030–1640 BCE), however, burials of many kinds were equipped with "coffin texts"—guides to life after death. Even individuals who did not belong to the court elite came to see the god Osiris as a kind of personal savior and to judge themselves and their careers by their success—so far as they could estimate it—in earning an afterlife.

For all its rich ritual, the Egyptian religious order could be burdensome. It demanded a life lived without feeling excessive desire or showing partiality, and it exerted pressure to find a god and win his or her favor. It provoked at least one great protest, led by the Middle Kingdom pharaoh Akhenaten in the fourteenth century BCE. When Akhenaten took responsibility for the divine and human order, he dismissed the ancient gods and all their works. Only the sun, he claimed, ruled the universe, and its only role was to provide the world with light. Akhenaten created a new capital city called Akhetaten (now Amarna), built new temples, and wrote new liturgies. When he died, he and his teachings were suppressed and literally removed from public memory by the destruction of many monuments and inscriptions that recorded what he had done. In this way, the dense and complex Egyptian religion successfully repelled the effort of the first great reformer in Western religious tradition to transform it.

EGYPTIAN SOCIETY

Life in ancient Egypt revolved around the Nile. Egyptian farmers used the fertile soil of the Delta to grow the barley, wheat, and other cereals needed for making bread and beer, as well as fruits, beans, and salad vegetables.

Egyptian Deities Representations of gods and goddesses in tombs, such as this relief of the goddess Isis, granted protection and safe passage to the afterlife for interred rulers.

EGYPTIAN FUNERARY STELES

Egyptian funerary steles were upright slabs placed as monuments in burial chambers. Through the period of the New Kingdom (1550–1070 BCE), they were carved in stone. Later steles, such as this one, carved around 946–712 BCE, were made of wood. Their purpose is still uncertain, but they may have served to immortalize the spirit of the deceased.

This stele commemorates a noblewoman supplicating Re-Harakhty, a form of the ancient Egyptian sun-god. Her sheer gown, trimmed in ornate detail, reveals her body, ideal according to the standards of Egyptian society. Her headdress of perfumed beeswax and a water lily demonstrate her wealth and high status. She pours a cup of wine on a table laden with food with one hand and raises the other in greeting and salute to a seated Re-Harakhty, who is taller than she is standing. The inscription behind them asks that the god present the food to Osiris, the god of the underworld, so that the noblewoman's spirit will be provided with the food it needs to survive in the afterlife.

This funerary stele portrays how Egyptians used the material aspects of their lives, such as clothing and food, to help them understand and navigate timeless, eternal questions of life and death.

QUESTIONS FOR ANALYSIS

1. How does this stele convey the noblewoman's social status?
2. What does the stele show about the relationship between the ancient Egyptians and their gods?
3. What does the noblewoman's request reveal about how ancient Egyptians understood the afterlife?

Irrigation systems kept the water from flooding specialized gardens and destroying the medicinal plants and other valuable flora that they contained.

The river was vital in other ways as well. The papyrus reeds that grew in the Nile were harvested and cut into long strips, which were then hammered into a smooth, durable writing material. Men were primarily responsible for this sort of outdoor work, toiling on the teams of builders and artisans that the kings mobilized for their projects. In the sandy soil of the upper Nile the Egyptians grew flax, a tall plant with extremely strong fibers. Once the flax was harvested and boiled, the fibers could be extracted. Men wound them into rope, and women, working indoors, carded the fibers and spun them into yarn. Both men and women worked in large-scale shops to make linen, a delicate fabric—normally white and often patterned—that was perfect for clothing in a hot, dry climate. Egyptians used it for many other purposes as well, including wrapping mummies.

The life of most workers was hard. Even those who worked directly for the kings lived in long rows of tiny, one-room houses, sleeping—probably—on the roofs. The linen weavers, male or female, crouching before their looms on little stools, suffered discomfort and other indignities. The words of an Egyptian text reveal much about attitudes toward gender as well as working conditions: "The weaver inside the weaving house is more wretched than a woman. His knees are drawn up against his belly. He cannot breathe the air. If he wastes a single day without weaving, he is beaten with 50 whip lashes. He has to give food to the doorkeeper to allow him to come out to the daylight." Vast quantities of linen were produced by these brutally efficient fabrication centers.

A DISTINCTIVE ORDER

Egypt astonished ancient visitors with its vast scale, enormous wealth, and immense ceremonial buildings. It offered a distinctive model of political and social order. Egypt sent expeditions to Nubia seeking cattle and slaves and intervened at times in politics in the Levant, but it was generally more oriented toward feeding its huge population and creating great temples and tombs than to conquering other lands—the enterprise that occupied so much of the energies of the Near Eastern states. Egypt often served as a target for its more aggressive neighbors. Most strikingly, in the Middle Kingdom period it taught its inhabitants, as we have seen, the powerful idea that individuals are responsible for their actions and will be rewarded or punished systematically for them—an idea in

sharp contrast with the determinist vision of the universe represented by the diviners and astrologers of the Near East. Strange though Egypt seemed, and sometimes vulnerable, it was also a brilliant experiment in social order and human values.

THE NEAR EAST: GREAT POWERS AND A DISTINCTIVE PEOPLE (1100–330 BCE)

Until almost the middle of the first millennium BCE, the great powers of the Mediterranean world continued to be located in Egypt and Mesopotamia. After sharing in the collapse of the Near Eastern powers in the twelfth century, the Assyrians, in northern Mesopotamia, reemerged in the eleventh. Their kings became the rulers of a mighty military empire that dominated much of Mesopotamia. Great military leaders like Shalmaneser III (r. 858–824 BCE) led organized, effective campaigns. The states that had succeeded the Hittites, and other states as distant as the Levant, were conquered and governed as provinces of a new Assyrian Empire.

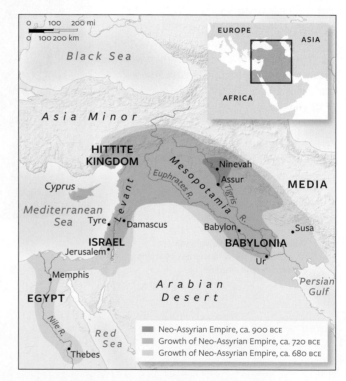

Expansion of the Neo-Assyrian Empire, ca. 900–680 BCE
Successful military campaigns propelled the Neo-Assyrian Empire. From the royal palaces at Assur and Nineveh, kings appointed governors to provinces as far away as Israel and Egypt.

WOMEN AND INHERITANCE

In ancient Egypt, women had certain legal rights, including the right of inheritance. A woman's inheritance was at least her dowry plus one-third of the property gained during the marriage. We know this from reading legal texts, which give a glimpse into women's rights and familial relationships. These wills from two brothers were recorded on a single papyrus scroll around 1900 BCE, during the Middle Kingdom. In the first, Ankh-renef bequeaths property to his brother Wah. The second will is Wah's; it in turn bequeaths to his own wife, Teti, the property given to him by his brother, which Teti may give to their children as she pleases. Wah also assures that Teti will be able to continue living in their house.

First Will

Copy of the will made by the Trustworthy Sealer of the Controller of Works Ankh-renef.

Year 44, Month 2 of the Summer Season, day 13. Will made by the Trustworthy Sealer of the Controller of Works Ihy-seneb, nick-named Ankh-renef, son of Shepsut, of the Northern District.

All my possessions in field and town shall belong to my brother, the Priest in Charge of the Duty-shifts (of priests) of (the god) Sopdu, Lord of the East, Ihy-seneb, nick-named Wah, son of Shepsut. All my dependents shall belong to my brother.

A copy of these matters has been given to the Bureau of the Second Recorder of the South in Year 44, Month 2 of the Summer Season, day 13.

Second Will

Year 2, Month 2 of the Inundation Season, day 18. Will made by the Priest in Charge of the Duty-shifts (of priests) of (the god) Sopdu, Lord of the East, Wah.

I am making a will for my wife, a lady of the town of Gesiabet, Sheftu, nick-named Teti, daughter of Sit-Sopdu, concerning all the property that my brother Ankh-renef, the Trustworthy Sealer of the Controller of Works, gave to me along with all the goods belonging to his estate that he gave to me. She may give these things as she pleases to any children of mine she may bear.

I also give to her the four Canaanites that my brother Ankh-renef, the Trustworthy Sealer of Works, gave to me. She may give (them) as she pleases to her children.

As for my tomb, I shall be buried in it with my wife without anyone interfering therewith. As for the house that my brother Ankh-renef, the Trustworthy Sealer, built for me, my wife shall live therein and shall not be evicted from it by anyone.

The Deputy Gebu shall act as the guardian for my son.

QUESTIONS FOR ANALYSIS

1. What kinds of property are handed from person to person within the family, and what does this exchange tell you?
2. What does Wah's will tell you about Teti's legal and social status?
3. What do these wills tell you about the strength of government in Egypt?

Source: William Ward, trans., Pap. Kahun I, 1 (ca. 1900 BCE), www.stoa.org/diotima/anthology/wardtexts.shtml.

THE NEO-ASSYRIANS AND NEO-BABYLONIANS (11TH–6TH CENTURIES BCE)

In this period, the kings of the Neo-Assyrian Empire built on a magnificent scale. Assurnasirpal II, early in the ninth century BCE, decorated his immense Northwest Palace at Kalhu with huge statues of winged elephants and lions, their heads human, carved from stone that had been carried from hundreds of miles away. His workers covered the palace walls with colorful glazed brick and spectacular sculpted reliefs. He also created schools of scribes and a vast library at Nineveh, a city north of Assur. Great powers, including Egypt itself in the seventh century BCE, fell to the Assyrians or fiercely resisted siege after siege.

But these wars and others—especially with the Medes, an Iranian people whose archers and cavalry could out-maneuver the Assyrians' slower infantry and chariots—eventually exhausted them. At the end of the seventh century, the Chaldeans, a Semitic people who had gained control of Babylon, formed an alliance with the Medes and defeated the Assyrians decisively, even though Egypt

Stele of Assurbanipal A stele from around 669–655 BCE depicts the king Assurbanipal in the traditional headdress of the Assyrian rulers. He carries a basket of earth on his head to symbolize his contributions to the rebuilding of Babylon, the great city sacked by his grandfather. A cuneiform inscription praising Assurbanipal runs over the stele.

Ishtar Gate Babylon's Ishtar Gate, built around 570 BCE, was decorated with glazed tiles forming designs such as this dragon, a symbol of Nebuchadnezzar II's power and authority. Merging features of various dangerous animals, including a viper, lion, and scorpion, the dragon stood as a warning to enemies of the city.

tried to help Assyria in an effort to maintain the regional balance of power. Under Nebuchadnezzar II (r. 605–562 BCE), the Chaldeans consolidated a Neo-Babylonian Empire that enjoyed a brief period of preeminence in the Near East.

Nebuchadnezzar made Babylon perhaps the greatest city in the world. The huge Ishtar Gate, covered with brilliant deep blue tiles and vivid images of lions, bulls, and dragons, was only one of the formal entrances to the city. During this period Babylonian astronomy and astrology reached their peak, as we know from the lists of accurately dated eclipses of the moon and sun, and conjunctions of the planets, recorded over hundreds of years.

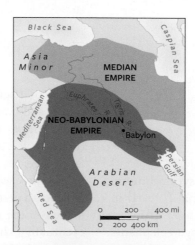

The Neo-Babylonian and Median Empires, 625–560 BCE

THE MEDIAN AND PERSIAN EMPIRES (678–330 BCE)

Yet Babylon in turn soon fell—as did the kingdom of the Medes, a short-lived Persian state established in 678 BCE—to the larger group of nomadic peoples who came together in the Persian Empire from the middle of the sixth century BCE on. Under the leadership of Cyrus the Great (r. 558–529 BCE), Persia would dominate more of the world than any other power before it.

The Persians settled in the area of modern Iran around 1000 BCE. By the end of the eighth century BCE, King Achaemenes founded the Achaemenid dynasty, whose later members built the empire. Persepolis became the ceremonial center of their realm, and other cities developed as administrative centers. The empire's vast armies, made up of peoples from many lands, were always anchored by highly trained Persian archers and infantry and supported by war wagons and scythed chariots. Cyrus and his successors wielded power that no other monarch could rival. He conquered the kingdom of the Medes and then the Neo-Babylonian Empire in turn, and his son, Cambyses II, conquered Egypt in 525 BCE. Their kingdom

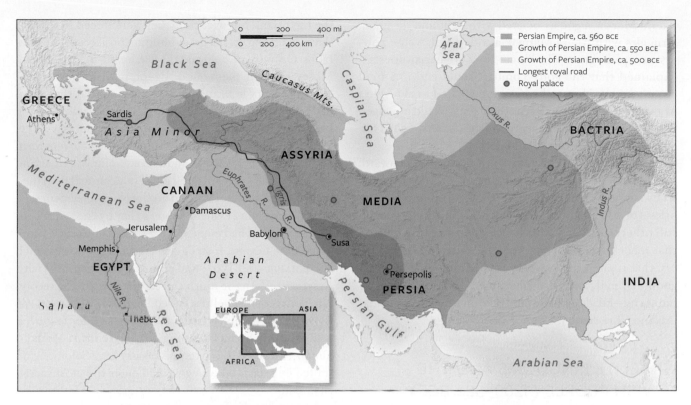

Expansion of the Persian Empire, 557–500 BCE Under the leadership of kings such as Cyrus the Great, the Persian Empire spread from its ceremonial center at Persepolis to cover a vast area, from the Nile to the Indus.

would remain a great power until 330 BCE, when it fell to Alexander the Great.

GOVERNANCE UNDER CYRUS AND DARIUS The Persian Empire at its height stretched from the Nile to the Indus. It was divided into administrative districts, each ruled from a palace by a Persian nobleman known as the satrap, who had his own staff of scribes and his own treasury. Royal roads, with rest houses to make travel easier, connected the satrapies to the capital: the longest one, from Sardis to Susa, stretched more than 1,550 miles. Personal representatives of the king, known as his "eyes," ensured that these local powers did not grow too independent. Every province had to contribute its share of tribute to the royal treasury. This payment chiefly took the form of gold and silver but could also include horses, grain, and eunuchs (men castrated as boys). The Persian kings were immensely rich: when Darius, the third king of Persia, built a palace in the decades around 500 BCE, he imported craftsmen from Egypt and Greece alike, while Babylonians were hired to make the bricks.

For all its demands, the Persian Empire seemed to many of its subjects a model of good government. Kings improved agriculture by maintaining and developing irrigation systems and promoted trade. More important, perhaps, it was Persian royal policy to leave each subject people in possession of its gods and customs, and to communicate with them in their own languages—or at least in Aramaic, the Semitic language that was gradually replacing Akkadian as the common language of the Near East. In the palace at Persepolis, reliefs showed representatives of multiple peoples carrying the royal throne. In Babylon, Cyrus had himself represented as a Babylonian king. Cultural sensitivity and language skills—as well as efficient and honest administration, stern policing, and good roads—made the Persians more desirable rulers than most.

ZOROASTRIANISM It was within Achaemenid Persia that Zoroastrianism, a new religion with a powerful vision of the universe, took shape. In its earliest form, Zoroastrianism identified the god Ahura Mazda as a single "wise lord" who ruled the universe. Certain lesser figures aided him; others, the *devas*, came to be seen as evil. Early Zoroastrianism is often considered to be one of the first monotheistic religions.

In its later form, Zoroastrianism became dualist.

Ahura Mazda, a god associated with light and the good, struggles with Angra Mainyu, a god of evil, whose powers are equally great. The Magi—the Zoroastrian priests—explained that the gods' combat would end in a final cosmic battle. Human beings were created to aid Ahura Mazda, and after their deaths their souls would be judged and sent to paradise (if their good deeds outweighed the evil ones) or to hell (if they did not).

From Darius I in the early sixth century BCE onward, the rulers of Persia claimed the support of Ahura Mazda. They supported the Magi, but they also supported the priests of other gods and allowed their subjects to worship still other ones. Their efforts helped to sustain a religion that made powerful claims on the loyalty of its followers, that treated the universe as a battleground between good and evil, and that envisioned individual souls as immortal—all ideas that would take on new forms in Judaism and Christianity.

ISRAELITE KINGDOMS AND THE JEWISH PEOPLE (1200–582 BCE)

In the later centuries of the second millennium BCE, a new Near Eastern civilization began to take shape in Canaan, part of the Levant. This area, once studded with relatively wealthy Canaanite cities, was now partly in decline. It was largely controlled by New Kingdom Egypt, though the **Phoenicians**, based on the coast, used their position and their skills as navigators and sailors to become prosperous as trading intermediaries between the empires to their east and west. Jerusalem was a Canaanite city that recognized Egypt as its overlord. In the years around 1200 BCE, new peoples—some of whom came from near the Aegean Sea—established settlements in Canaan. So, apparently, did another one: a Semitic people who called themselves the children of Israel.

ISRAEL AND JUDAH (1000–582 BCE) Centuries later, the children of Israel would recall that this arrival in Canaan was not the first. Their ancestors had already inhabited the Levant, but in the seventeenth century BCE, they believed, they had moved to Egypt, impelled by drought. There they had originally lived in peace with

the Egyptians, but over time they were forced to serve as slaves, working on the great building projects of the pharaohs. Only divine help and the leadership of a great man, Moses, brought them out of Egypt, perhaps in the thirteenth century BCE, and back to the land that their God had promised them. These stories are memorialized in the Five Books of Moses, the first part of the Hebrew Bible, which probably reached something like their current form in the period between 600 and 400 BCE, almost a thousand years after the events in question. They cannot be verified (or falsified) by historical and archaeological evidence.

Still, surviving evidence shows that by the tenth century BCE, Israel had emerged as a small but warlike kingdom in the Levant. It struggled with nearby powers such as Damascus and Tyre—and even more dangerously, with Assyria itself. In the ninth and eighth centuries, a second kingdom of the Israelites, called Judah, took shape in the south, centered on Jerusalem. There—so later tradition held—the inhabitants worshipped their God in a splendid Temple, ascribed to the tenth-century king Solomon and staffed by priests who alone could enter the most sacred chamber.

Originally, the Israelites lived simply, in families and tribes ruled by patriarchs. They supported themselves by a combination of pastoral activity and agriculture. Land was passed down through the male line, and women—who were often married off by their families for economic advantage—lived with their husbands' kin. As the kingdoms developed, Israelite society became wealthier and more sophisticated. Potters developed new skill in turning and polishing their wares. Families, which had once lived in small houses with several generations in three or four rooms, began to split up, and a distinct group of leading figures who served as warriors and royal counselors took shape. To some extent, the Israelite states came to look like much smaller versions of other Near Eastern societies.

Late in the eighth century BCE, the Assyrians repeatedly invaded and finally shattered the Israelite kingdom, transporting its population to other parts of the empire—a standard imperial policy. Judah survived, probably by becoming an Assyrian vassal state, and the city of Jerusalem grew rapidly as Judah's capital. The remains of walls, aqueducts, and jars with seals reveal an increasingly

PHOENICIANS

Mediterranean Sea

Tyre

Damascus

KINGDOM OF ISRAEL

Sea of Galilee

Jordan R.

PHILISTINES

Jerusalem

Jericho

Dead Sea

KINGDOM OF JUDAH

Sinai Peninsula

0   50   100 mi
0   50   100 km

Israelite Kingdoms, ca. 900 BCE

vibrant society. After Assyria finally collapsed, however, the Egyptian and Neo-Babylonian Empires fought over the Levant. Between 597 and 582 BCE, the Babylonians destroyed the kingdom of Judah. When Jerusalem fell, the Temple was destroyed—a calamity that Jews still remember and mourn today. Under Assyrian rule, Judah had been a major producer of olive oil, but the conquest destroyed this prosperity.

MONOTHEISM AND JEWISH RELIGIOUS CULTURE

In one vital way, the Jews differed from virtually every other people. They believed, passionately, in a single deity who ruled the entire universe. Their God was not simply the most powerful among many, he was their only deity, and a being so radically superior to humans that he could not even be imagined in human form. In a world in which most states acknowledged and sacrificed to many gods, even Jews found it hard to maintain an active commitment to their hidden, abstract deity. From Moses to the kings of Israel and Judah, leaders found their followers all too eager to set up idols and sacrifice to them. And yet, monotheism became the very core of the Jews' historic identity.

Priests and scribes held that God had chosen the Jews as his special people, leading them out of exile in Egypt and appointing the dynasty of Kings David and Solomon to rule them. The hand of God led and protected his people at all times. This vision of political theology gave the kings legitimacy and supported those kings and priests who insisted that their God was a jealous one who would not allow his people to worship idols at the shrines of the Canaanites.

By 582 BCE, once the Jewish states had been destroyed and the kings had been driven from their thrones and become vassals of the Babylonians, this comprehensive theology and history no longer matched reality. **Prophets**, priests, and scribes gradually came to grips with the new situation. Although they continued to believe in a single deity, the prophets asserted that it was wrong to expect that God would intervene at all times and places in favor of a single people, however dear to him they might be. According to the prophets, the Jews—as the histories that were woven together in exile showed—had often rejected their God and his teachings, and had suffered the punishment they deserved. The Jews must learn, so the prophets insisted, to maintain purity: to practice circumcision on all males, observe the Sabbath, and so on. Eventually God would send a Messiah, an anointed king, to rule over the world. For now, however, salvation lay in meticulous observance of the laws laid down by Moses and conveyed in his Five Books.

House of David An Aramaic inscription on a ninth-century BCE stele from Tel Dan in present-day Israel celebrates the victories of an Aramean king. It includes the words "House of David," the earliest archaeological evidence of the Davidic dynasty.

In a sense, two foreign rulers did as much as any Jewish ones to shape the religion of Israel and Judah. The Babylonian king Nebuchadnezzar II, who conquered Jerusalem in 587 BCE, forcibly transferred the Hebrew elite—from kings to priests and scribes—to his own country. The experience of Babylonian exile probably inspired these men to shape the Hebrew Bible into the series of richly human stories of departure and exile that it became in these centuries. They enriched it as well with the profound reflections of the prophets and the psalms—the sacred songs that the Israelites believed had been composed by King David.

The other foreign ruler who helped to shape Jewish tradition was the Persian Great King, Cyrus. In 538 BCE, for reasons that remain unclear, he released the Jews from their captivity in Babylon. Over time, the returned Jews reestablished their worship and compiled, from older sources, the books of the law of Moses, with which they tried to govern Jerusalem and Judah. The exact process by which scribes and priests restored these books is impossible to reconstruct in detail. But it seems likely that they gave the early books of the Hebrew Bible something like their final form. These books, and the larger Bible that took shape in Palestine over the next centuries, would influence the thinking and belief of readers in vastly different circumstances, as we will see, for thousands of years.

THE EMERGENCE OF GREECE: BUILDING A CULTURE (2700–600 BCE)

The kingdoms of the Near East were ancient by the early centuries of the third millennium BCE—the time at which the first substantial states took shape in what would later become Greece. Located on Crete, a large island in the Aegean Sea, the centralized Minoan state resembled, in some ways, the older and larger polities of the Near East. In contrast, Mycenae, the stronghold of a society based on the southern Greek mainland that flourished after the Minoan state fell, was one of several small states that cultivated alliances with similar states nearby. The Minoan and Mycenaean settlements marked the beginning of Greek society during the Bronze Age; but it was Mycenae, with its multiple small states, that first provided one of the central patterns of organization that the West would follow, in ever-changing conditions, through the centuries to come.

BRONZE AGE GREECE: MINOANS AND MYCENAEANS (2700–1200 BCE)

The Minoan and Mycenaean cultures were as complex and creative, in their own ways, as the empires of the Near East. By 2700 BCE, the Minoans had developed centers of trade and commerce on Crete, and built palaces at Knossos, Phaistos, and elsewhere. We know little about these early kingdoms, which went into crisis around 1700 BCE, when the palaces were destroyed and population fell. In the seventeenth and sixteenth centuries BCE, the Minoans rebuilt their palaces and developed a dazzling culture.

MINOANS Named after their legendary king, Minos, the Minoans were literate, but the script in which they kept records, Linear A, has not yet been deciphered. Their archaeological remains indicate that their society—the new as well as the old—centered on palaces. Centralized storehouses for grain ensured that there would be enough food for courts and for consumption in festivals. Gifted at crafts such as multicolored pottery and needlework, the Minoans were also skilled sailors. They traded with cities in Syria and Asia Minor, Egypt, and Sicily. But the products of their crafts were largely reserved for use in their own palaces.

Decorated with magnificent frescoes depicting dances and religious rituals, the Minoans' palace at Knossos rivaled the splendor, though not the size, of its Near Eastern and Egyptian counterparts. The palace incorporated an impressive stage for rituals and comfortable living conditions for its inhabitants: the Minoans devised ways of admitting fresh air and even created the first indoor plumbing. Smaller structures elsewhere on the island, especially along its coasts, indicate that the society had an extensive reach. In one respect in particular, Minoan society may have been distinctive: numerous statues of priestesses, and paintings of women taking part in the same sports as men, suggest that women's status was higher there than anywhere else—perhaps on an equal level with men.

Palace at Knossos The royal apartments in the Minoan palace on Crete (ca. 1500 BCE) were magnificently decorated with frescoes, such as this one of dolphins (right), and paintings, such as this portrait of women of high social status (left). The courtyards and patios were carefully designed to allow for the circulation of light and cool air.

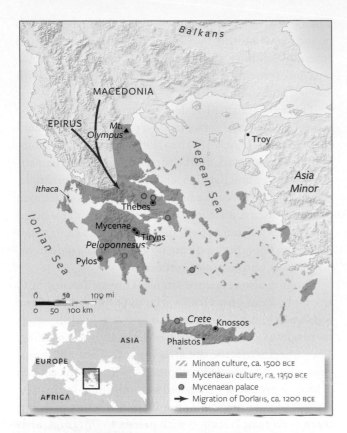

Minoan and Mycenaean Greece, ca. 1500–1200 BCE The Minoan people on the island of Crete had a strong centralized state, based primarily in the royal palace at Knossos. Later, the Mycenaean culture accumulated power by building alliances with similar, smaller city-states across the Peloponnesus and Greek mainland. But both civilizations collapsed around 1200 BCE, when the Dorian people invaded from the north.

MYCENAEANS Between 1450 and 1380 BCE, Knossos and the other Minoan palaces fell, probably to invaders from the Greek mainland. By then, however, another set of states centered on more modest palaces had come into being on the Greek mainland, in the Peloponnesus (the large peninsula that constitutes most of southern Greece), and on other islands in the Aegean Sea. At Mycenae, Tiryns, Thebes, and Pylos, the palaces—often heavily fortified—guarded the central administrations of small states. They were equipped with guardrooms and archives, and centered on a megaron (a great hall) surrounded by storerooms for oil, wine, and grain. The typical Mycenaean palace resembled nothing more than the large house Homer describes in the *Odyssey* as belonging to Odysseus.

The Mycenaean palaces, like those of the Minoans, were splendidly decorated, many with images of the Mycenaeans fighting wild men, a legend from a now-lost past.

On Crete, as well, the old palaces came back to partial life. This time, though, like the Mycenaean ones, they used Greek as their language of administration, perhaps because of conquest by or intermarriage with the leaders of the mainland states.

The inhabitants of these states worshipped some of the same gods who would emerge centuries later, in the writings of the poets Homer and Hesiod (ca. 750–700 BCE), as the gods of the Greek pantheon: Poseidon, god of the sea; the earth goddess, Demeter; and her daughter, Persephone. These Greek societies were aristocratic, ruled by men of high birth, and supported by sophisticated craftspeople and productive farmers. Artisans turned out handsomely decorated pottery, which would remain a specialty of the Greeks for centuries to come. Great men and women were buried sitting up, in beehive tombs (large circular chambers), with splendid gold masks and jeweled weapons.

These states were connected with the greater powers to the east and to the south by alliances maintained through complex diplomatic relations. And they made war, as those other powers did, with bronze arms and armor, using fighters on chariots as well as infantry and bowmen. Unlike the Near Eastern kingdoms and Egypt, however, the Mycenaean and Minoan kingdoms did not leave behind

Gods in Archaic Greece An early-seventh-century BCE bronze drum from Heraklion in Crete depicts the mythological ancestors of the Cretan people. The central figure's long hair and rectangular beard suggest an Assyrian influence.

any body of literature—no poetry, no religious texts, no fables, no codes of law. Interpreting sites without written texts to illuminate the beliefs of those who lived in them is very difficult. There is no way to know, for example, if any or all of these states actually mounted an expedition to Troy, as depicted by the eighth-century BCE Greek poets, though some scholars insist that they did.

We do know that the Minoan and Mycenaean kingdoms underwent a final, shattering crisis in the thirteenth and twelfth centuries BCE, in much the same period that crises brought down Kassite Babylon and New Kingdom Egypt. Centuries later, Greeks told the story that the Dorians—one of the main groups of Greeks in later historic times—had come south to Greece from Macedonia and Epirus during this period, and that their arrival had meant war and dislocation. Raids and invasions certainly took place, as did natural disasters. The fragmentary surviving evidence does not as yet support any single explanation for the simultaneous collapse of so many societies. One point is clear: the world that the eighth-century BCE bards looked back to had been dead for a couple of centuries before they began composing their poems about it. Until more documents come to light and are deciphered, we will not know the Mycenaeans and Minoans nearly so well as we know those who lived in the cities of Babylon and Egypt.

DARK AGE GREECE (12TH–9TH CENTURIES BCE)

Starting in the twelfth century BCE, the Greeks lived, for the next three or four centuries, on a far simpler level. This period is often called the Dark Age of Greece. The *Odyssey,* written at the end of this time, includes details that correspond in part with what archaeologists have learned from Greek sites of this period. Telemachus is the son of a chief. His house has servants—women who maintain supplies and ply their crafts, and men who cultivate the land and look after the livestock. Its rooms include his father's high-roofed treasure room, a broad space where bronze and gold lay in heaps

> with clothing in chests and much fragrant olive oil.
> There stood jars of old sweet wine,
> full of drink unmixed and fit for the gods—
> neatly laid out along the wall . . .

The Greeks' society was made up of clans, their chiefs bound to one another by complex family connections and rules of hospitality, and educated above all for war. Noble men and women were buried, like Mycenaean lords, with jewelry, arms, and gold.

This world of small-scale communities dominated by powerful noble families was not narrow. Men like Homer's hero Odysseus traveled both to trade and to raid. But communities were small, unlike the vast Mesopotamian cities of Nineveh and Babylon, and institutions were simple. After Telemachus calls a meeting in which the adult men of Ithaca discuss what to do about their king's absence, a herald gives his staff to each speaker in turn, as a sign that he has the floor. But there are no governors or monarchs, no generals, and no police authority.

Religion also remained simple. During Telemachus's assembly, Zeus—for Homer, the most powerful of the gods and the one who strives to preserve justice—sends two eagles as an omen after Telemachus finishes speaking. They wheel across the sky, attack one another, and disappear. Like other ancient peoples, Greeks saw the actions of birds as potentially freighted with meaning. In this case the poet leaves no doubt that Zeus had sent them. But there is no temple staffed with priests to interpret what the eagles' conduct portended. One member of the assembly, Halitherses, warns the others that the gods are displeased. But one of the suitors mocks him, insisting that not all the motions of birds mean something. By the end of the poem—when Odysseus returns, reestablishes his marriage, and slaughters the suitors—it becomes clear that Halitherses had been correct. From the historian's standpoint, though, the absence of institutions that could issue a strong verdict is even more striking. Families had their divine patrons, and family heads, rather than specialist priests, sacrificed to these patrons and invoked their aid.

THE IRON AGE AND REVIVAL: TOWARD ARCHAIC GREECE (1100–700 BCE)

From the tenth century BCE onward, the world of Dark Age Greece began to change, for reasons that are not entirely clear. Graves increased in number, showing that the mainland population, which had collapsed after the fall of the Mycenaean kingdoms, began to expand again. By the beginning of the eighth century, burials—which had traditionally taken place within community boundaries—were pushed to the margins of settlements

Proto-Geometric Pottery The development of new tools inspired precise designs, such as the concentric circles on this Proto-Geometric jar from Athens (ca. 975–950 BCE).

or beyond, as larger numbers of the living put pressure on the space once reserved for the dead. Cultivation of two crops that became central to Greek culture—olives and grapes—expanded. Pottery, which had degenerated after the collapse of the Mycenaean kingdoms, improved as well. Faster, more efficient wheels allowed potters to shape their vases more elegantly. New implements, such as compasses, enabled them to decorate their work with perfectly geometrical designs. Glazes became smoother and clearer. The pottery of this period, known as Proto-Geometric, was as elegant as it was simple.

A change in technology contributed to the general revival. In the Mycenaean world, as in the Near East and Egypt, the metal normally used for arms and armor had been bronze, an alloy of copper and tin. But new methods for molding bronze now developed. More consequential, smiths in Cyprus and the Levant learned how to smelt iron, which the Hittites had valued as a precious metal rather than for its practical applications. The Greeks adopted these techniques and began to make practical use of local deposits of iron ore. First weapons and then tools

such as plows were tipped with the new, harder material. They proved more effective and durable than those made with bronze had ever been. Farming became more intensive. Warfare became more violent, as iron weapons with their hard edges became available to more warriors. So began the Greek Iron Age, which extended from roughly 1100 to 700 BCE.

As the recovery proceeded, the texture of Greek life began to change. The noble households of the Dark Age described in Homer maintained substantial herds of cows and pigs, and the inhabitants sacrificed—and ate—a fair amount of meat. In the Archaic period, however, when populations grew, Greek communities turned increasingly to agriculture, raising the barley that was the staple of their diet and the flax that could be spun into linen cloth. The herds and the men who followed them decreased in number and moved into the hills.

Greek trade also revived. At the beginning of the first millennium BCE, Greeks were shipping their pottery to Cyprus and the Levant. Phoenicians and Greeks settled together in some trading stations. It is possible that the Phoenicians brought the Greeks back into international exchange networks in the tenth century and thereafter.

ARCHAIC GREECE (800–479 BCE): NEAR EASTERN AND EGYPTIAN INFLUENCES

The impact of Near Eastern and Egyptian developments on Greek society and culture, sometimes mediated by the Phoenicians, was profound. We have seen that the states of Mesopotamia and Egypt had created systems of theology and law, built temple complexes, and produced works of art on a vast scale. From the ninth century BCE at the latest, the Greeks began to emulate their neighbors.

PHOENICIANS AND THE GREEK ALPHABET The alphabet came early from the Phoenicians, who spoke a Semitic language. As early as the middle of the second millennium BCE, the Phoenicians had devised a nonpictographic alphabet to represent the consonants in their language. They used it in inscriptions—for example, on the sarcophagi (stone coffins) of their rulers. Phoenician merchants used their form of writing for recording their transactions, thereby bringing it to the attention of other peoples. The Greeks, who had traded actively with the Phoenicians for centuries, adapted the alphabet to the sounds of their own language, including the vowels, which

their ability to observe and raise questions about the universe and human society.

THE INVENTION OF AUTHORSHIP: HOMER AND HESIOD
It is possible that the poet of the *Iliad* actually invented the Greek alphabet, and it is certain that poets applied this new tool in a highly imaginative way. As bold and willing to experiment as the artisans and traders who were bringing Greek pottery to other peoples, the singers of tales not only wove stories far longer than ever before but also recorded them for others to read. Too long to memorize or to perform in one sitting, these **epics** were committed to writing. A new kind of literary creation had become possible—authorship, in which a single poet crafted a work, episode by episode, and then recorded it, word for word, for everyone else to read. This invention marked the origins of a development as astonishing as it has been fruitful—the beginning of a self-conscious, independent, rambunctiously creative society and culture in Greece.

The society that Homer describes in his epic poems is centered on older values of hospitality and courage in warfare, the values that had sustained Greek communities at a time of poverty in resources and technologies. But his

Intersecting Cultures On this tenth- or ninth-century BCE bust of a pharaoh, his name is inscribed in Egyptian hieroglyphs on the chest, surrounded by a Phoenician inscription dedicating the bust to the patron goddess of a Phoenician city.

made their written language easier to read and write than the Semitic ones. Soon they had worked out how to use these letters for everything from signing their names on pots to chiseling inscriptions into stone.

The Greeks' fuller set of letters proved easy to master. Within fifty years after the alphabet came to Greece, early in the eighth century BCE, it had been used to create and record great poems. By the end of its first hundred years of existence, ordinary Greeks were using it to keep records, to label the mythological figures represented on their clay pots, and to sign their names as graffiti on the structures in Egypt and elsewhere where they served as mercenaries. Greece never developed a class or order of professional scribes like those who taught and practiced writing in the older states. It never needed to. Texts were written and read by ordinary people—and almost certainly sharpened

Odyssey A jar from fifth-century BCE Athens vividly depicts an episode in Homer's *Odyssey* in which the Sirens, winged women with beautiful voices, attempted to lure Odysseus and his men into wrecking their ship on the rocks. Odysseus had his men plug their ears with beeswax and then tie him to the mast so he could listen to the Sirens' singing.

Geometric Pottery This eighth-century BCE terra-cotta krater, a large vessel used to mix wine and water, demonstrates the intricacy of designs found in Greek Geometric pottery. It is decorated with a common Near Eastern motif: two goats on either side of a tree.

characters have varied qualities, reflecting a more complex morality. In the *Iliad* the warrior Achilles shows a passionate determination to pursue honor and a burning capacity for anger. His enemy, Hector, displays resolute courage in the defense of his home. And in the *Odyssey*, Odysseus reveals a dazzling wiliness—as well as formidable strength—in his pursuit of the conquest of Troy and then during his journey home. The complicated, often ironic ways in which their fates play out make the two poems surprisingly accessible today.

Homer's work as a whole—and even more, that of his near contemporary Hesiod—also show what contact with older civilizations meant to the Greeks. The Greek writers composed and performed as individuals, supposedly inspired by goddesses (the nine Muses), but still speaking on their own authority and in their own voices. Hesiod even introduced his own name to his poems, making clear his personal responsibility for them. Some Near Eastern writers had done the same. But others had written as scribes and priests, explaining how the gods were related to one another, laying out the history and structure of the universe, and striving to convey the ways in which divinity and humanity interacted. The Hebrew Bible gives a sense of what this literature was like.

Greeks, so far as we know, had never attempted to put the stories of their many gods in any sort of formal order

before this time. Now Homer, in a poem aimed at aristocrats who loved to hear about family histories so complex that modern readers find them almost impenetrable, traced the connections among the Olympian gods in passing comments. Hesiod devoted one of his major works to explaining the generations of the gods and their relationships to one another, in a scripture, of a sort, for a people who lacked one. More striking still, in a bitter poem on the life of the farmer, he insisted as sharply as any Egyptian that the duty of the authorities was to maintain a moral order, to preserve justice in the universe. In their hunger for the bribes that only the rich could provide, Hesiod observed, they often failed to carry out this duty. In his poetry we can hear the voices of those who lacked status and power, and earned their living by the hard work of the plow or by risking dangerous voyages on ships.

GREEK ARTS AND CRAFTS: BUILDING ON NEAR EASTERN AND EGYPTIAN MODELS

Greek artists and artisans also explored the new possibilities that commerce with other cultures offered. In the age of Homer, as for centuries before, potters in Greece had decorated their wares with the abstract patterns that gave their style its name: Geometric. In the seventh and sixth centuries, by contrast, they followed models from the Near East

Athletics in Art A black pottery jar (525 BCE) from a Greek colony in Italy depicts two athletes engaged in a wrestling match.

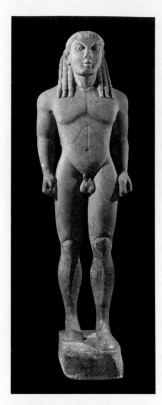

Kouros The rigid arms and advancing stance of this life-size sixth-century BCE statue reveal the influence of Egyptian sculpture.

and Egypt, and experimented boldly with new forms—animals, both real and imaginary, and humans engaged in rituals and social life. On the black vases of this period—so called because their figures were portrayed in black against the bright orange background of the clay—vivid figures of the gods appear. So do human athletes throwing the discus and the javelin to the sound of music made by a flute player, women gathering at a public fountain, and animals locking horns.

Greek sculptors, similarly, learned from their skilled Egyptian colleagues to create life-size statues, in bronze and stone alike, of human figures. Again, they rang changes on foreign innovations. Statues of young men—kouroi—were represented in the nude, and the sculptors dwelled with pleasure on every detail of the human form. Statues of women were clothed, the sculpted fabric falling in stiffly stylized drapes and folds. Using Egyptian conventions, Greek sculptors soon became astonishingly skillful at producing realistic figures that seemed balanced on the balls of their feet and ready to move.

In the eighth century BCE, Greeks began to build substantial temples to their gods. The same sculptural conventions they had developed to represent beautiful men and women served to represent the gods as well. For all their glorious wealth and all their ability to orchestrate the work of thousands of subjects, the rulers of the Near Eastern lands and Egypt had never imagined the gods so directly in their own image. When the poor seafarers and marginal farmers who clung to the bony slopes of Greece took this radical step, they revealed a cosmic self-confidence that would take them a very long way, as we will see.

GREEK EXPANSION: THE COLONIES (9TH–6TH CENTURIES BCE)
As the Greeks' social and intellectual universe expanded, they set themselves in motion. From the early ninth century BCE on, the old city-states began to establish colonies around the Mediterranean. The Phoenicians, whose trading cities survived and prospered during the Bronze Age Crisis, also founded trading posts in the western Mediterranean in the same centuries when the Greeks did. Apart from Carthage in northern Africa, which became a powerful city-state in its own right, they stayed largely aloof from local politics. They came to trade. The Greeks built some of their colonies as trading posts, but they also set out from their home cities looking for sites to settle as independent cities. They searched for harbors well protected from bad weather and flanked by high headlands that could easily be fortified. Though they maintained contact with their home communities, the new settlements were politically independent.

In two bursts, one in the eighth and one in the sixth centuries BCE, the Greeks established colonies on the coast of Asia Minor, on Sicily, and in mainland Italy and Gaul (modern France). Some of these, like the Sicilian city of Syracuse, would become bigger, richer, and more powerful than many of the home cities their inhabitants had left behind. Greek civilization thus expanded to the east and to the west alike—a process that would last, in different ways, for hundreds of years and play a central role in the making of Western history.

HELLENIC CULTURE: CONVERSATION AND COMPETITION
Even as Greeks scattered from the western coast of Asia Minor to the far western Mediterranean, new institutions were developing that helped them to form a collective identity. The Greeks called their lands Hellas and themselves Hellenes, and these new forms of sociability and competition came to define Hellenism. Some of these practices were rooted in the customs of the Dark Age communities, and perhaps in Mycenaean life before that. None was more durable or proved more fertile than the **symposium** (literally, "drinking together"), which became the central form of Greek social life.

The *Iliad* and the *Odyssey* already depicted groups of men and women reclining together on couches, drinking wine, and listening to a bard or talking. Over time, the symposium came to be a male event, one in which women appeared only as servants or entertainers. But it also became a model of free and open discussion in which philosophers and generals, men of inherited rank, and self-made men could take part. For centuries to come, Greeks were set apart by their passion for these meetings, which often launched new kinds of literature and new ideas.

Even more than the Greeks loved gathering to drink and argue, they loved to compete: "Strife," Hesiod

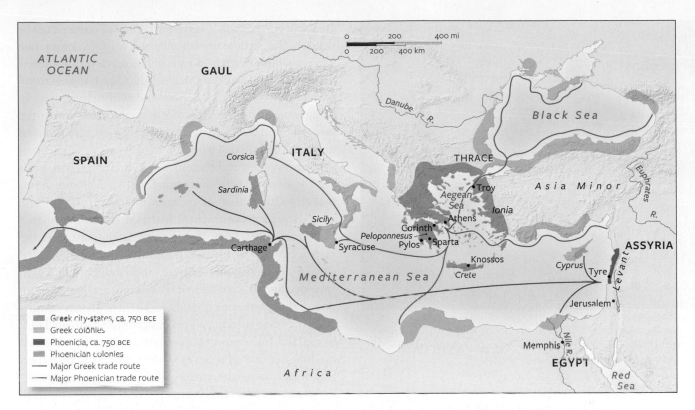

Greek and Phoenician Colonization, ca. 750 BCE From the early ninth century BCE, Greek city-states established trading posts, which ultimately became colonies, across the Mediterranean and the Black Sea. Together with the great maritime trading culture of the Phoenicians, the Mediterranean became a space in which goods, ideas, and even alphabets were exchanged, forming the basis of an enduring Greek linguistic and material culture.

explained, "is wholesome for men. And potter is angry with potter, and craftsman with craftsman, and beggar is jealous of beggar, and minstrel of minstrel." Homer has his heroes compete with all their strength, not only in warfare but also in the games that follow the deaths of their comrades, in which they race, wrestle, and box. In the ninth and eighth centuries BCE, these pursuits became the core activities at formal athletic competitions to which all Greeks were welcome. These were first held at Olympia, in the Peloponnesus, under the auspices of a great temple of Zeus, and then also at other sites.

Greek athletics took many forms, from boxing with hands wrapped in leather straps to racing chariots, and could be almost as dangerous as warfare itself. In 720 BCE, according to legend, one competitor lost his loincloth while running in a footrace. From then on, Greek athletes competed naked. As their contests began to occur regularly every two or four years, they developed into a pan-Hellenic institution. Special truces among warring groups enabled all contestants to attend the Olympics and other games. Poets celebrated the winners with elaborate verses of praise, and cities supported victors in comfort for the rest of their lives.

Conversation and competition both remained among the chief characteristics of Greek life for hundreds of years. Greeks were coming to have an identity as clear-cut as that of Babylonians or Egyptians—one centered on continual competition. The civilization that was beginning to take shape in the West already looked radically different from the older, wealthier, and more powerful societies with which it was in contact—and from which it learned so much.

GREEK CITY-STATES (12TH–6TH CENTURIES BCE)

In ancient times, most Greeks identified less as members of a great Hellenic world that stretched across oceans and continents than as citizens of individual communities. Independent city-states—settlements that recognized no superior and governed themselves—became the norm

Hoplites This detail from a seventh-century BCE jug depicts hoplite soldiers armed with spears and shields clashing in battle in their characteristic phalanx formations.

in Greece during the Dark Age and Archaic period, and would remain the standard form of Greek settlement until centuries later, when Greece finally became part of one larger empire after another. Called the **polis**, the Greek city—as we will see—followed a very different path of development than the cities of the Near East had.

HOPLITE WARFARE AND SOCIAL TENSIONS

Transformations in the city-state were the most consequential development of this consequential time. Bitter, prolonged warfare—consisting partly of pitched battles in which one side might rout and slaughter the other, and partly of long series of raids and crop-burnings in the countryside outside the enemy's walls—became the city's central activity during the Iron Age. The little communities controlled by noblemen now became larger settlements dominated by a class of fighting men called **hoplites**.

These soldiers mobilized in the warm weather to wage their campaigns and, in the fierce rivalry of Greek life, were called into action again and again. Each of them wore a helmet and carried a spear in his right hand and a large, round wooden shield in his left. Moving forward in a dense, coordinated formation called a phalanx, each hoplite was supposed to protect the man on his left with his shield, and trust the man on his right to do the same for him. These formations loosened as armies ran toward one another, but they still crashed together like waves until one side or the other broke, with many casualties. This form of warfare was not wholly new: the poems of Homer describe soldiers fighting behind walls of shields. But in the political world of the city, it had powerful social and political potential. In some cases, strife developed between the men of inherited rank who had traditionally claimed the right to command and the larger groups who now made war.

Between the eighth and sixth centuries BCE, polis after polis dealt with these tensions by developing a formal constitution—a set of rules, written or unwritten, that defined governmental institutions and regulated participation in them. Many cities, from Corinth in the eighth century to Athens in the sixth, either appointed a prominent person to serve as a monarchical ruler, or at least declared the wisdom of that policy. Laws were composed, though they were often ascribed to ancient lawgivers rather than to living men. Compromises provided for a partial sharing of power between the ancient families that had long dominated society and the wider group of soldiers who were now needed to defend the state.

Often these arrangements proved fragile. The sixth century BCE saw "tyrants" take power in Athens and many other cities. Not despots in the modern sense, tyrants were individual rulers who could not necessarily claim that their rule was legitimate, but who could offer efficiency in government. History now took place, at different tempos, on individual urban stages. Across the Greek world, as much in the colonies as on the mainland, Greeks thought of themselves first as Spartans or Athenians, Corinthians or Megarians, and only then as members of a coherent larger culture.

SPARTA: A DISTINCTIVE ORDER

The Greek *poleis* (cities) varied widely in physical form and political constitution. But a small city on the Peloponnesus in southeastern Greece—Sparta—stood out as a model that others could only aspire to. It developed a distinctive constitution—traditionally attributed to the lawgiver Lycurgus—in the eighth and seventh centuries BCE, after a time of civil strife. The city had two hereditary kings—members of ancient families who led its armies in wartime and performed religious rites. Another set of officials, called *ephors*, had the right to challenge royal decisions, and they often did so. A council of elders, the *gerousia*, also took an active part in making policies and negotiating treaties. In addition, an assembly of men of military age had the right to vote on enactments proposed to it, but not to stage formal debates. In Greek terms, Sparta exemplified **oligarchy**: the state was ruled by the few, rather than a single monarch or a mass of citizens.

What made the Spartan state distinctive, much more than these institutions, was its social order—and the sheer power that it enabled the city to unleash when the multiple governing bodies agreed to make war. The core of the city's strength lay in its fighting men, who called themselves *homoioi* ("men of the same kind"). Much of the social order was organized to train these men to be fighters of extraordinary skill and courage.

Spartan boys, who were taken from their families and raised for a time as members of age groups, were required to steal the food they needed to eat but punished severely if they were caught. For centuries after the city had ceased to exist, Greek writers told the story of a Spartan boy who, in his hunger, stole a live fox but had to come to the muster with it under his clothing. He proved his mettle by remaining silent, muffling his own cries, as the fox gnawed at his vital organs.

While growing up, each Spartan boy normally had his closest relationship with an older male lover, who would teach him the skills of warfare and the traditions of the city. Eventually the men would marry their female counterparts: Spartan women, who unlike those in the rest of Greece practiced gymnastics to make themselves fit wives and mothers for Spartan men. But even once they had reached adulthood, Spartan men lived more with one another in military messes—groups of men who ate together, feasting on the notorious Spartan blood sausage—than with their families. Male lovers marched into battle together, and their deep affection helps to explain the cohesion of Spartan armies, which astonished their enemies.

Sparta had its manufactures, but it never became an actively commercial society. The city never even minted its own coins, but used those of other states. The labor of slaves called **helots** provided the material support that sustained the system and the state. Tradition connected the helots to the wars that the Spartans waged in the eighth century against their Messenian neighbors in the southwestern Peloponnesus, though these accounts disagreed as to whether the helots were descended from the Messenians themselves or from Spartans who had not fought. The helots, who far outnumbered the free Spartans, worked at many jobs, from household service and sharecropping the farms of their masters to trade and crafts. Some reports stress how the helots were humiliated by their masters—for instance, being harassed by free citizens' youth groups, forced to wear demeaning clothing,

or made to drink wine with no water. Others point out that some helots owned considerable property and saved enough money to buy their own freedom.

Despite these uncertainties, it is clear that like later slave societies, Sparta was regularly threatened by rebellions of the helots. The city responded with ferocity. Young Spartans learned part of their craft as soldiers as they prowled Spartan territory, doing their best to terrify the slaves and catch and kill any who resisted. Rebellious helots were killed even when it meant removing them from shrines where they had sought sanctuary—itself a religious crime. Yet the Spartans also allowed helots to serve as soldiers, when numbers required it, and to deliver food and supplies to hard-pressed Spartan units—hardly the sort of duty one would normally assign to bitter enemies. Success at jobs like this often brought freedom.

In retrospect it seems an austere and frightening society. Yet for centuries most Greeks acknowledged that Sparta was the most virtuous society they knew or could imagine. Small though it was, without massive buildings or stunning works of art, Sparta took pride in the prowess of its relatively small class of citizen soldiers—who dominated most of the battlefields on which they appeared until the fourth century BCE—and in the stability of its social and political order.

Other Greeks respected Sparta, especially what they considered its excellent constitution. But the stability of the Spartan ruling class was an ideal to be admired rather than a model to follow. By the time the Spartan constitution took on its definitive shape in the sixth century BCE, Greece was embarking on a series of extraordinary experiments in every realm, from the state to speculative thought. The era of the mature Greek city-state had arrived. Forms of society and government unlike anything the Near East and Egypt had brought into being would take shape on Greek soil.

CONCLUSION

Imagine an observer using a retrospective form of Google Maps to survey the Mediterranean world sometime between 800 and 580 BCE. If the technology had existed, it would have been possible to survey the vast buildings of Babylon, the pyramids of Egypt, the enormous armies of the Neo-Babylonian Empire, and the even bigger ones of the Persian Empire that succeeded it. On the Mediterranean and in the Aegean Sea, Phoenician ships would have appeared, dominating the main traffic routes. In the Levant, the observer might have watched the downfall of Israel and Judah result in the siege and capture of Jerusalem and the exile of national leaders. In Greece, small cities would be rising, their expansion limited by geography. It would have been especially hard to see that Sparta, which lacked thick walls and large buildings, was already embarking on its aggressive program of expansion.

Yet the Greeks were learning from the older civilizations—learning, for example, how to fuse their ancient stories of the gods into a coherent form. And they were developing new forms of warfare, civic life, and colonial expansion that would soon transform the Mediterranean world. Their society afforded space for competition, for the unfolding of individual powers, and for the creation of institutions that are still with us today. In Babylon the exiled Jews were editing and completing what would eventually become the West's single central account of how the universe was made and how human beings should understand it and worship its creator. Though they would have been hard to discern, the roots of new institutions and beliefs were growing and taking hold.

[CHAPTER REVIEW]

KEY TERMS

civilization (p. 8)
domesticated (p. 8)
monotheistic (p. 8)
agricultural (p. 9)
city-state (p. 10)
ziggurat (p. 10)

cuneiform (p. 11)
polytheistic (p. 14)
divination (p. 15)
Code of Hammurabi (p. 15)
Epic of Gilgamesh (p. 17)
hieroglyphs (p. 22)

papyrus (p. 23)
ma'at (p. 23)
Phoenicians (p. 30)
prophet (p. 31)
epic (p. 36)
symposium (p. 38)

polis (p. 40)
hoplite (p. 40)
oligarchy (p. 40)
helot (p. 41)

REVIEW QUESTIONS

1. In the ancient Near East, what were the preconditions necessary for the development of agricultural societies?

2. What were the most important innovations of the early Sumerian city-states?

3. What distinctive features gave Egyptian civilization its relative stability from the Old Kingdom until its conquest by the Persians in the fourth century BCE?

4. What were the Egyptian views about life and death, and how did these ideas shape cultural practices?

5. What made the Hebrew religious tradition distinctive in comparison to other ancient belief systems?

6. What are the most notable similarities and differences between the Minoan and Mycenaean cultures?

7. What important developments helped to lead Greece out of its Dark Age?

8. What do the art and architecture of the Archaic period tell us about Greek values?

9. Why were conversation and competition such an integral part of early Hellenic culture, and how did they help to shape Greek identity?

10. How did the need for hoplite armies affect Greek politics and society?

CORE OBJECTIVES

After reading this chapter, you should have a solid understanding of the following core objectives. To strengthen your grasp of the core objectives, use the resources on the Student Site for The West.

- Identify cultural, technological, and political innovations that arose in the ancient Near East.

- Explain how Egyptian society remained stable for such a long time.

- Describe what made the Hebrew religion distinct from other ancient religious beliefs.

- Analyze how the Greeks adapted non-Greek art, culture, and technology during the Iron Age.

 GO TO **INQUIZITIVE** TO SEE WHAT YOU'VE LEARNED—AND LEARN WHAT YOU'VE MISSED—WITH PERSONALIZED FEEDBACK ALONG THE WAY.

CHRONOLOGY

621–620 BCE
Draco draws up first
legal code for Athens

594–593 BCE
Solon's reforms

6th century BCE
Athenian Agora established

561 BCE
Peisistratus establishes
a tyranny

510 BCE
Cleisthenes frees Athens
from tyranny;
lays foundations of democracy

490–479 BCE
Persian wars

465 BCE
Slave revolt in Messenia;
Sparta expels
Athenian soldiers

459 BCE
Athens allies with
Megara to fight Corinth

454 BCE
Athenians transfer Delian
League's treasury from
Delos to Athens

451–450 BCE
Pericles excludes nonnative
Athenians from citizenship

447–432 BCE
Athenians build
the Parthenon

2

"The School of Greece"

n the winter of 431–430 BCE, the Athenian statesman Pericles gave an unforgettable speech. Athens and a group of allied city-states had been at war with Sparta and its allies for a year, and the city's inhabitants were beginning to feel the impact of this conflict. Shut in behind the great walls that protected the city and its ports, Piraeus and Phalerum, a few miles away, the Athenians had seen the superior Spartan armies ravage their crops and property in the countryside while Pericles led a campaign against a Spartan ally. Frustrated, the Athenians had begun to question the wisdom of Pericles' strategies.

Pericles chose to meet his critics head-on at a prominent public occasion. Every year, the Athenians held a funeral ceremony for their fellow citizens who had died in battle. After a great procession in which the bones of the dead were carried in cypress coffins, "a man chosen by the state, of approved wisdom and eminent reputation," gave a speech. Standing on a high platform so that many could hear him, Pericles defended his decisions and described Athens as a city like no other in the world.

After praising the city's ancestors, Pericles singled out the city's distinctive form of government: democracy. Athenian citizens ruled their city collectively, and individuals who were born poor could rise to power so long as they showed ability in war or politics: "Our

---

The Parthenon Frieze Designed by the great sculptor Phidias around 438 BCE, the marble frieze that wound around all four sides of the Parthenon depicted a festival procession of horsemen, chariots, city elders, musicians, and religious celebrants. The animated beauty of these figures embodied the vitality, wealth, and power of Athens.

- What social pressures led to the transformation of Athens from domination by aristocrats to democracy?
- How did the Persian wars transform Athenian power?
- What caused Athenian defeat in the Peloponnesian War?
- How did the physical city embody Athenian political ideals?
- How was Athenian society democratic, and how not?
- How did Athenian culture express the basic social and political conflicts of the Greek world?

administration favors the many instead of the few; this is why it is called a democracy."

This unique constitution enabled Athens to surpass the rest of Greece in every vital area, Pericles claimed. Though the Athenians did not live in the sort of tyrannical city-state that forged the rugged Spartans, they remained just and honorable because they feared the law more than they feared men. Though the Athenians opened their city to strangers and spent their time as much on trade and holidays as on military training, they had shown repeatedly that they were also great fighters, unbeaten in battle. And although the Athenians discussed every important issue in public before deciding on a policy—and by doing so had earned the contempt of the taciturn and warlike Spartans— their love of debate made them independent thinkers, politically aware at all times and decisive when necessary. The Athenians' openness, their civic spirit, and their generosity, Pericles argued, made them supremely adaptable and effective in emergencies—so much so that they dazzled all rivals. "As a city," Pericles claimed, "we are the school of Greece."

But serving this democracy was hard. Pericles admitted that he could not praise the young Athenians who had died for their country in terms that could ever satisfy those who loved them. But he insisted that they had chosen to make their sacrifice and that they had been right to do so, and he urged all Athenians to continue to support the war as much as their age, position, and gender allowed. Fathers should produce more sons if they still could, and brothers should strive to match their fallen siblings' great deeds. Male citizens

and residents of Athens, in other words, could achieve heroism as the dead had—through sacrifice.

Many others, excluded from the public sphere, could not. Women, for example, heard only a message of self-discipline from Pericles: "Great will be your glory in not falling short of your natural character; and greatest will be hers who is least talked of among the men, whether for good or for bad." Even as Pericles uttered the grandest praise of democracy and the open society ever heard in the ancient world, he essentially admitted that public life excluded many.

Pericles had no doubt that the prize was worth all the suffering it required. For the city of Athens itself deserved no less. In giving up their lives or those of family members to serve it, the Athenians were showing something extraordinary: that they had learned to love their city above all else. Like Homer's Greeks of antiquity, the Athenians of the fifth century BCE saw valor in war as the highest of human virtues, and they prized the honor it could enable a man to win. But unlike Homer's Greeks, they practiced this virtue in the service of a higher, civic end. What gave the soldiers' sacrifice meaning was that they had made it to preserve a city that they loved.

In his speech, Pericles defined the new society that the Athenians had created, and he offered a new ideal of patriotism as the highest ideal that men could strive for. He thus helped to create a tradition that would last for millennia after his time. In every republic and democracy that the world has known, from the Roman Republic to the modern American one, language has been the most important tool in politics. The power of language has made it possible to create new states, defend old ones, negotiate changes in policy, and— in some ways most remarkable, and most like Pericles—to redefine constitutions in ways that transformed civic life. When Abraham Lincoln redefined Americans' vision of their country in his Gettysburg Address in 1863 and Martin Luther King Jr. did so a century later in his speech at the Lincoln Memorial, they drew on a tradition that began in Pericles' Athens.

Yet language is only as strong as those who create and use it, as the Athenians learned when Pericles died and they found themselves embarked on a long, bitter war that seemed to offer no way out. As civil strife broke out across Greece and politicians debated fiercely in Athens and elsewhere, political language degenerated into demagoguery. What Pericles had used as a tool to create a new consensus became a weapon for defaming and dehumanizing enemies.

The story of political language in the West—in both its creative and destructive forms—begins here.

ATHENIAN DEMOCRACY: THE FOUNDATIONS

The Athenians that **Pericles** addressed inhabited a sophisticated commercial society with complex institutions. They believed that they had always inhabited their land, and it is true that Athens was not invaded in the centuries after the fall of Mycenae and the other early states. The city ruled a substantial territory called Attica, a large triangular peninsula that juts into the Aegean Sea. With rich uplands and coastal plains for farming, Attica produced enough foodstuffs not only to support its population but also to enrich the elite landowners who dominated rural life. When its population expanded, it did not need to found colonies to provide for its citizens. The countryside offered room enough.

THE ANCIENT CONSTITUTION (900–600 BCE)

In the Archaic period, Athens was already rich. Its potters made the most elaborate and sophisticated vessels in Greece. It even attracted craftsmen from the wealthy lands to the east, such as Syria. During the eighth century BCE, the population of Attica exploded and Athens shrank in importance. A group of noble families, the Eupatridae ("the well-born"), dominated the city. Only members of this aristocratic group could serve as archons, the magistrates responsible for civic, military, and religious affairs. Nine archons served at a time in one-year terms. Noble ex-archons also filled the membership of the Areopagus, the city's council, which prepared legislation for the Assembly. This latter body could at this point only accept or reject laws and proposals, and cannot have been large.

Prosperity did not bring peace to Greece. In the second half of the seventh century BCE, the tribes that dominated particular parts of Attica fell out with one another. It also seems that conflict developed between older aristocratic families and newer groups—particularly, perhaps, those who were prosperous and bore arms for the city, but were excluded from power by the traditional constitution. As

city-states, such as Sparta and Thebes, competed for space and resources, wars regularly broke out, and Athens found itself compelled, somewhat later than many of its rivals, to adopt hoplite tactics. As elsewhere, the hoplites of Athens had to be rich enough to arm themselves and devote time to training. It is likely that many of these men, who were and saw themselves as the protectors of the city, were not able to participate in the Assembly and protested the power enjoyed by members of the older families.

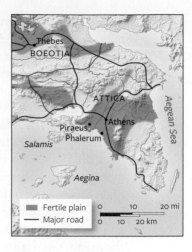

Attica, ca. 700 BCE

During this period of conflict, disturbances often took place at public events. Around 630 BCE, an aristocrat tried to establish a tyranny at Athens. He was defeated by heavily armed peasants from the countryside who entered the city and slaughtered his followers. Soon thereafter, in 621–620, a lawgiver (perhaps of noble birth) named Draco drew up a legal code for the city. Whether his legislation represented an effort to consolidate or to moderate the power of "the well born" is not clear. In later tradition, his code was remembered as extremely strict. The word *draconian* is still used for severe laws. In fact, Draco tried to make the legal system fairer and more efficient. His code was discriminating in its identification of crimes and assessment of penalties, distinguishing, for example, between murder and manslaughter.

SOLON: THE FOUNDATIONS OF A JUST SOCIETY (600–580 BCE)

Despite Draco's legislation, social conflict continued in Athens until **Solon**—an aristocrat who served as archon in 594–593 BCE—made a new set of laws. These were inscribed on wooden tablets and set into rotating frames so that everyone could inspect them.

The exact nature of Solon's reforms is uncertain. It seems likely, though, that they put an end to the system that had obliged many Athenian farmers to give a share of their produce to aristocratic landowners. Resentment of this duty, especially on the part of hoplites who were now key protectors of the city, had been growing until Solon ended it. He also divided the population into four categories according to property ownership, and allotted public offices to members of the three highest ones. He may even have created a new system for choosing archons by lot—a method that would later prove essential, in a different form, to Greek **democracy**. Though he gave the Areopagus the right to try certain major crimes against the state, he also created a second council that prepared legislation for the Assembly—a change that would lead to the Areopagus's gradual loss of power.

More important than the details of Solon's reforms were the ideals that motivated them. In poems describing his achievements, he made clear that his enactments were based on compromise and that he tried to serve justice by giving each side its due. He stated that he had protected the aristocrats' rights but had also given ordinary people the privileges that were theirs—a new concept in Greece. By doing so, he explained, he had brought about "good order"—a just constitution—and avoided civil war, which he described as the worst threat to any city. From now on, Solon claimed, Athenians could see their laws and institutions as the creations of human beings like themselves, and could examine them to determine whether they in fact preserved justice.

Solon's reforms did not immediately bring social peace. In 561 BCE, shortly before Solon's death, the aristocrat Peisistratus (against whom Solon had warned the Athenians) established a tyranny. Though Peisistratus was expelled from the city twice, he finally established power with the help of mercenaries (paid soldiers) from other cities. And yet, his rule was effective. He fostered the Athenian economy by expanding the use of money, developed the city's public spaces, and played a role in the wider sale of Athenian pottery. He promoted the city's public religion as well, building a temple to **Athena**, the city's patron goddess, and adding her image to Athenian coins.

It was only the incompetence of Peisistratus's son, Hippias, that brought an end to the regime he had created. The king of Sparta allied with another Athenian aristocrat to expel Hippias in 510 and tried to bring Athens under Spartan influence. But the Athenian aristocracy split, and a second faction, led by Cleisthenes, a member of a powerful noble family, successfully resisted the first faction's effort to disband the Areopagus. As a result, Athenian independence was restored.

CLEISTHENES: THE INSTITUTIONS OF DEMOCRACY (510–500 BCE)

Cleisthenes did much more than free his city from tyranny. Late in the sixth century BCE, he also transformed its institutions, laying the foundations of democratic government. He reorganized the population, which had traditionally been divided into four ancient tribes, into 139 **demes**—local units or wards of Athens. These were then organized into ten new tribes, each one reflecting a cross section of the population. By doing so, it seems, Cleisthenes broke the oligarchic power of the small group of aristocratic families that had traditionally ruled the city.

Cleisthenes also enlarged the council created by Solon to 500 members, with the ten tribes each supplying fifty representatives. It met every day, except for the many feast days. Fifty members at a time, tribe by tribe, lived and ate in a public building, acting as a standing committee. The council prepared the agenda and proposed laws to the Assembly, which was expanded to include all male citizens. Finally, Cleisthenes set up new courts, with juries ranging in size from 201 to 401 for private cases and 501 for public ones. Their members were chosen by lot from a pool of 6,000 potential jurors, drawn each year from the ten tribes. The newly chosen jurors swore an oath to uphold the laws, and each of them received a ticket (initially made of wood, and later of bronze) to indicate his status. Archaeologists have found many of these tickets in Athenian graves—evidence of the pride people took in their right to serve. The system demanded widespread participation. Over the years, thousands of citizens cycled through the council (on which they could serve only twice in a lifetime) and the juries.

One of Cleisthenes' radical innovations, **ostracism**, reveals the difference between the direct democracy of the Athenians and modern representative democracy. Nothing was more likely to poison the political life of a Greek city than the growth of factions—groups that were so unwilling to compromise that they might cause what the Greeks feared most: civil war. Cleisthenes found an ingenious way to let off these pressures, which might otherwise have undermined the constitution.

Ostrakon Members of the Athenian Assembly used clay tablets to record votes in favor of ostracizing prominent citizens who had become dangers to the state. This ostrakon from 482 BCE records a vote against the accused tyrant Themistocles.

The rules governing ostracism were simple. Once a year the members of the Assembly were asked if they would like to expel any prominent citizen who had become a danger to the state. Those voting yes scratched the name of the person on a piece of pottery called an *ostrakon* and placed it in an urn. Any individual who received 6,000 or more votes had to leave the city for ten years. No appeal was permitted, although the Assembly had the right to recall the ostracized man if public safety required it. Ostracism proved an effective way to resolve political tensions while avoiding violence. The ostracized citizen was not harmed or outlawed, simply forced to emigrate. The system rested on a popular consensus that did not require any individual to expose himself by bringing an accusation, as the courts did. Ostracism did not happen often, though archaeological evidence proves that it did take place. The practice itself indicates just how seriously the Athenians took the idea that the city and its laws mattered more than any individual did. And it commanded obedience even from the most prominent Athenians. Cleisthenes' own nephew was ostracized in 486 BCE.

THE DEVELOPMENT OF DEMOCRATIC INSTITUTIONS

Direct democracy found its fullest expression in the Assembly, which had ten annual meetings in addition to other sessions when necessary. All male Athenians older than twenty were eligible to take part in the Assembly and to speak. To vote, one had to be at the Assembly on the day when a measure was debated. Meetings took place on the Pnyx, a small hill in the center of the city, where the remains of the speakers' platform are still visible. The whole citizen body could not have assembled at the Pnyx or even heard the speeches that were given there. But the quorum of required voters for some measures was 6,000 — evidence that large numbers regularly attended.

The democratic changes that began with Cleisthenes had many causes. But a central one was the new military role played by ordinary Athenians in the fifth century. As we will see, when Persia invaded Greece at the beginning of the fifth century BCE, Athenians—many of them men of low rank—played a central role in defeating the Persians. The ordinary men who served as hoplites in the army and as sailors and marines in the navy were responsible for the victories and likely proud of their role in defending the state. The generals—ten military leaders who could come from any income level in society and were nominated for their abilities by their tribes and then chosen by lot—became more important as they won the great battles in the Persian wars. They took political power from the archons, the older officials who came from great families and who now served in religious and judicial roles. In

462–461 BCE Ephialtes, an Athenian politician who seems to have been a firm democrat, proposed to the Assembly that the old council of the Areopagus be stripped of its powers as a kind of appeals court and left in charge only of homicide cases and a few other crimes. His law passed.

ATHENS AND THE PERSIAN WARS (490–479 BCE)

Athens was becoming not only a democracy but also the most powerful city-state in Greece. For generations, Sparta had seen itself as the dominant power in Greece and had combined diplomacy with force to settle affairs in other cities—even Athens. But when the Greeks found themselves facing the much greater power of Persia, they experimented with new forms of cooperation, which served them well in combat. During the Persian wars, Athens came to regard itself as Sparta's equal and as the leader of the Greek states.

CONFLICT IN IONIA

Long before, in the tenth century BCE and after, Greeks had established numerous independent city-states in Ionia, at the far western edge of Asia Minor. These lively and sophisticated cities were on the border of the empire of the Medes and then, after it was conquered and absorbed by Persia, that of the Persians. The massive Persian Empire, centered on the magnificent royal ceremonial capital of Persepolis in southwestern Iran, was far wealthier than Greece and saw itself—as most Greeks saw it—as the greatest power in the known world. Later, in the 540s, the Ionian Greeks had watched as Cyrus, the king of Persia, defeated their overlord, Croesus, the powerful king of Lydia in western Asia Minor. With this defeat, the western edge of the Persian Empire encompassed all of Ionia, including the Greek colonies.

Late in the sixth century BCE, Persians and Greeks began to come into direct conflict. In 500, Darius, the Persian monarch, sent a naval expedition into the Aegean to invade the wealthy island of Naxos, which would have given him a base near mainland Greece. This expedition was actually proposed by a Greek: Aristagoras, tyrant of the Greek city of Miletus in Asia Minor. When it failed, Aristagoras feared that the Persians would attack his city. He urged the citizens of Miletus and other Ionian Greek cities to join him in rebellion.

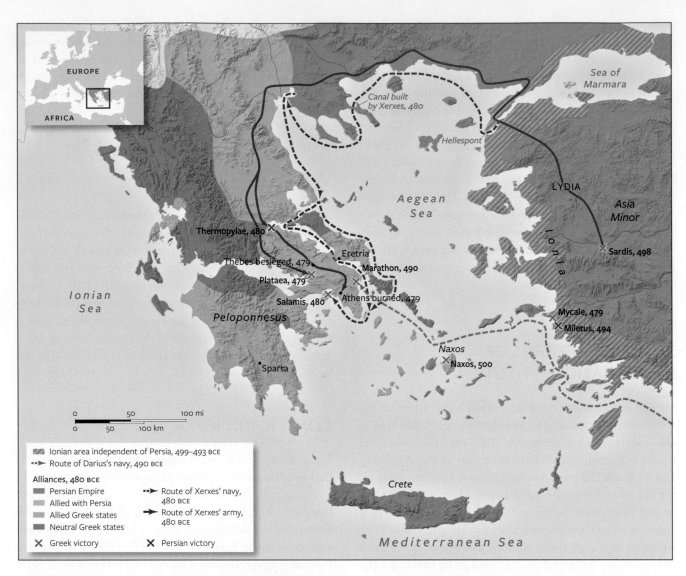

The Persian Wars, 499–479 BCE When the Persian king Darius invaded mainland Greece from the south with a navy of 600 ships, a Greek army decisively beat the Persians at the battle of Marathon on the southeast coast of mainland Greece. But when Darius's successor, Xerxes, invaded from the north, covering a vast amount of territory with a much larger army, the Persians won major victories—until they advanced far enough south to meet with Athenian naval power.

Despite the good advice of Hecataeus, a geographer who explained to the Ionian Greeks how powerful the Persians were, they went to war in 499 BCE. After destroying the Persian city of Sardis in 498, the Greek fleets and armies were decisively defeated. The Persians built vast siege mounds to take the Greek cities and also conquered several of the Greek islands off the Ionian coast. After their final victory in 493, the Persians burned the Ionian cities to the ground, made the Greek boys into eunuchs, and sent the girls to the royal harem.

The mainland Greeks took only a small part in this struggle. The Spartans had warned the Persians to leave their fellow Greeks alone, and the Athenians sent twenty ships to support their allies, the Eretrians, whose city, in mainland Greece, lay just across a narrow gulf from Athens. But after Darius crushed the Ionians' rebellion, he decided to invade mainland Greece to punish its inhabitants for their meddling, and in 490 BCE he crossed to Eretria.

WAR IN THE MAINLAND

Darius arrived with a massive fleet of some 600 ships and a substantial army. The Greeks were horrified by the scale of the invasion. Many years later, the poet and philosopher

Xenophanes described how Greek men would often ask one another when they first met, "How old were you when the Mede came?" Like the assassination of John F. Kennedy in 1963 or the attacks on New York and Washington, DC, in September 2001, the invasion became an unforgettable marker, a point at which time itself seemed to change.

The Spartans, whom the Eretrians asked for help, delayed until a religious festival was over. (Although they did not say so, they may still have resented the way that Cleisthenes had made Athens independent of them.) But Athens sent its hoplites, and one other city also sent troops. Apparently the Greeks were far fewer than the Persians—perhaps 10,000 Greeks arrayed against 20,000 or more Persians. After feeling out the enemy, the Greeks attacked, led by the Athenian general Miltiades, near the settlement of Marathon.

MARATHON New tactics gave the Greeks an advantage. The Persians, lightly armed, carried missile weapons—bows and slings. To avoid heavy losses early in the battle, the Athenian hoplites ran toward the enemy as soon as they came within missile range at about 200 yards from the Persian line. Giving the Persians little time to fire, the Greeks pressed their vulnerable enemies hard. The wings of the Greek army, deeper than the center, overran the Persian units that faced them. When the Persians pushed forward in the center, the Greek wings, instead

In Battle In a Persian cylinder-seal impression probably created at the time of the Persian wars, a lightly armed Persian soldier pierces the heavy armor of a Greek opponent.

of pursuing those they had beaten, enveloped the center and put the Persians to flight—as always, in Greece, the decisive moment of a battle.

Several thousand Persians died at Marathon, as opposed to only 192 Athenians and 11 allies, most of whom were hindered by their heavy armor as they chased the Persians. The Athenians then marched quickly back to Athens, ready to defend the city. Much later, a legend grew up that a single Athenian, Pheidippides, had run the whole distance from Marathon to Athens, announced the Athenian victory, and died—thus creating the legendary basis for the modern marathon run. The Athenians considered the victory a tremendous achievement and a testimony to the power of their people. They buried their dead under a great mound of earth at the battlefield. The war with Persia would continue, but soon after the victory at Marathon the Athenians showed their sense of political autonomy by carrying out the first ostracism of a powerful politician.

THERMOPYLAE AND SALAMIS Darius's successor, Xerxes—a harsher ruler than his predecessors, who campaigned brutally against the Babylonians when they rebelled against him—returned to the attack in 480–479 BCE. He brought a vast force against Greece: supposedly more than 1,200 ships and perhaps as many as 100,000 men. He had bridges built across the Hellespont (the strait between the Balkans and Asia Minor now known as the Dardanelles). The Spartans and a few of their Greek allies tried to cut off his advance at Thermopylae, where mountains on one side and the sea on the other left only a narrow, defensible pass. After a few days of savage fighting in which the Greek hoplites once again defeated the lighter Persian troops, a Greek traitor showed the Persians a path that led to the rear of the Greeks' position. This flanking tactic made the Greeks' situation hopeless, and most of them abandoned the fight. Three hundred Spartans, commanded by Leonidas, one of their two kings, remained with a few allies and died fighting heroically. Their epic last stand could not stop the Persian advance, though it may have bought the Athenians some time to prepare their ships for a decisive confrontation. But it became the first great model of what has remained the West's standard for absolute heroism: the last stand of a rear guard.

At this point the Athenians, led by Themistocles, an aristocrat who had served as archon, made one of those decisions that show how people of the past—even those who invented our system of government—often thought in ways that seem alien to us today. Leaders and common people routinely consulted **oracles**—sites where a god or a dead hero answered questions of all kinds, sometimes

The Greek Perspective The face of a terrified Persian soldier on the body of this drinking cup, made in Athens between 410 and 400 BCE, commemorates Athenian victory in the Persian wars. On the rim, a Persian servant ministers to her Greek mistress.

through the mouth of a priest or priestess. In this case an oracle predicted that wooden walls would someday protect the Athenians. So they followed Themistocles and left their city, which Xerxes burned, and entrusted their safety to their wood-hulled ships. In a momentous naval battle, a Greek fleet defeated the Persians at Salamis in 480 BCE. Xerxes then left the war in the hands of his commander, Mardonius, and returned to his capital, while the Greeks won a second victory at Mycale in 479. Greek hoplite armies did the same at Plataea and killed Mardonius. After his death, the Persians—although they continued their struggle with the Greeks in the Aegean for decades to come—would never again threaten the mainland.

MEANINGS OF WAR The meaning of these confrontations depends on the

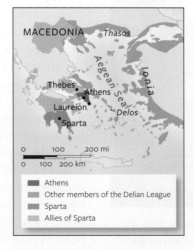

The Delian League, ca. 454 BCE

point of view of those who interpret them. Persia not only survived its defeat but prospered. The Spartans remembered the heroic example set by the 300 fallen at Thermopylae and commemorated their brothers-in-arms by an inscription: "O stranger, tell the Spartans that we lie here, obedient to their word." The Athenians saw themselves—especially their navy—as the saviors of Greece and set out to play the leading role in Greek affairs that they thought they had earned. By modern standards, they treated their triumph with modesty. The oldest surviving Greek tragedy, *The Persians*, is the work of Aeschylus, who fought at Marathon. Performed less than ten years after the battle, the play re-creates the response of Xerxes' mother, and then of Xerxes himself, to the news of the Persian defeat at Salamis. The play shows both disdain for the Persians and a remarkable ability to imagine their suffering. But the Athenians also rebuilt their devastated city on a grand scale and looked for ways to expand their power.

THE ATHENIAN EMPIRE (479–433 BCE)

Over the first half of the fifth century BCE, the Athenians made themselves the heads of what began largely as an alliance among equals but soon became an Athenian naval empire. After the Persian wars, the Athenians collected tribute from the other Greek states—supposedly to support expeditions to harry the land of the Persians. However, the Athenians seemed to do little with the gold that piled up on the island of Delos under the supervision of an Athenian treasurer. The "**Delian League**" came to seem increasingly like an instrument of Athenian power—especially after the Athenians, around 454 BCE, transferred the league's treasury from Delos to the temple of Athena at Athens, a powerful symbolic change.

TRADE AND POWER More than symbols were at issue. Athens was developing its military power in a new and dramatic way. In 482 BCE, rich silver deposits were discovered in Laureion, near the eastern coast of Attica. The Athenian government leased these to entrepreneurs, who used a workforce of some 20,000 slaves to dig and purify the silver. Most important, Themistocles persuaded his fellow citizens not to divide the new treasure among themselves but to invest the revenue from the mines in the navy, and they continued to do so throughout the century. The Athenians also continued to collect tribute from allied city-states in return for protection against the Persians. Athens now dominated the ocean as no previous power had.

Trade flourished. Athens built the "Long Walls," several miles in length, to ensure safe transport to and from its ports, Piraeus and Phalerum. Both ports were crammed with ships and swarmed with middlemen. Many of these were resident foreigners called *metics* ("co-dwellers") who specialized in the activities vital to maintaining international trade, such as the manufacture of jars, the shipment of grain and wine to Athens, and the payment of Athenian silver to its suppliers.

Observers noted the vast range of goods available at Athens. Some of these—such as timber, which the bare hills of Attica did not produce—had to be imported if Athens was to sustain its naval power. The city depended on the rulers of Macedonia to the north for this vital raw material. Trade therefore was a matter of state, and the Athenians did their best to ensure that no other power interfered with their ability to obtain the raw materials on which their power rested. These included not only timber but pitch, rope, and all the other materials needed to outfit their warships.

Other Greek cities within the Delian League, such as Thebes and the island city of Thasos, found themselves compelled not only to pay Athens tribute but also to obtain its permission to engage in trade. One resentful aristocrat observed, "If a city is rich in shipbuilding timber, where will it dispose of it unless it wins the consent of the Athenians? What if some city is rich in iron or bronze or cloth? Where will it dispose of it unless it wins the consent of the rulers of the seas?" Athens was a democracy and favored democratic governments in other cities, yet its conduct seemed increasingly imperial. The Spartans saw themselves as the leading power in Greece, but the Athenians now made clear that they claimed to be, at the very least, the Spartans' equals.

THE NAVY AND SOCIETY: TRIERARCHS AND OARSMEN

What really mattered—and what made the expansion of trade possible—was the powerful navy that the Athenians built with their new wealth. They created a fleet of armed **triremes**—large galleys powered by muscular oarsmen sitting in groups of three, one above the other, all working to the limits of their strength. The Athenians developed sophisticated naval tactics. They practiced rapid rowing, probably reaching speeds higher than ten miles per hour, and sudden changes of course. They used the rams at the front of their ships to break enemy fleets, attacking them from the vulnerable flank. The marines and archers whom they carried made each trireme an even more fearsome weapon.

Triremes In a fourth-century BCE Athenian relief of a trireme, the top row of oarsmen is visible, along with the oars of the second and third decks of rowers below.

Later in the fifth century BCE, the Athenian democracy devised a new social and economic system to sustain the navy. This system required both the rich and the poor to contribute, and ultimately gave the poor what critics of democracy described as a preponderance of power. The wealthiest Athenians were required to use their fortunes, for a year at a time, to provide public services. Some served as trierarchs, responsible for outfitting and commanding triremes. The trierarchs worked with expert contractors who took care of the technical and military details; but the trierarchs still had to see to it, at their own expense, that one or more ships provided by the state had all the necessary equipment, and that the most skillful officers were employed to command the crew.

Like Sparta, Athens defined itself largely by the military that it maintained. Equipped by the wealthy, Athens' military drew its forces from the populace. Poor Athenians rowed the galleys, and were paid for doing so out of the public revenues. Men who could afford arms served as marines, fighting from the ships, and they too were paid. In a society in which aristocrats still commanded armies and navies, men of low birth provided vital manpower and demanded respect for doing so. As a fifth-century critic of the regime explained, ironically expressing admiration for a system that he could neither accept nor change, "at Athens the poor and the commons seem justly to have the advantage over the well-born and the wealthy; for it is the poor who man the fleet and have brought the state her power."

THE PELOPONNESIAN WAR (431–404 BCE)

In the decades after the Persian wars, relations between Athens and Sparta—never easy—deteriorated. Sparta tried to prevent the Athenians from rebuilding their city's walls

RIACE WARRIOR STATUE

Although far removed from the Bronze Age, Hellenic artisans and their patrons retained a long-standing affinity for bronze, the alloy of copper, tin, and other metals that formed a key technology in the Near East and Greece between the fourth and second millennia BCE. In the eighth century BCE, the poet Hesiod spoke of men who not only used weapons of bronze but were themselves made of the metal. In Homer's epics, "brazen-hearted" men wield "pitiless" bronze weapons. In the fifth century BCE, Greek artisans favored bronze as a malleable material that could be sculpted to give full expression to the human form. They used chisels or tracing tools to carve lifelike details and added color by incorporating paint, other metals, and stone.

This rare example of a large-scale Greek bronze statue (many were later melted down so the metal could be used for other purposes) was one of two warrior statues recovered off the coast of Riace, Italy in 1972. It was completed at the height of Athenian power, around 460 BCE. A shield strap on the subject's left arm reveals him to be a warrior; the right hand might have held a spear. Greek artists of this period often depicted men in full-length sculptures because it was believed that the body was as expressive as the face. Here, the warrior's imposing musculature matches his fearsome facial features, which are accentuated by silver-coated teeth and copper lips and eyes. Though the hair and beard are sculpted in lifelike detail, their careful arrangement emphasizes the idealized nature of this figure.

QUESTIONS FOR ANALYSIS

1. In what ways does this sculpture strike you as realistic?
2. How does it also embody Greek ideals of masculinity?
3. In what ways does this sculpture represent the Athenian values articulated by Pericles in his funeral oration of 431–430 BCE?

after the Persians left, a decision that would have dramatically weakened Athens. The continuing buildup of Athenian naval power greatly worried the Spartans and their allies. In 465 BCE, a slave revolt broke out in Messenia, a region ruled by Sparta, and the helots seized a mountainside city that they could defend. The Spartans appealed to the Athenians, who were experienced in siege warfare, for help. The Athenians sent soldiers, but the Spartans ordered them away, fearing that they might join forces with the helots. This marked the end of the alliance between the two cities and the beginning of the final long slide into open conflict.

In 459 BCE Athens joined with a neighboring state, Megara, traditionally a Spartan ally, to fight Corinth, another Spartan ally. Sparta joined the war on Corinth's side. The war lasted until 446/5 BCE, and the peace that followed was continually disturbed by conflicts over the great powers' dependent cities. In 431, a full-scale war broke out, as Corinth pushed the Spartans to resist the growth of Athenian power.

SOCIAL AND POLITICAL CATASTROPHES

Agitation and argument were constant during the Peloponnesian War, which stretched from 431 to 404 BCE. Pericles, who first led Athens into war but also cautiously recommended that the Athenians not battle the Spartans on land, died in a plague outbreak soon after the war began. The plague killed thousands of other Athenians as well, perhaps enough to undermine the city's power and explain its eventual loss of the war. It also caused a breakdown in social customs. The great Athenian historian Thucydides tells us that the sick were abandoned, and the dead—in a radical violation of Greek tradition—were left unburied.

Yet even this disaster paled next to the other catastrophes that the Athenians endured. Through the second half of the fifth century, the pressures of the Peloponnesian War kept Athens in a state of agitation punctuated by emergencies. These occurred, for example, when the Spartans destroyed Athenian crops or when some internal enemy mutilated the statues of the god Hermes placed at crossroads in the city, causing a public panic. Although the wealthy, aristocratic general Nicias tried to carry on where Pericles had left off, he never won the favor of the people. They preferred Cleon, a politician who shouted and gesticulated in public, raised the pay of the jurors, and used the courts to attack his enemies.

ATHENS' DEFEAT

Cleon's aggressive policies scored some successes, but in 422 BCE he was defeated and killed by the Spartans in northern Greece. Nicias made peace with the Spartans, but the two cities and their allies continued to struggle. A young Athenian politician, the brilliant and aggressive Alcibiades, pressed for renewed conflict. The Athenians lost this encounter in 418, but Alcibiades continued to enjoy wide support. Politics in Athens was now pitched in a new key, in which demagogic forms of expression—violent words and gestures—seemed more effective than the more moderate language and gestures of a Pericles. War, as Thucydides would remark, proved to be a harsh teacher.

Athenian policy became more radical. In 415 BCE an Athenian army destroyed the city of Melos, which refused to become an ally, and massacred its male inhabitants. In the same year, Alcibiades persuaded the Athenians to undertake a bold but ill-planned expedition to help allies in Sicily against the powerful Greek city of Syracuse. Nicias, who thought the expedition foolish, was forced to take command, and the Athenian forces were defeated on both sea and land. Though weakened, the city fought on. During the last years of the war, Persian satraps forged an alliance with Sparta. A naval loss at Aegospotami in 406 was the final blow, and two years later the Athenians and their allies surrendered to the Spartans. The long conflict had cost the Athenians thousands of their fellow citizens, dozens of ships, and much of their wealth. The Spartans removed the Long Walls, which were torn down to music played by flute girls. Athens could no longer wait out sieges, confident that it could import the grain its population needed.

THE THIRTY TYRANTS

The period after the war's end was hard for the Athenians. The Spartans had damaged Athenian farms and destroyed olive groves, which took a generation to replace; and they had allowed many of the slaves who worked in the state silver mines to escape. Less prosperous than they had been for generations, the Athenians had to import more of their food than ever.

Moreover, after the Athenians begged for peace in 404 BCE, a short-lived aristocratic junta, the Thirty Tyrants, took over with Spartan backing. This oligarchical government did more than rule the city; it declared its opponents public enemies, executed them, and confiscated their goods. This was a radical form of attack on fellow citizens that would be repeated during hard times in the

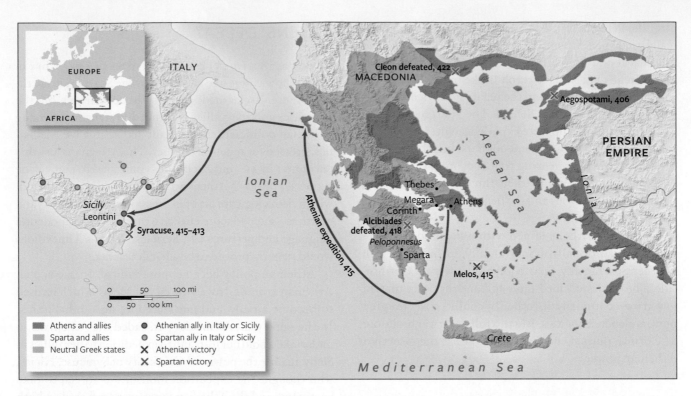

The Peloponnesian War, 431–404 BCE The Peloponnesian War mainly involved the two city-states of Athens and Sparta, but it raged across the entire Mediterranean region, from the massacre at the island of Melos in the Aegean Sea, to Alcibiades' ill-fated naval expedition to Syracuse, in Sicily, to the Spartan naval victory at Aegospotami.

Roman Republic and elsewhere. Opposition to the Thirty grew, and a small force of Athenian exiles seized a border fort. In bitter street fighting, the exiles defeated the leader of the Thirty, who died in the battle.

After further struggles, in 403 BCE the Thirty were expelled from Athens and the old laws and government restored. The democrats eventually declared an amnesty for the followers of the oligarchic regime, proclaiming that "we will remember past offenses no more." With its citizens reunited, Athens regained much of its strength. In the 390s the Athenians rebuilt the Long Walls under the protection of a fleet sent by the Persians, who wanted to counter the growth of Spartan power. The Athenian state began minting silver coins again, instead of the bronze ones issued during the war. Prosperity gradually returned, but Athens struggled against Thebes and other states for power over Greece. None managed to establish its power in a lasting way.

THE MEANING OF DEFEAT

The world's first great democracy was defeated in warfare by oligarchic Sparta. Those who have reflected on the

story, from the historian Thucydides onward, have often suspected that the city's ruthless pursuit of power over others brought about its defeat and the temporary overturning of its institutions—an outcome to worry supporters of democracy. The city and its institutions survived the turmoil, and a more or less democratic constitution lasted for some decades, but Athens would never again dominate the Greek world as it had.

THE ATHENIAN EXPERIMENT (490–406 BCE)

Culturally, the Athenian experiment succeeded beyond anyone's dreams. An extraordinary range of new artistic and intellectual forms, new ideas, and new ways of understanding the universe took shape in the city over the century that separated Cleisthenes' leadership from the end of the Peloponnesian War. The Athens of this period—in which, as we will see, Sophocles wrote his tragedies, Socrates inspired Plato to compose his dialogues, and Phidias and others created the magnificent complex of buildings and statues on the Acropolis—was not a quiet marble wonderland but a vast, messy debating hall, as agitated as Paris during the French Revolution of 1789.

THE AGORA

The city itself underwent a radical transformation during the sixth and fifth centuries BCE. When the Athenians began rebuilding after the second Persian invasion, they set to work on providing their city with public buildings worthy of a great power. The Agora had been established in the sixth century in a central area where three roads joined the city's main road, the Panathenaic Way. Peisistratus built a temple and a drainage system there. In the fifth century, the Agora became the site of a council chamber for meetings of the smaller body tasked with steering debate and legislation in the Assembly. Nearby, in a colonnade known as the Royal Stoa, the archon served as the state's chief officer of justice, and the laws of Solon, carved on stone, reminded Athenians that all men had the duty to take part in politics. By the end of the century other structures joined these buildings, including temples dedicated to Hephaestus, the blacksmith god, and Athena, the goddess whom the Athenians saw as their protector, as well as a debtors' prison. Perhaps the most splendid of all was the Stoa Poikile ("painted colonnade"), the walls of which were decorated with murals said to have been extraordinarily lifelike and beautiful. One of them depicted the battle of Marathon.

THE ACROPOLIS

Especially magnificent were the projects that the sculptor Phidias carried out, with the political and financial support of Pericles, on the **Acropolis**, the steep hill at the center of the city that is visible for miles and dominates the region. After they made peace with Persia in the middle of the century, the Athenians, between 447 and 432 BCE, built on the foundations of an earlier structure (destroyed by the Persians) what has come to be seen as the classic Greek building, the Parthenon. This structure was a subtly elegant rectangular temple to Athena Parthenos ("Athena the maiden"), one of the avatars of Athens' patron goddess. Built to house a huge gold and ivory statue of the goddess sculpted by Phidias, its roof was supported with columns of extraordinary elegance and its interior crowded with the treasures that belonged to the Athenian state—everything from Persian daggers and a gilt lyre to six thrones, more than seventy shields, and an

The Acropolis The steep Acropolis hill and its temple complex dominated the city of Athens from the mid-fifth century BCE on.

ivory figurine of a cow. The temple was also a strongbox—the Athenian counterpart to Fort Knox.

The same rebuilding campaign created other structures in Athens. One was the temple of the mythic hero Erechtheus, where graceful caryatids (columns carved in human form) supported part of the roof. Beneath it sheltered the ancient wooden image of Athena that the citizens had carried with them when they abandoned Athens to the Persians. In the same years, the theater on the southern slope of the Acropolis was rebuilt. Later still, after the crisis years of the late fifth century, the complex on the Agora was expanded further, with a mint, a new courthouse, and large inscriptions that evoked the city's democratic past.

GRAND STRUCTURES AND IDEALS

The public buildings of fifth-century BCE Athens resembled those of Near Eastern states in their scale and beauty. But their purposes, reflecting the society that created them, were different. For decades to come, Athenians described these public buildings as the clearest evidence of their ancestors' patriotism and virtue. In those days, as a fourth-century orator recalled, the Athenians' leaders had lived in modest houses exactly like those of their neighbors. In the orator's day, by contrast, wealthy men built themselves houses larger than the ancient public buildings—as clear a sign of ethical and political decay, in his view, as the public opulence of the old city had been indicative of ethical and political strength.

Yet Pericles' great buildings are ambiguous, at best, as symbols of the democratic state. They were built by a direct democracy, but the actual decisions were taken by Pericles and other male leaders, since the democracy excluded women, metics, and slaves from participation. The Parthenon served a religious purpose, showing that the Athenians felt gratitude to their gods for the victory over the Persians, who had burned the older temples and public buildings. But Pericles used the funds of the Delian League to pay for it. This must have given a clear sign to the other member cities that Athens saw itself as their leader—even, potentially, their ruler. Still, in this case, a city created public buildings on a scale that previously only monarchical states had constructed. The idea that a popular government should house itself and its gods with such grandeur also belongs to the heritage of Athenian democracy.

THE BOISTEROUS REALITY OF POLITICS

If the setting for public life was grand and orderly, its reality was often awkward and messy. The Greek comic poet Aristophanes (ca. 450–ca. 388 BCE) created the character of a poor countryman whom he used to describe what public life was like in the early years of the Peloponnesian War. Coming into the city at daybreak, the poor rustic finds the Pnyx, where the Assembly met, deserted because the city folk are still gossiping in the Agora. Bored and restless, he spends his time yawning, stretching, farting, and longing for his place in the country—only to be shocked at noon when the citizens, led by their tribes' representatives, crowd into the Assembly and fight for the places closest to the speakers' platform.

The boisterous process that Aristophanes ridiculed was the core of Athenian direct democracy. Every time a public debate broke out, the Assembly had to meet. This occurred, for example, in 406 BCE after the Athenian navy won a sea battle but failed to save the survivors from sinking ships. At a meeting of the Assembly, the commanders addressed the citizens and defended themselves. The council proposed a vote by tribes, which would allow the people to express approval or disapproval of the commanders' conduct. Savage debate broke out as to whether the motion itself was legal, ending only when the motion's author threatened to prosecute the officials who opposed it. After further debate, the Assembly voted to condemn the commanders, and six were executed. Soon after, however, the Assembly reversed itself and voted to prosecute those who had brought the commanders to trial.

Political and juridical processes in this system were noisy, chaotic, and subject to manipulation. Lies, threats, and unrealistic promises could sway the Assembly. No wonder, then, that Socrates' pupil Plato, the most brilliant and eloquent of ancient thinkers, despised his city's democratic government, especially after one of its juries condemned his teacher to death. And yet, as Pericles pointed out in his funeral oration, the Athenians' constant exposure to political and military debate, and their incessant involvement in deciding how the city should ensure its food supply or avoid secession by its subjects, gave even ordinary citizens a form of political education unique in the ancient world.

RELIGION AND CITY LIFE

Although it took the political genius of Pericles to rebuild the Acropolis, its buildings were dedicated not to public administration but to the gods who, Athenians believed, protected their city. The Greeks loved telling stories about these gods—from the traditional family of Olympian divinities headed by Zeus and including Ares, the god of war, and Aphrodite, the goddess of love, to the grimmer gods Hades and Persephone, who ruled the realm of the dead.

Oracle at Delphi On this fourth-century BCE vase fragment the god Apollo consults the oracle, a priestess in the Temple of Apollo, at Delphi in the southern Greek mainland. Even gods—but more often generals and statesmen—listened to the oracle's enigmatic advice.

The Athenian pantheon was never fixed. As one observer noted, "Just as in other respects the Athenians welcome foreign things, so too with the gods." Over time they continued to accept new divinities—from Dionysos, the god of wine, to Boreas, the wind god—as well as human heroes such as Theseus, the legendary king of Athens, and the two young men who killed the tyrant Hippias. Like other Greeks, too, Athenians recognized the gods of other cities and nations as divine. They were as eager as residents of any other city to consult the oracle of the god Apollo at Delphi, which gave notoriously ambiguous answers to the questions sent by rulers and ordinary people.

RITUALS The Greeks believed the gods inhabited the temples dedicated to them. They often referred to the statues of the gods, like the gigantic Athena in the Parthenon, as if they were the gods themselves. The interiors of these temples were not used for religious services, but important rituals were performed in them nonetheless. The old noble clans of Athens produced men and women who served as priests and priestesses, presiding over public rituals. Sometimes these involved dramatic sacrifices of animals. A young woman would carry a basket containing a sacrificial knife, and women would wail as the animal was killed, always by a male sacrificer. Occasionally the whole animal was burned; sometimes only parts, while the rest was shared out and eaten. In still other cases, the sacrifice involved no bloodshed but rather the offering of cakes, milk, and honey at the god's altar. Individuals also dedicated tripod vessels, vases, and even marble or bronze statues of young men and women, often with inscriptions explaining why they had done so.

Religious acts took place not only in temple precincts but throughout the city. When Greeks made a treaty or just organized a symposium (a party for drink and talk), they always began by pouring a little wine on the ground as a sacrifice to the gods. They also prayed, reminding individual gods of the long relationships between them and particular families, and expressing their hope for future favor. As one fifth-century Athenian wrote to the goddess Athena in an inscription that accompanied an offering, "Do you, daughter of Zeus, returning the favor, preserve [my] prosperity." Once a year, Athenians flocked to a massive shrine at nearby Eleusis, where they had the chance for a more personal religious experience involving rituals of initiation, after which the individual could lose himself or herself temporarily in a union with a divine being.

FESTIVALS The most striking feature of Athenian religion, however, was probably its public face. Life in any modern society is interrupted, throughout the year, for various purposes: holidays close schools, jury duty demands time away from work, and the like. But the interruptions are fairly uncommon. Ancient Athens, by contrast, enjoyed as many special days as normal ones.

Everyone knew that the calendar was thronged with religious festivals—as many as 150 in a year—and everyone knew, from the grand celebrations that accompanied

Religious Festivals At the annual festival of Dionysos, children aged two or three were given a first drink of wine from a child-size jug to celebrate their survival of infancy. These miniature wine jugs from Athens were made around 440–400 BCE.

them, when they took place. Varied in form and purpose, these rituals were dedicated to everything from celebrating the progress of the agricultural year to driving scapegoats out of the city. In some cases, they were as competitive as other Athenian activities, with teams competing in mock cavalry fights, exhibitions of skill at arms, and races. In other cases—especially those of the male and female groups that worshipped Dionysos—they practiced ecstatic rituals, leaving the city to do so. During these religious festivals the population did not work. The Athenian principle of equality also applied to the butchering of sacrificial animals, which were cut up into packages of equal size—some full of meat, others of bone and fat—and parceled out to every citizen for feasting. Although the public exercises of religion may have been more decorous than meetings of the Assembly, they embodied—and probably celebrated—the same democratic principle.

ATHENIAN SOCIETY

In the fifth century BCE, Athens dwarfed the other cities of mainland Greece. Covering some 1,000 square miles of Attica, its total population likely numbered more than 300,000 men and women: citizens, foreigners, and slaves. Much of its land was rural, with a large part devoted to the cultivation of staple crops such as olives, grapes, and barley. But the city depended on trade as much as cultivation. The Athenian climate made it hard to grow wheat, which was imported from the Black Sea region to the north through a system carefully overseen at tollbooths along the route. The richest citizens owned large amounts of land and earned their income by selling their surplus through middlemen in the city. The city also depended on a wide variety of artisans who constructed its buildings, adorned its temples, and manufactured arms and armor for its soldiers. Inscriptions on stone and passages in Greek comedy mention almost seventy different occupations, from the fullers who finished cloth to knife-makers and carpenters.

DAILY LIFE: DIVERSE GOODS AND PEOPLE

During the fifth century BCE, most of the 200,000 or so free Athenians lived and worked in the small households that were the basis of social life. The majority inhabited small stone houses with courtyards, constructed rapidly

Bounty of the Sea A fisherman holds small fish in his right hand and a basket of eel and oysters in the other. This Roman statue from the late first century BCE is likely a copy of a Greek original, suggesting the importance of the maritime economy to Greek city-states such as Athens.

after the Athenians reoccupied the city that the Persians had burned. Even the rich lived simply, as Athenians disapproved of excessive displays of private wealth.

With the seaport of Piraeus developing into the greatest market in the Aegean, Athens revived as a center of both manufacture and trade. Its workshops produced the goods for which the city had long been known, such as the red-figure pottery developed in the late sixth and fifth centuries, in which figures were left in the color of the clay, against a black background. Images on these vases show well-born men reclining and drinking at symposia, boys reading aloud from their books to their teachers and parents, women practicing mainly female crafts such as weaving, and the arms and armor that enabled the city to maintain its position in the Aegean.

Investors and traders saw to it that the city enjoyed all the goods it needed. A system of high-interest loans, which included an early form of maritime insurance, enabled traders to buy cargos of papyrus and rope from Egypt or

FIFTH-CENTURY ATHENS

> ❝ WE DO NOT COPY OUR NEIGHBORS, BUT ARE AN EXAMPLE TO THEM. . . . I SAY THAT ATHENS IS THE SCHOOL OF GREECE, AND THAT THE INDIVIDUAL ATHENIAN IN HIS OWN PERSON SEEMS TO HAVE THE POWER OF ADAPTING HIMSELF TO THE MOST VARIED FORMS OF ACTION WITH THE UTMOST VERSATILITY AND GRACE. ❞
>
> PERICLES, FUNERAL ORATION, FROM THUCYDIDES, *HISTORY OF THE PELOPONNESIAN WAR* 2.41.1

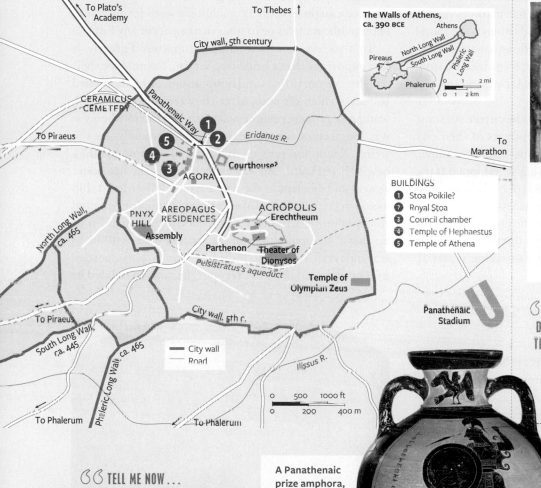

The Walls of Athens, ca. 390 BCE

Athens · North Long Wall · South Long Wall · Phaleric Long Wall · Pireaus · Phalerum

0   1   2 mi
0   1   2 km

BUILDINGS
1 Stoa Poikile?
2 Royal Stoa
3 Council chamber
4 Temple of Hephaestus
5 Temple of Athena

Map labels: To Plato's Academy · To Thebes ↑ · City wall, 5th century · CERAMICUS CEMETERY · Panathenaic Way · To Piraeus · Eridanus R. · To Marathon · Courthouse? · AGORA · AREOPAGUS RESIDENCES · ACROPOLIS · Erechtheum · PNYX HILL · Assembly · North Long Wall, ca. 465 · Parthenon · Theater of Dionysos · Peisistratus's aqueduct · Temple of Olympian Zeus · To Piraeus · City wall, 5th c. · Panathenaic Stadium · South Long Wall, ca. 445 · Phaleric Long Wall, ca. 465 · Ilissus R. · To Phalerum · To Phalerum

— City wall
— Road

0   500   1000 ft
0   200   400 m

Built atop the Acropolis in 447/6–433/2 BCE, the Parthenon was a magnificent temple dedicated to the goddess Athena, a storehouse for the city's wealth, and a monument to Athenian triumph. This detail from the Parthenon's frieze depicts the gods Poseidon, Apollo, and Artemis.

> ❝ THE GREEKS TEND TO HAVE THEIR OWN DIALECT, WAY OF LIFE, AND TYPE OF DRESS, BUT THE ATHENIANS USE A MIXTURE TAKEN FROM ALL, WHETHER GREEK OR BARBARIAN. ❞
>
> PSEUDO XENOPHON, *CONSTITUTION OF THE ATHENIANS*

> ❝ TELL ME NOW . . . OF THE GOOD THINGS THAT DIONYSUS BROUGHT HERE FOR MEN IN HIS BLACK SHIP. . . . FROM CYRENE HE BROUGHT SILPHIUM STALKS AND OX-HIDES, FROM THE HELLESPONT MACKEREL AND ALL SORTS OF SALT FISH, FROM THESSALY CRUSHED WHEAT AND BARLEY AND OX RIBS. ❞
>
> HERMIPPUS, *BASKET-BEARERS*

A Panathenaic prize amphora, showing Athena as goddess of military victory with spear and shield. The victor in the chariot race at the Panathenaic Games was awarded 140 of these vessels filled with olive oil (roughly five tons).

POPULATION

Approximately 300,000 (including 200,000 free inhabitants, 50,000 of whom were adult males; 25,000 metics; 80,000–90,000 slaves)

THE PANATHENAIC FESTIVAL

The most important of the 150 holidays in the city calendar, a week-long celebration of the city held every August with athletic competitions, musical performances, a male beauty contest, and a ceremonial procession through Athens to the Acropolis, culminating with the presentation of a sacred woven fabric to the city's patron goddess, Athena

QUESTIONS FOR ANALYSIS

1. What evidence do the quotations provide for the adaptability and grace that Pericles attributes to the Athenians?
2. Considering the map and the city calendar, what role do you think the Panathenaic procession and other festivals played in the life of the city?
3. How did the Parthenon and its remarkable art announce what it meant to be Athenian?

pork and cheese from Syracuse. If their ships returned and the traders sold the goods, they immediately paid off their creditors. If a ship sank (the floors of the Black Sea and the Mediterranean are littered with wrecked Greek ships), the trader was no longer liable for the money—a system that, like more modern ones, invited abuse.

Athens also became a center of consumption. Athenians loved to eat—especially fish—and they indulged in the rich eel, red snapper, tuna, and other delicious sea creatures that were available in Athenian fish markets. A poet of the fifth century listed the splendid things to be found on sale in Athens, as well as their far-flung sources: mackerel and salt fish from the Hellespont, frankincense from Syria, cypress from Crete, ivory from Africa, and colorful carpets from Carthage.

No wonder the Athenians, unlike the citizens of some other city-states, allowed foreign residents of their city to establish temples to their own gods—as, for example, local Egyptians did for Isis, whom they worshipped as the ideal wife and mother and the protector of the poor. The citizens of Athens expected to have access to a vast range of goods and were willing to accept the presence of many foreigners if that was necessary. This tolerance for diversity in goods and peoples gave the city a striking, if partial, resemblance to a modern metropolis.

WOMEN'S LIVES

Athens of the fifth century BCE was certainly no democracy in the modern sense. Women were formally excluded from all forms of public life and, so far as possible, from all male company. Women of the upper and middle classes (as we learn from the male writers and orators who are our chief sources) were supposed to remain confined to their houses. When Pericles praised the Athenian dead in the first year of the Peloponnesian War, he told the women in his audience that the best way for them to earn praise would be to not become the objects of gossip. Although this sounds horrifying now, he probably meant that women who were never mentioned in gossip would win reputations for virtue. Poorer women certainly could not have observed such traditional strictures.

THE FAMILY AND THE HOUSEHOLD Athenian men had considerable power over women. When a woman married, she and her dowry, the one substantial piece of property she was ever likely to own (even if only in a formal sense), were given by her father to her husband. If the

husband divorced his wife (divorce was easy to obtain in Athens), he had to repay the dowry to her father. If the husband died, she did not inherit his estate. Instead, one of his male relatives would marry her and administer the estate until his own male heir could inherit it. If a man caught another man having sex with a woman over whom he had authority—a wife or a daughter—he could kill the adulterer himself or inflict a variety of punishments, from taking his property to abusing him physically in public. Women caught committing adultery were forbidden to enter public temples or to wear ornaments of any kind.

In a society in which paternity mattered greatly, it was important that a bride be a virgin. To preserve their daughters from threats and temptations, Athenians tried to marry them off soon after they reached puberty. A woman of property might marry an older man when she was fourteen or fifteen years old. Immediately—as the writer Xenophon tells us in a manual on how to run a proper household—she was expected to make her house as neat and efficient as the captain of a well-ordered ship would make his cabin. Like Pericles, Xenophon insisted that women not attract attention outside the house: "Your business," his spokesman in the treatise said, "will be to stay indoors." Yet he also indicated that a woman needed a set of advanced skills to carry out the tasks mandated by

Women's Work This water jar, probably from fifth-century BCE Athens, suggests the gendered division of labor fundamental to Athenian culture. The seated woman is weaving, suggested by the wool basket at her feet, while a nursemaid hands her child to her.

Companions A detail from red-figure pottery (fifth century BCE), depicting a woman entertaining a man with music. Hetairai were professional women who provided elite men with music, conversation, and more intimate pleasures, and could count on a kind of social freedom that wives could not.

her separate sphere: she must keep the accounts, supervise indoor and outdoor slaves, look after slaves who became ill, and receive and store such necessities as wool and grain. Even as Xenophon praised the ideal household, he made clear that being in charge of it was a complex task.

Though women were confined, they worked at jobs that we know better from Athenian vase paintings than we do from any written texts. Most cloth, for example, was apparently made in the household. Paintings show women spinning raw wool into yarn and weaving it on looms. Even vessels made for men's symposia depict women making wool, which suggests that men esteemed this sort of work. Beautifully embroidered textiles might be displayed on cushions and chairs or as the clothing of statues of gods and goddesses to prove that the household's women were virtuous. Rich women would have been expected to supervise the female slaves who did this work.

PUBLIC APPEARANCES Naturally, not all women followed the purely domestic course that Pericles recommended. Young women marched together in some of the festival processions that Athenians loved to stage, and women of all ages attended funerals. **Hetairai** ("companions") were professional women who, from the sixth century BCE on, served as entertainers and companions for elite men. They appeared in public and attended symposia, where they played musical instruments, sang, and apparently took part in conversations. Collections of their witty remarks circulated in Greece. A hetaira named Aspasia was the chosen female companion of Pericles after he

divorced his wife. She bore him a son, entertained his friends, and supposedly gave him political advice. And he embraced and kissed her whenever he left or returned to their house, a warm gesture that other Athenian men are not recorded as offering their female partners.

Poor married women appeared in public by necessity. Those who had no slaves hauled their own water from the well and might have had to work as midwives or house servants. In less urban districts, women tended gardens and livestock. In the denser parts of the city, our sources offer glimpses of women assisting friends who had gone into labor, borrowing food and spices, helping to relight a lamp, and simply visiting one another as friends.

One exceptional source describes a woman named Hagnodike who cut off her hair, wore men's clothing, and trained as a doctor. After becoming a success at obstetrics, she was indicted for seducing her female patients. Brought into court, she raised her tunic to prove that she was a woman. Her prosecutors then denounced her even more fiercely—until their wives came to court and insisted that they stop bothering this woman who had helped so many others. Supposedly, the Athenians then changed their laws to allow women to study medicine. Stories like this are as rare as they are intriguing.

EDUCATION

Traditional Athenian education, which was chiefly aimed at boys, was not complex. They learned to read: vases show boys working with slates or scrolls in the presence of a tutor. As they grew older, they might go to a school. We know little about these, except that the law required they be open only between dawn and dusk. There or at home, boys would study the poems of Homer, from which, they believed, they could learn not only heroic ideals but also much practical information about everything from managing horses to fighting. From the seventh century BCE onward, music and movement formed an important part of many boys' education. Later accounts suggest that many learned to play the lyre and to set poetry to its music. Several hundred boys took part each year in formal choruses, and they were trained to sing and dance by *choregoi*— individuals from certain families chosen by the state to carry out this duty.

The point of all this preparation was to enable boys to emerge as young men able to play their roles in public life. Physical exercise was central to this form of training. Naked young men exercised at the gymnasium, learning

ATHENIAN FUNERAL LAW

This source from the late fifth century BCE, traced to the island of Keos near Athens, is a law governing burial practices in Athens. It is thought to be a copy of an earlier law enacted by the Athenian archon Solon. Throughout Greece, similar laws limited the expense of funerals and mourning at them. This was done partially as a democratizing measure: expensive or elaborate funerals could imply that the wealthy were more important in death than the poor. Another goal was to restrict women's attendance at funerals to the female relatives of the deceased, thereby reducing opportunities for women to gather outside the home. This source describes how Greek women washed the body and laid it out for burial, covering it with a shroud.

These are the laws concerning the dead: bury the dead person as follows: in three white cloths—a spread, a shroud, and a coverlet—or in fewer, not worth more than 300 drachmas. Carry out [the body] on a wedge-footed bed and do not cover the bier with cloths. Bring not more than 3 *choes* of wine to the tomb and not more than one *chous* of olive oil, and bring back the empty jars. Carry the shrouded corpse in silence all the way to the tomb. Perform the preliminary sacrifice according to ancestral customs. Bring the bed and the covers back from the tomb inside the house.

On the next day cleanse the house first with sea water, and then cleanse all the rooms with hyssop [an herb]. When it has been thoroughly cleansed, the house is to be free from pollution; and sacrifices should be made on the hearth.

The women who come to mourn at the funeral are not to leave the tomb before the men. There is to be no mourning for the dead person on the thirtieth day. Do not put a wine-cup beneath the bed, do not pour out the water, and do not bring the sweepings to the tomb.

In the event that a person dies, after he is carried out, no women should go to the house other than those polluted [by the death]. Those polluted are the mother and wife and sisters and daughters, and in addition to these not more than five women, the daughters' children and cousins; no one else. The polluted when washed with water poured out [from jugs] are free from pollution....

This law has been ratified by the council and the people. On the third day those who mourn on the anniversary of the death are to be free from pollution, but they are not to enter a temple, and the house is to be free from pollution until they come back from the tomb.

QUESTIONS FOR ANALYSIS

1. Why does the law limit the amount of money one can spend on funerals, and how might that restriction reflect Athenian democratic ideals?
2. What does "pollution" mean in this context, and how and why were women thought to carry that pollution?
3. What does this source tell us about Greek ideas about death?

Source: Mary R. Lefkowitz and Maureen B. Fant, "77. Funeral Law. Ioulis on Keos, Late 5th Cent. B.C.," *Women's Life in Greece and Rome* (website), www.stoa.org/diotima/anthology/wlgr/wlgr-greeklegal.shtml.

---

the arts of combat and competing in many forms of athletics. Eventually, an older man would become a young man's mentor and lover, teaching him the military skills of an adult and cultivating his mind. These relations were expected to follow a strict code. The older man had to maintain his dignity and not "fawn" on the boy or disgrace himself in other ways, and the boy was meant to learn to behave in a manly way. Unlike Sparta, Athens did not institutionalize these relationships in a formal, systematic way. But the similarities seem clear.

Technical education normally took place within the family. Healers and seers, carpenters and tailors taught their technical skills to their sons. Vase paintings show women reading scrolls, and many must have learned to do so. A few did that and more: Aspasia, the hetaira who was Pericles' companion, supposedly mastered and taught the art of rhetoric. Educated at home, most girls—at least according to the idealized description given by Xenophon—learned about diet and the various arts involved in making clothing.

Women Readers An olive oil jar from 450–425 BCE shows a woman reading a papyrus scroll. Women needed to learn to read, write, and do basic math in order to manage their households, but only a few exceptional women pursued their studies further.

METICS: RESIDENT ALIENS

As we have seen, many foreigners were attracted by Athens' wealth and power and settled there as metics. The city offered them work of every kind, especially when the great rebuilding program began after the Persian wars. At the same time, though, they were excluded from citizenship. In 451–450 BCE, Pericles introduced a citizenship law stating that no one who lacked two citizen parents could have "a share in the polis." Athenians, as a later historian put it, were the children of Athenians. Metics could and did serve as oarsmen and soldiers, but they could not own land, vote, hold office, or play any role in decision making. They could use the Athenian courts, but they were more vulnerable than citizens to summary arrest.

Citizenship could in exceptional cases be conferred on non-Athenians, as it was for the metic Pasion. A slave dealer who had been a slave himself, Pasion was freed by the bankers who owned him, and he prospered as a metic. He owned a factory that made shields. Showing an acute sense of diplomacy, he spent his profits freely on the needs of the Athenian people, who repaid him by making him a citizen. His son was an established Athenian who regarded himself as a guardian of the city's traditions. Most metics probably lived more modestly. Yet they too could win their way to citizenship. A list of men, probably metics, who were made citizens for helping to expel the oligarchic Thirty Tyrants in 403 BCE includes a farmer, a cook, a carpenter, a donkey driver, and a nut seller.

SLAVES

Even further from the status of citizens—and from enjoying the freedom and other rights that came with citizenship—were the thousands of slaves who kept the households and workshops of Athens functioning. Every bit as much as Egypt and Persia—as well as other Greek cities like Sparta—Athens was a slave society that depended on the work of unfree men and women. Most male slaves were purchased from a wide range of regions across Eurasia, from Syria to Scythia (the lands to the north and east, roughly from the Danube to the Don and Volga Rivers) and beyond. In the time of Pericles, Athens may have had as many as 80,000 or 90,000 slaves. Nicias, the aristocratic Athenian general who led the Sicilian expedition in 415 BCE, owned more than 1,000 slaves, whom he rented out to work in the mines. Even poor households probably had a few slaves, especially maids to perform basic household tasks.

Treatment of Slaves The working conditions of slaves varied widely: those depicted in this sixth-century BCE pottery fragment labored in a clay quarry.

COMPETING IDEAS OF SLAVERY IN HELLENIC SOCIETY

Slavery may be seen as a function of a society's cultural and political systems. Slavery was ubiquitous in Hellenic Greece, and some considered it necessary for the development of Athenian society. Most slaves were owned by and worked for Athenian families of all economic classes. These two sources, one from Athens and the other from a Greek outpost on the Black Sea, reflect differences in the ways slaves were defined and treated—socially, economically, and legally.

Constitution of the Athenians

The anonymous author of this treatise from the fifth century BCE is not Xenophon but is writing under his name. The treatise as a whole offers a critical interpretation of Athenian democracy. In this excerpt, Pseudo-Xenophon objects to the Athenian treatment of slaves as trusted and integrated members of society, and complains that it was essentially impossible to distinguish slaves, *metics* (resident aliens), and free persons.

Now among the slaves and metics at Athens there is the greatest uncontrolled wantonness; you can't hit them there, and a slave will not stand aside for you. I shall point out why this is their native practice: if it were customary for a slave (or metic or freedman) to be struck by one who is free, you would often hit an Athenian citizen by mistake on the assumption that he was a slave. For the people there are no better dressed than the slaves and metics, nor are they any more handsome. If anyone is also startled by the fact that they let the slaves live

luxuriously there and some of them sumptuously, it would be clear that even this they do for a reason. For where there is a naval power, it is necessary from financial considerations to be slaves to the slaves in order to take a portion of their earnings, and it is then necessary to let them go free. And where there are rich slaves, it is no longer profitable in such a place for my slave to fear you. In Sparta my slave would fear you; but if your slave fears me, there will be the chance that he will give over his money so as not to have to worry anymore. For this reason we have set up equality between slaves and free men, and between metics and citizens. The city needs metics in view of the many different trades and the fleet. Accordingly, then, we have reasonably set up a similar equality also for the metics.

Achillodoros, The Berezan Letter

This rare source, scratched on a thin piece of lead, comes from the Greek outpost on Berezan Island in the Black Sea. It was written by the merchant Achillodoros to his son Protagoras around 500 BCE. Achillodoros entreats his son to inform Anaxagoras of a dispute that has arisen between himself and Matasys about both the loss of property and the threat of enslavement.

Protagoras, your father sends you these instructions. He is being wronged by Matasys, because he is trying to enslave him and has deprived him of his cargo-vessel. Go to Anaxagoras and tell him, because he [Matasys] insists that he [Achillodorus] is the slave of Anaxagoras, claiming "[Anaxagoras] has my property, male and female slaves and houses." But he [Achillodorus] complains loudly and denies that he and Matasys have any business with each other, and insists that he is a free man, and [Matasys] and he have no business with each other. But if he [Matasys] and Anaxagoras have some business with each other, they know it between themselves. Tell this to Anaxagoras and his wife.

QUESTIONS FOR ANALYSIS

1. What does Pseudo-Xenophon mean when he says that Athenian society had "put slaves and free men on equal terms"?
2. Why might Matasys want to enslave Achillodoros?
3. How do these two documents illustrate the fluid status of slavery in Greece during this period?

Sources: Pseudo-Xenophon, *Scripta Minora*, in *Xenophon*, vol. VII, trans. E. C. Marchant and G. W. Bowersock (Cambridge, MA: 1925), pp. 479–81; Michael Trapp, ed., *Greek and Latin Letters: An Anthology, with Translation* (Cambridge: 2003), p. 51.

The conditions in which slaves labored varied widely. Many worked in agriculture at every level, from field laborer to overseer. Pericles owned a highly educated slave who kept "meticulous" accounts for his household.

Many slaves performed the same functions as free men and women, working beside them doing everything from weaving cloth to fluting columns. The workmen who built the complex on the Acropolis under Pericles included carpenters, metalsmiths, workers in gold and ivory, painters, and many more. Surviving records for one of the Acropolis buildings list eighty-six workmen whose status is clear: twenty-four citizens, forty-two metics, and twenty slaves toiled side by side, doing the same jobs. In theory, warfare was reserved for citizens. In practice, though, the Athenians were ready to abandon this rule in emergencies. In 406 BCE, when one fleet had been destroyed and another had to be fitted out by rapid improvisation, the Athenian Assembly used slaves to man the ships and granted them pay, freedom, and equality, not with Athenian citizens but with their allies, the Plataeans.

Other slaves worked in conditions as horrifying as those of the helots whose rebellions so worried their Spartan lords. Thousands, many of them children, not only worked in the Laureion silver mines in eastern Attica at terrible cost to their bodies but slept and ate below ground level. And in 413 BCE, when the Spartans invaded Athenian land in central Attica, some 20,000 slaves, mostly skilled workmen, deserted to the Spartan side—plausible evidence that they found their lives oppressive. All slaves, moreover, suffered indignities. Slaves belonged to their masters, who could sell them, rent them out, or bequeath them to others. Though they could marry, the master had an absolute right to break up their families. Protection from arbitrary violence and the legal right to purchase one's freedom, if one could assemble the necessary means, could not compensate for these hardships.

The prevalence of slaves in a state that stood for democracy and freedom seemed so awkward that the fourth-century philosopher Aristotle tried to explain it. Slaves, he insisted, naturally deserved their status because they were weaker and less intelligent than their masters. This argument would be revived almost 2,000 years later, during Europe's first age of colonial expansion.

ATHENIAN CULTURE: MASTERING THE WORLD

In the sixth century BCE the inhabitants of Ionian Greek cities, more quickly than their fellow Greeks on the mainland, became curious about the physical world and its many different inhabitants. Philosophers tried to understand how the physical universe operated: they offered explanations for earthquakes and the movements of the planets. Others tried to map the world and describe its peoples. After 500 BCE, philosophers and philosophy came to Athens, which gradually became the center of innovative thought in Greece. The Athenians learned much from Ionian thought, but they put their own twist on everything from poetry to philosophy.

This remarkable city created tragedy and comedy, and transformed rhetoric, philosophy, history, and more—forms of writing and thinking that have had lasting and pervasive effects. In medieval Baghdad and Paris, Athens was remembered only as the former residence of important thinkers. Even people who had no idea what the Parthenon looked like or any knowledge of Greek tragedy or history recognized words like *oligarchy* and *democracy* as keys to political life.

WAYS OF HEALING: HIPPOCRATES AND ASCLEPIUS

Athens in the fifth and fourth centuries BCE was a pressure cooker of political debate and intellectual inquiry. Native and foreign thinkers struggled to solve the problems of democracy and war and to understand their larger world. Medicine was one of the new ways of understanding that flourished in the fifth century BCE. The medical men—a group, rather than an individual, who wrote the works attributed to the single doctor Hippocrates (ca. 460–ca. 377 BCE)—were based outside mainland Greece. But they crossed and recrossed the Greek world in search of information about the human body and its ills, and of patients to treat.

Some of these medical men gradually developed new ways of dealing with disease. They insisted that a doctor must observe patients and record case histories precisely and unemotionally. They devised a system for explaining human physiology, which they claimed largely comprised four competing substances called humors: black bile, yellow bile, phlegm, and blood. Health depended on the balance among these, which the physician hoped to maintain. But because each city had its own seasons, winds, and water, the medical man must observe these closely to explain the illnesses that affected a particular people.

Hippocratic practitioners regarded all diseases as natural. Their empirical, fact-based method found a home in the skeptical, argumentative culture of the Athenians. Yet other sorts of healers also found a market there. After the plague of 430–426 BCE the god of healing, Asclepius, was eagerly received. A great shrine was built for him in Epidauros, where the sick, blind, and deaf could sacrifice, pray, and spend the night, in the hope that the god would visit them and heal their affliction. When he did appear, the temple priests interpreted his advice. More successes were

TRAINING FOR PUBLIC LIFE: THE SOPHISTS

The Athenians fiercely debated the diverse ways of understanding the world. In the homes of the well-to-do—especially in the *andron* ("men's room," the Greek version of the man cave)—guests lying two to a couch would drink wine and carry on discussions. Public argument was equally fierce and mattered more, at least in practical terms. Anyone who hoped to survive politically had to be able to speak effectively to the Assembly, in order to convince his audience that his proposals would serve their interests.

In 427 BCE, a brilliant orator named Gorgias arrived in Athens from the city of Leontini in Sicily, hoping to gain assistance in a struggle with a more powerful city, Syracuse. Athens agreed to help Leontini—a decision that would lead in the end to catastrophe, when the Syracusans routed the Athenian expedition in one of the gravest Athenian defeats of the Peloponnesian War. More important, Gorgias himself inspired fascination for the seductive power of his speeches, which were cast in language rich in alliteration. He became the first in a series of specialists who offered instruction in the art of public speaking.

These men, known as **sophists**, educated young statesmen for public life. They had a sharp ear for current debates over what sort of medicine or government worked best in which circumstances. And they knew

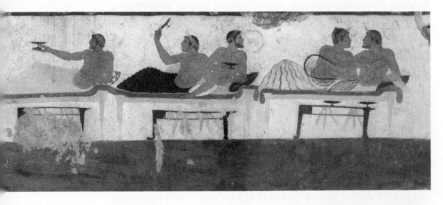

The *Andron* In this wall painting from 480–470 BCE, a group of men have retreated to the *andron* for a symposium, a gathering centered around wine-drinking and conversation. The men on the left are playing a popular drinking game, while the age-difference between the couple on the right suggests a kind of erotic relationship associated with the educated elite.

that absolute truths could rarely be established. So they trained their young pupils to argue both sides of almost any case and to be well informed, quick on their feet, and eloquent. Sophists also taught the technical skills needed to speak effectively: memory training for speakers who had no teleprompters to rely on, and elocution lessons so that they could be heard, unamplified, by a crowd of several thousand.

Education in rhetoric, the art of persuasive speaking, involved more than style and elocution; it emphasized content and form. Ideally, every statesman needed a grounding in moral philosophy and a treasury of historical examples at his fingertips, ready to cite at appropriate points. More important, he needed to know how to compose and deliver a speech. Aristotle (384–322 BCE) may have drawn on textbooks written and used by the sophists, which have not survived, when he divided speeches into three kinds: (1) deliberative or political, (2) forensic or judicial, and (3) demonstrative—straightforward praise or blame. Each kind of speech had a goal: to convince the audience where its advantage lay, in politics; where justice lay, in law; or who or what deserved honor and shame.

The sophists prepared their students to keep an open mind and figure out, as circumstances dictated, what approach to a problem would work best. At their most radical, the sophists denied that human beings could ever know absolute truths, and insisted instead that a practical education should limit itself to teaching students how to make arguments that others would find convincing. "Man," the philosopher Protagoras explained, "is the measure of all things." At their most ambitious, they claimed that they could master and teach all of the arts: one of them turned up at the Olympics wearing clothes that he had made himself and playing a musical instrument of his own manufacture. The sophists were the first Western teachers to offer what we would now call a liberal education, concentrated not on technical skills but on the range of arts needed by the free men who ruled Athens and other city states. Again and again, later societies from republican Rome to revolutionary America would treat the skills that the sophists taught as the core of a practical education for public life.

STAGING CONFLICT: CIVIC LIFE AS LITERATURE AND PERFORMANCE

Sophists wandered the roads of Greece looking for clients in all the city-states that welcomed political or judicial debates. Tragic and comedic drama, by contrast, were

Athenian inventions. They emerged during the late sixth and early fifth centuries BCE, when the great celebration of the god Dionysos underwent a slow transformation with extraordinary results. Like the Homeric epics of centuries earlier, Athenian drama became the common property of all Greeks, as theaters were built and performances of Athenian plays were held across the Mediterranean world.

THE FESTIVAL OF DIONYSOS The cult of Dionysos, the Greek god of the grape harvest, wine, and ecstasy, existed in archaic times and was celebrated by groups of men and women in rituals about which little is precisely known. In the sixth and fifth centuries BCE the festival of Dionysos became the grandest event of the Athenian civic year. It began with a procession of priests carrying images of the god, citizens, and metics, and involved sacrifices and offerings to the god. What made the occasion distinctive was that it came to include competitive dramatic performances. Every year, authors would compete to write the best tragic and comic dramas. Three authors would compose four plays each: three tragedies and a satyr play (a comedy involving imaginary wild men). Five more authors would enter comedies. Each would receive support from a sponsor, who paid for and trained the chorus and actors, and each one's plays were performed during the festival. A panel of judges selected the winners.

The plays were staged in the Theater of Dionysos, originally a simple dirt amphitheater that later became an impressive structure in the shape of half a bowl, its seats carved from stone, on the side of the Acropolis. The plays formed part of a civic ritual. The sons of Athenians killed in war paraded before the audience, and the tribute won in war was exhibited. Then, in front of a vast crowd that included women as well as men, actors and a chorus performed their parts. Formal and stylized, the tragedies never entirely lost their ritualistic character. Men took all roles and wore high shoes and masks, which defined the ways in which they could move and speak. Violent action took place offstage and was described as if witnessed by the characters in the play. And the choruses—groups of actors who danced, sang, and spoke commentaries on the action of the dramas—moved and pronounced their lines in an even more formal manner, befitting the origin of tragedy in religious ritual.

Yet these plays became works of art of great power and individuality, addressing many different subjects in radically different modes. Like the Jews in their exile, the Athenians at their cultural peak found ways to reflect on the relation between gods and humans, the nature of

Festival of Dionysos A large fifth-century BCE vase depicts a procession of followers of the god Dionysos, including a goat-tailed satyr. The grand religious festival in honor of Dionysos was the highlight of the Athenian year.

justice, and the weakness of humanity that retain their power even today.

TRAGEDY AND THE ANCIENT PAST Aeschylus (525–456 BCE), the first of the three great tragedians whose work survives, used **tragedy** to explore the meaning of human life and the origins of such institutions as law and justice. Setting a succession of plays in the world of Homer's poems, Aeschylus followed the sequence of events—as inevitable in his depiction as the cycle of seasons—that begin when Clytemnestra, wife of the Mycenaean king Agamemnon, murders him on his return to Troy. Orestes, their son, feels compelled to kill Clytemnestra in revenge, though he knows that he will be pursued by the terrifying Furies, the ancient gods of earth whose task was to avenge the spilling of blood—especially that of a blood relative. Only in the last play of the sequence, *The Eumenides* (*The Kindly Ones*, a euphemism for the Furies), does the goddess Athena intervene to create a human court, the Athenian Areopagus, which can judge cases of murder and declare them justified or not. Aeschylus's tragedies thus trace, in mythical form, the conflict between divine and human justice and the way in which a long chain of revenge killings was finally replaced by courts designed to reach just verdicts. Aeschylus's formal, often difficult language, like the plots of his plays, looked back to the mythical past and the foundations of those very Athenian institutions, such as the Areopagus, that lost or gained importance in the fifth century.

Sophocles (ca. 496–406 BCE) also set many of his plays in the deep past of myth, especially that connected with the city of Thebes. He portrayed Thebes as an imaginary, ancient Athens, a republic that had somehow come into being during an archaic age of kings and jealous gods. These gods tended to destroy any man who became too powerful by using his own abilities against him. As in the world of Aeschylus, curses—those imposed, for example, on individuals who kill their parents—are still effective.

In *Oedipus the King*, the main character unknowingly kills his father and marries his mother. Gloom hangs over Thebes. The smoke of sacrifice no longer rises to the gods, and the city's ancient, honest prophet can no longer interpret their messages. Oedipus is, in modern terms, not guilty, because he never intended to commit a crime. He killed his father, not knowing who he was, after severe provocation, and has ruled his state well. Yet he must tear out his too-sharp eyes, confess his crime, and leave the city to others in order to lift the curse he has brought upon the citizens whom he has tried to help. Oedipus—a good ruler who loves his people and proclaims his intention to punish whoever is polluting his country—finds that he himself is the source of the disaster and must suffer banishment. One wonders what implications Athenians—who often treated formal punishment as appropriate for political opponents—drew from this story.

Euripides (ca. 485–406 BCE), by contrast, concentrated less on questions of eternal justice and blood curses, and more on the psychology of individuals. His re-creations of ancient myth convey with shocking vividness the power of the gods to force those who worship them to commit terrible deeds. When Euripides decided to portray Orestes and Electra as the killers of their mother and her lover, in his own version he did so more to understand their emotions than to present them as adults struggling with the bloody commands of a human law that seems to conflict with the divine law.

TRAGEDY AND PUBLIC LIFE For all its apparent remoteness from contemporary themes and concerns, tragedy provided a way for Athenians to see, enacted on stage, some of the conflicts that provoked the sharpest political debates in their society. In *Antigone*, Sophocles depicts one of these through the actions of the brilliant ruler, Creon. Having just saved Thebes from chaos after an invasion, during which both the Theban leader Eteocles and his brother, the invader Polyneices, have died, Creon has taken command. Like a well-schooled sophist, he develops an elaborate metaphor—one familiar to thousands of Athenians from their time in the fleet—to justify his claim to absolute power: "Sirs, the vessel of our State, after being tossed on wild waves, has once more been safely

steadied by the gods." Creon demands (and here the tones of fifth-century BCE Athens can be heard) absolute loyalty to the state: "if any makes a friend of more account than his fatherland, that man has no place in my regard." Then he proclaims that Eteocles will receive the heroic funeral appropriate to one who has died for the city. The invader Polyneices, by contrast, will receive no burial, even though leaving the dead unburied, by Greek tradition, would pollute the city and invite the condemnation of the gods.

Antigone, the sister of Polyneices, insists that an ancient, divine law requires her to sprinkle dust on his corpse. Caught in this forbidden act, she accepts condemnation to death; this terrible fate, vividly described, is rapidly followed by the death of her lover, Creon's son, and the total collapse of his father. Both Antigone's sister Ismene and Creon denounce Antigone for violating the boundaries of female conduct. Yet the further progress of the play seems to show that she was right and they were wrong.

When read today, *Antigone*, first performed before the Peloponnesian War, seems a prophecy of central tensions in the Athenian polity: (1) the appropriation of the task of mourning for the war dead by male orators like Pericles speaking in public, and (2) the conflict between the Athenians' intention to defend liberty across Greece and the savagery of their actual conduct when smaller states refused to work with them. In its own time, it celebrated the woman's role as the guardian of sacred law in a society that seemed to be transforming some of its central customs and traditions.

Tragedy, then, did more than let individuals watch the terrifying but strangely gratifying stories of great men bringing themselves down by overreaching. It also made possible the literal staging—before a crowd of 15,000 that mirrored the population—of the dilemmas that afflict any organized society. Tragedy could not answer timeless questions such as how to reconcile the desire for revenge with the existence of a rational justice system. Its role was different: it literally dramatized the conflicts that no society could ever finally resolve.

COMEDY Unlike tragedy, comedy was set in the Athenian present, and it disregarded the complex rules that required tragedies to be dignified. The actors—all male—wore long phalluses to indicate the nature of the enterprise. The parts they played ranged from a slack-jawed yokel giving a comic perspective on the rituals of Athenian politics, to the politicians themselves.

Aristophanes (ca. 450–386 BCE), the greatest of the fifth-century BCE writers of comedy, offered commentary on the demagogic politics that corrupted Athenian

Comic Actors These terra cotta statuettes from the late fifth or early fourth century BCE, found near Athens, illustrate two characters commonly seen in comedies of the period: a grotesque, angry-looking man and a nurse holding a baby. All roles were played by men, who wore masks, and often padded costumes, to make the characters look bizarre and comical.

life as the Peloponnesian War raged on. At times, as in *Lysistrata*, he indulged in comic fantasy wild enough to convulse an audience. In this play, the women of Athens and other Greek cities, desperate for peace, conspire not to have sex with their husbands until peace is concluded. Their discussions—in which they decide to act as provocatively as possible, while still refusing to make love—parody the pragmatic arguments and calculations of Athenian political debate. At first the strike has ludicrous consequences (the actors' long phalluses play prominent roles in this particular comedy), but eventually the men of Sparta and Athens are forced to make peace. Like the tragedians, Aristophanes crafted models—indecorous and witty ones, rather than severe and tragic—that remain surprisingly powerful 2,500 years later.

HISTORY: CONNECTING PAST AND PRESENT

As grand and novel as Athenian drama, in its own way, was history—the effort, which came to center on Athens in this period, to explain the course of human affairs, using the same skills that had enabled the medical men to

understand disease and the sophists to forge the rhetorical tools of politics. In the poems of Homer and Hesiod, great households and important cities employed experts who could recite the genealogies of kings and aristocratic families. But in the fifth century BCE, history became something new: a form of writing cast in prose, not poetry, that connected the past to the present in a detailed, systematic way. Resting on inquiry as well as tradition, history was analytical as well as celebratory.

Like Hippocratic medicine, history began not in Athens but in the Greek cities of Ionia. Its name, the Ionian word *historie*, originally referred not to narrative history in the sense it does now, but to any systematic effort to understand the world through observation. The Ionian Hecataeus (sixth century BCE) not only made inquiries but recorded them, traveling as far as Egypt, known as a land with real historical records, to do so. And after learning about the deep past from Egyptian priests, he was a pioneer in subjecting earlier writers to sharp critique: "Hecataeus of Miletus speaks thus: I write what seems to me to be true. For the accounts of the Greeks are various and foolish, in my opinion." For Hecataeus, history would always be presented in the key of personal, human argument.

HERODOTUS: HISTORY ON A GRAND SCALE
The scale of the Greek wars against Persia and the Athenian war against Sparta called for a new sort of historical consciousness, cast in a new kind of writing. Herodotus (ca. 484–425 BCE), born in Halicarnassus, in Ionia, provided it. Cosmopolitan from birth, he had relatives outside as well as inside the Greek world. He tried to come to terms with the amazing Greek victories over Persia, not only as a tale-teller but also as a reporter of a new kind. Herodotus traveled throughout the Mediterranean world, interviewing everyone he could. Once he had established the complex background of alliances that led up to the wars, he completed his work—which he eventually read aloud at the Olympic Games, to the Athenians' vast satisfaction.

If Herodotus strove to match the ancient epics in the sheer size of his work and the range of characters it embraced, he made clear that unlike the poets, he had no Muses to inspire him: "Herodotus of Halicarnassus, his *Researches* are here set down to preserve the memory of the past by putting on record the astonishing achievements both of our own and barbarian peoples." He told the story of the Persian invasions and the victorious Greek defense with drama, irony, and wonderful descriptions of the decisive battles. But he also expanded his inquiry to the entire Mediterranean world, setting the wars in a vast

Persian Wars A fifth-century BCE drinking cup from Attica shows a swordfight between a Greek hoplite and a Persian soldier. Produced at the time of the Persian wars, it represents the Greek view of the conflict on an individual scale—similar to the approach Herodotus often took in writing his histories. The better equipped Greek soldier dominates the scene, looming over his ineffective Persian opponent.

geographical and historical context that included everyone from highly civilized Egyptians to Scythian nomads on the steppes of what is now Russia. Finally, he tried to explain why the wars had taken place—and found himself hard put to offer a hypothesis that went beyond the recitation of ancient myths.

Herodotus's work is a mixture of elements. At times—especially in his descriptions of the rise and fall of Croesus of Lydia, the overlord of the Ionian Greeks—he reads like the tragedian Sophocles. He explained the fall of Croesus's kingdom partly as the result of the gods' envy of great human achievement, partly as retribution for ancestral crimes. Yet when he narrated the events of the Persian wars, he devised vivid ways to represent the clash not only of individuals, as Homer had done so well, but of whole armies. And in setting out the background to the war, he managed to describe whole civilizations—for example, that of Egypt—in great depth, not only chronicling kings but also analyzing customs and institutions. He realized that peoples differed in what they ate, who they married or worshipped, and how they dealt with the bodies of the dead, all of which he recorded in detail.

As the first author of a political and military narrative on the grand scale of epic, Herodotus was the intellectual ancestor of all those who have since tried to document the history of great events. Herodotus was also the first writer we know of who used systematic, oral inquiry to find out what people thought, in his own world and outside it, thus making him the intellectual ancestor of all travel writers, ethnographers, and social scientists. At times, as in his dazzling narrative of the battle of Thermopylae, he managed to bring these forms of inquiry and writing together.

In his account of the brave Spartans' stand against the cowardly Persians at Thermopylae, Herodotus began to create what would be one of the longest-lasting and problematic legacies of Greek thought: the set of ideas and prejudices that depicted non-Greeks as less manly, less warlike, and less capable of free and civilized life than the Greeks. The term *barbarian*, which was originally just a description of non-Greek–speakers, gradually became pejorative in the fifth century BCE and after. Yet like Aeschylus, Herodotus, who had non-Greek relatives of his own, also considered events from the side of non-Greeks and made clear that, in the end, every civilization followed its own rules.

THUCYDIDES: HISTORY AS PAST POLITICS

Remarkably, another historian soon overshadowed the achievement of Herodotus. **Thucydides** (d. ca. 401 BCE), an Athenian, served as a general in the Peloponnesian War but went into exile when he failed to prevent the Spartans from taking a city held by the Athenians. Like Herodotus, he inquired as widely as he could, talking to participants on both sides in the war. Like Herodotus, he depicted the war on an epic scale, placing it in the broad context of Greek politics and tracing it across the Mediterranean to Sicily. And like Herodotus, he became a great writer whose prose retains its ability to move and shock.

Like many historians after him, Thucydides denied the debts that he owed to his greatest predecessor. Early in his work, he explained that he had set out to write his book "not as an essay which is to win the applause of the moment, but as a possession for all time"—a clear attack on the entertaining ethnographies and other digressions in Herodotus's work. By critically weighing each report against others, and by verifying so far as he could what his witnesses told him, he claimed to establish a reliable narrative of events—something Herodotus, in his view, had failed to do. And he made clear why it mattered to know the past.

Human nature would not change, Thucydides claimed. Accordingly, his history would provide not just a reliable narrative of the past but a key to understanding the events of the future. By collecting the speeches given by each side and inserting them into his work—or at least inserting the speeches that each side should have given—he made it possible, as Herodotus had not, to understand the real reason why the war had occurred. That reason was not divine retribution, but Spartan fear of growing Athenian power. At the same time, though he did not say this, he made his book a handbook for statesmen and generals who would have to meet similar challenges and would need to know what to say. It is thanks to Thucydides that we know, so far as we do, what Pericles said at the funeral of the first year's dead.

Thucydides' work established the principle—one still observed by leaders worldwide—that the most effective way to justify a policy or a decision is to cite an appropriate historical precedent. Along with rhetoric, the form of history forged at Athens by Thucydides became the core of elite education for centuries to come.

FINDING THE LESSONS THAT HISTORY CAN OFFER During the course of the Peloponnesian War, which we still portray more or less as Thucydides did, the Athenians started treating other cities in an increasingly tyrannical manner, demanding their support and destroying them if they refused it. In 416 BCE, the Athenians insisted that the tiny Spartan colony of Melos join them in their war against Sparta. When the Melians refused, in Thucydides' account, the two sides met to confer. Thucydides laid out the Athenians' demands and the Melians' reply. Every time the Melians appealed to justice or to the gods, the Athenians dismissed their arguments with outright contempt. The harsh tone of their remarks caused an ancient critic, in the first century BCE, to comment that it was "indecorous" for Thucydides to make Greeks address other Greeks in a fashion appropriate only for Persians.

Thucydides likely thought the same. The last books of his history describe the defeat of the Athenians in Sicily. During this debacle, the Athenians' leader makes the same ineffectual appeals to the gods and justice that the Melians had made when Athens was at the height of its power. In another section of the book, moreover, Thucydides draws one of his rare general conclusions. Just as he had described the plague to enable others to recognize it when it occurred again, so he described what happens in war to the language of politics: "Words had to change their ordinary meanings and to take those which were now given them. Reckless audacity came to be considered the courage of a loyal ally; prudent hesitation, specious cowardice; moderation was held to be a cloak for unmanliness; ability to see all sides of a question, inability to act on any."

In this first and greatest of military histories, Thucydides made clear the lesson that many later political and military historians have not been willing to face: that war, however necessary, can and often does destroy the moral and civil world of those who wage it. Sophocles had made a

similar point in his own way, but what tragedy portrayed as a dilemma, history narrated as a story that could have been given a different ending by wiser and more just decisions. To read Thucydides is to gain not only a training in the arts of rule but also a moral education in their destructive capacity.

PHILOSOPHY IN ATHENS

Perhaps the most distinctive and powerful Athenian creation of all was systematic philosophy. In the second half of the fifth century BCE, the city became the stage for a new kind of debate about everything from the shape of the universe to the purpose of human life. In the fourth century BCE, Athens became the home of permanent institutions for research and teaching founded by the most famous of ancient philosophers, Plato and Aristotle. The foundations for what they created were laid, however, in the great age of Athenian democracy—which, as we will see, ultimately proved unwilling to tolerate thought that accepted no bounds.

SOCRATES More critical of Athens than Thucydides—and more influential in the millennia to come—was another veteran of the wars, Socrates (ca. 469–399 BCE). He was not a member of the Athenian elite, although he inherited enough property to serve as a hoplite. In many ways he lived the ordinary life of an Athenian citizen, distinguishing himself for courage in battle and during political crises. But he turned his life into a unique quest to find the truth—or at least to establish how little of it humans could ever attain.

Supposedly inspired by the revered Oracle of Delphi, which once told a friend of his that no man was wiser than Socrates, he began to interrogate his fellow citizens. He expected to show that many were actually wiser than he. Gradually Socrates developed a distinctive approach that sought the truth by posing questions. This Socratic method showed, in almost every case, that the answers Athenians gave to the great questions about life and the universe were actually full of unstated assumptions and hidden contradictions.

Like the sophists, Socrates haunted the Agora at the center of the city. Trees, he contemptuously remarked, could not teach him anything, but his fellow humans might. Like the sophists, too, he knew how to apply the destructive tools of critical reason. During the Peloponnesian War he became the center of a group of aristocratic disciples that included the politician Alcibiades and two eloquent writers, Plato and Xenophon, whose works

Socrates This marble statue of Socrates from the Hellenistic or early Roman period suggests the continuing influence of Hellenic culture in the centuries that followed.

present him and his views in detailed (and contrasting) ways.

Unlike the sophists, however, Socrates refused to accept any payment for his teaching; at the end of his life he insisted that his special wisdom consisted only in the recognition of how little he knew. As happy to pose questions to a slave as to a sophist, he became the scourge of the respectable men who had never thought hard about the beliefs that they overconfidently professed. A passionately urban intellectual, Socrates seems never to have tired of the city squares where he could ask his questions.

It is difficult to know exactly what Socrates believed. At times, he seems to have believed that wisdom could be attained only by an intense process of ever sharper questioning; at other times, he seems to have felt that the gods might provide knowledge of certain kinds by direct revelation. According to Plato, Socrates disapproved of democracy and thought that the ideal society would be one ruled by a philosopher-king. But Socrates not only fought for democratic Athens; he also opposed the Assembly when it condemned a group of Athenian generals, in his view a violation of the law. Later he refused to obey the orders of the Thirty Tyrants when they commanded him to take part in a judicial murder, even though these aristocratic rulers included some of his supporters.

THE DEATH OF SOCRATES In the bitter years after the Peloponnesian War, Socrates became unpopular—so much so that he was brought to trial on charges of corrupting Athenian youth and introducing new gods to the city. Plato records in his *Apology* what he describes as Socrates' speech to the jury in his own defense: a brilliant exercise in defiance, in which Socrates not only refuses to apologize for his conduct but demands that the city support him for the rest of his life, as it supported other benefactors. Condemned to execution by a majority of the jury, he accepted the sentence and died (if we can trust Plato's account) among his friends, who wanted to spirit him away—a measure Socrates refused.

Socrates's death, like the example of his thought, has inspired artists and thinkers ever since his own time. His decision to die, like the inquiries to which he devoted his life, derived from one basic belief: that the philosopher must pursue wisdom not only with his mind but also in his life, which should become a disciplined, ascetic pursuit of virtue as well as wisdom. The tragic outcome of Socrates' decisions, moreover, has often been seen as a condemnation of the city in which he lived and which he criticized so sharply, demonstrating the limits of tolerance in the world's first democracy.

CONCLUSION

In a world dominated by great empires, and in a Greek mainland split among multiple states, the Athenians built a state ruled by its own citizens. Decisions about war and peace, life and death, hinged on speakers' abilities to convince ordinary people that they were right. Though women were excluded from public life and the city depended on slave labor for sustenance, Athens was a direct democracy for its free, native, male inhabitants. Athens was also Greece's dominant naval power, the leader of the coalition that had defeated Persia in two great wars. No other city could rival its private and public wealth, the splendor of its temples on the Acropolis, or the brilliance of the philosophers and orators who debated in its streets and assemblies.

Yet in later centuries the city has also been emblematic for its loss of equilibrium and tolerance. Its drive for power over the other Greek city-states in the years before the Peloponnesian War allowed demagogues to dominate the political scene. In the late fourth century BCE, Athens would fail to sustain its independence and its constitution against a brilliant conqueror, Philip of Macedon, and the democracy would come to an end. Still, for almost 200 years—a longer span than virtually any modern state except the United States—Athens remained both a working democracy and an unparalleled cultural center.

The fate of the Athenian experiment in politics has been a subject of debate ever since the time of Pericles himself—debates carried on in public speeches before the Assembly as well as in histories like that of Thucydides. For more than 2,000 years, Athens served as an example of the chaos that democracy can cause. Not until the nineteenth century did Athenian democracy win the admiration of political leaders and historians, which it still largely holds. In either perspective, the forms of expression created in Pericles' city have remained, like the word *democracy* itself, central to the Western tradition.

[CHAPTER REVIEW]

KEY TERMS

Pericles (p. 47)   deme (p. 48)   *metics* (p. 53)   sophist (p. 68)
Solon (p. 47)   ostracism (p. 48)   trireme (p. 53)   tragedy (p. 69)
democracy (p. 48)   oracle (p. 51)   Acropolis (p. 57)   Thucydides (p. 72)
Athena (p. 48)   Delian League (p. 52) hetairai (p. 63)   Socrates (p. 73)

REVIEW QUESTIONS

1. What specific steps led from aristocracy to democracy in Athens?

2. What drove Sparta and Athens to war in 431 BCE?

3. What types of activities took place in the Agora, and what do they tell us about Greek society?

4. How did Greek religious culture compare with that of other societies in the ancient world?

5. What roles did women play in Athenian society?

6. How important was slavery in Athenian society?

7. What was the key contribution of the sophists?

8. How did tragedy allow Greeks to explore the tensions in society?

9. What innovations did the Greeks make in the study of history?

10. What are the most lasting intellectual, social, and political innovations of Hellenic culture?

CORE OBJECTIVES

After reading this chapter, you should have a solid understanding of the following core objectives. To strengthen your grasp of the core objectives, use the resources on the Student Site for The West

- Describe how social pressures led to the growth of democracy in Athens.

- Analyze how and why Athens emerged from the Persian War in a position of political power and prestige.

- Explain the causes and the results of the Peloponnesian War.

- Show how the practices of Athenian political life differed from its lofty ideals.

- Evaluate the ways in which Athenian society was, and was not, genuinely democratic.

 GO TO inQuizitive TO SEE WHAT YOU'VE LEARNED—AND LEARN WHAT YOU'VE MISSED—WITH PERSONALIZED FEEDBACK ALONG THE WAY.

CHRONOLOGY

387 BCE
Persia imposes
"common peace"
on the Greek world

336 BCE
Philip II dies;
Alexander
succeeds him

334–330 BCE
Alexander invades
and conquers Persia

323 BCE
Alexander dies;
successor state
takes shape

3rd century BCE
Hebrew Bible translated
into Greek (the Septuagint)

274–168 BCE
Seleucid-
Ptolemy wars

338 BCE
Philip II of Macedon
defeats Athens and
Thebes at Chaeronea

335/334 BCE
Aristotle founds
his Lyceum

282–133 BCE
Pergamum flourishes

305–30 BCE
Ptolemies rule Egypt

238 BCE
Ptolemies call for new religious
feast in Alexandria, fusing Greek
and Egyptian religions

3

From Classical Greece to the Hellenistic World

CULTURES IN CONTACT

400–30 BCE

S ometime between 297 and 280 BCE, Demetrius of Phalerum, who oversaw the world's greatest library, sent a memo to his ruler, King Ptolemy II Philadelphus of Egypt. The library in question was a vast collection of Greek books stored in the new city of Alexandria, on the Mediterranean coast of Egypt. Demetrius thought that the collection also needed the laws of the Hebrews. The king agreed. He set free a number of Jewish prisoners and sent them as an embassy, bearing rich gifts, to the Temple in Jerusalem. There the high priest chose six men from each of the twelve tribes of Israel and sent them to Alexandria. Ptolemy spent a week discussing philosophical questions with them. They then translated the Hebrew Bible into Greek, taking exactly seventy-two days. The Jews of Alexandria examined the new version of their holy book and cursed anyone who would change it, indicating that they accepted it as authoritative. Then the translators returned home.

This story—though often repeated, in different versions, by Jews and Christians—is a myth, not history. Yet the core of the story is absolutely true. At some point in the third or second century BCE, the Hebrew Bible was translated into Greek, and the myth was popular enough to ensure that the most widely used version was called the Septuagint ("of the Seventy"). For centuries before this, Greek inquiries into other civilizations had

The Hellenistic World An 80 BCE floor mosaic from the Italian city of Palestrina depicts scenes of the animal and material wealth of the Nile River. The classical structures in this detail evoke the Greek-speaking people of Ptolemaic Egypt.

- How did Plato and Aristotle transform the Greek understanding of the world?
- How did the dynamics of power change in the Greek world in the fourth century BCE?
- How was Alexander able to conquer, and rule, so much of the known world?
- Why were the Hellenistic monarchies so vibrant economically?
- What were the most important components of social change in the Hellenistic period?
- What were the new elements of Greek culture in the Hellenistic period?
- In what ways did the meeting of Greek and non-Greek cultures produce new understandings and beliefs?
- How did the Jews respond to the social and cultural changes of Hellenism?

Mediterranean, began to give way. Greek became both a tool of empire and a language that crossed borders, enabling Greeks and non-Greeks to exchange objects, ideas, and beliefs. Greek institutions such as the agora (an open space, its sides lined with colonnades) and the gymnasium spread to new parts of the Mediterranean world and well beyond its borders. Athletic grounds and pillared temples made these cities look typically Greek, and the culture that developed in them derived from Greek religious, philosophical, and literary traditions. Historians call this period Hellenistic, both because it witnessed the high-water mark of Greek ("Hellenic") influence over the Mediterranean world and beyond, and because its societies and cultures differed in many ways from those of Greece's Classical period (fifth and fourth centuries BCE).

Greek culture did not simply replace long-held beliefs and traditions. Egyptian, Jewish, and Mesopotamian peoples tried to maintain their own beliefs and practices while under Greek rule. In this chapter we will focus on two examples: the society of Ptolemaic Egypt, which was the largest and richest Hellenistic state, and that of Israel. We will see that Greek understandings of the world penetrated both societies and mingled with their native traditions, with tremendous consequences for the development of the West.

NEW WAYS OF UNDERSTANDING THE WORLD

The original Greek cities would never again be so rich or so powerful as they had been in the fifth century BCE. But over the century that followed, one of them—Athens—continued to play a central part in Greek culture. Tragedies and comedies were still composed and performed; speeches were still delivered in the Agora; and charismatic teachers could still find brilliant, receptive pupils. For eight or nine centuries to come, ambitious young men (and a few equally determined women) from outside Athens and even from outside mainland Greece would come to the city in search of enlightenment.

PLATO AND THE ACADEMY

In the first half of the fourth century BCE, Athenian philosophy reached a high point of ambition and brilliance.

been the work of curious individuals such as Hecataeus and Herodotus. No Greek had managed to obtain a holy book from another culture, much less translate it. But in the Greek world of the third and second centuries BCE, as we will see, kings supported scholarship and science, and societies came into direct contact. The new understandings that emerged fundamentally transformed the development of Western literature, science, and religion.

These changes began in the course of the fourth century BCE, when the center of gravity of the Greek world shifted, slowly at first and then with a speed that stunned contemporaries. For hundreds of years, independent city-states had been the stages on which the political, social, and cultural dramas of Greek life had played out—not only in mainland Greece but also in areas as far-flung as southern Italy, France to the west, and the shores of the Black Sea to the north. By 300 BCE, though, foreign powers ruled many of these cities, as well as a range of territories outside the former Greek world. Massive kingdoms originating in Macedonia and incorporating Greek ways overspread the region.

Now Aramaic, which for centuries had been the language of trade and empire in Asia and much of the eastern

Socrates' disciples, above all Xenophon and Plato, departed from their teacher's model in vital ways after his execution in 399 BCE. Whereas Socrates, who feared that writing could harm the memory, had taught only orally, his pupils composed elaborate written dialogues and memoirs in which they offered vivid portraits of Socrates as he had lived, taught, and died. Theirs are the only works in which we hear Socrates speak. And although Xenophon (ca. 431–ca. 352 BCE) depicted Socrates as a great but rather conventional moralist, **Plato** (429/8–348/7 BCE) developed the dialogue into a powerful form of philosophical writing.

Plato also established philosophy on a new basis. Socrates had simply talked with anyone who wanted to listen to him. Plato turned the subject into a group pursuit with a firm location. When he inherited property in the 380s BCE, he created an institution for study at the site of an olive grove a mile or so outside the walls of Athens. Known as the Academy, a site sacred to the legendary hero Akademos, this club was a private association that admitted only an elect group to study. It became the ancestor of, and gave its name to, the long series of educational institutions—including the modern university—that have existed in the West.

Plato's Academy A mosaic from a house at Pompeii (early first century BCE) imagines Plato's Academy: men under a tree reading and talking, with the Acropolis distantly visible in the background.

THE WORLD OF FORMS

Building on Socrates but going far beyond him, Plato envisioned the universe of our daily experience as only the shadow of the true world of **forms**—the preexisting ideas that the creator of the universe used as patterns when assembling the planets and the earth. Human beings, Plato argued, were born with memories of this higher world that could be reawakened. In this ideal realm humans were ethically required to pursue truth and virtue, which for Plato, as for Socrates, were closely connected. But because people had to carry out this quest in the turmoil of the everyday world, they could never do more than approximate the highest truths and harmonies. And most would never even realize that a higher world existed outside daily reality.

In Plato's ideal world there is a form for the city, a society in which men and women carry out the tasks for which they are suited by nature. Most do humble, repetitive work. But women, as well as men, of high ability serve as the "Guardians," who see to it that justice is done for all. Plato was at times pessimistic about whether a society that approximated this ideal one could exist in reality. In his great work of political philosophy, *The Republic*, Plato has Socrates describe everyday humanity as the prisoners of illusion, their world a cave and their lives projected images on the wall. If a philosopher escapes the cave and reaches the light of the higher world, he will at first be dazzled; and even when he has achieved understanding, he will find it impossible to descend back into the cave and convince his fellows of what he has seen.

PHILOSOPHY IN THE WORLD

Yet Plato visited the great city of Syracuse in Sicily twice, hoping to convince the city's tyrant, Dionysius II, to restructure it on ideal lines. By teaching the ruler, an adviser suggested, Plato would introduce "the true life of happiness throughout the whole territory." But he could not persuade the ruler to listen, and his efforts ended in failure. In the end, the government of Athens, which he disdained, had to arrange for him to be freed from arrest.

In Athens, however, Plato's teaching won disciples. He argued that the study of certain disciplines, especially mathematics, could yield insight into the realm of pure forms. And he proposed that the heavens, in which the stars and planets moved regularly and permanently around the earth, were more perfect than the earth, and the animals and humans who live on it. Many of his followers—especially the pioneering astronomer Eudoxus (ca. 390–340 BCE)—were inspired by him to study the mathematical disciplines, which became a hallmark of the Academy.

ARISTOTLE AND HIS SCHOOL

Aristotle (384–322 BCE), a native of Stagira in what is now northern Greece, moved to Athens to become Plato's pupil in the Academy. But in the well-established Greek tradition, he soon disagreed with, and distanced himself from, his teacher. Whereas Plato emphasized formal argument and mathematics, Aristotle favored the **empirical** study of reality. A gifted student of biology, he waded into tide pools to study starfish. He discussed the habits of animals with expert hunters and fishermen, who taught him that sharks produce not eggs but baby sharks, as if they were mammals; and he conferred with beekeepers, who described the belly dance with which their bees deposited pollen. (These two observations were either mocked or misunderstood until they were verified in the nineteenth and twentieth centuries.) As a student of living beings, Aristotle believed that the forms governing their development existed within them, not in a separate world of perfect ideas.

THE LYCEUM Aristotle used the same basically empirical approach when studying other areas, such as literature and politics. In 335 or 334 BCE he, too, founded a school—in the **Lyceum**, a public meeting place in a grove outside Athens, which also housed a gymnasium where hoplites exercised. The school was dedicated to Apollo, the god of sun, light, and music. Aristotle equipped his new institution with a portico in which students could walk as they carried on their discussions and with a library, which became a research tool of a new kind. To understand the effects of tragedy, he inspected many examples and identified the formal qualities that could produce a purge of emotions in the viewer, called catharsis. And to understand the different forms of civic life, he and his pupils collected dozens of accounts of constitutions. Only one of these, a detailed investigation of the development of government at Athens, survives.

POLITICS Aristotle used these collected materials to create a systematic work, *Politics*. He argued that all governments can be assigned to one of six categories, three good and three bad: democracy, aristocracy, and monarchy on the one hand; ochlocracy (mob rule), oligarchy, and tyranny on the other. Even as the age of the independent city-state drew to a close, Aristotle stuck to the belief that the typical small Greek community, in which citizens all knew one another, was the natural, and thus the ideal, form of state for human beings. People were, he explained, "political animals"—beings whose natural dwelling place was the city.

TWO PHILOSOPHERS, TWO WORLD VIEWS

Plato and Aristotle disagreed on central points. For Plato, the deepest truths lay outside the universe that humans inhabited and could observe, whereas for Aristotle these truths could be found inside it. But both men envisioned the physical universe in terms of hierarchies and saw the world of the heavens as changeless, permanent, and more perfect than the world of matter below.

Both believed in social hierarchies as well. Plato imagined a perfect society in which everyone carried out the tasks for which nature had fitted him or her. Aristotle held that some peoples, especially the Persians, were servile by nature and therefore well adapted to monarchical states. But he also believed that many Greeks were destined by nature to be slaves. This argument would find eager acceptance in many slave societies over the centuries.

Above all, both men insisted that philosophy, as they pursued it, was a comprehensive—even encyclopedic—inquiry and a way of life. Over the centuries to come, their followers would accept this ideal even as they continued to comment on, and sometimes alter, the founding texts of their schools.

THE TRANSFORMATION OF GREECE IN THE FOURTH CENTURY BCE

The philosophers explained the world as if nothing had changed since the time of Socrates, or even before. In fact, though, the political and military world of the city-states had been transformed by the Peloponnesian War (431–404 BCE). In the years that led up to the war, local rivalries and quarrels were largely suppressed by the formation of the Athenian and Spartan power blocs, which most of the independent city-states joined. After the war, Athens and Sparta were both poorer and less powerful than they had been, and powerful smaller states such as Corinth and Thebes could change the balance of power by switching alliances. In this new situation, conflicts between city-states flamed up more frequently than in the past.

POWER IN THE REGION

In the 390s, Corinth, Argos, and Boeotia, the northern Greek region around Thebes, joined Athens in a league against the Spartans, whom they defeated at sea, thanks to a rebuilt Athenian fleet. In 387 BCE, however, the Spartans defeated the Athenian navy near Asia Minor. Thereafter the Spartan commander opened negotiations with the Persians, again a formidable power in the region. A year later, the king of Persia, Artaxerxes II (r. ca. 404–ca. 358 BCE), a ruthless ruler who was as deft at murdering rivals at court as he was at making war with the Greeks, imposed a "common peace" on the Greek world, with Sparta in a dominant position.

This settlement did not last long. Thebes soon asserted itself as a new regional power, rising to leadership in a confederacy of states grouped against Sparta. Its "Sacred Band"—an elite infantry corps comprising 150 pairs of male lovers supported by the state—played a particularly important role when the Thebans defeated the Spartans at Leuctra in 371 BCE. Theban forces killed more than half of the 700 Spartan hoplites who took part in the battle, a crippling blow. Between 371 and 362, a rebellion of some of the Persian **satraps** (provincial governors) and conflicts with Egypt occupied Artaxerxes. Thebes dominated Greece until the battle of Mantinea in 362, when an alliance of Spartans, Athenians, and others defeated a league led by the Thebans.

Sparta never recovered its former strength, however, and even Athens had only a fraction of the material and human resources it had possessed in the age of the Delian League. Athens now claimed fewer than half of the 200,000 or so citizens it had once boasted. The Persian Empire continued to be the greatest power in western Asia and the Mediterranean, incomparable in wealth and in the scale of its army and administration.

CHANGES IN THE CITY-STATE

In this period of decline, many city-state institutions survived. Athenians continued to serve for pay on state juries. A new system of indictments made the positions of

Greece in the 4th Century BCE

officeholders even more precarious than they had been in the fifth century BCE, when ostracism sometimes rid the city of overly powerful men. Professional orators still dominated public life and continued to address large crowds in the Assembly, where they evoked the glories of the ancestral democratic constitution of Athens.

In other respects, though, the city-state system was no longer what it had been. Persia regularly intervened in Greek affairs, threatening the autonomy of individual cities that the Greeks had preserved from Persian aggression, at least in the Greek mainland, in the fifth century. In the perpetual warfare of the period, Athenians and other Greeks who would once have served in their own cities' armies found themselves fighting as mercenaries for anyone who would pay. Whereas hoplites could fight only during the warm months, when they could leave their farms, mercenaries could fight all year, weather permitting. Moreover, new tactics—especially the use of *peltasts* (lightly armed foot soldiers equipped with javelins) and cavalry—began to prove more effective than the traditional hoplite army. Warfare now assumed a professional form and took place on a vast scale.

THE RISE OF MACEDON

As the Greek city-states struggled for preeminence, a new power was rising in the north, one that they could not resist even when they formed alliances against it. Macedonia was a kingdom ringed by mountains and endowed with rich natural resources, including gold, silver, and timber. Situated between mainland Greece and the Balkans, Macedonia developed around the capital at Aigai, which was less a city than a palace complex like those of Mycenae long before.

Archaeological evidence shows that the Macedonians built a wealthy warrior nation that produced arms and jewelry far more splendid than anything seen in the Greek cities. But they adopted the Greek gods of Olympus as theirs, and their rulers traced their ancestry back to the Greek hero Heracles. It was Heracles who carried out the miraculous task of cleaning the legendarily filthy Augean stables by diverting a river to run through them.

Macedonian Currency
A silver coin from fourth-century BCE Macedon bears the name of Philip II and an image of a horseman.

By the fifth and fourth centuries BCE, Macedonia had become part of the larger Greek world. The presence of precious metals made coinage possible, and trade developed with Greece. Timber and minerals were exchanged for red-figure pottery and other Athenian consumer goods. The Greek language came into common use.

In the middle of the fourth century, **Philip II** (r. 359–336 BCE), a brilliant ruler, united Macedon, treating Greek-speakers and non-Greek-speakers as of equal value to the state. He forged his subjects into a new kind of fighting unit: infantry schooled to drill and fight in a formation called by the traditional term *phalanx*. Two innovations made this particular version distinctive. Philip introduced a new kind of spear, the *sarisa*, thirteen to twenty feet long and made of flexible dogwood. Each spear extended several feet beyond the man who held it. When the rows of spearmen who made up the phalanx marched, the sharp-edged metal points of their spears preceded them, row after row, like a terrifying metal hedge. Equally vital was the intensive training that disciplined the Macedonians so that they could march or attack at great speed in any direction, or stick together and hold off cavalry attacks that would have scattered other infantry forces. The Macedonians became a tightly packed, swiftly moving, and powerful striking force. The phalanx could not turn easily, but when it attacked an enemy line, its force was almost irresistible.

Philip, moreover, coordinated infantry with cavalry in new ways. Once the phalanx had broken the front of an opposing army, the horsemen—too lightly armed and, because they had no stirrups, too lightly attached to their horses to mount an effective frontal assault—moved in and slaughtered the enemy infantry. In former times, the Macedonians had chosen their rulers for their prowess as soldiers. Philip followed this tradition. He served as a commander and fought ferociously himself, losing an eye as the price for one major victory.

THE CONQUEST OF GREECE

Military action in northern Greece won Philip access to still greater resources. Thrace, which he conquered, gave him rich gold mines. Thessaly, where he intervened in a civil war, provided him with the most skillful cavalry in the Greek-speaking world. A brilliant recruiter of talent, Philip assembled not only a superb mercenary army but also a new aristocracy of adventurers from all over the Greek world, many of whom he settled in conquered lands.

In 348 BCE, when he took Olynthus, a powerful ally of Athens in northern Greece, he confiscated its territory and enslaved its population. The Athenians tried to convince the other Greeks to ally with them against Philip, but they failed and made a grudging peace with him in 346.

Philip continued to expand his power and territory, moving steadily into southern Greece. Even the demonic energy and fiercely democratic convictions of the great Athenian orator Demosthenes (384–322 BCE), who denounced Philip in speeches that became proverbial for their intensity and power, were not enough to resist him. Demosthenes' contemporary, Isocrates, a brilliant writer

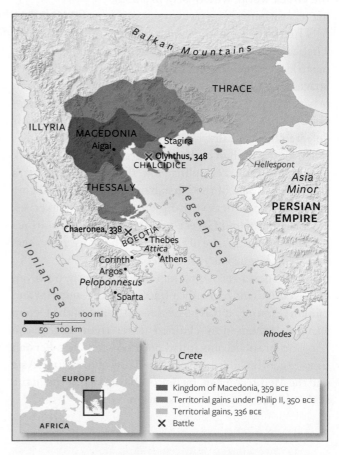

The Rise of Macedon, 359–336 BCE Philip II waged a brilliant military campaign to conquer Thessaly and Thrace, defeating Athens and its allies at Olynthus and Chaeronea and subjecting native populations to his control. By the time Philip was killed, his domain reached across Thrace, where he challenged the borders of the powerful Persian Empire.

and a renowned teacher of oratory, hoped to see Greece unified and at peace. He appealed to Philip, whom he tried to convince to make peace with the Greek states, and he may have helped to inspire in Philip the idea that he might eventually challenge Persia. But the outcome was far from the Greek union Isocrates had had in mind. In 338 BCE, Philip challenged and defeated Athens and Thebes at Chaeronea, in the northern Greek region of Boeotia.

Thereafter a conference in Corinth proclaimed the creation of a new league of Greek states, led by Philip. He now declared war against Persia and sent an invading force across the Hellespont, the strait between Europe and Asia that Xerxes had bridged when he invaded Greece in 480 BCE. From now on, foreign rulers would be the masters of Greece. Even Isocrates, who had hoped to see the Greek cities unified, acknowledged that this change was tragic and starved himself to death.

Alexander the Great A mosaic from Pompeii depicts Alexander leading the cavalry charge against Darius's Persian forces at Issus in 333 BCE.

ALEXANDER THE GREAT: THE WORLD TRANSFORMED

Philip was killed by an assassin in 336 BCE, and his son Alexander (356–323 BCE) took power at the age of twenty. Though he ruled for only thirteen years before his own death, the prodigiously talented Alexander transformed much of the known world—even areas that had previously been largely unknown to the Greeks.

THE YOUNG CONQUEROR (334–326 BCE)

Alexander began by establishing his position in mainland Greece. When Thebes rebelled against him in 335 BCE, he demolished the city and enslaved its citizens. This shocked the other Greek city-states and revealed the costs of resistance. In 334 Alexander crossed the Hellespont with an army of 32,000 infantrymen and 5,000 cavalry to attack Darius III of Persia (r. 336–330 BCE). An advance force of 10,000 more Greeks awaited Alexander in Persia. Still, he had far fewer soldiers than his opponent, who mustered as many as 100,000 infantrymen and 20,000 cavalry. But Alexander's mastery of tactics, speed in action, and determination gave him the advantage.

BATTLING PERSIA In his first confrontation with the Persian armies, at the river Granicus in northwestern Asia

Minor in 334 BCE, Alexander faced superior numbers on high ground across the river. But the Persians had put their cavalry in front of their 20,000 Greek mercenaries, who could otherwise have prevented Alexander's men from crossing. Alexander led a cavalry charge across the river, visible to all in polished armor and a helmet with a white plume. Though he risked and almost lost his life, he inspired his infantry, who punched through the Persian cavalry and slaughtered almost all of the Greek mercenaries. At this, most of the Greek cities under Persian rule came over to Alexander.

After much maneuvering, Darius himself confronted Alexander in 333 BCE at Issus, a narrow plain between the mountains and sea in southeastern Asia Minor. This time Alexander used his cavalry to flank and disrupt the Persian battle line. Darius fled in his chariot and then, when it stalled, on horseback. Alexander captured the treasures with which the Persian ruler traveled, as well as the women of his household, whom he treated with humanity and respect. Ignoring a peace offer from Darius, Alexander went on to conquer Egypt and then turned back eastward, intent on a final victory against the Persian king, who had regrouped his forces in Babylon.

In the autumn of 331 BCE, Greeks and Persians met in a climactic battle at Gaugamela in what is now northern Iraq. The Persians had war elephants and terrifying chariots armed with sharp scythes. But the disciplined Macedonians opened holes in their lines, let the chariots through, and then isolated them and slaughtered their crews. Alexander once again disrupted and annihilated the Persian line of battle, and Darius fled once more, leaving the Macedonian master of the field.

CONQUERING PERSEPOLIS (330 BCE) Alexander systematically stamped out opposition. When cities resisted him, as the Phoenician ports of Tyre and Sidon did, he stopped, laid siege, and did not move until he had crushed his opponents. He conquered not only the ancient cities of Babylon and Susa, which the Persians had ruled for centuries, but the ancient Persian capital of Persepolis, which he looted and burned in 330 BCE. From Persepolis he took the entire Persian treasury—a vast quantity of bullion worth the equivalent of more than $1 trillion today. He turned the bullion into coin, sharply expanding the money supply in the region. This not only strengthened Alexander's war machine but also transformed the economy of central and southern Asia. Realizing the futility of resistance, Darius's followers murdered their king, and

Alexander suddenly dominated the Mediterranean world and western Asia like a colossus.

Challenges soon arose—in the first instance, from the Persian who had killed Darius. But Alexander assigned his own satraps to deal with this revolt. He himself moved through the extraordinarily difficult terrain of what are now eastern Iran and western Afghanistan, crossed the high passes of the Hindu Kush, and invaded Bactria (modern Afghanistan).

TECHNIQUES OF RULE Though revolt followed revolt and Alexander suffered some major reverses, he soon developed an effective technique for establishing control of the nations he conquered. As the ruler of Macedon, he continued to rely on the Macedonians and Greeks who fought for him. But once he took control of Persia, he kept Persian officials in office as well, demanding that they prostrate themselves before him as they had done before their Persian rulers. At the end of his life, he supposedly

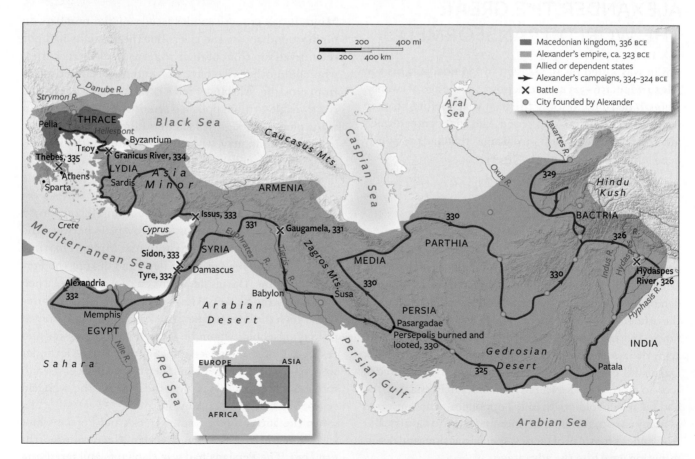

Alexander's Conquests, 336–323 BCE In 334 BCE Alexander crossed the Hellespont and engaged the Persian army in battle. His army defeated Darius III's forces repeatedly as they marched across the Near East and Central Asia, conquering Egypt, Babylon, and Persepolis, and territory as distant as Bactria (present-day Afghanistan). In just ten years, the entire area from Greece and Egypt to the borders of India was under Alexander's control, and contained many newly established cities, including several named Alexandria.

Hellenistic Affluence After Alexander conquered the Persian Empire, the taste for Hellenistic luxury goods spread as far as India. Jewelry like this delicate gold armband, decorated with the characteristically Hellenistic "Herakles knot," spread around the Greek-speaking world.

planned to move whole populations from Europe to Asia and vice versa to encourage intermarriage. He did establish many new settlements: about twenty new Greek cities, from Alexandria on the river Strymon in modern Bulgaria to Alexandria on the Indus in modern Pakistan. To these cities, a Greek ruling class brought not only the use of coinage but many other Greek customs. By working with different subject peoples and by fostering the spread of Greek culture in new territories, Alexander set the tone for the Hellenistic period.

Astonishingly, Alexander did not stop once he had defeated Greece's traditional enemies. Instead, following reports of the wealth and other marvels to be found at what Greeks considered the edge of the world, in India, he moved onward. In 326 BCE he defeated the Indian king Porus (d. 318 BCE), who ruled a state in what is now Punjab and whose vast army included war elephants, at the river Hydaspes. Even when his exhausted soldiers finally mutinied, Alexander continued his career of adventure. He turned south and fought his way, with great brutality, to the Arabian Sea. There he built a fleet, which he sent home under the command of a trusted admiral. He himself led his armies overland back toward the countries they had first conquered, in an epic journey through the deserts, to Persepolis and Susa.

RULING CULTURES (325–323 BCE)

From 325 BCE to his death in 323, probably from disease, Alexander established himself as absolute monarch of much of the known world: at least of Greece, Persia, and—as he claimed with more optimism than accuracy—Asia. Some modern historians have credited Alexander with a conscious policy of ethnic tolerance. He certainly showed none of the sense of Greek superiority that had established itself in the fifth century and that Aristotle, with whom he studied, had incorporated into his philosophy. Throughout his career Alexander worked effectively with men of many different origins. But the egalitarian interpretation of his thought goes beyond the contemporary evidence.

A PERSIAN GREAT KING What seems most likely is that Alexander saw himself as the successor of the Persian Great King. At the wedding ceremony that Alexander held in 324 BCE in the Persian city of Susa, where he married Barsine, eldest daughter of Darius, he wore court dress that was largely Persian. He also followed Persian court ceremonies and began to claim not only descent from Heracles but also divine status on the basis of his stupendous achievements. Persians had prostrated themselves before their king; now not only former Persian subjects but Macedonians and Greeks were ordered to prostrate themselves before Alexander, and only a few refused. His Macedonian supporters were married to Persian women and supplied with large dowries.

HELLENISM Even as Alexander emulated the manners of conduct of Persian Great Kings, the language and culture of his empire continued to be Greek, and his conquests spread the Greek language and Greek styles of city planning and religious observance, art, dress, and literature. This is what scholars mean when they call the last three centuries BCE **Hellenistic**: it was the time in which Greek language and culture extended farther than they ever had before, or would again.

Still, the new form of empire was not glued together by any clear common vision or ideology, or by any newer counterpart to the civic sentiments that had grown up with the rise of hoplite warfare in the Greece of the early city-states. Alexander ruled by force, and over time, force came to rule many of his actions. Always hot-tempered, he could become a despot when he felt challenged or provoked. He killed favorite commanders when they opposed him, and soon enough faced real enemies and their plots. In 324, when he issued a decree that required the Greek cities to take back many of their political exiles, he essentially forced them to rebel even though they knew the consequences that they risked by doing so. When Alexander died in 323, he was contemplating another invasion, this time of the western Mediterranean, where wealthy Syracuse and other Greek cities remained independent.

CULTURAL CHANGE

Alexander's conquests in Asia opened the way for thousands of Greeks to leave their homelands for cities in the East, bringing with them their language, religious beliefs, and cultural practices. The result was a Hellenistic culture that drew on Greek, Macedonian, Egyptian, Persian, and other Asian traditions. Alexander himself worked effectively with subjects of different origins. He adopted Persian court customs and married his Macedonian supporters to Persian women. He sparked controversy, though, when he ordered Greeks and Macedonians to prostrate themselves before him as his Persian subjects did. These two documents, written after the events described, illustrate the advantages and pitfalls of Alexander's cultural flexibility.

Arrian, *The Campaigns of Alexander*

Written in the second century CE by Arrian, a Greek-born Roman historian, this passage conveys the arguments of Kallisthenes, one of Alexander's advisers, against adoption of the Persian practice of bowing full-length before the ruler.

[Kallisthenes addressing Alexander:] "Perhaps, one must think like a barbarian[1] because our discussion takes place in a barbarian land. Even so I think it fit to remind you, Alexander, of Greece, for the sake of which you made this entire expedition—to annex Asia to Greece. And consider this: will you, on your return there, also compel the Greeks, the freest of men, to bow before you, or will you keep your distance from the Greeks but impose this dishonor on the Macedonians? Or will you make some final distinction when it comes to honors, and be honored by the Greeks and Macedonians in the human and Greek manner, while receiving barbarian honors only from the barbarians? But if it is said about Cyrus[2]…that he was the first man to have his subjects bow down to him, and that after him this indignity

became an institution among the Persians and Medes[3], one should bear in mind that the Scythians[4], men who were poor but independent, taught that very Cyrus a lesson—a lesson other Scythians later taught Darius[5], and the Athenians and Spartans taught Xerxes[6]…and Alexander—without having his people bow down before him—taught this Darius."

In making these and similar remarks Kallisthenes greatly vexed Alexander, though what he said pleased the Macedonians. Realizing this, Alexander sent word to the Macedonians telling them to think no more of the bowing ritual. But in the silence that followed these words, the most distinguished Persians stood up and one by one performed their bows.

Plutarch, From *Lives*

In this passage, Plutarch (46–120 CE), also a Greek-born Roman and author of biographical profiles of Alexander and other great figures of Greece and Rome, describes Alexander's purposes in cultural accommodation. Plutarch offers two examples of Alexander's prudent cultural policies.

Now, also, he more and more accommodated himself in his way of living to that of the natives, and tried to bring them, also, as near as he could to the Macedonian customs, wisely considering that whilst he was engaged in an expedition which would carry him far from thence, it would be wiser to depend upon the goodwill which might arise from intermixture and association as a means of maintaining tranquillity, than upon force and compulsion. In order to [do] this, he chose out thirty thousand boys, whom he put under masters to teach them the Greek tongue, and to train them up to arms in the Macedonian discipline. As for his marriage with Roxana, whose youthfulness and beauty had charmed him at a drinking entertainment, where he happened to see her, taking part in a dance, it was, indeed, a love affair, yet it seemed at the same time to be conducive to the object he had in hand. For it gratified the conquered people to see him choose a wife from among themselves, and it made them feel the most lively affection for him, to find that in the only passion which he, the most temperate of men, was overcome by, he yet forbore till he could obtain her in a lawful and honorable way.

QUESTIONS FOR ANALYSIS

1. Why does Kallisthenes object to Alexander's adoption of the Persian court practice in which subjects prostrate themselves before their ruler?
2. According to Plutarch, why was it wise for Alexander to accommodate the cultural practices of his foreign subjects?
3. How do these documents differ on the value of Alexander's adopting foreign ways?

---

[1] Barbarian: Non-Greek-speaker or foreigner, with a pejorative connotation.
[2] Cyrus: Persian King, mid-to-late-sixth century BCE.
[3] Medes: A Near Eastern people, conquered by Persia, mid-sixth century BCE.
[4] Scythians: A nomadic people living on the steppes of Eurasia.
[5] Darius: Darius III, Persian King, 336–330 BCE.
[6] Xerxes: Persian King, first half of the fifth century BCE.

Sources: Arrian, *The Campaigns of Alexander*, trans. Pamela Mensch, ed. James Romm (New York: 2010), pp. 168–9; Plutarch, *Lives*, vol. 4, trans. John Dryden, ed. Arthur Hugh Clough (Boston: 1888), p. 219.

THE ALEXANDER LEGEND

Decisive in real life, Alexander was portrayed as even more so in the myths that arose during his own lifetime. According to one legend, when challenged by an oracle stating that the conqueror of Asia Minor must untie a complex knot tied by a previous king of Phrygia (a region in central Asia Minor), Alexander could not find an end to pull, so he simply sliced the "Gordian knot" in half with a sword. This and other fictional exploits became the subject of hero cults and a vast body of art and literature. For centuries after the end of the ancient world, courtiers in Persia, Arabia, and medieval and Renaissance Europe grew up on a diet of Alexander's real and legendary adventures. He himself boasted that he had conquered the world, and he wept at the thought that there were no other worlds for him to conquer.

THE HELLENISTIC MONARCHIES (305–30 BCE)

Soon after Alexander's death, it became clear that only his energy and personal dominance had welded the vast range of peoples that made up his empire into a single political unit. Though a regent took control of the empire, the satraps of individual areas soon went to war, both with the emperor and with one another.

THE SUCCESSOR STATES

In the end, three large new states took shape among the ruins of the Macedonian Empire: (1) that of the **Ptolemies**, which extended from Egypt into Palestine, Libya, and Cyprus; (2) that of the Seleucids, in Palestine, Turkey, Mesopotamia, and parts of Afghanistan and India; and (3) that of the Antigonids, in Macedonia and northern Greece. But the crystallization of these larger states did not bring peace. Between 274 and 168 BCE, for example, the Seleucids and the Ptolemies fought no fewer than six wars in Syria.

Smaller states also sprang up, like that of the Attalids in western Asia Minor. One of Alexander's generals, Lysimachus, had built a small empire between the Black Sea and the Mediterranean, which he ruled from the city of Pergamum. He maintained independence by adroitly switching allegiances. On his death, his realm

fell apart. But the Attalids took over Pergamum and gradually built it up as a splendid city—a rival version of Alexandria, with great temples and libraries, and a fan-shaped upper city centered on the vast royal palace. Their kingdom survived until 133 BCE, when it was bequeathed to Rome.

AUTOCRACY AND AUTONOMY

The Hellenistic states basically followed the model that Alexander had sketched out—itself partly derived from the Persians. Unlike most of the Greek states of the last several centuries, all of the Hellenistic states were monarchical in form and sharply hierarchical in character. Greek elites, separated by language and customs from the natives, occupied the top levels, with native elites below them.

The workings of Hellenistic government are best known from the Egyptian kingdom of the Ptolemies (305–30 BCE). Emulating the ancient Egyptian pharaohs, whose kingdom the Macedonians had shattered, the Ptolemaic kings claimed godly status and used everything from public ceremony to coinage to teach subjects to see them in that light. The Ptolemies dealt with their Greek subjects as Greek rulers, communicating with them in Greek and allowing them to build and administer the normal Greek institutions, such as public gymnasia, in their cities. They dealt with their Egyptian subjects as the pharaohs had, using the Egyptian language for decrees that affected them. Two systems of justice applied—one Greek, and one Egyptian. The Egyptian state of the Ptolemies was thus bilingual and in large part bimodal.

The other successor states developed variants on this model. The Seleucids inherited the largest single share of Alexander's empire—Turkey, Syria, and Iran. With a population of 50 or 60 million, these lands were immensely rich. Unlike the Ptolemies, the Seleucids employed natives in the administration and the armed forces, and encouraged their soldiers and other Macedonians to marry Asians. The children of these unions served in the Macedonian phalanx that was the core of the Seleucids' army, along with native light infantry, archers,

Hellenistic Currency A silver talent issued by King Attalus I of Pergamum in the third century BCE carries a picture of Athena and an inscription in Greek. Pergamum, capital of the Attalid kingdom in western Asia Minor, was modeled on Athens.

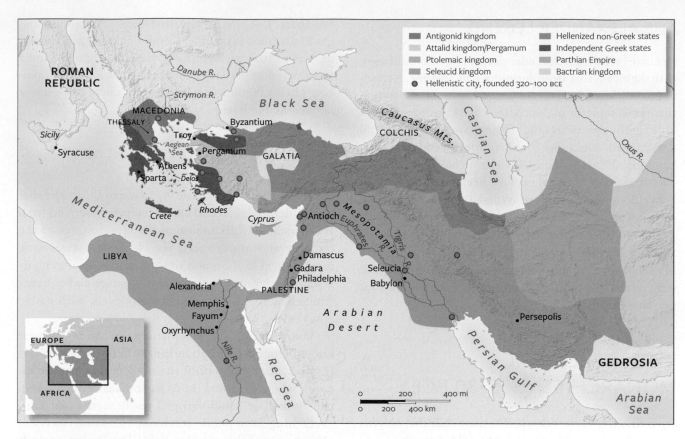

The Hellenistic World, Early 2nd Century BCE After Alexander's death, his empire broke up into three large kingdoms under the Ptolemies in Egypt, the Seleucids in Persia, and the Antigonids in Macedonia. These were joined by smaller states such as Attalid Pergamum in western Turkey and some of the original Greek city-states. Many new cities were founded in this period, particularly in Persia and Asia Minor.

and javelin-throwers. In 305 BCE, after initial efforts to establish satraps in the Indus Valley failed, Seleucus I (r. 321–281 BCE) made a deal with Chandragupta Maurya (r. 322–298 BCE), an Indian who was founding his own dynasty. Seleucus abandoned all claims to Indian territory in return for war elephants. Yet with all their military resources and native helpers, the Seleucids could not establish an effective administration for their immense domains. They established a ruler cult, in which cities worshipped the ruler "as if he were a god," and hoped that this could provide some of the unity that was imposed in Egypt by the nature of the Nile Valley.

The Antigonids, for their part, ruled as something like constitutional monarchs. Their authority was unchallenged because they respected the traditions of their Macedonian subjects. They had the strongest army of the successors and used massive fortresses not so much to dominate Greece as to ensure that it would serve as a buffer, preventing the Seleucids and Ptolemies from invading their territory.

THE ECONOMIC FOUNDATIONS OF POWER

AGRICULTURE The Hellenistic kingdoms, whether Ptolemaic Egypt or Seleucid Babylon, relied on the work of rural villagers to produce vast amounts of grain—the foundation of the state's prosperity. The Ptolemies considered themselves the true owners of all the land in Egypt. Lands outside their own estates, and those designated for use in the maintenance of temples, they assigned to officials who had served them well and to soldiers. Government officials introduced more effective agricultural methods, including irrigation, into the cultivation of especially fertile areas, such as the Fayum in north-central Egypt. They managed to push the desert back, improve yields, and create new settlements. Tax-farmers—entrepreneurs who bid for the right to gather taxes—maintained close oversight over the production, storage, and sale of wheat and other crops. Standing between landlords and villagers on the one hand and the kings on the other, tax-farmers made as much profit as possible by squeezing the taxpayers. The concerns of peasants reached the throne only in especially hard times, when mass flight from the land threatened the monarchy's economic foundations.

A MONEY ECONOMY The grain economy and its structures were in part ancient, determined as much by the climate and geography of the Mediterranean world as by human decisions. But they now functioned within a new framework. Alexander's successors followed his example by continuing to mint the Persian monarchs' fabulous hoards of bullion into coin which they used, as Alexander had, to pay their troops, who came mostly from the Greek cities in the mainland and elsewhere. As precious metals filtered into the economy, each state began to depend on large amounts of coinage to maintain its military power. To ensure this supply, states and their tax-farmers insisted on collecting taxes in money rather than in kind. State revenues swelled. Alexander's kingdom produced an income of 30,000 silver talents annually (a talent, during the Peloponnesian War, would pay the wages of a trireme's crew for a month); Egypt, almost three centuries later, had an annual income of 12,500 talents. Sophisticated systems of exchange developed, and it was possible to write a wheat check in one part of Egypt that could be drawn from a wheat account 300 miles away.

TRADE A lively trade developed across the Mediterranean. Roads were bad during the Hellenistic period, but ships were the major carriers of cargo, and their numbers exploded. In the three centuries after Alexander's death, the number of dateable wrecks on the floor of the Mediterranean went up 600 percent. Ship-borne commerce made possible the carriage of expensive goods from distant lands: African elephants for the Ptolemaic armies, spices from Yemen for the kitchens of the rich, olive oil and wine from Greece for homesick mercenaries and officials in Egypt, and other luxury goods from the Persian Gulf and southern Africa.

The monarchs taxed this trade, and by one scholar's calculation the Ptolemaic government controlled as much as 40 percent of the gross national product of Egypt—as much as a typical twentieth-century government. This enormous income stream enabled the Ptolemies to build the lighthouses, fortifications, docks, and warehouses needed to create safe and efficient ports. They also developed huge warships with many banks of oars and solid decks designed to hold catapults. As ships grew larger, armies did the same. Not all of the Hellenistic states could

match Egypt's resources. But all of them could muster more sheer military force than any previous Greek state had possessed—even Athens at the height of its power.

NEW GREEK CITIES

Within these powerful new states, Greek ways thrived as never before. The spread of the Greek language and the development of a money economy helped people, goods, and ideas to circulate rapidly. The Seleucids, in particular, encouraged immigration, and thousands of Macedonians and Greeks settled in Turkey and Mesopotamia, where they founded cities by the dozen. New cities, in fact, sprang up everywhere from northern Africa to northern Afghanistan, and some turned into metropolises, such as Alexandria in Egypt and Antioch in Syria.

These cities became models of Greek architecture and town planning as well as centers of administration and culture. Massive temples, their roofs supported by great columns and their precincts adorned with sculpture, honored each city's patron god or goddess. An agora was dedicated to public assemblies. Beside it stood a government building and a public auditorium. A second agora served merchants as a center for the exchange of goods and money. Often, the grandest complex in the city was a gymnasium or a theater, each a central Greek institution.

Alexandria, the Egyptian city founded by Alexander (who was buried there), had a Mediterranean port protected by an island, which made it a natural trading center. As the Ptolemies poured money into the city, massive public buildings took shape. These included the 400-foot-high lighthouse that took its place, in the first or second century CE, on the unofficial but widely circulated lists of the seven wonders of the ancient world. The city's rectangular grid design was in place by the first century BCE, and probably much earlier. Two main streets more than 100 feet wide crossed the city. Immigrants whose languages and ways differed sharply from those of the Egyptian residents poured in as well, especially from Greece but also from Macedonia and Persia. A substantial Jewish population worshiped in a massive, spectacular temple. With 300,000 free inhabitants, according to one ancient account, Alexandria dwarfed even the Athens of Pericles. So did Antioch in Syria and other Hellenistic cities.

URBAN NETWORKS Whereas the Greek cities of the fifth-century BCE Classical period regarded one another with suspicion or hostility, those of the Hellenistic world did their best to support one another. They recognized one another's gods, extended common privileges to one another's citizens, and copied one another's legislation. City walls fell into disrepair or were even torn down, and instead of joining military leagues, cities formed federations to maintain trading relations and protect one another against bandits and raiders. A group of Greek cities in Syria and Palestine, including Damascus, Philadelphia, and Gadara, formed the Decapolis (League of Ten Cities). Others formally recognized one another as friends, and when disputes and wars broke out, they sent their judges to serve as arbitrators. Cities also extended their power into the countryside around them, creating networks of substantial villages. The cosmopolitan urbanism of the Hellenistic period would have seemed strange to the Athenians and Spartans of the fifth century BCE.

URBAN BENEFACTORS Hellenistic cities drew creatively on Greek tradition. Athens had long depended on the trierarchs who fitted out its warships and the benefactors who staged and directed its plays. Now, in the Hellenistic period, cities also depended on "doers of good deeds." Greeks had always loved to compete; now rich men competed to do good for their cities. They might pay for gymnasia or theaters; give the city financial capital, the interest on which could cover public needs; or help to float a loan. Individual benefactors built fountains for people and animals, and endowed the massage oil needed by athletes. Public inscriptions recorded communal gratitude for these essential services.

SOFT POWER IN THE HELLENISTIC WORLD

The tradition of "doing good deeds" also governed relations among the Hellenistic rulers and their cities. Each king had a duty to support the cities in his realm, and as he did so, he set his stamp on each city. The Ptolemies, for example, made Alexandria a center for Greek thought and letters—a new Athens. Inspired in large part by Aristotle, they accomplished this by creating institutions for the pursuit of knowledge based on the model of his Lyceum, equipping them with the resources needed for research. Late in the fourth or early in the third century BCE, one of the Ptolemies founded a Museum—literally a temple of the Muses, the Greek goddesses who supposedly inspired poets, historians, and artists. There they established a learned society of literary men and philosophers who were paid not to teach but to carry out research on a broad range

of questions, from the size of the earth to the meaning of obscure passages in Homer's epic poems.

THE LIBRARY OF ALEXANDRIA The vast library that the Ptolemies created, and where some of these scholars worked, has become, like Alexander the Great, a legend—one far greater, in many of its versions, than the historical original. Yet the reality was extraordinary enough. The Ptolemies and their agents tried to assemble the entire corpus of Greek literature, and they succeeded in amassing some 700,000 papyrus scrolls. (Parchment—paper made from the skins of animals—was made from the second century BCE onward, but papyrus remained the normal writing material.) A law required ships calling in Alexandria to surrender all their books to the library. Those that were not already in the collection were kept, and the library provided copies for their original owners. To obtain the

Library of Alexandria From Ptolemaic Egypt around 285–250 BCE, this papyrus fragment is part of a copy of Homer's *Odyssey*. Alexandria's library was the most important repository of Homeric texts in the Hellenistic world, and its scholars sorted through variant readings to establish standard versions.

most accurate texts possible of the three great Athenian tragedians—Aeschylus, Sophocles, and Euripides—the library made a huge deposit, borrowed the official copies from the city of Athens, and then cheerfully forfeited the money in order to retain the precious Athenian books. Forged books, some created specially to meet the new demand for works of literature by the most famous Greek writers, accompanied the genuine ones into the library's warehouses, and then into the cupboards where scrolls were kept.

The Ptolemies found ways of dealing with efforts at deception. They appointed expert scholars to catalogue the collection—a first—and to sort the genuine from the forged works attributed to each author. One of these men, the poet Callimachus (ca. 305–ca. 240 BCE), is remembered as the patron saint of librarians for his remark, "A big book is a big pain." Several of them worked especially hard on the *Iliad* and the *Odyssey*, trying to correct the errors and remove the inauthentic verses that had entered both texts over the centuries.

FESTIVALS The Ptolemies undertook all this religious and literary activity partly because they, too, believed in the value of "doing good deeds." Yet they also saw such patronage as a way to establish the prestige and power of their royal line, which was a new dynasty, after all, in a land that prided itself on being ancient and never changing. From early in the third century BCE, the Ptolemies staged a spectacular procession in Alexandria every four years to honor the Olympian gods. The procession in honor of Dionysus, the god of wine, was particularly spectacular. Men dressed as creatures from Greek myth were sent out in scores to restrain the crowd. They were followed by the priest of Dionysos, musicians, and a train of decorated carts, each grander than the last. One bore an eighteen-foot statue of the god reclining on an elephant; another carried a mechanical contraption in the form of a woman who stood up, poured a libation of milk from a gold vessel, and sat down again. Hordes of animals—including birds, Indian and Ethiopian cows, a pride of lions, and an Ethiopian rhinoceros—and staggering crown jewels filled in the display.

Though costly, such festivals were effective ways for the Ptolemies to assert their wealth and power—both to the Egyptians who watched their new Greek masters and gods parade through the streets of Alexandria, and to foreign nations whose diplomats witnessed the magnificent show. The Ptolemies used such displays to support the cult of their dynasty, each member of which claimed the status of a god. This was the foundation of the loyalty they commanded from aristocrats, soldiers, and priests.

A NEW GREEK WORLD

Royal support and trade made Alexandria into something like an ancient counterpart to twentieth-century Paris or New York—a world city, rich, impressive, and cosmopolitan. No other city matched it. Throughout the Greek world, rulers saw, as the Ptolemies did, that the soft power of culture could solidify their hold on their thrones. The Attalids, for example, although they asserted their independence from the Seleucid dynasty, also emulated the direct descendants of Alexander. They built a vast temple complex and an enormous library at Pergamum. They, too, employed scholars to study the Greek poets. As Greek styles of building spread across Central Asia to India, across Egypt to northern Africa, and up into Afghanistan, Hellenistic institutions accompanied them.

Though Greek in language, systems of exchange, and literature, the Hellenistic world was genuinely new. Hellenistic states differed fundamentally from earlier Greek states. They were massive, exerted control over many spheres of activity, and squeezed vast resources from their subjects. The royal will was decisive in a way previously unfamiliar to the Greeks. The distance between subjects and rulers was greater than before. In some ways the Hellenistic states resembled those of the ancient Near East more than the earlier Greek states. In other respects, though, Hellenistic life offered new possibilities for segments of society—especially, as we will see, for well-born women.

HELLENISTIC SOCIETY

GLIMPSES OF THE EVERYDAY

The hundreds of documents, official and private, that have survived from Hellenistic Egypt paint a vivid portrait of urban life. Even a relatively small city such as Oxyrhynchus, with a population of some 20,000 about 100 miles southwest of Cairo near the Nile, had a lively, varied economy. The city maintained a central market with rental spaces for shopkeepers and artisans, including bakers; sellers of olives, rushes, and wool; makers of clothing and shoes; garland-weavers; and tinsmiths. Aristocratic women, who apparently enjoyed more freedom of movement than their Athenian counterparts, shopped for fine cloth and even ready-made clothing, rather than producing their own. Those with more money could go to a stall and drink "wine of Oxyrhynchos"; those with less money had to content themselves with "sour wine of Oxyrhynchos."

Some of these marketplace businesses became quite elaborate and needed a fair amount of equipment. Hellenistic bakers, for example, did everything from milling wheat into flour to baking coarse and fine bread and cakes to marketing them to consumers. Others, such as the fast-food sellers who offered customers bean and lentil pastes, worked on a tiny scale.

A sophisticated money economy, powered by consumption, offered commercial opportunities for nonelites with the energy and resources to capitalize on them, such as the third-century entrepreneurs Apollophanes and Demetrius. They were brothers who offered to set up shop in a new city and produce "cloaks, tunics, girdles, dresses, belts, ribbons, split tunics, everything to size," and promised that they could supply letters of recommendation to guarantee their abilities. Their documents were written in both Greek and demotic Egyptian, since the state used both languages. Greek proved especially helpful for the many craftspeople and merchants whose trade networks were not merely local. The spread of money and specialized trades carried the Greek language into new areas throughout the Hellenistic world.

SLAVERY

The Greeks, in modern times, have often been remembered as the defenders of freedom. But as we have seen, even the democracy of classical Athens depended on slaves at every level, from the ordinary household and farm to the silver mines that paid for the fleet. The societies conquered by Alexander and his successors also had slaves, especially in the temples, where they served the priests and sometimes engaged in a sacred form of prostitution. The people who worked the land in rural regions, however, were for the most part legally free, though they were often bound to remain on the ground they tilled unless they had official permission to leave (to attend the festival of a goddess, for example).

As Greek cities rose and Greek families settled in the conquered lands, slaves came with them. One in seven Greek families in Egypt—many of them recent settlers—owned slaves. Egyptian archives record that they were treated as property: bought and sold, bequeathed to others in wills, or set free (usually on condition that they remain with their master until he or she died). Laws established harsh penalties for any slave who dared to harm a free person. In Alexandria, a free man who threatened another

Slavery This third-century BCE fresco from a Hellenistic tomb in present-day Bulgaria depicts a slave leading a chariot and horses. Slavery was one of the many institutions that spread throughout the Greek-speaking world.

free man with a weapon of metal or wood had to pay a fine. A slave who did the same received 100 strokes of the whip, which could easily amount to a cruel form of execution.

Slaves were registered, like other forms of property, and sometimes they seem to have been marked on the face to make their status clear and indelible. Professional slave dealers brought cargoes of fresh workers from Syria and elsewhere to Egypt, and even bred some slaves especially for sale. An ancient geographer reported that tens of thousands of slaves came through the Greek island of Delos every day. A vast two-story colonnade, the largest structure on the island and situated conveniently near the harbor, has been identified by some scholars as the slave market, but others claim it was a park or a space for exercise.

For all their suffering, slaves were also vital to the economic expansion that made cities so prosperous. Many tax declarations and wills describe household workshops run by slave labor. For example, a Greek named

WOMEN'S LEGAL RIGHTS IN THE HELLENISTIC WORLD

This document is a legal complaint from a Greek woman living in the Egyptian village of Trikomia, which had a large Jewish population in the third century BCE. Lysias seems to have been a military settler there; his daughter Philista documents her injury in the baths, a Greek cultural practice exported to Hellenistic cities. Although addressed to Ptolemy, as most petitions were, it would have gone to Diophanes, the military general of the district. The bath attendant was turned over to the custody of the Egyptian police chief in the presence of Simon the *epistates*, an administrative official who was most likely Jewish. This document allows us to see not only the everyday practices of Hellenized Greeks but also gives us information about the mixed population of Ptolemaic cities.

To King Ptolemy, greeting from Philista daughter of Lysias, one of the settlers in Trikomia. I am wronged by Petechon. For while I was bathing in the bath of the aforesaid village on Tybi 7 of year 1 (he being bathman in the women's rotunda), and had stepped out to soap myself, when he brought in the jugs of hot water, he emptied one (?) over me and scalded my belly and my left thigh down to the knee, so as to endanger my life. On finding him, I handed him over to the custody of Nechthosiris, the chief policeman of the village, in the presence of Simon the *epistates*. I beg you, therefore, O king, if it please you, as a suppliant who has sought refuge with you, not to allow me, a woman who earns a living with her hands, to be so lawlessly treated, but to order Diophanes to write to Simon the *epistates* and Nechthosiris the chief policeman that they are to bring Petechon before him in order that Diophanes may inquire into the case, hoping that having sought refuge with you, O King, the common benefactor of all, I may obtain justice. Farewell.

QUESTIONS FOR ANALYSIS

1. This source includes a Greek woman, an Egyptian policeman, and a Jewish official. What does this suggest about Hellenistic society?
2. In addition to baths, what other Greek cultural and social practices were found in Hellenistic cities and villages?
3. What can you infer about Philista's status in relation to the male bath attendant, and what does this illustrate about the status of women in the Hellenistic world?

Source: Jane Rowlandson, ed., *Women and Society in Greek and Roman Egypt: A Sourcebook* (Cambridge, UK: Cambridge University Press, 1998), pp. 172, 174.

Apollonis, who managed the finances of Ptolemy II in the third century, owned small textile workshops in the Lower Egyptian city of Memphis, which had once been the national capital. One of them was operated by two male weavers, who may have been legally free, and three slave girls. Surviving letters show that one of the men had his master's trust and undertook voyages on his behalf, and that one of the female slaves gave orders to the men. When she suffered a robbery and lost a load of wool, she felt able to ask her master for help. Another will leaves the writer's property to his wife and children, but also sets free a female slave and her son, "whose father I am"—revealing another job that female slaves had to perform for their masters.

THE LIVES OF FREE WOMEN

In the cities of Hellenistic Egypt and Syria, free women enjoyed distinctive opportunities. Macedonian laws had given women far more freedom and power than Greek ones, and the laws did not change when men and women of Macedonian descent suddenly found themselves ruling much of the known world. Although the queens of the Hellenistic states often had to contend with dangerous court rivalries, court life also offered possibilities for attaining power. In the second and first centuries BCE, Egyptian queens became more powerful, until Cleopatra VII (r. 51–30 BCE) eliminated all of her siblings and became the last sole ruler of an independent Egypt.

Outside the Home Women in the Hellenistic world had more freedom than their Greek counterparts of the Classical period, and many worked outside the home. The dancing woman depicted in this bronze statuette from Alexandria (third or second century BCE) was likely a professional entertainer.

Queens amassed enormous amounts of property—much of which their husbands actually gave to them. And they used it for all the same things that kings did: to pay for great shrines to their favorite god, to sponsor chariots to compete for them in the Olympic Games, and to support poets who would praise them. Callimachus, the scholar at Alexandria, wrote a poem to celebrate the lock of hair that Berenice II, a Ptolemy by birth, had dedicated to the goddess Aphrodite to ensure that her husband would come back safe from Syria. He described Berenice's hair as ascending to the heavens and becoming a constellation. But Hellenistic queens also used their resources for purposes that reflected their gender, such as providing dowries for poor women.

Some Hellenistic women became poets, as a few Greek women had in the Archaic period. But they pursued many other vocations as well, often with the encouragement of fathers with careers in the same fields. Some became artists: Helena, the daughter of a painter who lived at the end of the fourth century BCE, painted a famous panorama of the battle of Issus that was taken to Rome and exhibited centuries after her death. Many women went far beyond elementary literacy, and some studied philosophy, especially within the tradition of Pythagoras, the mathematician and philosopher who lived in the sixth century BCE. Writers who called themselves Pythagoreans encouraged women to pursue wisdom. Some Pythagorean treatises, which emphasize that women must attain purity, avoid adultery, and lead a considered, moral life, are ascribed to female authors. A few women joined the Academy in Athens. Others became scholars and worked at the correction of texts. Many women worked at traditionally female jobs such as wet-nursing, textile production, and the production and sale of food. Some owned slaves and ran their own textile workshops.

All free women benefited from the Macedonian legal tradition, and in one sense ordinary women benefited more than queens. Perhaps because women as well as men had defined rights, marriage in the Hellenistic world came to be governed by contracts, many of which survive. These contracts regulated the conduct of both husbands and wives: husbands promised to take no further wives, and wives pledged to refrain from affairs with other men. Generally, women were more restricted than men in their movements. Contracts allowed husbands to travel freely, wives hardly at all. But in some parts of the Hellenistic world, such as the Fayum in Egypt, wives were as free as husbands to initiate divorce proceedings.

Literature reflected women's new freedom, if indirectly. It was in the Hellenistic period that poets began to compose love lyrics, and that both lyric and tragic poets began to imagine women as subject not only to duty (as Antigone had been in Sophocles' fifth-century BCE play) but also to personal passion. A more direct reflection appears in the world of legal documents, in which women often spoke—and still speak—for themselves, rather than being represented by men.

EDUCATION

For centuries, Greek cities had had their teachers—from slaves who taught children how to write on wax tablets to the sophists and philosophers who competed to train well-placed young men. In the Hellenistic period, official support enabled one kind of teaching—that of the Greek language and literature—to spread across the Mediterranean world and beyond.

In cities and towns, literacy offered vital possibilities: a way to emphasize the distance between city people and the illiterate peasants of the countryside, and a way to gain access to jobs in higher places. Hellenistic cities—and the kings and wealthy men who felt responsible for them—endowed positions for teachers, based in gymnasia. Public money paid for grammarians, who taught boys to read their way through the Greek classics, and rhetoricians, who taught them to compose speeches. There was no uniform system or curriculum, and each city had its own methods. But from Iran to the coast of Egypt, any cultured mother would have understood that when her son's teacher said he was reading the sixth book, this referred to what we call book VI of Homer's *Iliad*.

Greek theaters rose in Iran and Babylon, the epic poets were taught in Ceylon and India, and children in what is now Uzbekistan learned to love the story of the Trojan horse. Royal patronage enabled certain especially skillful poets and historians to make glamorous careers at court, while public contests gave poets and orators a chance to win fame. Greek education became one of the most widespread, shared features of Hellenistic society.

A COSMOPOLITAN CULTURE

The spread of public teachers and schools helps to explain how in many cities, both new and old, a Greek-speaking elite came into being. Its members were diverse in their origins but unified in their culture, and they exercised in the nude, practiced rhetoric and gymnastics, and produced a Greek literature of their own. This was a literature that never ceased to model itself on the great works handed down from classical Greece, but that also developed new ways of expressing the broadened experience of the societies formed by the Macedonian conquests.

NEW TYPES OF LITERATURE

From Athens to Alexandria, a new literature addressed the comic qualities of everyday life. Aristophanes, whose subversive, sometimes brutally personal comedies had amused and enraged the citizens of Athens in the fifth century BCE, had concerned himself with weighty issues such as war and peace. Menander (d. 290 BCE), his prolific successor in the late fourth and early third centuries, staged everyday life in exaggerated form. His gallery of characters included rude misers with pretty, marriageable daughters; eager, clumsy young lovers; and slaves deftly acting as intermediaries between lovers and maidens.

Menander responded shrewdly to the taste of his contemporaries. So did Theophrastus (ca. 372–ca. 287 BCE), a student of Aristotle's who applied his teacher's methods of classification to the characters of individuals, and the quirkier the better. He turned out Monty Pythonish character sketches of the fools and boors who people the streets of any big city: "The tiresome man is the one who will walk in when you have just dozed off and wake you up to have a chat. He will arrive for an appointment and then ask you to wait until he has taken a walk." Even at meals, this character can't stop talking about matters no one would want to hear about while eating: "You should have seen the color of the bile in my excreta," he says. "Darker than that gravy you've got." The city that Theophrastus observed was as funny, in its own way, as Athens had been when observed by Aristophanes.

This cosmopolitan new world inspired other sorts of literary exploration. Apollonius of Rhodes (third century BCE), from a Greek island in the eastern Aegean, devoted an epic poem to the mythical expedition that Jason and other heroes undertook in a ship named the *Argo* (which gave them the collective name Argonauts). To win a throne in Thessaly, Jason had to bring back the golden fleece of a winged ram from Colchis on the Black Sea. Apollonius took a deep interest in human psychology, especially in extreme situations. Building on the precedents set by Euripides centuries before, he developed complex internal monologues in which his characters revealed the emotions that wrenched them. Medea, daughter of the king of Colchis, pondered her plan to betray her father for the sake of her lover, Jason: "this pain of mine, it burns without end: how I wish / I'd been killed already by the swift shafts of Artemis." Hellenistic poets did not address great political and religious themes as often as the tragedians of classical Athens had. But they staged difficult emotional situations with a precision, insight, and empathy that lent their work much charm.

Charm, in fact, became one of the central characteristics of Hellenistic literature. The Sicilian Theocritus (310–250 BCE), whose talent took him from Syracuse to Alexandria, created a new genre called pastoral, the escapist literature of a sophisticated urban society. In Theocritus's dreamy idylls, shepherds and goatherds played reed pipes and told sad stories of unhappy lovers tormented by the gods. Allusive, sophisticated poetry like this appealed to the rulers and courtiers of the new cities. It attracted readers whose education enabled them to recognize allusions to older texts and who appreciated word games and riddles. The fifth-century comedies of Aristophanes were packed with allusions that called attention to the physical

Laocoön and His Sons According to Greek legend, the Trojan priest Laocoön and his sons met with a painful death from venomous snakes. This statue, a Roman copy of a Hellenistic original, displays the visceral emotion that found expression in Hellenistic literature as well.

appearance and personal foibles of public figures, as his audience knew. Poetry at that time had been part of a local, public life. In the Hellenistic world, by contrast, poetry was written for the highly cultivated members of courts. No Hellenistic thinker could have blamed a comic playwright, as Socrates had once blamed Aristophanes, for destroying his reputation.

NEW PHILOSOPHIES: EPICUREANS AND STOICS

However artificial, this elegant new literature speaks of a Greek culture that stretched across the Mediterranean, one in which poets and playwrights read and responded to one another. This new environment fostered Greek philosophy as well. Athens was still a central spawning ground for new ideas. Plato's Academy and Aristotle's Lyceum existed through the Hellenistic period, but new schools of philosophy flanked them. These schools addressed themselves to Athens and to the great monarchies and sophisticated cities of Egypt and the Near East.

The philosopher Epicurus (341–270 BCE) founded a school in Athens called The Garden. He and his followers insisted that the entire universe consisted of matter in motion. They traced the creation of the cosmos back to an accidental collision of primary particles, some of which swerved by chance as they fell through the great emptiness that preceded the universe. As more and more particles hit one another, the original chaos dissolved, and the earth, planets, and stars took shape. This vision of the world, radically different from the ordered, hierarchical ones that Plato and Aristotle had imagined, filled the **Epicureans** not with despair but with hope. They found no reason to fear the vengeful gods of earlier Greek myths, or the Furies that had appeared so terrifying on the Athenian tragic stage. Instead they devoted themselves to the pursuit of pleasure—rationally understood, of course.

Zeno (ca. 335–262 BCE) and Cleanthes (ca. 331–232 BCE), who taught in the Athenian building known as the Stoa Poikile ("painted colonnade"), came to be known as **Stoics**. Unlike the Epicureans, they saw the universe as animated by a divine spirit. They, too, however, insisted that the reasonable person should abandon fear and all other excessive emotions. Once one realized that the universe is ordered by a superhuman fate, one could cease to hope for mastery or struggle for the unobtainable.

Epicureans and Stoics differed in more ways than this one. The Epicureans formed something like a religious brotherhood, whose members followed detailed instructions for dress and diet. The Stoics, more loosely organized, insisted on the brotherhood of all men, in theory at least, and formulated natural laws that they held as superior to human laws. Yet both offered their followers not only an intellectual system but a guide to life. Like Socrates, they saw the pursuit of wisdom as a disciplined way of life to which the philosopher must dedicate himself, doing his best to put aside lesser concerns. Unlike Socrates, they derived strikingly similar moral codes, precise and humane, from their radically divergent underlying principles. They taught their followers to pursue their human duties so far as possible, and to avoid emotions that might spoil the calm enjoyment of the world that was the proper pursuit of a philosopher.

HELLENISTIC SCIENCE

In Alexandria, Syracuse, and other great Hellenistic cities, royal patronage enabled scholars to devote themselves for years at a time to solving highly technical problems in their fields. This fostered something like research centers

LADY OF KALYMNOS

The "Lady of Kalymnos" is a magnificent Greek sculpture whose features express values shared across the cultures of the Hellenistic world. This larger than life bronze sculpture, found on the seabed near the Greek island of Kalymnos in 1994, is a variation on the Herculaneum Woman, a type of draped, gracefully poised female figure found in Roman and Greek culture beginning in the fourth century BCE. The head of this sculpture also resembles the portrayal of Ptolemaic queens on coins, particularly in the framing of the face and hair by a veil.

The pose and clothing of the figure suggest that she is a noblewoman. She possesses a calm dignity as she seems to gaze at a distant point. Her dress, with its voluminous folds, makes the strongest statement of her wealth and social position. The shimmering drapery of her tunic wrapping around her full-length skirt indicates her domesticity and sober modesty.

QUESTIONS FOR ANALYSIS

1. How does this sculpture portray an ideal view of femininity in the Hellenistic period?
2. How does this statue represent the way cultures intermixed in the Hellenistic world?
3. Do you see in the sculpture signs of the greater autonomy that women experienced in this period? Explain.

Hellenistic Inventions Built in Athens around 150 BCE, the Tower of the Winds drew its name from the friezes of the wind gods at the top of its eight walls. Its weather vane and sundial—both since removed—indicated wind direction and the time of day, respectively, while an intricate system of pipes inside fed a water clock, which could keep track of the hours at night.

and an international scientific community. Greek mathematicians had already developed their subject to a high level by Plato's time, and in the following centuries they composed systematic treatments of individual branches of the field. One of their textbooks, the *Elements* of geometry of Euclid (ca. 325–250 BCE), remained the standard for centuries to come.

These scholars also innovated radically, posing and solving problems that could not be directly answered by the mathematical means available. The Syracusan mathematician and scientist Archimedes (ca. 287–212 BCE), for instance, reckoned the number of grains of sand that would be needed to fill the universe and found ingenious ways to explain the behavior of objects in water. One of his principles, still named after him, holds that when

an object is placed in a fluid, it is subject to an upward pressure, known as buoyancy, equal in magnitude to the weight of the fluid it displaces. Eratosthenes (third century BCE), an Alexandrian scholar with an interest in quantification, ingeniously calculated the circumference of the earth by extrapolating it from the lengths of the shadows cast by the sun at noon.

In their quest for knowledge as well as power, Hellenistic rulers sponsored new forms of inquiry. Medical men in early-third-century Alexandria received permission to dissect human bodies and even to vivisect condemned criminals. A dizzying amount of new information emerged from what must have been investigations of unspeakable cruelty. The Alexandrians did not realize that the veins and arteries formed a single circulatory system, but they did establish that the arteries transmitted not air, as Aristotle had thought, but blood. At the same time, and in the same city, other scholars used royal support to craft ingenious devices. Inventors devised spectacular machines that used water or water vapor to make artificial birds sing and statues move. Archimedes not only worked on the theory of statics and mechanics but also created practical military devices such as the burning mirrors with which he supposedly reduced invading Roman ships to cinders in 212 BCE.

CONVERSATIONS ACROSS CULTURES

For centuries, Greeks had traveled around the Mediterranean world and the Near East, marveling at the age of Egyptian and Babylonian tradition. As knowledge of the Greek language spread, it now became possible for scholars and scientists to draw ideas and information from the vast catchment area that the Greeks ruled. These learned men began to engage in substantive conversations across cultures—for example, with the teams of astronomers and diviners who had worked competitively in Mesopotamian temples over the centuries.

CULTURAL FUSION: ASTRONOMY

Since the time of Plato, many Greek thinkers (though not the Epicureans or Stoics) agreed that sets of hard, nested, transparent spheres carried each planet around the earth, while also accounting for the apparent irregularities of its motion. These thinkers, less interested in predicting than explaining planetary events, had not tried to correlate their geometrical models with the observed positions of the planets. As early as the eighth century BCE, in contrast, the priests who predicted eclipses and planetary positions for the rulers of Mesopotamia had decided that the planets and their movements determined the fates of kingdoms and individuals on earth. They based their predictions on mathematical tables that enabled them to forecast the positions of the known planets, the sun, and the moon for any given day and time.

On a day—and in a century—that we cannot precisely specify, a momentous conversation must have taken place. This exchange, in Greek or perhaps in Aramaic, was between a Greek who could use geometry to explain why the planets move as they do and a Mesopotamian diviner who could work out their future motion from tables. They realized that the tables drawn up in Mesopotamia could map onto the geometrical models of the Greek tradition. Conversation and inquiry continued. By the second century BCE, Hipparchus, an astronomer from Rhodes, and others fused these two sets of methods into a single, comprehensive mathematical theory that offered both explanations and predictions of planetary motion. For the first time in human history, at least in the West, precise statements about how the natural world works were cast in the language of mathematics and tested and refined against the results of observation.

Alexandria became the central place for the application of the new quantitative skills to astronomy, cartography, musical harmony, and many other fields. The methods created in Alexandria would continue to be employed for almost two millennia in the Islamic world to the East as well as in the West. As in early Greece, so in the Hellenistic world: the fusion of Western with non-Western skills, methods, and beliefs created what came to be seen, in retrospect, as the core achievements of the Western tradition.

NON-GREEK PERSPECTIVES

Greeks and non-Greeks did not confine their contact to the dining hall of Alexandria's Museum and similar spaces, where scholars literally compared notes. Sometimes their meetings were indirect. Few, if any, Greek scholars in Alexandria learned to read Egyptian hieroglyphs or cuneiform tablets from Mesopotamia. Interpreters—many of them Egyptians and Mesopotamians who had learned Greek—explained the histories of their peoples and traditions to the literate, Greek-educated elites who ruled their kingdoms.

These non-Greeks keenly felt the loss of political independence, even if their rulers adopted local customs and rituals. They tended to insist, as the Egyptians had done some centuries before, on the age, stability, and profundity of their cultures. By showing that their historical records stretched far back in time, long before Homer or the Trojan War, Egyptians and Mesopotamians could avenge, in the study, the defeats their kings had suffered on the battlefield. And though only a few Hellenistic Greeks read these works attentively, and they did so in Greek translations that they could not verify, many of them came to understand themselves as newcomers to ancient lands, which they ruled but whose mysterious religions and traditions they might not be able to understand.

THE PTOLEMIES: MANAGING RELIGIOUS DIVERSITY

When the Macedonian dynasty of the Ptolemies took charge of Egypt, they introduced the Greek language and Greek cults. But, like the Persians and other ancient rulers before them, they made no effort to abolish the existing public religion. On the contrary, they accepted responsibility for it, made massive contributions to the priests and temples of the ancient Egyptian gods, and even created

Hellenistic Egypt Along with retaining Greek language, laws, and institutions, the Ptolemaic kings incorporated Greek stylistic influences in their architectural projects. Along the colonnade of the Isis Temple, built by a Ptolemaic king in 358–345 BCE, the carved faces gaze forward, rather than in traditional Egyptian profile.

Religious Diversity A grave stele from the Ptolemaic period combines Greek and Egyptian elements: from the bottom, the goddess Isis in the form of a snake; the Greek god of silence, Harpocrates, a Hellenization of the Egyptian god Horus; and an image of the deceased.

new temples—like a spectacular one built late in the third century BCE and graced during its construction, according to its hieroglyphic inscriptions, by the presence of the Ptolemaic king and queen.

In the course of the third century BCE the Ptolemies began to transform the religious and cultural systems that they began with, one Greek and one Egyptian, into something more coherent. Greeks in Memphis, south of what is now Cairo, had already begun to worship at the great temple of the god Apis, whom the Egyptians connected with Osiris, their god of fertility and the underworld. Osiris was a mysterious figure whose identity and attributes the Greeks did not fully grasp. Within a few years, however, this divinity took on a new, Hellenic form as Sarapis—a being whom the Greeks came to identify with their own fertility god, Dionysos, the very one who formed the focus of the Ptolemies' magnificent celebrations. Ptolemy I (r. 323–283 BCE) had a temple built in honor of Sarapis in Alexandria. Equipped with bilingual inscriptions that identified its founding god and goddess, the temple also held a massive library of Greek texts—a kind of annex to the main Alexandrian library. As the center for the cult of a divine couple, it soon became strongly identified with the Ptolemaic royal cult.

A few decades later, Ptolemy III (r. 246–221 BCE) went much further in the same direction. By now it was customary for the Egyptian priests to meet once a year in solemn assembly with their Greek king. In the winter of 238 BCE, the priests came to Alexandria to celebrate the king's birthday. The assembly yielded a series of decrees, recorded in both Greek and hieroglyphs, that called for the creation of a new religious feast in honor of the Ptolemies. It would take place, significantly, just when the Nile flooded and the land's fertility was assured for another year. From this point on, the priests identified themselves and their religion ever more strongly with their Greek rulers, whose epithets and titles were translated into Egyptian and frequently celebrated.

Lords of a double society and culture, the Ptolemies made a point of issuing their decrees in Greek as well as in Egyptian. This tradition gave rise to, among much more, the Rosetta Stone, an Egyptian record inscribed in 196 BCE on a massive piece of black stone in Egyptian hieroglyphs and demotic script, as well as ancient Greek. When unearthed in the late eighteenth century CE, the stone provided scholars with the key to deciphering the long-forgotten hieroglyphs. Even the Persians of the fifth century BCE had not managed religious and cultural diversity more skillfully than the Ptolemies.

CULTURAL TENSIONS AND NEW BELIEFS

Despite the Ptolemies' tolerance of diversity in Egypt, the Hellenistic world was hardly peaceful. The Seleucids, who inherited Syria and parts of Asia Minor from Alexander, warred with the Ptolemies over and over again. The origins of the Greek dynasties in conquest often aroused terrible bitterness. Some writers adopted the Persian belief that history would end in a great confrontation between good and evil and turned to prophecy. They put into the mouths of the Sibyls, prophetesses known throughout the Mediterranean world, the prediction that at some future date history would reverse itself and the hated Greek invaders would either be cast out and the ancient kingdoms restored, or the great kingdoms would finally disappear in flood or fire.

The Greeks, as we have seen, had always been curious about the peoples they encountered. Herodotus learned much about the nomadic Scythians who lived in the steppes of Eurasia from Greek traders settled around the Black Sea. But this interest had never been universal or systematic. During the Hellenistic period, however, some Greeks began to believe as fervently as the Persians and Egyptians that non-Greek traditions might harbor vital teachings unknown to Greek thought. Alexander the Great himself is said to have been deeply impressed by the austere, loincloth-clad Brahmins whom he encountered in India and whom the Greeks called gymnosophists ("naked philosophers"). Still other Greeks collected mysterious stories and magical recipes associated with "thrice great Hermes," the ancient sage who had supposedly taught the Egyptians how to write, or the Persian prophet Zoroaster, about whom Plato and others spun rich fables.

Many inauthentic texts came into circulation—supposed revelations of the non-Greek gods and prophets, stuffed with fragments of genuine Egyptian or Persian tradition but designed to show that these had anticipated, or were the source of, the Greek philosophies of Plato and Aristotle. Small sects formed, creating pseudo-Persian and pseudo-Egyptian rituals. Magical practitioners and astronomers who offered predictions of the future often described themselves as "Chaldeans" (Mesopotamians), even when they were Greek by birth, and sprinkled their writings with foreign words that gave them a mysterious appeal. The culture of the Hellenistic Mediterranean, for all the rigorous and lively scientific experimentation and scholarly debate that took place in Alexandria, also fostered abundant crops of new superstitions. These were as loosely connected to the peoples with whom they supposedly originated as the "Druidic" and "Egyptian" magical texts in a modern occult bookshop. This mixture of beliefs and practices became fertile ground for

Rosetta Stone From 196 BCE Ptolemaic Egypt, the Rosetta Stone is inscribed with a decree from King Ptolemy V written in the kingdom's three official scripts: Egyptian hieroglyphs, demotic (or "popular") Egyptian, and Greek.

the development of new religions—including, as we will see, Christianity itself.

THE JEWS IN THE HELLENISTIC WORLD

One of the ancient Near Eastern peoples, however, did learn to speak for itself, even under Hellenistic rule. Jews and Greeks had come into contact for centuries, especially in Egypt, where both nations' mercenary soldiers served. In the second half of the sixth century BCE, Cyrus, the king of Persia, had conquered Babylon and allowed the Jews, who had been forced to migrate there earlier in the century, to return home to Judah. There, as we will see, they were brought for a time under the control of one of the Hellenistic monarchies, the Seleucids, with explosive results.

SECOND TEMPLE JUDAISM (6TH–2ND CENTURIES BCE)

Jerusalem, the former capital of Judah, became the center of Jewish life and worship in the fifth and fourth centuries BCE. There, on a hill called the Temple Mount, the Jews had rebuilt their Temple. This **Second Temple**, an impressive structure, gradually became a vast complex of buildings. At the end of its existence, in the first century CE, it grew big enough to encompass some twelve modern soccer fields.

The Second Temple was uniquely central to Jewish life. It was the only place where Jews could perform sacrifices to their god, as their law mandated. Three times a year, at Passover, Pentecost, and Sukkot, Jews came to the Temple to make ritual sacrifices. For the rest of the year, the priests carried on services and made sacrifices. The Temple bustled with people, especially on the three great holidays, when moneychangers and butchers offered travelers help in buying and slaughtering ritual animals. This large and richly decorated house of God, which only Jews were deemed clean enough to enter, was also a central slaughterhouse where thousands of animals were butchered and

The Second Temple This Roman public notice displayed in the Second Temple is in Greek, the most common written language shared by Temple visitors from outside of Palestine. It reads, "No Gentile may enter beyond the dividing wall into the court around the Holy Place; whoever is caught will be to blame for his subsequent death."

eaten at every holiday. By charging for its services and soliciting donations, the Temple became as rich as it was elaborate.

THE PEOPLE OF THE BOOK Splendid though the Temple was, it did not dominate all of religious life in Israel. The Jews had long stood out as monotheists, bound to a single god by a national covenant, which they believed their ancestors had entered, and forbidden to worship others. Like other Near Eastern peoples, they had created some texts that recorded their laws, but as late as the fifth century BCE there was no set body of texts that corresponded to what we know as the Hebrew Bible. The Persian monarchy, however, pushed subject peoples, including the Egyptians and the Jews, to systematize their laws. A plan of this kind likely led the Persians to send Ezra, a professional scribe trained in Babylon, to Jerusalem in the middle of the fifth century BCE. He was instructed to collect and organize the laws of his people.

Ezra, so it seems, compiled what is now the first part of the Hebrew Bible: the Pentateuch, or Five Books of Moses (Genesis, Exodus, Leviticus, Numbers, and Deuteronomy). By doing so, he provided an authoritative account of the origins of the universe and the history of the Jews, as well as a summary of their laws and observances. He also brought the Jews together and presented their law to them, dramatically reading it aloud from a platform, after which a great celebration took place. Jewish worship after the Babylonian exile still revolved around sacrifice and prayer, but it added something radically new as well: the public reading of "the book of the law," presumably the Five Books of Moses, which was assembled in official copies and made accessible to the whole people, women as well as men.

Over the coming centuries, the Hebrew Bible took shape as further texts—especially the writings of the prophets and the Psalms—were added to the Five Books of Moses. Bible scrolls were kept in the Temple, and other copies in synagogues—religious gathering places that became increasingly central to Jewish life. On the Sabbath, Jews came together in synagogues to read from the Bible, first in Hebrew and then in Aramaic, the language of everyday Jewish life in Babylon. By the third century BCE, when the massive Hebrew Bible was translated into Greek, even Greeks could find out that the Jews were "the people of a book."

JUDAISM TRANSLATED—AND REVISED The Temple, with its wealth and power, and the scriptures, with their authoritative narrative of early history and their detailed codes and commandments, helped to maintain the unity of the Jewish tradition. Yet in this culturally fertile period, religious beliefs continued to change. The Bible could divide as well as unite. In a culture in which every text was produced by copying, it took centuries to stabilize the Hebrew Bible completely. And whereas most Jews in Palestine encountered the Bible through readings in Aramaic, others there and many in other areas spoke, read, and worshipped in Greek. They also needed a Bible in the familiar language that they could follow. By the second century BCE, a Greek translation of the Hebrew Bible was in circulation.

From translation to interpretation was only a short step. The **Septuagint**, the Greek translation of the Five Books of Moses made in the third century BCE, incorporated changes that rationalized and softened parts of its message. Writers whose identity we do not know went so far as to add new books of history, prophecy, or reflection, which they claimed also deserved to be treated as scripture. From Genesis 6, for example, writers in the third and second centuries BCE crafted the book of Enoch. This new book tells the story of the fall of the Watchers—angels sent by God to watch over the universe—and Enoch's efforts to intercede on their behalf with God. Over time the sacred history of Israel became more complex and rich than the narrative of it in the Five Books of Moses. The mental universe that believing Jews inhabited gradually filled up with superhuman beings not explicitly mentioned in the Bible.

SOCIAL AND ECONOMIC CHANGE IN HEBREW SOCIETY

The Hellenistic period was fertile materially as well as culturally for the people of Palestine. Though Judea itself, the area around Jerusalem, was rocky and poor, other parts of the country lent themselves to cultivation of grapes and olives. The peaceful conditions fostered by the Ptolemies encouraged trade with Egypt, and the vast expansion of money set loose by Alexander and his followers expanded economic activity. Lending came to be seen not as usury (a sin) but as a normal transaction. Caravans brought trade goods to Jerusalem, which became by the second century BCE, as a contemporary noted, a city "skilled in many crafts." Using devices for scattering seed and irrigating crops—technology well established elsewhere but new to

Palestine—successful landlords accumulated extensive holdings and became rich.

The fast-moving, trade-centered Palestine of the third century BCE appears in Ecclesiastes, a later book of the Hebrew Bible. Kohelet, the author of the text, describes his decision to invest in vineyards and olive groves, which were far more profitable than fields of grain: "I made me great works; I builded me houses; I planted me vineyards: I made me gardens and orchards, and I planted trees in them of all kind of fruits." In this world, successful entrepreneurship on the land could make one, literally, as rich as a king.

Like other moralists, Kohelet dismissed his gains as "vanity and vexation of spirit." In memorable words he called for the restoration of a simple, traditional morality that would teach men to love God, enjoy their lives, and do good. Yet the world he described, and took for granted, was one in which rich men like him ground the poor under their feet: "If thou seest the oppression of the poor, and violent perverting of judgment and justice in a province, marvel not at the matter." Many of the new rich had slaves to work their land or serve in their households.

WOMEN'S LIVES The status of women changed as radically in Jewish society as it did in Egypt in the third and second centuries BCE. The older books of the Bible describe a polygamous society in which the prospective groom offered his future father-in-law a bride price: cattle and other goods, or money, which could support the bride if the marriage did not last. In the Greek world, brides brought property and money with them to their marriages in the form of a dowry. During the third century BCE, Jewish women also began to bring dowries with them to their marriages: goods and money to be managed by the husband and used, with his resources, to support the family. Scribes now drew up contracts to regulate this complicated system and to ensure that the interests of both sides were protected—for example, by ensuring that widows had the right to inherit their husbands' property. The new Jewish system of marriage was monogamous, and contracts required husbands to promise not to take further wives.

Women did not attain full equality, and only men could initiate divorce proceedings. But as the development of the marriage contract shows, women now had more property and power than ever before in Jewish history. Some were richer than their husbands and maintained them in better style than the men could have afforded on their own. And some women worked. Chapter 31 of the biblical book of Proverbs, written in the Hellenistic period, describes the ideal wife: she plants vineyards and trees, spins wool and weaves cloth, makes fine linen and sells some of it to merchants. Instead of eating "the bread of idleness," she rises before dawn to work, and the fine things she makes "praise her in the gates."

Other biblical passages written in this period praised women for their intelligence as well as for their beauty. And still others warned fathers to watch their daughters carefully, because too much independence could make them wicked. Unlike the soil of Egypt, that of Palestine has not preserved individual legal documents and contracts to illustrate these changes. But they mattered greatly—especially when a new prophet, named Jesus, began to preach a radical new message in Palestine.

ADOPTING GREEK WAYS As trade and migration brought Jews into regular contact with the Greek world, the Greek language—and Greek culture—inevitably attracted them. Jews who moved to Egypt and elsewhere, as tens of thousands did, began to use Greek as well as Aramaic. Not only did Jews read their Bible in Greek, as we have seen, Greek eventually became a language of Jewish prayer in the great synagogue at Alexandria and in others across the Mediterranean. In the second century CE, rabbis in Palestine would hear the holiest Jewish prayer, the Shema, recited in Greek. In Palestine itself, moreover, the Greek language and Greek customs began to spread. For example, families that could afford it began to bury their dead in lavish above-ground tombs, which they equipped with Greek inscriptions praising the virtues of their dead relatives.

Greek artistic forms and ideas followed the language and infiltrated every area of life. The biblical book of Judith is a narrative originally written in Hebrew in the second century BCE, which survives now only in Greek. It describes how the virtuous widow Judith and her loyal maid enter the camp of an Assyrian general. Judith promises him sexual favors, tricks him into becoming drunk, and beheads him, maintaining her chastity and saving her fellow Jews. An inspiration to painters and musicians for centuries, the story clearly shows the impact both of the new position of women in Israel and of Greek tragedy.

Jews also came to appreciate the Greek custom of the symposium—the evening meeting at which men, and sometimes women, reclined, drank, recited poetry, and argued about philosophy. Eventually they took it over for themselves, and the Passover seder, which had been a rapid

ritual, performed standing up, in memory of the ancient Jews' escape from Egypt, became a long celebration performed by Jews who reclined at the table and debated every aspect of the Passover experience.

SELEUCIDS AND MACCABEES: THE LIMITS OF CONVERGENCE (2ND CENTURY BCE)

What did it mean to live as a Jew? The Seleucid rulers of Palestine, like their Persian predecessors, allowed their Jewish subjects to follow their own ways of life and worship. But in the third and second centuries BCE, many Jews began to believe that turning away from the beliefs and practices of the rest of the world had been a mistake, the origin of centuries of misfortune. Young men began to practice athletics in the nude, as the Greeks did. Others began to worship the gods of the invaders. At the request of these Jewish reformers, in 176 BCE the Seleucid ruler of Syria, Antiochus Epiphanes, imposed the worship of the god Baal—a Semitic name for Zeus—whose idol he introduced into the Temple itself.

DANIEL'S VISION: RESISTANCE TO CULTURAL MINGLING A resistance movement sprang up, one powered (at first) by the hope that divine vengeance would put matters right. The unknown author of the prophetic book of Daniel, horrified to see "the abomination of desolation" in the Temple, looked back to the earlier history of Israel and Judah for precedents to follow. Like the earlier prophets, he denounced the sin, corruption, and irreligion that he saw around him, and insisted that God would avenge himself.

The text of Daniel also offers a dramatic vision of the future. The king of Babylon dreams of a gigantic statue of a man, its head made of gold, its chest and arms of silver, its belly of bronze, its legs of iron, and its feet of iron and clay. A stone smashes the statue, whose remains are swept away by the wind while the stone fills the whole earth. The prophet explains that the metals of the statue represent the different kingdoms that succeeded one another in the past. The great stone stands for the new, universal kingdom that God will create.

Daniel and other Jewish writers found consolation for their present sorrows in the belief that history would soon come to a magnificent, terrifying close, as God smashed the oppressors of the true God and his people

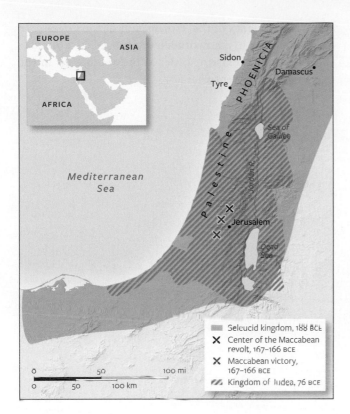

The Seleucids and Maccabees in the 2nd Century BCE

Map legend:
- Seleucid kingdom, 188 BCE
- X Center of the Maccabean revolt, 167–166 BCE
- X Maccabean victory, 167–166 BCE
- Kingdom of Judea, 76 BCE

in one climactic confrontation or battle. Paradoxically, these opponents of cultural mingling between Jews and non-Jews may have drawn this vision from the Zoroastrians, with their visions of cosmic confrontations between good and evil. The Jews' convictions underpinned resistance, first to the Seleucids and then, as we will see, to Rome. They also provided a vital part of the framework on which Jesus and his followers created what would become the Christian church.

THE MACCABEES The **Maccabees**, a group of pious Jewish rebels, resisted the Seleucids in a more practical way, rising up against Antiochus Epiphanes in 167–166 BCE. Using guerilla tactics they defeated the Seleucid armies, cleansed the Temple, and reestablished worship there. Antiochus's death in 164 BCE prevented him from trying to regain control, and the Maccabees founded the Hasmonean dynasty, which ruled Judea for the next century. Religious ideology could, evidently, rally a people as effectively as the political ideologies that had long before united Athenians and Spartans.

The books of Maccabees, which recorded these events, offer the earliest testimony to beliefs that would become central to Judaism. In one of these books, the Jewish mother of seven sons, whom Antiochus puts to death for refusing to betray their religion, encourages the last one to die rather than to violate the commands of Judaism: "Accept death, so that in God's mercy I may get you back again with your brothers." He dies well, and she does the same. Belief in the sanctity of martyrdom—that a heroic death in defense of religious purity is the highest imaginable fate and means certain salvation for the martyr's soul—would become a central feature of Jewish tradition, and then of Christian and Islamic religious life as well. It was not only the belief in one god that these monotheistic religions had in common.

The victorious Maccabees did not prohibit all Greek influences. They issued public documents in Greek and minted coins that followed Greek models. They also used Greek to recount their own history in the second book of Maccabees. Even as the Maccabees restored the Temple and the worship of the God of Israel, Jews were beginning, for the first time, to think about how to explain themselves to non-Jews.

CONCLUSION

By the end of the second century BCE, the world had changed. A single, Greek-speaking culture had spread across the entire Mediterranean world and beyond it. A single pattern of urban settlement, a uniform kind of temple to the gods (though not the God of Israel), and a clearly chosen set of literary classics had imposed themselves from Bactria to Marseilles, and from Egypt to the Black Sea.

Greek culture had immense prestige. Everyone from the rulers of Egypt to the leaders of Jewish society in Palestine wanted to exercise in gymnasia, take part in athletic contests, write poetry in Greek, and—in most cases—worship Greek gods. Thanks to Persian gold and Macedonian conquest, the market society pioneered by the Phoenicians and expanded by the Athenians and other Greeks had become the normal form of urban life. The Greek language had spread across the Mediterranean world with the conquering armies and merchants, enabling distant peoples to communicate and supporting the creation of great states. A policy of tolerance, coexistence, and multilingual government had enabled the survival, in Egypt and elsewhere, of native priesthoods, religions, and customs.

At the same time, another power—one almost as old as

the Greek city-states and far stronger—had risen to challenge the Hellenistic states and some of their rivals. The Romans, whose state had grown up over the centuries in the center of the Italian peninsula, regarded themselves as the descendants of the Trojans, not of the Greeks. In that respect, as in many others, they posed a formidable challenge to the existing order as they entered it in the third and second centuries BCE.

[CHAPTER REVIEW]

KEY TERMS

Plato (p. 79)
forms (p. 79)
Aristotle (p. 80)
empirical (p. 80)

Lyceum (p. 80)
satrap (p. 81)
Philip II (p. 82)
Alexander (p. 83)

Hellenistic (p. 85)
Ptolemies (p. 87)
Epicureans (p. 96)
Stoics (p. 96)

Second Temple (p. 102)
Septuagint (p. 103)
Maccabees (p. 105)

REVIEW QUESTIONS

1. In what ways did Plato establish a new basis for philosophy?

2. What are the most important differences between Plato's and Aristotle's thinking?

3. What steps did Philip II take to conquer the Greek city-states?

4. How did Alexander consolidate his rule over the eastern Mediterranean and western Asia?

5. How did trade and commerce help to connect the Hellenistic world?

6. What types of "soft power" were used by Hellenistic monarchs to solidify their rule?

7. How were the lives of women different in the Hellenistic kingdoms as compared with those in fifth-century Athens?

8. How did the Hellenistic world contribute to the development of science and philosophy?

9. How did the Ptolemies draw on Egyptian and Greek traditions in their rule of Egypt?

10. What were the most important developments in Hebrew religious culture during the Second Temple period?

CORE OBJECTIVES

After reading this chapter, you should have a solid understanding of the following core objectives. To strengthen your grasp of the core objectives, use the resources on the Student Site for The West.

- Identify the distinctive approaches of Plato and Aristotle in understanding the world.

- Explain Alexander's approaches to non-Greek cultures as he conquered and ruled foreign lands.

- Analyze the causes of economic prosperity in the Hellenistic kingdoms.

- Describe the transformations in Greek culture brought about by contact with foreign cultures during the Hellenistic period.

- Evaluate the intellectual and religious innovations that arose from the mix of Greek and non-Greek thought in the Hellenistic period.

- Explain how Jewish culture and religion both accepted and resisted Hellenism.

 GO TO inQUIZITIVE TO SEE WHAT YOU'VE LEARNED—AND LEARN WHAT YOU'VE MISSED—WITH PERSONALIZED FEEDBACK ALONG THE WAY.

CHRONOLOGY

753 BCE
City of Rome is
founded as a monarchy

509–508 BCE
Romans establish Republic

ca. 500 BCE
Law of the Twelve Tables
Early fifth century–ca. 287 BCE
Struggle of the Orders

280–276 BCE
Romans defend against invasion
by Greek King Pyrrhus

264–241 BCE
First Punic War

218–201 BCE
Second Punic War

214–140 BCE
Romans war against
and defeat Macedonians
and Greeks

149–146 BCE
Third Punic War

Rome

MONARCHY, REPUBLIC, AND THE TRANSITION TO EMPIRE

1000 BCE–14 CE

31 BCE
Octavian assumes sole
power as Augustus

133–121 BCE
Gracchi brothers
attempt reforms

91–87 BCE
Social War

73–71 BCE
Spartacus leads
slave revolt

63 BCE
Cicero delivers orations
against Catiline

After 50 BCE
Caesar becomes
sole ruler of Rome

44 BCE
Brutus and Cassius murder Caesar

n the autumn of 63 BCE, the politician Marcus Tullius Cicero stood before the Roman Senate, the city's official body of elders, at a special meeting held in the Senate House, located in the Forum at the center of the city. Rome was an old city, traditionally dominated by great aristocratic clans that had been established for centuries. But it was also a republic, in which politicians of lower origins who had a gift for public speaking and organizing could attain power. Cicero was born to a rich family with noble status, but one based in the hill town of Arpinum, sixty miles southeast of Rome. As a so-called new man (the first in his family to win high office), he had established his authority through his accomplishments as a lawyer, orator, and official. In a series of fiery speeches, powerfully delivered, he now denounced the aristocrat Catiline, whom he had beaten in an election for consul, the supreme office in the Roman Republic. For the last century, as Rome became more and more prosperous, the poor had suffered and thousands lost their farms. Catiline, like other Romans of high standing before him, had wooed them by offering a program of land distribution.

Cicero proclaimed that his spies had caught Catiline and his followers conspiring to assassinate Cicero and take over the city of Rome. He described Catiline as a

Pompeian Frescoes Well-preserved objects and artwork from the city of Pompeii, which was buried under ash after the eruption of Mount Vesuvius in 79 CE, offer some of the best clues to everyday life in the Roman world. This colorful fresco in a lavish Pompeii villa constructed around 40 BCE may show an initiation ritual in the cult of the Greek god Dionysos. It indicates how closely the gods were entwined in ordinary life, and how much the Romans embraced Greek culture.

- What do Roman myths and modern archaeology reveal about the origins of Rome?
- How did social tensions find expression in Roman politics?
- Why did the Roman Republic expand throughout the Italian Peninsula and beyond?
- What were the core Roman values, and how were they transmitted through society?
- Why did the republican system become increasingly unstable in the second and first centuries BCE?
- What led the Republic into its century of crisis?
- How did Rome make the transition from republic to empire under Augustus?

create—wielding words as if they were edged weapons to practice the politics of personal destruction.

But if Cicero won his battle against Catiline, he lost the war, which he and others waged, to preserve the Roman Republic. In the end, Cicero would die by violence, assassinated by the agents of one of his political enemies, Mark Antony. A great empire would replace the Republic that he claimed to stand for, the largest state in the ancient world that was ruled by a group of citizens rather than a monarch. In his speeches against Catiline, Cicero argued that the keys to understanding and solving Rome's problems lay in Roman history, which offered a rich set of models for emulation and precedents for prudent action. Let us follow his example and turn back to the Roman past, to see how the Republic took shape, and why—in the end—it could not be sustained.

monster in human form, a murderer of his own wife and son, a violator of the Senate's rules, a political assassin, and a reprobate—someone so visibly marked with the stamp of evil that his fellow senators shrank away as he walked among them. Cicero went on to compare the Rome of his own day, gripped by terror as political murders spread fear among the population, with the city in its former days, when "brave men did not lack the courage to strike down a dangerous Roman citizen more fiercely even than they struck down the bitterest of foreign foes." And he insisted that the Senate was at fault because it had tolerated the presence of a criminal: "This man still lives! Lives? He walks right into the Senate. He joins in our national debates. He watches and notes and marks down with his gaze each of us he plans to assassinate."

Catiline, overwhelmed by Cicero's opposition, left Rome and eventually died fighting alongside his followers. Cicero's speeches became classics, translated and memorized by schoolchildren for more than 2,000 years. His words deserved the fascination of posterity. Like the politicians of fifth-century Athens—but working in a far larger society and state—Cicero showed how a leader could win support and stamp out opposition by mobilizing effective language and using it to appeal to historical traditions that still had deep meanings for his fellow citizens. And like the Athenians, Cicero could use language to destroy as well as to

ORIGINS (1000–509 BCE)

The rise of Rome is different, in crucial ways, from the histories we have followed up to this point. Like Athens and Sparta, Rome began as a city, and though it was a monarchy at the start, it became, like them, a republic. But where the Greek cities fought and developed alliances with other city-states, Rome expanded into a vast national state, merging first with local peoples and slowly filling the entire Italian Peninsula. And whereas the Greek republics were eventually subjugated by the Macedonian monarchy, Rome not only remained independent but also became a world empire that long outlasted Alexander's. Like the Hellenistic empires, it had a common language—Latin—that spread as far as England, Spain, North Africa, and Syria; unlike them, it retained its possessions in all of these lands. But even as the Romans became masters of the world, they lost the republican liberty that they had prized for centuries, as Julius Caesar and those who followed him transformed their society into the greatest empire the world had known.

THE ITALIAN PENINSULA

Early in the first millennium BCE, many peoples inhabited the Italian Peninsula, a landscape that favored the development of multiple societies. In this narrow landmass stretching from the Alps in the north to a heel only one

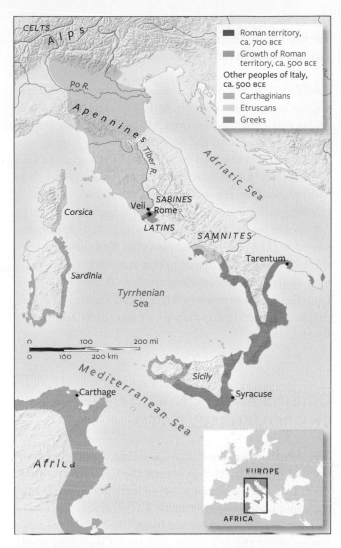

The Italian Peninsula, 700–500 BCE The Latin people shared the Italian Peninsula with several other peoples: the Etruscans to the north; the Greeks to the south; their allies, the Sabines; and the Samnites, with whom they warred for centuries. Carthage and its colonies also proved a threatening local power. Rome was founded around 1000 BCE, but only slowly expanded its territory over the centuries.

hundred miles from the coast of North Africa, landscapes and ecologies vary sharply. The Apennines—the mountain chain that forms the peninsula's spine—divides east from west. Navigable rivers such as the Tiber, and wonderful natural bays, favor trade and exchange.

THE LATINS

The Latins, an Indo-European people, lived in Italy from the early centuries of the second millennium BCE. They settled a central Italian plain punctuated by hills that could be fortified, and bordered by the Tiber as well as the Tyrrhenian Sea to the west. They became the founders of Rome, and their language and traditions

would reach the far-flung borders of the Roman Empire. In the early centuries of the first millennium BCE, however, the Latins had many other peoples as near neighbors, including the Sabines, an Italic people, most of whom would eventually join the Latins; and the Samnites, who spoke a now-lost language and would fight the Latins for centuries.

THE ETRUSCANS

The **Etruscans**—a highly sophisticated people governed by aristocratic families—founded cities from the Po River valley in the north and what is now Tuscany down to the area around Rome. The Etruscans' language is not yet fully understood, and their origins are uncertain. But archaeologists have shown that they developed an urban culture with massive buildings, sophisticated painting, and free-standing sculptures of human bodies. They had a special gift for elegant metalwork that served for everything from fine hand mirrors to delicate dental bridges. Women enjoyed greater equality in the family and beyond. A Greek historian of the fourth century BCE remarked that "Etruscan women take particular care of their bodies and exercise often, sometimes along with the men, and sometimes by themselves. It is not a disgrace for them to be seen naked. They do not share their couches with their husbands but with the other men who happen to be present, and they propose toasts to anyone they choose."

The Etruscans worshipped multiple gods, believed in an afterlife in which the virtuous feasted and the vicious

Etruscan Houses Etruscan cremation urns—like this one from the seventh century BCE—were often modeled as houses, giving us an idea of what Etruscan and early Roman dwellings may have looked like. These homes were typically oval and made of clay, with a wooden roof in which a hole was cut to let the smoke from the central hearth escape.

An Etruscan Couple This Etruscan sarcophagus (ca. 600–500 BCE) depicts in expressive detail a married couple on a banqueting couch. It is an example of the Etruscan culture's relative gender equality: the couple are the same size and assume similar postures, with the woman in the foreground, and they participate together in a banquet, which in the Greek tradition was a distinctively masculine activity.

were punished, and possessed elaborate techniques for warding off evil in the present and divining the future. Their traditions were recorded in verse scriptures, some of which survive and can be read in part. Etruscan kings ruled Rome in the sixth century BCE, and over time many Etruscan cities became Roman.

GREEK COLONIES To the north, Celtic peoples, moving out from the area of modern Austria, expanded over the Alps into Italy. In the deep south, on the tip of the peninsula and in Sicily, Greek cities founded colonies as early as the eighth century BCE. In the fertile soil of Sicily, olive trees and grape vines grew readily, and the island soon began to produce oil and wine. Some of the colonies were as large and powerful as any city in the Greek homeland—especially the port of Tarentum, on the southern coast of Italy, and Syracuse, in Sicily, which as we have seen defeated an Athenian invasion during the Peloponnesian War. Hoplite warfare, magnificent temples to the Greek gods, and massive amphitheaters, all built in the

best Greek style, spread across the lower portions of Italy. To this day, southern Italy possesses Greek ruins as magnificent as any in the Greek mainland.

CARTHAGE For all their wealth, the western Greeks did not control all of southern Italy. **Carthage**, a Phoenician settlement on a North African peninsula, sent its trading ships around the Mediterranean to import vital goods such as wheat and metals. The Carthaginians were brilliant navigators—around 500 BCE they sailed ships southward along the western coast of Africa, eventually reaching what is now Senegal. They aggressively set up colonies in Sicily and Spain that, unlike Greek colonies, were designed to serve the home city. And they defended these colonies with their expert seamanship and the military skills of their Numidian cavalry—Berbers who came from the region of modern Algeria and Tunisia. The Carthaginians would eventually prove the most dangerous of Rome's rivals.

ORIGINS AND MONARCHY: WHAT THE ROMANS BELIEVED

The city that became Rome—and that would eventually dominate or defeat the Etruscans, the Carthaginians, and many other Italic peoples, often learning from them at the same time—was first settled around 1000 BCE. The Romans themselves did not know this. They told two stories about the origins of their city. Like other Mediterranean peoples who wished to show that they were as venerable as the Greeks, the Romans traced their ancestry to the Trojan exiles who, led by the hero Aeneas, had left the city in Asia Minor after it fell to the Greeks and eventually settled in Italy. There, in the twelfth century BCE, or so they thought, the Trojan leader and his followers intermarried with the Latins who already inhabited the center of the peninsula. The other story held that the real founding of the city had taken place later, in the middle of the eighth century BCE, when Romulus—who was supposedly reared, along with his brother Remus, by a she-wolf—brought male settlers together at what would become Rome and then stole wives for them from the Sabines and the Latins.

From the start, these legends claimed, the Romans both fought and allied with other Italian peoples. The traditional narrative held that seven kings ruled the city for two and a half centuries, from 753 to 509 BCE: Romulus, Numa Pompilius, Tullus Hostilius, Ancus Marcius,

Lucius Tarquinius Priscus, Servius Tullius, and Lucius Tarquinius Superbus. This story cannot be literally true, as there is no known case in which an unbroken series of rulers all lived so long. And according to the stories, each of the early monarchs supposedly contributed something vital. Numa, for example, created the state's calendar and its public religion, and Servius Tullius built the wall that ringed the entire city. The last king, Lucius Tarquinius Superbus ("the Proud"), infuriated the city's inhabitants by taking tyrannical measures—starting, supposedly, with the assassination of his predecessor. When his son forced a virtuous woman, Lucretia, to sleep with him, she revealed the crime and then killed herself. In 509 BCE a rebellion broke out, led by Lucretia's husband and Lucius Junius Brutus. The rebels not only defeated the king but also transformed the state into a republic.

These vivid stories would be told and retold for centuries by everyone interested in the history and fate of Rome. They were created by well-born Roman writers centuries after the events they purported to describe, and they offer a mixture of myth and history, the original components of which are hard to pull apart. Yet it is possible to tease out of these stories the values that meant the most to the Roman elite—for example, that the survival of the state mattered more than any individual life. And behind those values one can sense something of the historical struggles, some of them violent, that led to the creation of Rome's republican institutions.

ORIGINS AND MONARCHY: WHAT THE RECORD SHOWS

In keeping with these narratives of the city's past, early Rome did reach a peak of grandeur in the sixth century BCE, which Romans remembered as a time of Etruscan kings. And the Romans did adopt central customs from the Etruscans: from the wearing of the toga, the long woolen garment that adult males wrapped around themselves, to the fasces—the bundle of rods, sometimes surrounding an axe, that was carried before Roman officials as a sign of their authority.

The period of the monarchy did witness the creation of the city's calendar and the building of the Cloaca Maxima, the great sewer that helped drain Rome's swampy central region. From the start, the city's public life revolved around a central marketplace, the Forum. But archaeologists and historians have discovered a great deal more, in the last several decades, about the rise of Rome.

Romulus and Remus Many Romans believed that twin brothers, Romulus and Remus, had founded their city. According to legend, they were abandoned at birth but rescued by a she-wolf. A medieval Italian artist added suckling infants to an ancient sculpture of a wolf to create this evocative visualization of the founding myth.

Though much remains uncertain, it seems clear that settlement in Rome began around the year 1000 BCE, when villages were founded on some of the seven hills surrounding that low-lying, swampy area. Much later—in the eighth and seventh centuries BCE—Rome's advantageous position near the mouth of the Tiber, which made it a natural center for trade, may have been decisive in transforming the small settlements into a single, larger city. Rome's craft production became more sophisticated, its trade more developed. A colony of Phoenician merchants from Tyre lived there, selling valuable silver and ivory objects to the Romans and to the Etruscans to the north.

The population was mixed: it included Latins and Sabines, and by the sixth century BCE there was also an Etruscan quarter. But Latin provided a common language, and inscriptions carved on stone show that some Romans were literate by the sixth century. Even before that, the city's inhabitants had collaborated on projects. A wall on the Capitoline Hill was raised in the eighth century (exactly the period in which legend set Rome's founding), and later projects included the paving of the Forum and construction of the first public buildings.

By the end of the sixth century BCE, Rome had taken on the form of a full city, though not one as grand or as elegantly laid out as a Greek city of comparable wealth and power. The Romans found ways to obtain vital resources: their city was on an existing road that the Sabines used to transport salt, essential for city life, from marshes at the mouth of the Tiber. Trade brought in luxury goods,

Fasces A sixth-century BCE relief depicts an Etruscan official holding *fasces,* a bundle of rods carried as a symbol of a ruler's authority—a custom the Romans later adopted.

including Greek vases of high quality, and local artisans began to construct temples out of stone with elaborate terra-cotta ornaments.

THE EARLY REPUBLIC (509–146 BCE)

From the traditional narratives we know that sharp tensions developed between the last kings, whose actions were seen as tyrannical, and some well-born and powerful Romans. When the last king of Rome, Lucius Tarquinius Superbus, was forced to leave the city in 509 BCE, Rome was transformed from a monarchy, as the much later historian Livy wrote, to "a free Rome under magistrates elected for a year and under laws whose authority exceeds that of men."

The first decades of the Republic were anything but peaceful. The city fought a long series of wars—with

Tarquinius Superbus and his supporters (508 BCE); with the Latin League, a confederation of villages outside Rome; and with the powerful Etruscan city of Veii. The wars caused crises at home that threatened to divide Roman society. In the end, though, the city survived, making a treaty with the Latin League in 493 in which both sides were recognized as equals. Rome began to develop a constitution that could accommodate the stresses that came with expansion.

POLITICAL INSTITUTIONS AND SOCIAL TENSIONS

Some of republican Rome's central institutions took shape in this early period. Roman tradition held that the **Senate** came into existence with the city, as a body of 100 who advised Romulus, the city's mythical founder. Its membership was mixed, consisting of aristocratic men and men of lower birth. The Senate met in or near Rome when magistrates summoned its members. Meetings were private. After the presiding officer explained the issue to be discussed, each senator spoke in order of rank. The senators enjoyed complete freedom of discussion, each addressing the assembly from his seat. The right to wear a special striped tunic and boots, as well as other privileges, set the members of this great assembly apart from other Romans. Once the kings were expelled, the Senate took on greater responsibility for the state as a whole—but also proved unable to manage the social and political conflicts unleashed by the fall of the monarchy.

Rome's population as a whole was divided at an early stage into **patricians**, members of aristocratic families that enjoyed special political privileges, and **plebeians**—that is to say, everyone else who was free. Patricians were easy to identify: they derived their rank from their birth and held the monopoly, for example, on priestly positions. The category of plebeian was less neatly defined. It included both owners of small properties, who probably farmed their estates for a living, and providers of the crafts and services necessary to maintain the city. Many artisans and small shopkeepers were based on the Aventine Hill, near the Tiber, which became Rome's first river port.

The creation of the Republic was only the beginning of a long contest between these two social classes. The plebeians were excluded from priesthoods, magistracies, and the Senate. Over time the conditions in which they lived became harder: bad harvests and accumulated debt harmed small landholders. Continued wars with

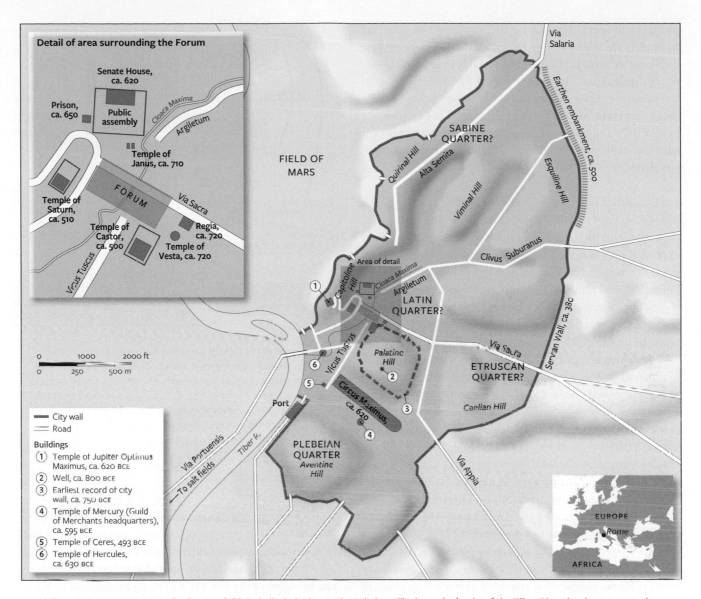

Detail of area surrounding the Forum

Senate House, ca. 620

Prison, ca. 650

Public assembly

Cloaca Maxima

Argiletum

Temple of Janus, ca. 710

FORUM

Via Sacra

Temple of Saturn, ca. 510

Temple of Castor, ca. 500

Regia, ca. 720

Temple of Vesta, ca. 720

Vicus Tuscus

Via Salaria

FIELD OF MARS

SABINE QUARTER?

Quirinal Hill

Alta Semita

Viminal Hill

Esquiline Hill

Earthen embankment, ca. 500

Clivus Suburanus

Area of detail

Capitoline Hill

Cloaca Maxima

Argiletum

LATIN QUARTER?

Via Sacra

Servian Wall, ca. 380

Palatine Hill

Vicus Tuscus

ETRUSCAN QUARTER?

Caelian Hill

Circus Maximus, ca. 620

Port

Via Portuensis

Tiber R.

To salt fields

PLEBEIAN QUARTER

Aventine Hill

Via Appia

EUROPE

Rome

AFRICA

0   1000   2000 ft
0   250   500 m

— City wall
= Road

Buildings

1 Temple of Jupiter Optimus Maximus, ca. 620 BCE
2 Well, ca. 800 BCE
3 Earliest record of city wall, ca. 750 BCE
4 Temple of Mercury (Guild of Merchants headquarters), ca. 595 BCE
5 Temple of Ceres, 493 BCE
6 Temple of Hercules, ca. 630 BCE

Republican Rome, ca. 350 BCE The Romans initially built their city on the Palatine Hill, above the banks of the Tiber River, but it soon spread outward to cover seven hills with densely packed roads and apartment buildings. In the center of the city, significant public buildings such as the Senate House and temples to deities such as Hercules, Jupiter, and Mercury were clustered around the Forum.

Rome's neighbors were also costly. The resulting conflicts between the plebeians and the patricians—known as the **Struggle of the Orders**—shaped the city's development. The history of Rome's political assemblies enables us to follow these tensions and their sometimes creative effects over time.

THE ASSEMBLIES The earliest Roman assembly, the *comitia curiata,* rested on a division of the entire population into thirty groups, or *curiae*, ten for each of the three tribes that Romulus had fused when founding the city. Each was headed by a magistrate called the *curio*, who mustered the city's armies. Later, a second, more complex organization,

the *comitia centuriata* ("assembly of the centuries"), was created, supposedly by the next-to-last of the legendary kings. This assembly took responsibility for enacting laws, choosing senior magistrates, and inflicting the death penalty on Roman citizens.

Citizens in Rome were divided into five classes by property and assigned to centuries (groups of 100 men) for military purposes. As in most Greek cities, only male property-holders could serve in the army. The smallest and richest of these five groups voted first in the assembly, and voting ended when a majority agreed. Thus, though all males who bore arms had a formal right to vote, the system gave predominant power to the wealthiest property-holders. Those who did not have the property to qualify for membership in one of the five classes were confined to a single tribe and effectively disenfranchised. By contrast, those wealthy enough to enter the first of the property classes and serve as horsemen, whose equipment and training were especially costly, held enormous power over the city's fate. In a time of almost constant warfare, military men gained a firm foothold in Roman government.

THE STRUGGLE OF THE ORDERS AND THE ROMAN CONSTITUTION Early in the fifth century BCE, the plebeians' resentment of patrician power exploded into action. The government tried to buy grain from farmers in the Pomptine Marshes south of Rome, but failed, and famine raged among the poor. In 494 BCE, the plebeians refused to march against the city's enemies. Instead, they seceded, possibly to the Aventine Hill, where many of them would eventually live and work.

The patricians gave in. They freed plebeians from some of their debts. More important, a third assembly came into being: the *comitia plebis tributa*, or assembly of the tribes. Unlike the assembly of the centuries, it gave no special power to men of wealth and standing. Men voted in their tribes, artificial divisions of the people, twenty-nine of which existed by the fifth century. This assembly also developed important powers. It elected "tribunes of the people," eventually ten in number. They were declared "sacrosanct"—that is, immune from injury or attack—and they had the right to enforce the decrees of the assembly as well as veto power over the actions of other officials. Eventually extended to include thirty-five tribes, this body became Rome's legislative assembly. After a long series of further struggles, the Hortensian Law (ca. 287 BCE) gave the acts of the plebeian assembly, known as plebiscites, absolute authority over all Romans.

From early on, the Roman constitution took shape in the course of political struggles between groups that saw themselves as pursuing separate interests—and whose differences were sharpened when, as often happened, they were waging war with other peoples. To that extent, the Greek general and historian Polybius (ca. 200–ca. 118 BCE) was perfectly right when he said, in a passage later quoted by Cicero, that the Roman constitution differed from the others known to him. It was not, he explained, the

Voting On a coin we can date to 63 BCE, a man—presumably a propertied one—casts a vote in a legislative assembly.

Magistrates

| **Censors** Conduct censuses, lease state properties, identify men to be removed from the tribes or Senate | **Consuls** Two heads of state serve one-year term, lead army |
| | **Praetors** Rank high in army; serve as governors |

Advises

Have veto power over

Elects

Senate Senators (including senior magistrates) debate proposed laws

Assembly of the Centuries Citizens enact laws, serve in the army, impose the death penalty

Tribunes of the people Ten tribunes enforce decrees of Assembly of the Tribes

Elects

Hold imperium

Hold lesser imperium

| **Plebeian assembly** Plebeians enact plebiscites | **Assembly of the Tribes** Plebeians and patricians pass acts of the assembly |

Government of the Roman Republic The political structure of the Roman republic was based on the principle that power was to be shared, and temporary. Roman citizens elected magistrates—consuls, praetors, and censors—whose administrative power was regulated by the Senate, the assembly of the centuries, and the tribunes of the people. Consuls and praetors wielded power in the military as well as the state. They served one-year terms and were reelected only in unusual circumstances.

work of a single statesman, like the Spartans' constitution, but the result of generations of trial and error, a product of history and experience that never stopped developing. The Romans themselves noted this when they spoke of the Struggle of the Orders and its significance.

MAGISTRATES From around 509 BCE administrative and legal power lay in the hands of the magistrates—and would remain there until the end of the Republic half a millennium later. Two consuls—elected once a year by the centuriate assembly, which continued along with the plebeian assembly—possessed imperium, or supreme power. This was symbolically represented by the bundles of twelve rods, or fasces, that were carried before officials in public. The consuls—some of whom were patrician, others plebeian—ruled the state and led Rome's armies in the field, where they had almost unlimited authority.

Below these two rulers, a hierarchy of additional magistrates carried out other administrative and legal duties. Praetors, who held a lesser level of imperium, also wielded impressive power in the state and army. Later, as Rome came to rule other states as provinces of a single empire, praetors served as governors. Censors not only carried out formal censuses but also identified men of bad character, who were removed from their tribes and from the Senate. The censors also took responsibility for leasing the state's properties so that they brought in revenues. A patrician "king of the rituals" oversaw the sacrifices carried out on the Kalends, or first of the month, and announced the dates of other holy days. Other patricians continued to dominate the city's priesthoods. Meanwhile, the tribunes of the people represented the popular interest and gradually won a place of their own in the state's constitution.

MANAGING SOCIAL TENSIONS AND CONFLICT

Yet even as these institutions helped to stabilize the Roman Republic, it found itself enmeshed in conflict with other peoples. The causes of war varied. At times Rome acted when it saw a chance to gain more territory and resources. In the 440s, for instance, while helping to arbitrate a dispute between Latin powers, Rome annexed a town to the south that opened the way to the rich grain-producing area of the Pomptine Marshes. During the period of 437–434 BCE, Rome fought with the Etruscans at Veii to secure a city needed to protect the salt road. But later wars with Veii and other Etruscan cities seem to have been motivated more by the two sides' distrust of one another's designs for the future. In the early fourth century, Celtic peoples drove rapidly south over the Alps, sacked Rome, and held it for ransom—a traumatic event that destroyed the city's early records and shattered its citizens' confidence. Yet the city recovered rapidly from this shock, leaving new and skillful leaders in charge and giving their soldiers a new sense of self-confidence.

The Roman Republic continued to expand by either destroying enemy cities or offering them a place in the Roman state, and their inhabitants Roman citizenship. By the early fourth century BCE, it had become by far the largest state of its kind ever seen and too big to be considered a city-state in the classical sense. Aristotle had believed that a true state could not be much larger than a normal Greek city; otherwise its citizens could not all know one another. The Roman Republic occupied a vast amount of territory in central Italy, and the number of males legally entitled to take part in the assemblies approached 35,000.

Formal citizenship continued to expand, and

The Census In this second-century BCE relief, an official conducting the census registers young men for the army as a soldier looks on.

throughout Roman history many talented men born in the countryside, like Cicero himself, would rise to power and wealth in the city. But even as expansion and opportunity did much to power Rome's rise, problems remained. In practice, most of those who lived in the countryside outside Rome would not have been able to join in the actual voting, which was always held in the city. As stresses worsened in the centuries ahead, opportunities to manipulate the aging institutions of republican politics also expanded.

THE LAW OF THE TWELVE TABLES In the mid-fifth century BCE, the continuing struggles between patricians and plebeians led to the creation of the *decemviri*, a board of ten men charged with drawing up a law code that both groups could adhere to. Supposedly the board sent an embassy to Greece to study the laws of Solon at Athens; more likely they examined the laws of nearby Greek cities in southern Italy. After further struggles and another secession of the plebeians, the laws were finally passed and published, around 450 BCE, as the **Law of the Twelve Tables**. They were a set of definitions of legal rights and procedures posted in the Forum on twelve tablets of ivory or bronze, so that all Romans could see them.

The Twelve Tables prohibited intermarriage between patricians and plebeians, and dealt with general problems of marriage, inheritance, and real estate law. They defined the power of the Roman **paterfamilias**, or head of household, as absolute: the life and death of his children and his wife were in his hands. The Tables did not put an end to the Struggle of the Orders: the ban on intermarriage was abrogated as early as 445 BCE, and conflict continued for two more centuries. But the Tables showed the way to an eventual resolution: the creation of formal laws, which came to be a central feature of Roman government.

THE ROMAN LEGIONS Rome was also becoming more skillful at managing conflict with other peoples. As part of its response to the Celtic sack of Rome and the second invasion that followed half a century later, the Romans founded military colonies, settling citizen soldiers farther and farther from the seven hills. At times, these provocative measures sparked wars, as with the Latins and Volscians from 340 to 338 BCE. But Rome was also ready to respect and support the power of local elites if their members were willing to join the Roman state. After 338 BCE, all Latins shared the so-called **Latin right**: they could marry and trade with Romans, and even gain citizenship if they settled in Rome, while Romans who settled in Latin cities could become citizens there as well. Rome's continued growth gave opportunities to the poor and ambitious who lived far beyond the city's perimeter. Military service was one way for those ambitions to be realized.

The Roman armies grew with the city. Gradually they developed an organization that would remain standard, even as it evolved, until the end of the empire. The army was divided into detachments known as **legions**, which enrolled around 5,000 foot soldiers each. Soldiers of the same rank had uniform clothing and equipment, which a small allowance helped them to purchase. Each legion made camp in the same way, laying out its tents in the form of a square with streets to divide them and a ditch and palisade to protect them from attack. Uniform commands and a body of experienced noncommissioned officers, the centurions, gave the legion coherence and enabled it to march and take up positions for battle in a uniquely disciplined way. Archers and other support troops were mercenaries, paid for their service.

In 282 BCE the city of Tarentum, a Greek colony in southern Italy, appealed to King Pyrrhus of Epirus in northwestern Greece for help against the Romans. Pyrrhus knew that the Romans were powerful, and he hoped that once he had defeated them he would be able to conquer Macedonia. He arrived in Italy at the head

Legions This gold coin, issued sometime between 225 and 212 BCE, shows a Roman soldier and a soldier from an Italian ally swearing an oath of alliance.

Pyrrhus This bust of King Pyrrhus of Epirus—whose invading army Rome eventually defeated, thereby establishing authority over the Italian Peninsula—is a first-century BCE copy, but the original, made during Pyrrhus's lifetime, is one of the earliest-known portraits of a Roman historical figure.

of a professional Hellenistic army with 25,000 infantry and 3,000 cavalry. At first Pyrrhus was surprised by the discipline the Romans showed as their infantry and cavalry crossed a river to meet him in good order at Heraclea. Though the legion proved able to fight Pyrrhus's phalanxes on more or less even terms, his twenty war elephants broke up the Roman lines and made them vulnerable to attack by his cavalry. Still, the Romans continued the war. Four years later, Pyrrhus (whose name became proverbial for winning victories too costly to be justified, known ever after as "Pyrrhic victories") found himself so low on resources that he had to leave Italy and return to Greece, with only a remnant of his original force. Once Rome defeated this major Hellenistic Greek opponent, it was generally recognized as a great power in the Mediterranean, sovereign over the entire Italian Peninsula.

THE WARS WITH CARTHAGE

The peninsula, however, was not enough. Needing more land for agriculture and more citizens for soldiers, Rome was soon involved in wars in Macedonia and Greece. But the rival power of Carthage, the great Phoenician trading city in North Africa, challenged the Romans most powerfully—and did the most to make them the rulers of an empire. Because the Latin word for Phoenician is "Punic," Rome's long, exhausting series of wars with Carthage is called the **Punic Wars**.

THE FIRST PUNIC WAR (264–241 BCE)

For centuries, Rome and Carthage had coexisted without major conflict. But in the 260s, the tyrant of Syracuse made war against the Mamertines, mercenaries from the Italian mainland who had seized the Sicilian city of Messana. The Mamertines appealed for help, first to the Carthaginians and then to the Romans. In this case, most of the senators hesitated to go to war, but the plebeian assembly, eager for booty, voted to intervene. Syracuse allied with the Carthaginians, relying on the power of their fleet to protect them against Rome.

The war proved grueling. The Romans, inexperienced in naval matters, lost a series of fleets to storms and to the Carthaginians, whose seafaring skills were renowned. Though the Roman general Marcus Attilius Regulus, who was sent to North Africa with a small army, scored initial successes, at length he was defeated and captured. Yet the Romans persisted, and eventually they ground down the Carthaginians' brilliant commander in Sicily, Hamilcar Barca. In 241 BCE, after a war of twenty-three years, the Romans forced their enemies to make peace, and Rome was left in command of Sicily. This vast island, famous for its grain and other natural products, and rich in minerals as well, became Rome's first official province—the beginning of what would soon grow into an empire. Rome had also become, for the first time, a naval power—a development that would prove crucial for its empire.

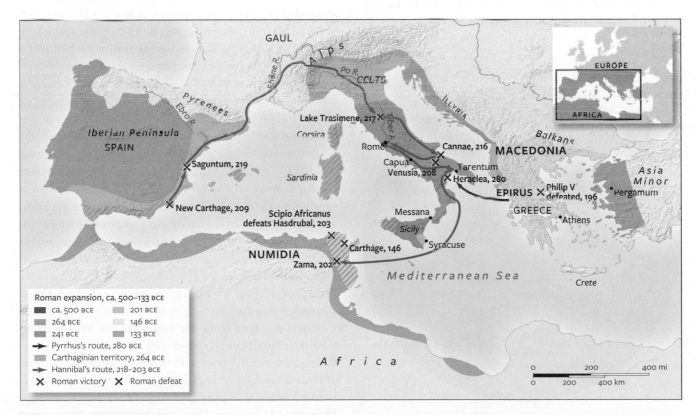

Expansion and War, 390–133 BCE In the later centuries BCE, Rome expanded rapidly, sparking conflict with Carthage. In the ensuing series of wars, Rome gained control of Sicily and, ultimately—despite Hannibal's land invasion over the Alps and numerous Roman defeats—territory as far east as Macedonia and Asia Minor, as well as much of the Iberian Peninsula.

THE SECOND PUNIC WAR
(218–201 BCE)

Soon after the end of the First Punic War, Carthage recovered enough strength to wage a long war against rebellious mercenaries. Rome, though it aided Carthage at first, became increasingly concerned at the signs of revival, especially as the Carthaginians began to negotiate with Celts in the Po River valley in northern Italy. The Romans used a rebellion in Sardinia as a pretext to take that island, which had been Carthage's granary. In response, the Carthaginians, anxious to ensure their supply lines and to regain leverage, invaded Spain—not a nation as yet, but a vast region inhabited by Celts, Greeks, and Phoenicians.

There Hamilcar Barca, his son-in-law Hasdrubal, and his eldest son, Hannibal, established a strong Carthaginian presence. According to tradition, Hannibal swore an oath to his father never to be a friend to Rome. For a time, peace held; but in 219 BCE Hannibal besieged and took the city of Saguntum in Valencia, in eastern Spain. Although Rome ignored the city's appeals for help, Hannibal decided that war was inevitable; moving with a speed and determination that shocked the Romans, he rapidly made his way from Spain to Italy.

The Second Punic War involved a confrontation between two of history's most brilliant commanders. Hannibal is still famous for his decisiveness, speed in action, and willingness to take great risks. His Roman opponent, Publius Cornelius Scipio Africanus, was equally renowned, not only for his absolute commitment to Rome and his tactical daring but also for his humanity. Hannibal led a powerful force, including elephants and, according to tradition, more than 100,000 infantry and cavalrymen. Dodging Scipio, who came to meet him in Gaul (modern France), Hannibal crossed the Alps, though his forces suffered terrible losses in doing so. He routed the Romans at Lake Trasimene in 217 and at Cannae in 216, where he encircled and killed tens of thousands of Romans and their allies. The losses were devastating: almost as many Romans died in one day at Cannae as British soldiers died, under a hail of German artillery and machine-gun fire, on the first day of the Somme, one of the deadliest battles of World War I.

A brilliant tactician, Hannibal was also politically gifted. He made a point of releasing all the Latins whom he took captive. Impressed by his generosity, several cities—including Capua, the second largest in Italy—seceded from Roman rule and joined him. He also formed an alliance with the king of Macedonia. But the Romans once more showed their powers of recovery. A Roman commander, Fabius Maximus, nicknamed Cunctator ("the Delayer"), kept Hannibal busy without allowing him many chances for formal battle. Hannibal scored tactical successes, defeating Roman armies at Herdonia and Locri in southern Italy. But he never managed to conquer the critical port city of Tarentum. Moreover, newly developed Roman sea power prevented Carthage from sending reinforcements to Italy.

Eventually, Scipio gained permission to take the war to Africa—a stroke as brilliant as Hannibal's march across the Alps. After Scipio defeated Hasdrubal, Hannibal was recalled to defend the homeland. Scipio had learned to leave open spaces in his battle array to avoid letting Hannibal's elephants throw his soldiers into confusion, and to coordinate Numidian cavalry with his Roman foot soldiers. In 202 he defeated Hannibal at Zama, in Carthage. Hannibal advised his masters to make peace, and they surrendered in 201.

Rome emerged from the Second Punic War, as from the first, as undisputed victor, with an enormous military. Rome commanded more than 100,000 soldiers by the end of the war and faced engagements in new areas, such as the Balkans, where they had fought an ally of Carthage, Philip V of Macedonia. Carthage, by contrast, had to hand over all but ten of its ships and all of its elephants, and to pay an enormous fine. The crushing burden of this peace did much to ensure the coming of a third and final war.

Hannibal's Elephants A Roman plate from the third century BCE depicts an elephant carrying soldiers and a military fortification, conveying an idea of the terror that Hannibal's elephants may have inspired.

Rome's expansion continued, now on a far grander scale. In 196 BCE a Roman general who shared what would soon be a fashionable attitude of warm respect for the Greeks defeated Philip V, confined him to the Macedonia north, and proclaimed that Greece was free. Warfare continued intermittently until the 140s, when the Romans, having defeated the Macedonians and the Greeks themselves, declared the former Greek world another province of their empire.

THE THIRD PUNIC WAR (149–146 BCE)

In the years that followed Rome's victory in the Second Punic War, Carthage came under continuing attack by Massinissa, king of Numidia and a Roman ally in North Africa. Rome tried at first to mediate, but then sided more and more with Massinissa. In 153 BCE, a Roman embassy led by the censor Cato was struck by Carthage's wealth and by its efforts to rearm. Cato led a campaign for invasion in the Senate, and in 149, after the Carthaginians attacked the Numidians, the Romans invaded the attackers' homeland. The invasion started poorly. But Scipio Aemilianus, the adopted grandson of Scipio Africanus, became consul in 147, and his leadership proved decisive. Carthage fell after a long siege and some vicious street fighting. The city was partly burned, but the Romans did not, as legend holds, sow salt in its territory so that nothing would ever grow there again. Eventually Carthage recovered to become a prosperous regional capital in what was now the Roman province of Africa.

Through the next decade and after, Roman armies carried out massive operations in Spain and Gaul, conquering most of each. The city that had been hamstrung by civil strife two centuries before found itself the ruler not only of Italy but also of an empire that stretched across much of the Mediterranean world. For the next century and more, Rome would never be at peace: a long series of wars, abroad and in the Italian Peninsula, would continue to reshape the Roman state and society.

THE EXPANDING REPUBLIC: CULTURE AND SOCIETY

Rome's rise to regional dominance brought with it vast cultural change. Romans began to write about their past. And Greeks realized that they were face to face with something they had not experienced before: a state as aggressive and powerful as Macedonia had been, but ruled as a republic rather than a monarchy. Their efforts to understand how this was possible also help us to understand the nature of the Roman Republic as it rose to dominance in the time of the Punic Wars and after.

POLYBIUS: EXPLAINING ROME

In the third century BCE, members of the Roman elite were beginning to learn Greek and write in the forms that the Greeks had created. By the second century, young Romans—some, but not all of them, patricians—were studying grammar and rhetoric in the Greek manner and using their skills to compose tragedies, comedies, epics, elaborate formal histories of the city, and technical treatises on subjects as dry and practical as husbandry.

In the mid-second century BCE the Greek general Polybius (ca. 200–ca. 118 BCE), who became a close friend of the younger Scipio during a long stay in Rome as a hostage, decided to learn how Rome had become great. Roman leaders could now entertain—and impress—a visitor with their long experience of politics and warfare. A sophisticated and widely read man, Polybius believed that one could survive the trials of the present only by finding patterns in the past—patterns created not, as the Jewish author of the book of Daniel thought, by divine intervention, but by human nature in action. Polybius set out to take apart Rome's institutions, in order to work out exactly what made them function so well.

POLITICS Following Aristotle, Polybius noted that all states seemed to fall into six types: monarchy, aristocracy, and democracy, and their evil twins, tyranny, oligarchy, and mob rule. Whatever form a society took, it had little hope of attaining real stability. Human nature destined most cities to move through the entire set of forms of government in sequence, as each of the sound forms gradually failed and gave way to its own dark side.

Rome, however, seemed to have worked out a uniquely stable form of government. By allowing monarchical and democratic elements to temper its basically oligarchical constitution, it

Polybius A second-century BCE stele depicts the Greek general and historian Polybius, whose writings illuminated the history of Roman society and politics.

had hindered the processes that normally made governments deteriorate from working as quickly and destructively as elsewhere. When foreign powers menaced Rome, the consuls, the Senate, and the plebeian assembly competed to serve the public good by cooperating as effectively as possible. And when the consuls or the Senate tried to make the state serve the one-sided ends of a monarchy or an aristocracy, the other elements in the constitution resisted. Rome's unique constitution created a system of checks and balances, one so smoothly machined and precisely balanced that it might preserve the city for a long time against the corruption that was inevitable in the long run.

SOCIETY Roman society as a whole, moreover, was organized in ways that promoted courage and patriotism. Family rituals, for example, helped to initiate the young into the values that made this republic uniquely durable. Great houses displayed masks that reproduced the features of their accomplished men. These served not only, like modern family photographs, as a record but also as an educational tool. At funerals, living men who resembled the distinguished dead donned these masks, and speakers connected the achievements of the deceased with those of his ancestors.

The experience of growing up in such families, Polybius explained, was powerful: it explained why Roman heroes had proved willing, over the centuries, to sacrifice their lives or even those of their sons, "setting a higher value on the interest of their country than on the ties of nature that bound them to their nearest and dearest." The virtues that the Spartans tried to instill in young men by taking them out of their families, and that Pericles had tried to teach by oratory in Athens, were integrated into Roman domestic life in a way that no Greek city had achieved. This helped to explain how the Romans could recruit enormous armies and navies not from mercenaries but from citizens, who fought "for their country and their children."

A MIXED CONSTITUTION Polybius was not starry-eyed, though. He found the Romans greedy and cruel. When they captured a city, he observed not only human corpses but also those of dogs and other animals, cut to pieces. His understanding of Rome, moreover, was that of a foreigner, who sometimes applied Greek ways of thinking about society inappropriately to what remained a foreign world. He did not see—as we soon will—that Rome was undergoing an economic transformation while he lived there, which would add new sources of strength and strain to those he appreciated. Nonetheless, Polybius's

vision of the Roman constitution and of Roman society captured something that would fascinate readers and political philosophers for centuries. When the American Founding Fathers needed a model for the constitutional order of their new country, they found it—so they believed—in the Roman mixed constitution that Polybius described.

ROMAN VALUES

Few if any Romans could have rivaled Polybius in producing a sophisticated explanation of what made their state so special. But most would have agreed with his emphases, and by the mid-second century BCE, Romans themselves were giving expression to what they considered distinctively Roman beliefs and values.

THE INTERESTS OF THE STATE Just as Polybius argued, special traditions nourished Roman abilities in politics and warfare. Like Athenians and Spartans, ordinary Roman men served as their country's soldiers, and men of family and position as cavalrymen and officers. The great Roman commanders saw the giving of counsel as an essential duty, and tradition held that they were bound to advise the Republic to the best of their ability, even if doing so might lead to their own deaths. When Regulus, the Roman commander sent to attack Carthage during the First Punic War, was captured by Spartan mercenaries, the Carthaginians sent him back to Rome on parole. They demanded that he advise the Romans to make peace or exchange prisoners. Instead, Regulus told the Romans to continue waging war against their enemies. He then returned to Carthage, although he knew that he would be savagely put to death for doing so. (The Carthaginians supposedly placed him in a barrel full of spikes and rolled it down a slope.)

Central to the exalted behavior of Romans like Regulus was the belief that the state and its good health mattered most, individual ambition not at all. True, the ancient families that dominated the Senate and the consulship were the ones that celebrated their members' accomplishments with the funerals that so impressed Polybius. But Romans imagined themselves as a people of virtuous farmers, more or less equal.

Tradition heralded heroes like Cincinnatus (b. ca. 519 BCE). A consul, a patrician, and a staunch opponent of all efforts to improve the standing of the plebeians, Cincinnatus had lived plainly, so the story went, farming his own land. When an emergency arose during one of

Rome's wars, he agreed to serve as military commander at the request of one of the consuls and the Senate. Cincinnatus carried out his task brilliantly and defeated the enemy, against whom he himself led the infantry. But as soon as the enemy surrendered, he spared them; and as soon as he had accomplished his task, he returned to his farm.

THE TRIUMPH   Though the story of Cincinnatus is a bit too good to be true (and probably took shape some centuries after the events it describes), it accurately conveys the values of those who told it. So did many of the rituals that the Romans used, along with tales of the mighty dead, to give expression to their values. For example, the triumph—a great procession derived from Etruscan ritual—was held in honor of Roman generals who returned from the field after defeating the city's enemies. Only commanders who had killed some 5,000 of the enemy and held the rank of praetor or consul could enjoy a triumph.

Those who did receive this signal honor—starting, according to Roman tradition, with Romulus himself—might ride in a four-horse chariot through the city to the temple of Jupiter on the Capitoline Hill. Accompanied by his sons, if any, as well as the members of the Senate, enemy captives dressed for sacrifice, musicians, torchbearers, and colorful banners and paintings, the *triumphator* passed through large public places where the entire city could see him. Nothing could have emphasized the primacy of military virtue more effectively.

RELIGION

Rome was also a devout city. It revered a rich panoply of gods, both the older Roman ones and newer ones from

Roman Gods A second-century CE relief—perhaps part of a model of the temple of Jupiter on the Capitoline Hill—portrays the three gods most central to Roman religion: Jupiter, ruler of the universe, in the center; Juno, mother of the earth, on the left; and Minerva, goddess of wisdom, on the right.

Vestal Virgins This first-century CE relief depicts the goddess Vesta (seated on the left) and her Vestal Virgins, full-time priestesses who took vows of chastity and who could be punished by death if the vows were broken.

Hellenistic Greece. At the start of the Republic, the cult of the three great Roman gods, Jupiter Optimus Maximus, Juno, and Minerva, was moved to the Capitoline Hill, where a stone temple with terra-cotta decorations, in the Etruscan manner, was built for them. Jupiter was officially worshipped as ruler of the universe; Juno as mother of the earth; and Minerva, the goddess of wisdom, presided over the arts and crafts. Temples to other gods—Saturn, Ceres, Mercury—spread out below the Capitoline Hill. Of these the temple of Janus was especially important. Janus was the two-faced god of beginnings and endings, war and peace. The gates of this small, rectangular temple in the Forum were opened when Rome was at war and closed—a rare event—only when it was completely at peace.

Priests and priestesses were organized into groups called colleges: the Vestal Virgins served Vesta, the Roman goddess of the hearth. Male specialists scrutinized every piece of evidence they could find to determine what the gods desired them to do and had in store for them. Priests charged with divining the future used ancient methods to interpret the entrails of sacrificial animals, as well as certain forms of animal behavior. Eclipses, earthquakes, and the births of strange fetuses, human or animal, were recorded and then connected with later events to show that the gods had sent omens in advance. Ancient ritual brotherhoods continued to perform their rites, and new priesthoods—like those of the orgiastic mystery religion of Dionysos, imported from Greece—offered new forms of religious experience. Like the Athenian calendar, the Roman one was dotted with holy days—some forty-five of them.

In some ways, though, the core of Roman religion was private, not public, based in the household, with its own lares and penates—the gods who protected households and certain other realms. The head of the family was responsible for seeing to it that these gods were fed by sacrifices, and their statues attended banquets and other family occasions. A wealthy household might include a handsome shrine to its gods, with fine reliefs sculpted to represent the protector and the protected. Even the poorest plebeian house would have its own more modest version.

THE FAMILY

The family—the large kin group that Polybius had seen as essential to the preservation of Roman values—was the core of Roman society. Each head of household, or paterfamilias, ruled his family, at least in theory, absolutely. The Roman father had the power of life and death over his children, as the Twelve Tables had stated (in practice, he exercised this only when deciding if a particular baby, perhaps one born with a deformity, should be exposed—left outdoors to die—or accepted). Yet mothers also mastered the stern tradition of Roman virtue and lived by it when called on to do so—as Regulus's wife supposedly did by torturing Carthaginian prisoners to death on learning of her husband's fate.

Sons and daughters grew up listening to the same tales of family tradition, and both passed to maturity through carefully marked stages of life. For sons, this meant changing from the boy's toga with its purple stripe to the manly toga, which was all white, at the age of fourteen, when they might also receive permission to attend their fathers, if they were senators, on official business. Girls entered maturity by marrying, for which they were considered ready by the age of twelve.

EDUCATION

The sources do not tell us much about the ways in which Roman children were educated in the first centuries of the Republic. Though the state provided no official schools, it seems that schools of some kind existed by the second century BCE, and that girls as well as boys attended them. The children apparently studied Greek poetry, which probably means that their families could afford tutors to teach them the elements of the language. Formal education became one more way in which the boys and girls of the upper class were separated from the rest of society. The early teachers were men of low status, slaves, or freedmen—one reason, probably, that we know relatively little about them.

Boys engaged in physical education: not the naked gymnastics of the Greek tradition, which the Romans tended to look down on, but training in horseback riding and the use of weapons. Hunting was highly valued as both a form of exercise and a training in boldness and dexterity. Both boys and girls, finally, learned by watching their parent of the same sex: boys about the public life of politics, law, and war-craft; girls about the skills of household management.

WOMEN'S LIVES

When Roman men spoke about women—for example, in the stone epitaphs with which husbands celebrated the virtues of their honorable, loving wives—or represented them in paintings and sculpted reliefs, they emphasized female docility and removal from economic life. In fact, though, many women lived more active and visible lives in Rome than had been possible in Athens. In the Greek city, women were supposed to occupy separate quarters, or at least to seclude themselves when male visitors arrived. In Rome, by contrast, women and children inhabited every corner of their houses. When guests arrived, the mother of the family might be working at her loom—a useful occupation and a symbol of her virtue and commitment to overseeing

An Ideal Wife This grave marker from around 80 BCE includes a portrait of a Roman husband and wife. The husband is identified by his trade as a butcher; the wife, by feminine virtues typically valued by Roman men: she is "chaste, modest, and not gossiped about."

POMPEII'S VILLA OF THE MYSTERIES

This painting is part of a large fresco featuring life-size figures that decorates all four walls of a grand room in the Villa of the Mysteries in Pompeii. The name of the house reflects the idea that the fresco depicts the "mysteries" of initiation into the religious cult of Dionysos. Scholars disagree on this interpretation of the fresco, however; some believe that it shows preparations for marriage rites. In any case, this lavish wall decoration clearly indicates that the household was a prosperous one. The red color of the background was made from cinnabar, an expensive pigment, and its extensive use announced the prestige of the villa's occupants.

In the detail shown here, a fully dressed, veiled woman enters a room at left. A naked boy reads from a papyrus scroll under the watchful eye of a female figure, perhaps his mother, who also holds a scroll. Another woman, wearing a wreath and carrying a plate of what may be bread, glances back while she walks out of the scene. Throughout the fresco, the use of shading and perspective creates an illusion of depth.

QUESTIONS FOR ANALYSIS

1. What clues to everyday life in ancient Rome do you see in this section of the fresco?
2. What details in the fresco suggest that the family living in the villa were of the elite?
3. Historians disagree about the fresco's meaning. Drawing on your reading of the chapter, what is your interpretation of it?

her household. But she would speak to male visitors and might well join them, reclining, at the banquet table. Roman women could own property and initiate divorce proceedings. Many women owned agricultural land, and some of them chose their tenants and collected the rents. And although paternal authority could weigh heavily on them, many had no father by the time they married: most women married by the age of twenty, whereas men waited until they were around thirty—and were thus likely to die before their daughters reached marriageable age.

Poorer women worked at every imaginable job. They served as nurses and as maids; they became butchers, fishmongers, and bakers; they wove cloth or laundered clothing. Others sold everything from beans to nails. Many were employed as waitresses in taverns, jobs that may have included prostitution as a side activity. Anyone who walked through Rome, or any Roman city, passed dozens of *tabernae*—little square rooms, with open fronts facing the street, where artisans and merchants had their shops—in which women earned their own livings. Roman law assumed in theory that women were weak-minded

Women's Work Women whose families relied on their income worked in a wide range of jobs. In this relief from second-century BCE Rome, a woman in a butcher shop writes on a wax tablet—perhaps recording the shop's accounts.

and needed male protection; Roman writers argued at length that women were fickle and unreliable. But the social reality was more complicated than law or literature portrayed.

SLAVERY

In one case especially, social reality came close to undermining Roman ideals. The Punic Wars transformed the Roman state, as we have seen. But they also transformed Roman society. Romans had always owned slaves, but after the Punic Wars their numbers rose dramatically. Slaves began to play vital roles in almost every sphere of Roman life.

Rome's victories produced captives by the thousands. The wars against the Samnites in the early third century BCE, for instance, were said by the historian Livy to have yielded 50,000 slaves. Scipio Africanus sent 2,000 skilled artisans back to Rome after he captured New Carthage (Cartagena, in Spain). This enormous stream of captives was swelled by a second one provided by brigands and pirates, who kidnapped men and women—including Roman citizens who ventured onto lonely roads—and sold them to feed the labor market.

Slaves—and freed slaves—were soon working throughout Rome and the other Roman cities. Town slaves probably worked shorter hours than farm slaves and were normally paid a wage. In households, they served as stewards, cooks, and maids; in shops, they worked as artisans and salespeople. Those with particular talents, or whose callings required them to master special skills, could become famous and rich: Publius Terentius Afer, a slave from Africa who became a successful playwright, ended his life as a free Roman. So did star actors, who used their earnings to buy their own freedom. Town governments bought slaves, who served as clerks, attendants at baths and temples, and assistants to the officials charged with maintaining buildings, roads, and sewers.

Amid these variations were important uniformities: Roman slaves had no civil rights. They could not serve in the armed forces, vote, or own property (slaves who saved their salaries did so with their master's permission). Marriage was also prohibited, though again, if the master permitted them, they could enter a form of marriage. On funeral monuments, slaves sometimes spoke of their dead partners as husbands or wives, but they did so at the sufferance of their owners. Discipline was harsh, especially for those who worked in the most dangerous jobs,

THE REPUBLIC IN FLUX: ECONOMIC AND SOCIAL CHANGE (218–180 BCE)

No Roman spoke more powerfully for what had become the city's values in the second century than Marcus Porcius Cato (234–149 BCE). A disciplined and effective military commander of humble origins, he served in Spain but accepted none of the loot from his conquests there. Austere and demanding of others, he wore the simplest Roman clothing and normally drank only water, or wine of the same quality that he gave his slaves.

Cato's *Origins* was the first account of Roman history written in Latin by a Roman. More revealing of a new Rome, though, is his book on agriculture. Also written in Latin, this impressive manual on how to run a farm presents farming as a primary business for Romans, one that they should enter while young. But what Cato offered readers was not advice on how to cultivate one's own small plot, in the manner of Cincinnatus. Rather, it was a handbook on how to flourish in the new economic and social world that was taking shape.

Slave Society This first-century CE Pompeian fresco depicts a mythical scene with an element of everyday life included: to the left, a slave washes the floor, a common occurrence in wealthy Roman households.

as gladiators or in the mines. A well-ordered farm was supposed to have an underground prison where masters could confine slaves who displeased them.

In some cases, masters developed warm relationships with their slaves. Cicero worried when his slave secretary, Tiro, was sick, and sent him another slave to keep him company. Eventually he gave Tiro his freedom and made him—as Cicero's brother Quintus wrote in a congratulatory letter—"a friend rather than a slave." The two men in fact continued to be close. Women, similarly, could feel real affection for their maids.

But as the number of slaves rose—to 10 percent or more of Rome's total population—Rome showed all the features of a slave society. Masters were told to treat their slaves gently in order not to provoke them, as that could result in their own murder. Runaway slaves who were recaptured could be branded on their foreheads or have metal chains forged around their necks, and when slave revolts broke out, as we will see, they were put down without mercy. The new Roman household, with its slaves for cleaning and serving, and its income from farms run by slave labor, had little in common with the ancient Roman ideal of virtuous poverty.

THE LATIFUNDIA: INEQUALITY IN THE COUNTRYSIDE

Rome's new society and economy had its roots in the long wars against Carthage and Macedonia, which transformed the nature of military service. Instead of joining the army for the duration of a short, traditional campaign, soldiers now spent decades traveling and fighting with their commanders. When they finally returned home, some found that a neighboring landowner had appropriated their family's small farm; others, unable to settle back into rural life, sold their plots of land and moved to Rome or another city. The farms of the wealthy became larger and larger, requiring newly massive labor forces to herd flocks, tend vines and olive trees, and plant grain.

These large agrarian estates, known as **latifundia**, were assembled by entrepreneurs, many from the class known as *equites* ("knights"), below the senatorial aristocracy. On these properties, using free tenant laborers as well as slaves, the equites cultivated the crops that the army, and the growing city of Rome, needed. Reaping machines and other technology were essential to farming on this scale. In his plainspoken book, Cato describes

Latifundia Vast estates outside Rome cultivated the crops and livestock needed to feed the city's growing population. This first-century CE mosaic from present-day Algeria possibly depicts such an estate, with laborers cultivating its grapevines.

a substantial estate, well equipped and staffed, run by a manager and designed to yield cash crops in substantial quantities.

Cato's inventory of the people and equipment needed to make olive oil on this estate conveys a large-scale operation with specialized craftsmen whose products support the ongoing work. Cato lists everything: staff members, draft animals, oil presses, other equipment and tools, all the way down to mattresses, pillows, and towels. His recommendation that slaves too old to work simply be discharged, so that they do not burden the estate, reveals more cold-eyed efficiency than old-fashioned Roman values. Cato, the heroic defender of Roman tradition, was a precise, passionless modernizer when it came to extracting money from the land. He and others like him helped to turn Rome into a more cash-centered society, in which rich and poor were widely separated.

CITY LIFE

Rome was changing not only in the countryside but in its cities as well. By 100 BCE the city of Rome itself had as many as 750,000 inhabitants. The new urban life that took shape in this period had little in common with Rome's vision of its past. Improved building technologies that made use of stone, brick, and concrete spanned the valleys that separated the city from mountain springs with aqueducts and brought fresh, clean water to Romans. But as they grew, Rome and its subject cities were anything but neat and clean. City dwellers had to navigate labyrinths of narrow streets caked with dirt and animal dung, frequently blocked by benches and shop stalls—features of a newly vibrant economic life.

URBAN INEQUALITY In this bustling urban setting, wealthy families lived in individual houses built around an atrium, or open space, with a pool in its center where the head of the house would meet visitors. An opening in the roof let in light and air as well as rain to fill the pool, channeled by ornamental downspouts. One room might be given over to the household gods and to images of distinguished ancestors; another to the library and records of the paterfamilias. Well beyond the atrium, in the public part of the house, the family would enjoy its own garden, very likely with pools for fish and swimming. A lavatory with running water awaited those who needed to relieve themselves after the many courses of a banquet, which the guests, reclining on couches, would eat in the garden in warm weather.

Most Romans, however, lived on a much more modest scale than the rich. Republican Rome became a city of *insulae* ("islands")—apartment houses built of wood and mud bricks that took their name from their appearance: they stood out like islands in the city. Often five or six stories

Aqueducts Improvements in technology allowed Rome to create irrigation systems that spanned vast distances. The Pont du Gard aqueduct was part of a thirty-mile irrigation system in southern France built in the mid-first century BCE or CE.

high, these apartment houses were built, like the houses of the wealthy, around central courtyards. Their ground floors were pierced with niches, in which shops operated. From the courtyard, stairways gave access to corridors on the higher floors. Even the bigger, more expensive apartments on the second floor had no lavatories or kitchens, and little privacy, since rooms opened into one another. On higher floors, the corridors were lined with single rooms, each of which might have a small balcony and a single window, unglazed or covered with thin sheets of mica, and each of which might house an entire family. Inhabitants could buy cooked food from shops or prepare their own meals on small coal braziers—a risky process that often caused fires. Collapses were also common, even though building regulations limited the height of these structures and mandated the thickness of their walls.

GRAFFITI, URBAN VOICES Craftsmen and small merchants lived high in the air—except when they had to run downstairs to buy food or relieve themselves. Their wishes, beliefs, and political ideals were expressed not in eloquent speeches but in passionate and often ungrammatical graffiti, which are still a major Roman art form. The walls of another large Roman city, Pompeii, preserved by volcanic ash after the eruption of Mount Vesuvius in 79 CE buried the city, bear every kind of message—from homespun wisdom ("A small problem gets larger if you ignore it") to wild boasts ("Floronius, privileged soldier of the 7TH legion, was here. The women did not know of his presence. Only six women came to know, too few for such a stallion"). There are humble confessions ("We have wet the bed, host. I confess we have done wrong. If you want to know why, there was no chamber pot") and messages

Wealthy Households The House of Menander in Pompeii, likely owned by a rich merchant, includes all the hallmarks of a Roman mansion, including a central atrium with a pool, a skylight, and vivid mosaics decorating the walls.

of support for candidates in elections. As one unusually critical writer put it, "O walls, you have held up so many tedious graffiti that I am amazed that you have not already collapsed in ruin."

The lives of the urban poor—small shopkeepers and laborers, to say nothing of slaves—had little to do with traditional Roman values, the virtuous life of the farm, or even the lives of established plebeian families. The upper classes saw them less as fellow Romans to be helped than as mouths to be fed and voters to be manipulated—and as potential support for revolutionary movements.

SPECTACLE AND ENTERTAINMENT

Like other great cities, Rome devised its own public spectacles—partly designed to divert city-dwellers from the difficulties of daily life.

GLADIATORS As early as the third century BCE, great men in Rome sponsored what became a central form of urban amusement: combats between matched pairs of professional fighters, or gladiators. These were held at

Urban Voices Graffiti covered the walls of Pompeii, giving popular expression to views on all kinds of issues, from sex to politics. This inscription endorses a local political candidate.

GRAFFITI AND WALL INSCRIPTIONS FROM POMPEII

Graffiti provide an unexpected and delightful source for social, economic, and even political history, as evident in these inscriptions from the Roman provincial town of Pompeii, destroyed by the eruption of Mount Vesuvius in 79 CE. They offer an intimate look at the everyday concerns of Pompeii's people, sometimes expressed in poignant ways. The wall inscriptions were used as bulletins and notices, campaign posters, message boards, and confessionals to express emotional declarations and pieces of advice.

Market days: Saturday in Pompeii, Sunday in Nuceria, Monday in Atella, Tuesday in Nola, Wednesday in Cumae, Thursday in Puteoli, Friday in Rome.

A copper pot is missing from this shop. 65 sesterces reward if anybody brings it back, 20 sesterces if he reveals the thief so we can get our property back.

Take your lewd looks and flirting eyes off another man's wife, and show some decency on your face!

Anybody in love, come here. I want to break Venus' ribs with a club and cripple the goddess' loins. If she can pierce my tender breast, why can't I break her head with a club?

Twenty pairs of gladiators of Decimus Lucretius Satrius Valens, lifetime flamen of Nero son of Caesar Augustus, and ten pairs of gladiators of Decimus Lucretius Valens, his son, will fight at Pompeii on April 8, 9, 10, 11, 12. There will be a full card of wild beast combats and awnings [for the spectators]. Aemilius Celer [painted this sign], all alone in the moonlight.

The dyers request the election of Postumius Proculus as Aedile.

Vesonius Primus requests the election of Gaius Gavius Rufus as duumvir, a man who will serve the public interest—do elect him, I beg of you.

His neighbors request the election of Tiberius Claudius Verus as duumvir.

The worshipers of Isis as a body ask for the election of Gnaeus Helvias Sabinus as Aedile.

The inhabitants of the Campanian suburb ask for the election of Marcus Epidius Sabinus as Aedile.

At the request of the neighbors Suedius Clemens, most upright judge, is working for the election of Marcus Epidius Sabinus, a worthy young man, as duumvir with judicial authority. He begs you to elect him.

The sneak thieves request the election of Vatia as Aedile.

The whole company of late drinkers favor Vatia.

Inn to let. Triclinium [dining room] with three couches.

Here slept Vibius Restitutus all by himself his heart filled with longings for his Urbana.

To rent from the first day of next July, shops with the floors over them, fine upper chambers, and a house, in the Arnius Pollio block, owned by Gnaeus Alleius Nigidius Maius. Prospective lessees may apply to Primus, slave of Gnaeus Alleius Nigidius Maius.

To let, for the term of five years, from the thirteenth day of next August to the thirteenth day of the sixth August thereafter, the Venus bath, fitted up for the best people, shops, rooms over shops, and second-story apartments in the property owned by Julia Felix, daughter of Spurius.

He who has never been in love can be no gentleman.

Health to you, Victoria, and wherever you are may you sneeze sweetly.

Restitutus has many times deceived many girls.

If any man seek / My girl from me to turn, / On far-off mountains bleak, / May Love the scoundrel burn! / If you a man would be, / If you know what love can do, / Have pity and suffer me / With welcome to come to you.

At Nuceria, I won 855½ denarii by gaming—fair play!

On October 17 Puteolana had a litter of three males and two females.

The smallest evil if neglected, will reach the greatest proportions.

If you want to waste your time, scatter millet and pick it up again.

QUESTIONS FOR ANALYSIS

1. How can these graffiti help us to discover what life was like in this Roman provincial town?
2. What kinds of information do these notices give us about political life in the late Republic and the early empire?
3. How do the rental notices illustrate how and where people lived and worked?

Sources: Naphtali Lewis and Meyer Reinhold, eds., *Roman Civilization: Selected Readings*, 3rd ed., 2 vols. (New York: 1990), p. 276ff; William Stearns Davis, ed., *Readings in Ancient History: II. Rome and the West* (Boston: 1913), pp. 261–4.

Gladiators A terra-cotta relief from the first century BCE depicts one of the public spectacles staged throughout the empire: gladiators fighting lions in an arena.

first as games to commemorate the death of a male relative. Armed with fearsome weapons—some with short swords and shields, some with net and trident, some with scimitars—the gladiators fought to the death. They were recruited in many ways. Some were criminals or prisoners of war, sentenced to fight; others were volunteers, both slaves and freemen, who fought as professionals and were trained by experts. With increasing frequency, gladiatorial combats were held in the Forum and other public places, and the tickets distributed, as a sign of favor, to prominent plebeians. Men and women sat together to watch the blood flow.

In 186 BCE, another form of public slaughter was introduced to Rome: the *venatio* ("hunt") of animals, the rarer and wilder the better: lions, tigers, bears, elephants, leopards, and crocodiles. Crowded into amphitheaters, the citizens of Rome could now enjoy watching the sort of exciting combat between men and beasts that had once been accessible to the rich and powerful alone. Rome's new public culture of violence spread throughout the rest of the Roman world. Schools for gladiators opened in Capua, in southern Italy, and other cities. We cannot know exactly what these combats meant to those who watched them, but they were almost certainly seen as celebrating the military virtues that were central to Roman society. Perhaps they also helped exorcise the fear inspired by the massive defeat the Romans had suffered at Cannae in 216 BCE during the Punic Wars.

THEATER Another form of public entertainment also took shape in the third and second centuries BCE: Roman theater. As Romans traveled to and traded with the Greek

cities of southern Italy, they saw Greek plays performed. By the mid-third century BCE, the Greek poet Livius Andronicus was translating and adapting Greek works into Latin, notably Homer's *Odyssey*. In 240 BCE he staged the first of what became a series of plays in Latin, both tragedies and comedies.

Following Livius Andronicus, the Roman Plautus (who may have begun life as a stage technician) and the African Terence (who, like Andronicus, came to Rome as a slave and was eventually emancipated) composed massive series of plays. Theatrical performances became a standard element in Roman religious festivals, taking place at first in temples. Typically, the actors were slaves and the plays were produced by officials of patrician blood who hoped that they could rise, with popular support, to higher office.

Plautus (ca. 254–184 BCE) made comedy Roman. He filled the stage with characters who were familiar to Romans, from boastful soldiers to slaves who often outwitted their masters. Terence (ca. 186–ca. 159 BCE), whose comedy was less broad than that of Plautus, adapted Greek plots and cast them with characters who were more complex, though his female characters tended to be stereotypically submissive. The plays of Plautus and Terence were enormously popular with Roman audiences. These grew from the couple of thousand who could have seen the original comedies in temples to much larger assemblies. Roman theater attracted patricians, equites, ordinary men and women, and slaves, seated (or standing in the case of the slaves) in positions determined by their status.

Roman Theater Vast audiences flocked to see the plays of authors such as Plautus and Terence. This second-century BCE relief of a scene from a Terence comedy suggests the rudimentary stage set and the masks the actors wore, conventions borrowed from Greek drama.

THE CRISIS OF THE REPUBLIC (133–31 BCE)

As ordinary Romans in their thousands left the land and large, unruly cities took shape, the Republic entered what would prove to be its last century—a century of crisis. Rome's new imperial reach had introduced instability into the constitution that Polybius had praised for its balance. Thanks to the Hortensian Law that had concluded the Struggle of the Orders around 287 BCE, decisions made by the plebeian assembly carried the force of law. Nonetheless, the great aristocrats continued to dominate politics, maintaining a near monopoly over high office. Of the 256 consuls elected between 262 and 134 BCE, only 16 were "new men": the rest belonged to an inner circle of some twenty families. The aristocrats who, despite the growing numbers of slaves and poor city dwellers, remained committed to the belief that they were best qualified to manage Rome's political and military affairs were known as *optimates*. Others, known as *populares*, argued that it was vital to help the poor, to whom they turned for support.

Roman officials also incited disorder in the provinces. For many years, Roman governors could extort cash and booty from the provinces entrusted to them, almost at will. Even if convicted of extortion, they would only have to reimburse what they had taken. Meanwhile, Roman tax-farmers (officials, often from great families, appointed to collect the taxes as contractors) extracted not only the legally required revenues but much more—from Sicily, from Spain, and after 167 BCE, from Macedonia. Those in a position to enrich themselves became wealthier, and their interests increasingly diverged from those of ordinary Romans.

THE GRACCHI

The members of one noble family, **the Gracchi**, set out to reform the system—to recast Roman society on lines more in keeping with the austerity and general egalitarianism of the city's traditional beliefs and values. Or so they claimed.

TIBERIUS Tiberius Gracchus (163–133 BCE), the son of a man who had served more than once as consul and won a triumph, introduced legislation when he was tribune in 133 BCE to restore the limits on how much of the state's public land any Roman could own, and to redistribute the land thus freed to landless men. The measure passed the plebeian assembly, but another tribune, Marcus Octavius,

vetoed it; and when it went to the Senate for adjudication he vetoed it again, both times violating the traditions of Roman politics.

Tiberius promptly removed Octavius from office—another innovation, but one that the other tribunes did not contest—and created a land commission that began work on a redistribution project. When the ruler of Pergamum in Asia Minor left his kingdom to the Roman people in 133 BCE, Tiberius accepted the legacy without consulting the Senate and proposed to divide it among the landless. He then broke with tradition even more sharply by running for the office of tribune again, in order to gain immunity from a charge of treason. Terrified by these radical measures, the *pontifex maximus* ("chief priest") led a crowd of senators and others to the Capitoline Hill, calling on them to save the Republic. They murdered Tiberius and some of his followers, though the land commission continued to operate.

GAIUS A decade later Tiberius's younger brother Gaius Gracchus (153–121 BCE), elected tribune in 123 and 122 BCE, introduced even more systematic legislation. This included a grain law designed to ensure that the people received a guaranteed supply of wheat at subsidized prices, as well as regulation of recruitment into the military and expansive public works programs. No radical, Gaius seems to have been most concerned with spreading the risks—and the responsibilities—of government more widely among the inhabitants of what had become essentially a Roman Empire. He fought to have senatorial legislation exempted from control by the tribunes. But he also sought to give the equites, who were ineligible for service in the Senate but whose wealth gave them considerable power, a monopoly over membership in criminal juries. He did this to ensure that they exercised real control over the notorious abuses of Roman governors in the provinces, by judging them when accusations of corruption or cruelty arose. Finally, he tried to extend the political rights of full citizenship to all Latins, and Latin status to all allies, who would thus be protected from the worst horrors of Roman government and made eligible for the land distribution that his brother had introduced.

At this point Gaius's allies began to defect. He failed to win reelection as tribune in 121 BCE and raised an armed revolt. The Senate responded by passing, for the first time, the *senatus consultum ultimum* ("final decree of the Senate"), which allowed the consul to deal with enemies of the state violently, if necessary, without worrying about strict legality. Gaius and his followers were killed—as the *popularis* Catiline would be, just over half a century later. Ironically, one effect of Gaius's legislation was to put the vast wealth of the province of Asia (southwestern Turkey) into the hands of the already wealthy publicans, or tax-farmers, who collected taxes for the state and paid a fee for the right to do so. The Gracchi, in other words, failed. But their policies would be revived again and again by later *populares*.

CONTINUING UPHEAVAL (108–51 BCE)

The suppression of the Gracchi and their programs did not restore order and tranquility. Warfare continued. Slaves rose against their Roman masters from 138 to 132 BCE and 104 to 101 BCE. The senatorial elite performed feebly against Numidian forces who fought hard against Rome's armies in North Africa in the last two decades of the second century BCE. An even tougher opponent was Mithridates of Pontus, an area on the southern coast of the Black Sea in Asia Minor. Known for his command of languages (he could speak those of all twenty-two countries he ruled), Mithridates (r. 120–63 BCE) played effectively on local discontent with Roman taxes. He began hostilities by organizing the slaughter of some 80,000 Romans and Italians living in Asia Minor. And when he represented himself as the defender of Greek freedom against Roman oppression, he gained support from Athens and other Greek cities.

THE SOCIAL WAR Most threatening of all was the **Social War** of the early first century BCE. Over time, the inhabitants of Italy had come to be classified in three ways: (1) as full Roman citizens, with all the attendant rights, including freedom from direct taxes; (2) as "Latins," who had an intermediate status, enjoying the civil and legal but not the political rights of citizens; or (3) as "allies," who supplied many of Rome's soldiers but were not allowed to possess the lands they helped Rome to conquer. When Gaius Gracchus proposed, in 123 BCE, to grant the Latins full citizenship and the allies Latin status, the Senate rejected the measure and expelled the Latins and allies who did not have voting rights from the city of Rome. In 91, a nobleman who belonged to the populares, Marcus Livius Drusus, proposed a law that would have made the Latins citizens. The senators, furious, rejected his proposal and murdered him in his own house.

At this point the Marsi (a Latin people who had sent soldiers, ineffectively, to help Drusus), the Samnites, and soon most of central and southern Italy erupted in a bitter revolt against the Romans. They even created their own state, which they called "Italia," with a new capital and its own coinage. Atrocities were committed on both sides. Though Rome sent its best generals to deal with the enemy, the elite decided in the end to compromise, and in 89 BCE Latins and allies who had not risen against Rome or who were willing to lay down their arms were granted citizenship. For the rest of the history of the Republic, Rome would struggle to assimilate these new citizens, some of whom became prominent.

Social War The Latins and their allies minted this coin in the early first century BCE. The Italian bull trampling and goring the Roman she-wolf is a metaphor of the Social War.

MARIUS AND SULLA As confidence in Rome's future and its safety dimmed, great military bosses began to play central roles in public life and politics—and not only, in the traditional way, as holders of elective office. Gaius Marius (157–86 BCE), a "new man" from outside the Roman elite, and Lucius Sulla (138–78 BCE), an aristocrat who started out as one of Marius's officers, fought more successfully than the older members of the elite. But they did so by abandoning traditional restraint. Marius gave up on the ideal of the citizen army. With the latifundia expanding, fewer citizens could afford to serve, and recruitment dwindled. Marius set no property qualification for military service and enrolled his own forces, whom he paid and who were

Sulla Lucius Sulla, who won a reputation for his violent methods of "proscribing" and hunting down his enemies, is portrayed in this bust from about 50 BCE.

loyal to him alone. Suddenly, Romans were joining the army less to preserve what they and their fellow citizens had than to win property and money. Marius's campaigns in Africa and against the Cimbri (Germanic tribes that invaded Italy in 102 BCE) proved so successful that equites and members of the senatorial elite supported him and helped to elect him consul time after time. Sulla, for his part, fought brilliantly against Mithridates, whose armies he destroyed, and against the Latins in the Social War.

But in addition to winning great victories for Rome, Marius and Sulla introduced a new level of violence into Roman politics. Each in turn found himself expelled for a time from the city. Sulla actually fought his way back in. And each responded by massacring his opponents. Marius simply had them killed. Sulla used a more terrifying means: like the Thirty Tyrants of Athens, he "proscribed" his enemies, listing their names on tablets in the Forum and sending squads of soldiers to hunt them down. Sulla promised rewards to slaves and members of their families if they would betray the outlaws, and barred their descendants from holding office. Though Sulla proscribed and killed only a few hundred people, no citizen could feel secure in the protection of laws and officials after these extralegal measures had been taken. He consolidated his power by settling his veteran soldiers on confiscated lands in Italy. This was the world in which Cicero would grow up and form his political convictions.

In the end, Marius voluntarily gave up his dictatorial power. Sulla, who turned out to be a genuine traditionalist, did his best to prevent imitation of the radical Gracchi. He ruled that men who had served as tribunes could not take on more prestigious magistracies and that they could no longer veto legislation—an effective way to discourage would-be tribunes of the people. He also increased the number and activities of the courts, doubled the size of the Senate and enhanced some of its powers, and then retired—to die, almost immediately. Yet violence continued. The most alarming outbreak came in 73 BCE when a former Roman soldier named Spartacus, who had become a gladiator, led a small group of hard-bitten followers who soon raised a massive slave revolt. Spartacus destroyed a number of Roman legions before he was finally defeated and killed in 71 BCE.

THE FIRST TRIUMVIRATE Although the forms of republican government continued to exist and function, all efforts to stabilize Roman politics seemed to have failed. Politics looked more and more like a game dominated by power and money, as great men fixed elections by telling their many dependents, known as clients, how to vote. At last, three of the great Roman military bosses—Julius Caesar, Pompey (Gnaeus Pompeius Magnus), and Marcus Licinius Crassus—formed an informal alliance in 60 BCE, retrospectively known as the First Triumvirate. These men were powerful generals and effective diplomats who had fought in all corners of the Roman world and beyond. Their massed military power enabled Caesar to force through legislation. But this alliance also fell apart as the ambitions of its three leaders clashed.

MODELS OF LEADERSHIP

In the continuing efforts of Roman elites and ordinary citizens to stabilize the chaotic situation, two powerful models of leadership emerged, each best personified by a single man.

CICERO The statesman and orator Marcus Tullius Cicero (106–43 BCE), whom we met at the start of the chapter, fought to preserve what he saw as the core of Roman tradition. A new man himself, he could not point to distinguished ancestors when he sought public office. Instead, he honed his skill in using language. This was the art that he deployed against Catiline in 63 BCE, in speeches that utilized every tool in the rhetorician's kit with matchless brilliance. It enabled him to defend the traditional preeminence of the Senate—and the power of the families that had dominated it for centuries—against those who sought to transform Rome. It gave him the ability to flatter those whose views he opposed, such as Caesar, one of the aristocratic populares.

CAESAR The general and statesman **Julius Caesar** (100–44 BCE) represented the other great model of political action. Born in Rome to an ancient family, Caesar could call on the distinguished ancestors that Cicero lacked. As gifted a writer as Cicero ("Avoid an unfamiliar word," he advised, "as a sailor avoids the rocks"), Caesar practiced a very different craft: the precise, lucid, and matter-of-fact description of his achievements on the battlefield. Caesar made those achievements the basis of his authority. His conquests were quick and dramatic: in the years between 58 and 50 BCE, his forces killed more than a million Gauls, enslaved a million more, and conquered the whole vast area they inhabited (basically all of modern France and Belgium). Caesar's powerful histories of the wars he waged against the Gauls and his fellow Romans were exercises in propaganda that became literary classics.

Like Marius and Sulla, Caesar took personal

Julius Caesar This bust may date from 46 BCE and could be the most reliable indication of what Caesar might have looked like.

command of what became not the armies of the Republic but his own armies. Locked in a tense alliance with the other members of the First Triumvirate, he broke with them and then defeated and killed Pompey. (The Parthians, who controlled a vast territory in western Asia, did as much for Crassus: showing a sense for poetic justice,

they made the fabulously rich general drink molten gold.) Caesar made himself master of Rome just after 50 BCE. Like Cicero, Caesar often looked back to past precedent. As *pontifex maximus* ("chief priest") of the city, he did his best to reestablish traditional Roman morality in what many saw as a decadent time. But Caesar picked very different precedents to follow. Like the Gracchi, he saw that stability could be obtained only if the thousands of poor men whom military service and economic growth had thrown off their lands were granted new lands by the state. After he conquered Gaul in 50 BCE, he resettled almost 200,000 poor Romans there, to the fury of the natives.

CAESAR IN POWER

Over time, Caesar secured his hold on power through a series of bold innovations. In 49 BCE he entered Italy, famously crossing over the Rubicon River, in defiance of the law that forbade a commander with imperium, the right of command, to come into Italian territory with soldiers. Leading his legions, Caesar used military

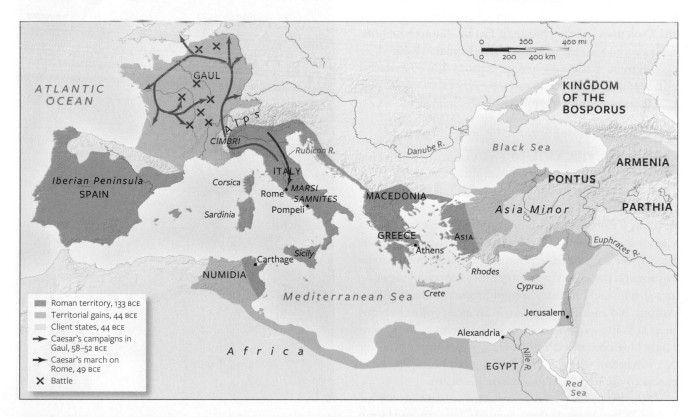

Rome in 44 BCE Under Julius Caesar, the Roman army conquered large territories, including all of Gaul, and Numidia in North Africa. The rulers of several client states, such as Egypt, also owed allegiance to Caesar. By the time Caesar was assassinated in 44 BCE, Roman territory encircled the Mediterranean Sea.

force, and the threat of force, to dominate Roman politics. He depended on men whose loyalty was not to the state but to him alone, even giving his former slaves official positions in the mint. He enlarged the Senate to 900 members, inviting allies from as far as Gaul to join, in order to solidify his base of support. Caesar expanded the public games to include such magnificent spectacles as mock naval battles—a precedent that the emperors would build on for centuries to come. He replaced the republican Roman calendar—a complex system that had been manipulated for political purposes by the Roman priests—with a new one based on the observed course of the sun through the heavens. His Julian calendar is basically the one still in use today in most of the world.

More generally, Caesar began to treat Rome in a new way: not just as the ancient capital of what had become a new empire but as a world city, as Alexander had treated his new city of Alexandria in Egypt hundreds of years earlier. In 47 BCE Caesar restored Cleopatra, the last of the Ptolemies, to the throne of Egypt. Though he himself rejected the title of king, which Romans disliked, he agreed to be made a god (Mark Antony, his relative and ally, became his priest). There was every reason to suspect that Caesar meant to turn Rome into a monarchy.

THE SECOND TRIUMVIRATE

In 44 BCE, Marcus Junius Brutus and Gaius Cassius Longus, senators and politicians as loyal to the old Roman order as Cicero had been, but more decisive, murdered Caesar in the Forum and tried to reconstruct the Republic. Unable to find wide popular support, they lost the ensuing civil war to Caesar's nephew Octavian (63 BCE–14 CE), who had formed a Second Triumvirate with Mark Antony and another patrician, Marcus Aemilius Lepidus in 43 BCE. Proscribed after Caesar's assassination, Cicero might have been saved by Octavian, who admired him; but Mark Antony, whom Cicero had denounced as the chief threat to the Republic, insisted on his death.

Over time, Octavian eliminated all threats to his power. When Mark Antony married Cleopatra and began to act independently, suspicion grew that he hoped to set himself up as ruler of the Roman Empire, using the wealth and power of Egypt to rule the rest. Though the fleets and armies that Octavian and Mark Antony mustered were comparable in size, Octavian defeated his rival in a naval battle near Actium in Greece in 31 BCE. Mark Antony was a highly competent general and even won one victory on land at Alexandria, but his troops melted away, and first he and then Cleopatra committed suicide.

OCTAVIAN: LAST REPUBLICAN OR FIRST EMPEROR?

Octavian created a new system, known to historians as the principate: the rule of a single chief, or *princeps*. From 31 BCE on, a single ruler would hold the reins of power in Rome. Yet it would take a century and more before Roman rulers were ready to abandon the pretense that the Republic still functioned.

Throughout his life, Octavian insisted that he was no

Cleopatra This is a first-century BCE marble portrait of Cleopatra VII, whom Julius Caesar restored to the throne of Egypt in 47 BCE.

more than the first among Roman equals. As a sole ruler, he preserved and respected the institutions of the Republic, above all the Senate; lived simply, in the manner of Cato and other earlier Roman heroes; and expanded the empire. Even more than Caesar, **Augustus**—as Octavian was renamed—set the style for the transformed Rome that would rule the western Mediterranean world for almost 500 years. His Rome was a full-scale empire ruled from a court rather than the republican capital of a territorial empire formed by conquest. Historians and poets, politicians and pundits have debated the lessons of this transformation for centuries—ever since the greatest Roman historian, Tacitus, writing in the early second century CE, identified Augustus as the one who subverted the Republic while pretending to maintain it.

AUGUSTUS: BUILDING AN EMPIRE (31 BCE–14 CE)

Augustus's policies were the most potent mixture of tradition and innovation that Rome had seen. Dignified and austere in the old Roman way—one of his favorite sayings, according to his ancient biographer, was the homely "quicker than you can boil asparagus"—Augustus cut a powerful figure. At first he held only traditional offices, such as the consulship, and insisted on showing deference to the Senate and to the ancient customs of the Republic. Many important responsibilities actually remained with the Senate: for example, the administration of large parts of the empire, from Asia Minor and North Africa to nearby Sicily and Sardinia. Just as under the Republic, praetors governed all of these. But the city of Rome panicked when he threatened to cease serving as consul, and he eventually took on a new role, accepting the powers of a tribune, but without the formal title.

RESTORING ORDER

Augustus made massive efforts to restore order at all levels. Newly precise rules of dress sorted out the "orders" of Roman society, distinguishing senators from equites by the decoration of their cloaks and togas. He paid special attention to religion. Augustus brought back ancient orders of priests, served in them himself and urged others to do so as well, and started a massive program to restore the formal temples of the city of Rome. In one year, he

Augustus In monumental public statues, Augustus expressed different visions of his authority: as a heroic warrior, with the figure of Cupid suggesting his divine lineage; and as a somber statesman, wearing the toga of the Roman citizen.

rebuilt some eighty-two of them, which had fallen into ruin during the civil wars, and he created particularly magnificent temples to Jupiter on the Capitoline Hill, and to Apollo, whom he saw as his special patron, on the Palatine Hill. The private worship performed in Roman families had never ceased, but Augustus put new emphasis on the public cults of the state, which would become central to the empire.

Following the example set by Caesar, Augustus insisted that he stood for peace. In his monumental autobiography he noted that he had ended wars in region after region: Gaul, the Iberian Peninsula, Germania. Nothing pleased him more than the moment in 29 BCE (and two other occasions) when the doors of the temple of Janus were formally closed, indicating that no war was being waged anywhere in the Roman world. One of the most splendid structures with which he enriched the city of Rome was an altar to the goddess of peace (Ara Pacis), decorated with splendid friezes showing the whole city in procession to celebrate his safe return from Gaul and the Iberian Peninsula. These measures were not mere gestures. After two centuries of almost continual conflict, Augustus's reign ushered in the long period of peace traditionally called the **Pax Romana** ("Roman Peace"), which lasted from 27 BCE until 180 CE.

Augustus reinforced the cult of peace by taking care, in the late-republican tradition, to display the value of clemency in his own conduct. He treated his political opponents with far more tolerance than the previous generation had shown. He refused to hunt down the authors of political lampoons against him posted around the Senate, though he did refute their charges and suggest that anonymous authors of such works should be condemned.

EXPANSION AND CONFLICT

Even as he celebrated his ability to keep the peace within the empire, Augustus spent vast energy and resources on expanding and consolidating its borders. Sometimes, he was able to do so without engaging in conflict. In 25 BCE, when the ruler of Galatia in central Asia Minor was assassinated, it was transformed into a Roman province without bloodshed. Following the death of Herod the Great, the client king who ruled Judea, Augustus deposed his successor and imposed direct Roman rule through an appointed prefect. But Augustus's vast armies waged war again and again: in the Iberian Peninsula, where Augustus himself took command in the field for the last time, from 27 to 25 BCE; in Africa, where Ethiopian and Berber

raids had to be met and retaliation proved necessary; in the east, where Armenia—a client state of Rome, important as a buffer between Roman-controlled Asia Minor and the Parthian Empire—fell into turmoil in 2 BCE, calling forth a massive Roman response.

Above all, though, it was in the western territories that Roman armies fought. A series of invasions between 12 BCE and 6 CE pushed deep into the land of the Germanic peoples, to the Elbe River and beyond. Publius Quinctilius Varus, who commanded Roman forces on the Rhine River, was deputed to establish the empire's authority in the new province of Germania, across the Rhine from Gaul. He was opposed by the Marcomanni and other Germanic tribes, led by Arminius, son of the chief of the Cherusci. In 9 CE Varus provoked a revolt in Germanic territory. Led by Arminius (ca. 19 BCE–21 CE), who had learned the craft of war serving in the Roman armies, the Germanic forces annihilated Varus's three legions in a running battle in the Teutoburg Forest. The bones and armor of the Romans slaughtered there have recently been recovered by archaeologists, scattered over several miles. Augustus, stricken with grief and fury, beat his head against the wall of the imperial palace, demanding that Varus give back his lost

First among Equals On this section of a frieze from the Ara Pacis ("Altar of Peace") a procession from left to right includes a group of priests; Augustus's son-in-law, Agrippa, his toga covering his head; and other members of Augustus's family. The size and detail of these figures match that of Augustus (not shown), echoing his pretense of being simply first among equals.

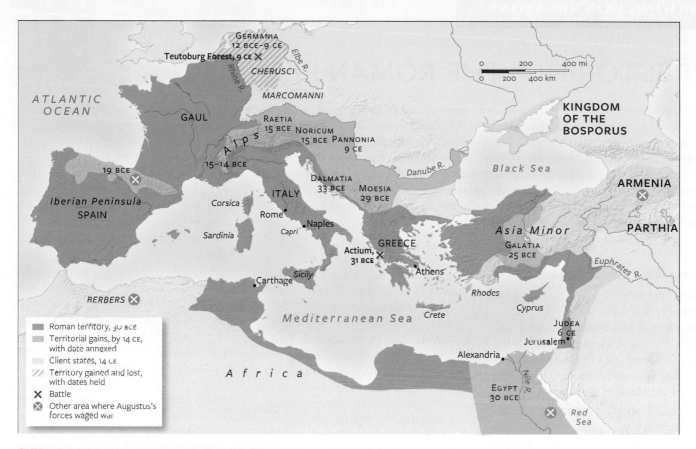

Building an Empire, 30 BCE–14 CE Augustus consolidated and expanded Roman rule, bringing Egypt and large parts of central Europe and Asia Minor under imperial control. Between 12 BCE and 6 CE, Augustus's forces engaged in protracted, bloody battles with Germanic tribes, but never fully succeeded in bringing their territory under Roman control.

legions. Augustus never admitted that this terrible defeat led him to abandon plans to make the Germania province Roman. In practice, though, he and his successors accepted that Roman power could not move far beyond the Rhine. The borders that Augustus established would remain the effective borders of the empire for some 300 years after his time.

AUGUSTAN ROME

The traditional Roman respect for established law and restraint in dealing with other nations—a tradition that had been deeply strained in the last years of the Republic—continued to exist. But it did so, from now on, less as the expression of a consensus than as the decision of a single, all-powerful individual. Even as Augustus and his counselors insisted that nothing basic had changed, he was laying the foundations for a fundamentally different constitution: an autocratic one, ruled by a court, in which once-great institutions like the Senate gradually became marginalized.

ECONOMIC REFORMS Augustus developed the operations of the empire on a new scale. He created a permanent imperial treasury. He developed a modest administrative apparatus for those parts of the empire, like Gaul and the Iberian Peninsula, that Caesar and he had conquered and that still had military garrisons. These Augustus claimed as imperial property and ruled directly. And as Augustus became responsible for the welfare of the Roman people, he regulated the city of Rome with a new precision. A massive program of resettlement, which Augustus worked on throughout his reign, provided land and livings for thousands of those who had been thrown off their original properties to provide land for Pompey's and Caesar's military veterans: Horace and Virgil, the greatest poets of the time, both of whom celebrated Augustus in powerful verse, were among those whose families he saved from homelessness and destitution.

"RESTORING" THE ROMAN REPUBLIC

Octavian Caesar, better known by his honorific title Augustus (meaning "great" or "venerable"), was praised as a politician who repaired the most grievous political, economic, and social problems of Roman society and who "restored" the Republic after the assassination of his uncle and adoptive father, Julius Caesar. In actuality, Augustus created a monarchy by taking titles and ruling independently of other magistrates and even the Senate, while at the same time claiming to have preserved Roman identity and unity. Suetonius's text records the widely held view of Augustus as protector of the Republic, whereas Tacitus illustrates the more complex view of Augustus as both political savior and despot.

Suetonius, "Life of Augustus"

Gaius Suetonius Tranquillus, commonly known as Suetonius (ca. 69–ca. 122 CE), was a Roman equite and biographer who wrote *The Twelve Caesars* in 122 CE. In this excerpt, Suetonius frames Augustus's political actions as done for the good of the state and the happiness of the people.

His good intentions he often affirmed in private discourse, and also published an edict, in which it was declared in the following terms: "May it be permitted me to have the happiness of establishing the commonwealth on a safe and sound basis, and thus enjoy the reward of which I am ambitious, that of being celebrated for molding it into the form best adapted to present circumstances; so that, on my leaving the world, I may carry with me the hope that the foundations which I have laid for its future government, will stand firm and stable."

He corrected many ill practices, which, to the detriment of the public, had either survived the licentious habits of the late civil wars, or else originated in the long peace. Bands of robbers showed themselves openly, completely armed, under color of self-defense; and in different parts of the country, travelers, freemen and slaves without distinction, were forcibly carried off, and kept to work in the houses of correction.... The bandits he quelled by establishing posts of soldiers in suitable stations for the purpose; the houses of correction were subjected to a strict superintendence; all associations, those only excepted which were of ancient standing, and recognized by the laws, were dissolved. He burnt all the notes of those who had been a long time in arrear with the treasury, as being the principal source of vexatious suits and prosecutions....

He was desirous that his friends should be great and powerful in the state, but have no exclusive privileges, or be exempt from the laws which governed others....

The whole body of the people, upon a sudden impulse, and with unanimous consent, offered him the title of Father of His Country. It was announced to him first at Antium, by a deputation from the people, and upon his declining the honor, they repeated their offer on his return to Rome, in a full theatre, when they were crowned with laurel.

Tacitus, *Annals,* Book I

Publius Cornelius Tacitus (56–117 CE) was a Roman senator and historian. In his *Annals* (ca. 109 CE), Tacitus discusses the emperors who succeeded Augustus, but here he describes Augustus's funeral and reign. Tacitus records the popular ambivalence about Augustus's deeds, a mixture of praise and scorn that contradicts the idea that his actions were universally lauded.

Then followed much talk about Augustus himself.... People extolled, too, the number of his consulships ... and his other honors which had been either frequently repeated or were wholly new. Sensible men, however, spoke variously of his life with praise and censure. Some said "that dutiful feeling towards a father, and the necessities of the State in which laws had then no place, drove him into civil war, which can neither be planned nor conducted on any right principles.... The only remedy for his distracted country was the rule of a single man.... The ocean and remote rivers were the boundaries of the empire; the legions, provinces, fleets, all things were linked together; there was law for the citizens; there was respect shown to the allies. The capital had been embellished on a grand scale; only in a few instances had he resorted to force, simply to secure the general tranquility."

It was said, on the other hand, "that filial duty and State necessity were merely assumed as a mask. It was really from a lust of sovereignty that he had excited the veterans by bribery, had, when a young man and a subject, raised an army, tampered with the Consul's legions, and feigned an attachment to the faction of Pompey. By a decree of the Senate he had usurped the high functions and authority of Praetor ... wrested the consulate from a reluctant Senate, and turned against the State the arms with which he had been entrusted against Antony. Citizens were proscribed, lands divided, without so much as the approval of those who executed these deeds.... No doubt, there was peace after all this, but it was a peace stained with blood.".…

No honor was left for the gods, when Augustus chose to be himself worshipped with temples and statues, like those of the deities, and with flamens and priests. He had not even adopted Tiberius as his successor out of affection or any regard to the State, but, having thoroughly seen his arrogant and savage temper, he had sought glory for himself by a contrast of extreme wickedness.

QUESTIONS FOR ANALYSIS

1. What kinds of problems does Suetonius tell us that Augustus corrected, and what effect did his actions have?
2. Tacitus gives us two views of Augustus. What are they, and on what actions and ideas are they based?
3. What can these two documents tell us about Augustus's impact on the development of imperial Rome?

Sources: Suetonius, "Life of Augustus," in *The Lives of the Twelve Caesars*, trans. Alexander Thomson, rev. T. Forester (London: 1893); *Annals of Tacitus*, trans. Alfred John Church and William Jackson Brodribb (London: 1876).

Desiring to control the obligations of the state, Augustus limited the number of those entitled to distributions from the public granaries to 350,000. But to ensure supply, he had to create a formal system of grain imports and distribution, supported by fleets of transport ships and storehouses. It was ruled at the top by a new official—one of many whose posts Augustus created—from the equites. Because Italy itself could not supply the vast amount of grain that Rome required, it had to be imported, especially from Egypt and North Africa, which between them supposedly provided 80 to 90 percent of the city's needs. Docks, warehouses, and mills also had to be provided, and supplementary stocks of grain bought in Gaul and elsewhere in the empire.

SOCIAL CHANGE Under Augustus, divisions between the rich and the poor, the free and the unfree, became starker than ever before. Men like Marcus Vipsanius Agrippa, a general and statesman who became Augustus's son-in-law, amassed unlimited fortunes. With these they assembled properties on a vast scale, including urban palaces and magnificent villas in the Bay of Naples, on Capri, and elsewhere, where slaves staged elaborate banquets. Equites and freedmen who amassed fortunes by supplying the legions and the state also enjoyed lives of display.

By contrast, hundreds of thousands of ordinary Roman citizens lived on what they could bake from the three pounds or so of grain they received each day, with perhaps a little cheese or meat, or worked in the thousands of menial jobs that the city provided: cooks, porters, hairdressers, and other poorly paid positions. Near the bottom of the social scale, butchers and fishmongers, tanners and fullers (cloth-finishers) faced tasks that required them to work with the bodies of dead animals, apply noxious chemicals, or spend whole days standing in tubs of dirty water. Only the public baths provided by the state, which were freely available to all, enabled them to clean their bodies. Yet they and their families walked streets that were carpeted in animal dung and lived in tiny, ill-ventilated spaces.

In Augustus's time, as many as half of Italy's more than 7 million inhabitants may have been slaves. Though no longer seen as the threat they had been in the time of Spartacus, they were still subject to brutal discipline and were legally unfree. Even those who attained freedom, moreover, continued to be obliged to carry out certain tasks for their former masters.

WOMEN'S AUTONOMY In one respect at least, the changes that this period brought actually loosened the established structures of authority. For most of the history of the Republic, wives came under the absolute power of their husbands: their property was surrendered to their husbands, and they themselves could be divorced for any cause—including, in the case of the elder Cato, his desire to pass his wife on to a potential benefactor. In the late Republic, more and more families objected to the loss of property that the marriage of their daughters entailed. New legislation transferred power over dowries to wives, giving them a new independence of action. Meanwhile, the growth of a court society offered a few women of high standing a new level of freedom and authority. Augustus's own wife, Livia Drusilla, who divorced her previous husband to marry him, exemplified the traditional Roman matron and enjoyed his full confidence, so much so that her son from her previous husband, Tiberius, became Augustus's heir. Some suspected her of being a ruthless political intriguer.

Augustus did his best to exert paternal authority in the old way over the younger women in his family. His biographer Suetonius wrote: "In bringing up his daughter and his granddaughters he even had them taught spinning and weaving, and he forbade them to say or do anything except openly and such as might be recorded in the household diary. He was most strict in keeping them from meeting strangers, once writing to Lucius Vinicius, a young man of good position and character: 'You have acted presumptuously in coming to Baiae to call on my daughter.'" But his measures failed: he felt compelled to banish a daughter and a stepdaughter for their promiscuity and other vices, and wished that his daughter had committed suicide, as a more virtuous friend did, when disgraced.

THE CITY OF ROME Nothing was more obviously dramatic in Augustus's policies than his effort to transform the city of Rome. He laid special emphasis on improving the city's infrastructure. Augustus divided the city into fourteen administrative districts for more effective management. He gave the prefect of the city the power to supervise all guilds and corporations and to ensure that all necessary practical measures were taken. The city's walls, towers, and gates were rebuilt, and the roads that connected it with the rest of the empire repaved. Another official oversaw the dredging and draining of the Tiber and the maintenance of the aqueducts and sewers that were vital to Rome's public health. He also commanded the city's police force and its fire brigade—an innovation inspired by the example of Alexandria in Egypt. A special tax on the sale of slaves made it possible to station seven detachments of night watchmen (*vigiles*), who patrolled the city for fires, equipped with grapnels, ladders, and even with pumps pulled by horses. For more than half a century, Augustus's fire brigade prevented the outbreak of large-scale fires.

But Augustus's vision embraced more than the city's practical needs. As he also remarked, he turned the brick Rome that he inherited from his predecessors into a brand-new city of gleaming marble. His temple of Apollo, with its colonnades and public library, became a favorite meeting-place for the Senate. Grand as it was, though, it could not compete with the magnificent complex he built on the Campus Martius ("Field of Mars"), a spacious area in a bend of the Tiber that Augustus had embanked and graded. With a dazzling exhibition of the Roman mastery of resources and technology, he had an Egyptian obelisk floated across the Mediterranean and installed, upright, so that citizens could follow the shadow cast by the sun through the signs of the zodiac, which were inlaid on the pavement.

In addition to the new Forum that the emperor built, the statues of a dignified Augustus that appeared everywhere, and the Pantheon (temple of all the gods) and baths built by his son-in-law Agrippa, these projects turned the city into one great stone demonstration of the emperor's power and benevolence. Like Periclean Athens, Augustan Rome seemed to visitors almost to speak aloud of its greatness. But whereas the buildings and sculptures of Athens told a civic story, those of Rome celebrated a single person.

At age seventy-six, Augustus recorded his life in a testament written in Greek, copies of which he had set up around the empire—itself a practice of Julius Caesar and other great men of the Republic. Augustus boasted that he had refused the title of dictator when it was offered to him. In the conclusion, after reviewing a life of achievement that had begun with avenging Caesar's murder and led to the extension of the empire deep into Africa, far north into Germania, and far to the east, he stated proudly that he had never called himself a monarch. He insisted that the Senate continued to rule Rome, while he merely held traditional offices such as the consulate and did his best for his fellow Romans: "I exceeded all in influence," he admitted, "but I had no greater power than the others who

Mausoleum of Augustus Completed long before his death, Augustus's mausoleum was enormous in comparison to other elite tombs, and was fronted by bronze pillars that listed his many accomplishments. Despite Augustus's statement "I had no greater power than the others who were colleagues with me," the mausoleum, like so many other buildings he erected, proclaimed his power and importance.

were colleagues with me in each magistracy." No wonder that the Roman people had given him what he described as his proudest title: father of his country.

LATIN LITERATURE IN ITS GOLDEN AGE The last decades of the Republic and the first ones of the empire were remembered for centuries as a golden age of Latin literature. Highly educated Romans could now make creative use of Greek models. Writers like Catullus, Tibullus, and the female poet Sulpicia created a new kind of personal love poetry, which described in vivid detail what it was like to feel desire for a hard-hearted woman (or young man)—and, on occasion, to have it gratified. Ovid wrote in graphic detail about the techniques needed by a lover—and succeeded in irritating Augustus, who exiled him. As comedy had reflected the new social world of Rome during the Punic Wars, love poetry reflected that of the late Republic and early empire, in which wealthy Roman women enjoyed splendid educations and a remarkable freedom from constraint. But the highest praise—and the richest rewards—went to the poets and prose writers who used Latin to describe the epic rise of Rome to its new position. Horace (65–8 BCE), another very sophisticated poet, adapted many forms of Greek verse. A satirist and a philosopher, he also found ways to celebrate Rome's virtues of military heroism, piety, and moderation in power.

The most spectacular achievements were those of the poet Virgil and the historian Livy—both of whom turned their talents, so it seemed, on the Roman past. Virgil (70–19 BCE) made his name with short poems in the pastoral mode, modeled on Hellenistic verse, and a longer poem on farming. But his great achievement was the *Aeneid*—a magnificent epic, left incomplete at his death, in which he built on the models of Homer's *Iliad* and *Odyssey* to tell the story of how the Trojan Aeneas brought a remnant of his people to Italy and founded Rome. Livy (59 BCE–17 CE), for his part, wrote in prose, in which he produced a monumental survey of Roman history. He also drew heavily on earlier writers, especially Polybius. Both men's lives were shaped, like so many others, by Augustus's career and accomplishments. Virgil thought Augustus had revived Rome. A prophecy in the *Aeneid* proclaims that he, "born of the gods, will again found the golden ages." A republican himself, Livy shared Augustus's love for Roman traditions, and treated the emperor as a restorer of the Republic.

For centuries, across the Roman Empire, ambitious young men and women would learn what it meant to be Roman by reading their way through these great depictions of the glorious present and past. Yet neither author simply praised everything that Rome had done. Virgil made clear, as he followed Aeneas through his wanderings and then through his bitter war with those Latins who refused to join the Trojans, how much suffering it had taken to create Rome. Livy indicated, as he looked backward to early Rome, that its society had been far purer and more virtuous in the distant past than it was in his own day: "the less wealth men possessed the less they coveted."

CONCLUSION

During the first centuries BCE and CE, Roman society and culture flourished, in some ways, as never before. Thanks to the Pax Romana and the vast wealth that emperors and other patrons could deploy, architecture and art blossomed: the most astonishing relics that the visitor sees today in Rome, from the Roman Forum and Colosseum to baths and theaters, come from this period.

Yet to Tacitus, the historian from the senatorial order who held many public offices, the story of the early empire was one of republican virtue lost under autocratic rule, as the free oratory of the Republic was transmuted into the gossip and flattery practiced in the imperial court. Augustus, in his view, had begun this process. As Tacitus wrote in his *Histories of Rome*,

> Many authors have written of the earlier period, the 820 years from the founding of the city of Rome, and they recorded the history of the Roman people with both eloquence and freedom. But after the fight at Actium, when it seemed vital that all power be granted to one man, those great minds disappeared. Truth was harmed in many ways: first of all, by growing ignorance of public affairs, which were seen as strange to them; then by the passion to flatter the masters, or, on the other hand, by hatred of the rulers. Some were opponents, others were servants, and between the two, neither worried about posterity.

Whereas Polybius had described the Roman constitution as a great balancing apparatus, Tacitus believed it had completely lost its equilibrium. And whereas the Romans Polybius knew taught their sons about their past so that they would become virtuous citizens, the Romans Tacitus knew turned away from their past and pretended it had not happened. They had ceased to worry about making Romans.

The terms Tacitus used here are important. He did not argue that there could have been another way to escape the calamities of the late Republic, another path that Augustus or other leaders could have taken. Peace could be restored, he admitted, only when one man held power in the state. The Republic had proved mortal, and the city that had freed itself from monarchs was a monarchy again.

The limited freedoms that survived under the empire depended on the will of absolute rulers. Yet Tacitus argued that Augustus and his rivals could not have preserved republican liberty in any measure without allowing the Republic itself to fall. No wonder that the story of Rome's tumultuous final century as a republic and first century as an empire has troubled citizens of all modern republics.

[CHAPTER REVIEW]

KEY TERMS

Etruscans (p. 111)

Carthage (p. 112)

Senate (p. 114)

patricians (p. 114)

plebeians (p. 114)

Struggle of the Orders
(p. 115)

Law of the Twelve Tables
(p. 117)

paterfamilias (p. 117)

Latin right (p. 118)

legion (p. 118)

Punic Wars (p. 119)

latifundia (p. 127)

populares (p. 132)

the Gracchi (p. 132)

Social War (p. 133)

Julius Caesar (p. 134)

princeps (p. 136)

Augustus (p. 137)

Pax Romana (p. 137)

REVIEW QUESTIONS

1. What peoples inhabited the Italian Peninsula before the founding of Rome, and how did they influence its origins?

2. What were the central political institutions of republican Rome, and how did they work together?

3. How was the class system reinforced in the Roman Republic?

4. What propelled the expansion of Rome under the Republic?

5. What were the benefits of being a Roman citizen, and how did Rome use the promise of citizenship to its advantage?

6. How did family and religious rituals help to foster such Roman values as courage and patriotism?

7. What types of inequality were prevalent in republican Rome?

8. What were the most important reforms of the *populares,* and what tensions were they responding to?

9. How did Julius Caesar seize power and create stability?

10. Was Augustus a republican or an emperor? Explain.

CORE OBJECTIVES

After reading this chapter, you should have a solid understanding of the following core objectives. To strengthen your grasp of the core objectives, use the resources on the Student Site for The West.

- What do both Roman myths and modern archaeology reveal about the origins of early Rome?

- Explain how Rome's strength and political skill enabled it to conquer the Mediterranean region.

- Evaluate how Roman cultural and political ideals were expressed in its social and cultural institutions.

- Explain why the republican system became unstable in the second and first centuries BCE.

- Describe what made Julius Caesar's rise to power distinctive.

 GO TO **inQuizitive** TO SEE WHAT YOU'VE LEARNED—AND LEARN WHAT YOU'VE MISSED—WITH PERSONALIZED FEEDBACK ALONG THE WAY.

CHRONOLOGY

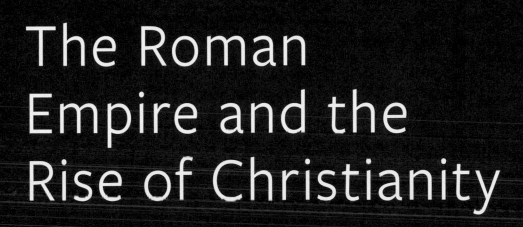

The Roman Empire and the Rise of Christianity

14–312 CE

A Christian woman named Perpetua died in 203 CE during an outbreak of persecution at the rebuilt city of Carthage. She recorded her experiences in prison as death approached. A well-born young Roman matron with a new baby, perhaps in her late teens, Perpetua belonged to a group of converts who were preparing to be baptized. Other members included one of her two brothers and a female slave named Felicitas. When Perpetua's father demanded that she leave the group, she explained to him, in the most graphic terms, that she now had a new identity and a new family: "'Father, can you see this vase that is lying here, for example, or waterpot or whatever?' And he said, 'I see it.' And I said to him 'Well, can this be called by any other name than what it is?' And he said, 'No.' 'That's it: I can only call myself what I am, a Christian.'" As Perpetua encountered it, Christianity was less a set of formal doctrines than a thick web of lived experience and loving community—a set of relationships far richer than those that bound her to her family. Nothing could make her abandon her beliefs and make offerings—as the authorities demanded—to the well-being of the emperor. The group was first subjected to surveillance and then arrested by Roman officials.

Arrest horrified the young mother: "I was terrified, because I had never experienced

312 CE
Constantine defeats Maxentius at Milvian Bridge

284 CE
Diocletian's reforms

Late 3rd century CE
Diocletian establishes tetrarchy

Mid-3rd century CE
Goths and Sasanians threaten empire's southern and eastern borders

303 CE
Great Persecution

A Mighty Empire As Roman troops conquered territory across Europe and the Mediterranean, they built grand and lasting infrastructure. This relief from Trajan's Column, erected in Rome in 113 CE to commemorate Emperor Trajan's victory against the Dacian people near the Black Sea, shows the ceremony at the opening of an arched bridge built over the Danube. The emperor himself stands to the right, preparing to sacrifice a bull.

FOCUS QUESTIONS

- What caused the disorder in the first century of the Roman Empire?
- What factors promoted stability across the empire during its second century?
- How did the lives and beliefs of the Jews change during the early imperial period?
- What were the origins of the Jesus movement?
- How was the Christian movement transformed in the middle of the first century?
- How did the emergence of Christian scripture contribute to the movement?
- How did Christianity crystallize into a formal church in the second and third centuries?
- How was Roman power challenged in the second and third centuries, and how did it respond?

such darkness. What a terrible day! The crowds made it unbearably hot. The soldiers demanded money. And then I was torn apart by worry about the baby." Partial relief came soon. Deacons—officers of the Christian community—bribed the guards to let the Christians go to a more comfortable part of the prison for a few hours. Later Perpetua gained permission to have her baby with her and to nurse him. More important, her brother made a request—one that shows that a Christian woman in 203 CE could be a figure of power in her church. He told her "you are highly honored," and asked her to request a vision. Perpetua complied. She asked for—and received—visions: a comforting vision of a heavenly shepherd, and an empowering one in which she defeated an Egyptian wrestler. She told her companions that martyrdom awaited them—but also, after that, victory over their enemies. Perpetua did not bend. When her father was beaten at an official's order, she "was as sorry for my father's plight as if I had been struck," but her pity for his wretched old age did not change her mind. Christianity somehow dissolved the paternal authority that had traditionally been a central feature of Roman society.

Perpetua and Felicitas died in the arena, their flesh torn by beasts and their throats cut. These were experiences of unimaginable terror, which they bore, according to the record, with remarkable dignity. Their story—including Perpetua's diary—became part of the church's official history, celebrated with sermons by great bishops.

Nothing is harder for historians than understanding the convictions that gave Christians the strength to do what Jesus had told his original followers that he expected: to leave their parents, spouses, and children and follow him. Roman Christians—many of them free, some of high standing—turned their backs on their families and their positions in society. They had to defy those whose authority they had been taught since birth to acknowledge: parents, officials, the emperor himself. And they had to do so in cities built to display the power of Rome and in courts and arenas that dealt out punishments that now seem inhuman. Unfortunately, most of the documents that describe events like these, accounts written in retrospect and designed to celebrate the triumph of the new church, give little sense of what Christianity meant to its first followers. But the words of Perpetua and other, anonymous, Christian writers—rare survivals, with the immediacy of everyday life—take us with them along the streets of the late Roman city, and into the courts, prisons, and circuses where they suffered. From them we can glean a sense of how effective the Christian message was, even as Roman authorities tried to stamp it out.

THE EARLY EMPIRE (14–96 CE)

By 203 CE, when Perpetua and her friends died in the amphitheater, the Roman Empire bestrode the Mediterranean world like a colossus, as powerful in Africa as in Italy or Gaul. Go back two centuries, and this development seems even more astonishing. For the early empire was as much a tangle of contradictions as a massive, powerful state.

Although republican traditions mattered deeply to Octavian and his subjects, they slowly became accustomed to thinking in monarchical terms. Octavian accepted new titles—including "emperor" and "Augustus"—that revealed, whatever his claims to the contrary, that he was more than the first citizen of Rome. His vast resources and his habit of micromanagement meant that the emperor dominated even in the older republican conquests, such as North Africa, which were legally subject to the Senate. Resistance to Augustus disappeared after the defeat of Antony and Cleopatra, and the empire, despite its unsuccessful effort to expand in Germania to the river Elbe, was now immense. It almost completely surrounded the Mediterranean, from Egypt and Judea in the east to Gaul and Spain in the west. The lands Augustus conquered in Africa stretched from the Sinai Desert all the way to Numidia, and the enormous income from land rents in Egypt, which effectively belonged to the emperor, supported the projects of many of Augustus's successors. Many areas that the empire did not directly control—such as Mauretania, on the northwestern tip of Africa—were ruled by Roman clients.

But like all monarchies, the Roman Empire faced difficult problems. It would have to maintain a vast population and an extensive apparatus of roads, fortifications, and officials, but it could not rely indefinitely on the enormous wealth that Augustus disposed of. And it would have to arrange for peaceful succession—a problem especially difficult if the emperor in question was not popular with the Senate or the people, or if the identity of the proper heir was problematic.

THE JULIO-CLAUDIANS (14–68 CE)

Until 68 CE, the emperors—four of them after Augustus—were chosen from two imperial families, the Julii and the Claudii. Their ability to follow the example set by Augustus varied. So did their claims to the throne, which depended on a complicated combination of adoption, marriage, and actual shared blood. None of them was succeeded by his own son. As their fortunes indicate, the great structure that Augustus reared was in part quite shaky, despite appearances.

No emperor could hold his throne in security unless he had the support of multiple parties: the Praetorian Guard, a special unit that the Claudian emperor Tiberius settled on the outskirts of Rome and tasked with protecting the palace; the armies, mostly on the frontiers; and the old senatorial elite, which supplied emperors with their chief administrators. Even a powerful ruler could find himself—or think himself—threatened if one or more of these pillars seemed to wobble.

For example, Tiberius (r. 14–37 CE), whom Augustus designated as his successor, was a man of high intelligence and education who shared Augustus's respect for Roman traditions, but he was hampered from the start by financial problems. Many of these were caused by a long and expensive series of campaigns in Germany. There his nephew Germanicus failed to take back the territories lost by Varus in 9 BCE. The growing suspicion that others

Praetorian Guard A marble relief from the second century CE depicts members of the Praetorian Guard, the special military unit tasked since the reign of Tiberius with protecting the emperor.

were plotting against him, made worse by his passion for astrologers' predictions, led Tiberius to institute trials in the Senate, sometimes for far-fetched reasons, and eventually to withdraw from Rome.

Tiberius's heir, Caligula, became emperor in 37 CE. He was also highly cultured, but after a popular start he demanded the sort of preeminence that Hellenistic rulers had enjoyed. He insisted on his own divinity, humiliated courtiers and senators, and even demanded that a statue of him be placed in the Jerusalem Temple—exactly the sort of humiliation of subject and allied peoples that republican Rome had traditionally avoided. The Praetorian Guard assassinated him in 41 CE and replaced him with his uncle Claudius (r. 41–54 CE), whom they found cowering behind a tapestry. An erudite man with a rich sense of Roman history and tradition, Claudius achieved considerable successes—he conquered much of Britain, enlarged the citizenship, and built a great harbor north of Ostia, at the mouth of the Tiber, southwest of Rome. But he did not win much love or respect. Dominated by his third and fourth wives, Messalina and Agrippina, Claudius allowed his only

Nero's Palace In 64 CE, Emperor Nero began construction of his extravagant palace on the Palatine Hill, the Domus Aurea ("Golden House"). Its lavish design drew on all the latest architectural advances, from concrete walls to a mechanical system operated by slaves that allowed this central courtyard's domed ceiling to revolve.

surviving son to be pushed aside by Nero, Agrippina's son by a previous marriage.

Nero (r. 54–68 CE) won golden opinions in the first part of his reign—during which he allowed his mother and then his chief advisers, the philosopher Seneca and the freedman Burrus, to counsel him—and made clear his desire to work with the Senate. But when Agrippina opposed his affair with the daughter of the Roman proconsul in Greece, he had his mother killed. Treason trials for Burrus, among others, soon followed. Nero's passion for the arts and for sport—he played musical instruments and competed in the Olympic Games—won him respect from the Roman crowd, as did his magnificent building program. However, after much of Rome burned in 64 CE, Nero used 125 acres of private land near the Palatine Hill to build a magnificent palace, its rooms decorated with glorious frescoes and a colossal statue of himself. Though always popular with the Roman plebeians, Nero gradually lost the senatorial elite and the armies. After a revolt in Gaul against his tax policies, Nero's support dwindled until he committed suicide, and the Senate acclaimed a governor in Spain, Servius Sulpicus Galba, as the next emperor.

THE FLAVIANS (68–96 CE)

Cruel, lazy, and unwilling to bribe soldiers for their support, Galba lasted only seven months of 68 and 69 CE

before being assassinated. After a chaotic period in which four emperors succeeded one another within a year, the Flavians—Vespasian, Titus, and Domitian (all successful military commanders)—restored order. Vespasian (r. 69–79 CE) reformed the public finances, instituting new taxes. When his son Titus complained that it was undignified to charge for entrance to public urinals, Vespasian, a cold, efficient man, replied, "Money has no smell." He also began construction of the Flavian Amphitheater (now known as the Colosseum), the largest in the world, where crowds of 50,000 and more could watch gladiatorial combat, mock naval battles, and public executions. Titus, though he died in 81 after only two years in office, also won respect for the efficiency and generosity he showed in dealing with a great public disaster, the eruption of Mount Vesuvius in 79, which destroyed the cities of Pompeii and Herculaneum.

Domitian (r. 81–96 CE) avoided wars of aggression, managed trade and taxation effectively, and won popularity with the plebeians. But the price was high. Augustus had made Julius Caesar a god and became one himself, after his death in 14 CE. The Flavians took office after office, demanded to be called "lord and god," and formed a court society more docile than anything Rome had seen before. Domitian infuriated the senatorial aristocrats. After court officials assassinated him, the Senate formally condemned his memory, destroying all memorials to him.

The Colosseum In 72 CE, the emperor Vespasian began building the Flavian Amphitheater, now known as the Colosseum, just east of the Forum. When completed eight years later, it could hold more than 50,000 spectators and was the stage for many public events, including gladiatorial contests.

THE EMPIRE AT ITS HEIGHT

The emperors who came after Domitian—starting with one of his advisers, Nerva—were childless and appointed their successors, who consistently attained high levels of prosperity and military success. After the disorder of the first century, their rule through more than half of the second century reassured members of the aristocracy, who came to believe that a virtuous emperor could still preserve the core virtues of the Roman order. The hard-working, conscientious rulers of the Nerva-Antonine line—Nerva, Trajan, Hadrian, Marcus Aurelius, and Antoninus Pius—preserved the borders of the empire, maintained the roads and armies, and enabled the citizens of the empire to enjoy peace and prosperity for decades.

This long period of basic tranquility, interrupted by two brief civil wars, was a true Pax Romana. The empire's cities grew and prospered. Rome itself dwarfed the rest, but some ten other cities reached 100,000 or more inhabitants. The elite of every great city, moreover, tried to make its habitat over in the most up-to-date Roman image. They built gymnasia and baths, forums, colonnades, and amphitheaters. Their houses featured fine tiles, their tables wine, oil, and fish sauce. From these bright centers where members of the elite met in city squares to argue, there stretched sprawling suburbs where the much larger number of prosperous craftspeople and merchants lived and worked. And beyond these lay huge tracts inhabited by

Imperial Cities Throughout the empire, local elites designed their cities after the Roman model. This second-century theater in Palmyra, in present-day Syria, was built with ornate columns and terraced seating in the Roman style. The main entrance was even decorated with a bust of the emperor.

peasants cultivating extensive estates as sharecroppers or tilling small farms of their own.

SOURCES OF UNITY

The stability of the second century made it possible for the Roman economy to grow—and, more particularly, for members of local elites to prosper. A uniform currency, a massive road system, and the protection of Roman arms fostered trade in regions from Gaul to Asia Minor.

Currency Gold coins, minted only in Rome but circulated throughout the empire, united all subjects under the image of the emperor. This coin bears Emperor Hadrian's name and profile.

COINAGE Local authorities were allowed to mint the small bronze coins of low value needed to purchase everyday necessities. But silver and gold coins were minted, for the most part, only in Rome. From Caesar on, coins carried new images: not the traditional bust of the goddess Roma, but a portrait of one of Rome's rulers, represented as a god on earth. These reinforced the legitimacy of the empire and the emperors, often connecting the latter with divine or heroic ancestors. But they also afforded help of a less transparent kind. Italy lacked precious metals, which had to be mined or captured elsewhere. Successive imperial governments debased the quality of the standard coin, the denarius, slowly but steadily—and thus managed to stretch their official budgets for the military and public works further than they could have done had the purity of the coinage been maintained.

ROADS An effective system of public transport—ports and docks on seacoasts and the enormous network of Roman roads—enabled Rome to stay in touch with its distant provinces. A permanent magistracy created by Augustus saw to the building and repair of this huge system, which at its height included some 50,000 miles of stone roadway, cemented in place and laid on top of a bed of stones to allow for drainage. Sometimes as straight as a ruler for miles, sometimes curving to follow the countryside, the roads enabled the legions to move their enormous baggage trains across the empire, a vital logistical support for Roman power. A postal system that could pass letters and information from the western end of the empire in Britain to Antioch in Syria had stations every twenty-five

Roman Roads This detail from Trajan's Column shows Roman soldiers building a road. Rome's excellent roads linked the empire from end to end, facilitating the movement of troops and supplies, and speeding up communication. They were crucial to the expansion of Roman power.

to thirty-five miles, and even more frequent points for changing the horses that pulled its carriages. The roads were never perfectly safe—brigands threatened travelers even in peaceful times. But the system was an immense achievement, longer in total than the American interstate highway system.

EVOLVING LEGIONS The empire supported massive armies to protect and occasionally to extend its borders. The Roman legions, always seen as the core of the military, were recruited in the first instance from citizens, the elite of the Roman plebeians, or from noncitizens who received citizenship when they joined up. Members of auxiliary infantry and cavalry forces received citizenship when they left the army after serving for twenty-five years. Gradually recruitment became more local. One African legion, for example, was made up of Italians and Gauls in the first century. In the second century, foreign recruits from Asia Minor, Syria, and eastern Europe dominated, but Africans joined as well. By the end of the century, most of the soldiers in the legion were Africans, from Mauretania and Numidia (where the legion was stationed). These disparate groups underwent rigorous training. In theory they had to remain single while they served. But though they slept in what were supposedly single-sex barracks, archaeologists have shown that women and children lived with them, evidence of long-term relationships.

The army not only maintained Roman power but also carried out vast engineering works, building camps, roads, and dykes from North Africa to northern Britain. When necessary, a legion could hunker down for as long as a year to build the siege ramp and equipment needed to take a fortress. And all members of the army learned to live as Romans, with Latin as the common language. In many areas—though not all—the army succeeded in Romanizing large numbers of subject peoples.

IDENTITY The empire continued to take in peoples whose identity was very far from Roman. Add up the importation of slaves, the recruitment of soldiers, and the movements of those engaged in trade, and it is likely that Roman populations were more mobile than any other before modern times. Yet there were limits to Rome's openness and flexibility. Like the Greeks, Romans spoke readily of "**barbarians**": in their case, members of the tribal societies that dominated Scandinavia, much of the Germanic world, and the steppes to the east. Some of them—such as the Gauls and the inhabitants of what is now England—proved willing to take up bathing, eating bread, and other Roman habits, along with Roman dress. But many of them—above all the Germanic peoples—seemed impossible to socialize in Roman ways. They clung to their gods, their languages, and their accustomed practices. Romans admired the courage of these "barbarians"

Barbarians A second-century CE sarcophagus depicts two barbarians—identifiable from their long beards and cloaks—surrendering to a group of Roman soldiers.

in battle, as Tacitus explained when he wrote a short treatise about Germania—but not their refusal to engage in commerce or productive work. Over time, the empire's Germanic neighbors would put immense pressure on its structure, opening what proved to be decisive cracks in its defenses.

REVENUES Support for this vast imperial system came from multiple sources. The empire taxed most of its subjects systematically. Indirect taxes were universal: customs duties on trade, a 5 percent inheritance tax, taxes on selling or freeing slaves. Outside Italy, in the first and second centuries CE, direct taxes were also imposed. Periodic censuses established the numbers of inhabitants in particular areas and the distribution of property in them—including slaves and houses as well as land. These served as the basis for a head tax and a property tax, which were paid in coin in the large mercantile cities of the Greek east, but paid in kind in the great agricultural provinces of North Africa and Sicily.

In addition, the emperors themselves contributed to the budget, sometimes—as in the case of Augustus—on an immense scale. During peaceful times, the treasuries of empire and emperor alike grew rich. Tiberius claimed that he saved more than Augustus himself had spent on gifts for citizens and veterans. But Caligula spent what Tiberius had hoarded, and major wars could empty the treasury rapidly. Nerva and Marcus Aurelius both had to sell off palace furniture and other imperial possessions to finance their campaigns. The evidence is fragmentary, but it seems that on the whole, taxes and duties on trade did not seriously damage the imperial economy in its first two centuries.

ROMAN LAW Equally important in constructing and maintaining the authority of the emperors was the legal system that reached its definitive shape in this period. For centuries, Roman lawyers had stated and generalized legal principles. Augustus licensed certain officials to give formal interpretations of legal questions, on his authority as *princeps* (ruler). By the second century CE, emperors treated the law as a central part of their function. The emperor was the source of law, which his edicts and instructions to provincial governors promulgated and clarified. His counselors included legal experts and he himself served officially as the final court of appeals (though these became so numerous by the third century that an assistant had to handle them). Roman law could be harsh, but it also recognized certain vital principles: for example, that one must assume a given person was free in status unless there was clear proof to the contrary. Even in the provinces, where Roman law coexisted with foreign systems—such as the law of the Jews—it was often seen as fair and incorruptible, even by citizens who had been raised by other customs.

THE REIGN OF THE "GOOD EMPERORS" (96–180 CE)

The talented emperors of the Nerva-Antonine line continued, on an even vaster scale, the Augustan program of transforming Rome into a city that spoke of the power of its rulers and inhabitants. Hadrian (r. 117–138 CE), for example, built a new palace on a plot of land almost as large as the city itself. He also designed and built a huge

The Pantheon Hadrian's ambitious transformation of Rome included the rebuilding of the Pantheon, with its vast dome, in 118–125 CE—a great achievement of Roman construction technology.

temple to Venus and Roma in the Forum. And he rebuilt the Pantheon—the enormous temple to all the gods that Augustus's son-in-law Agrippa had raised in 27 BCE. Hadrian equipped it with what was for centuries thereafter the largest dome in the world, a vast coffered expanse with a round window at its summit to admit the rays of the sun. To celebrate his conquest of Dacia, in what is now Romania, Hadrian used as many gladiators in four months of games as Augustus had used in forty years. The enormous structures built in Rome by Trajan and Hadrian, many of which survive, were the greatest civic benefactions that had ever been seen in the Roman world.

Working with the Senate, dozens of whose members served him as military commanders and provincial governors, Hadrian devoted most of his attention to the imperial provinces. Traveling most of the time with a large retinue of soldiers, officials, and technical specialists, he inspected legions, negotiated with both local inhabitants and the empire's neighbors, and expended funds and effort on massive public works. Across the northern expanse of Britain after 122 CE, he built an eighty-mile wall to separate the "barbarians" of Scotland (defeated in battle but impossible to conquer) from the Romans to the south. This ambitious project—with towered gates at intervals of a mile, and sixteen larger forts to protect it—housed a multinational, multi-ethnic force of Roman soldiers who watched their lively frontier for more than 200 years.

A passionate enthusiast for Greece and Greek traditions, Hadrian attended the Eleusinian mysteries more than once and supplied the funds to complete the enormous Temple of Olympian Zeus at Athens.

Like his predecessors, Hadrian found that the person of the emperor was a great source of authority. He spent relatively little time in Rome, but crossed and recrossed the empire from Britain to the frontier of the Parthian Empire, with which he made peace. When necessary, he went to war—as in Judea, where Simeon bar Kokhba led a massive revolt in 132 CE, which Hadrian suppressed only with difficulty and the loss of many soldiers. Still, he held the loyalty of the Roman armies, and when he died he was entombed in the vast mausoleum that he had created for himself on the bank of the Tiber.

Antoninus Pius and Marcus Aurelius smoothed the rough edges of Hadrian's imperial system. Antoninus (r. 138–161 CE) pushed farther north into Scotland, even building a new wall; mended some fences with the Senate; and tried for economies in public expenditure. Marcus Aurelius (r. 161–180 CE), the first emperor to be challenged seriously by barbarians, fought bitter but eventually successful campaigns against peoples from what is now Romania. Eventually he established and fortified the northeastern frontier of the empire. He also spent much time away from Rome, touring the eastern provinces and defending the frontiers.

A SYNTHESIS OF ROMAN AND GREEK TRADITIONS

As the imperial frontiers expanded, the great emperors of the second century CE increasingly saw themselves as representing—even embodying—a synthesis of the Roman and Greek traditions at their best. Devoted to the Roman gods, they maintained both ancient and recent traditions. Hadrian dedicated his Temple of Venus and Roma on April 21, traditionally celebrated as the day of Rome's founding. Marcus Aurelius had his successful campaigns against the barbarians recorded in stone reliefs, as Trajan had, on a monumental column. But they also pledged allegiance to Greek culture with a dedication that some of their predecessors had lacked. Hadrian completed the Temple to Olympian Zeus at Athens, which the Athenian ruler Pisistratus had begun several centuries before. Marcus Aurelius studied and wrote Stoic philosophy, in Greek. His *Meditations* expressed in pregnant, short passages his overwhelming sense of duty, his deep feelings of debt and gratitude to those who had trained him—and his

Marcus Aurelius's Campaigns Marcus Aurelius erected a monumental column in Rome in 180–195 CE to memorialize his victory in battle against Germanic tribes. This detail shows Roman soldiers beheading Germanic nobles, an undeniable symbol of the emperor's conquest.

IMPERIAL ROME

> OTHERS, I AM SURE, WILL FORGE BRONZES THAT LOOK EVEN MORE LIKE BREATHING FLESH, / WILL PULL FACES THAT SEEM ALIVE FROM THE BRONZE, / WILL PLEAD THEIR CASES BETTER, WILL CHART THE MOVEMENTS OF THE SKY / WITH THEIR RODS, AND PREDICT WHEN THE STARS WILL RISE. / YOU, ROMAN, REMEMBER TO RULE THE PEOPLES WITH SUPREME POWER. / THESE WILL BE YOUR ARTS, TO CIVILIZE THE LIFE OF PEACE, / TO SPARE THE DEFEATED AND TO CRUSH THE PROUD.

VIRGIL, *AENEID*

> THE PEOPLE, WHICH USED TO GIVE OUT MILITARY COMMANDS, CONSULSHIPS, LEGIONS AND THE REST, NOW PAYS NO ATTENTION AND EAGERLY DESIRES ONLY TWO THINGS, BREAD AND CIRCUSES.

JUVENAL, *SATIRE 10*

Emperors mobilized extensive resources to build massive public baths, the largest of which could accommodate a few thousand guests. By 52 CE, Rome used 200 million gallons of water a day, much of it supplying public baths for a population of 1 million.

> WHAT WORSE THAN NERO? WHAT BETTER THAN NERO'S BATHS?

MARTIAL, *EPIGRAMS*, BOOK VII

This coin (97 CE) shows Annona, goddess of the grain supply, and Ceres, goddess of agriculture. The grain dole, established in 58 BCE and distributed at the Temple of Ceres, provided free grain for all citizens older than ten in the city of Rome, some 220,000 tons of wheat per year.

The Circus Maximus (first century CE), with a capacity of 250,000 spectators, was the largest site for public games in Rome.

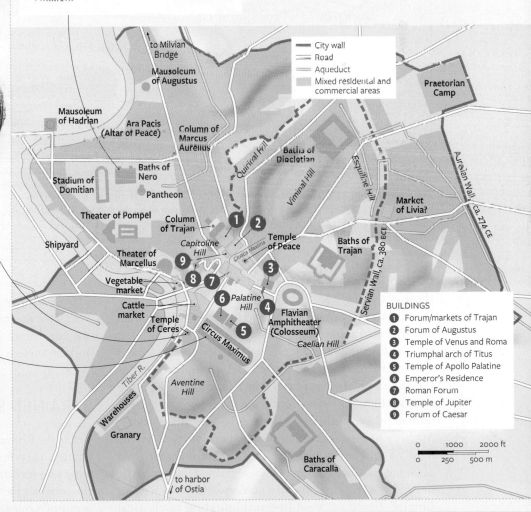

City wall
Road
Aqueduct
Mixed residential and commercial areas

to Milvian Bridge
Mausoleum of Augustus
Mausoleum of Hadrian
Ara Pacis (Altar of Peace)
Column of Marcus Aurelius
Baths of Diocletian
Praetorian Camp
Stadium of Domitian
Baths of Nero
Pantheon
Quirinal Hill
Viminal Hill
Esquiline Hill
Market of Livia?
Theater of Pompei
Column of Trajan
Capitoline Hill
Temple of Peace
Baths of Trajan
Shipyard
Cloaca Maxima
Theater of Marcellus
Vegetable market
Cattle market
Temple of Ceres
Palatine Hill
Flavian Amphitheater (Colosseum)
Caelian Hill
Circus Maximus
Tiber R.
Aventine Hill
Warehouses
Granary
to harbor of Ostia
Baths of Caracalla
Aurelian Wall, ca. 274 CE
Servian Wall, ca. 380 BCE

BUILDINGS
1. Forum/markets of Trajan
2. Forum of Augustus
3. Temple of Venus and Roma
4. Triumphal arch of Titus
5. Temple of Apollo Palatine
6. Emperor's Residence
7. Roman Forum
8. Temple of Jupiter
9. Forum of Caesar

0   1000   2000 ft
0   250   500 m

QUESTIONS FOR ANALYSIS

1. How did the power of the emperor shape the physical city of Rome?
2. How did basic aspects of everyday life in the city depend on Rome's imperial power?
3. How would you assess the opening quotation's comparisons of Rome to other cultures during this period?

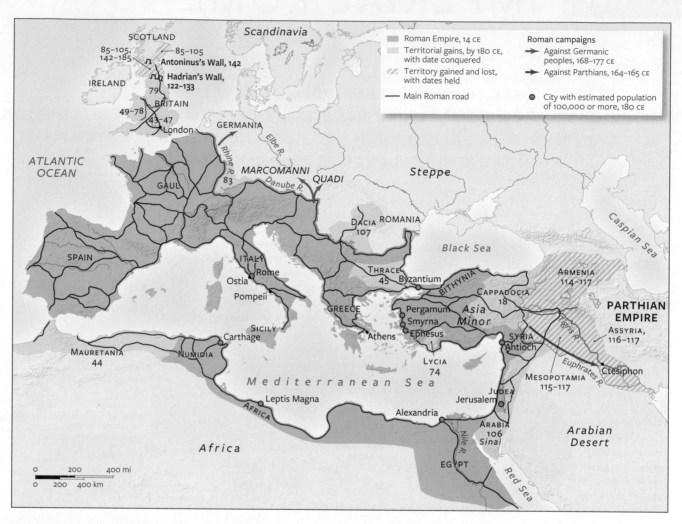

The Roman Empire at Its Height, 14–180 CE In the first century and the early years of the second, the Roman Empire expanded, pushing farther into Britain, North Africa, central Europe, and Asia Minor. Not all territorial gains were lasting. But during the long second-century period of stability, many cities grew—particularly in Asia Minor and the Sinai Peninsula—and emperors built new roads and other infrastructure projects that connected the vast empire.

fundamental pessimism about all human affairs, including those of the empire.

As the cosmopolitan men and women of the Roman world looked about them, they could feel confident that the civilization of ancient Greece still flourished. Athens and other Greek cities—above all, the vast and prosperous Greek cities of the Near East, from Alexandria in Egypt to Antioch in Asia Minor—continued to exercise a magnetic pull on people with intellectual and political ambitions. Mastery of Greek prose and verse continued to be the mark of cultivation. Oratory, once the common medium of Greek civic life and diplomacy, remained the key to the halls of power, even in the vast public world of the Roman Empire. Based on word-by-word imitation of classical Athenian orators such as Demosthenes, the oratory of the second century was a virtuoso exercise in reviving the past

that could serve real political purposes in the present. In Athens, Romans and Greeks also formed clubs that celebrated the ancient gods. And across the Roman world, the ancient shrines continued to make sacrifices to the gods and the ancient oracles to offer messages.

STRAINED BORDERS

Yet as the Romans consolidated their rule over their vast empire, they found themselves confronting new challenges on its borders. In 161 CE the Parthians—rulers at the time of much of Persia—attacked the Roman protectorate of Armenia and Roman territory in Syria, defeating the legions that mustered against them. Marcus Aurelius had convinced the Senate to accept his adopted brother,

Lucius Verus, as co-emperor, on an equal footing with him. Verus marched against the Parthians, transferring legions from the Rhine and Danube borders. He chose his commanders well, and they drove the Parthians out of Syria and invaded Mesopotamia. The Romans signed a peace treaty with the Parthians in 166 CE. In the same year, though, a plague struck one of the armies that had carried out this campaign. It spread rapidly through the Roman armies and eventually drove Marcus Aurelius from Rome. As much as 10 percent of Rome's population died.

The empire had no respite from border attacks and other afflictions. In 168, population pressure from Germanic peoples in Scandinavia forced the Marcomanni and Quadi tribes west across the borders into the empire. Verus died in 169, leaving Marcus Aurelius in sole charge. Faced with an empty treasury and a depleted army, he auctioned the imperial flatware to raise money and recruited brigands and slaves to serve in the army. War with the Marcomanni and Quadi continued until 175, when peace was made, but then broke out again in 177. Recurrences of the plague also hit the Romans hard. Marcus was about to begin yet another campaign when he died in March 180. In some ways, the empire never recovered from this series of strains.

THE JEWS OF IMPERIAL ROME

Yet it was a different set of enemies—the Christians—who would eventually undermine, and transform, the Roman Empire. Christianity was, originally, a Jewish sect. The Jews—some of them settled in what they saw as their divinely promised homeland, Palestine, under rulers indirectly controlled by Rome; others scattered across the world—had created a distinctive and powerful religion. By the end of the first century CE, the Jews of Palestine had fought and lost a disastrous war against the Romans. But they had also created the conditions under which a new, universal religion—Christianity—came into being.

PALESTINE

In the first century CE, there may have been as many as 5 million Jews. History had scattered them everywhere, from Babylon (where a large community flourished, descended from the ancient Judeans who had gone into exile there in the sixth century BCE) to Egypt (where another large community, partly descended from Jewish mercenaries, maintained an immense synagogue in

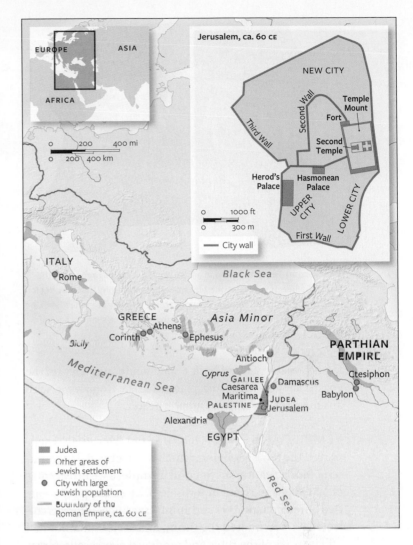

Jewish Settlements in the Roman Empire, 1st Century CE Millions of Jews lived throughout the Roman Empire, but particularly in Babylon, Egypt, and Palestine, where Jerusalem remained the center of Jewish life and worship. The old walled city surrounded the Hasmonean king Herod's palace, and the enormous Second Temple on the Temple Mount—which Herod rebuilt—towered over everything.

Alexandria). The center of Jewish life and worship, as it had been since the middle of the fifth century BCE, was Jerusalem, the largest city in Palestine. In the second century BCE, the revolt of the Maccabees against the Seleucids had won independence for Palestine, first as a semiautonomous monarchy and then as an independent one, ruled by the Hasmoneans. In 63 BCE, however, the Romans conquered Palestine, turning it into the province of Judea. After decades of troubles, Herod, the son of a Hasmonean official from southern Palestine, was made the king. He married a Hasmonean princess, murdered the last male heir of that dynasty, and embarked on an ambitious career that involved romanizing Palestine as

The Second Temple Found in a first-century CE synagogue near the Sea of Galilee, this large stone block bears iconography that may depict the Second Temple. Classical columns frame a seven-branched lamp, or menorah, and jars of oil like those kept in the Temple's inner chamber.

far as possible. Herod built a spectacular new city on the coast, Caesarea Maritima, planned in the Roman way with an aqueduct, forum, and amphitheater.

TEMPLE AND SYNAGOGUE But Herod also supported the Jewish religion, which he practiced. He reconstructed the enormous **Second Temple**, a wealthy center of learning and ritual in Jerusalem. Here the priests carried out regular prayers and animal sacrifices, officials collected and accounted for tithes, and scribes maintained official texts of the Bible and produced new scrolls. Great baths enabled women to undergo ritual purification. At the national festival of Passover, as many as 400,000 people flooded into the city from Palestine and beyond to take part in the Temple's public rituals. Perhaps only such modern pilgrimage rituals as the mass journeys of Muslims to Mecca every year can give a sense of the scale and drama of these celebrations.

For all its size and wealth, however, the Temple was by no means the Jews' sole religious institution or the dominant one in daily life, and others had a very different tone. Many communities in Palestine, including some Jerusalem neighborhoods—and all of the larger Jewish communities outside it—had synagogues, which were public halls where congregations held meetings, offered public prayers, and studied the Hebrew Bible. In synagogues built after 70 CE, archaeologists have discovered pulpits—evidence that a community member led the service and perhaps preached to the congregation. Unlike the Temple priesthood, the wealthy community members who built

synagogues did not necessarily see it as their job to set off and cleanse separate spaces or to keep them absolutely free from non-Jewish words and practices. Unlike modern Orthodox synagogues, ancient ones do not seem to have divided their congregations by gender. Jews simply met, prayed, and studied—at times using Aramaic, at times Greek. Sometimes their discussions led to new varieties of religious belief and practice.

VARIETIES OF JUDAISM

The Jews themselves exhibited diverse practices and beliefs. Rabbis (teachers) were beginning to formulate new ways of thinking about the requirements of Jewish law, but at this time they seem to have enjoyed limited authority. Judaism itself, after all, was divided into a variety of groups. The relatively wealthy Sadducees, a small group, saw the Bible as the sole religious authority and insisted that no human being had the right to interpret the text in any way. Sadducees served in important Temple offices, and they saw the Temple and its sacrifices as the core of religious life.

More numerous than the Sadducees—and more influential, in the long term—were the **Pharisees**. The Pharisees saw the observance of the Law—the maintenance of purity that set Jews apart as the people of a single, unique God—as central to Judaism. They formed associations whose members ate together to ensure that all the food they consumed met the highest standards of purity. But the Pharisees found that the text of the Hebrew Bible was too brief to tell them exactly what these standards required. Instead, they learned to interpret the scriptures and devised rules for doing so properly. The Pharisees, for example, extended the biblical prohibition against eating a calf boiled in its mother's milk into a firm rule against ever mixing meat and dairy products in a single meal—the basis of the system of kosher foods that many Jews still follow.

Another group, the Essenes, developed codes of diet and conduct even stricter than those of the Pharisees. Repelled by what they saw as the corruption of the Jerusalem Temple, they founded their own communities, which only those who committed themselves to their beliefs and practices were allowed to join. Some lived in cities, others withdrew into the Palestinian desert. Eating only vegetables prepared by their community's strict codes, using latrines far outside the perimeter of the inhabited space, refraining from sexual intercourse, and praying regularly by their own calendar, the Essenes dedicated themselves to the pursuit of purity and holiness. Those who could not sustain the discipline that the community demanded were excluded from it. Some starved, unable to bring themselves to eat foods not prepared by Essenes.

Groups like this one—coherent, strictly regulated, walled off from normal society—often teach the rejection of existing authorities in both politics and religion. The Essenes argued that the Temple and the ruling house of Herod had become so corrupt that the existing order would soon be overthrown. Only what one text called the "War of the Sons of Light against the Sons of Darkness" could restore righteousness. Drawing on the prophets of the Hebrew Bible, they awaited the end, not rebelling but praying.

OTHER JEWISH GROUPS

The Sicariots ("assassins," so called because they carried small daggers known as *sicae*) and Zealots took a militant political position. Convinced that Roman rule over Palestine represented, as the rule of Alexander's successors had, a violation of the divine order, they called for armed resistance and revolution. Meanwhile other prophets, especially in Galilee, north of Jerusalem, preached the coming of a new order, and magicians claimed their own kind of supernatural power, drawn not from divine help but from their sovereign abilities to command demons and transform the order of nature.

In Palestine as well as across the Roman Empire and beyond, finally, there were "Hellenists"—Jews who spoke Greek and used the language in their worship. No language barrier separated Hellenized Jews from their neighbors. They maintained a rich ritual life and an attractive set of communal institutions. Their scriptures offered a powerful account of the cosmos and history and a profound ethical literature. Though many pagans continued to mock the Jews for their stubborn insistence on parochial customs such as circumcising male babies, and their refusal to eat pork or fight on Saturdays, others found Jewish religion and custom magnetically attractive. Thousands converted or became "God-fearers"—sympathizers who attended synagogue services or even participated in communal institutions without formally converting to Judaism. Sometimes these sympathizers were wealthy and enjoyed prestigious positions as benefactors of the synagogues that they frequented.

In the decades around the beginning of the Christian era, Judaism was complicated and full of conflicts, expansive and vital. It was in this world—in a Palestine ruled by Rome, most of whose inhabitants practiced what claimed to be a universal religion—that the tiny Jesus movement began to grow into a new religion.

THE LIFE AND DEATH OF JESUS

Jesus, whose life and death inspired Christianity, was born in Bethlehem, a city not far from Jerusalem, a few years before the beginning of the Common Era. He was a Jew, not only by birth but by upbringing and lifelong practice. Recognized early for his wisdom, he taught by giving direct advice and by offering parables (stories with a moral). According to those who knew him, he also performed wonders: at different times he healed the sick, raised the dead, and cast out the demons that haunted many of his contemporaries. So far, Jesus did not stand out. Other men of power—such as Honi the Circle-Drawer, a wise man who conjured rain from the skies when the sun baked the fertile soil of Galilee—walked the roads and villages where Jesus spent his early life. Other preachers, such as John the Baptist, urged men and women to forsake their sins and repent.

A RADICAL MESSAGE

Over time, however, Jesus became more radical than these other preachers of righteousness—even more radical than other dissidents among the Jews. Like the Essenes, he taught that the end of time was approaching rapidly, that the men and women alive in his own time would witness the final struggle between good and evil. Like them, too, he formed a small community of his own, one made up of men and women who acknowledged his spiritual power and followed him as disciples—though unlike the Essenes, his followers did not immediately establish settlements. They continued to live as other Jews of the time did: they followed the elaborate rules codified in the Law, which had become central to Jewish life after the return from the Babylonian exile, and which offered detailed rules for most aspects of life. But Jesus demanded more of them, much more. He forbade them to divorce their spouses, told them never to use violence against others, and urged them to give up their own families and follow him.

CONFRONTING AUTHORITY Jesus evidently could not make his peace with the priests of the Second Temple. He came to believe that he was the Messiah—the anointed king whose coming the Hebrew prophets had predicted

Jesus's Origins One of many sacred images from a third-century CE catacomb in Rome used for Christian burials, this mural of Christ as a shepherd is one of the earliest artistic portrayals of Jesus.

and whose reign would bring history to its conclusion. A central reason why this change was necessary, for Jesus, was that the Temple itself was corrupt. One spring, probably around 33 CE, he went to Jerusalem, as did thousands of others, for the great Passover ceremony—but in his case, also with the intention of confronting the religious authorities. In the immense forecourt of the Temple, Jesus denounced and attacked the moneychangers who helped pilgrims from abroad make their contributions to the priests. He also seems to have threatened the Temple itself with destruction at God's hands. Arrested and tried by the Romans—for reasons that historical sources do not directly state—he was executed in the Roman manner, by crucifixion.

EXECUTION As he hung on the cross dying, Jesus seems to have thought that he had failed: he cried out, "Lord, lord, why have you forsaken me?" But on the third day after his death, when his disciples came to claim his body—so they reported—it had vanished from the tomb. Soon Jesus appeared to many of them, apparently alive, inviting those who doubted his resurrection to touch his wounds. The terror and misery caused by his death made way, among his relatives and disciples, for new emotions: joy, excitement, and renewed commitment to his cause.

HISTORICAL QUESTIONS

Even this brief outline of Jesus's story—one based on generations of scholarly effort to analyze all the sources that survive in the same way that a historian would analyze any other source—is debatable at every point. All of our sources—the narratives that became the four **gospels** (literally "good news") in the **New Testament**, other rival gospels, the short and problematic account in the work of the Jewish historian Josephus (37–100 CE)—were written decades after Jesus's time. Their authors depended on earlier written accounts, which do not survive. In normal circumstances, eyewitness testimony could not have lasted unchanged until the gospels were written. The particular traditions about Jesus that went into the gospels were altered as they were retold and first written down, and each of the authors of the gospels selected and edited his material in a unique way.

When the gospels disagree, as they often do, and when they all diverge from what is known from other sources, no other historical authority can give certain guidance. Scholars disagree, accordingly, on whether Jesus was tried by the Jews or by the Romans; on the role played by Pontius Pilate, the Roman governor, in Jesus's condemnation and execution; on whether Jesus saw himself as an anointed human king of the Jews, a son of God, or a Jewish prophet like those of the Old Testament; and on whether any of these events actually took place.

THE JESUS MOVEMENT

It is certain, however, that after Jesus's death he became the beloved founder of a larger movement within the Jewish world—one led by his brother James and others in Jerusalem. His followers clearly believed that he had been chosen by God to transform the world. And when the heavens did not open up and the Temple did not fall after his death (as Jesus had warned would happen), they reinterpreted his call for change as the demand to begin a mission.

CHRISTIANS Some of Jesus's immediate followers and others who had not known him in the flesh began to preach in his name. By the late 60s CE, they would be known as "Christians"—followers of Christ, a word that means "the anointed one." With that choice of term they claimed divine status for Jesus. Like him, they healed the sick, raised the dead, and fed the hungry, and these wonders established their charisma and authority. Soon a number of Jews from different sects—and some non-Jews (known as Gentiles), including a few Roman "God-fearers"—joined the movement. Small congregations formed, meeting to celebrate the common meal—to eat bread and drink wine—in his memory. Before long they began to encounter opposition, and then persecution, from other Jews. Christian missionaries were denounced and stoned. At the same time, they began to debate certain issues: for example, the role of non-Jewish converts within the new movement. Should they be required to follow the Jewish law? Or could they simply accept Jesus and his teachings? After Jesus's death, the movement was tiny—so tiny that its growth seems to have stirred no discernible interest among the Roman authorities, ever alert for any signs of subversive meetings. How did this tiny seed take root?

A SPIRITUAL REVOLUTION Historians no longer invoke the power of miracles to explain events in human history. But it is not irrational to think that the triumph of Christ over Rome had something miraculous about it. It was, in fact, the culmination of a unique and seemingly inexplicable sequence of events—a spiritual revolution that unfolded over the last two centuries before and the first three centuries of the Common Era.

A generation or two ago, historians argued that Christianity, like other revolutionary movements, appealed chiefly to outsiders caught in tumultuous social and economic change. In fact, however, Christianity appealed almost from the beginning to a strikingly wide range of individuals. And the church spread through the Roman Empire not only in the troubled first-century times of Nero and his immediate successors, but also in the prosperous and peaceful second century—the empire's high point of power and wealth. To find the sources of Christianity's strength, we must look within. Its success was the result of a shift in the way men and women understood the universe, and its past and its immediate future—and in the ways they hoped to find their own paths through the dark labyrinth of life on earth to a higher existence elsewhere.

EARLY CHRISTIANITY

In the fourth decade of the first century CE, the Christian movement underwent its first radical transformation—a world-shattering change that took place in the realm of the spirit and was the work, to a great extent, of one person. Saul, a Roman citizen and educated Jew who had helped to persecute the Christians, became one of them, changing his name to **Paul**. Soon he became a leader, one who unhesitatingly took positions on the great questions of organization and theology on which, like so many jagged rocks, the small Christian vessel seemed likely to founder. Paul's official letters to other Christians and Christian congregations are preserved in the New Testament, along with a number of letters that scholars agree he did not write. Paul's letters are the earliest Christian texts, older than the gospel retellings of the life of Jesus. The early history of the church can be traced in them and in the book of Acts, the New Testament book that describes the spread of Christianity after the death of Jesus.

THE CONVERSION OF PAUL

Saul was born in Tarsus, a bustling city near the Mediterranean coast of what is now southern Turkey. A mercantile center, Tarsus lay at the intersection of many trade routes, and it had a mixed and cosmopolitan population. Saul himself was a Pharisee. According to the book of Acts, Saul studied the Jewish law not only in his native city but also in Jerusalem. By his own account, he was "a Hebrew of Hebrews," passionately loyal to Jewish tradition, and worked against the first Christians whenever he encountered them.

Then one day, as Saul and his companions traveled to Damascus, they saw a brilliant light. Saul also heard a voice say: "Saul, Saul, why do you persecute me?" When Saul asked for the identity of the being who addressed him just as God had addressed the ancient Hebrew prophets, he learned that Jesus himself was speaking. Stunned by the experience and struck blind for three days, Saul was cared for by Ananias, a Syrian Christian who had also had a direct revelation. Ananias healed Saul by laying hands on him, and informed Saul of his mission as the prophet of Christianity. The bitter defender of Judaism suddenly became Paul, an eager, eloquent missionary who crossed and recrossed the entire Mediterranean world, converting many men and women to Christianity and helping the new churches overcome the problems they encountered.

A change of heart as radical as it was unexpected, the conversion of Paul is one of the exemplary dramas of Western history. For centuries, writers and painters have portrayed the moment of transformation—Saul, prone on the dusty Syrian road, struggling with his divinely assigned mission—as a metaphor for true conversion to any faith. Many Christians in much later times—one famous example is Martin Luther, the religious reformer who in 1517 began the Reformation—have seen Paul's conversion as the standard by which all decisions to join the Christian church should be measured.

PAUL AND THE TENETS OF EARLY CHRISTIANITY

Jesus's followers, as we have seen, believed that Jesus had come back to life and appeared to them. Paul never met Jesus in the flesh, but he understood his own conversion in the same terms. He was certain that he had encountered a living Jesus and that the meeting had changed him completely. Again and again, in his magnificent first letter to the Christian community in the Greek city of Corinth—a church Paul himself founded—he insisted that Jesus had literally risen from the dead and that his resurrection was the central guarantee of the truth of Christianity. The promise of eternal life, verified by Jesus's return, made clear, for Paul, that the Christian revelation was true.

What did it mean, then, to follow Jesus, the son of God? Must his followers also practice Judaism? Many of them—especially Jesus's brother James, who developed the church of Jerusalem—thought so. Paul never lost his respect for the Jewish law, which had provided a canon of upright conduct and belief for the Jews over the centuries. He seems to have remained an observant Jew himself. But when he saw the disorder and confusion caused in early Christian communities by those who insisted that the Jewish law continued to bind them—and that horrified

others who came to Jesus from the pagan world—he began to believe that those who accepted the new faith from the outside had no obligation to follow the Jewish rules of diet, conduct, and rest. After all, those rules, as the prophets and Jesus had both taught, were made by human beings, not for them.

Paul developed a powerful new theological doctrine to justify this argument, and he maintained it in the teeth of opposition from the family of Jesus himself. Sin, in traditional Judaism, required atonement, and atonement in turn required sacrifice. It was by making offerings that the Jews, as the Five Books of Moses explained, had reconciled themselves to God after they slipped back into idol worship on their way from Egypt to the promised land. In fact, Judaism revolved as much around ways to make amends as it did around obedience to positive commands. The willingness to sacrifice what was dearest to one, moreover, was the highest proof of one's love—as the biblical patriarch Abraham showed when he made clear, in the book of Genesis, that he would sacrifice his son Isaac at God's command.

Jesus, Paul now argued, had been the son of God—not just an anointed king, but a divine being. The human race, God saw, had become so corrupt, had committed so many sins, that it could never reconcile itself with him through ritual or prayer. He decided, accordingly, to sacrifice his only son and, by doing so, to make his son atone for the sins of the human race. All that one needed for salvation, now that this epoch-making event had taken place, was to have faith in Jesus and his sacrifice. Any non-Jew who had faith would be saved and had no need to follow Jewish laws or perform Jewish rituals. Any Jew could be saved as well, so long as that individual shared the faith.

A NEW MESSAGE, A NEW MEDIUM

This message proved sharply controversial, and Paul embraced the controversy. He argued with Jewish Christians who insisted on the necessity of following the Law, and with Christians who tried to combine the new teachings with such traditional practices as magic and astrology. And he argued with those who did not show enough respect for the Jewish law and its crucial role in the drama of human salvation—to teach people that they were sinners. Jesus had said that he came bringing not peace but a sword, and Paul repeatedly confronted, and overcame, opposition. He made himself an extraordinarily effective organizer and missionary, in perpetual motion around

Peter and Paul A second-century CE sarcophagus from the Roman Christian catacombs depicts Paul, the church's first leader; and Peter, one of Jesus's disciples. The imagery also includes the Greek letters *xi* and *rho*, the first two letters of "Christ."

People of the Book Christians were early adopters of the codex, which resembles the modern book. This second-century CE Greek-language manuscript, the oldest known copy of the Gospel of John, is written on separate, stacked sheets of papyrus instead of on a long, continuous scroll.

the cities of Asia Minor and beyond. After his arrest, he appealed, as a Roman citizen could, to the emperor, and traveled to Rome and elsewhere before he met his eventual martyr's death. Even after he died, his writings carried on his arguments with opponents on all sides.

Christians very soon began to copy Paul's work, and other texts, in a new kind of book—not rolls of vellum or papyrus, of the sort that had been used for centuries, but codices. The Romans had traditionally strung together wooden tablets and written on them. Soon they began to fold parchment and papyrus, their two forms of paper, and make books of the form we still use. Protected with bindings of wood and leather, codices could hold more content than scrolls and were easier to refer to if a debate sprang up. Such books were in use by the end of the first century, when the poet Martial described them: "If you want to have my books with you at all times on a long trip, buy the ones with small pages made of parchment." Paul's little books—which explained how Jesus had come to complete the historical experience of the Jews—and other texts began to make Christians, too, a people of the book.

SPREADING THE MESSAGE: THE HOUSE CHURCHES

Paul wove his way up and down the trade routes of the eastern Roman Empire, moving from city to city in Asia Minor, Syria, Palestine, Greece, and Italy. He worked intensively with groups of those he called the Brothers—fellow believers. When Paul reached a new city, he began by preaching Jesus's message in the synagogue. Jewish responses were often harsh: "Five times," he told the Corinthians, "I have had forty lashes less one [thirty-nine blows of the whip] from the Jews. Three times I was beaten with rods; once I was stoned." At Damascus, he had to have himself lowered down the city wall in a basket to escape Jewish opponents. Evidently, then, Paul began each mission within the Jewish world from which he came, only to be expelled from it.

Yet the cities that Paul knew also harbored associations

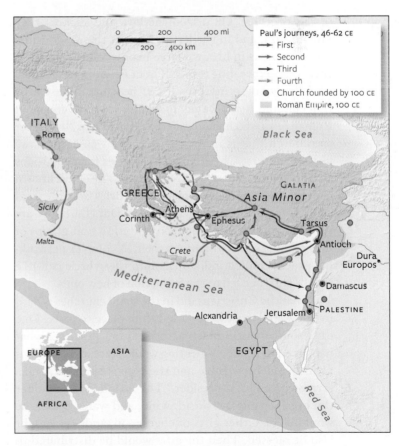

Paul's Travels through the Eastern Roman Empire, 46–62 CE
After Paul converted to Christianity, he traveled repeatedly on the Mediterranean trade routes to spread its tenets. At first his journeys did not take him far from his native Tarsus, but later he went as far as Rome. He visited the Christian communities in the cities he passed through, and founded churches, such as the one at Corinth, himself.

An Early Church The house-turned-church at Dura Europos in present-day Syria, the earliest known church building, dates from 235 CE. The frescoes in its meeting room are probably the oldest existing Christian paintings. This one depicts Christ as a shepherd (on the left), accompanied by his flock.

of the Brothers. He prized the love and support they offered him, and in the letters he sent them, scrawling his postscripts in his own large handwriting, he singled them out in revealing terms: "Greet Priscilla and Aquila, my fellow workers in Christ Jesus," he wrote to the Christian community in Rome, praising a married couple of Roman Jews who had migrated to Asia Minor, "and greet the church that is in their house." This passage shows us that the first Christian communities formed groups small enough to meet in private homes. The oldest known church buildings—one of them, which dates from the third century, is in the ancient Syrian city of Dura Europos—are private houses that were reconfigured so that groups of fifty or more could worship in them. A complex networking process pulled individuals into these little cell-like groups and then led to the formation of new ones.

What the Christians did in the small churches is hard to know, and must have varied from place to place. One early source, Justin Martyr (100–165 CE), describes what happened in Rome. A meeting would start with readings from the Hebrew Bible and the New Testament, and a sermon given by a "presider." The members would offer the presider gifts of bread, wine, and water, which he would bless. Other gifts of cheese, oil, and wine might also be blessed. Then the gifts would be distributed to those present, and deacons would take them to those who could not come. It was a simple service, with very little set ritual or formal prayer, and it included the offering of the Eucharist—the holy meal of bread and wine at which Christians recalled the sacrifice of their savior by partaking, spiritually, of his body and blood.

EARLY CHRISTIAN SOCIETY

Paul's travels on the trade routes took him to cities of very different kinds. In Greece, he went from Athens, still grand and rich, where he found no footing, to Corinth, which the Romans had destroyed in 146 BCE. Julius Caesar had recently reestablished the city, and in this rapidly changing society Paul seems to have found many who were eager to hear his message about Jesus. The men and women who joined these early Christian communities, some of whom Paul identified by their callings, belonged to different social levels. Paul himself earned his living by making tents. This was a craft that he could pursue as he moved from city to city, since it required only skilled hands, a curved needle, and a few other tools. Many of those to whom he preached and with whom he worked also practiced modest crafts. But many of the Brothers to whom he sent greetings by name in his letters to the Romans and Corinthians were of higher social standing. Crispus, for example, whom Paul baptized at Corinth, had been the "ruler" of a synagogue—a wealthy man, entrusted by the congregation with responsibility for the upkeep of the building. Others held positions as local officials or engaged in what may have been quite substantial businesses. Some of them owned slaves.

What seems most striking about the individuals Paul singled out for greeting is the variety of their origins and fortunes. They included Jews like Paul, but also Hellenist Jews and non-Jewish God-fearers like the Roman centurion Cornelius, who is mentioned in the book of Acts. "There is neither Jew nor Greek," Paul told the Brothers of Galatia in central Asia Minor, "there is neither slave

The Eucharist From the Greek word for "thanksgiving," the Eucharistic meal was part of the ritual of early Christian churches. One of the first representations of the Eucharist is this early-third-century CE mural from the Roman catacombs. It shows men and women sitting together at a table to share the ceremonial bread and wine.

THE CHRISTIAN CATACOMBS

The proper burial of its members was an important function of the early Christian community. Since only Roman aristocrats could be buried in the city of Rome, Christian leaders arranged with Roman officials to bury their dead in tunnels constructed in the soft volcanic rock beneath the city. Beginning at the end of the second century, the Christian catacombs spread over some sixty-eight square miles and eventually housed almost a million burials.

The frescoes on the walls of the catacombs, which may have been indicators of the wealth or social status of the dead, depict episodes in the life of Jesus and the narratives of the New Testament. This wall painting shows a miracle in which a suffering young woman is healed by merely touching Jesus's clothing. As Jesus passes, she reaches out to catch a trailing thread of his simple white cloak, similar in appearance to her own. He then turns and blesses her with his right hand. Jesus appears as a youthful, clean-shaven, and compassionate figure.

Recent scholarship contends that Christians gathered in the catacombs to eat meals, worship, and celebrate Mass among their departed. The scenes depicted in the frescoes provide important evidence about the customs and beliefs of the young church.

QUESTIONS FOR ANALYSIS

1. How would an image like this have helped in the spread of Christianity?
2. What significance do you see in the similarities between these two figures?
3. What does the image of the woman suggest about women's status in the early church?

Women in the Church Paul's letters revealed that women numbered among the leaders of the early Christian church. Their importance was reflected in religious imagery, such as this fourth-century CE wall painting from the Roman catacombs. It illustrates a story from the Gospel of John in which a Samaritan woman gives Jesus a drink from a well, even though the Samaritans were traditional enemies of the Jews.

nor free, there is neither male nor female: for you are all one in Christ Jesus." Paul's letters show that he believed this passionately, and that the early church corresponded in many ways to his idealistic vision of an all-embracing spiritual community.

Women as well as men actively supported the movement. When Paul wrote to the Romans, he thanked a fair number of men by name for their help. But he showed equal gratitude and affection for Priscilla, who, with her husband Aquila, had risked her life to save him, and "Mary, who has done much work among you." Most striking of all are his warm words for Phoebe, "a deacon of the church at Cenchreae" (the eastern port of Corinth). Paul urged the Romans to "receive her in the Lord in a manner worthy of the saints, and help her in whatever she may need from you, for she has supported many, including me." Evidently, women played a very active part in the first years of the Christian movement.

And when Paul sent greetings to "those of the household of Aristobulus" and "those of the household of Narcissus," he was offering fellowship—not by name, and less warmly than he offered it to free men and women—to the domestic slaves who shared the religion of their Christian masters and mistresses. At the beginning of his first letter to the Corinthians, Paul noted that "not many of you were wise according to the flesh, not many were powerful, not many were of noble birth." As usual, he chose his words with care, to describe a loose set of congregations whose members could be found at all points on the social and cultural ladders of the time.

IMPROVISATION AND ORDER

As Paul moved from city to city and from synagogue to house church, he confronted a kaleidoscopic world of beliefs and practices, one in which even what later came to be seen as basic Christian ideas and institutions had not yet crystallized. His own first letter to the Corinthians describes the general order of services: "When you come together, each of you has a psalm, a lesson, a tongue, a revelation, an interpretation"—a varied, flexible, and unpredictable ritual. With complete acceptance, Paul notes that members of the congregation might speak in tongues— that is, give testimony in strange languages unknown to them or anyone else, a phenomenon still widespread today in evangelical Christianity. He cautions the Corinthians only that they should restrict the number of these testimonies in any given service, and reserve time for precise discussion of or quiet meditation on their meaning.

Whereas Judaism emphasized tradition, as embodied in what had become a fairly set canon of sacred books that were read and interpreted in the synagogue, the new house churches of the Brothers rang with improvisations and hummed with the silence that accompanies deep thought. A modern Quaker meeting may give some idea of the tone and quality of their services. No wonder that these lively churches, which offered fellowship to women and slaves, spread so rapidly throughout the empire.

In time, Paul and other leaders decided that they must formulate clearer rules to maintain order and discipline in the new church. Paul explained to the Corinthians that although it was important to have Christians who spoke in tongues, other offices and gifts mattered as well. Christians needed prophets to tell of the future, deacons to oversee community funds, and apostles to preach. Gradually, Christian worship took a coherent shape, centering on the Eucharist.

Paul himself clearly respected female colleagues—as we have seen in his support for Phoebe, a female deacon. Yet his first letter to the Corinthians demanded that women cease playing a public role in Christian services: "The women should be silent in the churches. For they are not permitted to speak, but to be subordinate, as the law also says. If they want to learn something, let them ask their own husbands at home. For it is shameful for women to speak in church." It is possible that Paul decided that women must keep silent—but more likely that a later writer, seeking as Paul had to impose order, inserted these words. Slowly, the church was developing a spiritual hierarchy.

ROME'S EARLY RESPONSES

As pagans became more aware of the existence of the Christians, they also grew more suspicious about the Christians' secret meetings, normally held at night, and the barbarous deeds that were rumored to be carried out in them. Wild accusations flew. Pagans whispered that Christians met, for example, to devour the flesh of babies and engage in promiscuous sex.

When in 64 CE the city of Rome suffered a devastating fire, which destroyed three of its fourteen districts completely and badly damaged seven more, the emperor Nero blamed the Christians. Many of them were put to death—some in a circus (an arena for sports and spectacles), wrapped in bloody animal skins and torn apart by wild beasts, and others nailed to crosses and set on fire. Tacitus (d. after 117 CE), the great historian of Rome who tells us this, also notes that many onlookers began to feel sympathy for the Christians who suffered so terribly.

Similar accusations against the Christians reached the emperor Trajan in the second century CE. Pliny the Younger, his official in Bithynia, a rich and strategically important province in northern Asia Minor, was puzzled by the apparent contradiction between the unpleasant but harmless rituals that the Christians actually performed and the savage deeds attributed to them. He asked his emperor for advice on how to treat the denunciations. Trajan replied that though he should not seek out individual Christians and should discourage anonymous denunciations, he should certainly punish zealous Christians with death. Although most Christians lived in relative personal safety much of the time, they often found themselves accused of overturning traditional beliefs and engaging in barbarous conduct. The accusations were hard to bear and harder to defend oneself against in a conservative society.

NEW SCRIPTURES

The last decades of the first century witnessed radical changes in the situation of both Jews and Christians. A Jewish rebellion against Rome in Palestine resulted in a disastrous defeat—including the destruction in 70 CE of the Second Temple, which Jesus had prophesied. Christians inside and outside Palestine responded to these events, drawing up accounts of the life of Jesus and other books that contrasted their traditions, beliefs, and practices with those of the Jews. These became, with Paul's writings, the core of their own new Bible.

THE JEWISH WAR (66–73 CE)

What gave the Christian movement its final push toward self-definition was a series of transformative events in the history of the Jews. In 66 CE, the Zealots, a faction of Jews in Jerusalem advocating rebellion against the Romans, slaughtered several hundred soldiers and drove out the Roman proconsul. Nero assigned the general Vespasian—later to be emperor himself—the task of conquering Palestine. The Jews mounted such powerful resistance that the Romans needed some years to conquer Jerusalem, which fell in 70 to Titus, Vespasian's successor in command. The Romans destroyed the Second Temple and carried away its great seven-branched candelabra, which they later paraded in triumph through the streets of Rome. Pockets of Jewish resistance elsewhere were eventually wiped out; at the rocky citadel of Masada, the Jewish garrison committed mass suicide when it could no longer resist. By 73, however, the Romans had completely defeated the Jews.

The consequences of this war—and the later outbreaks that followed it—were many. Jewish religious authorities lost their taste for religious war. The Sadducees and Essenes gradually disappeared. The Pharisees, at first few in number, survived to become the leaders of a new kind of Jewish life in which there was no Temple, the synagogue took its place as the center of Jewish communities, and the rabbis became the chief interpreters of the Law. As to the Jews more generally, they lost their independence in what they saw as their native land. Though they remained

Spoils of the Second Temple A relief on the Arch of Titus in Rome (82 CE) records the fall of Jerusalem and the destruction of the Second Temple in 70 CE. Here, Roman conquerors carry away spoils from the city, including the golden menorah that was lit every night in the Second Temple.

ROMAN POLICY ON CHRISTIANS: MEMO TO AN EMPEROR

When Christianity emerged in the Roman Empire in the first century CE, it aroused the suspicion of emperors and officials. Though Christians were often blamed for fires and natural disasters, the empire varied in its responses to those accused of practicing the new religion.

This exchange of letters between Emperor Trajan and Pliny the Younger, governor of the Roman province of Bithynia from 111 to 113, conveys the unsettled nature of Roman policy toward the early Christians. In the first letter, Pliny anxiously asks whether his various actions toward Christians have been proper in the emperor's opinion. Trajan's response, no doubt to Pliny's great relief, approves of his decisions. The emperor also stresses that former Christians who repent should be spared, and that anonymous accusations are improper.

Letter of Pliny the Younger to Emperor Trajan

Pliny's letter on the Christians (112 CE) was one of dozens he wrote to Trajan, describing matters ranging from the upkeep of aqueducts and theaters to public celebrations of the emperor's rule.

It is my normal practice, my lord, whenever I am not sure how to deal with a matter, to refer it to you. For who could be better to guide me when I delay or to instruct me in my ignorance? I have never taken part in the trials of Christians. Accordingly, I do not know what is normally investigated, or punished, and how far. I have also been uncertain whether any distinction should be made because of age, or whether the young should be distinguished from those who are fully grown; whether those who repent should be pardoned, or if it does not help a man, once he has been a Christian, to stop being one; whether the name Christian itself deserves punishment, if no crimes come with it, or the crimes that belong to the name. Meanwhile, in the cases when Christians were brought before me, I acted in the following way. I asked them formally if they were Christians. If they confessed, I asked them again and a third time, and threatened punishment. If they persisted, I ordered their execution. For I did not doubt that, whatever they might confess, obstinacy and unbending stubbornness deserve punishment.... An anonymous pamphlet was published, which contained many names. I thought that those who denied that they were

or had been Christians, and at my dictation venerated the gods and worshipped your image, which I had ordered to be brought here with the statues of the divinities, with incense and wine, and cursed Christ—none of which those are truly Christians can be coerced into doing—should be released. Others whom the informer named said that they were Christians and then denied it. They said they had been but had ceased, some three years before, some many years, some even twenty years. All of them also worshipped your image and the statues of the gods and cursed Christ. They claimed that the sum total of their guilt or error had consisted in this: that they had regularly assembled on a particular day, before dawn, and sung responsively a hymn to Christ, and bound themselves by an oath, not to commit some crime, but not to commit fraud or theft or adultery, lest they break their word or refuse to repay their deposit when called upon to do so. After doing this it had been their custom to depart, and then to come together again to take food, but ordinary, innocent food. And they claimed that they had ceased to do this after my edict, by which, following your commands, I had forbidden associations. Therefore I considered it all the more necessary to find out the truth from two maids, who were called deaconesses, by torture. All I found was a wicked and wild superstition. Therefore I postponed the trial and immediately consulted you. It seemed worthwhile to consult you about the matter, because of the large number of those at risk. For many people of all ages, of all ranks and of

both sexes are being, and will be, put in danger. And the plague of this superstition has spread not only through the cities, but also through towns and fields, and it seems possible that it can be stopped. For it is clear that the temples, which had almost been deserted, have begun to be frequented, and that the established rituals, which had ceased, are being performed again, and that the meat of sacrificial victims, for which hardly any buyers could be found, is coming from all sides. From this it is easy to grasp how many people may be freed from error, if there is some possibility of repentance.

Letter of Emperor Trajan to Pliny the Younger

Trajan was one of the conscientious, hard-working rulers of the Nerva-Antonine line. He governed effectively with his officials in the provinces, as this letter from 112 CE demonstrates.

You followed exactly the right procedure, my dear Pliny, in dealing with the cases of those who were denounced to you as Christians. For it is not possible to lay down any absolute, general rule. One should not go looking for them. If they are denounced and accused, they should be punished—with the proviso that anyone who denies he is a Christian and demonstrates that clearly, by worshipping our gods, should receive pardon because of his repentance even if he came under suspicion in the past. But anonymous denunciations should play no part in a prosecution. For this is a terrible precedent and does not fit our times.

QUESTIONS FOR ANALYSIS

1. Why does Pliny give alleged Christians several chances to reject their faith?
2. According to Trajan, under what circumstances should suspected Christians be punished?
3. How do these letters convey the unsettled policy of Rome toward the early Christians?

Sources: Translations by Anthony Grafton.

more numerous in the diaspora—the world of Jews scattered from East Asia to Gaul and Britain—their interest in the conversion of others died away. Jewish religious life became, as it has been ever since, an effort to live a virtuous and holy life in the absence of the Temple and—until recently—a homeland.

Above all, the consequences of the Jewish revolt against Rome proved dramatic for the Christians. Suddenly, the vast changes that Jesus had predicted seemed to have taken place. The Temple lay in ruins as he had said it would, its priests dead or scattered. In the decades after the Jewish war, Christians began to write down the first narratives of Jesus's teachings and life. As they did so, they redefined their Messiah. Collections of sayings attributed to Jesus were set into contexts in his life. At some time before 100 CE, the **gospels** took shape: accounts of Jesus's life, ascribed to many different writers. Four of them, which bore the names of Matthew, Mark, Luke, and John, were collected in what became the Christian scriptures.

THE GOSPELS

The Gospel attributed to Mark, probably the earliest of the four, portrayed Jesus as a prophet sent to preach to unbelievers—one who deliberately adopted a language they could not understand so that they would condemn themselves. In Mark, Jesus tells his followers, for example, a parable about a man who sowed seed—some of which was eaten by birds, some of which fell on rocky soil and died, and some of which "fell on good ground, and gave fruit that sprang up and increased; and one seed yielded thirty, and one sixty, and one a hundred." The story seems simple. Modern readers often see in Jesus's decision to speak in parables evidence of his homely, accessible approach to moral and theological teaching. In fact, Mark represented Jesus's stories as one tactic in a spiritual war that he waged against much of his original audience.

According to Mark, even Jesus's disciples found the parable about the seed puzzling. Jesus explained that the story referred to the ways in which different individuals received the word of God. More important, he told his disciples that only they, the few, would hear his message as they should: "To you it has been granted to know the mystery of the kingdom of God." Unbelievers would hear his stories but not understand them, and by failing to understand, they would condemn themselves. A remnant would understand and be saved—and even they would not share the disciples' direct access to the mysteries Jesus taught. The gospels described the Jesus movement itself

as hierarchical, as the church had in fact become already in the course of Paul's career.

Later writers conveyed Jesus's teachings in different ways. The author of the Gospel attributed to Matthew, for example, set out to show that the wisest of the pagans, the three Magi—eastern kings who came bringing gifts for the infant Jesus in the manger—had used their skills in astrology and other occult forms of knowledge to predict the birth of a Jewish messiah and then to find him. The Gospel of John used the terminology of Greek philosophy to argue that Jesus, as the son of God, was no mere holy man but a divine being who had existed from the very creation of the world. These later evangelists placed less emphasis on the rapid approach of history's end—which Mark saw as imminent, after the Temple's fall—and more on the individual Christian's duty to prepare his or her soul for death.

Christianity gradually created a rich religious literature of its own, one that combined in beautiful and original ways the sayings attributed to Jesus and the stories, developed from them, about his life and works. Christian beliefs continued to develop, with many branches of theology and ritual sprouting from the original trunk. But by the end of the first century a loose movement with tenuous borders had given way to a more structured organization.

Christianity had slowly begun to set itself apart from its Jewish roots. The Jewish branch of the early church would have largely died out by the early second century. The Christian gospels, moreover, as they were written and incorporated into what became a coherent and powerful new set of scriptures, made clear that Jesus had come not to fulfill but to replace Judaism. The gospel accounts also held the Jews—above all, the Pharisees and the Temple authorities—responsible for Jesus's death. The firm distinction between Jews and those who accepted Jesus became a condition of existence for the new religion—a condition that would, over the centuries, have some lasting and terrible results, especially for the many Jews who continued to live in Christian societies.

REVELATION: THE POWER OF THE WORD

Although Christianity defined itself against Judaism, it still retained many Jewish practices and traits. None of these proved more fundamental to the new religion than the belief that history was nearing its end.

PAUL AND THE END OF TIME   Paul clearly believed that he was living in the last years of the world. "Behold," he told the Corinthians, in words that ring in the mind like the magnificent trumpet music that accompanies them in Handel's *Messiah* (1741), "I show you a mystery. We shall not all sleep, but we shall all be changed, in a moment, in the twinkling of an eye, at the last trump: for the trumpet shall sound, and the dead shall be raised incorruptible, and we shall be changed."

Paul expected to see the just fly through the air to greet the second coming of the Messiah, and the dead rise, in his own lifetime. But he also warned against any effort to compute the date and time when the last act of history's drama would take place, or to anticipate the transformation of the state and society by human action. In the perfect world to come, all would be different, starting with the bodies of the saved, and all believers would be equal in their saving faith. For now, though, slaves should remain slaves, and free men and women free, awaiting the moment when the mystery would be revealed in the heavens.

Others, however, were less content to wait, and more intent on the nature of that second coming and what it would mean for Christians and others. The expulsion of the Jews from Rome by Claudius around 50 CE, the catastrophic Jewish war against Rome from 66 to 73 CE, and the fall of Jerusalem in 70 all made these questions even more urgent. This series of disasters evidently suggested to many Jews and Christians that the end of time was near.

JOHN'S VISIONS Sometime in the second half of the first century, a Christian named John, who believed this, wrote another of the open letters that make up so much of the New Testament—the book of Revelation. A writer full of hatred against Rome and other centers of sin, John described himself as living in a time of trouble—an age when a "synagogue of Satan" (perhaps a group of Jewish Christians) flourished in Ephesus, a Greek city on the coast of Asia Minor, where John himself may have lived, and a prophetess named Jezebel told Christians that they were permitted to commit fornication and eat food that had been sacrificed to idols. Addressing himself to seven churches, John explained to them, as an angel had explained to him, how Jesus would return in splendor and violence to judge and then transform the world.

In Revelation, a spectacular series of visions explodes upon the page—of "one like the son of man, in the middle of 7 candlesticks ... and he had 7 stars in his right hand, a sharp sword emerging from his mouth. And his face was as when the sun shines at its full strength"; of a royal figure with a sealed book, worshipped by beasts and elders; of a lamb with seven horns and seven seals, and many more

strange figures. The angelic revelation makes clear that the future holds a time of destruction, as the four horsemen of the apocalypse—terrifying mounted figures named Conquest, War, Famine, and Death—slaughter humanity. The martyrs, or "witnesses"—those who have died for the truth—emerge from their graves to cry for vengeance, and a cosmic war is waged in heaven. Finally Babylon, the great city of commerce, withers; Satan is chained for a thousand years and Jesus is resurrected; and then, after a still more terrible time of tribulation, the devil is loosed, to be destroyed in a final combat. Then, and only then, can the Last Judgment take place and a new heaven and earth take shape.

Neither the date when Revelation was written nor the identity of its author is certain. But John, whoever he was, clearly found beauty and consolation in the idea that Jesus was the Messiah and would come back, in the course of a cosmic war, to judge the dead and the living and to create a perfect society. In many ways, he harked back to Jewish writers of the last centuries BCE. John shared with them the conviction, perhaps drawn from the Persian Zoroastrians (who, as we saw, had similar beliefs), that the true history of the universe took the form of a battle between powers of good and evil. Like the Zoroastrians, John knew that in the course of history, God would right the wrongs inflicted by evil rulers on those who had remained faithful to the true religion.

WORDS TO OUTLAST STONE In other respects, however, Revelation marked something new in sacred literature. In the vividness with which John evoked the sufferings that would lead to the transformation of the world, and in the gloating passion with which he contemplated the mass deaths of those he condemned, he forged a new kind of religious feeling: steely, powerful, and deeply and absolutely self-righteous. His rich imagination enabled him to call up, from the language of biblical prophecy, a vision of the future, cast in words alone, that would outlast the marble and concrete of the imperial world around him, which he despised. The Roman Empire, from Augustus on, used urban complexes and great structures to tell stories about its power and glory to its subjects: monuments like the Testament of Augustus in Asia Minor, temples to the imperial cult, forums, and triumphal arches. The author of Revelation imagines away these massive stone symbols of power, offering believers a countervision of the future. His work—still read by millions of Christians, long after the Roman Empire is dust—attests to the evocative force of the word. The book of Revelation framed the Christian millennium in such powerful terms that it would become a permanent force in Western culture.

THE DEVELOPING CHURCH

The fiery visions of Revelation notwithstanding, Christian beliefs in the second century CE sometimes seemed as fragile as the empire seemed eternal. Even success created new problems. As more educated people joined the church, they began to read and respond to the scriptures in new ways.

VARIETIES OF BELIEF

All Christians believed that there was one God and that Jesus was his Son, but they understood what that meant in different ways. Was Jesus the same as God the Father? And what of the Holy Spirit, who was also mentioned in the Gospels? Opinions differed and debates broke out.

THE TRINITY Gods who died, as Jesus had, were nothing new. Plenty of lesser divinities in Greek myth died, usually from unnatural causes, and plenty of Greek rulers and Roman emperors became gods once they were safely dead and out of office. But these were minor deities. Paul and other Christians, by contrast, insisted that the true God and Creator of the universe had become flesh and died. But some who saw themselves as Christians could not accept the notion that God had actually humbled himself to put on human flesh and undergo the torment and humiliation of the Crucifixion. Some insisted that Christ had not actually died on the cross.

One dissenting school devised a radical hypothesis: Jesus was divine; but like the Greek and Roman demigods whose mortality he shared, he had been a lesser god. Only in the early third century did Christians frame what became the definitive view for most of them: that God the Father, God the Son, and the Holy Spirit were the same yet different. Tertullian (ca. 160–ca. 225 CE), a Christian from Carthage, became the first writer to use the term *Trinity* for this God who was three in one.

GNOSTICS Another group of early Christians known as **Gnostics** left a rich and sometimes wildly imaginative body of religious texts, many of them recovered in the twentieth century from the jars in which they had been buried in the Judean desert. Inspired by the philosophy of

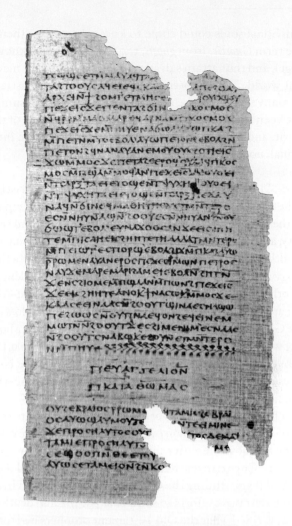

Gnostic Texts In the centuries after Jesus's death, accounts of his teachings were not limited to the texts preserved in the Bible. This is the first page of the gospel of Thomas, a record of sayings attributed to Jesus, from a papyrus codex of fourth-century Gnostic gospels.

the Platonists, which strictly separated the material world from the ideal, many Gnostics refused to believe that the true Creator could have anything to do with evil or suffering. They elaborated visionary cosmologies and theologies of great beauty.

The true Creator, the Gnostics believed, brought forth not the universe itself but emanations of himself—subsidiary beings. One of these was the feminine Wisdom, which they defined as the creator spirit. Wisdom, deluded and believing that she was the universal ruler, created the material world. Human souls roamed this world, with all its error, confusion, and darkness, like fireflies in a forest—pinpricks of light against a vast, turbulent, and threatening background. With the help of the Savior and other emanations from the divine Creator, individual souls could come to know themselves (hence the term *Gnostic*, from *gnosis*, the Greek word for knowledge), and thus attain salvation by rising out of the material world. The Gnostics challenged other Christians in many ways—by the radical separation they assumed between the world of matter and the higher world of the spirit, and by their insistence that salvation was an individual, not a collective, matter.

MARCION Even the most solid pillars of Christian belief and conduct sometimes shook under the impact of these controversies. In the first half of the second century, a Gnostic named Marcion (ca. 85–ca. 160 CE), son of a wealthy merchant family in Asia Minor, established a theology all his own—a revelation with which he challenged all other authorities. The God of the Old Testament—the Creator—Marcion insisted, could have nothing to do with the God of the New Testament. For the Creator was a bungler who had brought pain and suffering—for example, the pain of childbirth—into the world. The God of the New Testament, by contrast, promised salvation to those who had faith in him.

The Gospels and parts of Paul's Epistles seemed to contradict Marcion's version of Christian truth. But he overcame this obstacle with a simple application of his mighty scissors. Christian teachers, he insisted, had falsified their central texts, stuffing the Gospels and Epistles with irrelevant, deceptive efforts to show that the life and death of Jesus verified what the Old Testament prophets had foretold. In fact, Marcion claimed, the true New Testament consisted only of a few chapters from Luke's Gospel and the central letters of Paul, in which he had dwelt on the unique, saving nature of Jesus. All the rest was not only padding but ugly growths, grafted onto the authentic core texts by teachers of darkness. The new church that Marcion organized did not last long: his strict insistence that all members remain celibate ensured that.

MONTANISTS In the late second century CE, another creative misreader—Montanus, a cleric from Phrygia in central Asia Minor—posed a more serious challenge to those who would build an orderly church. In his thought, the established Christian expectation that the world would soon end took on new urgency. The city of God— New Jerusalem—would soon descend on the Phrygian hills, and those Christians who did not accept his revelations would be destroyed, along with the unbelievers. Montanus preached the coming of the end and attracted female prophets who had their own ecstatic visions and preached as effectively as he did. Their message appealed

to many, including the formidable theologian Tertullian. Montanist churches sprang up around the Roman world, and unlike those of Marcion, they survived for centuries.

SUFFERING AND STRENGTH

Christians not only disagreed with one another on central issues, they also had to contend with harsh treatment from outsiders, as they had earlier under Nero and other emperors. In 177 CE, for example, Christians in the cities of Lyon and Vienne, both on the Rhône River in Gaul, were rounded up, dragged into the city forum, imprisoned, and interrogated. One of them, Sanctus, repeated in Latin "I am a Christian" and held out even when red-hot metal plates were pressed against him. A tiny woman, Blandina, resisted with equal courage even though "her whole body was mangled and her wounds gaped." Later the two of them and others were sent to the circus, where they were

Early Christian Martyrs Early Christians venerated those of their number who held to their faith despite persecution. A fourth-century catacomb fresco celebrates the martyrs Marcellinus and Tiburtius, both executed in the early fourth century CE. Marcellinus was a priest; Tiburtius was a wealthy man who donated all his wealth to the poor when he became a Christian.

whipped, attacked by wild animals, and finally burnt to death. Even the ashes of their bodies were scattered to prevent proper burial.

A firsthand report of their death somehow survived, but it is not clear how literally we can take this and later accounts, few of which offer the graphic details found in the partly first-person documents about Perpetua. Martyrdom came to have its own scripts, and we cannot tell, at this distance, whether martyrs actually performed these as they were tortured and killed, or whether the patterns of heroic suffering were imposed on them by pious writers in retrospect. What is clear, though, is that the sense of identity and loyalty that these groups displayed was one of Christianity's chief sources of strength and stability. The tradition of the martyrs' deaths suggested that however sharply Christians might disagree about the nature of God or the proper order of the service, they could unite to resist the challenges presented by an empire that treated them as subversive.

THE CHURCH AS AN INSTITUTION

Yet even during this time of debate and persecution—the former of which never ended—Christianity crystallized into a church, a formal institution with a complex hierarchy of officials. During the second and third centuries CE, the local clergy in great cities such as Rome, Alexandria, and Antioch chose clerics to lead them. These men took chief responsibility for doctrine and worship in their city and in the smaller communities around it. They also represented their communities to the wider Christian world, exchanging letters with the heads of other communities. Gradually the term for their office, *episkopos* ("overseer" or "bishop"), took on a new meaning. These **bishops** established themselves as the formal leaders of the new Christian church.

CHRISTIAN LEADERSHIP
Christian leadership soon became a specialized calling that required a range of skills and knowledge. In the first instance, the bishop preached. Indeed, for some centuries he was normally the only one to preach in a given cathedral, or main city church. His sermons became the preeminent source of religious instruction for ordinary Christians. But the bishop did more than that. He also chose young men to follow careers in the clergy, and he organized the collection of a treasury from his parishioners to cover the church's expenses. Gradually, too, certain bishoprics—especially that of Rome, which claimed that the apostle Peter himself had established it—developed a special preeminence in the church. Their

Early Bishops In the second and third centuries CE, the clergy in large Christian cities increasingly chose leaders—bishops—to oversee all of the priests in their region. This fifth-century CE mosaic from Naples depicts a Carthaginian bishop carrying a holy text as a symbol of his authority.

bishops came to have special titles as "archbishops" or "metropolitans." They not only administered their own dioceses, but also presided over all the others in a given district.

MATERIAL SUPPORT
Once episcopal leadership was established, Christians became immensely successful at raising funds. Whereas the imperial government, when it promoted the ransoming of Roman citizens from captives, could only watch with regret as these citizens became the slaves of those who had paid for their freedom, Christian communities could pay for the release of their fellows and afford to impose no further bonds on them. By the middle of the third century CE, Christians were feeding some 1,500 poor people a day in Rome. In this and other ways, the church took over, for its flock, one of the traditional duties of the emperor—something that the "good emperors" of the second century would never have allowed.

THE CATACOMBS
The church had also begun to take responsibility for proper burial of the dead. In Rome, by the end of the second century, the church had won permission to bury Christians in underground galleries called catacombs. Over the next several hundred years, almost 900,000 Christians would be interred in the Roman catacombs, which stretched over sixty-eight square miles. Christians did not fear the dead, and early services sometimes took place in small churches near these cemeteries.

Hundreds of years later, in the sixteenth century, Christian scholars would imagine that the early Christians had hidden underground from their persecutors. In fact, though, the government had allowed the Christians to create their buried city of the dead, long before they were permitted to build public churches for the living. Gradually, the church had developed a structure of institutions, a hierarchy of officials, and a body of art and literature—all before its existence won official approval from the empire.

INSTABILITY IN THE EMPIRE (180–312)

To Christians, the empire must often have seemed like a vast and immovable structure. In fact, however, the crises of the mid-second century had weakened it in crucial ways. For decades to come, military commanders competed with one another to seize power. Arbitrary rule sapped the empire's institutions and debased its coinage, leaving it without the resources to meet new threats on the borders.

MISRULE AT THE TOP

The emperor Commodus (r. 180–192 CE), who succeeded Marcus Aurelius, was the first emperor in decades not to be chosen for his abilities, but because he was the emperor's son. He brought with him a return to the frightening days of the Julio-Claudian emperors. Commodus ruled through favorites, had senators executed, and performed as a gladiator. When he renamed himself Hercules and gave other signs of megalomania, including an effort to transform the city's calendar, he was murdered. After a year of crisis in 193, during which five emperors claimed the throne, Septimius Severus became emperor and ruled until 211.

In this period the empire's main institutions continued to function: some of the greatest jurists in Roman history worked and wrote under Septimius Severus and his successors. But the vast system that had supported the empire was beginning to weaken. Septimius expanded the army and raised its pay, straining the treasury. He deliberately debased the basic Roman coin, the silver denarius, resulting in a rapid inflation that weakened the urban economy. The Severan emperors pushed urban elites hard to collect and pay the taxes the state badly needed, and Septimius tried experiments in border defense, but with little positive effect. Septimius's sons Geta and Caracalla

Septimius Severus This portrait of Emperor Septimius Severus, his wife Julia Domna, and his sons Caracalla and Geta was painted in Roman Egypt around 200 CE. Geta's face has been erased—perhaps after Caracalla had his brother assassinated in 211.

inherited the empire, but Caracalla had his brother murdered, and ruled until he was assassinated in turn by one of his bodyguards. For three-quarters of a century, emperors won their office and lost it at the point of a sword. In one period of forty-five years, the armies created twenty-seven emperors, only one of whom died a natural death.

AN ORGANIZING THREAT AT THE BORDERS

The same period saw the Germanic tribes along Rome's borders develop into a greater threat. The origins of these Germanic peoples are uncertain—late legends traced them back to Scandinavia, but the archaeological record connects them to northern Poland. When Rome first encountered them in the expansive years of the early empire, they were relatively few, poor, and disorganized: once they had used up the soil around a particular settlement, they moved on. But in the course of the second and third centuries CE, the **Goths** and other Germanic peoples who moved toward Roman territory learned to keep cattle and use manure to fertilize their farms. Their settlements grew larger and they began to trade more effectively with the Romans, providing them with slaves, military recruits, and amber (coagulated tree sap) for jewelry. Eventually, the tribes mastered the new ways of working iron to make tools and weapons, and of turning pottery on wheels.

Their society, once relatively egalitarian, became dominated by increasingly powerful and wealthy elites: burials, in which arms and armor appear ritually mutilated, suggest that warriors played an increasingly prominent role. Bands of young warriors—young men who had no land, or too little to cultivate—led their movement to the west, but women and children followed. By the second century they had reached the eastern shores of the Black Sea, and in the third century they spread through the region, raiding the Aegean coasts of both Asia Minor and Greece. They raided up to the walls of Thessalonica in northern Greece and planned to invade Greece. A Roman army defeated them at Naissus in Serbia, probably in 269,

but they remained in large numbers in parts of modern Ukraine and Poland.

Most important, permanent coalitions of the tribes came into being, with powerful leaders. We know relatively little about these small kingdoms, such as the Tervingi and the Greuthungi, but the confederations stayed together and posed an unmistakable threat to the empire. And to the east a new dynasty in Persia—the Sasanians—mounted newly aggressive campaigns against Rome.

PULLING APART

During this period the Roman armies assigned to prevent border incursions rebelled against imperial control more than once. Military commanders formed alliances, only to

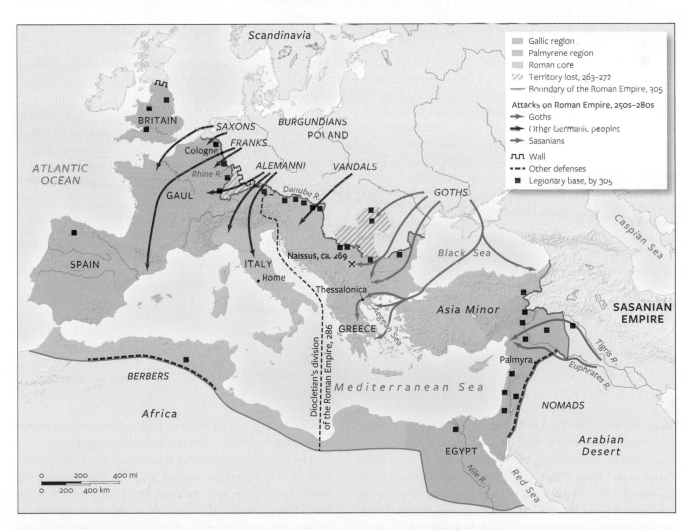

Instability in the Empire, 180–305 CE From the late second century on, the territorial integrity of the empire was increasingly under strain. Those with rival claims to territory, particularly the Goths and other Germanic peoples from northern Europe, pushed at the borders, clashing with the Roman armies despite defensive fortifications, and in some cases taking territory. In 286, Emperor Diocletian permanently split the empire in two.

PETITION OF PEASANTS TO EMPEROR MARCUS JULIUS PHILIPPUS

The crisis of the mid-second century had lasting effects on the empire. One result was a debasing of the coinage, causing inflation and difficulties for the tenant farmers living on agricultural estates. High-ranking political and military officials and soldiers took advantage of the weakness of these poor peasants to extort money, resources, and labor from them. In this document from 245 CE, peasants from Phrygia, in Asia Minor, petition Roman emperor Marcus Julius Philippus (r. 244–249) to protect them from such abuses, which he had apparently attempted to do previously as prefect of the Praetorian Guard.

Petition to the Emperor Caesar Marcus Julius Philip Pius Augustus and to the most noble Caesar Marcus Julius Philip [Philippus's son] from Aurelius Eclectus for the community of …your tenant farmers in…Phrygia, by the soldier Titus Ulpius Didymus.

Most reverend and most serene of all emperors, although in your most felicitous times all other persons enjoy an untroubled and calm existence, since all wickedness and oppression have ceased, we, alone experiencing a fortune most alien to these most fortunate times, present this supplication to you. The burden of the petition is as follows.

Most sacred emperors, we are your property, an entire community, that has fled to you and has become supplicants of your Divinity. We are unreasonably oppressed and we suffer extortion by those persons whose duty it is to maintain the public welfare. For although we live remotely and are without military protection, we suffer afflictions alien to your most felicitous times. Generals and soldiers and lordlings of prominent offices in the city and your Caesarians, coming to us, traversing the Appian district, leaving the highway, taking us from our tasks, requisitioning our plowing oxen, make exactions that are by no means their due. And it happens thus that we are wronged by extortions.

Once before, Augustus, when you were praetorian prefect, we appealed to your Highness about these matters, showing what was happening. And the enclosed epistle shows that your godlike spirit was disturbed about these matters: "We have sent to the proconsul the complaints that you have included in the petition and he shall provide that there be no further ground for the complaints."

Now since this petition no benefit has resulted and since it has happened that undue exactions are made in regard to our farm work when people descend upon us and tread us underfoot unjustly, and since we are oppressed willfully by the Caesarians, our possessions are spent on them, our fields are stripped and laid waste, and we live remotely and dwell far from the highroad.

QUESTIONS FOR ANALYSIS

1. What abuses do the peasants describe, and what do these abuses indicate about the conditions of those who worked the land?
2. What does this document tell us about how the peasants felt about political and military officials?
3. Did the petitioners believe that Emperor Philippus could and would help them?

Source: Allan Chester Johnson, Paul Robinson Coleman-Norton, and Frank Card Bourne, *Ancient Roman Statutes* (Austin, TX: 1961), p. 232.

break with one another and wage civil wars. The empire split briefly into three regions—a Roman core ruled by Gallienus (r. 253–268 CE), an eastern region ruled from Palmyra by Odaenathus, and a Gallic empire ruled from Cologne by Postumus. Zenobia, the daughter of a Roman governor of Syria, married Odaenathus, who claimed to be both "king of kings" in Palmyra and the holder of a Roman office. In 267, when he was assassinated, she took command, calling herself Augusta and her child Augustus. She rapidly built up an empire, controlling Roman trade routes in the eastern Mediterranean and taking Egypt.

The strongest emperor of this period, Aurelian (r. 270–275 CE), responded in creative ways to the threatening new situation. He met invasions with massive shows of force, brutally quelled a rebellion of the mint workers in Rome, and defeated and captured Zenobia, putting an end to her rival empire. To protect Rome—since the armies usually remained at the frontiers—he surrounded it with enormous brick and concrete walls, parts of which survive. Yet Aurelian was murdered by his own officers while marching to meet a Germanic invasion, and it took some weeks before an elderly commander named Tacitus (r. 275–276 CE) was chosen to replace him.

DIOCLETIAN

What remained of the old senatorial elite of Rome gradually disappeared, and provincial commanders dominated the empire. Only in 284 CE did the uncultured but effective **Diocletian**, a hard-bitten soldier, take office and restore order. Diocletian (r. 284–305 CE) defeated the Sasanians and other enemy peoples, and reinforced the empire's borders with a massive program of fortress building.

REFORMS Diocletian reorganized the administration of the empire's provinces, dividing the responsibilities of military and civil officers. He recast the tax system to take account of the productivity of land: more fertile areas and larger estates paid more than poorer ones. And he tried to stabilize the coinage by producing a new pure gold coin, the aureus. Diocletian also supported the codification of the law—an enterprise that later emperors would continue. Formidable though his energy and skill were, however, he brought on severe difficulties when he legislated wages and prices across regions. By eliminating the regional differences in wages and prices that had encouraged specialization and trade, these measures did fundamental harm to the Roman economy. Diocletian also tried to bind members of many occupational groups, such as soldiers, *coloni* (tenant farmers), and bakers, to their jobs and towns. In the end, he was reduced to accepting payment in kind, rather than coin, for taxes.

THE TETRARCHY At the same time, he began the process that would eventually split the empire. Diocletian appointed an able co-emperor, the general Maximian, who ruled the west while Diocletian ruled the east. Each emperor, or Augustus, was soon flanked by a caesar, who assisted him. The new form of imperial government—carefully designed to avoid many of the weaknesses of the old—was known as the **tetrarchy**, or rule of four. It was meant to provide effective administration of the empire by splitting it into coordinated regions.

SYSTEMATIC PERSECUTION From the beginning of the third century CE, imperial persecutions of Christians, long intermittent, became systematic in their execution

and serious in their impact—perhaps reflecting recognition of the power that the church had attained. In the middle of the third century, when the emperor Decius (r. 249–251 CE) ordered persecutions, Christians in many areas were forced not only to make sacrificial offerings to the emperor but to obtain certificates attesting that they had done so. Individuals found themselves compelled to make frightening and dangerous decisions, sometimes on the spur of the moment, and even those of greatest authority in the Christian world could not always be consistent in their actions. Cyprian, the bishop of Carthage, fled persecution under Decius. Afterward, however, Cyprian argued that those who had obtained certificates should be expelled from the community of Christians. Under the emperor Galerius (r. 305–311 CE) he gave himself up and suffered martyrdom. Confusion spread: How far could a Christian yield to the pressure of the persecutors and remain a Christian?

Diocletian's Tetrarchy A sculpture from Constantinople from around 300 CE personifies the tetrarchy Diocletian introduced. The two Augusti, with beards signifying their seniority, consult closely with the caesars who assist them.

In 303 CE, moreover, Diocletian launched the most sustained of the persecutions. After attacking the Manicheans—a group of dualists whose missionaries competed for a time, in the third and fourth centuries, with the Christians—he set out to eliminate the alternate hierarchy and authority of the Christian churches. In Palestine, a center of Christian activity, Christians were arrested, held for many years, and then enslaved in the copper mines or publicly executed. Throughout the empire, Roman authorities destroyed churches, confiscated Christian books, and rounded up Christians. By the time this **Great Persecution** came to an end in 311, it had cost the lives of half the early Christian martyrs whose names are known. The church had never faced a more serious threat.

THE ASCENT OF CONSTANTINE

Within a few years, however, the empire was transformed once more, in a way that thoroughly altered the condition of the church. The process began with a period of political turmoil. In 303 and 304, Diocletian's health collapsed, and he and Maximian abdicated in 305. The caesars, Constantius and Galerius, became the new Augusti. But civil war broke out between Constantine, son of the senior Augustus, whose mother was a Christian; and Maxentius, son of Maximian, who had ruled with Diocletian. In Rome in 306 the Praetorian Guard declared Maxentius *princeps*, and he then usurped full power. Constantine's power rested on the Roman legions in Britain, where he ruled. After long negotiations and struggles with Maximian and a series of

Battle of Milvian Bridge The triumphal Arch of Constantine in Rome, built to celebrate the victory at Milvian Bridge, includes this frieze of Maxentius's troops drowning in the Tiber River.

campaigns against the Franks, who were threatening the empire's Rhine frontier, Constantine invaded Italy.

Once there, he defeated Maxentius's forces in the north and marched on Rome. Before a final confrontation on October 26, 312, near the Milvian Bridge across the Tiber, Constantine saw—or so he claimed late in life—a cross above the sun in the sky, with the words "Be victorious in this." His troops went into battle with crosses on their shields and won a decisive victory. Maxentius drowned and Constantine became the unquestioned senior emperor.

Convinced that he owed his victory to the Christian God, Constantine (r. 306–337) immediately put an end to persecution. On the site of what had been a military barracks, he built a church for the bishop of Rome—a vast, dark basilica, or hall, in the form traditionally used in Rome for public buildings. Crises would return in later years; but Christianity itself would become, as we will see, the religion of the empire and of regions far beyond it. The little movement of Jesus and his followers had transformed the world.

CONCLUSION

The Roman Empire, in its centuries of growth and consolidation, left a deep imprint on the Mediterranean world and the lands to the north and west. The Latin language, which spread with empire, would gradually develop into the Romance languages. Roman roads and fortifications survived, often in continued use, for centuries. And the memory of a great power that had stretched across what is now Europe would remain—and inspire repeated attempts at revival, not only in western Europe, but in many other lands as well.

In some ways, though, Christianity—modest though its institutions were in these centuries—proved even more durable, and even more powerful. The dramatic new understanding of the self and its place in the universe, and the vivid promise of salvation, amounted to a spiritual revolution, which also reshaped society across the Mediterranean world and beyond. What began as the creed of small groups of outsiders like Perpetua and her fellow martyrs became the theology of an institution that spread more widely than the empire itself, and that took over, as the empire fell on hard times, tasks that had once been central to the emperor's office. There is no Roman Empire today, and no one is trying to revive it. But Christianity continues—sometimes, as in Rome, within the same churches built by Constantine, the first Christian emperor.

[CHAPTER REVIEW]

KEY TERMS

barbarians (p. 152)   **gospels** (p. 160)   **Gnostics** (p. 171)   **tetrarchy** (p. 177)

Second Temple (p. 158)   **New Testament** (p. 160)   **bishop** (p. 173)   **Great Persecution** (p. 178)

Pharisees (p. 158)   **Paul** (p. 161)   **Goths** (p. 174)

Jesus (p. 159)   **Trinity** (p. 171)   **Diocletian** (p. 177)

REVIEW QUESTIONS

1. What were the most important sources of unity within the Roman Empire?

2. What made the "good emperors" of the Nerva-Antonine line so successful?

3. What was the importance of Greek culture in imperial Rome?

4. What made Jesus's message more radical than that of other dissident Jews?

5. Why did Christianity find such a receptive audience within the Roman Empire?

6. How did the apostle Paul help to shape Christian theology?

7. What were the hallmarks of early Christian communities?

8. How did Rome's persecution of Christians help make the early church stronger?

9. What threats did Rome face at the empire's borders in the second and third centuries?

10. What were the most important reforms made by Diocletian?

CORE OBJECTIVES

After reading this chapter you should have a solid understanding of the following core objectives. To strengthen your grasp of the core objectives, use the resources on the Student Site for The West.

- Identify the factors that contributed to the Roman Empire's stability and prosperity during its first two centuries.

- Trace the emergence of new sects and new beliefs among the Jews of the imperial period.

- Identify the major steps in the development of the small Jesus movement into early Christianity.

- Describe the characteristics of the mature Christian church of the second and third centuries.

- Evaluate the internal and external challenges to Roman power starting at the end of the second century, and Rome's response to them.

 GO TO **inQuizitive** TO SEE WHAT YOU'VE LEARNED—AND LEARN WHAT YOU'VE MISSED—WITH PERSONALIZED FEEDBACK ALONG THE WAY.

CHRONOLOGY

Early 3rd century
Origen and other Christian scholars
create canonical Old and New Testaments

325
Council of Nicea

324–330
Constantine founds
Constantinople

By 346
Some 3,000
monasteries
exist in Egypt

363
Jovian
reestablishes
Christianity

395
Theodosius I divides the
empire between west and east

380
Edict of
Thessalonica

313
Edict of Milan

337
Constantine is baptized
as a Christian

360–363
Julian re-creates paganism

378
Roman defeat at Adrianople;
Alaric unites the Goths

390s
Augustine writes
his *Confessions*

Late 4th century
Jerome begins
the Vulgate Bible

6

The Late Roman Empire and the Consolidation of the Church

312–476

Byzantium, a small Greek city, had stood for centuries, a prosperous trading center on a peninsula at the well-placed point where Asia and Europe meet. There, between 324 and 330, Constantine founded a magnificent city that he named Nea Rom ("New Rome"). Soon renamed Constantinople ("Constantine's City"), it celebrated its official birthday on a day chosen by astrologers as propitious. Constantine, who considered raising great buildings to be central to his imperial role, equipped his new creation with every architectural feature of an important Roman city. He built a forum, a circus, and a splendid imperial palace, which subsequent rulers would enlarge and rebuild for centuries. Later, in 413–14, the emperor Theodosius II would construct twelve miles of thick walls around the city, with eighty-six gates and hundreds of towers, which protected Constantinople from invasion for almost a thousand years.

Constantine's city was a Christian capital, equipped with fifty churches, but its location made it something else as well: a shopping mall for the whole Mediterranean world. The city's arcaded main street was laid out on two levels, an upper one for pedestrians and a lower one for shops that sold everything from precious stones and purple silks to spices. Traders from all over the world came to Constantinople to exchange their goods—many

From Palace to Church When the fourth-century consul Junius Annius Bassus decorated his palace in Rome, he included this marble inlay showing him at the head of a procession of chariots. Around 150 years later (ca. 470), a Germanic general occupying Bassus's palace donated the building to the pope. It remained a church until the seventeenth century, with this image as a reminder of its pre-Christian history.

FOCUS QUESTIONS

- How did Constantine strengthen Christianity in the empire?
- How did Constantine and his successors attempt to fortify the empire?
- What factors weakened the empire in the later fourth century?
- What major beliefs and philosophies competed in late imperial culture?
- How did Christianity respond to the rival beliefs of the period?
- What new developments in Christianity strengthened its position?
- How did imperial authority come under challenge?
- How did Jerome and Augustine set a new foundation for the Latin church?
- How can an empire fall and no one notice?

having traveled the Silk Road west from China across grassy steppes, mountain passes, and desert oases. They arrived to be astonished by the city's magnificent white marble buildings, which seemed to float above the waters of the Bosporus strait. For centuries, Constantinople would be the central node on trade and information networks that stretched over land and sea from Asia to western Europe. Apparently, the Roman city—one of the chief building blocks of the empire—still had life in it.

In some ways, Constantinople was simply the newest and largest of the great cities of Asia Minor, such as Antioch and Ephesus, in which Greek literature and culture flourished under Roman imperial rule. In other ways, though, it was distinctive: not exactly like the old imperial capital of Rome or the Greek cities of the empire. Its institutions, though Roman, were less elaborate than those of Rome. Constantinople was governed by a proconsul, one of the officials who normally governed provinces of the empire, and though it had a Senate, its members carried a lower status and less grand titles than their counterparts in Rome. The complex web of institutions that looked after streets and sewage, cared for temples, and preserved public order in Rome did not exist in Constantinople. Constantine himself used grants

of land to encourage settlers and provided free food for citizens. For all its wealth, Constantine's great city had an improvised character. The columns and statues that made the city so splendid were, for the most part, brought from elsewhere in the empire rather than fabricated there. Constantinople's mixture of public grandeur and institutional weakness was typical of the late Roman Empire as a whole, from its restoration in the decades just before and after 300 until it finally flickered out of existence a few centuries later.

Constantinople was typical of its period, also, in the way in which cultures and traditions mingled in it. The city's inhabitants spoke Greek, but Latin continued to be used in the legal system, and bureaucrats prided themselves on their knowledge of ancient Roman and Etruscan customs. Constantine, who favored Christianity, prohibited the building of new pagan temples, but the existing temples continued to be active, and the goddess of Fortune was not only invited into the city but celebrated. The statue of Constantine atop a colossal column held a smaller statue of Fortune in his hand. The emperor cared for the preservation of other Roman customs, such as chariot racing, for which he greatly expanded the city's existing racecourse, the Hippodrome. Like the eastern empire that would eventually have its capital in Constantinople, the city was a newer and more distinctive community than its inhabitants liked to admit.

CONSTANTINE AND CHRISTIANITY

Constantine himself is a mysterious figure, his embrace of Christianity ambiguous. He held off from formal baptism until 337, when he was nearing death. He destroyed a few pagan temples and eventually prohibited sacrifice, yet he generally allowed temples to remain. His image continued for many years to appear on coins decorated with the image and name of the sun-god. The arch built in Rome to commemorate his triumph discreetly omitted the names of both the pagan gods and the Christian God. Historians have sometimes been quick to point out what look like contradictions in Constantine's policy, and to condemn him as a hypocrite—someone who chose to throw his weight behind the new church for solely political reasons. But they overlook the fluidity of belief in this period, when as we will see, pagan and Christian practices often overlapped. They also overlook the differences between modern and ancient customs, both Christian and non-Christian. Many Christian converts postponed baptism until they were near death, and rulers in the ancient world often chose to follow a particular divinity for pragmatic reasons. Seen in this framework, Constantine's decision to cast his lot with the divinity that had led his troops to victory at the Milvian Bridge was a plausible response to his own experience. What we can say about Constantine is that from 312, he supported Christianity.

BUILDING NEW CHURCHES

That support came first of all in material form. The **Edict of Milan**, which Constantine issued in February 313, ordered the return of meeting places and other property that had been confiscated from Christians during the Great Persecution initiated by Diocletian. In the years

Constantinople and Other Cities in the East, 324 Founded by the emperor Constantine on the site of the Greek city of Byzantium, Constantinople was located at a key point along networks of trade, ideas, and Christian beliefs.

to come, he endowed the church with more lands and properties.

At the same time, he set out to build the first great public churches for what had been a persecuted religion—for example, the Lateran and the Vatican churches in Rome, which he began and his successors completed. These basilicas were immense halls modeled on the public spaces of Roman political life and designed to give the church the visible authority of great Roman institutions. As the faithful entered through the basilica doors, the bishop and the priests, standing at the altar at the opposite end, looked like high Roman officials. Brilliantly colored mosaics portrayed the members of the Holy Family and the saints and retold in visual form the stories of the Hebrew Bible and the New Testament. These new churches became centers of Christian life, teaching, and worship, some of which have remained to the present day.

Constantine This sculpture of Constantine's head was part of a colossal statue that once stood in the basilica the emperor built in Rome to commemorate his victory at the battle of Milvian Bridge.

As Rome's prestige grew, the bishops of Rome came to see themselves as the successors of Saint Peter, the apostle who had evangelized Rome and died there in or after 64 CE. They began to claim precedence over other bishops: eventually the title *papa* ("pope"), originally used for all high clerics, became exclusively theirs. And the Roman church began to use Latin, not Greek, as its language—and not just any Latin, but that of the Roman Empire, in which the **pope**, like the emperor, spoke of himself as "we."

The Church of the Nativity and the Church of the Holy Sepulcher, which Constantine had built in Bethlehem and Jerusalem, respectively, also became centers of the Christian cult. And Palestine itself became, for the first time, the imaginative center of Christianity—the goal for those who embarked on a new sort of travel, known as pilgrimage, to see the great sites of Christianity's early dramas, and for thousands more to dream about.

A NEW STATUS

Constantine did more than make the church richer and grander. Like Augustus, Constantine reoriented time itself, ordering the empire to adapt its public calendar to the seven-day week of the church and respect the Christian day of rest, on Sunday. By doing so, he dramatized the new status of Christianity in the empire. He did the same, as we will see, even more effectively in 325 when he convoked a council of the church at Nicea. Arius (ca. 250–336), a priest in Alexandria, had been arguing, in defiance of his own bishop, that only God the Father (and not Jesus) had existed eternally. On this and other points, the council laid down what would become central beliefs of Catholic Christianity.

Yet even the emperor could not impose unity on the entire church. The position that only God is divine, which came to be known as **Arianism**, remained influential in the empire and beyond, and compromise positions continued to be proposed. The late empire remained home to a lively and diverse array of religious beliefs and practices. For all his power and his capacity to innovate, Constantine could not change that.

THE EMPIRE RECAST: FROM CONSTANTINE TO THEODOSIUS I (312–395)

The late empire, as Constantine consolidated it in the early fourth century, rested on foundations laid by Diocletian. His policies had enriched the imperial treasury, and Constantine used the accumulated wealth for his own enterprises. Diocletian had also been a great builder, who provided Rome with an enormous new public bathhouse and reared a grand palace for himself in Split, in modern Croatia. He, too, had spent much of his time campaigning and ruling in the eastern territories of the empire. Above all, Diocletian set the tone for the reconfiguration of the empire. Whereas Augustus and other early rulers of Rome had refused titles that reflected their power, Diocletian took the title *dominus* ("lord") and wore a diadem.

Solidus On this gold coin from 326, Constantine wears the laurel wreath crown, an old Roman symbol. The Latin inscription proclaims that his power is ordained by God.

A VAST BUREAUCRACY

Constantine and his successors continued to make the empire more splendid, formal, and elaborate. The civil service had been small and rickety in the age of Augustus and his immediate successors. Local notables across the empire had mostly concentrated on their home cities, which they defended at court when necessary and enriched with gifts of public buildings. After the violence and dislocation of the third century, however, this local elite was slowly replaced by a new one of imperial servants, who looked to the emperor and his representatives. The late empire employed some 30,000 administrators, divided into military and civil services and responsible for oversight of everything from the imperial armies to the local affairs of cities. A detailed gazetteer lists them all, with their titles and duties, the hierarchy of their offices, and even the postal privileges each of them enjoyed. The empire had become a vast bureaucracy.

The emperor himself became a grander and more distant figure than ever before. Only foreign rulers, diplomats, and members of the imperial family could gain access to the emperor and his successors, figures as stately and splendid as animated statues in their official costumes, richly worked in purple and gold. As the court moved, the cities where it came to rest—Arles, in what is now the south of France, and Trier, in western Germany, as well as Constantinople—became splendid ceremonial centers.

ECONOMIC REFORMS

Constantine worked hard to promote prosperity. Drawing gold from the treasuries of pagan temples, he created a new gold coin, the solidus, which stabilized the currency and continued to be minted for centuries. Through legislation he provided tax exemptions for cities that had been hit especially hard by the disturbances of the last century. Constantine did his best to restore agricultural labor forces where civil war had created "deserted fields," as abandoned lands were called. He settled military veterans in some areas and gave tax concessions to help landlords in others.

PROSPERITY Romans in many regions of the empire prospered for much of the fourth century. In Britain, Romans living both in towns and in country villas laid down splendid mosaic floors in their houses. Favored cities in the western empire grew with stunning speed. So did the cities of Asia Minor, stimulated by the building of Constantinople. In North Africa and in Palestine as well, landowners prospered as the eastern cities boomed. And trade flourished, as indicated by the new wrecks full of wine and wheat that joined the dozens of older ones on the floor of the Mediterranean, and by the continued distribution around the empire of goods such as pots made in Gaul.

STRESS Yet there were signs of stress as well. Constantine's government weighed heavily on its subjects. The solidus, which made the imperial currency the literal gold standard for all transactions, also, as contemporaries noted, increased the gap between rich and poor. Higher taxes were needed to maintain armies large enough to protect the frontiers and to support the massive civil service. And because the armies had to be mobile to combat threats on the frontiers, the government needed its revenues in currency rather than grain, so far as possible. Some provinces of the empire—Asiana, for example, in western Asia Minor—were overwhelmed by garrisons of soldiers and demands for taxes in the form of tithes on locally produced grain. A new tax on business transactions, collected every four years, and a new head tax brought choruses of complaint that the government was stifling enterprise in every field.

THE *COLONI* Most consequential in the long run, though, was Constantine's decision to bind many groups of Romans to the places where they lived and worked. Again following Diocletian, he required that *curiales* (local officials) make up any shortfalls in the expected tax revenues. As notable families began to try to evade these offices, legislation tied them—and their descendants—to their posts. Agricultural workers were legally bound, first on imperial lands and then throughout the empire, to the land they cultivated. Forced to stay in place as laborers on the great estates, liable to taxes as well as exactions from their landlords, these *coloni* were legally free, but substantively as confined as slaves. So were artisans in the cities, who were bound to their crafts.

CONSTANTINE'S SUCCESSORS

Some of the fourth-century emperors carried on the fratricidal tradition that Diocletian had tried to end with the advent of the Tetrarchy in 293. After Constantine died, two of his nephews were murdered. But other emperors worked as intensively as Constantine to improve their inheritance. Julian (r. 360–363), another of Constantine's nephews, reversed what seems in retrospect the normal pattern of conversion. He left Christianity, in which he had been raised, for paganism, which he tried to restore

Coloni A detail from a fourth-century Carthaginian mosaic shows agricultural laborers—possibly *coloni*—delivering ducks and other produce to the owner of the estate, a lounging, richly dressed woman. In the background, child workers harvest olives from a tree.

throughout the empire. The version of pagan religion that Julian favored was much tighter and less tolerant than paganism had traditionally been—a religion in a new sense: more like Christianity, which demanded more than formal adherence. After dismissing the Christian bishops and priests who had received official support from Constantine, Julian reestablished the pagan temples that had ceased to function. Splendidly educated, he took pleasure in using his excellent classical Greek to denounce anyone who ventured to criticize or disagree with him. Julian also set out to stabilize Rome's frontiers. But in 363, in the course of a border war with the Sasanian Empire, he received a mortal wound, and the revival of paganism came to a halt, though not quite to an end.

Julian's successor, Jovian, who ruled for less than a year, reestablished Christianity as the imperial religion. Jovian's successor, Valentinian I (r. 364–375), was an effective soldier who seemed to restore the prestige and power of the empire everywhere at once. A long series of campaigns across both the Rhine and the Danube repelled threatened invasions and enabled Valentinian to strengthen both frontiers with further fortifications. Through effective mobilization of resources he defeated a massive invasion of Roman Britain by three allied Germanic peoples, and ran his own successful campaign in North Africa. By the end of his reign, Rome was again the greatest power in the Mediterranean world.

THEODOSIUS I

Theodosius I (r. 379–395), Valentinian's chief general, was almost as effective when he himself became emperor

THE OBELISK OF THEODOSIUS

In 390, the Roman emperor Theodosius I raised an ancient Egyptian obelisk in the Hippodrome, the racetrack in Constantinople. Two inscriptions on the monument's base proclaim the power of Theodosius. The writing on the southeast side, visible from the seats of the emperor and his officials, is in Latin, the official language of Roman law, government, and the army. The northwest inscription, facing the crowd, is in Greek, the common tongue of the eastern empire. The obelisk also features hieroglyphs that commemorate the victory of an early Egyptian king.

The southwest side, pictured here, shows a chariot race on its lower half. Above the race, orderly rows of officials and guards occupy the imperial box. Although damaged, the four seated figures are probably of high rank, as every other figure is standing. Two officials flank what may be a staircase that leads from the Hippodrome up to Theodosius's box. The obelisk's inscriptions and imagery announce the stability of the emperor's rule at a time of declining imperial strength.

QUESTIONS FOR ANALYSIS

1. What cultural and class intersections are present in the inscriptions on the obelisk and its base?
2. Why was the Hippodrome a politically useful place to raise this obelisk?
3. Why would the message of the obelisk have been particularly important in the context of the declining Roman population and the pressures on the empire's borders in the late fourth century?

in 379, not long after the death of his old master and his brother Valens. (Valens ruled the eastern empire from 364 to 378, when, as we will see, he died in combat against Gothic invaders.) Like Valentinian, Theodosius was a ruthless and effective commander. He defeated and killed Magnus Maximin, a western commander who usurped power in Gaul and Italy. Like Valentinian, too, he moved back and forth between Constantinople and Milan, now the capital of the western empire, and maintained his power in the west by promoting Latins and wooing the

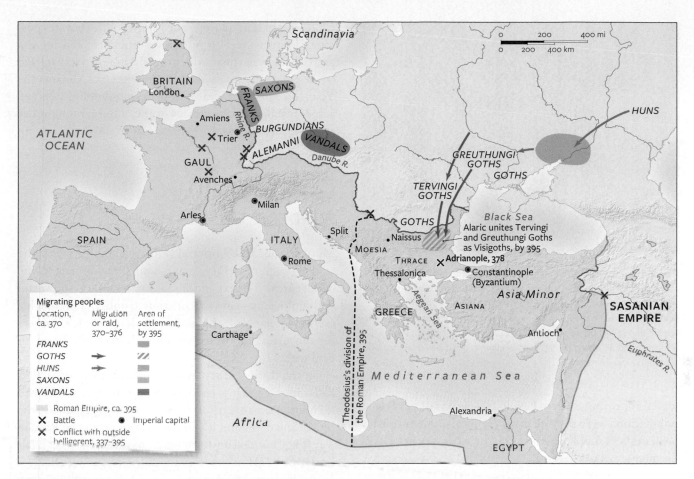

The Empire in Reverse, ca. 337–395 Beginning in the late third century, rival forces began to put pressure on the Roman Empire's borders. The Sasanian Empire was a major threat in the east, while Germanic tribes such as the Goths, Franks, and Vandals began to push into Roman territory from the north. In 378, Roman forces suffered a devastating defeat at Adrianople after confronting a group of Goths who had moved into Roman territory.

old senatorial families in Rome—even those that had supported Magnus Maximin. The Edict of Thessalonica, which Theodosius issued in 380, declared the form of Christianity that had been established by the Council of Nicea the official religion of the empire. He deposed Arian bishops and declared the pope in Rome—Damasus, who held office from 366 to 384—the guardian of orthodoxy. Though Theodosius did not destroy pagan temples by direct action, he did not punish those who did, and he abolished the order of Vestal Virgins at Rome and the Olympic Games.

Yet even Theodosius could not always impose his will. Unable to defeat the Germanic peoples who had entered imperial territory, he settled them as allies in Thrace and Moesia (Serbia). He also made a treaty with the Sasanian Empire. Though he celebrated both events as military victories, they showed the limits of his power. It may have been his realization of those limits that led him to divide the empire again, at his death in 395, between his sons Arcadius (in the east) and Honorius (in the west).

THE EMPIRE IN REVERSE

Slowly, over the later fourth century, the great imperial project went into reverse gear. The area of settlement in many cities shrank—Amiens from 250 acres to 25, Avenches from 370 to 22. Large-scale projects such as Diocletian's baths were few, and such resources as were available were often spent on surrounding the shrunken city cores with walls. By the end of the fourth century, even areas that had recently shown great prosperity—such as Roman Britain—saw their cities shrink. Archaeologists have found evidence of squatters in possession of buildings, blocked ditches and sewers, and urban land being

Agricultural Estates When cities declined, wealth moved to the countryside. This fourth-century Carthaginian mosaic indicates the vast number of people necessary for the operation of a large-scale landed estate, from those who grew vegetables and fruit to those who hunted and raised domesticated livestock. The structure at center is a reminder that all the estate's profits belonged to the wealthy elites who owned it.

used for farming, even in London—a clear indication that populations were diminishing. Coins also seem to have been in short supply, a disruption caused by the attacks of Germanic tribes.

POVERTY AND WEALTH IN THE COUNTRYSIDE

On the land, latifundia, large agrarian estates with bound labor, continued to develop, and small-scale farming to decline. More and more of the poorer population found itself attached to the land. Conditions varied: in some cases, laborers voluntarily agreed to become coloni in return for protection; others tried to escape. In 419, it was discovered that a number of high imperial officials were runaway coloni. The restrictions on them were tight. Male coloni had to marry daughters of coloni. They could not sell their property without their landlord's permission. They paid their taxes through the landlord, as well as paying him rent. And they could not sue him. In the ninth and tenth centuries and after, the majority of Europe's agricultural workers would become serfs, legally unfree and bound to the land. Though the coloni were not their direct ancestors, their attachment to the land marked the beginning of a period of many centuries during which most of Europe's inhabitants would be unfree.

The great senatorial families, far from the imperial court even in Italy, played little role in politics but still possessed immense wealth. Wherever cities declined, money, power, and even the production of art and poetry moved to the great villas of wealthy landowners like Melania the Younger. This aristocratic woman's landholdings, spread across five distinct provinces of the empire, brought her as much revenue as two North African provinces paid in taxes.

PRESSURES ON THE BORDERS: THE GOTHS

More serious, the imperial borders established by the soldier-emperors Diocletian and Constantine came under threat. The expanding Sasanian Empire—powerful and ambitious—caused constant trouble. The Goths, Germanic peoples who had lived along Rome's borders for centuries, continued to prove difficult for Rome to deal with.

By the third century, as we have seen, the Goth tribes had consolidated into lasting confederations and launched raids into Roman territory. They also adapted to life in the remaining cities and learned how to fight in the Roman way. They wielded uniform weapons produced in specialized workshops, as the Romans did. A missionary bishop, Ulfila, had converted them to Christianity—though they adopted a theology that was close to Arianism—and even provided them with an alphabet, with which a translation of the Bible could be written down. Constantine and later emperors made them *foederati*—formal allies.

Goths As the Goths moved into western Europe, they increasingly encountered and came into conflict with the people of the Roman Empire. This chaotic marble relief from a mid-third-century sarcophagus shows Romans locked in fierce combat with Germanic tribesmen, identifiable by their thick beards and bare chests.

ADRIANOPLE In the later fourth century, the **Huns**, horse-borne nomads from the east who were skilled archers, began to devastate the Goths' settled agrarian communities, situated outside the Roman walls and fortresses. In 376 the Goths asked for permission to cross the border and enter the Roman Empire. The eastern emperor Valens agreed. Two years later he decided that he had made a mistake and confronted the Goths—and perhaps some of the Huns—in Thrace. He did not wait for the troops of his western fellow emperor, Gratian, to reach the field, and faced an army as large as his near **Adrianople** in 378. Pulled out of line and surprised by the cavalry of the Goths' allies, the Romans suffered a devastating defeat. Valens himself died in the rout, along with 20,000 of his 30,000 soldiers. It was in the aftermath of this decisive battle that the Goth leader Alaric united the Tervingi, the Greuthungi, and others into a single people, who came to be known as the Visigoths.

THE AFTERMATH From now on, even such strong emperors as Theodosius I had to treat the Goths more or less as equals, using their military power to supplement that of the shrinking Roman armies. Gothic kingdoms began to develop inside what had been Roman territory.

The emperors found no way to resist any given group of "barbarians"—as the Romans of the time of Augustus or Marcus Aurelius would have called them—except by forming alliances with other ones. By the end of the fourth century, Vandals, Franks, and other Germanic peoples warred with one another in northern Gaul. Over the next hundred years, they took over more than half of the former territory of the empire. Meanwhile, the Huns continued to harry Romans and Goths alike. The western empire—with longer and more dangerous borders to defend than the east, and poor revenues with which to pay for its armies—was in clear decline.

The eastern empire had its share of defeats. The army that the Goths destroyed at Adrianople belonged to the east, and the Huns sacked the eastern fortress city of Naissus in Serbia in 441. Eastern emperors paid a heavy tribute to Attila, leader of the Huns—so heavy, according to one source, that providing the revenue for it drove some hard-pressed taxpayers to commit suicide. In the end, though, the sea and the walls of Constantinople protected the heartland of the eastern empire in Asia Minor from the resettlements, invasions, and wars that transformed the western empire.

Gothic Alliances As the Goths became more powerful and settled inside the boundaries of the empire, Romans had to make alliances with them to ensure peace. Even the daughter of Emperor Theodosius I, Galla Placidia—shown wearing a pearl necklace and earrings in this fifth-century portrait with her son and daughter—was briefly married to a Gothic king after she was captured by Alaric.

A DYNAMIC CULTURE: COMPETING BELIEFS AND RIVAL PHILOSOPHIES

In these conditions, it did not come as a surprise to the well-informed clerics and senators of Rome when the Visigoth leader Alaric besieged their city in 408 and sacked it in 410. But some found in this event confirmation of their fears that the empire was collapsing. After Julian, the emperors had sided more and more completely with the Christian church. Pagan sacrifices were prohibited. The great altar of the goddess Victory, at which Roman senators had been initiated into their duties for centuries, was removed. Some of those who had never converted blamed Christians for the city's fall from its former greatness. As we will see, the same period in which the western empire lost so much of its power and cohesion saw the church reach a new level of organization and stature. But even as Christianity became the imperial religion, it faced competition at every level—from long-established forms of philosophy and from newer revelations that circulated through the vast and rapid communications systems of the empire.

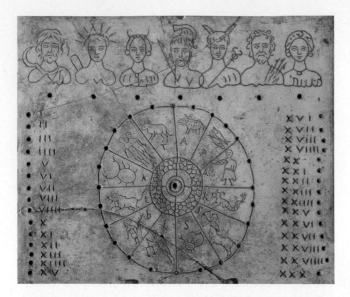

Roman Astrology A first-century Roman calendar associates each month with a sign of the zodiac, and each day of the week with a god from the Olympian pantheon linked to one of the planets, indicating the importance of astrological symbolism in daily life.

ASTROLOGY: GODS IN THE PLANETS

In the Hellenistic centuries, Babylonian diviners, who used the positions of the planets to predict the future of everything from individuals to nations, brought their techniques into the Greek kingdoms, where they fused with Egyptian ideas about time and Greek astronomical methods. By the first century BCE, astrological beliefs and practices were rapidly spreading through the Roman world as well. Learned Greeks and Romans practiced astrology as a complex, demanding art, and even men and women of great power turned to astrologers for advice on critical matters. The emperor Tiberius (r. 14–37 CE), for example, relied on the counsels of a professional astrologer, Thrasyllus, who may not have read the stars but certainly understood his employer. When Tiberius had him stand at the edge of a cliff, next to a powerful slave, and asked what he thought of his own future, Thrasyllus replied that everything looked dark. Struck by the accuracy of the astrologer's prediction, the emperor relied on his advice, which sometimes moderated Tiberius's cruelty.

THE SEARCH FOR PERSONAL REVELATION AND GUIDANCE

People at every social level sought advice not only from diviners, but also from traditional oracles like the one at Delphi in Greece, from specialists in explicating dreams, and from magicians and charmers. Many searched for gods who could provide them with a satisfactory understanding of the universe and intimate personal guidance. In the middle of the second century, for example, a previously successful Greek orator named Aelius Aristides became ill. For twelve years he lay in bed unable to move, tormented by strange dreams. When Aelius did manage to get up, he subjected himself to violent exercise routines, running barefoot in the mud or swimming in the ocean in midwinter. He did all this because the god Asclepius, who specialized in healing, appeared in his dreams and gave him instructions. Asclepius comforted Aelius and prescribed mild therapies as well as the violent ones: suffering from a sore throat, Aelius dreamed that the god instructed him to gargle.

Aelius tried to lead an old-fashioned life. Like most Greek writers during this period, he did his best to use the traditional vocabulary and language of Greek prose at its classic height. In religion, too, he saw himself as a traditionalist. Yet he forged a personal relationship with his protective divinity, whose immediate presence he felt, while Zeus and the other Olympians remained distant figures, irrelevant to his everyday needs and problems. Many other residents of the vast Roman Empire felt similar needs and, like Aelius, found themselves unable to fulfill them by joining in the traditional temple cults.

EASTERN CULTS

The search for insight into the larger meaning of life, moreover, took place at a time when individuals—not only well-born Romans, but also much poorer men and women—could see and experience a wide range of religions. They could watch animal sacrifice and listen to prayers being offered at the ancient cult centers of their own cities, since the Romans allowed traditional priesthoods to carry out their rituals so long as they acknowledged the supremacy of Roman gods and the Roman emperor.

And while emperors battled to keep foreign powers from invading Roman territory, the imperial borders yielded to individual travelers and their beliefs. Egyptian and Syrian temples enticed pilgrims with spectacular rituals couched in mysterious Eastern languages. Newer Eastern cults and Westernized versions of them, like the Egyptian cult of Isis, also spread. Often these revelations rested on little direct knowledge of the traditions that had spawned them. After the defeat of Antony and Cleopatra

Eastern Cults Religious practices from distant reaches of the empire also shaped belief at its center. A fresco from first-century Naples portrays Isis-Fortuna, a Roman interpretation of the Egyptian goddess Isis. She is decorated with celestial motifs and attended by a winged cupid and by her son, Harpocrates—a Hellenistic rendering of the Egyptian god Horus—on horseback.

in 31 BCE, the Egyptian priests gradually lost their command of the ancient hieroglyphic texts that preserved the rituals and beliefs of their ancient nation. Few priests could write a text, even when a Roman emperor wanted one to adorn an obelisk.

Around the second or third century a new cult, centering on the revelations of an ancient prophet named Thrice-Wise Hermes, found adherents in Egypt and elsewhere. Its founding texts were stitched together in Greek from mixed remnants of Egyptian religion, recalled in fragments, and Greek philosophy. Throughout the Mediterranean, at the same time, magical texts attributed to Hermes provided readers with astrological, alchemical, and magical recipes. It was an extraordinary moment. Any citizen of a fairly cosmopolitan Roman city in, say, Asia Minor could read about, and some could experience, half a dozen revelations and their associated rituals. Christianity developed—and soon found its most learned and powerful supporters—amid this extraordinary cultural ferment.

RIVAL PHILOSOPHIES AND THE VIRTUOUS LIFE

Those in search of guidance could find philosophies, as well as cults, that offered what they needed. The search

for an understanding of the universe, and the passion to lead a virtuous life, were deeply rooted in the civilization of the Romans. For centuries, Greek philosophers had offered their own form of guidance to the virtuous life. From Pythagoras and Socrates on, they had not only offered definitions of virtue but provided examples of it in action, and even organized communities whose members could pursue the truth and the good life. Romans such as Cicero offered introductions to the beliefs of Platonists and Aristotelians, Stoics and Epicureans, in accessible Latin works. Here, too, inhabitants of the empire could hope to find personal guidance.

Two forms of Greek philosophy in particular—Stoicism and Epicureanism—were popular in the Roman world. In his *Meditations,* Marcus Aurelius, one of Rome's highly effective "good emperors," examined his daily life and work in the light of his Stoical convictions. Doing so, he learned how little his grand military successes mattered in the universe at large. Warfare, he realized, was nothing more than "dogs fighting over a bone." By learning to see his own deeds from a critical distance, he shaped his self as rigorously and virtuously as—and more effectively than—he shaped his larger society. And the Stoic emperor was only one of many who tried to live a life of both action and contemplation.

NEOPLATONISM: PHILOSOPHY AS CULT

The Platonic tradition also drew thought and action together in ways that remained influential in Rome. In the centuries after Plato's death, the members of his Academy explored philosophical positions very different from Plato's own. In the second and third centuries, a new version of Platonism took shape that owed as much to Aristotle as to Plato.

Plotinus (204/205–270), the most charismatic advocate of **Neoplatonism**, believed that he was restoring the ancient core of the philosopher's teachings. His synthesis would dominate the reading and teaching of Plato for centuries to come. Deeply committed to living the tenets of his philosophy, and idealistic in the extreme, Plotinus regretted that he even had a body. Still, he saw the universe as a great and beautiful chain that stretched, each link in place, from the divine being that had created it all the way down to the earth. The gods, Plotinus held, ruled this universe, as its symphonic beauty made clear. The sage should seek an understanding of the cosmic order and its purpose by mastering mathematics and the other central disciplines, and by learning to apply them with discipline and imagination. Knowledge, for Plotinus, must be pursued not only for its own sake but also because it was the path to virtue. As the wise had long understood, philosophy was not only an intellectual but also a moral discipline, one designed to lead those who followed it to the good life. So far Plato himself might well have agreed.

But Plotinus's practices were not all traditional. The philosopher, as Plotinus embodied him, still used reason to seek the truth, but he was now a holy, as well as a wise, man. Gods spoke to him directly, and he used techniques of incantation to exploit their powers. The form of philosophy that he and his followers stood for, moreover, was very different from Plato's. Plato had cast his arguments as dialogues, which mimicked the form of living speech and suggested that there might be more than one side to a debate. Plotinus, by contrast, read widely in many traditions beside his own and, like Aristotle, composed formal treatises. His chief disciple, Porphyry (245–ca. 305), arranged his teacher's works in systematic form and used it to wage war against rival revelations—notably that of the Christians.

Other Neoplatonists followed up on hints in Plotinus and argued that his thought was the culmination not only of Greek but also of ancient Near Eastern history—that it encapsulated the revelations of the ancient Egyptian and Babylonian priests. In the Mediterranean world of the third century, antiquity was still the source of authoritative patterns in thought, in literature, and in the arts. Philosophy itself now became a learned, encyclopedic pursuit.

PAGAN CRITICS OF CHRISTIANITY

Over the second and third centuries, these multiplying philosophies and cults, with their many rewards, posed a serious challenge to Christianity. Though Christian numbers grew, the majority of Romans were still pagans, who had never regarded Christians with special favor. Like the Jews, after all, they practiced a religion whose tenets prevented them from taking part, as all citizens and subjects should, in the public forms of sacrifice and ritual staged in great temples across the empire. Neither group was willing to sacrifice to the emperor. Like the Jews, the Christians observed a day of rest. Worse still, rumor held, they emulated the worst deeds of the heroes of ancient Greek myth: they had sex with their mothers, like Oedipus, and ate their children, like Thyestes. What more could one expect, some pagans asked, from men and women whose God had died the most humiliating death, like a slave, on a cross?

Better-informed pagan critics of Christianity, such as Porphyry, wielded more sophisticated weapons. A trained scholar, Porphyry studied the Old and New Testaments as if they were Greek histories. The results were striking. The biblical books, he argued, swarmed with obvious errors and contradictions. It was clear, for example, that the book of Daniel, with its prophecies of events to come, had actually been written in the second century BCE, long after the events it described. As to Christ's commandments, they were perverse and foolish. To follow them, Porphyry stated, would be in itself clear evidence of folly.

FORGING A NEW CHRISTIAN CULTURE

From the second century on, Christian writers had found ways to answer at least some of these attacks. But in the third and early fourth centuries, a new Christian culture took shape—one that applied the tools of ancient scholarship and philosophy to defend the church. Throughout the Roman world, Christian communities were growing in towns that also harbored Greek and Roman temples, their cults in full operation, as well as Jewish synagogues, many of whose members saw the new religion as a perversion of their true one. Certain cities offered special opportunities for Christian missions—for example, Caesarea, a port town in Palestine that Herod had rebuilt in the first century BCE as the model of a Roman urban paradise with fine roads, temples, baths, a circus, and a theater. Caesarea had lively communities of every kind: Greeks and Romans loyal to their gods, Jews who prayed and read their Bible in Greek, Jews who prayed in Aramaic and read the Bible in Hebrew, and Christians.

These people of different languages and ideals lived side by side, walked the same streets, and argued in the same markets. In one case they even witnessed the same miracle—an outbreak of perspiration on temple pillars, which was reported independently by a Christian and a Jewish source, who interpreted the event very differently. In Caesarea, throughout Palestine, and in other eastern areas where many traditions intersected and interacted, Christianity took on new ideas and practices that redefined its relation to ancient culture.

ORIGEN OF ALEXANDRIA

If Porphyry became the charismatic leader of a new pagan philosophical school, his counterpart, **Origen** of Alexandria, became one of the first Christians who wielded the pagans' weapons as effectively as they did. Born into a Christian family around 175, Origen received traditional training in Greek scholarship and philosophy in his native city. A passionate Christian whose father died a martyr, he was devoted to the teachings of Jesus—so much so, according to some accounts, that when he found himself tortured by lust, he castrated himself to remove the cause of the problem. Steeped in the writings of the Jewish philosopher Philo (ca. 13 BCE–ca. 45 CE), as well as the works of Greek thinkers, Origen became a profound reader of the scriptures and an original theologian. In Alexandria, he mastered pagan learning but seems to have found little support. Once he moved to Caesarea, however, Origen set out to show that Christianity represented not the denial but the culmination of the best parts of ancient culture, Greek and Jewish alike.

To make this case, Origen had to clarify what Christianity stood for. Heretics, Gnostics, and even conventional Christians disagreed about what belonged in the Bible. During the second and third centuries, most Christians read not what we now call the Bible—a set group of texts, presented in a systematic order—but a more or less random collection of biblical books that circulated independently in scrolls. These were too small to hold more than a fraction of the New Testament, to say nothing of the Old. Many read texts that did not become part of the Christian biblical canon, or that were even declared heretical in later centuries, but which they had no particular reason to exclude from study and contemplation.

ASSEMBLING THE BIBLE Origen was one of many Christian scholars who collaborated to establish a canon: a set of texts generally recognized as orthodox. In twenty codices, Origen laid out the Old Testament, word by word, in Hebrew, then in Hebrew transliterated into Greek, and in four different Greek versions, none of them his own. And he dressed the texts of the Old and New Testaments in the protective garment of his commentaries, which were designed to lead readers who were not theologians through difficult passages to the hidden truth. The Bible,

Caesarea and Alexandria, 3rd Century

as Origen tried to recast it, became a source of central authority—authority of a new kind, in an organization that was equally novel.

But bringing the texts together caused new problems, for it showed that the Hebrew Bible and the Septuagint, the most widely used Greek translation made by Jews long before, often disagreed, as did manuscripts of the New Testament. If, as Origen believed, the Hebrew Bible and the New Testament were God's divine revelation, they could not contain serious mistakes or real contradictions. Wherever they seemed to err, accordingly, he read them as Greek scholars of his time often read Homer: allegorically. The tale of Jonah and the whale that swallowed him might seem problematic in the literal sense—but this meant only that it stood for a hidden, higher sense, which the puzzling narrative challenged the Christian reader to discover. In a massive series of editions and commentaries derived from his famous lectures on the biblical text, Origen assembled the first systematic Christian explication of the Bible.

A CHRISTIAN VIEW OF HISTORY Origen's reading of the Bible, in turn, underpinned an account of the order of the universe as stately and beautiful as those of the pagan Neoplatonists, with whom he had much in common. God, he explained, though one in nature, had three persons. Origen used a different terminology, but he accepted and defended the earlier Christian doctrine of the Trinity—the Father, the Son, and the Holy Ghost. He went on to connect God to the created world in novel and powerful ways. In the beginning, God had created not only the universe, but minds worthy to contemplate it and know it—and, by knowing it, to attain salvation. These created minds had had free will, which enabled them to choose not to know the truth and to fall into error in their ignorance. Like fallen stars, they lost their brilliance as they plunged into the darkness of the world of matter. But over time, Origen argued, as these souls lived and died (and he firmly believed in reincarnation), they would come to know the truth and then to follow it.

World history, accordingly, followed a clear arc—one that led from the confusion and disorder of the present to a future "restoration" when all things would be made simple and true once more. This idea, which Origen borrowed from the Stoics, he generalized into the first Christian

EARLY CHRISTIAN VIEWS OF MARRIAGE

Early Christians were adult converts who came from different social classes and backgrounds, and often combined their previous beliefs with their new ones. Clement of Alexandria was an early "Greek Father" and a Neoplatonist who was able to meld his knowledge of Greek Platonic philosophy with ideas from Christian belief and even some mysticism. Tertullian, a Latin church father from Carthage in the Roman province of Africa, saw Greek Platonic philosophy as misleading and suspect. This pairing of sources illustrates the presence within Christianity of competing social and religious views.

Clement of Alexandria, *Stromateis*

In *Stromateis* ("Patchwork"), Clement of Alexandria (150–215) discusses a variety of topics, including the scriptural exhortation to marry for procreation. He believed that marriage was a good and necessary institution, providing order in love and in the Christian's life.

Marriage is a union between a man and a woman; it is the primary union; it is a legal transaction; it is a spiritual transaction; it exists for the procreation of legitimate children.... So there is every reason to marry—for patriotic reasons, for the succession of children, for the fulfillment of the universe (insofar as it is our business). The poets regret a marriage which is "half-fulfilled" and childless, and bless the marriage which is "abundant in growth." Physical ailments demonstrate the necessity of marriage particularly well. A wife's care and her patient attention seem to surpass all the earnest devotion of other family and friends; she likes to excel all others in sympathy and present concern; she really and truly is, in the words of Scripture, a necessary "helper."...

It is a sign of weakness and unmanliness to try to escape from a partnership in life with wife and children. A state which it is wrong to reject must be totally right to procure. So with all the rest. In fact, they say the loss of children is one of the greatest evils. It follows that the acquisition of children is a good thing. If so, so is marriage. The poet says, "Without a father there could be no children, without a mother, not even conception of children." Marriage makes a man a father, a husband makes a woman a mother....Marriage must be kept pure, like a sacred object to be preserved from all stain.

Tertullian, *Ad Uxorem*

Tertullian (ca. 160–ca. 225) produced an extensive body of literature in defense of Latin Christian beliefs and practices. He praised marriage but considered the celibate, unmarried state of Christians like the apostle Paul to be superior, arguing that though it is "better to marry than to burn," chastity is preferable because it allows a Christian to remain more pure and be closer to God. *Ad Uxorem* ("To His Wife") was written on the occasion of the remarriage of a Christian widow to a non-Christian, a union abhorrent to Tertullian.

[T]here is no place at all where we read that nuptials are prohibited; of course on the ground that they are a good thing. What, however, is *better* than this good, we learn from the apostle [Paul], who *permits* marrying indeed, but *prefers* abstinence; the former on account of the insidiousnesses of temptations, the latter on account of the straits of the times. Now, by looking into the reason thus given for each proposition, it is easily discerned that the ground on which the power of marrying is conceded is *necessity*; but whatever *necessity* grants, she by her very nature depreciates. In fact, in that it is written, To marry is better than to burn, what, pray, is the nature of this good which is (only) commended by comparison with evil, so that the reason why marrying is *more* good is (merely) that burning is *less*? Nay, but how far better is it neither to marry nor to burn?

But if we listen to the apostle, forgetting what is behind, let us both strain after what is before, and be followers after the better rewards. Thus, albeit he does not cast a snare upon us, he points out what tends to utility when he says, the unmarried woman thinks on the things of the Lord, that both in body and spirit she may be holy; but the married is solicitous how to please her husband. But he nowhere permits marriage in such a way as not rather to wish us to do our utmost in imitation of his own example. Happy the man who shall prove like Paul!"

QUESTIONS FOR ANALYSIS

1. In *Stromateis*, how does Clement of Alexandria argue in favor of marriage and the family?
2. In *Ad Uxorem*, why does Tertullian argue that although marriage is good and a necessity, abstinence is better?
3. How and why do the early Christian writers feel conflicted about the relative values of marriage and celibacy?

Sources: Clement of Alexandria, *Stromateis* 2.23.137(1), 140(1), 142(3), 145(1), trans. John Ferguson (Washington, DC: 1991), pp. 249–54; Tertullian, *Ad Uxorem* 1.3, trans. S. Thelwall, in *The Ante-Nicene Fathers*, vol. 4, ed. Alexander Roberts, James Donaldson, and A. Cleveland Coxe (Buffalo, NY: 1885), p. 40.

philosophy of history. The great restoration, though inevitable, would happen only in the future—perhaps only after centuries. In the meantime, the Christian should lead, as Origen did, a life of extreme austerity, ideally in celibacy, poverty, and dedication to one's fellow Christians.

In Origen, the Christians at last had an exponent equal in learning and eloquence to the greatest of their opponents. He and his disciples—who were many and passionate—found that their faith sustained them through persecutions. During a savage campaign that the emperor Decius (r. 249–251) mounted against Christianity in the middle of the third century, Origen was arrested and tortured, and his sufferings probably hastened his death. But his books and his model of a new kind of Christian thought and scholarship survived.

INTERNAL DIVISIONS: MANICHEISM

By the third century, Christianity was becoming a learned, even a cultured, religion—the sort of religion that could appeal to highly educated men and women. But it was also threatened by new internal divisions. Even as Christian scholars debated with those pagan scholars who noted their existence—probably still a small minority—they also found themselves challenged, yet again, by rivals from within their ranks. The most powerful challenge came from the east—from outside the Roman Empire.

Mani (216–276), a Persian Christian a generation younger than Origen, began in the mid-third century to preach what he believed God had revealed to him. He knew the traditional Persian religion of Zoroastrianism, according to which the cosmos was the object of a great struggle between two great powers, being and not-being. In the course of his travels, which took him as far as India, he encountered Buddhism and Hinduism as well. Drawing on all of these traditions, as well as Christian Gnosticism, Mani explained the cosmos in a much more pessimistic way than Origen or the Zoroastrians had. His dualist vision distinguished sharply between the realm of spirit, which was good, and that of matter, which was evil. Before the world was created, matter had invaded spirit: the realms were mingled. Since then, souls had been locked in matter, and humans had been doomed to commit sins and then to expiate them by being reborn in the same condition, again and again, rather than escaping to the realm of pure spirit.

As the successor to Jesus, who had been pure spirit, Mani claimed, he could offer his followers not only an explanation of the universe, but a guide to life, which could release them from matter. He demanded that the "elect"—his most loyal followers—lead an ascetic life, for which he provided detailed rules. Prohibitions against eating certain foods, for example, enabled the Manichean to avoid harming any human spirit that might have entered a lesser being, such as a plant, in the course of reincarnation. These views and precepts had something in common with Origen's. Mani presented them, however, as the culmination not only of Christianity, but of the teachings of all wise men at all times. And he charged his ordinary followers, known as "hearers," not only with learning the true doctrines but also with providing for the elect.

Mani and Manicheans
The Persian mystic Mani used this rock-crystal seal to sign documents. Its design shows Mani flanked by two followers, and the Syriac inscription reads, "Mani, apostle of Jesus Christ."

Mani himself seems to have been executed by the Persian king. But Manichean monks, male and female, put his teachings into practice. A Manichean church grew up, with its own structure and offices. Missionaries soon took to the roads, bearing the scriptures and teachings of Mani everywhere from Spain, Italy, and Roman North Africa to China, where for hundreds of years Manichean churches continued to teach their dualist method and prescribe their rules for a truly holy life. In city after city, the Manicheans and other opponents from within the Christian camp challenged conventional Christians and their beliefs in public debates.

CHRISTIANITY: NEW SOURCES OF STRENGTH

In the fourth century the Christian church grew and changed rapidly. New bishops and clerics, called to replace those who had died in the persecutions and convulsions of the last hundred years, needed training. New churches needed correct, orthodox books with which to conduct services. And many Christians sought new, more intensive forms of spiritual life, which required further innovations. From Constantine on, emperors (except for Julian) transformed Christianity from a dissident sect—in radical opposition to official culture if not engaged in political rebellion against it—to the official religion of the empire. But it still needed defense against enemies, especially those, like the Manicheans, who seemed to have much in common with the Christians.

EUSEBIUS: ENVISIONING THE CHRISTIAN EMPIRE

Eusebius (ca. 260–ca. 339) was the most prominent of the Christian thinkers and writers who met these needs. A cleric from Caesarea, the cosmopolitan city in Palestine where Origen flourished, he came to maturity under the guidance of the saintly Pamphilus, with whom he corrected manuscripts of the Bible, even as his teacher awaited martyrdom in prison. Eusebius assembled all the information he could about the pagan and Christian past, and collected manuscripts of the Greek Old and New Testaments, the acts or records of the sufferings of martyrs, and the writings of Christian teachers. In Caesarea, a wealthy town and diocese, Eusebius had access not only to books but also to skilled scribes who could make multiple copies of them on command. He used these resources effectively to outdo all of his predecessors—including Origen, whose library he used intensively—in fashioning versions of the Bible and accounts of the Jewish and Christian past for Christians to use. He turned the local church into something like a media center for the new Christianity and the Christian empire.

REIMAGINING HISTORY Even before Constantine's victory in 312, Eusebius drew up the *Chronicle*, a long and complex series of comparative tables of world history—Egyptian, Assyrian, Persian, Jewish, and Roman. These showed Christianity—and its elder sibling, Judaism—to be far older than the culture of the Greeks. The tables also showed, in graphically clear form, that after older empires rose and fell, Rome had unified the world under a single empire just in time for the message of Christ to reach all of its citizens. Evidently, the Christian God was guiding the course of history.

After Constantine rose to power, Eusebius composed an equally innovative history of the church. This work, which unlike pagan histories was largely made up of older documents that gave it the ring of absolute authenticity, argued that true Christians had always accepted a core of canonical texts and doctrines. It vividly portrayed the sufferings of Christian martyrs, often in their own words, and it dismissed even the most serious challenges to Christian orthodoxy, such as the Manicheans, as madmen who "patched together false and godless doctrines." Two more works, both compiled from a vast range of pagan sources, argued that the best pagan thinkers had agreed with Christianity on basic points. A generous God had given

them partial revelations of the truths made fully accessible only to Jews and Christians.

THE EMPEROR AS CHRISTIAN HERO Faced with the need to explain how the Roman emperor could be not a figure of darkness but a hero of the true religion, Eusebius took advantage of ideas first developed during the Hellenistic age of Alexander the Great and his followers. In an elaborate biography, Eusebius portrayed Constantine as the ideal monarch. This almost superhuman figure, as pious as he was strong and virtuous, deserved the help of God and the loyalty of his Christian subjects. The new rhetoric that Eusebius developed, which portrayed the emperor as a godlike figure who ruled the church as well as the state, remained standard in the Eastern world for

A Christian Ruler Many sources other than Eusebius highlight Constantine's devotion to his faith. On this sarcophagus from the late fourth century, Constantine holds a crucifix and what may have been an orb, a symbol of office carried by Christian rulers since Constantine's time.

hundreds of years to come. And the novel texts that he composed became the models for Christian writers for generations.

MONKS AND HERMITS: NEW WAYS OF CHRISTIAN LIFE

Imperial support and theological scholarship were not the only foundations for Christianity's new strength in the fourth century. For some time, individual Christians had left their communities and families to live an especially religious life. Such men and women pursued holiness by dedicating themselves to disciplined and celibate lives. As they did so, they provided the church with new and lasting forms of organization and of spiritual life.

CHRISTIAN MONKS In Upper Egypt, early in the fourth century, a military veteran named Pachomius organized new Christian communities: groups of men, and then of women, who lived together, wore uniform clothing, and followed a simple set of rules for life. Some, like Pachomius himself, had been conscripted into Roman armies and needed a place to settle once peace returned and they were released. Some were poor farm workers seeking a life with meaning. But some were men and women of high family who read Pachomius's writings and sought him out. Whatever their origins, they joined a rigorously ordered community—one perhaps modeled in part on the camps Pachomius had known in the army.

Their day began at dawn, with prayer. Thereafter the members worked, weaving ropes and baskets from rushes, or gardening and baking to produce the simple bread and cooked vegetables that they ate twice a day, in silence, at common meals. At evening came further prayers and a brief discourse by the head of the house, which the others would then discuss among themselves in small groups. A humble, quiet existence, the new **monastic** form of Christian life spread quickly. By the time Pachomius died in 346, some 3,000 monasteries dotted Egypt. These modest houses were the direct ancestors of the thousands of monastic houses, with their extensive libraries and rich liturgical life, that would become one of the central institutions of Christian Europe for centuries.

DESERT HERMITS In Lower Egypt, by contrast, a different sort of Christian life took shape: that of the so-called Desert Fathers and Mothers, many of whom

A Desert Monastery These frescoes of Christ (bottom), Mary (left), and John (right) date from the eleventh century, but the church itself was built in the fourth century for a monastery founded in Lower Egypt by one of the Desert Fathers, at a time when Christian monks in the region became known for their asceticism.

actually lived on the borders of towns. Like the Pachomian monks, the hermits of Lower Egypt chose a life of hard and unremitting work. They, too, wove ropes to earn their keep. But they led severely ascetic lives, often choosing to live entirely on their own, outside civilization, or in tiny groups of individual cells, rather than in communities. They found a strange comfort in the stark lands on the edge of the desert. Syncletica, a fourth-century female ascetic born to wealth, lived in a crypt, among tombs. And they devoted themselves with a silent, radical passion to the pursuit of holiness.

Those who stood out for their piety became spiritual masters, to whom apprentices would come in search of an apparently simple spiritual instruction, which might take years to explore. Their experiences found a unique record in the so-called *Sayings of the Desert Fathers and Mothers*—a long series of stories about the masters, their practices, and the ways in which they initiated younger and less certain believers into the full demands of the desert life. The most stringent of these demands was that the desert way be lived not only in the body but in the spirit. "There are many who live in the mountains," Syncletica told her disciples, "and behave as if they were in the town. They are wasting their time. It is possible to be a solitary in one's mind while living in a crowd." Here was a faith for the toughest of Christians, those men and women who could settle into desert ravines on the edge of cultivated land

and master the snakes and scorpions, demons, and attacks of temper and indigestion that haunted all who tried to live this scrupulously pure Christian life, scraped clean of all temptation. "Those who are great athletes," Syncletica warned, "must contend against stronger enemies."

The dedicated lives of these monks and hermits exercised something of the same magnetic attraction on a particular kind of believer that the small, persecuted groups of the early church had had for believers like Perpetua and Felicitas. Many hoped to make God the center of their lives on earth, thereby finding a peace of the spirit that no other life could offer. For centuries to come, male and female ascetics would serve as core supporters of the church. They offered an example of a more consistently Christian life than anyone could hope to attain in the public life of cities, and of a deep emotional commitment to one another that turned the desert caves they inhabited into a warm and loving community. The desert, the biographer of the hermit Antony wrote, became in their settlements a kind of city.

SIMEON STYLITES The new asceticism was not, of course, for every Christian. This was true even of the more

Simeon Stylites A fifth- or sixth-century Byzantine relief carving depicts Simeon Stylites atop the column where he spent much of his life. The man ascending the ladder, perhaps a priest, carries a censer, the container in which incense is burned during the Mass.

modest forms in which it was practiced by the Egyptian monks of Pachomius or the Palestinian monks who later filled the outskirts of Jerusalem and other cities with their clustered cells. But it could be witnessed and appreciated by thousands, such as the crowds drawn to a curious spectacle in the desert near the Syrian city of Aleppo.

There Simeon Stylites—a Syrian Christian of the late fourth and early fifth century—devoted himself to an increasingly harsh regimen that included fasting and wearing clothing so tight as to cause severe pain. He began to live on increasingly tall pillars (Stylites means "of the pillar") and took up permanent residence on a small platform atop an ancient column some thirty feet high. Simeon stayed there for thirty-six years, leading a stunningly austere life. Though Simeon insisted he was an ordinary mortal, the fascinated crowds that gathered under his pillar regarded him as a man of superhuman purity and power. They cheered and counted as he prostrated himself over and over again, and listened eagerly to his twice-daily sermons urging them to fight heresy, repress the Jews, or demand greater dedication and piety from the leaders of the church.

THE RELIGION OF EMPIRE

When Constantine defeated his chief rival and established his imperial power under the sign of Christianity in 312, the religion that he sought to favor and regulate was complicated and contentious. Holy men rivaled bishops for authority, and heretics challenged orthodox theologians. Moreover, Christianity was but one feature of the late empire's rich and fluid culture, which was still steeped in the pagan practices and classical learning of the Roman Republic and early empire. How was the first emperor to give Christianity legal standing to deal with these pressures?

ARIANISM AND THE COUNCIL OF NICEA It was one of the many challenges to orthodoxy that moved Constantine, as we have seen, to take a direct hand in governing the church. A priest from Alexandria named Arius had been putting forward arguments about God and Jesus that troubled many. Arius had challenged his bishop, who argued for the absolute divinity of Jesus, with the argument that God the Father had, in fact, created his Son. If the Son was created, then he was not eternal and could not be identical in his essence to the Father. The compelling logic of this position, called Arianism, appealed to a

Council of Nicea A twelfth-century fresco from a monastery in present-day Bulgaria imagines the Council of Nicea in 325. Constantine, flanked by members of the clergy, passes judgment on the Alexandrian priest Arius, who lies prostrate in the foreground.

number of respected thinkers, including Eusebius himself. A local gathering of bishops suggested to Constantine that he assemble the senior clergy to debate it. He did so, assembling the first general council of the church in 325 at Nicea, not far from Constantinople.

At this **Council of Nicea**, the vast majority decided against Arius, and almost all of the bishops who had supported him accepted their opponents' view. The view of Jesus as divine, after all, had the authority of tradition behind it, as Origen and other Christian writers had generally espoused it. The council fathers hammered out a formula—one account holds that Constantine proposed it—according to which God the Father and the Son were "of the same substance," and they inserted this into the statement of the Christian creed that the council promulgated as an official statement of the church's core beliefs. This came to define the core beliefs of Catholic Christianity. Arius went into exile in Palestine.

Unity, however, was never fully achieved. Constantine gradually moderated his position, allowing Arius and his followers to return home. Constantine's last surviving son, who ruled as Constantius II from 337 to 361, was strongly attracted to Arianism and tried to establish a compromise position between it and what had become orthodoxy. The questions at issue would continue to be debated over the centuries.

THE DONATIST CHALLENGE More serious—and much more threatening to the church's unity—was a second spiritual war, one that blazed up after the Great Persecution begun under Diocletian came to an end in 313. North Africa had long been a central area of the church, as it was of the empire: wealthy, productive, and closely connected to the western center of the empire in Italy. When the persecution of Christians ended there, debates raged about the status of those Christians who had surrendered books and other church properties to the authorities without seeking martyrdom. Donatus Magnus (d. ca. 355), who became bishop of Carthage in 313, insisted that sacraments administered by the clerics who had compromised themselves in the years of persecution were invalid. In Carthage and elsewhere, bishops who had managed to survive by making what they saw as necessary concessions were denounced by Donatist purists, who insisted that they should have died for the faith.

From the Donatist challenge a second church began to emerge—a church, like the earliest Christian ones, that admitted the faithful only, excluded all others, and chose its own bishops and clerics. Donatists had the moral and theological authority that comes with absolute adherence to a narrow, tautly drawn line of principle. Their preaching seems to have had a special appeal for the peasants of Roman North Africa. Their church challenged the imperial church to a competition that an established religion could hardly hope to win if it had to rely on the human qualities of its servants alone. The orthodox church was still trying to force the Donatists back into the fold by systematic persecution when the Vandals invaded Africa in 429 and conquered it within a few years.

CHRISTIANITY IN A DIVERSE CULTURE

In the late fourth century, as emperors fought unsuccessfully to keep Rome united, the religious and cultural scene in the empire was above all diverse. From the city of Rome to cities deep in the western and eastern provinces, a great many people continued to observe pagan rituals,

Hypatia of Alexandria A fifth-century terra-cotta statue portrays Hypatia, a scholar who was representative of the great intellectual and cultural diversity of the later Roman Empire. This diversity was dealt a blow when, caught in the middle of a conflict between Christians and Jews in Alexandria, she was murdered by a Christian mob.

to consult and sacrifice to pagan gods, and to believe that they lived in the religious and moral world of the great republican writers Virgil and Cicero. Education, after all, still centered on the study of the republican and early imperial classics. Grammar schools and state-supported public professorships of rhetoric trained ambitious young men in the skills of oratory. In the houses of great urban families, and in the villas of Roman aristocrats in Britain and Gaul, young men copied and corrected manuscripts of the Roman poets and historians under the severe eyes of tutors who insisted that they master every fine point of grammar, rhetoric, mythology, and history. In the cities of the east, the Greek classics were studied with equal care. Hypatia (d. 415), a female scholar and philosopher who learned mathematics and much more from her father, the mathematician Theon of Alexandria (d. ca. 405), corrected and edited the works of the greatest ancient astronomer, Claudius Ptolemy.

This way of life, with its passionate loyalty to the old texts and the old gods, coexisted surprisingly well with the Christian churches in much of the empire. Many—perhaps the majority—of members of the old pagan families attended churches, even as they also committed themselves and their children to a regime of purely classical literary education. Learned Christians studied Plato and his followers, consulted astrologers about the future, and had their villas frescoed with mythological images.

Ordinary Christians also studied the New Testament texts in the new kind of book—the codex—that Christians now preferred. One way to study was simply to copy the text, and women sometimes acted as scribes as well as men. Those who could not read the New Testament—and those who could read a little, but had no access to the works of learned authorities such as Origen and Eusebius—were mostly dependent on what they could learn when a bishop preached to the city's entire Christian community in simplified language. Christians sometimes married pagans,

Mixing Christianity and Paganism A third-century mosaic from a cemetery beneath Saint Peter's Basilica in Rome reflects the interwoven religious practices of many communities. The intermingling Christian and pagan imagery conflates Christ with the sun-god Apollo, who is drawn through the sky on a chariot.

and even pious ones engaged in practices that resembled those of the pagans. Monica, the North African woman whose son, Augustine, would become the greatest Christian thinker of the late empire, still brought small gifts of flowers and food to the shrines of Christian martyrs, as her ancestors would have to pagan temples. In many areas, though not all, the religious situation seemed diverse but stable—perhaps more stable than the empire itself as imperial authority came under increasing threat internally and externally.

IMPERIAL AUTHORITY UNDER THREAT (MID-4TH– MID-5TH CENTURIES)

Attacks at the borders continued to command the armies and resources of the empire over the mid- and late fourth century. What had been a network of great cities that stretched from Britain to Asia Minor was gradually

New Testament Codices In this fifth-century Italian mosaic, bound codices of the Gospels of Mark, Luke, Matthew, and John are displayed in a cabinet. Codices, the new literary technology so important to the spread of Christian texts, were stored flat to prevent warping.

reduced to a skeleton of more or less intact roads sustained by the tax collectors and garrisons who traveled them. City governments relinquished some of their traditional functions of public support to the church, especially as elite families departed for the countryside. And public disorder became a more serious threat in the cities of the empire.

VIOLENCE AND AUTHORITY

Never gentle to its subjects, the imperial state in the fourth century became increasingly violent to anyone who broke the law, threatened public order, or simply angered an emperor. Constantine, hailed by Christians for his tolerance, showed zeal and ingenuity in inflicting pain. He revived the old Roman punishment for parricide (the murder of a parent or close relative): sewing up the guilty

party in a sack, with snakes, and throwing the bundle into a river. He also devised ingeniously appropriate penalties for other crimes, such as pouring molten lead down the throat of a slanderer. Members of the imperial court who fell into suspicion and public enemies were crucified or burned at the stake.

One document gives the flavor of this new imperial world. A conversational manual for Latin speakers who planned to travel in Greek-speaking parts of the empire in the fourth century includes in one of its vocabulary exercises this description of Roman justice in a provincial town: "The governor arrives to take his place on the platform between the guards. The platform is prepared. . . . The accused man stands, a brigand. He is interrogated as his doings deserve. He is tortured. The interrogator hammers him, his breast is torn. He is hung up . . . he is beaten with rods, he is flogged . . . he is led off to be beheaded." Imperial authority, in the world of this textbook dialogue, was not an abstraction. But enforcement of this kind required consistency: any sign of weakness could undercut such public shows of strength and provoke further resistance.

CHALLENGES TO IMPERIAL AUTHORITY

Yet the threat of official violence was not strong enough to maintain order. In the face-to-face world of the ancient cities, where news traveled quickly, crowds assembled on little notice: Christian flash mobs materialized when a Manichean and a Christian, or a Donatist and an orthodox bishop, were to debate. Sometimes they took it into their own hands to create, or restore, what they saw as true public order.

CROWD ACTIONS Early in the fifth century, some 500 Egyptian monks entered the city of Alexandria en masse. The two patriarchs of the local Christians were locked in confrontation with Orestes, the imperial prefect tasked to run the city. Amid these tensions brawls broke out between the city's numerous Jews and the local Christians. Orestes seemed to take the Jews' side when he ordered the arrest of a Christian teacher they detested. Violence on both sides followed, and eventually the Christians expelled at least a large part of the Jewish population from the city. They even attacked Orestes, himself a Christian, who barely escaped with his life. The crowd also murdered Hypatia, the female scholar and philosopher. Christians, once the victims of Roman crowds and imperial authority, now themselves challenged the empire's public order.

THE BISHOP AND THE EMPEROR Emperors could use such mob actions to confront enemies and carry out policies, but they could also respond with savage punishments. In 390, the citizens of Thessalonica murdered an imperial official who had arrested a popular charioteer, along with some of his colleagues. Ambrose, a famously learned bishop of Milan, and others begged the emperor Theodosius I, who was then in Italy, to spare the sinners. He did so at first, but then decided to avenge the murders and massacred some 7,000 citizens.

The horrified bishop wrote formally to the emperor, to tell him that he must repent—and that he, Ambrose, could not allow the Christian emperor to attend Mass or take Communion until he did so: "I dare not offer the sacrifice if you intend to be present. Is that which is not allowed after shedding the blood of one innocent person, allowed after shedding the blood of many? I do not think so." Theodosius thus became the first in a long line of secular rulers who would, through the centuries to come, find themselves confronted by the demand of a religious authority that they recognize it as the higher power. Unlike some of those who came after him, Theodosius, after mourning for several months, accepted his punishment and did penance in public. Christians wept to see the emperor humbly repenting his sins in this way.

Theodosius, as we have seen, formally established the empire as Christian with the Edict of Thessalonica in 380. But the location of spiritual—and political—authority was less clear than ever. In the days of the Julio-Claudian emperors, the historian Tacitus had remarked that the "secret of empire" was that soldiers outside Rome could make an emperor. In the age of Theodosius I, it seemed that the Christian God and his human servants might be able to unmake one.

Saint Ambrose A fourth-century chapel mosaic depicts Ambrose, the influential bishop of Milan who convinced Emperor Theodosius I to repent for his massacre of citizens of Thessalonica.

CODIFICATION OF THE LAWS

Both the accomplishments and the weaknesses of the late empire are starkly visible in the figure of Theodosius II, emperor in the east from 416, when he took power in his own right, to 450. In 438, Theodosius issued a codification of the laws: 2,700 enactments of the emperors from Constantine to his own time, topically arranged. He made clear that part of the purpose of this legal project was to attack heresies, which he defined in some detail. Self-confident and pious, Theodosius thus completed what many would have seen as a project that began with Constantine: the full Christianization of the empire. For all his piety, though, Theodosius did not succeed in infusing the vast majority of the laws in his code with any Christian content. His own wars against Rome's enemies, from the Persians to the Vandals, were only indifferently successful. He could not prevent the loss of North Africa and other onetime imperial heartlands.

THE EMERGENCE OF THE LATIN CHURCH: JEROME AND AUGUSTINE

As the western empire disintegrated, great churchmen settled, in a definitive way, the church's organizational and theological problems. Having mastered the works of earlier Christian scholars and theologians, they confronted the rivals of Christian orthodoxy, from pagan philosophers and Manichean missionaries to the churches that claimed to enroll only true believers. Two late Romans in particular—Jerome and Augustine—placed what would become a distinctively Western, Latin church on its long-term foundations.

Both men were born far from what we now think of as the centers of the West—Jerome in Stridon, in what is now Eastern Europe, and Augustine in Thagaste, in North Africa. Both mastered the classics brilliantly, and both soon attracted favorable attention from those in higher positions. **Jerome** (ca. 347–419/420), a Christian from birth, achieved prominence in Rome, where the cultivated Pope Damasus (366–384), grateful for Jerome's support when his election was challenged by a rival and violence ensued, made him his secretary. But Jerome had to leave the city after Damasus died, when he was charged with having illicit relations with well-born female disciples. **Augustine** (354–430), the son of a Christian mother and a pagan father, became a highly successful orator, poet, and teacher of rhetoric, and he climbed the Roman career ladder from Carthage, to Rome, to the imperial capital of Milan.

Both men struggled, throughout their lives as Christians, to accommodate their love for the ancient writers with their commitment to the church. Jerome expressed this conflict in his account of what became a famous dream, in which he was dragged before the divine seat of judgment, flogged, and told that he was "a Ciceronian, not a Christian." Augustine portrayed it even more memorably in his spiritual autobiography, the *Confessions*, in which he tried to understand and explain why his younger self had loved Virgil's pagan heroine Dido so much.

HUMAN NATURE AND SALVATION

In the struggle to define Christian doctrine that continued to occupy much of the church's attention, both men came down, as they thought Paul had, firmly against those thinkers who held that the innate good qualities of human nature entitled at least some men and women to the award of divine grace. As Paul had preached, only faith in Jesus, given by divine grace, could save unworthy humans from the damnation that they deserved. Humanity without grace, Jerome and Augustine insisted, was a disgusting spectacle. With his customary ability to find the vivid detail that no reader can forget, Augustine remarked that a baby, glaring and shrieking in its furious desire for its mother's breast, feeling no desire to help or love anyone else, was a reflection of human nature after the sin of Adam and Eve, and only Christ could ransom it. Jerome would certainly have agreed.

Augustine went on to elaborate the doctrine of predestination. God, Augustine insisted, chose of his own volition both the elect, who had faith, and the reprobate, who did not. Yet the elect could still fall and the reprobate could still rise, if they willed it: "It depends on you to be elect," Augustine told his congregation. True, God knows who will be saved and who will be damned, but this is because he knows what each person will do. Predestination, Augustine believed, did not do away with human freedom.

Jerome and Augustine Despite their differing approaches to their faith, this miniature seventh-century painting of Jerome (left) and Augustine (right) places them side by side, emphasizing their shared pursuit of Christian scholarship. Both hold a book, symbolizing their notable learning.

AUGUSTINE'S CONVERSION

The two men differed in many ways and did not get on particularly well with one another. Jerome did not have to undergo anything like Augustine's protracted struggle to become a Christian in the first place. Augustine, though exposed to Christianity early in life by his mother, followed a long and winding spiritual journey. At one time a convinced Manichean and astrologer, he later decided that the canonical Manichean texts and those who taught them were superficial. Even then he dedicated himself at first to the reading of pagan philosophical works by Plato and others. Long attached to a woman whom he loved and with whom he had a son, he gave her up for a more

AUGUSTINE AND MONICA

In his *Confessions* (397–400), Augustine, Bishop of Hippo, describes the death of his mother, Monica. He conveys the sadness of the universal experience of losing a parent, but also the solace of his Christian faith in her salvation. Torn by these responses, he seeks to reconcile his identities as a Christian and his mother's son.

On the ninth day, then, of her sickness, the fifty-sixth year of her age, and the thirty-third of mine, was that religious and holy soul set free from the body.

I closed her eyes; and there flowed a great sadness into my heart, and it was passing into tears, when mine eyes at the same time, by the violent control of my mind, sucked back the fountain dry, and woe was me in such a struggle! But, as soon as she breathed her last, the boy Adeodatus burst out into wailing, but, being checked by us all, he became quiet. In like manner also my own childish feeling, which was, through the youthful voice of my heart, finding escape in tears, was restrained and silenced. For we did not consider it fitting to celebrate that funeral with tearful plaints and groanings; for on such wise are they who die unhappy, or are altogether dead, wont to be mourned. But she neither died unhappy, nor did she altogether die. For of this were we assured by the witness of her good conversation, her "faith unfeigned," and other sufficient grounds.

What, then, was that which did grievously pain me within, but the newly-made wound, from having that most sweet and dear habit of living together suddenly broken off? I was full of joy indeed in her testimony, when, in that her last illness, flattering my dutifulness, she called me "kind," and recalled, with great affection of love, that she had never heard any harsh or reproachful sound come out of my mouth against her. But yet, O my God, who madest us, how can the honour which I paid to her be compared with her slavery for me?

As, then, I was left destitute of so great comfort in her, my soul was stricken, and that life torn apart as it were, which, of hers and mine together, had been made but one.

QUESTIONS FOR ANALYSIS

1. What does Augustine mean when he says that his mother did not "altogether die," and why then was it unfitting to cry at her funeral?
2. Why was Augustine so "full of joy" about her testimony of his dutifulness?
3. What does Augustine see as the real source of sadness after the death of a loved one?

Source: *Prolegomena: St. Augustine's Life and Work, Confessions, Letters*, trans. J. G. Pilkington, in *The Nicene and Post-Nicene Fathers of the Christian Church*, 1st ser., vol. 1, ed. Philip Schaff (Buffalo, NY: 1886) pp. 138–39.

---

advantageous marriage and found it achingly difficult to renounce his sex life and become celibate. It was only by traveling mentally through the harmonious universe of the Neoplatonists that Augustine finally found himself, in Milan, living with Christian friends and exposed to Christian classics.

Augustine described these spiritual adventures in his *Confessions*, written in the 390s. His story reaches its climax in a famous scene in a garden. Here Augustine recounts how he heard a child chant *Tolle, lege* ("Take, read"); opened the life of Saint Antony; and found inspiration for a new kind of meditation and, ultimately, a full and final conversion. Augustine's experiences, and his narrative of them, became the preeminent model of Christian conversion in the Western church. Jerome, for all his eloquence and erudition, wrote no comparably classical work of Christian spirituality.

JEROME AND AUGUSTINE AS LEADERS

Their careers as leaders of Christian communities also diverged. Jerome had problems with male authority figures, from Pope Damasus, whom he criticized sharply, onward. He benefited from the patronage of wealthy Christian women, which enabled him to found a learned, monastic community in Palestine. With their help Jerome became one of the models of the Christian life of retirement and contemplation. He admired two of his benefactors, Paula and Eustochium, so much that he wrote letters under their names, which powerfully demonstrated their piety and learning. Augustine, by contrast, found mentors in the public men who led the church—above all Ambrose, whose learning, eloquence, and unshakable poise impressed him deeply. He watched as Ambrose regulated Christian life for the great city of Milan, admiring the rigor with which Ambrose enforced what he saw as pure Christian devotion. Augustine also noted the sharp sense of what worshippers needed that led Ambrose to introduce communal singing into the service. Women, in Augustine's vision of Christianity, played a more subordinate role than in Jerome's.

Later, Augustine was chosen by popular demand, first as a priest and then as bishop of Hippo in North Africa. There he spent the last three decades of his life administering a large diocese and defending his flock against heretics and invaders. Augustine's lived Christianity was active and engaged in the world: a model for later bishops, not for contemplatives.

JEROME AND AUGUSTINE AS SCHOLARS

Nonetheless, the two men's achievements were closely related. Both of them, to begin with, set out to establish Christian scholarship and theology, in the Latin-speaking western empire, on a still deeper and more solid foundation than the one Origen and Eusebius had provided in the east. Jerome, a scholar trained in Greek and even, to some extent, in Hebrew, set out, as Origen had, to provide his church with a reliable Bible. Working with the Hebrew original of the Old Testament, as well as the Greek version of it and the Greek New Testament, he produced an extraordinarily beautiful work in Latin that became, somewhat altered, the **Vulgate**—the Bible that came to be used throughout the Western church.

Augustine lacked Jerome's mastery of Greek, to say nothing of Hebrew. But he shared the same commitment to applying the finest tools of ancient philosophy and rhetoric to the needs of the Christian church. In *On Christian Doctrine*, he showed how each of the main disciplines of the ancient curriculum could be applied to the study of the Bible and the preaching of Christian doctrine. Augustine acknowledged that even the wisest pagans had not fully anticipated Christian truth. But he still found a place for their ideas and methods in the Christian curriculum. The Jews had robbed the camp of the Egyptians on their way to freedom, he argued, and made Egyptian treasure serve their needs. In the same way, Christians could rob the pagans of their ideas and methods, so long as they saw to it that these were used only for proper religious ends. Augustine himself used the philosophical skills he had learned from the Neoplatonists to show how inferior the wisdom and eloquence of human writers were to the simple, inevitable truths that his Christian mother, who may have been illiterate but whose piety was unshakeable, had always known.

A UNIVERSAL CHURCH

The more sharply Augustine was challenged, the more original and brilliant were his responses. When Rome fell in 410 to Alaric and the Visigoths, members of the senatorial aristocracy complained that the city had lost the favor of its ancient gods by adopting the Christian religion. Augustine replied with a massive and magnificent rereading of history, *The City of God*, in which he denied any effort to glean simple, providential lessons from historical events. Christians, he argued, could never be certain, in this world, who was saved and who damned. The two groups coexisted, in state and church, like good and bad fish hauled out of the ocean in a single net, all gasping, all sparkling, but only some of them edible and healthy. Only on the Day of Judgment would God's decisions be announced. Until then, Augustine argued, God's servants on earth—his priests and civil governors—must do their best to rule the church and the state.

As bishop of Hippo, Augustine scored some dazzling successes. The Manichean Faustus acknowledged his defeat in debate with Augustine and converted to Christianity. But when persuasion failed, as it did with the Donatists, Augustine urged the state to apply coercion. Even forced conversions were better than persistence in heresy and error. In Milan, Augustine had seen the great archbishop Ambrose at work—a bishop who did not hesitate to call the emperor himself to account when he thought it necessary. In Hippo, Augustine defined the church as a mixed body—a universal, not a gathered church limited to the saved—and made clear that the state must serve and protect it.

As Augustine lay dying, enemy Vandals who had invaded Christian North Africa and would eventually destroy its deeply rooted Roman civilization were besieging his city. The church he served had developed over two centuries from an archipelago of tiny communities spread across an empire that disliked, and sometimes tried to exterminate, them, into a great public institution, one that possessed buildings, treasuries, and libraries. Christian doctrines, built on but radically different from the philosophy and scholarship of the pagan empire, had reached a high level of precision and sophistication. The ablest men and women in the western empire, in fact, were choosing—for all sorts of reasons—to place their lives in the service of the church. Their decisions proved wise. For centuries to come—indeed, even now—their successors would continue to hold religious services and offer spiritual support to Christians in Europe and beyond.

THE FALL OF ROME (5TH–6TH CENTURIES)

Look up the fall of Rome and you will learn that it happened in 476, when the Gothic leader Odoacer removed Romulus Augustulus from the throne and took him captive. It sounds like the end: the leader of a Germanic tribe topples a Roman emperor—and one named after the founder of the city of Rome. In the fifth century, however, the fall of the last Roman emperor attracted very little attention: neither contemporary observers nor historians said much about it. Romulus Augustulus survived his downfall in good condition. Odoacer gave him a pension, and he lived on in a lavish villa built centuries earlier by a wealthy Roman. Can an empire fall if no one notices?

DEFEATS IN THE WEST

In fact, the quiet transformation of 476 was one in a long string of misfortunes that struck the city of Rome and the territories around it in the fifth century. These events definitively separated the declining western half of the Roman Empire from the eastern, which continued to flourish under the rule of Constantinople. Some of these events spread fear throughout the Mediterranean world. In 408, the Visigothic ruler Alaric besieged the city of Rome, holding out successfully for a massive ransom.

In 410, he returned, stormed one of the city's gates, and allowed his troops to sack and pillage. (As Christians, the Visigoths generally spared churches but ransacked the tombs of the pagan emperors.) In the 450s, Attila, leader of the Huns, a terrifying force of Eurasian warriors on horseback, ravaged Italy. Attila decided not to attack the city of Rome itself, and he died in 453 before he could attack Constantinople. But in 455 the Vandals, a Germanic tribe that had moved west from Poland to Spain and had taken North Africa from the Romans, sent a fleet that sacked Rome as effectively as Attila could have.

Disasters like these made clear that the massively fortified borders created by the emperors of the second and third centuries could no longer protect Rome's citizens and subjects. Roman Britain, suffering raids by another Germanic tribe, the Saxons, and unable to gain help from the imperial government in Italy, ceased to exist in 409 or 410, when Roman magistrates were expelled. Roman Spain fell to Germanic invaders in the same years. Life changed dramatically and permanently for the inhabitants of these former Roman provinces. Although the empire continued to mint new coins in the fifth century, they evidently did not circulate in the Iberian Peninsula and Britain, where these coins have not been found. Older coins were also taken out of circulation, hoarded, and buried by fearful owners desperate to preserve what they had and no longer able to buy the sorts of goods they had once routinely imported. Even before the Romans first invaded Britain, the British had regularly bought wine and pottery in large quantities from Gaul. In the fifth century, this trade ceased. The economy of Britain functioned at a lower level after the turn of the fifth century than it had 450 years before.

THE LAST GARRISON

As defeats multiplied, borders crumbled, and conditions inside the imperial heartlands worsened, it became clear that a definitive change had taken place. Long before 476, many realized that the western empire was no longer the powerful entity that it had been even in the fourth century. Surviving sources give us a glimpse of the end on the ground.

Severinus, a Christian from the east who became a saint, arrived in Noricum, near the Danube, an area that now belongs to Bavaria and Austria, in 453 and spent the next three decades there. Another Christian, Eugippius, wrote Severinus's biography. Eugippius was more

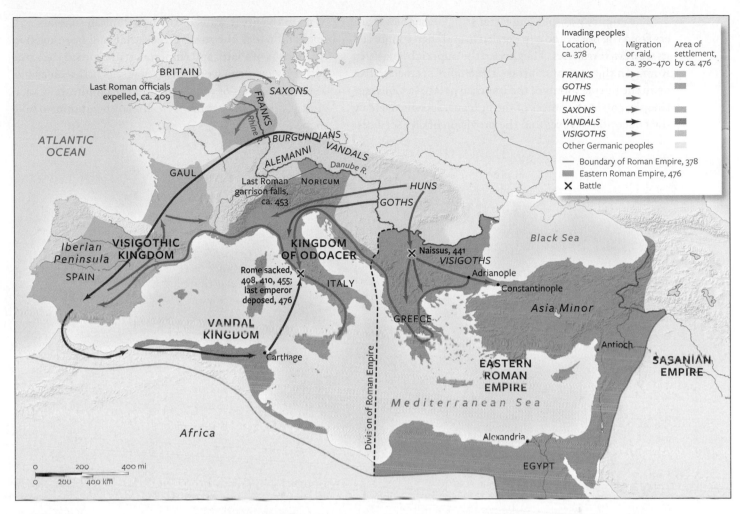

The Fall of Rome, 378–476 After the division of the empire, Roman rule gradually became less stable. Saxons invaded England, expelling Roman forces by 410. Franks, Vandals, Huns, Goths, and Visigoths pushed into Roman territory on all sides. Germanic tribes sacked Rome repeatedly, while the Huns made it as far as Constantinople. The last Roman garrison on the Rhine fell around 453, and by 476 the Gothic leader Odoacer ruled Rome.

interested in Severinus's holiness than in the melting away of Roman authority and power, but he described that as well. Eugippius's account of the last Roman garrison to guard the Danube frontier is especially revealing. Far too small to cover the entire stretch of frontier in any case, this garrison ceased, in the course of Severinus's life, to receive any pay. The empire, based in Italy, no longer maintained the old safe courier service to all its provinces. Detachments of soldiers were sent to collect the money owed, and for a while they succeeded. But a last group was killed by local barbarians, who threw the soldiers' bodies in the river, where they eventually washed up on the shore. This is the last we hear of the garrisons on what had been the Germanic front. Not with a bang but with a whimper, the imperial frontier ceased to exist.

CONCLUSION

In the fourth and fifth centuries, church and empire were both transformed. Christianity became the official religion of the whole vast territory Rome had ruled. The church found ways to take on the learned traditions of the Greco-Roman world, using scholarship and philosophy for its own ends. Its bishops became civic as well as religious leaders, capable of standing up to an emperor when Christian values demanded it. And the church had begun to create new institutions, which enabled Christians to pursue holiness outside the bonds of normal life, in ascetic communities or in solitude. Yet the church was also showing multiple fault lines, as disagreements over theological questions hardened.

The empire was splitting faster still. Germanic invaders from the north and east settled in and then conquered its western territories. They ended the imperial dynasty in Rome. In the east, by contrast, the empire seemed to live on in the purple rooms of the imperial palace in Constantinople, and in the offices of the bureaucrats who oversaw the collection of taxes and the provision of city services.

Within the great walls of the new capital, scholars still read and wrote the same Greek that had been used in the Athens of Plato, and emperors still claimed the same authority over the world that Augustus had seen as his. Yet in both parts of what had been the empire, new societies and new civilizations were already beginning to take shape.

[CHAPTER REVIEW]

KEY TERMS

Constantine (p. 182)
Edict of Milan (p. 183)
pope (p. 183)
Arianism (p. 184)
coloni (p. 185)

Huns (p. 189)
Adrianople (p. 189)
Neoplatonism (p. 191)
Origen (p. 193)
Mani (p. 195)

Eusebius (p. 196)
monastic (p. 197)
Council of Nicea (p. 199)
Donatists (p. 199)
Jerome (p. 202)

Augustine (p. 203)
Vulgate (p. 205)

REVIEW QUESTIONS

1. How did the city of Constantinople exemplify Roman traditions and new departures?

2. What role did Constantine play in the rise of Christianity?

3. What was the relationship between Rome and the various Germanic tribes during the late empire?

4. What other religions and philosophies competed with Christianity in the religious marketplace of the late empire?

5. What criticisms were leveled at Christianity by the pagans, and how did the Christians use scholarship to defend their faith?

6. How was the Christian Bible assembled?

7. How did the late empire use violence to assert its authority?

8. How did religious leaders try to assert their authority over secular rulers?

9. What role did Jerome and Augustine play in the development of the early church?

10. What weaknesses eventually led to the fall of the western Roman Empire?

CORE OBJECTIVES

After reading this chapter, you should have a solid understanding of the following core objectives. To strengthen your grasp of the core objectives, use the resources on the Student Site for The West.

- Analyze the religious and political changes introduced by the Roman emperors from Constantine to Theodosius.

- Identify the causes and effects of economic and social decline in the late Roman Empire.

- Describe the spiritual and philosophical movements and innovations in late Roman society.

- Analyze the evolution of Christian theology and practices in the late imperial period.

- Evaluate the political changes, and the ultimate collapse, of the western Roman Empire in the fourth and fifth centuries.

 GO TO **InQuizitive** TO SEE WHAT YOU'VE LEARNED—AND LEARN WHAT YOU'VE MISSED—WITH PERSONALIZED FEEDBACK ALONG THE WAY.

CHRONOLOGY

527
Justinian becomes
Byzantine emperor

483
Clovis I establishes
Frankish kingdom

529
Benedict creates his monastic *Rule*

529–534
Justinian issues *Corpus Iuris*

532
Nika riots

590
Romans unanimously
proclaim Gregory pope

By end of 6th c.
Saxons conquer
much of Britain

672 and 711
Muslim troops fail to
conquer Constantinople

726–729
Byzantine emperor
Leo the Isaurian
forbids worship
of icons

523
Boethius composes
*The Consolation
of Philosophy*

493
Theodoric the Great founds
a Gothic kingdom in Italy

540
Persian king Chosroes I
attacks eastern
Roman Empire

610
Heraclius ascends to Byzantine throne;
reforms and strengthens military;
Muhammad first receives his revelations

622
Hijra to Medina

By 720s
Umayyad Caliphate
extends from
Asia to Spain

Early 8th century
Bede writes his *Ecclesiastical
History of the English People*

Between Worlds

LATE ANTIQUITY AND THE MAKING OF THE MIDDLE AGES

476–900

I n 949 an Italian priest named Liutprand arrived in Constantinople, the capital of the Byzantine Empire. He represented a prince who effectively ruled Italy, and he was well prepared for the mission. Unlike most of those who now lived in central and northern Italy, Gaul, and the Iberian Peninsula, Liutprand not only spoke Latin but also learned Greek, the language used in Constantinople and the provinces it ruled. Well informed about the world, he could discuss the threats to peace in Italy and elsewhere in the west that were posed both by the Islamic rulers who controlled North Africa and the Iberian Peninsula, and by the barbarian peoples of northern Europe. By Liutprand's time the Vikings, seafarers from Scandinavia, were harrowing Atlantic and Mediterranean seacoasts and establishing settlements of their own. The great empire established in the west by Charlemagne was falling apart.

A sophisticated traveler, Liutprand was nevertheless astonished by Constantinople and the magnificent imperial court it housed. The immense buildings, obelisks, and columns that crowned its central ridges stunned visitors. Liutprand saw the Hippodrome built in antiquity for chariot races, the Senate House, and the great domed church of Hagia Sophia ("the Holy Wisdom") as he followed the central processional road that led to the imperial

Ravenna Mosaics After Byzantine forces led by Justinian's general Belisarius recaptured Ravenna, the capital of western Rome, from the Ostrogoths in the mid-sixth century, the city's bishops initiated the construction of magnificent churches decorated with colorful, intricate mosaics. This panel, from The Basilica of Sant'Apollinare in Classe, shows a group of holy virgins following the Magi to welcome the baby Jesus. Their beautifully patterned clothing was popular among noblewomen at the time.

[FOCUS QUESTIONS]

- What political and cultural initiatives invigorated Byzantium?
- What were the most important characteristics of early Islam?
- What were the cultural interactions of the Islamic world and Byzantium?
- In what ways were the societies of the Latin west rebuilding in this period?

palace complex. There he passed through the Chalke Gate, a large gatehouse covered with statuary, and entered the multiple suites of rooms for receiving visitors—the largest of which could accommodate 228 guests for dinner. The crowds in attendance maintained strict order, coordinated by officials called *silentiaries*—who, as their title suggests, were responsible for warning guests to keep the proper, respectful quiet as they ate.

When Liutprand entered the throne room of the Magnaura Palace, where the emperor awaited him, he saw the most breathtaking spectacle of all. Next to the emperor's throne was a metal tree on which mechanical birds perched and sang. Beside the throne, moving statues of lions roared and lashed the floor with their tails. Following the proper etiquette, Liutprand prostrated himself before the emperor. When he rose, the Byzantine ruler had apparently disappeared. Dazed, Liutprand looked around. Slowly he realized that the emperor, Constantine VII Porphyrogenitus ("purple-born"), and his throne had shot upward toward the ceiling. The emperor, who had somehow managed to change from one set of ceremonial clothing to another, now sat high in the air at a level with his mechanical singing birds—a feat of stagecraft that dramatized his power as no ordinary ceremony could have. The technology that amazed Liutprand had in fact first been developed in Hellenistic Alexandria, though the elaborate court rituals preserved in Constantinople had disappeared in the west. Liutprand could only wonder if the mechanism was something like that of a wine press.

After the death of Theodosius I in 395, the Roman Empire split definitively into its eastern and western components. As the western empire collapsed, the eastern empire gradually evolved into a new organism. Its name comes from the ancient city of Byzantium, and its transformation from Rome to Byzantium took a couple of centuries, from the fifth to the seventh, to reach completion. Historians used to mark the beginning of the Middle Ages with the formal fall of Rome in 476. Now they refer to the fifth through seventh centuries, when ancient legacies in the East and West were creatively adapted into new forms of political and religious life, as "late antiquity," followed by the long process, from the seventh to ninth centuries, in which a new, medieval civilization took shape. The most dynamic force in this period of adaptive change was Islam, a faith that quickly established a political and cultural foothold in the western and eastern lands where Rome's legacies continued to unfold.

BYZANTIUM: EAST ROME TRANSFORMED (527–630)

Byzantium, as we have seen, was refounded by Constantine as New Rome, the eastern capital of the Roman Empire, in 330 CE. Constantine had equipped it with the aqueducts and roads, forums and law courts that a great Roman city needed, and after his death it came to be called Constantinople—"Constantine's city." Over the centuries to come, Constantine's successors expanded on what he had begun. They provided the city with palaces, churches, holy images, and miracle-working relics—objects that had come into contact with Jesus. One central institution was the Hippodrome, greatly enlarged by Constantine. Chariot races took place there six times a day, preceded by parades and interspersed with performances by singers, acrobats, and mimes. As at Rome, four teams—Reds, Greens, Blues, and Whites—competed, and factions of fans supported each of them with an enthusiasm that often bordered on mob violence. The most important long-term addition to the city's infrastructure came about in the fifth century, when the entire city was surrounded with two sets of immense limestone and brick walls, strengthened by a moat and 192 battlemented towers. These formidable defenses would protect the city from external enemies for some 800 years.

JUSTINIAN: REBUILDING AUTHORITY

The real transformation of Constantinople—and the empire it ruled—took place in the sixth century. For almost forty years, **Justinian** (r. 527–565), nephew and counselor

A Charioteer of the Hippodrome This funerary monument from the Hippodrome memorializes a famous charioteer, Porphyrius, who competed there in the late fifth and early sixth centuries. The relief shows Porphyrius in his chariot, flanked by two winged victories.

of the previous emperor, the childless Justin, ruled the empire. Justinian was an innovator—he took advantage of a new law permitting marriage between people of different rank to wed his mistress, an actress named **Theodora** (ca. 500–548). Of the many institutions he transformed, the central one was the law.

A NEW LEGAL CODE For centuries Roman law had grown, slowly and unevenly, as the Senate and the emperors issued edicts and jurists interpreted them. There were schools, at Berytus (modern Beirut) and elsewhere, to train future lawyers, but only a few collections of the laws existed. In 425 Theodosius II, worried that legal skills were declining in the eastern empire, founded a new law school in Constantinople. More important still, four years later he set up a committee of twenty-two jurists who organized and edited the decrees of the Roman emperors from

Constantine to Theodosius himself. This was the first official law code that the empire had issued in centuries.

Justinian, however, went much further than his predecessors. He declared that making and interpreting the law formed a central part of the emperor's job: "The imperial majesty should be armed with laws as well as glorified with arms, that there may be good government in times both of war and of peace, and the ruler of Rome may not only be victorious over his enemies, but may show himself as scrupulously regardful of justice as triumphant over his conquered foes." Justinian created a committee of jurists that, in only five years, updated the body of imperial legislation in a new *Code*; collected and edited the opinions of authoritative Roman jurists from over the centuries in the *Digest*; and compiled a textbook of legal principles, the *Institutes*. This book offered statements of basic principle, such as "Justice is the set and constant purpose which gives to every man his due. Jurisprudence is the knowledge of things divine and human, the science of the just and the unjust." The ***Corpus Iuris*** (*Corpus of Law*) as a whole was intended to embody these principles as well as to provide, in one place, the body of Roman law as emperors and jurists had developed it.

Like the codes of the ancient Near East, Roman law was not gentle. Following the precedent set by Constantine, Justinian introduced many new forms of penalty, notably bodily mutilations, into Roman legal practice. But the law still aimed at justice. It acknowledged the continued existence of slavery, but taught that men and women should be considered free until their slave status was demonstrated. Divorce, which Christianity condemned, was restricted more severely than ever before. Women's control of their own property was confirmed, and they were allowed to make bequests directly to their children, even if still minors. Though the *Corpus Iuris* was compiled in a Greek-speaking city, the laws and opinions it contained were in Latin. The continued use of Latin for legal purposes perpetuated the belief that the eastern empire was still Roman—a belief that Justinian's successors would cling to for centuries.

Yet the codification of the law transformed the nature of the empire. Copies of the *Corpus* were sent to provincial capitals. Barbarian rulers in the west, such as the kings of the Lombards, whom we will soon meet, took it as the model for compilations of their own laws. Imperial and royal authority was more solidly founded than ever before. It was rooted, the law made clear, in the sovereign power of the people, but that had passed, irrevocably, to the emperors. In time, as we will see, the mere statement that the people had once exercised power proved radical in its implications. For the moment, however, the emperor claimed a new kind of ideological supremacy, based in the first instance on law.

FISCAL REFORM Justinian also rebuilt the fiscal foundations and administrative organization of the empire. John the Cappadocian, a close ally who rose, as Justinian did, from relatively modest origins, served him as Praetorian prefect and legal adviser. John did his best to transform the existing tax system in the east, which had concentrated on collecting vast amounts of grain and other agricultural products, into one that brought in cash instead. He let no one—even the wealthy—escape their obligations. John's efforts aroused anger, even from some fellow members of the official service. John the Lydian, a learned lawyer and bureaucrat from Philadelphia in western Turkey, recalled those years in savage terms, with a nice classical allusion to the ancient myth of the Greek underworld (Hades) and the three-headed dog that guarded it: "This shark-toothed Cerberus, though he was the common plague of mankind, chewed up my Philadelphia so finely that after him . . . it became bereft not only of money, but also of human beings." Archaeological evidence confirms that in the area of Asia Minor that John the Lydian came from, agriculture and city life both contracted in this period—though, as we will see, taxation was by no means the only destructive

force at work. Still, by the early 540s, when John the Cappadocian was dismissed, the state enjoyed far larger means than ever before.

THE NIKA RIOTS (532) Justinian's efforts to establish imperial authority and power on deeper foundations provoked resistance. In 532 he scheduled public executions of a member of each of the leading circus factions, the Blues and the Greens. Crowds gathered and a riot started. While faction members chanted "Nika, nika" ("Win, win"), much of Constantinople burned, including the massive old church of Hagia Sophia. The only account we have—the *Secret History* by Procopius, a contemporary historian who recorded the emperor's achievements but despised his character—claims that the emperor was terrified that the mob would murder him in his palace and almost abandoned the city. At this point Theodora played a crucial role.

In Byzantium—as in other court societies—women of high position could be central in political and social life. Theodora came of age as an actress, playing mythological characters in revealing costumes. The law forbade actresses, who had low status in Byzantium, to change their occupation or to marry men of higher standing, such as an heir to the empire. But Justinian fell in love with this tough, witty woman. When he became emperor, she became his partner, and when a new law permitted it, they married. Some later historians described their reign as a double monarchy.

Despite court gossip describing her as a prostitute, Theodora became essential to Justinian's success. Never losing her fellow feeling for poor women, she tried to eliminate prostitution in Constantinople and helped women who had been forced into that life by providing them with dowries. When Justinian wrote, in one law, that there was neither male nor female in the service of Christ, he showed his respect for her views. In the Nika riots crisis of 532, it was Theodora who stiffened her husband's back. "An empire," she supposedly remarked, "makes a beautiful shroud." Justinian held fast. His favorite commander, Belisarius, bribed one faction to leave the circus, then entered it at the head of an army and massacred thousands of members of the other factions. At the end of the day, public order was not only restored but more firmly founded than ever.

Justinian This mosaic in the Basilica of San Vitale in Ravenna from 547 depicts Justinian in all his imperial grandeur, dressed in purple and accompanied by numerous courtiers. The halo around his head and his position beside a bishop (in the gold robe) symbolize that the Christian church sanctioned Justinian's rule.

IMPERIAL GRANDEUR Justinian, moreover, deployed his wealth in creative ways, building on foundations that previous emperors had laid. Over the last two centuries, Roman men of power had abandoned their distaste for rich colors and fabrics. Silk became the fabric of choice, and

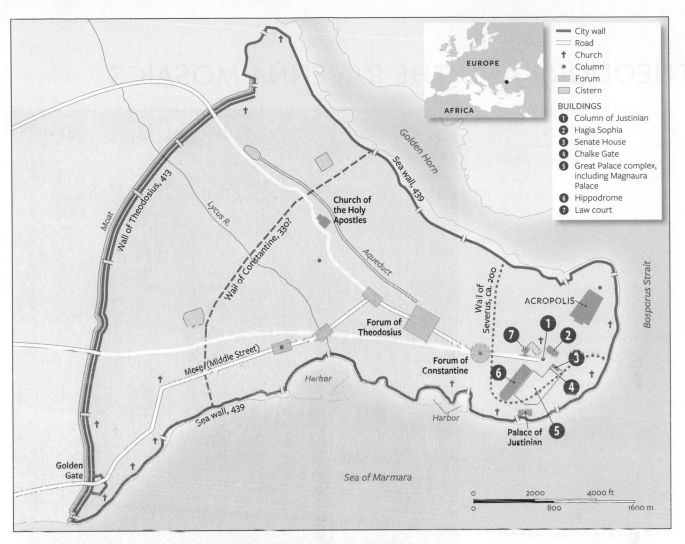

Constantinople under Justinian, ca. 560 Situated on a peninsula overlooking the Bosporus, Constantinople had expanded considerably since it was founded, with Theodosius's fortified wall of 413 marking the ultimate border of the city. The Roman institutions built by Constantine, such as the Hippodrome and law courts, were located in the old city center, at the tip of the peninsula. Roman infrastructure—roads, aqueducts, forums— spread throughout the city. When Justinian rebuilt Constantinople in the mid-sixth century, he added monumental building projects of his own, such as the Great Palace and the church of Hagia Sophia.

purple, the deep, glowing dye made from crushed shellfish, the most desired and enviable of colors, used only by members of the imperial family. Palace life became grander. The corps of eunuchs—men castrated as boys, who had long served as a buffer between the imperial family and the rest of the world—grew in number and importance. These beardless men held many positions in the imperial bureaucracy, in which they had their own career hierarchy. Narses, a court eunuch, would eventually become Justinian's second great commander.

Justinian played to the new respect for extravagance as he rebuilt Constantinople, making it the grandest of capitals. He placed an equestrian statue of himself on an

immense column in the center of its largest square to celebrate his military achievements, all of which had been the work of his generals. Magnificent mosaics on the same themes sprawled across the walls and ceiling of the huge palace gate. By the end of his reign, the city had around half a million inhabitants—a radical contrast to Rome, where fewer than 50,000 inhabited a city that had been built for a million people. Like Hadrian and other successful emperors of ancient Rome, Justinian acted as a benefactor across his territories. As he fortified cities such as Athens and Corinth, which had become vulnerable to invaders from the north, and equipped them with baths and other public structures, the emperor seemed to be everywhere.

THEODORA AND THE RAVENNA MOSAICS

In 540, armies dispatched by the Byzantine emperor Justinian captured Ravenna, the capital city of the Ostrogoths in northeast Italy. Between 540 and 600, the bishops of Ravenna built magnificent monuments to the Christian empire, including the Basilica of San Vitale. The walls of the church are decorated with grand mosaics, completed in 547, depicting Justinian and the empress Theodora as imperial rulers and defenders of the Christian faith.

This detail of the mosaic of Theodora shows the empress adorned with jewels, her head encircled by a halo. Attended by a courtier and a handmaiden, she presents the gift of a bejeweled golden chalice to the courtier. The striking placement of the sacred chalice in front of the courtier's contrasting white robe accentuates its importance. All three figures are richly and elaborately dressed, and the bottom edge of Theodora's gown is embroidered with the three Magi bearing gifts to the baby Jesus. The mosaic captures the integration of imperial power and Christian faith that was so central to Byzantine rule.

QUESTIONS FOR ANALYSIS

1. How does this mosaic convey Theodora's faith?
2. How does it represent Theodora's power?
3. How does the image of Theodora suggest the strength of character she showed during the crisis of the Nika riots?

THE CHRISTIAN EMPIRE

Justinian strengthened the imperial embrace of Christianity. In 529, shortly after becoming emperor, he attacked pagan learning through a decree that forbade the teaching of philosophy at Athens; he also made it illegal for pagans to hold public office. This decree resulted in the closing, after almost a thousand years, of the Academy at Athens. Its philosophers, who saw themselves as carrying on the ancient tradition of Plato himself, supposedly went into exile in Persia.

From the start of his reign, Justinian also tried to impose religious unity on the church. Beginning in 325 with the Council of Nicea, the church had been attempting to identify the core doctrines that every Christian must accept. But debates continued. In Rome, and in the west more generally, official doctrine held that Christ was fully God, as well as fully human. In the east—which had been the heartland of Arianism—many disagreed, holding to the position that only God was divine. Since 451, when an ecumenical council had taken place at Chalcedon, near Constantinople, disputes over the relation between Christ's human nature and his divine nature had racked the church. Justinian did his best both to find a theological compromise and to expel heretics. In the end, he failed to stamp out the Monophysites, who held that Christ had only one, divine nature—and whose supporters included his wife, Theodora, as well as many bishops. Eventually, the term *catholic* (literally, "universal") would come to designate the Latin church of Rome. The churches of the east, whose chief officials were called patriarchs, would eventually declare independence from it.

THE CHURCH OF HAGIA SOPHIA
Above all, Justinian made Constantinople the grandest center of Christianity. The city already boasted many churches, a few of them imposing. But the church of Hagia Sophia, rebuilt by Justinian in the wake of the destruction caused by the Nika riots, not only outdid them but even surpassed the great domed Pantheon in Rome itself. Justinian imposed the task of creating the vast structure on two experts in both mathematics and architecture, Isidore of Miletus and Anthemius of Tralles. Setting some 10,000 men to work, they imported materials from all around the empire: porphyry from Egypt, marble of many colors from Thrace and elsewhere, columns from Hellenistic temples in Asia Minor. On an enormous square nave they reared an extraordinary dome, more than 100 feet across and almost 200 feet, at its peak, from the floor of the church.

A high arcade with forty windows let in a flood of

Hagia Sophia The great church of Hagia Sophia in Constantinople is a monument of architectural mastery. Its vast dome and many windows let in far more light and air than had been possible in earlier basilicas. The Arabic calligraphy was added after the church was converted to a mosque in the fifteenth century.

sunlight and made the golden dome, for all its size, seem, as Procopius wrote, "not to rest upon solid masonry" but to be "suspended from Heaven." Traditional basilicas were imposingly dark. Hagia Sophia, by contrast, was so bright it seemed that it was "not illuminated from without by the sun, but that the radiance comes into being within it." The multiple colors of the stones pulled the eye from surface to surface: "One might imagine that he had come upon a meadow with its flowers in full bloom. For he would surely marvel at the purple of some, the green tint of others, and at those on which the crimson glows and those from which the white flashes." The splendid marble blocks were smoothed and fitted together not with lime or mortar but with melted lead, which made the divisions barely visible. This delicate craftsmanship enhanced the beauty of the church and overpowered visitors. When Justinian himself first entered the church, he cried out, "Solomon, I have outdone you."

Hagia Sophia was indeed larger and more spectacular than Solomon's Temple at Jerusalem, as described in the Old Testament. Equally splendid were the services led there by the patriarch of Constantinople and often attended by the emperor and his court. When emissaries from the prince of Kiev, in Russia, came to Constantinople a few years after Liutprand, they reported that during services in Hagia Sophia, they could no longer tell if they were on earth or in heaven.

Justinian built and repaired churches and raised basilicas across the empire, from Jerusalem, to Ephesus in

Asia Minor, to Carthage in North Africa. In the church in which the monks of the fortified monastery of Saint Catherine at Sinai still worship, a millennium and a half later, the roof beams still bear the names of the church's patrons, Justinian and Theodora.

EMPEROR OF STATE AND CHURCH By creating so many structures in honor of God, and by supporting, as he did, the power of the bishops, Justinian represented himself as a Christian emperor in a new sense: one who held power of the same kind, divine in origin, over state and church. He introduced more and more religious elements into court art and ceremony. Sometimes he appeared to defer to religious authority. In processions, he walked while the patriarch rode. On the whole, though, the emperor emerged as the dominant figure. Hymns of a new kind were composed, which emphasized the unity of Christ and emperor. Images also celebrated the emperor in a new way. A double panel of ivory, carved in the 530s

Icons Divine images painted on wood or pieced together in mosaics became associated with the Christianity of the Byzantine Empire. This sixth-century icon of Mary and the baby Jesus comes from the Monastery of Saint Catherine in Egypt.

Barberini Diptych An intricate ivory carving from the 530s shows a triumphant Emperor Justinian on horseback. The heavenly realm of angels above him and the laboring peasants below suggest a divine order of creation.

and known as the Barberini diptych after its later owners, shows Justinian as a classical warrior on horseback, triumphing over his enemies. Angels appear above the emperor, holding a bust of Jesus, to emphasize the religious sanction that underpinned his authority.

RELIGIOUS ICONS: THE EASTERN TRADITION In the long term, the effects of the new emphasis on religious images were profound. Eastern Christians had long created icons: flat panel paintings that depicted Jesus, the members of the Holy Family, or saints. The earliest surviving examples come from the time of Justinian, from the monastery of Saint Catherine at Sinai. Soon Constantinople became a city of icons, as well as relics, and the icons came to be charged with a miracle-working power. Many thought that the Virgin, images of whom were displayed during sieges, saved the city from barbarian armies. Later emperors went to war carrying icons of this divine protector. Theologians explained that when worshippers prayed before an icon, they should venerate not the image but its subject. In practice, though, many came to these images to beg them for help in having children or healing illness. Images permeated personal as well as public religious life, and the religious practices that surrounded them deviated more and more from formal theological principles.

Even as the empire became solidly Christian, with the emperors clearly established as protectors of and authorities in the church, Christianity became imperial. The images of Jesus that Justinian's brilliant mosaic workers pieced together from millions of colored stones and tiny pieces of glass represented him not as a suffering human on the cross but as an exalted ruler in heaven, the Pantokrator, or ruler of the universe. A new form of Christianity—the ancestor of modern Orthodox Christianity—had come into being: one that identified rulership with holiness and treated the emperor as godlike.

ECONOMY AND SOCIETY

Constantinople was created as a ceremonial center and a fortified base for the rest of the eastern empire. Home to a thriving sector of artistic and craft production, the city also supported a massive population that had to be defended and provisioned even in difficult times. These identities did much to determine the ways in which the ordinary people of the city lived, worked, and died.

WORK Constantinople, the empire's capital, housed not only the court and the church, but the large population of artisans who realized Justinian's vision of what a church should be. Few made enough to own their own shops. Many earned wages, instead, in large workplaces owned by the imperial government or by churches. Some worked in the mint, creating coins that not only served as a medium of exchange but also enhanced the image of the emperor, shown being crowned by Christ or in the company of the Holy Family and the saints. A whole series of specialized crafts collaborated to make silk. The silk filaments had to be unraveled from cocoons, put onto reels, made into cloth, and finished and dyed—each step requiring a different craft workshop. Mosaics were the most painstaking of crafts. As many as 20,000 pieces were needed to compose one square meter of an image that, when complete, would cover an enormous wall. Foreign merchants traveled to the city from east and west, armed with safe-conduct documents. Glass, linen, and African ivory came from Greece

and Egypt; luxury goods, carried by Arab traders, came from China and India. A system of investments and loans financed large trading expeditions.

Outside the capital, most Byzantines worked the land. They sowed wheat in the late fall to take advantage of the rainy season, allowing half of their land to lie fallow each year to restore its fertility. As always in the Greek world, olive trees and grape vines were widely cultivated, as olive oil was used for cooking and for fuel in lamps. Life in the country was, for the most part, poor and simple. The tools farmers used had changed little, if at all, since Roman times, and crop yields were relatively low.

WOMEN'S LIVES Women's lives were sharply separated by their places in society. Noblewomen lived in palaces, traveled in litters (seats carried by servants), and seldom if ever saw the world outside their luxurious habitats. Like the women of ancient Athens, they were expected to remain at home except when joining a religious procession, going to the public baths, or mourning a death or celebrating a birth in their family. They were accompanied by male escorts and covered their faces with veils. Poor women lived and worked in shops and fields. When a wealthy woman lost her husband, she might enter an aristocratic convent. A poor woman in the same situation would go on working as she always had, unless a grown child could support her. Whatever her rank, a Byzantine

Byzantine Noblewomen In a mosaic from the early sixth century, a female figure is clad in the richly decorative clothing, jewelry, and hairstyle suggestive of the luxurious (though cloistered) lives of Byzantine noblewomen.

woman's destiny was normally assumed to be marriage and childbearing. Girls as young as seven could be engaged, and most married at thirteen or fourteen. Only women from the higher ranges of Byzantine society became literate. Yet—as the case of Theodora shows—the empire's extremely hierarchical order enabled empresses, and a few other highly born women, to shape public policy and religious life.

IMPERIAL STRENGTH AND DECLINE

As Justinian's triumphs in the east grew, he also tried to reunite the Roman Empire as a whole. He sent his general Belisarius, who had won his and Theodora's trust when he crushed the Nika rioters in 532, to North Africa the next year. There, with an armada of ships and a small army of some 15,000 men, Belisarius defeated the Vandals, a Germanic tribe, who had invaded the region in 429 and founded their own kingdom. Awarded the consulship and other honors, Belisarius then conquered Italy, taking Naples, Rome, and finally the capital of Ravenna back from their Gothic rulers. His later career was less dazzling

and he lost Justinian's confidence, retiring to Constantinople in 548. But he survived to defend the city in 559 against another set of invaders, Huns from north of the Danube. His clever tactics convinced them that the ragtag militia he had managed to raise was a massive army. Meanwhile, the eunuch general Narses, who followed Belisarius into action in Italy in 551, conquered the Goths and restored Byzantine power. He remained in Italy, rebuilding fortifications and defeating another Germanic tribe, the Franks, until he was dismissed and given a high title in 568.

Although the capital that Justinian built was still the city that astonished Liutprand four centuries later, the unified empire that Justinian thought he had brought back into existence in the 530s could be maintained only at the cost of long and destructive wars from Italy to Syria—and by paying subsidies to barbarians, which in turn engendered resentment, and even assassination plots, against the emperor. For much of Byzantine history, the great capital in Constantinople was the head of a much smaller political body than its architects had expected.

PLAGUE (541–542) Like his successes, Justinian's failures show that history often turns on unpredictable

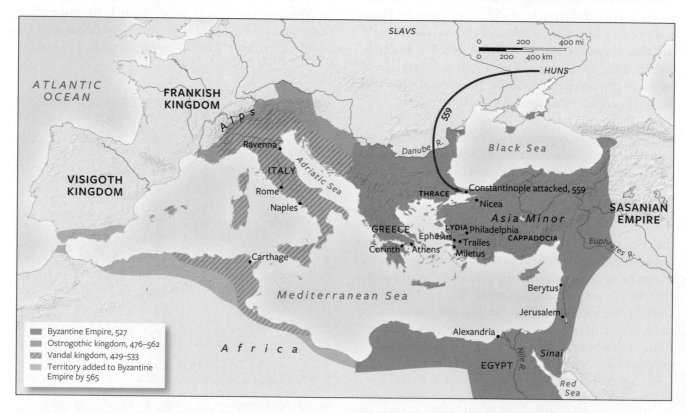

Byzantium, 527–565 In 527, the Byzantine Empire held sway over the former eastern Roman Empire, including Greece, Asia Minor, and Egypt. By 565, it had expanded across North Africa, subsuming the Vandal Kingdom; gained territory as far as the southern coast of the Iberian Peninsula; and conquered former Ostrogothic lands in Italy and around the Adriatic Sea. Constantinople even withstood an attack by the Huns in 559.

events, big and small. Without Belisarius, for example, the timid Justinian would never have had a chance of winning back the western empire, even temporarily. Another contingency proved even more powerful and, in fact, decisive. In 541, plague struck the empire. Procopius recorded the terrifying, and puzzlingly varied, symptoms that manifested themselves: black swellings in the groin, armpits, and elsewhere, followed in some cases by deep coma and in others by wild excitement as patients threw themselves out of their beds onto the floor or tried to hurl themselves into the sea. The disease raged for three or four months in Constantinople, where mortality rose to 5,000 and then to 10,000 a day, and returned in later years.

Normal morality disappeared in these terrible conditions: "Now in the beginning each man attended to the burial of the dead of his own house, and these they threw even into the tombs of others, either escaping detection or using violence; but afterwards confusion and disorder everywhere became complete." Justinian appointed an official to see to the burial of the dead and put the army at his disposal. But the mounds of corpses grew too quickly for orderly disposal. Funeral rites were abandoned, corpses piled in ditches and fortifications, and finally the emperor himself fell ill. Throughout the empire and outside it, in Persia and elsewhere, the plague emptied farms, left crops unharvested, and harrowed the cities. Slaves melted away, and many houses were completely deserted. Although Justinian recovered, Theodora died. He never regained the energy and creativity of his early years, and his reunited empire soon cracked apart once more.

THE REVIVAL OF PERSIA Another—and equally unexpected—cause for Byzantium's decline came, as the plague probably did, from outside the empire. In 224 a Persian nobleman, Ardashir I, overthrew the Parthian kingdom with which Rome had long waged war and created what became the Sasanian Empire (224–651), centered in Iran but encompassing much of the Near East and Central Asia at its height. This new, tightly organized Persian state now spread from the Euphrates to the Indus. It had its own Zoroastrian religion; its own priesthood, the Magi; and its own spectacular capital at Ctesiphon (not far from modern Baghdad), one of seven central imperial cities. An immense brick arch, more than 100 feet high, is all that remains of what was once a structure as spectacular as anything in Constantinople—an imposing palace, its floors covered with splendid carpets and its walls with mosaics and more carpets. Supplicants came here from all corners of the Sasanian Empire to plead their case to the *shahanshah*, an absolute monarch who ruled his empire,

as the kings of ancient Persia had, through satraps. He received them wearing a crown so heavy that it had to be suspended from the ceiling. In this tolerant kingdom, not only Zoroastrians but Christians, Manicheans, and Jews lived together peacefully. Under Sasanian rule, the Jewish academies of Babylon assembled the great body of legal principles and debates now known as the Babylonian Talmud, which would become the core of Jewish tradition and education in later centuries.

WAR WITH SASANIAN PERSIA (540–630) The Romans warred with Persia from 230 to the end of the third century, and again from the 330s to the 380s and in the 520s. In 540 Chosroes I, the ruler of Persia, attacked the empire from the east, forcing Justinian to strengthen his frontiers. The Persians' heavily armed cavalry and skilled archers hit hard and fast, so terrifying the eastern Roman legions that they sometimes refused to fight. Chosroes reached Mesopotamia and Syria, where he sacked the ancient city of Antioch. In the second half of the sixth century, though, Persia—like Constantinople—suffered from plague and invasion by migrant peoples, as the Slavs, followed by the Avars, warrior nomads from the steppes north of the Black Sea, spread into the Balkans and beyond. Divided and relatively weak, the Sasanian Empire now posed little threat; in 591, the Byzantine emperor Maurice (r. 582–602) won concessions from the son of the monarch, Chosroes II, in return for installing him on the Persian throne.

But Maurice became unpopular with the troops when he insisted on cutting military pay and campaigning through the winter, and eventually an officer deposed and executed him. Civil war broke out in Byzantium just as Sasanian Persia was recovering strength. Persian armies moved into Roman territory, conquering Egypt and Syria and taking their great cities, Alexandria and Damascus. In 614 Persian troops captured Jerusalem, taking the True Cross—on which, tradition held, Jesus had been crucified—from its place in a Christian shrine. When the Byzantine emperor Heraclius (r. 610–641) asked for a peace treaty, Chosroes II imprisoned his diplomats. Soon the Persians besieged Constantinople itself.

REFORM UNDER HERACLIUS In a whirlwind of activity following his accession in 610, Heraclius reorganized the empire. By cutting official pay, raising taxes, and melting down the treasures of the churches, he found the resources to buy off one set of enemies, the Avars, for a time. He remade the Byzantine army into an effective force. He schooled his soldiers in the belief that they

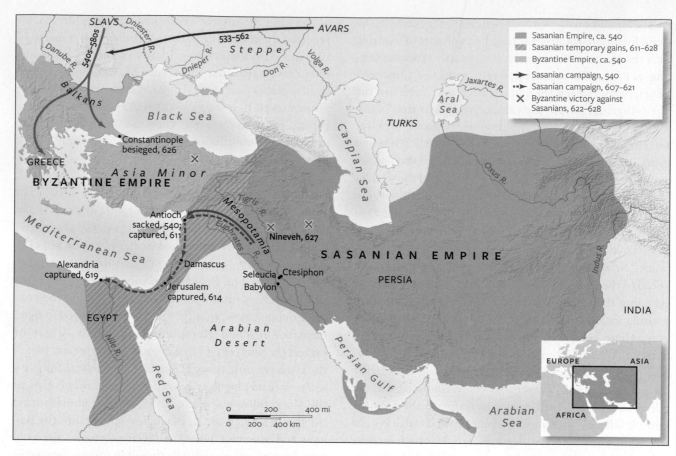

The Sasanian Empire and Its Wars with Byzantium, 540–628 From the mid-sixth century, the powerful Sasanian Empire put renewed pressure on Byzantium's eastern borders, conquering significant territory in Syria and Egypt and even besieging Constantinople in 626. To the west, Byzantium was threatened by the Slavs and Avars invading from eastern Europe and Central Asia. These migrant peoples also caused instability in Persia, and Heraclius's campaigns in the 620s succeeded in reversing Sasanian territorial gains.

represented Christianity against infidels—an idea that would have a long history—and trained them intensively in traditional Roman tactics. In a brilliant series of campaigns, Heraclius defeated three separate Sasanian Persian armies and formed an alliance with the Turks, a Central Asian people. Meanwhile, in 626 the great walls of Constantinople held off a siege force consisting of Persian ships and an Avar army. As Heraclius and the Turks ravaged the central lands of Persia, news came of a plot against Chosroes II, who was deposed and killed in 628. The previous frontiers of the Byzantine Empire were restored, and in 630 Heraclius brought the True Cross back to Jerusalem.

THE ORIGINS OF ISLAM (600–650)

The eastern empire had survived its most demanding test. Or so Heraclius believed. But he could not have been more

wrong. In their search for allies, both Byzantium and Persia had dealt with Arabs—inhabitants of the coastline and, in some cases, the central desert of the Arabian Peninsula. These lands now produced a new and lasting civilization, centered on a new religion: one whose quick expansion threatened the survival of the eastern empire far more radically than the Persians had.

ARAB SOCIETIES

The new religion of Islam took shape around oases in the Arabian Desert. The peninsula had been divided, for centuries, between coastal inhabitants and desert peoples. Along the eastern and southern coasts, great states grew up in the first millennium BCE. Once navigators mastered the Indian Ocean monsoon cycle, around the beginning of the Christian era, they used the winds that could take ships across the ocean in both directions to play a central role in world trade routes. Ivory and other goods were brought across the Red Sea from Africa and transported north to Persian and Roman territory. The **Silk Road**—the 4,000-mile-long series of trade routes along which goods and beliefs traveled from China and India to Constantinople and Rome, was reaching the peak of its activity, with caravans passing through Persia and the northern territory of the Arabian Peninsula. The Arabian kingdoms controlled the trade in spices, which were carried in ships across the Indian Ocean and north up the Red Sea. They also produced goods of their own—notably frankincense and myrrh. Readers of the Gospels would have understood that the Magi who came to see the baby Jesus were Persian wise men bringing precious gifts from Arabia.

Foreign cultures strongly influenced these coastal Arab societies. In Bahrain, an archipelago in the Persian Gulf, archaeologists have found villas and temples built in the styles of the Hellenistic Greeks, with fine stone pillars and

Cultural Exchange on the Silk Road Connecting Rome and Constantinople to far-flung China and India, the Silk Road enabled more than goods to circulate. This Buddha figure from third-century Gandhara (present-day Pakistan) combines Eastern religious imagery with a toga-like garment and tightly curled hairstyle indicative of Roman influence.

mosaics. Jews from Palestine and Christians from Ethiopia, as well as polytheists whose temples honored many gods, settled in these communities. Many religious messages circulated through the oases and along the caravan trails.

By the fifth century CE and after, however, these centers of trade were in decline. The west, in the last centuries of the Roman Empire, could buy fewer goods. Power in the Arabian Peninsula now rested not with traders but with the inhabitants of the desert: the many tribes of the Bedouin, migrants who lived as shepherds. Domesticated camels, which could move quickly through the arid center of Arabia living on stored water for days at a time, carried the desert migrants across country with a speed and security usually reserved, in the premodern world, for travel by water. Organized in kin groups and linked by polygamous marriages, the desert Arabs valued courage and honor above everything else. They dominated the caravan trade and settled at oases, where deeply buried water sources enabled them to build stable clusters of fortified houses and to raise idols to their gods. At Mecca, a busy and successful oasis and mercantile center, a group of them dominated the town. Like most Bedouins, they were polytheists, but they paid special reverence to a small, square shrine—the wall of which encased a meteorite—one of the typical forms of local religious practice. Here, in 610, a merchant named Muhammad began to receive messages from an all-powerful God. At first, these revelations terrified him. Gradually they became the core of a new religion and inspired the creation of a new society.

"THERE IS ONE GOD AND MUHAMMAD IS HIS PROPHET"

A boy of noble descent who was left a poor orphan when his father died, **Muhammad** (ca. 570–632) worked as a merchant. His success leading a caravan for a wealthy older woman won him her respect and affection. They married, and he grew in prominence. A traditional story records that when the four tribal groups that ruled Mecca wanted to repair the **Kaaba**, their square shrine, they could not agree on which of them should lift the sacred stone back into place in the structure. Muhammad suggested that they place the stone on a cloak and that members of each group should lift one corner of it. Then he himself set the stone back into place. The story—like the many others that grew up around Muhammad's early years—may not be literally true. But it makes clear that he developed a reputation as a man of fairness and integrity, one whom all

The Kaaba The Kaaba shrine in Mecca, the holiest place in Islam, is the most important destination for Muslim pilgrims to this day.

could trust. He and his wife had four daughters and two sons, both of whom died very young.

Gradually, Muhammad began to retreat to a cave not far from Mecca, where he camped on an arid hill for periods of several days to meditate and pray. One day, apparently when he was home in Mecca, a voice spoke to him, saying in Arabic, "You are the messenger of God." His experience seems to have been as dramatic—if not as unexpected—as the vision that transformed the Jew Saul into the Christian Paul on the road to Damascus. Terrified, Muhammad begged his wife to cover him. Eventually he began to receive regular visits from what he regarded as a powerful spirit, traditionally identified in the Islamic world as the angel Gabriel. He ran away and even thought about throwing himself off a mountain. But God himself confirmed the truth of the messages that Muhammad received. Soon the messenger commanded him to recite, and he found himself beginning to offer teachings in the form of rhymed verses.

EARLY TEACHINGS Scholars believe that when Muhammad began to address the people of Mecca after 610, he started by announcing that the world was out of joint. God, whom he now called Allah, was eternally just and omnipotent. All should hear and follow the teachings of this true God. But many—especially the wealthy polytheists who controlled Mecca—did not do so. They attributed their gains to their own gods, when in fact Allah

"has provided them against hunger and kept them safe from fear." They made no effort to maintain justice or to use their riches to help the poor. And they were oblivious to God, who had showed them "the two ways"—the hard way of justice and the easy one of vice.

Muhammad often spoke of the future. Like the ancient Hebrew prophets, he used it as a weapon, claiming that the sins that he saw everywhere in the present would be avenged in the future. A day of judgment awaited those who refused to believe in and obey Allah: "For when the trumpet is sounded, / That, at that time, shall be a difficult day, / For the unbelievers, anything but easy." Those who rejected Allah would have "an entertainment of boiling water / and burning in hell." Those who accepted God's teachings and followed them, in contrast, would enjoy an eternal life in paradise, which Muhammad vividly described. His teachings challenged the whole social world of Mecca and its merchants, with their worship of many gods. Soon Muhammad began to gain a reputation—a mixed one. Some, like his cousin Ali, found him and his teachings deeply impressive; others rejected his teachings. And as Muhammad gained followers, they attracted more and more unwelcome attention from the ruling groups.

FROM MECCA TO MEDINA At first, Muhammad appealed to members of more than one group. His religious ideals clearly resembled those of the monotheists who already lived near him in Arabia and whose traditions he respected. Muhammad not only regarded the Jewish prophets and the messengers of the Christian revelation as divinely inspired, but also hoped he might win their followers to his message. Accordingly, he adopted certain Jewish customs, such as facing east while praying. Soon, however, he realized that Mecca's inhabitants were incurably hostile to his beliefs. His criticisms of the worship of idols apparently enraged local men of wealth, who mistreated those of his followers who could not retaliate. Though Muhammad's clan protected him from violence, the other inhabitants of Mecca boycotted his followers and finally began to threaten Muhammad himself.

After some exploration he found a new home a couple of hundred miles to the north, at an oasis called Yathrib. It was a community with many Jews, where a fair number of people already saw themselves as monotheists. After making preparations, he sent his followers there ahead of him. Only when all had left Mecca safely did he and Ali depart, moving at first in the opposite direction, and finally join their friends. This journey, or *hijra*, to the city that came to be called Medina, took place in 622. As soon as they could, Muhammad's followers built a small complex where the Prophet, as they now knew him, could live and develop his revelations. They also established in Medina a place where he and his followers could prostrate themselves before Allah: Islam's first shrine. For centuries, these events have been taken as the real beginning of Islamic religion, and of practices that would remain characteristic of it for centuries. It was in Medina, for example, that Muhammad received the revelation that he and his followers should worship facing Mecca, rather than Jerusalem. Muhammad also approved polygamy by his example in this period. After the death of his first wife he married two others, one of them a scholar and religious thinker in her own right, whom he brought with him to Medina; there he married another four women.

THE FORMATION OF ISLAM

During the next ten years, Muhammad built both a religion and a community in Medina. The process was not easy or peaceful—nor did Muhammad expect it to be. The term for the religion he founded, *Islam*, is connected to the Arabic word for peace. It means "voluntary submission to God," and the word *Muslim*—which comes from the same root—refers to one who engages in that form of religious activity. But like Jesus, Muhammad did not come to bring his followers an easy or a peaceful life. His revelations included the concept of jihad ("effort," or "labor"): Muslims, he told them, had the duty to strive, to struggle. The word could refer to an internal effort to fight evil and do good—or to an external struggle against those, whether Muslims or not, who refused followers of Islam the right to practice their religion in the proper way. Muhammad himself led an attack on a Meccan caravan, which provoked efforts at retaliation. His new city had to hold off more than one attack, including a full-scale siege in 627 known as the Battle of the Trench, after the defenses that the Medinans dug.

By 632—when Muhammad moved back to Mecca, on the invitation of the leading clans, only to die shortly after his arrival—the new religion had taken on many features of what would become its permanent form. Shaped by persecution and then by exile, the new faith was now not accommodating to older gods and other deities. Although it is common to identify the three faiths as "Abrahamic" because of their shared origins and principles, the followers of Allah now set themselves apart from Jews and Christians, even though they continued to respect those traditions and revere their prophets. Allah demanded sole allegiance. As Muhammad uttered the verses that went into the Qur'an and the Hadith (the body of "traditions"

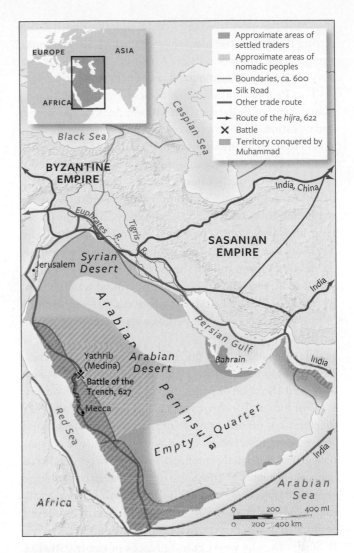

The Rise of Islam, 600–632 Islam took shape in the busy and diverse atmosphere of the Arabian Peninsula. Populated by Bedouin nomads as well as Arab traders settled in oasis towns such as Mecca, Arabia was crisscrossed by trade routes to Europe and Asia.

also acknowledged as authoritative), his statements became longer and more complex, and the system of belief and conduct they commanded developed into an articulated whole. The Kaaba in Mecca—once a pagan shrine—became the central place of worship for Islam, the new faith.

LIVING BY ALLAH'S COMMANDS Muhammad taught a rigorous code of belief and conduct. In the central command of the **Five Pillars of Islam**, the followers of Allah must acknowledge that God is supreme in goodness, knowledge, and mercy, incomparable to any other being, and that Muhammad is his messenger. But worshippers of Allah must do far more than proclaim God's greatness and loving kindness. The Five Pillars of Islam also required that Muslims pray five times daily; practice charity; fast during Ramadan, the ninth month of the year; and make a pilgrimage to Mecca. Every Muslim knew that his day, his year, and his lifetime must reflect these commands.

The Prophet called for a radical transformation in many areas of behavior. The inhabitants of the desert had traditionally followed a code that required immediate action to redress any slight to one's honor. If one member of a clan killed or injured a member of another, acts of retaliation followed—often for years. By contrast, Islam called for self-control and submission to God. Whereas the members of tribes had been fearless, Muslims feared God and disciplined their actions to reflect that fear. The tables of penalties that Muhammad and his followers devised shared the harshness of ancient Near Eastern and Roman law: the amputation of a hand was the punishment for theft. The tables reflected a systematic effort to impose an economy on violence that had often spread without limit.

Islam shared some requirements with the other Abrahamic religions. Like Jews, Muslims were forbidden to eat pork. But the code of Muhammad imposed rules on new areas of human life. Muslims must not drink wine. They must not cut off one or more of their children from their estate. Men must treat women with respect, and women, though not the equal of men, possessed rights even in what became the established system of polygamy: they retained control of their dowries and, under certain circumstances, they could initiate divorce. Like Christians, Muslims could own slaves. But the teachings of Muhammad aimed at mitigating the worst consequences of the institution. Concubines were automatically freed on their master's death, and the child of a free man and a slave woman was automatically free. Islam treated manumission of slaves as a highly meritorious act. Slave owners were warmly encouraged to free their slaves when they themselves died, if not before, and many did—though other Muslims continued to trade in slaves.

AN EXPANDING STATE

Muhammad's demanding code, and the community that strove to live by it, rapidly attracted followers. Muhammad himself was a gifted diplomat and politician as well as a prophet. During his years in Medina and after returning to Mecca in 632, he acted not only as the head of a sect but also as the ruler of a state. Subsequent rulers of the Muslims bore the title of **caliph** ("successor"), meaning

that they had taken on Muhammad's authority. And worshippers began to see themselves as members of a single *ummah*, or nation—a community constituted not by membership in kinship groups but by adherence to a common set of religious beliefs and practices. By the end of Muhammad's lifetime, effective preaching and clever diplomacy had won him power over all of Arabia.

THE QUESTION OF SUCCESSION But the question of succession to the position Muhammad had occupied introduced a measure of instability into Islam. Who was to become caliph? Those who had had personal connections with the Prophet? Those who were formally related to him? Those who showed the greatest ability? Muhammad's first two successors, Abu Bakr (632–634) and Umar (634–644), had been his close associates. They argued that Islam meant that all followers of the religion were bound not only to Muhammad but also to one another, and after a short civil war their position was generally accepted. During Umar's term as caliph, the Muslims made the conquests in Persia, the Levant, and Egypt that turned their society into an empire. Uthman (644–656), whom Muhammad inspired to become one of the first converts to Islam, continued to expand Islamic territory and encouraged economic activity. He also presided over the production of a full written text of the **Qur'an**, Islam's scripture. But some of his policies—especially his habit of granting his own family lucrative positions—stirred opposition. In 656, rebels entered his house and assassinated him. The next caliph—Ali, the Prophet's cousin and son-in-law, whom the rebels put in place—tried to reestablish what he saw as the purer principles of Muhammad. But he also confronted rebellious armies and was murdered after five years in office. From that time on, faithful Muslims have disagreed radically, and sometimes violently, about who is the rightful successor of the Prophet.

SHIITES AND SUNNIS The Shiites, who derived their name from the term *shia* ("party"), held that only someone directly descended from Muhammad through his daughter Fatima (and her husband, Ali) should be caliph. Gradually they came to believe that the true caliph should also be a holy man, or *imam*. But agreement among them broke down after Ali's sons Hasan and Husayn struggled for the succession and Husayn was put to death. The Sunnis, who gradually became the dominant group in most of the Islamic world, saw the caliph as a political leader appointed by a general consensus. Though they agreed that Ali had been the legitimate caliph, they insisted that his status was no different from that of the other caliphs before and after him. They supported the **Umayyads**—the family that took over the caliphate in the later seventh century and consolidated the creation of imperial Islam.

THE EARLY CONQUESTS (633–719)

Though struggles beset the caliphate from the start, it expanded with great force, and it is not hard to see why. The original armies of Islam were made up entirely of Arabs and believers. United by their religion and their world view, ready to combat injustice and irreligion, they moved with great speed. Unlike the heavily armed Byzantine forces, Muslim soldiers traveled light, using camels to carry everything they needed over their desert highway. The early caliphs devised a military system that effectively

bound the tribal warriors to them. Regular salaries and gifts of conquered land won their loyalty and ensured that support for the caliphate spread into new territories. The continued prominence of tribal chiefs—and the practice of relocating members of the same tribe near one another in new lands—were also important in ensuring loyalty.

The Byzantine and Sasanian Empires—exhausted by their recent conflicts—could put up no effective resistance. Muslim forces invaded Syria in 634 and controlled the Levant within a year. Sasanian Persia, invaded twice, in 633 and 636, fell in 651. So did the breadbasket of the Mediterranean world, Egypt, which Muslim armies attacked in 639, and North Africa. As a result of these conquests, Byzantium and Rome were cut off from the ship-borne supplies that had supported the growth of the great cities since the conquest of Carthage by the Roman Republic in the third and second centuries BCE. By the second decade

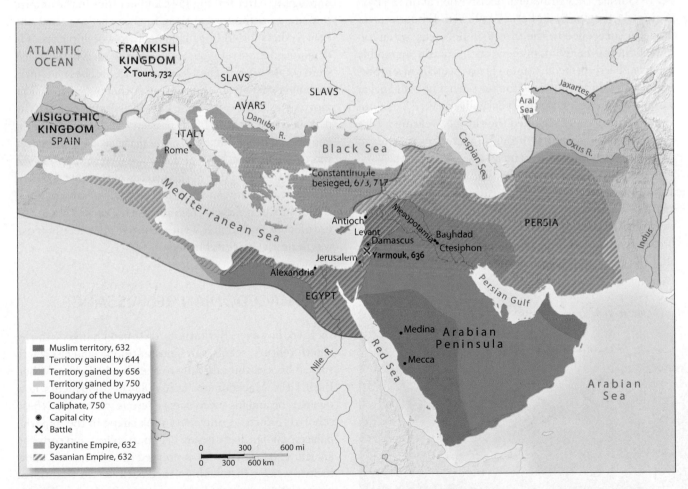

The Expansion of Islam, 632–750 Not long after Muhammad's death, the Islamic caliphate began to expand. Muslim armies spread first across the Arabian Peninsula into Egypt and southwestern Persia. By the middle of the seventh century, they had conquered the rest of Persia and large territories formerly ruled by Byzantium. By 750, the Umayyad Caliphate spanned from the Indus River in Asia to the Iberian Peninsula.

of the eighth century, the Islamic world, organized as the Umayyad Caliphate, extended from Asia to modern Spain. Eventually the faith and its followers would expand still farther, into sub-Saharan Africa, China, and India. Already, however, Islam had conquered all of the lands that would make up its core for centuries to come.

ISLAM AND BYZANTIUM: CULTURAL ADAPTATION (7TH–10TH CENTURIES)

As much of what had been the eastern empire, including the Holy Land itself, fell to the Arabs, Byzantium grew unstable. In the 620s, Heraclius had saved Byzantium from conquest by Sasanian Persia. But the armies of Islam proved superior to his. In 636, at Yarmouk, east of the Sea of Galilee, they inflicted a decisive defeat on the Byzantines. A long period of crisis followed. Emperor after emperor succeeded to the throne in his teens, often following the murder of his predecessor. After the incredibly tough and determined Justinian II was overthrown in 695, his enemies slit his nose and tongue so that he could never assume power again. But he eventually sneaked back into Constantinople and regained the throne, wearing a false nose of gold and speaking through an interpreter—only to be overthrown once more, and assassinated, in 711.

The Byzantines employed a mixture of tradition and innovation to keep the Muslims at bay. In 673 and again in 717 and after, Muslim efforts to conquer Constantinople failed. The great walls proved impossible to breach, and Greek fire—an oil-based incendiary weapon that the Byzantines shot, through siphons, onto enemy

Greek Fire A twelfth-century manuscript depicts the use of Greek fire by Byzantine forces. The Byzantines used this oil-based weapon to destroy the ships of Muslim invaders in 672 and 711.

ships—destroyed the Arab fleets. But the Muslim conquests continued in what is now Spain (711–718) and southern France (718–719). By this time, the Umayyad Caliphate ruled one of the greatest empires ever created. After these years, the westward progress of the caliphate's border slowed, and finally stopped, as the military situation in France grew stable.

ICONOCLASM

The challenge posed by Islam sent tremors through Byzantine society and culture. The emperor Leo the Isaurian (r. 717–741) fought the Umayyads to a standstill. He invited Slavs to settle in depopulated areas of the empire, freed large numbers of agricultural workers who had been tied to the soil, and reformed systems of taxation and law.

One of his most powerful innovations lay in the realm of religion. After forcing Jews and heretics in the empire to undergo orthodox baptism, in the years 726 to 729 he issued edicts forbidding his subjects to worship icons. He denounced these religious images as the sorts of idols that were condemned in the Hebrew Bible, and began efforts to remove them from churches and other holy places. The movement he led came to be known as **Iconoclasm** ("the destruction of images"). The patriarch resigned in protest, and a revolt broke out in Italy, where the worship of images was deeply rooted. Though Leo managed to suppress the revolt, it would be one of the origins of the long series of theological debates and political struggles that separated Byzantium definitively from the west. Debates about the use of icons in churches went on until 843, when their use was definitively reestablished.

THE MACEDONIAN RENAISSANCE

By then, however, Byzantium itself had changed. In the eighth century, scholars in Constantinople and elsewhere turned back enthusiastically to the Greek classics. When Basil I the Macedonian (r. 867–886) established a new dynasty, he and his successors generously supported these scholarly efforts. A university took shape in the imperial palace. Scholars had already begun to collect and copy the ancient texts, which were preserved in codices with a new form of writing that distinguished between the traditional capital letters and new, lowercase ones. In almost all cases, surviving texts of ancient Greek books descend from the copies made in this period. With official support, these scholars compiled immense encyclopedias of information about history, geography, technology, and other subjects useful for imperial purposes. The wealthy, technologically sophisticated Byzantium that Liutprand visited in the tenth century did not descend directly from the city of Constantine. Its culture was the product of deliberate efforts to revive and use the past—efforts so systematic that scholars have called this period the Macedonian Renaissance.

CALIPHATE CULTURE

The Umayyad Caliphate (661–750) founded its capital at Damascus in Syria—a place that had been inhabited for millennia and had the natural resources, as the oases of Arabia did not, to support a court and all that came with it. At first the Umayyads maintained the administrations of the lands they conquered, working with local officials of the former Byzantine government. They showed tolerance to Christians and Jews, even allowing churches to be built. By the end of the seventh century, however, their policies were changing. Arabic, which had been written for centuries, now became the official language of government. With administrators and judges appointed, and coins struck, the Umayyad Caliphate had become a massive, well-organized state. As its armed forces expanded—thousands of Persian soldiers converted to Islam and joined the Umayyad armies—the need for revenue increased, and government developed to cope with it.

SCRIPTURE AND INTERPRETATION Within the new state, a new culture took shape. Like the other Abrahamic religions, Islam developed a set of core texts: the fixed, canonical scripture of the Qur'an, and collections of the sayings and deeds of Muhammad not included in it, called the Hadith. Unlike the Hebrew Bible or the New Testament, the Qur'an does not follow a narrative structure. In rhythmic prose, it calls for worship of the one god, Allah; lays out his teachings and the code of conduct that his followers must accept; and evokes a future day of judgment. After Muhammad's death, as questions of interpretation arose, scholars gained prestige for their ability to solve these problems. Schools grew up around them—not only in Arabia but also in Syria, Palestine, and Egypt. More like Judaism in this respect than Christianity, Islam had no central religious authority, no pope or patriarchs who could claim widespread support for their own supreme status. Rather, the ulema, the body of learned men who forged theological and legal principles from the Qur'an and the Hadith, came to have a collective authoritative status.

Umayyad Mosque A mosaic from the western colonnade of the Umayyad Mosque in Damascus applies Byzantine style to new Islamic themes. The harmonious intertwining of huge trees, flowing water, and ornate buildings strung with hanging lamps or pearls evokes a heavenly or terrestrial paradise.

THE MOSQUE Formal religious services—and a system of institutions to support them—also came into existence as the caliphate became wealthy and powerful. As the Christians had taken over both Roman temples and the standard Roman form for a large public building, the basilica, so the Muslims began—in seventh-century Damascus, for example—to take over for worship the parts of a temple that had become a church, inside a vast enclosure. The temple structure was torn down, but its outside walls were preserved. Inside this enclosure and to the south, a vast prayer hall was erected. Facing it, a courtyard, surrounded by arcades, became the central space of the **mosque**—a new worship center that could easily expand when the need arose. Fountains cooled the air and enabled worshippers to wash. Magnificent mosaics depicted the landscape of paradise, a place of gardens and rivers. Muezzins called the faithful to prayer five times a day, led prayers, and in many cases became famous for the power with which they recited the rhythmic lines of the sacred text.

THE DOME OF THE ROCK Islamic architectural projects soon became at least as ambitious and splendid as Byzantine ones. As early as 685, the Umayyad caliph Abd al-Malik ibn Marwan began construction of a great shrine, the Dome of the Rock in Jerusalem. An octagon with an immense wooden dome, designed to rival the domed Church of the Holy Sepulcher built by Constantine, the Dome of the Rock was meant to house Muslim pilgrims on the Temple Mount. Its location was carefully chosen. For Jews, it was the site of the Second Temple, destroyed by the Romans in 70 CE during the siege of Jerusalem. For

Dome of the Rock Around 685, the Umayyad caliph Abd al-Malik ibn Marwan built the magnificent Dome of the Rock, its rotunda meant to rival the architecture of great Christian buildings. It still stands on the Temple Mount in Jerusalem, a site sacred to Muslims, Christians, and Jews alike. The complex tilework and the golden covering of the dome were added later.

Christians, it was the site of the Church of the Holy Wisdom, which Constantine's mother Helen had founded. For Muslims, however, it was the place where Muhammad had ascended to heaven, guided by the angel Gabriel.

The caliph rivaled the emperors of Byzantium as he exploited technology and art to create a new and spectacular sacred space. A work of engineering wondrous enough to compare to Hagia Sophia, the dome's gilt exterior reflected the sun so brilliantly "that no eye could look straight at it." Inside the shrine were brilliant marbles and mosaics—the latter executed by craftsmen from Byzantium. Inscriptions emphasized that Islam regarded Jesus as a true prophet but also denied that he was the Son of God. They stated that "God has no companion"—a clear attack on the Christian doctrine of the Trinity—and quoted the Qur'an for the first time, so far as is known. A century and a half after the Byzantine emperor Justinian's death, Islam had not only taken over much of his empire but also achieved a comparable mastery of art and nature. For all the questions about where authority did and would rest, the caliphate was clearly the most powerful, expansive organism in the bitterly competitive political ecosystem of the eighth- and ninth-century Mediterranean world.

THE HOUSE OF WISDOM Late in the eighth century, the caliph Haroun al-Rashid—perhaps imitating the rulers of Persia—created the House of Wisdom in Baghdad, a new city founded in 762 as the capital of the Abbasid Caliphate, successors to the Umayyads. In this institution, Muslims, Jews, and Christians studied a wide range of fields. They devised astrolabes and other tools for observing nature, collected maps and drew up new ones, and looked in books for ancient models of knowledge. Some of the inspiration for this work very likely came from a sense of rivalry with Byzantium, where scholars were also working to recover ancient texts. Many exchanges took place between Greeks and Muslims, with scholars from Constantinople taking part in diplomatic missions from the emperors to the caliphs. Collections of medical remedies and manuals on the interpretation of dreams were translated from Arabic into Greek: they may even have been commissioned by the imperial court.

ISLAMIC SCHOLARSHIP In the ninth and tenth centuries, scholars at the House of Wisdom and elsewhere collected, read, and translated many of the basic works of the ancient Greeks. This movement was first pursued systematically by Syrian Christians like Hunayn ibn Ishaq

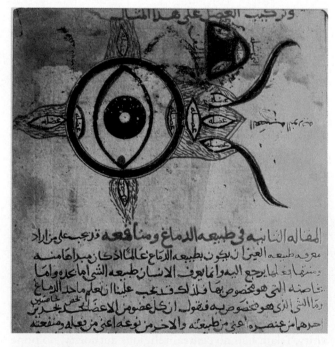

The House of Wisdom This illustration of the anatomy of the eye comes from a twelfth-century copy of the ninth-century *Book of the Ten Treatises on the Eye* by Syrian physician Hunayn ibn Ishaq. Like other members of the House of Wisdom, he translated the work of Galen and other Greek writers into Arabic, often adding important scientific insights of his own.

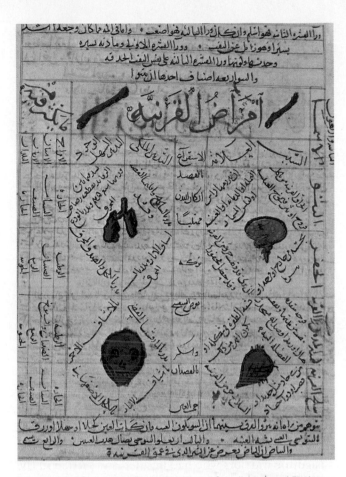

Islamic Learning A page from *The Canon of Medicine* (1025) by the Persian physician and scholar Avicenna (Ibn Sina) details the anatomy of the skull, lungs, stomach, and heart.

(809–873), who studied medicine in Baghdad and became the physician to the caliph. His interests embraced ancient Greek philosophy as well as medicine, and he translated Aristotle's works as well as those of the great Greek medical writer Galen. Islamic scholarship and teaching never embraced the whole of Greek thought: poetry, history, and tragedy did not win much interest in the Islamic world. Instead it developed its own forms of imaginative literature, such as the fantastic tales collected in *The Thousand and One Nights* and the philosophical novel written by Ibn Tufail in the twelfth century, *The Self-Taught Philosopher*. But the translation movement of the Abbasids brought the basic texts of Greek logic and philosophy, and the technical works of Greek astronomers and astrologers, cartographers, and medical scholars, into Arabic.

Within a few decades, Muslim philosophers were adding new ideas, methods, and discoveries to those of the Greeks. The Persian scholar Avicenna (Ibn Sina; ca. 980–1037), for example, wrote exhaustively on philosophy and medicine. His *Canon*, a massive medical textbook,

brought together the heritage of Greek medicine. Where theories differed—Aristotle had insisted on the central role of the heart in human physiology; Galen on that of the liver—he weighed them and suggested solutions. His work became the standard textbook not only in Islamic but also in Christian medical schools, where it was studied for centuries. The Muslim mathematician Muhammad ibn Musa al-Khwarizmi (ca. 750–ca. 830) and his colleagues formulated many of the rules of algebra, the very name of which (from *al-jabr*, "restoration") still records its origins. Christian administrators and businesspeople learned from translated Arabic works how to do computations rapidly and simply and how to keep accurate quantitative records.

THE WEST IN LATE ANTIQUITY (475–843)

In the eighth century, the Umayyads, who held on to power in most of the Iberian Peninsula, except for a couple of northern regions, were hoping eventually to push north into the former territories of the western Roman Empire. Byzantine emperors, as we have seen, still hoped to regain the lands in Italy and North Africa that Justinian had managed, for a time, to rule. Neither would have seen the little monarchies and impoverished churches that still existed in their time in Italy, Gaul, and the British Isles as even potential rivals. Yet, for all their weaknesses, the western lands were already constructing a new social order and political and religious institutions that would, eventually, underpin their own claim to world power.

The societies of western Europe had been undergoing a slow transformation from the fourth century on. Relics of the Roman past—and many members of the old Romano-British and Gallo-Roman aristocracies—survived for centuries. Roman roads continued to serve for travel and transport of goods; Roman aqueducts, sewers, and baths continued to function; and leading men in Britain and Gaul continued to aspire to Roman ideals of both social life and government. Germanic peoples were also present in the former Roman territories, normally because they had provided paid military service. Late in the fourth century, in response to a king's request for aid in a dispute, Saxons, Angles, and Jutes from northern Germany entered Britain with threatening force. The Roman Empire did not respond to requests for help, and though the British won a number of battles, by the end of the sixth century these so-called Saxons had conquered most of Britain and established a number of small kingdoms there. By then most vestiges of Roman social and economic life were gone.

THEODORIC'S GOTHIC REALM

The first systematic effort to re-create institutions in the Latin west—the kingdom of Theodoric the Great—was a remarkable attempt to continue and transform the Roman state. **Theodoric** (r. 475–526) led the eastern branch of the Goths, or Ostrogoths. Empowered by an agreement with the emperor in Constantinople to recapture Italy, which had been conquered in 476 by the Germanic leader Odoacer, Theodoric conducted an effective campaign. He defeated Odoacer with the help of the Visigoths, the western Goths who had established themselves in the Iberian Peninsula earlier in the century. Isolated in Ravenna, which he had made his capital city, Odoacer made peace with Theodoric in 493 and agreed to split Italy with him— only to have Theodoric murder him, with his own hands, at the banquet held to celebrate their pact.

From 493 until his death in 526, Theodoric ruled with considerable skill. Officially he served as *patricius* ("noble of senatorial rank"), representing the emperor in Constantinople, but effectively he ruled his own lands independently. Through astute marriage alliances and generalship—in military affairs Theodoric relied exclusively on the Goths and their allies—he made himself, in effect, the ruler of a Gothic realm that stretched from modern France to the Balkans, and included for a time the Vandal kingdom in Africa as well. Romans loyal to tradition appreciated Theodoric's support for the circus and its games. Like most Goths, Theodoric was an Arian—a believer in the view that because God the Father had created the Son, Jesus could not be divine. But Catholics and Jews were grateful for the tolerance that he extended to their forms of worship: "We cannot," he wrote to the Jews of Genoa, "order a religion, because no one can be forced to believe against his will."

Members of old Roman noble families—Symmachus, his son-in-law Boethius, and Cassiodorus—served Theodoric, combining such traditional offices as the consulship with the post

Theodoric the Great The Ostrogothic king Theodoric drew on memories of Roman authority to consolidate his reign in Italy. Following the Roman model of including an emperor's portrait on coins, he minted a solidus that was a close copy of a contemporary Byzantine coin.

of *magister officiorum* in the Ravenna court. They composed official rulings and drafted official correspondence for him. Early in the sixth century, when the pope and the Eastern Orthodox Church split on theological grounds, Theodoric even found himself allied with his theological opponents. By the end of Theodoric's reign, the synthesis he had brought into being was already showing deep signs of wear. His treaty with the Vandals broke down, the Visigoths reasserted their independence, and he left no adult heir. Angry, paranoid, and very likely surrounded by real enemies, Theodoric had Boethius and Symmachus arrested on suspicion of treason. Charged with aiming to restore the power of the Senate and with conspiracy with Constantinople, Boethius was executed with extreme cruelty in 524. Theodoric himself died soon after. Neither the female regent he left in command nor her cousin, who deposed her, proved capable of rallying the Gothic nobility against Justinian. Byzantine authority was restored in Italy and much of the west.

In most of the Iberian Peninsula, however, the Visigoths who had supported Theodoric maintained their independence. Leovigild (r. 568–586) fought fiercely against the Byzantines, and toward the end of his reign began to bring his people back into the Catholic fold. He also began the long, slow process of removing barriers between the Visigothic warriors who had invaded and settled in the peninsula and the older Roman families who had long cultivated the land. In the course of the seventh century, the Visigoths elaborated a sophisticated legal code. The king was described as a holy ruler, and though he did not interfere with the church on matters of doctrine, Visigothic kings not only appointed bishops but also excommunicated criminals. Fierce regulations and severe physical punishment were brought into play to force the peninsula's Jews to convert: failing to observe the Christian day of rest on Sunday, for example, could result in a Jew's being flogged and scalped. This warrior society, with its violent code of law, survived until the Islamic invasions transformed the Mediterranean world.

LOMBARD DUCHIES IN ITALY

But the Byzantine government in Ravenna did not enjoy authority for long. In the 540s, a Germanic people known as the Lombards—whom a Roman history memorably and paradoxically described as "a people fiercer than the fierceness of the Germans"—moved into Pannonia (now part of Hungary). In 568 a bold and effective ruler,

Germanic Kingdoms in 500 and 650 By the end of the fifth century, Germanic tribes ruled most of western Europe. Jutes, Angles, and Saxons had invaded Britain from northern Germany; the Gothic king Theodoric the Great controlled a large region reaching from Spain to the Balkans; and the Franks, Visigoths, and Vandals had established other independent territories. From 568, the Lombards invaded much of the Italian Peninsula, and the Franks began to significantly expand their rule in Gaul.

Alboin, led them and several other tribes across the Alps into Italy. They soon established what they called a Lombard "duchy" in the northeast and then proceeded to move south through Italy. Byzantine resistance was weak, and Milan fell in 569.

The Lombards terrified the Romans. With their striped clothing and long hair, they looked like the very image of barbarians. They starved out the Roman cities of Tuscany. Only ports, which the Byzantine navy could defend and supply, remained independent. Christian authorities claimed that the Lombards rifled churches and confiscated all the valuables. They established their capital at Pavia, while other communities, such as Naples

and Benevento, became the seats of the thirty-six Lombard dukes who ruled almost the entire Italian Peninsula. Groups of Lombard families, organized at first for combat, spread through Italy.

Some Italians decided it would be possible to live with the Lombards, and surrendered to them. Gradually the Lombards themselves became, to some extent at least, recognizably Romanized. Impressed by the coherence of Roman law, they began to codify the elaborate rules that regulated crime and the vendettas that followed, the manumission of slaves, and the relations between landowners and those who served them, in Latin codes of their own. Though they were Arians, one of their queens, the Bavarian Catholic Theudelinda, did her best to support the Latin church. At first her efforts met mostly with resistance. By the end of the eighth century, however, a Lombard monk from Monte Casino, Paul the Deacon, could write the whole history of his people from an impeccably Catholic point of view.

THE HERITAGE OF THE ANCIENTS IN THE LATIN WEST

Through the sixth and seventh centuries—while the Roman senatorial elite slowly lost its wealth and power, the Senate itself was disbanded, and such central Roman institutions as the circus ceased to exist—the foundations of a new culture were being laid. Members of the old elite played a crucial role in this project.

THE WORKS OF BOETHIUS When Boethius (ca. 480–524), superbly educated in Greek and Latin, was imprisoned by Theodoric in 523, he composed a great dialogue, *The Consolation of Philosophy*. In it Philosophy, personified as a woman dressed in splendid clothing that has become worn and ragged, visits him in prison. In a magnificent set of speeches, she leads him through arguments that ease his suffering, not by improving his condition but by showing him the truth. As Boethius and Philosophy examine key moments in his past and stories from ancient history and literature, he learns that Fortune, the fickle force that bestows wealth and position, takes them away just as arbitrarily. In an image that painters and poets would elaborate on for centuries, Philosophy depicts Fortune as a goddess who turns a wheel that first raises the men who ride on it but then throws them down: "As thus she turns her wheel of chance with

Wheel of Fortune In this fifteenth-century French manuscript of *The Consolation of Philosophy,* Boethius encounters the goddess Fortune—portrayed here as a queen—and her wheel of fate.

haughty hand... fortune now tramples fiercely on a fearsome king, and now deceives no less a conquered man by raising from the ground his humbled face."

Happily, Boethius learns, it is not this frightening being but God who rules the universe. Being eternal, God has foreknowledge. Since all time—past, present, and future—is the same to him, he knows everything that will happen, including human mistakes and sins. But God does not cause these sins. From their own standpoint, humans, who live in time, freely choose between good and evil. Philosophy, in other words, teaches us both that the universe is ruled by divine Providence, and that humans make their own fates and have the duty to live virtuously.

Boethius's dialogue—composed in a mixture of prose and verse—is one of the most culturally revealing products of late antiquity. From the third and fourth centuries on, Christians searched for ways to make creative use of the ideas and writings of the best pagans. Boethius was definitely a Christian, but in *The Consolation of Philosophy* he never mentions the Christian God or Jesus. Instead, he argues that there is a divine order behind the apparent chaos and injustice of this world. The study of the liberal arts and of philosophy allow humans to understand this order and to live virtuously within it. As Latin Christianity began to develop a formal theology in the eighth century and after, Boethius's work remained essential.

CASSIODORUS: LEARNING AS THE PATH TO GOD Even more significant was the work of another Roman aristocrat and government official, Cassiodorus (ca. 490–ca. 585). After the struggles that followed the death of Theodoric, he spent time in retirement in Constantinople and then, after 550, moved to his ancestral lands in southern Italy. There, on an estate that he named Vivarium ("fish-pond") after the ponds that Roman aristocrats stocked with fish on their estates, he created a monastic community. Cassiodorus's writings touched on many subjects. Like other writers in the fifth and sixth centuries who drew up compendia and syntheses, as if they glimpsed that the world would soon change and many of the books to which they had access would disappear, Cassiodorus wrote a history of the world. But his central achievement—the one that proved formative for the culture of the Latin west—was to define Christian culture, especially monastic culture, as bookish.

Cassiodorus had tried to establish a center of Christian higher learning in Rome but failed "because of continual wars and raging battles in the Kingdom of Italy." Accordingly, he set out to create with words what he had failed to build in three dimensions: a guide to learning that would lead Christians to "ascend without hesitation to Holy Scripture through the praiseworthy commentaries of the Fathers." In his *Institutes*, a treatise on the disciplines and their uses, Cassiodorus showed the reader how to master not only the Bible and its commentaries but also the ancient liberal arts, for each of which he provided a brief description and a bibliography. Cassiodorus adopted a classification created by a scholar from North Africa, Martianus Capella, who divided the seven liberal arts into two categories: the humanistic arts of language, grammar, and rhetoric, and the "scientific" arts of arithmetic, geometry, astronomy, and music. Cassiodorus added that dialectic, the art of argument, had both humanistic and scientific aspects.

The library that he assembled in his own monastery disappeared during the troubles that later afflicted the Italian Peninsula. But Cassiodorus made clear that the Christian life must center on a systematic, intensive encounter with the sacred texts: "Therefore, pray to God, the source of all that is useful; read constantly; go over the material diligently; for frequent and intense meditation is the mother of understanding." And he explained that Christian scholars must not just collect the scriptures and other texts but do their best to copy texts for future generations and ensure that they were correct. The path to God—for Cassiodorus, and for generations of later Christians—thus lay through learning.

FOUNDING THE MEDIEVAL LATIN CHURCH

In an age of invasion and political upheaval, late antique thinkers in the West worked hard to preserve classical texts, arts, and ideas in a form in which Christians could use them. Two more men, both of them as deeply connected as Boethius and Cassiodorus to the old Roman world, transformed the Christian church. Benedict of Nursia and Pope Gregory, later known as Gregory the Great, are fought over by historians precisely because they belong to two different worlds: the surviving ancient one that formed them and the early medieval one that they helped to create.

BENEDICT AND THE BENEDICTINES
Benedict (ca. 480–ca. 547), born to a substantial family and educated at Rome, decided while young to follow the monastic life. In 529 at Monte Cassino, on a hill overlooking the road from Rome to Naples, he created a new kind of religious community and drew on existing models to compose his *Rule*, a book that set down its principles. Benedict saw the monastery not, as the eastern Desert Fathers had, as a collection of brilliant spiritual soloists, each ascending to God in his own cell, but as a choir singing in harmony, a community governed by an abbot or father and linked in their pursuit of holiness.

Abbey of Saint Scholastica A sixth-century fresco from the Abbey of Saint Scholastica in Italy provides an early view of monks and nuns who, in their uniform clothing and plain surroundings, conformed to Benedict and Scholastica's prescriptions for a holy, ordered life.

Benedict at Monte Cassino This illustration from an eleventh-century Italian manuscript imagines Benedict seated in front of the Abbey of Monte Cassino, where the abbot presents him with books produced by the abbey's monks, symbolizing the lasting influence of the religious order that Benedict inspired with his *Rule*.

The monks were to lead an ordered life, divided into periods devoted to manual labor, study of the Bible and other texts, and performance of the liturgy—which was, and would remain, the central task of Benedictines over the centuries. Again and again through each day and night, at each of the eight canonical "hours" that began at midnight with Matins (the morning service), the monks would rise and chant the service, sometimes for hours. These prayers did not come to an end until nine in the evening, with Compline. The Lombards destroyed Monte Cassino, along with the other Italian monasteries, not long after Benedict died. But his model—which soon became an order, whose members founded houses across the Latin west—turned into the first great Latin model of the religious life, one that still survives.

SCHOLASTICA
Monasticism was not confined to men. According to Pope Gregory, whose *Dialogues* depicted many incidents from Benedict's life, Benedict's sister Scholastica was, if anything, more of a miracle-worker than her

brother. She founded a community of nuns not far from Monte Cassino, which was probably directed by Benedict as well. In the following centuries, double monasteries, in which a convent for nuns accompanied a monastery for monks, spread across Europe. Such houses attracted many women of high birth, like Scholastica, and it was common for the abbess to take charge of both houses, the male as well as the female. Some abbesses claimed to possess the power to hear confession and grant absolution. Nuns, like monks, sang psalms, fasted, and kept vigils at night; like monks, too, they carried out the administrative jobs that their houses required, such as overseeing the wine cellar, the making of cloth, and the gate where visitors were admitted. Those who could read were expected to teach the illiterate. Some became scribes. According to the life of a sixth-century French bishop, "the virgins of Christ lettered most beautifully the divine books." Others wrote lives of holy men and women. The abbey offered women of different origins the chance to pursue spiritual lives as systematically and intensively as male monks.

GREGORY: SUSTAINING THE CHURCH If Benedict created one of the medieval church's central institutions, **Gregory** (ca. 540–604) rebuilt the church as a whole. Born into an aristocratic Roman family whose ancestral house was near the Colosseum, he served as prefect of Rome. When he turned, still early in life, to the monastic vocation, he transformed his family estates into monasteries. Later he represented the Roman church to the Byzantine imperial court in Constantinople. In 590, Gregory was proclaimed pope unanimously by the clergy, nobles, and ordinary people of Rome. A man of great personal humility, Gregory preferred the title bishop of Rome to the grander one of pope. But he devoted unremitting energy to the interests of the church he worked for as *servus servorum Dei*—"servant of the servants of God."

As an experienced administrator, Gregory knew the importance of maintaining and preserving the church's lands and other properties, and he defended these by every means at his disposal against Lombard invaders and everyone else who hoped to dispossess the church. His motive for doing so was deeply Christian. As the Lombard invasions destroyed public order and thousands of once solid citizens and farmers found themselves wandering the roads of Italy, homeless and impoverished, Gregory used the church itself to sustain them. He organized public distributions of bread and other forms of poor relief and created hospitals to help cope with the devastation wrought by plague.

Gregory Pope Gregory, portrayed in this ninth-century Italian fresco, was celebrated for his humility and service to the church. He converted his family estates into monasteries, created hospitals in response to plague, and organized the distribution of bread among the poor.

To support all this activity, and to ensure that the church had the resources to sustain it, Gregory also created a new administrative structure. Elaborate records carefully kept by officials provided a foundation for the church's claims to lands and income. Always better equipped than any rival institution in Italy with records, and always better able to produce public documents, the church became the chief heir in the west to Rome's mastery of filing and control systems. Gregory was passionately committed to the church's spiritual tasks as well. He made long-lasting changes in the order of the Catholic Mass and helped to create the form of plainchant that came to be known as "Gregorian chant." He also collected the miracles of Benedict and other saints, and told their stories dramatically in his *Dialogues*—a work that represents the beginning of one of the church's most durable projects and one that goes on to this day: its massive effort to record, evaluate, and classify the deeds of the saints and identify those that were genuinely miraculous.

Finally, in his *Rule of Pastoral Care*, Gregory put forward a new ideal of the priestly life, aimed not at those who lived as monks in closed communities but at those who served Christians in the world. For centuries to come, most prelates such as bishops and archbishops, abbots and abbesses, would be, like Gregory himself, men and women of high birth. But Gregory insisted that social standing on its own did not make a bishop. The true prelate, like the true monk, must aim high: "The conduct of a prelate ought so far to be superior to the conduct of the people as the life of a shepherd is accustomed to exalt him above the flock." This was, of course, an ideal, but it inspired Gregory himself. He had hoped to go to Britain as a missionary when his career was interrupted by his elevation to the bishopric of Rome. By the end of the sixth century, despite the disruptions of the Lombard invasions, he was sending missionaries to bring the Christian message to the Angles and Saxons living in what is now England.

CHRISTIANITY IN IRELAND By Gregory's time the church's missionary enterprise was well established. Rome's effort to enlarge the frontiers of Christianity in northern Europe centered on Ireland, which was converted to Christianity when missionaries—most famously a Briton, Saint Patrick—reached the island in the fifth century and began to preach. An effective advocate, he ordained priests and presided over them as a bishop. Soon, noblemen and noblewomen founded monasteries, and the Irish monks mastered Latin with enthusiasm. They developed great skill in copying texts, which they wrote out in splendid calligraphic scripts and decorated with magnificent illustrations—everything from full-page portraits to drawings of technical concepts to whimsical flora and fauna sprawling in the margins. These illuminated manuscripts were beautiful to look at and made texts more accessible to readers. They also began to write their own Latin poetry—verse of great wit and skill in which they deployed an immense vocabulary in the service of acrostics, puns, and other forms of wordplay, as well as in the praise of God. Their work even shows acquaintance with Hebrew and Greek words—an extraordinary phenomenon at a time when most western clerics in Italy and Gaul knew only Latin.

Irish monasteries attracted students from England as well as their own land. In 563, Saint Columba transplanted their monastic system to Scotland, and from there it spread through the British Isles and to Gaul. To help

The Book of Durrow Irish monasteries became famous for their illuminated manuscripts. The Book of Durrow, a colorfully decorated text of the Gospels, was likely created in the second half of the seventh century by Irish monks. In this full-page illustration, a detailed geometric design interlaces various animals.

ordinary Christians come to terms with their sins, Irish monks composed penitentials: short treatises that listed the sins and prescribed prayers for repentance. This new spiritual tool made the Irish priests highly effective as missionaries and counselors.

BEDE: A NEW CHRISTIAN CULTURE Irish monks and Roman clerics disagreed, however, on vital points: for example, when to celebrate the central Christian feast, Easter. Each side claimed to follow the accounts in the

Gospels and the traditions of the church, and each found followers. Debate led to a synod, held at Whitby in northern Britain in 665, where the Roman side won—as Bede, a monk of the nearby Benedictine house of Jarrow, recorded with some satisfaction.

The Venerable Bede (d. 735) himself was an expert on time and the calendar, on which he wrote a detailed and useful book. More important, he had the intellectual resources to write, in the first decades of the eighth century, a magnificent *Ecclesiastical History of the English People*. This dramatic book recorded not only the debates about the calendar but the whole course of the Christianization of Britain, in rich and sometimes poetic detail. As Irish, Italian, Gallic, and British monks argued and swapped texts, a new Christian culture was taking shape: one that could do more than preserve the Bible and its commentators. Gradually—as Bede made clear in his history—the Roman church established its authority over the larger structure of the church's calendar and liturgy. But appointments to the important offices in the church remained in the hands of local rulers, whom clerics served as counselors.

THE FRANKISH KINGDOM: THE MEROVINGIANS (483–561)

As a new Christian culture spread through Britain, a new authority took hold in Gaul that blended Roman and Germanic traditions. Bands of **Franks**—Germanic warriors—had crossed the Rhine into Gaul since the third century. Some of them the Romans wiped out; others, however, joined the Roman army, and many of their leaders eventually gained high positions in the Roman administration. In the fifth century, Roman authority faded, and the Franks began a series of conquests that put them, by the end of the century, in control of northern Gaul, while the Ostrogoths still ruled in the south.

CLOVIS The Franks' historical tradition crystallized around a figure called Merovech, supposedly the founder of the Merovingian dynasty who led them in the fifth century and after. But the solidly attested part of their history begins with Clovis I (466–511), supposedly Merovech's grandson, who came on the scene in 483. Merovingian power rested on the ability to mobilize a large number of skilled and ferocious warriors. Clovis did this with exceptional skill. He defeated Visigoths, Ostrogoths, and Burgundians and created a Frankish realm that stretched,

at its farthest extent, from the Pyrenees to the Danube. Paris served briefly as his capital, though he was always in motion. Even the Byzantine emperor recognized Clovis's rule over vast areas of the west. After Clovis's death in 511, his four adult sons divided the kingdom and established four separate capitals, in Reims, Orléans, Paris, and Soissons. Though Clothar, the son based in Soissons, reunited the kingdom in 558, a new division into three parts followed his death in 561.

FUSING GERMANIC AND ROMAN INSTITUTIONS In the Frankish kingdoms, Germanic and Roman practices and organizations were fused into something new. Roman landowners continued to operate their great villas, using a labor force tied to the land. Members of the Frankish nobility also accumulated wealth and power. Free Roman and Gallic small farmers, arms-bearing men who had the right to settle their own quarrels in their own Roman courts, dominated the landscape in large parts of northern Gaul. Other cultivators were legally classified as "half free" and possessed only limited rights. Roman cities such as Lyon and Bordeaux, which continued to serve as centers of exchange, dwindled into small local capitals, their populations sharply reduced from what they had been in the first and second centuries CE.

The personal power of the Frankish kings continued to rest on their ability to mobilize a large retinue of free warriors. But they also took over vast amounts of public land, where estates cultivated by bound peasant labor had provided the basic revenues for the Roman administration. With this new wealth, and with the many Gallo-Roman inhabitants who continued to possess resources and influence, the Franks erected courts that followed Roman models in key ways. High officials who bore the title *comes* ("count") oversaw the royal treasury, transportation, and other practical matters, and administered the districts of the kingdom, independently for the most part. The *maior domus* ("head of the household") oversaw the royal court—a position that would become increasingly powerful in the sixth century, as king after king died leaving minors as their only heirs. Yet Frankish kings were still formally acclaimed by being raised on shields, in accordance with the ancient custom by which the assembly of free warriors had elected and proclaimed war-leaders. The traditions of the Franks were still preserved in songs, and their rulers—as we will see—did not master the writing of Latin, though they understood it. They concentrated on the traditional skills of hunting and fighting.

The church had survived more or less intact in the

ROMAN AND GERMANIC LAW

The Germanic kingdoms had their own ancient laws, but their earliest written collections of laws were only created after contact with the Romans. When read in full, Roman and Germanic laws provide a wealth of information about regulations, everyday concerns of fairness and justice, and methods of dispute resolution in the societies that created them. Just the section titles alone, like the sampling given in the two sources here, provide a strong sense of each society's priorities.

From *The Digest of Justinian*

The *Digest* is a collection of writings over many centuries by Roman jurists, organized by topic into fifty books. It was promulgated by Emperor Justinian in 533.

I.
   I. On justice and law
  II. On the origin of law and of the different magistracies, as well as the succession of those learned in the law
 III. On statutes, decrees of the Senate and long usage
 IV. On Imperial enactments
 IX. Concerning Senators
  X. On the office of Consul
XXI. On the office of one to whom jurisdiction is delegated

II.
 III. Where a man refuses obedience to the magistrate exercising jurisdiction
  V. Where one who is cited fails to appear; also where a man cites one whom, according to the Edict, he has no right to cite
  X. On one who contrives that a defendant shall not appear
XIII. On statement of particulars and discovery of documents etc.

III.
 IV. On proceedings taken on behalf of any corporation or against the same

IV.
 II. Acts done through fear
 IV. On persons under twenty-five

V.
  I. On trials at law; as to where a man ought to take proceedings or be sued
 III. On the action for recovery of an inheritance
 IV. On suits for parts of an inheritance

VII.
VII. On the Services of Slaves

VIII.
 II. On Servitudes of Urban Estates
 III. On Servitudes of Rustic Estates
 IV. Rules common to Urban and Rustic Estates

XI.
 III. On Corrupting a Slave
 IV. On Fugitive Slaves
  V. On Gamblers
 VI. When a Surveyor makes a false report as to Dimensions
VII. On Things Religious and Funeral Expenses and on the right to conduct funerals

From *The Laws of the Salian Franks*

The laws of the Salian Franks, a Germanic group living in what is now the northern Netherlands, were probably recorded during the time of Clovis I in the sixth century, then later revised and expanded under the Merovingians and Carolingians.

   I. Concerning a Summons to Court
  II. Concerning the Theft of Pigs
 III. Concerning the Theft of Cattle
 IV. Concerning the Theft of Sheep
  V. Concerning the Theft of Goats
 VI. Concerning the Theft of Dogs
 VII. Concerning the Theft of Birds
VIII. Concerning the Theft of Bees
 XI. Concerning Thefts or Housebreaking Committed by Freemen
 XII. Concerning Thefts or Breaking-in Committed by Slaves
XIII. Concerning the Abduction of Freemen or Free Women

 XIV. Concerning Waylaying or Pillaging
  XV. Concerning Homicide or the Man Who Takes Another Man's Wife While Her Husband Still Lives
 XVI. Concerning Arson
XVIII. Concerning Him Who Accuses Before the King an Innocent Man Who is Absent
 XIX. Concerning Magic Philters or Poisoned Potions
  XX. Concerning the Man Who Touches the Hand or Arm or Finger of a Free Woman
XXIII. On Mounting a Horse Without the Consent of Its Owner
XXIV. On Killing Children and Women
 XXV. On Having Intercourse with Slave Girls or Boys
XXIX. Concerning Disabling Injuries
XXXII. On the Tieing-up of Freemen
XXXIV. Concerning Stolen Fences
XXXV. Concerning the Killing or Robbing of Slaves
XXXIX. On Those Who Instigate Slaves to Run Away
  XL. Concerning the Slave Accused of Theft
 XLI. On the Killing of Freemen
XLVIII. Concerning False Testimony
  LV. On Despoiling Dead Bodies
  LX Concerning Him Who Wishes to Remove Himself from His Kin Group
 LXIV. Concerning Sorcerers
LXVe. On Killing Pregnant Women
 LXX. On Cremation
LXLVIII. Concerning the Woman Who Joins Herself to Her Slave

QUESTIONS FOR ANALYSIS

1. How important were politics and civic life to the Roman jurists whose writings were consolidated into the *Digest*?
2. In what ways do the laws of the Salian Franks demonstrate an interest in limiting violence and vengeance in Germanic society?
3. What are the most significant areas of similarity and difference between Roman and Germanic law?

Sources: Charles Henry Monro, trans., *The Digest of Justinian* (Cambridge: 1904–9), pp. vi–xi; Katherine Fischer Drew, ed., *The Laws of the Salian Franks* (Philadelphia: 1991), pp. 59–63.

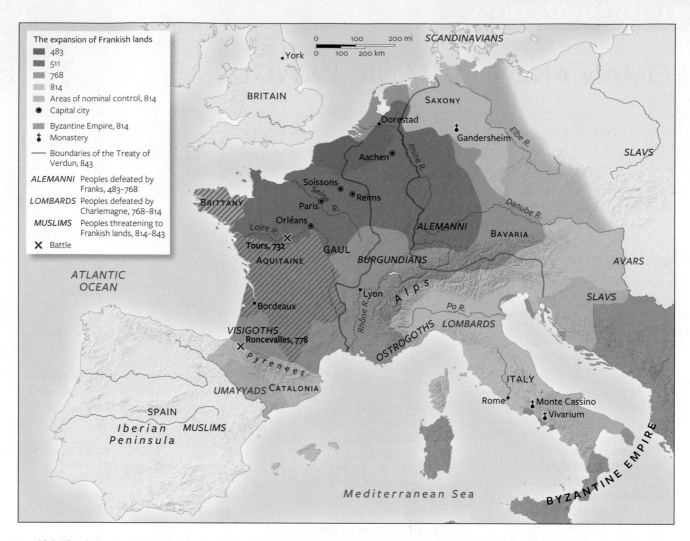

Frankish Kingdoms, 483–843 By the early sixth century, the Merovingian king Clovis I had defeated rival Germanic tribes to gain control of northern Gaul. His four sons divided the kingdom, governing separately from their capitals of Orléans, Paris, Soissons, and Reims. In 732, the Carolingian king Charles Martel defeated Umayyad forces at Tours. When his great-grandson Charlemagne acceded to the throne in 768, he began a program of expansion, ultimately controlling Frankish territory from the Umayyad borderlands in Catalonia, to the Italian Peninsula as far south as Rome, and to the Elbe and Danube Rivers in the east.

Frankish lands, and bishops based in cities still administered its dioceses. Inspired by his wife Clothilde, a Burgundian princess and a Catholic, Clovis converted to Christianity. A tradition, perhaps based on the life of Constantine, holds that he did so after praying for and winning a victory over the Alamanni, another Germanic tribe. From his time on, the Frankish rulers effectively exercised power over the church within their realms, more or less as the Byzantine emperors did in theirs. But though the Frankish churches were Catholic, they were also locally controlled. The lords who ruled their lands also appointed their clergy, without practical input from the pope.

THE FRANKISH EMPIRE: THE CAROLINGIANS (768–843)

In the course of the eighth century, the kings of the northeastern Franks—the Merovingians—gradually ceded more and more of their power to another family, the **Carolingians**, descended from noble Frankish clans. The Carolingians took possession first of the office of mayor of the palace, becoming dominant figures in the court and building a powerful army. In 732, one of them, Charles Martel ("the hammer"), defeated the forces of the Umayyad Caliphate that had crossed the Pyrenees between Tours and Poitiers, at what came to be called the battle of Tours. Though no one could have known it at the time, this eventually turned out to be the end of Islam's expansion from the Iberian Peninsula into Gaul. Charles also encouraged and protected missionaries from Britain, notably Saint Boniface (d. 754), who set out to convert the Germans. Charles's grandson, Pepin the Short, became king of a larger Frankish realm in 751. And Pepin's son, Charlemagne ("Charles the Great"), turned the Frankish kingdom into the largest and most successful empire the west had seen in centuries.

CHARLEMAGNE **Charlemagne** (r. 768–814) cut an impressive figure—in a world of relatively small men and women, he was more than six feet tall—and was an effective warrior. Though officially he shared his inherited crown with his brother Carloman, his preeminence became clear. He added vast stretches of territory to the domains of the Franks—from Aquitaine (eastern France), through Saxony and Bavaria (Germany), to Hungary.

Passionately committed to Christianity, Charlemagne

Charlemagne A ninth-century bronze statue of Charlemagne on a horse shows him wearing the crown and stately clothing befitting an emperor. The globe in his left hand is a symbol of his own power and of the new Holy Roman Empire's historic reach.

not only conquered the Saxons and Bavarians but also destroyed the shrines of their gods. He continued to recruit missionaries from Britain, though his own efforts took the form of smashing and burning idols and executing those who continued using pagan practices. He also defeated the Avars, nomads from Asia who had settled in and fortified much of what is now Hungary. By the 770s, Charlemagne was campaigning successfully in Italy, where he conquered the Lombard cities. He also moved forces across the Pyrenees into the Iberian Peninsula, most of it still ruled by the Umayyad Emirate of Córdoba. Though his rear guard was wiped out at Roncevalles, he and his sons took territory in Catalonia, beginning a struggle between Christians and Muslims for the Iberian lands that would last for hundreds of years.

VASSALS AND ENVOYS Charlemagne did his best to organize the vast territories that he ruled. Under the Merovingians, great lords were connected to lesser ones through a ritual. The vassal—the lesser nobleman or warrior who was to be the subject—placed his hands inside those of the lord. Then he swore an oath to serve the lord, who in turn swore to protect the vassal and to rely on him, both as a warrior and as a counselor. Charlemagne made intensive use of this practice, which came to be called **fealty**.

At the same time, though, Charlemagne used special officials called *missi dominici* ("the lord's envoys"). Traveling in pairs—one of them was normally a cleric, one a layman—they visited both the lords and communities ruled by Charlemagne and his own possessions. They systematically examined the administration of the laws, the collection of revenues due the ruler, and the governance of Charlemagne's own manors. They reported back directly to the emperor, who threatened severe punishment for anyone who harmed them or interfered with their work. As we will see, both of Charlemagne's ways of securing his power—the swearing-in of loyal vassals and the construction of new institutions such as his envoys—would be vital for centuries to the states that came after his.

A NEW EMPEROR At the end of the eighth century, Pope Leo III, supposedly mistreated by the Romans, appealed to Charlemagne for help. Charlemagne responded, calling a church council at Rome. On Christmas Day in 800 CE, the pope crowned him emperor. The act was dramatic: it indicated that the Roman Empire—which should mark, according to the book of Daniel, the last stage of history before the end of time—could be continued, as authority over it passed to a new dynasty. But the pope also saw himself as creating something new: a **Holy Roman Empire** that would act as the protector of the church. From this point on, Byzantium could no longer claim sole rights to be Rome's successor state. Charlemagne had become not only a claimant to power but also a world figure—one recognized both by the ruthless empress Irene of Byzantium, who proposed marriage (which he prudently declined), and by the learned Abbasid caliph of Baghdad, Haroun al-Rashid, who sent him an elephant (which he appreciated). Yet debates would also rage for centuries to come. Who was the master—the pope who crowned the emperor or the emperor who protected the pope? Was the emperor himself a holy figure, responsible for the church in his domains? The Holy Roman Empire that began—as later historians argued—with Charlemagne would confront these questions again and again.

ECONOMIC AND SOCIAL LIFE In many ways, the Carolingians laid the foundations on which European prosperity would rest for generations to come. Pippin set a precedent by legislating the exact quantity of silver that a denarius had to contain. Charlemagne, thanks to successful efforts at mining silver in what is now western France, was able to impose a new and heavier standard for the denarius, which he proclaimed legal tender in 794. This new currency—like that of the Byzantine emperor—advertised the power of the rulers who issued it. It also made possible the spread of trade. In the ninth and tenth centuries, public markets sprang up, held usually once a week, encouraged and protected by local lords. Wool cloth from England and high-quality weapons made by the Franks in the east could be bought in western towns like Dorstad, on the Rhine in what is now Holland. Rulers and clerics did their best to encourage trade and commerce by building bridges across the Seine and other rivers and repairing roads. They assembled craftsmen and artists, who worked on churches and palaces or on great estates, and consumed food, clothing, and other goods.

Women of noble birth played a central role in social and economic life. They were responsible for vital duties in the sizable households of estates and palaces: the provision of appropriate hospitality to guests, the preparation of food and drink, and the distribution of charity. Women oversaw the proper treatment of domestic animals and the cultivation of gardens. They took full charge of childbirth and the treatment of what were seen as women's characteristic ailments. And they specialized in one of the period's central art forms: the creation of the richly varied embroidered fabrics used for the decoration of churches, the proper vestments of priests, and gifts for hosts and

Saint Radegund and Charity Many noblewomen undertook charity as part of their household duties, but the sixth-century Frankish queen Radegund went so far as to found a monastery. An eleventh-century manuscript of an account of her life shows her washing the feet of the poor and serving them food.

guests. In the extraordinary colors and designs of these fabrics, we see one of the first art forms created by European women.

In the thousands of peasant households found on the great estates of the Franks, wives joined with husbands to work the land. Women produced and sold cloth, cheese, and milk, and raised and sold chickens and eggs, in large enough numbers that the laws took notice of them. A statute condemning those who violated rules for coinage included separate physical punishments for women, "because women too are in the habit of engaging in market transactions." Under the law, husbands had absolute power over their wives, whom they could repudiate or even kill. In everyday life, however, families recognized the nurturing and guidance of women by the appointment of godmothers for children, which became more common. And the vision of marriage offered by the church emphasized that spouses should both consent before wedding one another.

A CAROLINGIAN MOTHER'S HANDBOOK FOR HER SON

We know about the Frankish aristocrat named Dhuoda only through a short book she wrote in the 840s, during a period of discord and war, for her absent teenage son William. This text, called a handbook after its Latin title, *Liber Manualis*, is a book of religious education and moral advice, as well as a kind of literary mirror into which William could look to evaluate his faults and contemplate the salvation of his soul. It includes sections on God, death, prayer, proper relations within the family, and even interpreting numbers. Her writing shows that Dhuoda was highly educated. This excerpt is about the importance of able counselors.

There are some people who consider themselves advisors, and who really are not, for they believe they are wise although they are not. "If I speak as a person who is less wise, I am wiser." But this is not the fault of God, in whom all possible usefulness thrives. There are those who give good advice, but who do not give it well. This is of no use to them, nor does it inspire the other person. Why? Because such advice does not aim at the highest and principal virtue. And many give bad advice which has no bearing on the problem. There are different ways of reacting to various questions. In the old days there lived many honorable, practical, truthful people. Folk nowadays certainly differ from them in many respects. What is its relevance to us? The world reveals many things. Scripture says, "Evil abounds and charity is grown cold among many." In these turbulent times, a man doesn't know whom to choose as counselor, or someone he can trust above all. For many people the hope of finding help from any one remains dim….

But all the same, do not despair on that account, my son. There are still, among the descendants of our elders, several people who with God's help are good at and capable of giving advice, which I believe is useful, appreciated, and pertinent to them and their lords. All these things are unfolded in the One who is called the Most High. For Scripture says, "Is there no physician in Egypt, no balm in Gilead," no flowing water in Canaan, nor any counselor in Israel? and so forth. Surely there is. It's evident that many people have common sense. "The Lord knows his own." He is the light of the world, "angel of great counsel," dispenser of beneficent words and salvation to his own people. He existed then and now, he dwelt with the men of old and today he dwells among the living. He is in you as you go and come, and he exhorts you, as companion-at-arms to this noble and illustrious king, to accept the dominion of your overlord. May God lead you onward to become this king's high and upright counselor! Amen….

For you to become such a counselor, everything depends on the will and power of the Almighty God. If with help of the supreme Creator you reach the time of life I spoke about earlier, be on guard against the dishonest, choose the worthy. Shun the wicked, associate with the good. Don't take advice from a malicious, cowardly or wrathful man. Such a man will gnaw at you like a ringworm and he will never remain firm in his counsels. Wrath and his habitual envy very easily drag him headlong to his plunge into the abyss….

And you, son William, be wary, and so on. Flee from the type of wicked men I have described. Associate with wise people who pursue the good, those who with true submission to the will of their lords proffer good counsel, and so have earned from God and the world an honorable and great recompense. What was true for them in their time, I pray that now, today and always, may increase in you, dearest son.

QUESTIONS FOR ANALYSIS

1. According to Dhuoda, what are the qualities of good and bad counselors?
2. Why is it so difficult to distinguish between the two kinds?
3. What do we learn from this excerpt about the importance of good counsel in the Carolingian world?

Source: Dhuoda, *Handbook for Her Warrior Son, Liber Manualis*, ed. and trans. Marcelle Thiébaux (Cambridge: 1998), pp. 101, 103, 105.

IMPROVEMENTS IN AGRICULTURE The work life of the peasants was changing too. In parts of the Frankish world, peasants learned in the eighth and ninth centuries how to break the heavy, wet soil of northern Europe using a moldboard plow with a coulter, or vertical blade, that cut deeply into the ground. This device was not new: it had been used in parts of the Roman Empire. The deeper furrows made by the metal coulters allowed rainwater to drain away without drowning the seeds. Too hard for oxen to pull, the moldboard could be drawn effectively by horses, once proper harnesses were invented. Anonymous innovators brought plows and horses together in this period. Some of them began to rotate fields as well, planting both spring and winter wheat in different seasons, and devoting the rest of their land to beans and legumes, which provided vital protein for their diets and restored the soil's fertility at the same time.

After centuries in which European farmers recouped barely three times their original investment of seed—and thus had little more than enough to plant again and feed themselves—agricultural productivity probably rose, propelling the rise in population that becomes visible in the late tenth century. The agricultural foundations for Europe's eventual revival were laid in this period. But their full adoption would not be quick. Field rotation worked best if peasants could pool most of their lands and plow and cultivate them together. But it would take centuries for new forms of community to develop, in which the forms of collaboration necessary to support field rotation could be mastered, and for landowners and peasants to devise ways of making the investments in costly iron and draft animals that were needed to spread the new agriculture.

ALCUIN AND THE CAROLINGIAN RENAISSANCE

Though Charlemagne's empire did not prove durable, the changes that he introduced touched many areas. Illiterate himself, he loved to hear books read, and he deeply respected learning. He imported learned men from Britain, who created a palace school for him at Aachen, in modern Germany, where he established his capital. Alcuin of York was one of many learned clerics who came from England to the Continent and joined other erudite men to teach Charlemagne, his sons, and his courtiers. It was Alcuin who convinced Charlemagne that he should seek not only to kill pagans but also to convert them.

Charlemagne's scholars also created new traditions of learning at monasteries across Europe. Alcuin made clear that to become learned, one had to "hoist himself up with the help of seven pillars or steps"—that is, master the seven

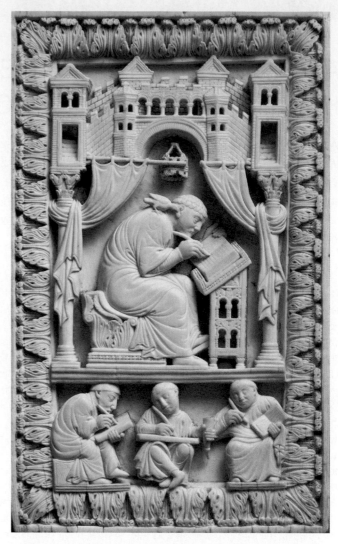

Scriptoria This ninth-century Carolingian ivory relief depicts Saint Gregory and a group of monks working together in a scriptorium, the monastery's dedicated room for the production of manuscripts.

liberal arts. Monasteries, in earlier times, had not had special spaces dedicated to producing and storing books: this helps to explain why the original collection of Cassiodorus at Vivarium and the library of the Benedictines at Monte Cassino were eventually lost. Alcuin convinced his pupils—and his patron—that they needed to gather the ancient texts and ensure their survival. Charlemagne created a court library, where he had the classics collected so he could enjoy listening to them being read aloud. More important, in the late eighth century, monasteries began to devote fixed spaces, known as scriptoria, to the writing of books. Here scribes could devote themselves, over the years, to the slow, careful work of copying.

Alcuin's pupils, and their pupils in turn, collected

strenuously. They brought together almost all of the ancient Latin texts that we possess now, corrected them where they seemed corrupt, and multiplied copies of them. And they gave these copies a new form, producing the model of the book that we still use more than a thousand years later. This was not just a codex, but one with a single block of text on each page, with word divisions and punctuation to help readers who were not native speakers of Latin. The Carolingian scholars equipped ancient texts with their own commentaries and drew up textbooks on complicated subjects, such as the form of the universe and the nature of the calendar. And they used the Latin models creatively. Alcuin himself wrote a Latin life of Charlemagne, in which he cleverly adapted the life of Augustus written by an ancient Roman historian, Suetonius. The energy and intelligence with which these scholars used the ancient texts they knew has earned their work the title **Carolingian Renaissance**.

One of the many disciples of the Carolingian scholars was Hroswitha (ca. 935–1002), a German noblewoman who became a canoness of the Abbey of Gandersheim in northern Germany. She studied the ancient Latin comedies of Terence—himself an African who had become Romanized by culture—and wrote witty comedies in his manner about Christian martyrs. But Hroswitha's female characters defied authorities with a wit and independence more reminiscent of characters in Greek drama than of the submissive women in Roman plays.

In the end, the Carolingians studied the classics for religious ends. Alcuin himself argued that Saint Paul, whom he took as a model, had found Christian pearls in "the dregs of the poets." His followers used their new learning to draw up a massive commentary on the Latin Bible, which was also copied repeatedly and became the basic text used for educating priests in cathedral schools.

COLLAPSE OF THE FRANKISH DOMAINS When Charlemagne died in 814, the political structure that he had assembled soon proved to be more fragile than it had seemed. His son, Louis the Pious, tried to preserve the empire while dividing it into semiautonomous areas ruled by his own three sons and a nephew. But he soon found himself confronting multiple problems: bitter rivalry among his sons; frontier attacks from Scandinavia, the Slavic peoples, and Muslim Iberia; and disaffection among some of his followers. He defeated his opponents and seemed to have settled the empire solidly when he died in 840. In fact, though, his surviving sons soon went to war with one another.

Carolingian Scholarship Charlemagne's enthusiasm for books and learning helped establish a tradition of collecting, studying, and updating the classics and religious texts. This illustration (845) celebrates the presentation of the Bible in which it appears (left) to King Charles the Bald, one of Charlemagne's grandsons, by the monks who painstakingly created the book.

The Treaty of Verdun, signed in 843 by the three grandsons of Charlemagne, ratified what now seemed inevitable: the permanent fission of Charlemagne's unified Frankish domains into smaller realms, which would eventually become the cores of modern France and Germany. For the first—but not the last—time after the fall of Rome, the immense difficulty of combining the many peoples of what is now Europe into a single empire or nation became clear. As the Frankish realms fell apart and Vikings and other nomadic peoples harried the coasts and borders of what had been Charlemagne's empire, the times seemed dark indeed. Yet like the action of the moldboard plow, these divisions prepared the ground for another revival soon to come.

CONCLUSION

By the tenth century, the Roman Empire that had once stretched from northern Britain to Syria and Egypt had been divided, more or less permanently, into three distinct civilizations: Byzantium in the east, the expansive realm of Islam, and the societies of western Europe. Each had its own vision of spiritual life, its own language of high culture, and its own ways of organizing politics and society. Each was, as we have seen, at times eager to borrow from the others. Though ancient texts continued to hold the keys to the kingdom of knowledge, new ways of organizing society, new forms of worship and religious life, and new forms of production had begun to take shape. We have moved from a late antique world, still largely shaped by the inheritance of Greece and Rome, into a new world—that of the Middle Ages.

[CHAPTER REVIEW]

KEY TERMS

Justinian (p. 212)
Theodora (p. 213)
Corpus Iuris (p. 213)
Silk Road (p. 223)
Muhammad (p. 223)
Kaaba (p. 223)

Five Pillars of Islam
    (p. 225)
caliph (p. 226)
Qur'an (p. 226)
Umayyads (p. 227)
Iconoclasm (p. 228)

mosque (p. 229)
Theodoric (p. 232)
Benedict (p. 235)
Gregory (p. 236)
Franks (p. 238)
Carolingians (p. 240)

Charlemagne (p. 241)
vassal (p. 241)
fealty (p. 241)
Holy Roman Empire
    (p. 242)
Carolingian Renaissance
    (p. 245)

REVIEW QUESTIONS

1. What were the most important reforms undertaken during the reign of Justinian?

2. What role did Justinian play in both strengthening the institutional church and furthering the connection between church and state?

3. What are the core tenets of Islam?

4. Why was Islam able to expand with such great force?

5. How did Muslim society utilize the knowledge of classical antiquity?

6. What peoples conquered the Italian Peninsula in the century after the fall of Rome, and how were they influenced by the empire's legacy?

7. How did Benedict create the blueprint for monastic life in Europe?

8. What is Pope Gregory's legacy in the history of the Christian church?

9. How were Germanic and Roman institutions and customs fused in the Frankish kingdoms?

10. What were the most important innovations of the Carolingian dynasty?

CORE OBJECTIVES

After reading this chapter, you should have a solid understanding of the following core objectives. To strengthen your grasp of the core objectives, use the resources on the Student Site for The West.

- Assess the political and cultural transformations of the eastern Roman Empire from the fourth through the seventh centuries.

- Analyze the threats and crises that affected the Byzantine Empire beginning in Justinian's reign.

- Describe the origins and spread of Islam.

- Compare the culture and scholarship of the later Byzantine Empire to that of the Islamic caliphates.

- Evaluate the intellectual and religious changes that took place in western Europe in late antiquity.

- Describe the political and social evolution of western European society in the early Middle Ages.

 GO TO **inQuizitive** TO SEE WHAT YOU'VE LEARNED—AND LEARN WHAT YOU'VE MISSED—WITH PERSONALIZED FEEDBACK ALONG THE WAY.

CHRONOLOGY

8

Europe Revived

900–1200

Mid-12th century
King Henry II establishes common-law precedent in England

1147–1149
Second Crusade

1137
Louis VII begins to unify territories that would become France

1154–1155
Holy Roman Emperor Frederick Barbarossa establishes military authority in Italy

I n January 1077, the Holy Roman emperor Henry IV trekked south from Germany over the Alps to the fortress of Canossa, on the summit of a steep hill in northern Italy. Bare foot in the snow, dressed as a penitent in a hair shirt (a rough garment that abraded the skin), he spent three days outside the gates. Inside, Pope Gregory VII had taken shelter with Countess Matilda of Tuscany, a formidable ruler and one of the few successful female military leaders of the Middle Ages. She had offered to protect the pope from the emperor's troops. Like his predecessors, the emperor had insisted on the right to choose and install clerics in his dominions, a process known as investiture. But Gregory fought back, supported by a party of reformers within the Roman church who asserted its independence from imperial control. Gregory excommunicated the emperor (made it unlawful for him to take Communion) and declared him deposed. Though Henry resisted, German princes and aristocrats took advantage of the situation to push for greater independence from the empire. Henry decided to concede, for the moment, so that he could consolidate his position. After three days of public humiliation, Henry was allowed inside the gates. He begged the pope's forgiveness, Henry's excommunication was lifted, and Gregory, Matilda, and Henry shared Communion in the fortress's cathedral.

Medieval Court Culture In the Middle Ages, courts shaped new customs and expectations for the behavior of nobles and their retinues. The characters that populate these medieval playing cards include a lady-in-waiting—an attendant to a queen or noblewoman—plucking a musical instrument (left); an extravagantly dressed young man posing with a falcon trained to hunt (center); and a horseman blowing a trumpet adorned with a flag (right).

[FOCUS QUESTIONS]

- How was medieval society organized?
- In what ways were cities gaining in importance?
- What new features and powers did European states develop?
- How did the power of the Church find expression in this period?
- What were the major sources of cultural change in medieval Europe?

and intellectual expeditions to learn what the Muslims knew about ancient philosophy and science. It was a time of radical innovation, desperate struggles, and fierce debates.

Yet most people who lived in this time did not think of their age as one of rapid change. In theory, at the end of this period as at the beginning, society consisted of three orders or estates: those who prayed (clerics), those who ruled and fought (nobles and armed knights), and those who worked (peasants, servants, merchants, and artisans). Each group had its own purpose and its own place in what was seen as a larger divine plan. And even when one group called for change—as many clerics did when they demanded reforms in the relationship between state and church—they often did so by insisting on a return to an ideal past or following the authority of ancient books. In the medieval world, even revolutions often began by looking backward.

Making the journey to Canossa became a proverb, in more than one European language, for undertaking public penitence. Yet this dramatic moment had only limited practical consequences. Within a few years Henry reasserted his power to appoint clerics, and Gregory excommunicated and deposed him again. The Holy Roman Empire and papacy were locked in a contest that would last for more than two centuries, leaving both sides exhausted. Still, the meeting at Canossa indicated that radical changes had taken place in Europe in the late tenth and eleventh centuries. The papacy and the empire were now great powers, determined to assert their autonomy and authority. Both could muster resources, spiritual or political, from allies and supporters across Europe. They were flanked, moreover, by revived smaller powers—from the princes who owed allegiance to the emperor and the cities of Italy, to the states that were developing across Europe.

In the years from 1000 to 1200, the European world showed an expansive vigor that no one, observing the collapse of Charlemagne's successors and the harrying of Europe's borders a century or two before, would have expected. Trade and industry began to develop, cities grew and pushed for independence, and new states—large, coherent, and powerful—began to take shape. Religious men and women explored new forms of the devout life and helped build new kinds of churches. New ways of thinking about God, nature, and humanity developed and became established parts of the curriculum of Europe's first universities. Europeans mounted military expeditions to retake the holy lands of early Christianity from Islamic powers,

THE SOCIAL ORDERS

Europe in the year 1000 was a society of scattered farms and tiny towns. Within the town walls, as well as just outside, large patches of ground were cultivated. The towns were inhabited not only by people but also by animals of many kinds, from the cows and pigs kept for milk and meat to the oxen and horses that served as beasts of burden. Noisy and chaotic during the day, towns were quiet and dark at night, when their gates were closed, street doors locked, and windows shuttered.

Between settlements there stretched vast tracts of forest—tangled masses of living and fallen trees and thick vegetation, home to bears, wolves, and wild boar, as well as smaller animals. Here and there a hermit or a group of monks might have built a small house. In clearings, fires burned all day as charcoal makers turned wood into coal. These patches of open space were more important than they probably looked. Slowly, tree by tree, the great forests of Europe were felled. As it became available, a lord would install serfs to farm the new land.

MANORIALISM: SERFS AND LORDS

In much of Europe, the way of organizing agriculture that had taken shape in Carolingian times—called

manorialism by historians—was spreading. Lords—nobles vested with local power by their overlords—ruled a population that consisted, more and more, of **serfs**: peasant laborers, male and female, bound to the land they cultivated. Serfs were not slaves—in fact, the percentage of slaves in the population gradually shrank. And the status of the farming population was never entirely uniform. The children of serfs sometimes gained permission to marry individuals who were legally free, for example. But the vast majority of peasants could not move from their land or marry without the permission of their lord. They paid their lord taxes on the crops they grew for themselves, and provided labor for their lord's farm.

In the central regions of France, in northern and western Germany, and elsewhere, serfs worked together, planting crops twice a year and rotating fields to maintain fertility. They rarely produced sizable surpluses in the thick, hard soils, but their shared fields yielded enough to sustain their communities and provide seed for the future. Meanwhile, intensive cultivation of the small areas around peasant houses, fertilized by human and animal manure, provided the variety that kept a diet healthy: legumes such as beans and peas, and vegetables.

Women worked beside men. They helped glean wheat and make hay in the lords' fields. Women also looked after poultry and cows, made cheese and other dairy products, and sold some of what they produced in village markets. Houses were small—usually one or two rooms, in which a whole family would share a single bed. But the village

Serfs at Work A richly illuminated page from a fourteenth-century English book of psalms includes an illustration of serfs laboring in the fields. Three women are harvesting grain with sickles, while a man gathers the cut grain into bundles.

well, where women drew water, and the village laundry, where they washed their family's clothes, offered spaces for sociability. This was the life of those who worked. It imposed many burdens.

The lords and ladies who ruled the land and lived on the work of others had demanding tasks of their own. In return for the right to establish and profit from their manors, they owed obedience to a higher ruler, whom—as we will see—they served in multiple capacities. In their own domains, they were expected to provide protection against raiders and thieves, and to offer justice when crimes took place or families fell out over the division of the lands assigned to them. Nobles used their revenues to build small fortresses—the castles that began to dot the European landscape—and to equip themselves and some of their followers with arms and armor.

Men of the knightly class, often nobles who as younger sons did not stand to inherit lands and wealth, learned to fight as boys. They prepared for lives as warriors in the service of kings or great nobles, which—if they were skillful and lucky—might earn them manors and titles of their own. Noblewomen learned to administer a complex household, maintaining stocks of everything from linens to spices and organizing feasts for visitors of high status.

Across Europe, members of this second order, those who ruled and fought, mastered similar skills and provided similar services for those bound to their lands. But the formation of a military class across Europe did not ensure peace. For knights, the normal way of settling disputes, after all, was by combat, and a simple slight could easily lead to a formal feud that involved all members of two houses and their allies. They also plundered and harried peasants and clerics who could not defend themselves.

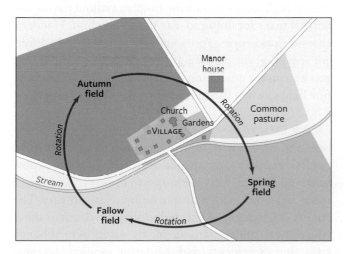

A Medieval Manor A manor might have consisted of the lord's house, a cluster of serfs' cottages surrounded by vegetable gardens, and three fields. Each year the fields were rotated: one field was planted in the spring and another in the fall, with the third lying fallow to restore its fertility.

THE PEACE OF GOD: THE CLERGY

As the end of the first millennium since the birth of Jesus approached, clergy in southwestern France devised what they hoped might be a way to prevent continual violence against the innocent. Local clergy and nobles met in councils called peace assemblies, which gathered around the relics of the saints that every church and monastery possessed. The presence of these bones and garments, charged with the sacred electricity generated by their onetime owners and vested with the power to do miracles, galvanized the crowds. The councils—made up, in many cases, of the same local authorities that had been responsible for at least some of the violence—called for a **Peace of God**. They issued rules and threatened those who broke them with powerful spiritual sanctions—the interdict (prohibition of divine services) or excommunication. In 989, one of these councils met at the Benedictine abbey of Charroux in western France. It condemned those "who break into churches," those "who rob the poor . . . of a sheep, ox, ass, cow, goat, or pig," and anyone who "attacks, seizes, or beats a priest, deacon, or any other clergyman, who is not bearing arms (shield, sword, coat of mail, or helmet), but is going along peacefully or staying in the house."

The peace movement won impressive support, and the coming of the year 1033—marking a thousand years since the Crucifixion—aroused new forms of religious enthusiasm. The formal rules became more precise: the Truce of God, for example, forbade warfare in the period from Thursday to Sunday. Yet it also became clear that spiritual commands alone would not stop the nobles from engaging in their feuds or doing violence to those who could not resist, and the movement gradually lost its force. Over time, as we will see, new political forms took shape that tasked those who fought to guard and protect the members of the other two orders.

THE REEMERGENCE OF CITIES (900–1200)

In 900, imperial Rome was a ghostly ruin. Some 20,000 inhabitants clung to parts of the historic city center and to the great churches—Santa Maria Maggiore, the Vatican, and the Lateran, where the popes actually lived. The Forum was deserted, as it would be for centuries, except for flocks of animals and their shepherds. Ancient monuments such as the Colosseum served mostly as quarries for *spolia* ("spoils") such as columns, dozens of which were taken from Roman temples and basilicas to be reerected in the naves of churches.

TRADE AND MANUFACTURING

Outside Rome, though, cities began to grow and take on new functions. On Italy's western coast, Amalfi had developed trade in the eighth and ninth centuries, selling local grain and timber in Egypt for gold, with which the merchants bought silk and other luxuries in Byzantium. In Genoa and Pisa, which rivaled and then overtook Amalfi, coins came back into circulation in large numbers—gold dinars from Egypt and Syria, and coins from Byzantium as well. Trade needed protection, especially from the raids launched by the Muslim Caliphate of Córdoba (Spain) on Christian ports, including Pisa itself. The cities developed fleets of galleys—long, narrow ships propelled by oars and manned by trained fighters. In 1015–16 Pisa and Genoa defeated Muslim efforts to invade Sardinia—only to fight over the island themselves, with the Pisans ending up victorious.

On the other side of the Italian Peninsula, Venice—a new city that had taken shape in the ninth century on islands and marshes in a lagoon on the Adriatic Sea—began to build trading networks in the central and eastern Mediterranean. Late in the eleventh century it entered into alliances with Byzantium. In return for its military aid against expanding Norman and Muslim power, Venice received support for its churches and the privilege of trading throughout the Byzantine Empire without paying the normal taxes for doing so. Far to the north, in Flanders, cities such as Bruges, Ypres, and Ghent developed a different specialty: the manufacture of cloth. Soon the region was known for producing fabric of many kinds, from the fine light cloth of Bruges to the scarlet cloth of Ghent.

FAIRS Also in the eleventh century, inland trade slowly began to revive, with new institutions to support it. In twelfth-century Champagne and Brie, in what is now northern France, fairs grew up where surviving Roman roads and rivers made transportation relatively easy. The counts of Champagne granted special privileges to those who came to trade, guaranteeing the safety of merchants, enforcing agreements, and regulating weights and measures. What began as local centers for exchanging produce and livestock turned into trade fairs for many different kinds of goods. The spice trade played a central role, though not—as used to be thought—because spices preserved food or disguised the taste of meat and fish that had

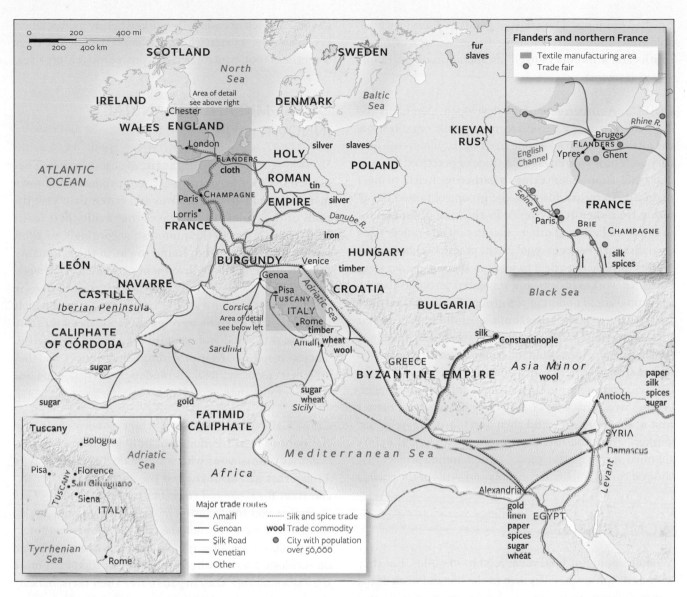

The New Cities and Commerce, ca. 1000 From the eighth century, new trade routes connected Europe's growing cities. Valuable commodities such as sugar and gold crossed the Mediterranean, while spices and silk came from farther east through Constantinople. Cities in Tuscany benefited from being at the center of this Mediterranean commerce. In Flanders, France, and England, trade fairs sprung up along major waterways, where townspeople could buy goods from across Europe and even Asia.

gone bad. Europeans in this period liked strongly flavored food, and almost all the spices that served their needs were produced in Asia. Italian merchants brought spices and silk (another Asian luxury product) overland to the fairs, where they could trade for Slavic and Baltic slaves, furs from the north, and the fine cloths of the Flemish. Once again—but now in a new way—western Europe was connected to trading networks that spanned Eurasia.

NEW TOWNSCAPES European towns, often sited where ancient Roman roads or more recent trails met,

gradually took on a new and characteristic form. Towns from Chester in western England to Bologna in Italy were identifiable from a distance by the walls that protected them and the gates where guards and city officials controlled traffic. In the town center, a market square offered space for the sale of food and other goods. Along the central streets, merchants and craftsmen built houses of a new pattern. On the ground floor a shop or workplace, open to the street, offered the space to produce and sell goods. The family that owned the shop normally lived above it, using attic space, if available, to store raw materials and finished products. The range of goods and services available grew: apothecaries sold medicines and spices, blacksmiths and armorers banged out metal products, tailors sewed garments.

GUILDS As urban economies developed, merchants and craftsmen created a second form of public organization: the **guilds**, which took shape from the later eleventh century on. Those who engaged in trade or practiced a particular craft, from shoemaking to barbering, began to meet regularly. In return for fees, the groups obtained recognition from their legal overlords: the king of France, for example, in Paris and other cities in central France. They used these privileges to regulate the practice of their trade. Guilds forbade outsiders to work in their trade, set standards for workmanship, and regulated prices so that no individual could undercut the group. They imposed fines for violations of the rules, built splendid halls for their formal meetings and feasts, and gave their dead members lavish funerals. Sons could inherit membership, but a man who married the widow of a guildsman needed to pay for his own place in the guild. A boy who did not inherit membership would have to work his way up, serving a master first as an apprentice and then as a journeyman (a "day worker," from the French word for day, *journée*) before submitting his "master-piece"—a demanding project that showed command of all the tools and skills of the trade.

WOMEN'S LIVES

Women could not hold membership in guilds, but they were as deeply engaged as men in the life and work of the towns. Sermons and books of advice for women instructed them to confine themselves to their homes and, if they needed to leave home at all, to keep their eyes modestly fixed on the ground. Their main job, according to these books, was to administer their households—a complicated and demanding task for the wife of a prosperous merchant or craftsman. She had to see to it that the house's chests were full of clean linens, the kitchen stocked with food and utensils, and her own medicine chest fully equipped with remedies. These duties, though limited, were demanding enough. Maintaining the household took long hours and required expert knowledge of everything from washing fine cloth to overseeing childbirth (sometimes with the help of a paid midwife) to nursing sick children. Despite the advice books, the realities of city life placed women in many other roles as well. Poor women sold food and clothing in markets, carded and spun wool, wove cloth in shops, and even occasionally worked beside men as laborers. Wealthier women whose husbands died before them sometimes took control of large, prosperous enterprises.

ECONOMIC AND FINANCIAL INNOVATIONS

Wealthy landowners made the rise of cities possible. They needed the goods that town artisans produced and town merchants sold—from the arms and armor that were the tools of their trade to the spices that made their feasts appetizing. It was in their interest, accordingly, to allow traders and craftsmen to found towns in their domains, to protect them, and to give them permanent privileges. In 1155, King Louis VII offered the citizens of Lorris in north-central France a set of privileges that were widely imitated. The citizens were guaranteed freedom from taxes on their food and on grain they raised themselves. They were released from providing labor services, and they and their customers were allowed to trade without paying tolls—or more than a fixed rate.

CITY FREEDOM Most important, townspeople won the right to legal freedom, not only for themselves but, eventually, for anyone who could make his or her way to a town that had been granted the normal privileges and stay there for a year and a day. The medieval proverb "City air makes you free" commemorates this system. It also suggests the ways in which the rise of trade and manufacture tended to dissolve the older landed economy based on serfdom. Lords realized that they needed cash more than labor. Slowly, they began to free their serfs, making them tenants—charging them rent rather than requiring specific tasks—and allowing some of them, and their children, to leave the land.

FINANCE As trade grew in scale, so did costs and profits, calling forth new means of financing these activities. By the tenth and eleventh centuries, merchants in Italian cities were joining together to create ventures larger than any one of them could have financed alone. A form of contract developed in the Islamic world, the *commenda*, offered a template for an effective kind of association. Investors became "sleeping partners," venture capitalists who raised the money that enabled an active partner to outfit ships and buy trade goods. Liability was limited: if the enterprise failed, a ship's captain did not have to repay his investors. The very existence of these contracts shows that a new society was taking shape—one whose members were used to calculating prices in different currencies and knew about the goods that were for sale in cities hundreds of miles apart on the coasts of distant lands.

One new group of specialists, the notaries, produced the contracts and other forms without which a commercial society could not function, and maintained registers of them to document commercial agreements. Eventually banks took shape, often with headquarters in an Italian city and multiple branches in distant regions. Instead of carrying coins, always a risky business, a merchant could deposit money with the Bardi or Peruzzi banking families in Florence, receive a letter of credit, and withdraw the cash when needed—for example, to buy pepper in Alexandria or furs in Champagne.

THE COMMUNES: INDEPENDENT CITY GOVERNMENTS

As cities grew richer and more powerful, a second transformation took place. In the centuries after Rome fell, local bishops often ruled cities. But their powers were limited and the new cities proved violent—so violent that they undermined trade and defied control. In Italy, extended kin groups banded together to build towers in which members of allied families could take refuge and defend themselves during civil strife—notably by dropping tiles from the lofty roofs on their enemies. From a distance, these cities looked like forests, as San Gimignano in Tuscany and a

Italian Towns In San Gimignano, in Tuscany, fortified towers—built between the eleventh and thirteenth centuries by noble families for defensive purposes—still dwarf the town's other buildings.

few others still do. But these developments only worsened the dueling and feuding.

Throughout the eleventh century, groups of local noblemen came together in Pisa, Siena, and other cities, determined to devise a more stable form of government. When necessary, they negotiated or fought to remove themselves from the political and legal control of their bishops or local lords. They declared themselves **communes**, ruled by officials called consuls and by assemblies of "law-worthy men"—men whose noble status enabled them to seek redress for grievances in court. The city was coming back to political life—and not only as a central cog in a much greater machine, as in the Roman world, but as an independent organization, as it had been in ancient Greece.

The earliest form of city government did not last long in most cases. The merchants and bankers who were becoming increasingly prominent in urban economies generally found themselves excluded from the assemblies and public offices populated by noblemen. Struggles ensued, and by the first decades of the thirteenth century, new and more settled forms of government took shape. In some cities, such as Florence, members of the old noble families were legally excluded from political life. In others, such as Venice, nobles and merchants merged into a single ruling class. Whatever their decisions on this point, most Italian cities created central governments and housed them in fortified palaces that dominated the urban landscape. Foreign professionals, usually trained as lawyers, were hired to manage city finances, administer justice, and even lead their armies in war. After a one-year term, each incumbent, known as a *podestà* (chief magistrate), and his staff would leave for another city—but only after the books had been audited. Other tasks were carried out by committees of citizens who were chosen by lot and lived in government buildings while they served. Creativity was a hallmark of this new urban society.

THE MEDIEVAL STATE

The Middle Ages also saw the creation of territorial states: cohesive polities that gradually developed all of the powers we now ascribe to governments, from raising taxes to providing justice. In some cases—France, for example—these states began as mosaics, as rulers hastened to bind lesser nobles to them, though at the expense of giving them lands of their own to exploit and govern. In other cases—especially in England—right of conquest enabled the king to divide up the whole territory as he wished. In theory, subjects had to obey ultimate royal authority. In practice, obedience could be difficult or even impossible to compel. But over time, as we will see, new institutions took shape that could provide rulers with tremendous power and resources.

ORIGINS

Building on precedents that went back to Charlemagne and before, kings and great nobles constructed states, at first, not by creating institutions but by building networks of fighting men who could help them wage war or defend the realm. A nobleman or a knight was both a person of status and, in almost every case, a subordinate whose superiors might include a great noble, such as a duke or king. Like serfs, lords and knights were bound to their superiors. A dramatic ceremony sealed the pact: the inferior party placed his hands within the superior's, swore fealty, and entered a relationship—like the serf's relationship with his master—defined by a complex web of rules. A noble vassal would usually owe his lord defined obligations: thirty days' military service each year, for example, and help with large expenses, such as a daughter's dowry. In return, the vassal might be granted an estate, with its revenues, and a castle. Such compacts were endlessly modified: one vassal of the

Swearing Fealty An illustration from a thirteenth-century English book of psalms depicts a knight—equipped with armor, sword, and horse—kneeling before a king and extending his hands as he swears his oath.

king of England was bound to hold the head of his seasick lord as he vomited on Channel crossings. But all of these agreements were designed to provide the lord with the array of trained soldiers he would need to face an armed enemy in the field, and to provide those soldiers with the financial support they required to maintain themselves as fighting knights.

EARLY STATES: THE DUCHY OF NORMANDY

The supple system of political organization, grounded in the loyalty between lords and vassals, was even enlisted by former enemies of Christian Europe. From the ninth century onward, Vikings from southern Denmark, Norway, Sweden, and the island of Gotland in Scandinavia sailed the Baltic and Norwegian Seas in their slender long-ships. They sacked cities—Rouen fell to them in 840—and raided monasteries. In the ninth century, warriors from Denmark invaded England and conquered three of the four Anglo-Saxon states—Northumbria, East Anglia, and Mercia—leaving only Wessex under Anglo-Saxon rule. The territory they held, which came to be called the Danelaw, was gradually reconquered by the Anglo-Saxons, who drove them out of their last holding, Northumbria, in 954. In the early tenth century, after raiding and forming small colonies, warriors from Denmark and Normandy founded the duchy of Normandy in northwestern France. There they found their place in the local structures of authority. The Viking Rollo, appointed the first Norman duke by the king of France in 911, agreed to protect France from further raids. In the same period, the Vikings who had remained in Scandinavia created the kingdoms of Denmark, Sweden, and Norway.

Gradually the Normans adopted Christianity and became experts in the European form of warfare. From Normandy, warriors and traders soon moved out into the Mediterranean and Atlantic worlds. In the late ninth century and after, Norman traders played a role in the creation of the medieval state of Kievan Rus', while others settled Iceland.

Throughout the late tenth, eleventh, and twelfth centuries, rulers expanded the effective power of their states, finding ways to enforce the obligations of their vassals and to develop new powers alongside them. By the end of the tenth century, Richard II, Duke of Normandy (r. 996–1026), had the best-organized small state in Europe. His courts offered justice to subjects in all parts of his domain. Taxes and tolls gave him dependable revenue. And a

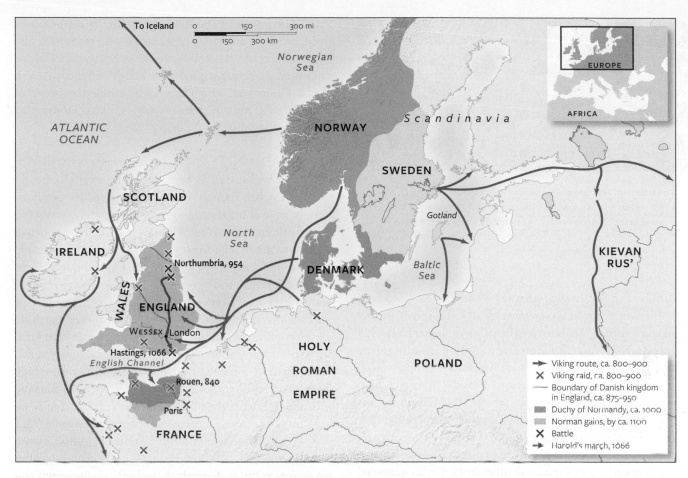

The Vikings, the Duchy of Normandy, and the Conquest of England, ca. 800–1100 In the ninth century, Vikings sailed out from Scandinavia to colonize new territories, from Iceland to Kievan Rus'. They raided towns and monasteries on the English, Irish, and French coasts, establishing the Duchy of Normandy in France in the early tenth century. In 1066, William II, Duke of Normandy, gained control of England after his military victory at Hastings.

precise set of rules governed the number of horsemen that each of his vassals was required to provide in times of war.

EARLY STATES: THE KINGS OF WESSEX

By contrast, the kings of Wessex in southern England ruled a much weaker state than the duchy of Normandy. Though they had also begun to extend their justice to all parts of the realm, they had little dependable revenue. More important still, many of the farmers who worked the land were free peasant landholders (as their descendants would remain until the Norman conquest). In wartime, the Wessex kings had to rely on a large but poorly trained militia of free farmers and a much smaller group of elite soldiers. Locally, the kingdom was divided into districts called shires and administered by "shire-reeves"—officials whose title would eventually evolve into the familiar word

sheriff. These men, powerful and hard to control, were responsible for local defense and the collection of revenues. Even more difficult to handle were the powerful lords of the realm, who gave little support to most English kings and took no interest in strengthening the realm as a whole. Though large and rich, England could not raise an army of armored men on horseback who were bound to their king by personal ties. A strong individual king such as Canute the Great (d. 1035), who was himself of Danish and Slavic rather than British descent, could assert royal authority for a time, but in the end the noble families reasserted their power.

Over time, the Normans developed tight connections with the Anglo-Saxon rulers of the House of Wessex—especially Edward the Confessor (r. 1042–1066), whose mother was the sister of a Norman duke. William II, Duke of Normandy (r. 1035–1087), seems to have thought that Edward, who had no children, promised to make

The Battle of Hastings A scene from the Bayeux Tapestry (1067)—an embroidered cloth that tells the story of the Norman conquest of England in 1066—shows Norman armored cavalry charging toward the English. Archers, who played a key role in the battle of Hastings by killing King Harold, follow on foot.

him heir to the English throne. When an Anglo-Saxon nobleman, Harold Godwineson (ca. 1022–1066), in fact became king, William built an armada and invaded England in 1066. After defeating another invading army from Norway, Harold and his men made a forced march to a hill near Hastings, in Surrey. Harold's infantry, armed with axes, formed a shield wall that resisted the Normans and their allies successfully. When the continental invaders retreated and the English pursued, breaking up their strong formation, the Norman cavalry rallied and counterattacked, supported by skillful archers who managed to kill Harold. Suddenly, Duke William II of Normandy was King William I of England, known thereafter as **William the Conqueror**.

ENGLAND: ESTABLISHING CENTRAL AUTHORITY

Over the next century and a half, England became a strong state. Because William had taken the entire country by conquest, he could parcel it out to his vassals in a single, coherent system. He carefully divided the land holdings given to his followers to prevent any of them from becoming too mighty. His court, made up of his chief noblemen and clerics, supported him in taking control of the new territory. In 1085, William's counselors took part in his decision to send agents throughout England and make a comprehensive assessment of the wealth of the whole land. The survey that resulted, though incomplete (London, for example, was omitted), was 2 million words long. It registered 13,418 settlements by order of their landholder—from the king, the clerics and religious houses, and the noble tenants-in-chief, down to the lesser servants of the

king. The power of the English monarchy rested on its deep, precise knowledge of its rights and resources, and those of its subjects—knowledge no other state in Europe possessed. In 1179, a royal official compared the survey to the Last Judgment, which "cannot be avoided by any art of subterfuge." This is why it was, and is, called **Domesday (or Doomsday) Book**.

ROYAL ADMINISTRATION Although resistance to Norman royal authority continued, the twelfth century saw the English monarchs—who continued to rule Normandy as well until 1204—grow increasingly powerful. King William's fourth son, Henry I (r. 1100–1135), began to transform the court into a royal administration. One group of specialized royal servants, settled in London's Westminster district, took responsibility for collecting and auditing the king's revenues. Known as the Exchequer—a name supposedly derived from the checkered cloth on which counters were moved to compute sums—the treasury was an early adopter of Arabic numerals. (Its French counterpart continued to use Roman numerals, which were far harder to add and subtract without making mistakes.) The Exchequer's permanent records of royal accounts became vital instruments of royal power. This was strengthened even more by another group of royal servants: the judges whom Henry sent on circuit to offer royal justice throughout the kingdom. Though civil war followed Henry's death, his grandson Henry II, Count of Anjou, not only restored the structures that Henry I had built but substantially improved them. During the Angevin Henry II's reign as king of England (1154–1189), the court became a royal council, whose support the king called on when he made legislation.

JUSTICE BASED ON LEGAL PRECEDENT Even more systematically than Henry I, Henry II exploited royal power to give justice to his subjects. In the eleventh century, most trials in England were conducted by ordeal or battle. The outcome revealed the judgment of divine Providence as to which side was in the right. But Henry II promoted the growth of juries—a dozen free men brought together at first simply to state whether a given person was lawfully in possession of particular lands. Henry sent out more justices to preside over the ordinary courts as well. By the end of the twelfth century, many English people thought of justice as something provided by juries, who determined questions of fact, and royal judges, who offered a form of justice based on legal precedent rather than divine intervention. The system seemed fairer and more transparent than the old one, and it extended royal

THE SURVEY OF HUNTINGDONSHIRE FROM DOMESDAY BOOK

Domesday Book was an extensive land survey commissioned by King William I of England in 1085 and conducted throughout the following year. The information collected allowed the king to estimate the revenues he could expect from his newly conquered lands and how many fighting men he could call up. It also helped him to settle land disputes between lords. All in all, it was an important tool for the administration of good governance.

The following excerpts are from the entry on Huntingdonshire, a county north of London. It describes the economic value of lands held by the king and by the Abbey of Ely, a prosperous Benedictine monastic community of importance to the Norman kings.

The land of the king

A manor.[1] In Hartford King Edward [r. 1043-1066] had 15 hides[2] assessed to the geld.[3] There is land for 17 ploughs.[4] Rannulf the brother of Ilger keeps it now. There are 4 ploughs now on the demesne[5]; and 30 villeins and 3 bordars[6] have 8 ploughs. There is a priest; 2 churches; 2 mills rendering 4 pounds; and 40 acres of meadow. Woodland for pannage,[7] 1 league in length and half a league in breadth. [In the time of King Edward the Confessor] it was worth 24 pounds; now 15 pounds....

[The land of the abbey of Ely]

In Spaldwick the abbot of Ely has 1 manor assessed at 15 hides to the geld...15 ploughs can plough this land.... Now the abbot of Ely has there 4 ploughs; 7 beasts; 30 pigs; 120 sheep...4 beehives; and 1 mill worth 2 shillings. There are 50 villeins and 10 bordars. Among them all there are 25 ploughs and 160 acres of meadow; 60 acres of woodland for pannage. It was worth [in the time of King Edward the Confessor]...16 pounds; and now it is worth 22 pounds.

QUESTIONS FOR ANALYSIS

1. What types of economic information are recorded in these excerpts from Domesday Book?
2. What comparisons can you make between the two properties described?
3. How did Domesday Book enhance the power of the Norman kings?

[1] manor: an estate or unit of lordship   [2] hide: the amount of land that would support a household   [3] geld: a tax collected by the Normans   [4] plough: the amount of farmland that could be plowed by a team of eight oxen   [5] demesne: the part of the manor held directly by the lord or farmed for the lord's profit   [6] villeins and bordars: unfree peasants who owed labor services to their lord and farmed some land for themselves   [7] pannage: food given to pigs in the autumn

Source: "The Survey of Huntingdonshire in Domesday Book," in *English Historical Documents 1042–1189*, 2nd ed., ed. David C. Douglas and George W. Greenaway (London: 1981), pp. 1036, 1075.

---

authority across the land. Though still a medieval monarchy, Henry II's England offered a new and powerful model of good government.

MEDIEVAL MONARCHY ON THE CONTINENT

The largest continental monarchies did not develop new institutions as quickly as England, partly because they did not have the unique opportunity to reorganize their institutions that the Norman conquest provided William I and his successors.

FRANCE France, for example, developed slowly. When Hugh Capet, a Frankish landowner, was crowned king in 987, he was actually chosen by his fellow noblemen in preference to a candidate from the Carolingian line. A weak monarch, he had to give away some of his own lands to win supporters. His successors, though often no stronger than he, benefited from good genetic luck: they had long reigns and produced sons to continue their line. Forgetting the

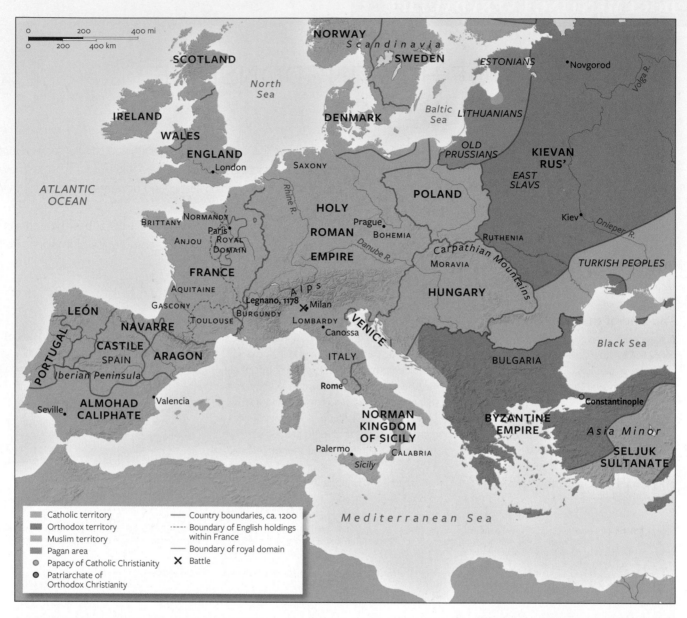

Continental States, 1200 In the eleventh and twelfth centuries, new Christian monarchies developed across Europe. Catholicism held sway from the Iberian Peninsula, where Spanish kings had begun to push back the Islamic caliphate, to the Norman monarchies of England and Sicily, the Holy Roman Empire in central Europe, and networks of towns ruled by nobles in Poland and Hungary. The Orthodox Kievan Rus' and Byzantine Empire were strong, centralized states, though Turkish peoples pressured their borders from the east.

older principle of election, they came to see themselves as monarchs by inheritance, and more and more of their subjects agreed. Slowly, the French kings built up their control over what became the royal domain: the territories in and around the Île-de-France, which included the city of Paris, and for a time the duchy of Burgundy.

Slowly, too, other great nobles in Burgundy, Anjou, and elsewhere emulated the dukes of Normandy and established firmer states. French landholders loved to fight, but gradually they settled into a more orderly existence as a landed aristocracy. Though the French king Louis VII (r. 1137–1180) was less successful than England's Henry II, his contemporary and rival, he did manage to establish connections with vassals across France, and the court began to employ more educated men. For his part, Henry applied ferocious energy to holding and expanding the Angevin territories. In 1152, after Louis VII had his marriage to Eleanor of Aquitaine (ca. 1122–1204) annulled, Henry married her, and by doing so became duke of Aquitaine and Gascony. French armies attacked, but Henry fought them off and added Brittany and Toulouse to his holdings. He also conquered a large tract of Ireland and invaded Wales. Modern historians have sometimes described this vast collection of territories as an Angevin empire, though it seems more likely that Henry planned to distribute parts of it to his sons: he gave Aquitaine to Richard and Ireland to John to rule. By the end of the twelfth century, this "empire" was beginning to dissolve.

SPAIN In Spain, a number of small Christian kingdoms—Navarre, Aragon, Castile, and León, which ruled parts of the northern Iberian Peninsula from the ninth and tenth centuries onward—engaged in a long struggle to regain territory from the Muslim states. Effective warriors such as Sancho III of Navarre (1004–1035) and Ferdinand I of León (1037–1065) pushed the boundaries of Christian power to the west and south. They also encouraged Christians to settle on the land and developed networks of vassals. By the middle of the eleventh century, the northern half of the Iberian Peninsula was largely in Christian hands.

SICILY The best organized of the continental European states—Sicily—was, like England, governed by Normans. Two adventurous Norman brothers, Robert Guiscard (ca. 1015–1085) and Roger de Hauteville (d. 1101), had already conquered much of Calabria, in southern Italy, by 1061, when one of the three Muslim rulers of Sicily appealed to them for help against a rival. They captured the city of Palermo in 1072 and controlled the whole island by 1091. Drawing on the skills of Greek shipbuilders and sailors, Robert used Sicily, without much ultimate success, to war against Byzantine settlements. As the count of Sicily, Roger set up a unique government, partly based on the existing foundations of Muslim rule. He followed his predecessors' example in granting Greeks and Muslims, as well as the much smaller Latin population, free exercise of their religion, and their own courts and tax system. He ruled as absolute monarch over all.

THE HOLY ROMAN EMPIRE The Holy Roman emperors, in theory the superiors even of their fellow monarchs, claimed lands that stretched from Saxony in far northern Germany to Lombardy in northern Italy, and from parts of eastern France to the borders of Hungary. In practice, strong emperors such as Henry IV (r. 1084–1106) and Frederick Barbarossa (r. 1152–1190) a century later exercised power over vast areas, while official servants, called *ministeriales*, collected revenues and offered justice in parts of the empire that the emperor ruled directly. But when struggles with the Roman church engaged imperial attention, or weak rulers inherited the title, the power of local princes and noblemen increased.

Henry faced many challenges after his submission to the pope in 1076. He spent much of his reign on inconclusive wars in Italy and the empire, and near the end of his life he was deposed by his son. But he retained strong support—made stronger by papal efforts to intervene on behalf of his enemies. He ended his days back on the throne, having established the imperial house as a center of loyalty, and in 1101 created the Landfrieden—a general peace agreement designed to eliminate feuding between local rulers and nobles.

Frederick Barbarossa In an illumination from a twelfth-century German chronicle, Frederick Barbarossa is depicted as emperor, crowned and seated on a throne, flanked by two of his sons.

Frederick advanced imperial authority beginning in 1154–55 with the first of what would eventually be six expeditions to Italy. He helped the papacy put down a rebellion in Rome, conquered the rich and strongly fortified city of Milan, and reasserted some of the imperial powers over the appointment of clerics that Henry IV had claimed. Fascinated by the traditions of Roman law, he hired jurists who described him as the lord of the world and the inheritor of the great Romans. But as Frederick grew older and the northern Italian cities became wealthier and more independent, the balance of forces changed, and in 1176 he was defeated by the cities of Lombardy at Legnano, not far from Milan. In the empire itself, he achieved considerable success at a more pragmatic level, pacifying and uniting the princes who ruled the German lands—only to drown in 1190, when crossing a river at the head of a military expedition to regain the Holy Land from Muslim rule. Frederick left behind the myth of a great emperor, whom many Germans believed would someday return to rule them again, but relatively few strong institutions.

POLAND East of the Holy Roman Empire's German territory and north of Austria, Catholic central Europe was divided into massive kingdoms. Poland, which stretched south all the way from the Baltic Sea to the Carpathians, had been Catholic since the tenth century, when the first ruler of Poland, Mieszko (r. 963–992), adopted the religion of his Christian wife, Dobrava, who came from the empire's kingdom of Bohemia (now part of the Czech Republic). Once Mieszko and his court were baptized, determined preaching gradually brought the previously pagan Polish tribes into the Christian church.

Boleslaw, the duke of Poland from 992 to 1025, mounted an ambitious program to unify Poland and Bohemia. Over the next two centuries, however, Poland collapsed into rival duchies fragmented by a powerful peasants' revolt and the grinding pressures exerted by the Holy Roman Empire to the west and Kievan Rus' to the east. Poland was also the target of raids by Old Prussians and Lithuanians, Baltic tribespeople from the north and east, and threats by the crusading order of the Teutonic Knights, who conquered the Old Prussians and settled Prussia in the thirteenth century. During this period, Poland gradually developed towns, partly thanks to the immigration of German merchants and artisans. Though many formerly free Polish peasants were forced into servile dependency on their lords, others in border areas to the south were able to gain their freedom in return for settling new lands. Under Casimir III (r. 1333–1370), the last king of Poland from his dynasty, the state managed to consolidate its authority internally and began to expand successfully into Kievan Rus' and Lithuania.

HUNGARY Hungary, too, had been Christian since the tenth century, but had been slow to develop the characteristic forms of western European urban life. A Christian chronicler who passed through in the first half of the twelfth century saw more tents than houses. But in Hungary as in Poland, the twelfth and thirteenth centuries witnessed German immigration; the development of towns, in which Muslim and Jewish as well as Christian merchants contributed to a flourishing economy; and the spread of manors and servile labor. As in parts of western Europe, struggles for supremacy between the king and the nobility led to the issuing of charters that began as statements of noble privileges and gradually came to be seen as statements of the rights of all free men. The invasion in 1241 of Mongol nomads from Central Asia destroyed the Hungarian army and devastated the country.

BOHEMIA The most powerful and prosperous of these central European Catholic states was Bohemia. Cities grew rapidly there, powered in part by the success of local silver mining and supported by royal charters that specified the liberties citizens enjoyed. Prague, well situated on the Vltava River, became the largest city east of the Rhine, with more than 30,000 inhabitants after 1300. It developed skilled crafts and manufactures—notably that of arms and armor—and in 1348 it became the seat of the first university in central and eastern Europe, which soon attracted more than a thousand students. The rise of merchant capitalism affected rural as well as urban Bohemia. As in the west, peasant families lived in widely varied conditions, and the most successful and ambitious purchased their freedom.

KIEVAN RUS' Farther east the Viking merchant-raiders who took part in the founding of Kievan Rus' moved south from Scandinavia along the Volga River, seeking to exchange slaves and furs from eastern Europe for Islamic silver coins. There they came into contact with the East Slavs, tribes driven from the lower Danube River basin in the sixth century into the vast forested lands that stretched from the Dnieper River in the south to the Baltic Sea and Volga River in the north. Russian tradition assigns the foundation of the first state, in the northern town of Novgorod, to Rurik (r. ca. 860–879), a Viking, and his followers, the Rus'. Some of Rurik's warriors moved south to Kiev. His successor, Oleg (r. 879–912), followed them, killed their leaders, and made Kiev his capital.

Cyril and Methodius This fifteenth-century manuscript shows Byzantine brothers Cyril and Methodius at their writing desks, inventing the Cyrillic alphabet used to record the Slavic language. The text below their portrait is written in Cyrillic.

For the next century, the Kievan state expanded, subjugating the East Slavic tribes and forcing them to pay tribute. Raids on Byzantium in 907 and 941–44 persuaded the emperors to make trade agreements with Kiev. Nomadic incursions and civil war slowed the growth of the Kievan Rus', but Grand Prince Vladimir I (r. 981–1015) consolidated the state. He also brought it into the world of Eastern Christianity.

In the ninth century, two Byzantine brothers, Cyril and Methodius, had invented a new alphabet for writing in the Slavic language. They translated Greek biblical and liturgical texts for the inhabitants of Moravia (now part of the Czech Republic) inhabited by Slavs. There they met with opposition from Franks who used a Latin text for the Mass and did not think the liturgy should be translated into the vernacular. The Byzantine emperor and the Orthodox patriarch, however, supported these efforts, and the Slavonic liturgy spread in Bulgaria and elsewhere. Eventually, Vladimir decided—perhaps in hope of unifying the diverse peoples in his enormous realm—to convert Kiev to the Orthodox Christianity of Byzantium, which became the state religion of Kievan Rus'. Grand Prince Yaroslav I (r. 1019–1054) encouraged the building of cathedrals in Novgorod and Kiev, and the Russian church eventually began to assert its independence from the patriarch of Byzantium.

Most Russians lived as free peasants, by farming and gathering fish and furs. What once had been a ruling order of merchant-warriors divided into a group of noble landholders, or boyars, and another of professional merchants. Fortified towns spread, and artisans began to supply a wide range of goods and services. For all its sophistication—under Vladimir, a law code was committed to writing—the unified Kievan state, beleaguered by raiders from the steppe, began to undergo fission into multiple principalities. The power of Kiev declined. Though a newer Baltic trade based in the wealthy and powerful city of Novgorod prospered, Kievan Rus' never regained the prominence it had possessed before 1050.

COURT CULTURE: CHIVALRY

The elaborate courts of the Holy Roman Empire and the new states of France, England, and Spain helped to create a culture that cultivated and celebrated the virtues of the nobility. Supported by monarchs who believed in military values—but also wanted their courts and retinues to live in a reasonable, disciplined way—knights and nobles of higher standing developed a new code, called **chivalry**. They began to describe the life they followed as a calling, blessed by God, for which one required formidable skills and elaborate training. The prospective knight had to learn his craft by serving an older knight as a squire. Then he must pray and hold vigil over his future arms before he could be formally dubbed a knight.

CODES OF CONDUCT Combat, and the skills it required, mattered most—as it always had—to younger sons who had to make their way as soldiers. But the knight also had to learn the pursuits of peacetime. Hunting, falconry, and the artificial combat known as jousting, which soon became a highly regulated and vastly popular practice, provided ways to maintain combat readiness. Weddings, visits from one monarch or noble to another, and diplomatic missions required skills of a different kind: the knight had to know how to stand, speak, dance, and sing with poise and elegance. Codes of knightly conduct were enforced by specialists such as heralds, who laid down the rules for what arms a nobleman could bear.

Women of the noble order had to master the skills of peacetime as well. Women usually did not fight, and they ruled, for the most part, only when no mature male heir was available. But in the world of the court, they presided at tournaments and feasts, and performed in public before large, attentive, and critical audiences. Books of advice—and satires of those who failed to meet the new standards—set the rules. Every aspect of the noblewoman's life—dress, movement, eating—became an art to be cultivated in a systematic way. Noblewomen must be at once lively and decorous, open and demure; must speak courteously with men of their own rank without doing anything to harm their reputations; and must certainly never be seen, as more than one book warned, eating greedily or smearing their mouths with food.

Courtesy, honor, love: these complex terms, rich and ambiguous, denoted the codes of conduct that developed to regulate aristocrats' conduct toward fellow warriors and noblewomen. The change was marked: the nobles of Europe learned to discipline their movements, restrain their appetites, and keep themselves clean—skills that would gradually spread through the rest of the European population.

COURTLY LOVE Most remarkable of all, the nobility began to practice a new form of love—courtly love. Marriages, as we will see, were typically arranged for political or financial advantage. But at courts, love blossomed between women and men of high rank. They modeled their relationships on that of lord and vassal. The woman was the sovereign: her will ruled, and her favors—from the award of a glove to a tournament victor, to the award of a kiss or an embrace—were the highest compensation a man could hope for. Perhaps these relationships were seen as a parody, an inversion of the natural order; or perhaps they were seen as a challenge to it.

What is certain is that conflicts arose. Many noblemen were vassals of more than one master, a situation that put the ties that supposedly bound society under intolerable stress. In the close-knit, ceremonious world of the court, conflict was common, and love—between a knightly vassal and his lord's wife, whose favor he might wear at a tournament—apparently even more so. What was a chivalrous man to do when his duties—or duty and "courtesy"—conflicted?

Courtly Love Enameled figures on this twelfth-century chest enact scenes from chivalric love poetry. At left, a troubadour plays a stringed instrument for a dancing woman; at right, a woman restrains a suitor with a leash, symbolizing the complex rules that governed relationships at court.

LITERARY INNOVATIONS These dilemmas could not be solved. But they found expression in what seemed a new poetic form, the epic, composed in the modern languages that were then taking shape—French, Spanish, and a type of German. As early as 1066, Norman knights waiting to fight at Hastings heard "The Song of Roland"—a poem about the defeat of Charlemagne's rear guard by Muslims at Roncevaux in 778. In the song, Roland, leader of the rear guard, dies heroically—but only after putting himself and his friends at the mercy of their enemies by his rashness. Even at this early stage, the epic form not only celebrated but also questioned noble values. Roland's courage was clear at every point, but it brought him to disaster. Wisdom and good counsel, which he lacked, would have served him, his men, and his king better. A Spanish epic, *The Poem of the Cid*, composed in the twelfth century, celebrated the deeds of Rodrigo Díaz (ca. 1043–1099), a Castilian nobleman who fought for both Muslim and Christian lords. In 1094 he captured the city of Valencia in eastern Spain, where he founded his own short-lived principality. The poem praises him as a great warrior, but it also elevates him fictionally, through the marriages he arranges for his daughters, into the catalyst of unity among the Christian kingdoms of Spain.

Chrétien de Troyes (ca. 1135–ca. 1190) explored the potential conflicts between skill at love and valor in war. In a series of romances—episodic poems based on ancient stories about King Arthur and his followers—he made clear his own view: the good lover could not be a good fighter. The brave Lancelot, obeying the orders of his lady, finds himself unhorsed and unconscious again and again. Marie de France (fl. late twelfth century) emphasized the violence implicit in the chivalric order. In the first of her lays, short romances that derived from a Breton tradition, the wife of a royal servant stuns the king with her beauty. She plots with him to kill her husband, only to have the knight turn the tables and kill them both.

Even more novel were the poems that celebrated love, especially illicit love, despite its violation of Christian codes of law and conduct. New conventions of behavior recognized that women, as well as men, nourished passions not recognized, much less accepted, by the formal codes of state and church. The troubadours—the love poets of southern France—recognized, as Marie de France did, that women harbored strong desire:

Fair, agreeable, good friend,
When will I have you in my power,
Lie beside you for an evening,
And kiss you amorously?

COURTLY LOVE

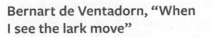

Fin' amor, or courtly love, was the name given to a form of chivalric love that was supposed to improve the lover by joining romantic passion to a reverence for the beloved. The ideal of courtly love had its origins in earlier Arabic and Latin love poetry, recent trends in Christianity toward a spiritual adoration of God, attempts by the Church to regulate marriage, and the formal relationship between lord and vassal. It was most clearly articulated by the troubadours of southern France, such as Bernart de Ventadorn and Marcabru. Both selections reveal the element of social power underlying professions of courtly love between men and women.

Bernart de Ventadorn, "When I see the lark move"

Bernart de Ventadorn was one of the most popular troubadours of the twelfth century, and his descriptions of courtly love were often imitated by other medieval poets. In this song, his love causes a loss of power over himself, for which he seems to blame all women.

When I see the lark move
for joy his wings in the sun,
and disappear and swoop
for the delight that comes to his heart,
great envy comes upon me
at one so joyful,
and I wonder that in an instant
my heart does not faint for desire.

Ay, alas! I thought I knew much
of love and I know so little!
for I cannot forbear to love her
from whom I shall have nothing.
She has stolen my heart and my being,
and for herself the whole world;
and when I am parted from her, there is
    nothing
other than desire and my yearning heart.

Never more have I power over myself
nor was I myself from the moment
that my eyes saw her
in a mirror that pleased me much....

Of ladies I despair;
never more shall I trust them
and as I once defended them,
so shall I forsake them.

Since I see that none help me against her
who destroys and confounds me,
I fear them all and mistrust them,
for I know they are all alike.

In this does show herself true woman
my lady, for which I blame her,
since she wants not what she should
and does what is forbidden.
I am fallen in disgrace
and have acted like a fool on the bridge;
and I do not know what is happening to me,
unless I have aimed too high.

Marcabru, "The other day, beside a hedge"

The troubadour Marcabru often used satire as social criticism. In the humorous "The other day, beside a hedge" (ca. 1130–50), the protests of a peasant woman against a nobleman's advances expose flaws in the ideal of courtly love. This excerpt is a prose translation of the original verse.

The other day, beside a hedge, I found a common little wench brimming with joy and wisdom: just like the daughter of a peasant woman, she wears a cape, a tunic lined with a pelt, a coarsely woven blouse, shoes and woolen stockings.

…

"My sweet, dear pretty one" said I, "I turned off the road to keep you company, for such a peasant wench as you ought never to have been looking after so many beasts without a suitable companion in such an isolated place as this."

"My lord," she said, "whoever I may be, I know wisdom or folly when I see it. Let your 'companionhood,' sir," thus said the peasant woman to me, "remain where it is fitting, for she who thinks she is the mistress of it has nothing more than the vain illusion of it."

…

"My pretty one," said I, "a noble fairy fashioned you when you were born: there is in you a pure and rarefied beauty, and it would be easily doubled with just one union, me on top and you underneath."

"Sir, you have praised me too much that I am very angry about this. Since you have exalted my reputation so much," thus said the peasant woman to me, "because of this you shall have me as your reward when you leave: gape fool, gape in your mid-day siesta!"

"Wench, one tames a cruel and savage heart with practice. I well know that a man can have a mighty good time when he has a chance encounter with such a little peasant wench, with noble affection, as long as one does not cheat the other."

"My lord, a man excited by the heat of folly swears and makes pledges and guarantees. You would pay such homage sir," thus said the peasant woman, "but I, for a small entrance fee, do not wish to exchange my maidenhood for the title of whore."

QUESTIONS FOR ANALYSIS

1. How does the lover in "When I see the lark move" connect matters of love and power?
2. In what ways does the woman in "The other day, beside a hedge" challenge the social assumptions of chivalry?
3. What do these poems tell us about the ideals and realities of romantic relationships between men and women in the twelfth century?

Sources: Bernart de Ventadorn, "When I see the lark move," *Music of the Troubadours* (CD liner notes), trans. Keith Anderson (Munich: 1999), pp. 10–11; Marcabru, "The other day, beside a hedge," in *Marcabru: A Critical Edition*, ed. and trans. Simon Gaunt, Ruth Harvey, and Linda Paterson (Cambridge: 2000), pp. 379, 381.

Marie de France An illumination from a thirteenth-century French manuscript depicts the poet Marie de France writing at a desk.

Within the complex codes that governed every aspect of noble life, some men and women refused to let any rules dictate what they desired and felt. As we will see, they were not the only twelfth-century Europeans who refused to subject themselves to the rules that normally governed Christian society.

THE MEDIEVAL CHURCH

Europe remained deeply Christian in the tenth, eleventh, and twelfth centuries, but the Roman church was evolving rapidly. The long-standing differences between the Greek church in Byzantium and the Latin church in Rome sharpened into a schism. On the doctrine of the Trinity, the western church held that the Holy Spirit proceeded through the Father and the Son, the eastern church that the Spirit proceeded through the Father alone. In 1014 Pope Benedict VIII (r. 1012–1024) added the Nicene Creed, which in 325 had affirmed the co-divinity of the Son, to the Mass. By the middle of the eleventh century, the papacy was insisting that Greek churches in southern Italy either conform to Latin practices or close. In response, the Orthodox patriarch Michael Cerularius closed the Latin churches in Constantinople. A papal legate sent to Constantinople in 1054 demanded that the patriarch recognize the supremacy of Rome. When he refused, the papal legate excommunicated him, and he excommunicated the legation in return. Reconciliation proved impossible, and from this time forward the Roman and Orthodox Churches were divided by what is known as the **East-West Schism** or the Schism of 1054.

CHURCH AND STATE

Relations between the Catholic Church and developing state authority were also changing. In the tenth century, as we have seen, the Holy Roman emperors, though far weaker than Charlemagne had been, routinely followed his example in choosing and installing popes, not to mention the bishops and abbots in their realms. Kings and other local lords also claimed the right to appoint clerics in their domains, as they had for centuries. Some saw themselves as heirs to the legacy of the Roman emperors as holy kings who were as much representatives of God on earth as any cleric. All rulers regarded high positions in the Church as powerful offices in the state and believed it vital to staff them with men, often of noble birth, who would offer good counsel and reliable assistance in crises—including military crises. For their part, many clerics saw it as normal to pay for their offices, as was often required.

Investiture On this twelfth-century enamel plaque, the Holy Roman emperor, carrying the cross and orb of royal authority, invests a monk as a bishop.

In the eleventh century, circles of reform-minded clergy who studied the scriptures and the historical record decided that these practices violated what they now saw as basic standards. They found it frightening that many clerics obtained their high positions by paying for them, for in doing so they were committing a clear sin, that of simony (named after Simon Magus, a character in the New Testament book of Acts who tried to buy the powers of Jesus's disciples). Priests who came to see themselves as God's representatives on earth, members of a separate and high estate, could no longer accept that even the highest clerics—most eleventh-century popes—were appointed by secular lords. They looked back to the Christian Roman Empire and saw, as they wanted to, that the clerical estate had then stood higher than the nobility, higher even than the emperor himself. When Ambrose had first condemned and then absolved Emperor Theodosius I in 390, he had set a precedent that should be revived. It was a pope, they noted, who in 802 had invested Charlemagne with his imperial crown.

Changes were made. In 1059, when Holy Roman Emperor Henry IV was still a boy and could not intervene, the College of Cardinals—a group of priests and bishops in Rome that would become increasingly central to the Church—elected the pope without consulting Henry. This firm move was intended to take the whole question of clerical election out of secular hands.

THE INVESTITURE CONTROVERSY (1075–1122)

Henry IV had assumed his full powers by the time a Roman cleric named Hildebrand, famous for his learning and holiness, was proclaimed Pope Gregory VII in 1073, to the wild enthusiasm of the Roman populace. Gregory strongly advocated clerical independence of secular authority. Two years later, conflict flared in Milan, a republic within the Holy Roman emperor's dominions. A candidate for the important archbishopric of Milan requested recognition of his appointment from Henry IV and paid a fee. Gregory condemned the transaction. Henry's clerical supporters condemned Gregory. Soon bishops and theologians on both sides were hurling anathemas (condemnations) and excommunications at the other side's leader and at one another. This **Investiture Controversy** became one of the great ideological disputes in European history.

POPE GREGORY VII Papal records claim that at the time of the Milan dispute, in 1075, Gregory VII drafted a document entitled the Dictatus Papae ("papal dictation"). With radical simplicity he confirmed the preeminence of the pope over all others, both in the Church and outside it. Gregory claimed that only the pope, as the sole universal ruler appointed by God, could depose or reinstate bishops, divide or unite bishoprics, and use the imperial insignia, and even "that it may be permitted to him to depose emperors." These ferocious axioms, though not made public at the time, served as the basis of Gregory's policies. Gregory and his associates in the Church tried systematically to put his principles into effect—an enterprise that has come to be known as the **Gregorian Reform movement**. His views soon found their way into one of the Church's earliest written codes of ecclesiastical law. Imperial theologians drew up equal and opposite codes. They stressed the absolute authority of secular rulers, appointed by God.

Though Henry IV's penance at Canossa in 1077 gave Gregory a victory in the first skirmish, the war ran for another century and a half. Both sides won victories from time to time, and compromises were forged—above all in 1122, when Emperor Henry V (r. 1111–1125) and Pope

The Investiture Controversy A twelfth-century manuscript illustration captures a key moment in the drama of the investiture dispute: Henry IV kneels in supplication to the abbot of Cluny (left) and Countess Matilda of Tuscany (right), asking them to intercede with Pope Gregory on his behalf. Matilda and the abbot are larger than Henry to emphasize their power in the negotiation.

Calixtus II (r. 1119–1124) agreed that although rulers could invest bishops with their powers as secular lords, only the pope could confer spiritual authority on them by presenting them with a ring and a staff. This agreement, called the **Concordat of Worms**, ended the formal Investiture Controversy, but the great struggle between church and state continued.

THE CONTINUING CONFLICT: THOMAS BECKET

In England the conflict pitted the powerful monarch Henry II against Thomas Becket (ca. 1120–1170), a brilliant lawyer and state official, as well as Henry's personal friend. Becket rose to be Henry's chancellor, and in 1162 the king followed tradition and appointed Becket archbishop of Canterbury. Once a worldly man, Becket turned ascetic in his new office—another sign of the reforming inspiration so widespread in the Church. At a meeting in 1164 of the English clergy at Clarendon Palace in southwestern England, Henry demanded that the Church accept limitations on its privileges—especially the jurisdiction of its courts. Becket refused to sign the constitutions Henry issued. Summoned for trial, Becket fled to the Continent.

After the pope brokered Becket's return to England in 1170, four of Henry's knights made their way to Canterbury and murdered the archbishop. Tradition holds that he was wearing a hair shirt under his splendid official raiment. Within two years Becket had been made a saint,

Thomas Becket The story of Thomas Becket's assassination spread far beyond England. This Italian church fresco shows Henry II's soldiers murdering Becket in Canterbury Cathedral, with the cathedral's altar and columns clearly visible in the foreground.

and his shrine at Canterbury became a central focus of Catholic life in England. The murder cost Henry much of his popularity, and helped to trigger a revolt of the English barons against him in 1173–74. Though he did penance for Becket's assassination and defeated his enemies, the monarchy was left in a weakened position at his death in 1189. When church and state came into conflict, not even the most skillful of secular rulers could count on victory.

CHURCH AND STATE COLLABORATION: THE EARLY CRUSADES

For all their struggles, church and state often found it possible to cooperate. Great clerics never stopped serving as royal counselors and ministers. And church and state collaborated on some major enterprises. The first of these joint ventures was called into being by the Church's new energy and received strong support from secular rulers. For centuries, as we have seen, the original heartlands of Christianity in Asia Minor and the Levant had been in Muslim hands. In the course of the eleventh century, the era of the Peace of God, many Christians seem to have taken an increasingly strong interest in the Holy Land. Pilgrims traveled to Palestine sometimes in groups thousands strong, and parents named their daughters Jerusalem.

ORIGINS At the same time, the papacy actively encouraged the reconquest of Spain from the Muslims—an enterprise that began with the expansion of Christian kingdoms in the northern half of the Iberian Peninsula and that came to be known as the **Reconquista**. As early as 1064 Pope Alexander II (r. 1061–1073) offered an indulgence (remission of the normal penance for one's sins) to those who participated in the campaign to take the city of Barbastro in northeastern Spain. The expedition succeeded, but only temporarily; the city was retaken by the Muslims a year later. Christians of every social level shuddered as they heard about the sufferings of their fellows in the Holy Land and in Spain, where, Christians claimed, in 1086 Muslim soldiers had filled carts with the heads of the Christians they had defeated at Zallaqa.

The Muslim great powers—the Abbasid Caliphate in Arabia, Iraq, and Central Asia; their rivals the Seljuk Turks in Asia Minor; and the Fatimid Caliphate in North Africa, Egypt, and the Levant—could easily be represented as the natural enemies of all Christians. In Christian eyes, the Seljuk Turks posed an especially powerful threat. The

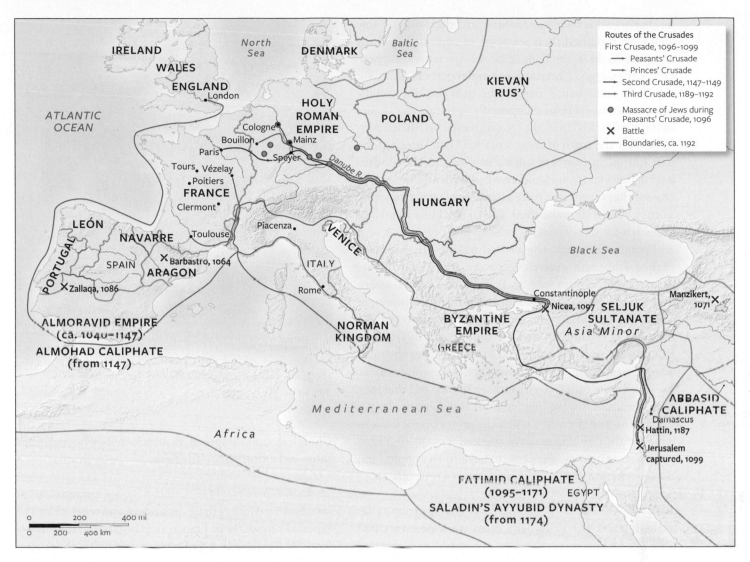

The Early Crusades, 1096–1192 In 1096, the Peasants' Crusade traveled from Cologne to Constantinople with the goal of retaking the Holy Land from Muslim rule. Along the way, they attacked communities of Jews, whom they also saw as enemies of Christianity. Later crusaders fought many battles in Asia Minor and the Arabian Peninsula, conquering the Seljuk Turks' capital at Nicea in 1097 and Jerusalem in 1099.

Byzantine Empire was beleaguered on many sides, from Norman invasions of Greek territory and rebellions by Christian sects and Turkic groups. In 1071 the Seljuks defeated the Byzantine army decisively at Manzikert in eastern Asia Minor, conquering almost all of the peninsula. The Byzantine emperor Alexius I (r. 1081–1118) managed to regain control of some coastal areas in the west, and courted the papacy in the hope of finding help against the Seljuks, whom the Byzantines represented as a common enemy.

In these same years, the Gregorian Reform movement inspired many nobles, especially in France, with the desire to serve Christianity. But the desire to serve the faith, as they interpreted it, did not always imply giving

up their arms. Sometimes it implied adventure—as when they themselves undertook pilgrimages to the Holy Land. Sometimes it implied armed conflict. Princes, prelates, and nobles began to devise ways of arguing that a given war was itself just and pious—a campaign undertaken for Christian ends.

It seems probable that Odo of Lagery, the reforming cardinal who became Pope Urban II in 1088 and served until 1099, already had some kind of Christian expedition to the Holy Land in mind when he took office. In 1095 an embassy from the Byzantine emperor to the Council of Piacenza asked Urban for help against the Seljuk Turks. Later that year, at the Council of Clermont, Urban preached a sermon. The historical sources that report Urban's words on that occasion were written later, and their authors may well have modified their accounts of what he urged his audience to do in the light of later experiences. Supposedly, Urban urged Christians to band together and attack the "base and bastard Turks" who held the Holy Sepulcher, the tomb of Jesus. Supposedly, spontaneous shouts of "God wills this" from the crowd greeted his call to arms. Whatever the truth of these stories, Urban launched the first European efforts to wage a holy war: the **Crusades**, a term derived from cloaks marked with silk or woolen crosses that Christians from all orders of society donned as they vowed to make their way to the Holy Land and redeem it for Christians.

Preaching spread the crusading impulse through France, Italy, and western Germany. It was usually targeted on large cities such as Poitiers and Tours, where multiple churches could provide support and information. Crusaders had mixed motives. They wanted to strike a blow for the Church—and, by doing so, win freedom from their sins and the necessary penalties. But they also wanted to fight an enemy whom they increasingly saw as hateful. Two brothers from southern France said that they took the cross "on the one hand for the grace of the pilgrimage and on the other, under the protection of God, to wipe out the defilement of the pagans." For the first time in Christian history, war came to be defined as holy—and the destruction of a particular enemy as a virtuous act.

THE PEASANTS' CRUSADE

The first groups that actually took the crusader's cross were peasants and knights of low stature, badly organized and most of them poorly armed. They were led by Peter the Hermit, a preacher famous for his ascetic life and personal piety. This Peasants' Crusade, a mixed group of Franks and Germans, made their way in 1096 from Cologne to Constantinople, where the Byzantines transported them to Asia Minor. There they attacked the outskirts of Nicea, once a Christian center and now the Seljuk capital, and raided other cities. When they marched out to conquer Nicea, the Turks slaughtered most of them. Peter, who was in Constantinople when the battle took place, survived, as did a few thousand of the crusaders.

Another crusader group, led by a count named Emicho, made its way through the cities flanking the Rhine River. Emicho and the Christian citizens of Cologne and other German towns were struck by a powerful thought. On the way to deal a blow for Jesus against the Muslims who had taken the Holy Land away from Christianity, they decided it was both reasonable and proper (although the official

The Peasants' Crusade In an illustration from a twelfth-century French manuscript, Peter the Hermit stands at the head of a crowd of crusaders, boldly leading them forward—presumably to the Holy Land.

Church sharply disagreed) to attack those who had killed Jesus in the first place—the Jews.

THE JEWS AND THE CRUSADES

Communities of Jews had lived for centuries in western and central Europe, especially in southern France and the cities of the Rhineland. Well established, prosperous, and pious, they maintained synagogues, ritual baths, and the other necessities of Jewish communal life. For the most part they lived in an uneasy peace with their Christian neighbors, attending the same markets and practicing the same crafts. As cities developed and laws and guild ordinances were written, however, Jews were forbidden to engage in the same trades or crafts as Christians. Jews were allowed to serve as moneylenders—an activity that Church law prohibited Christians from practicing, and not one calculated to soften Christian attitudes toward Jews. Violence against the Jews began to spread into regions that had not known it. In Toulouse in southern France, a Jew was publicly slapped every year in retribution for an imaginary betrayal—hard enough that one of the victims died. Now the Jews realized that they were under threat, and they turned to the traditional ways by which Jewish communities had survived in the past. They prayed and fasted in the hope that God's anger might be turned aside. They asked local bishops for help—and in Speyer and other Rhineland cities, the bishops protected them.

But even bishops could not provide safe refuge everywhere. In 1096 in the Rhineland city of Mainz, where 700 Jews crowded into the bishop's great hall for protection, Emicho and his followers broke in and slaughtered them all—men, women, and children. Some of the Jews, reviving the ancient precedent of Masada, the last Jewish stronghold to fall to the Romans, killed their own families, "preferring them to perish thus by their own hands rather than to be killed by the weapons of the uncircumcised." The crusaders plundered their bodies and piled them in heaps. The stories of these Jewish martyrs would be commemorated for centuries to come on Yom Kippur, the Jewish Day of Atonement.

THE CRUSADER KINGDOMS   The Peasants' Crusade of 1096 was only the beginning of what is called the First Crusade. In the same year, noblemen such as the pious, hard-bitten warrior Count Raymond of Toulouse (d. 1105) and the Frankish knight Godfrey of Bouillon (d. 1100) led better-organized groups of professional soldiers to the East in what came to be called the Princes' Crusade. Helped by the element of surprise and by extraordinary luck, the crusaders won battle after battle, taking Nicea in 1097 and marching through Syria toward Palestine. In 1099 a much reduced crusader army succeeded in taking Jerusalem itself after a short siege. A brutal massacre of many of the Muslim and Jewish inhabitants of the city followed. Godfrey became the first king of a Latin Christian kingdom based there, though he died almost immediately after in battle.

Four new Latin Christian territories took shape in the East between 1098 and 1104: Edessa, Antioch, Jerusalem, and Tripoli. Each had its own aristocrats and knights who built castles on the best European models to serve as their bases of power. They captured ports—Haifa, Acre, Beirut, and Tyre—that enabled them, through Italian merchants and navies, to remain in contact with Europe. The spice trade, vineyards, and olive groves of the region provided valuable goods that they sold and shipped to Europeans. Venetian and Genoese merchants not only provided transport but in return for military help to the colonists, negotiated the right to build and fortify settlements of their own. Meanwhile, the Latin lords came to an accommodation with the inhabitants of their new lands—Jews, Muslims, and Eastern Orthodox Christians—whom they not only ceased to attack but treated, in the case of the Jews, better than they would have at home. Though the capture of the Latin East was motivated by religious zeal and hatred of

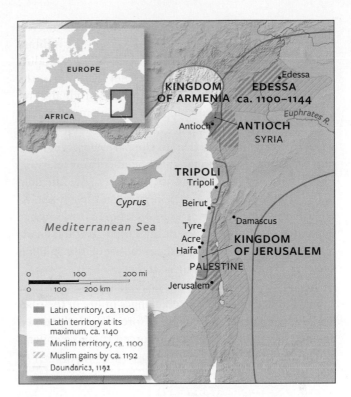

The Crusader Kingdoms, ca. 1100–1192   After conquering Jerusalem in 1099, Latin Christians established the kingdoms of Edessa, Antioch, Jerusalem, and Tripoli. Controlling port cities allowed them access to the Mediterranean and Europe. These kingdoms had expanded by 1140, but were never stable. By 1192, Saladin and other Muslim rulers had retaken almost all of these Latin Christian territories.

non-Christians, some Latins discovered there the pleasures of a cosmopolitan life.

The four Crusader kingdoms never became as solidly rooted as those of western Europe. A high mortality rate meant that male heirs were not always available for thrones or major fiefs. In such cases, lordships reverted to the rulers of the four settlements, reducing the power of nobles to resist their rulers—but also weakening the rulers' ability to muster the resources to defend the realm. Women from ruling families took advantage of this situation to take power. When the king of Jerusalem Baldwin II (r. 1118–1131) died, his eldest daughter, Melisende, and her husband, Fulk, were crowned. Though Melisende could not command in war, she successfully insisted on ruling with Fulk, and kept her son Baldwin III out of power for seven years after he came of age in 1145. Her younger sister, Princess Alice, made a similar effort to rule Antioch after her husband died, and succeeded for seven years.

Though the Latin kingdoms in the East cooperated effectively, they could never count on being strong enough to fight off the hostile forces that surrounded them. New institutions were created to help—above all the military orders. The Templars took their name from the building in Jerusalem where they met, which they identified as the Temple of Solomon. The Hospitalers had originally created the Hospital of Saint John in Jerusalem before the First Crusade even took place. Soon enough both orders were providing military help to the Latin East, guarding ports and borders. Although their members were relatively few—each could field around 300 soldiers in the kingdom of Jerusalem—they were expert fighters and deeply knowledgeable about local conditions. As religious orders, they depended on—and received—a stream of gifts and charitable bequests that enabled them to buy equipment and systematically recruit young men for service.

For all the improvisatory skill that western Latins showed in dealing with the challenges of life in the eastern Mediterranean, the balance of forces regularly turned against them. They were often forced to make appeals to the Latin West or, in desperate circumstances, to Byzantium.

SALADIN AND THE CRUSADES When one of the Crusader kingdoms fell in 1144, Pope Eugene III announced a Second Crusade (1147–49) to restore the territory to Latin control. Popular enthusiasm for this crusade—though perhaps less intense than for the first—was still widespread. To mobilize Christian forces, the French cleric Bernard of Clairvaux and King Louis VII of France held a public meeting at Vézelay in central France, at which the king appeared wearing his cross. The audience grabbed all of the premade crosses that Bernard had brought with him, and he had to tear his monastic habit into strips to meet the further demand. But both the French and imperial armies were defeated by the Seljuk Turks in Asia Minor, and an assault on Damascus failed as well.

The Crusader kingdoms faced even greater danger when Saladin (Salah al-Din Yusuf ibn Ayyub; 1137/8–1193), a Muslim of Kurdish ancestry, first became vizier of Egypt and then took over the state, ruled until then by the Fatimid Caliphate. Allying himself with the Abbasid Caliphate in Baghdad, Saladin invaded and conquered Syria between 1174 and 1182. In 1187 he defeated a crusader army and retook Palestine. A chivalrous ruler who granted amnesty to Christian soldiers (once they paid a substantial ransom), Saladin won the respect of opponents as well as allies. The English king Richard I, known as Richard the Lionhearted (r. 1189–1199), joined in a Third Crusade (1189–92) against Saladin, along with Holy Roman Emperor Frederick Barbarossa and Philip II (r. 1180–1223)

Saladin's Soldiers A mid-thirteenth-century history of the Crusades includes this illuminated initial "B," in which Saladin's troops take a group of Europeans prisoner while a city burns behind them.

of France. But Barbarossa accidentally drowned along the way, leaving Leopold V, Duke of Austria, to lead a much reduced imperial force. The others joined Guy of Lusignan, the king of Jerusalem, and once Richard arrived, they used the full range of medieval siege technologies to take the port of Acre. Quarrels broke out among the Christian rulers, and Philip and Leopold eventually left. Richard, a brilliant warrior, managed to defeat Saladin at Arsuf in 1191 and took Jaffa. Divisions in the Crusader army prevented Richard from retaking Jerusalem, which remained in Muslim hands, though unarmed Christian pilgrims and merchants were guaranteed the right to visit the city. Richard was captured by a Christian enemy on his way home and died soon after, as did Saladin.

Gradually the Crusader kingdoms were ground down. Still, Latin states and Roman popes continued to see themselves as having a vital stake both in the Holy Land and in other areas where Christians and Muslims confronted one another. As we will see, serious crusading enterprises continued for centuries to come, most successfully in Spain.

THE NEW CHRISTIANITY

As novel as the Crusades—and in some ways more durable—was the vast outpouring of religious feeling that inspired them. The old monastic houses that looked back to Benedict—with their well-born monks; their slow, stately life of religious services and manuscript copying; and their great wealth—had become hard to distinguish from other centers for the noble and rich. Newer and more energetic religious establishments flanked them. The Benedictine monk Bernard of Cluny drew up a massive indictment of the sins of his time in the long poem "On Contempt for the World." Bernard threatened his fellow monks and nuns—as well as the corrupt priests who lived in the world and pursued glory and gold there—with the wrath of the Savior, who would soon return and punish them: "The times are very bad, the hour is late, we must take heed: For the final judge will soon arrive." The monastery of Cluny in eastern France became the center of a federation of Benedictine houses devoted to piety and prayer and to the reforming ideals of the Gregorian movement.

THE CISTERCIAN ORDER Not everyone agreed with the monks of Cluny, who held that monks should abandon physical labor for prayer. At Cîteaux, not far from Dijon, a Benedictine abbot and some twenty followers founded a new house in 1098. They called for a return to strict observance of Benedict's *Rule*. To pursue holiness as Benedict had hoped, they argued, monks must abandon the collecting of rents and the gathering of appointments to well-endowed priestly offices and go back to working the land.

Though these **Cistercians**—they drew their name from the location of their first house—regarded themselves as "perfect Benedictines," under the inspired leadership of Stephen Harding (d. 1134) they soon developed rules and customs of their own. They replaced the black Benedictine habit with a new one of white wool, which signified their commitment to lead an "angelic" life. They insisted that they would accept only gifts of unimproved land, which they would cultivate themselves. The Cistercians' rigorous pursuit of holiness inspired enormous enthusiasm. Gifts multiplied as Europe's prosperity rose, and by the middle of the twelfth century Cistercian houses had appeared everywhere—from Britain in the north, to the Iberian Peninsula in the south, to the Holy Roman Empire, Hungary, and Poland in the east. All houses sent representatives to the general chapters of the order, which took place once a year, and which maintained discipline throughout the new order.

Women of many social levels—daughters of minor nobles and urban merchants and craftsmen, but poorer women as well—looked for a way to turn from the world and live an "apostolic" life. In the twelfth and early thirteenth centuries, many formed small communities, living in houses on the edges of cities and tending the sick in hospitals or the lepers in their leprosaria. They sang hymns, prayed, and sometimes adopted habits. These initiatives could stir disapproval from the Church, but in rich towns such as Troyes in northern France, many of these small, informal women's religious organizations became Cistercian convents, whose members were allowed to frame their own austere lives in search of purity.

The leaders of the Cistercians—above all Bernard of Clairvaux (1090–1153)—promoted new forms of Christian spirituality and devotion. In profound treatises on pride and humility, Bernard explored the religious experience of monks like himself. More important for ordinary Christians, he believed passionately in the spiritual power of the Virgin Mary and helped to spread a new form of Christianity in which her intercession—and that of her Son—became central to religious experience. Many Christian men and women appealed to Mary and Jesus for help—just as they would have appealed, in ordinary life, not to the king but to their local lord or lady. Alongside the militant piety of the crusaders, a more personal piety took shape in the twelfth century.

Bernard of Clairvaux In this twelfth-century French woodcut, the Cistercian leader, wearing his order's white habit, composes a sermon while young monks study at his feet. The hand of God reaching down from heaven symbolizes that Bernard has received divine favor.

HILDEGARD OF BINGEN Ordinary Christians regularly interpreted experiences—especially those that seemed outside the order of nature—as evidence of supernatural intervention. And they valued, and searched for, sincerity and sanctity in those around them. Evidence of these qualities could enable their possessor to transcend what might otherwise have been the overwhelming limitations of birth and sex, and gain recognition as a teacher and scholar.

Hildegard of Bingen (1098–1179), the tenth child of a German noble family, was given as a "tithe" (a tax of 10 percent) to a Benedictine house in the Rhineland, where she was enclosed (cloistered). At the age of five she began to have visions "while awake and seeing with a pure mind and the eyes and ears of the inner self, in open places, as God willed it. How this might be is hard for mortal flesh to understand." At first, she talked about the revelations she received only to a trusted few. But gradually she developed a reputation for piety and began to gather supporters. A male cleric became her first secretary and recorded

Hildegard's Visions In a twelfth-century edition of Hildegard's *Visions*, a small portrait shows her sitting at a writing desk (bottom left), while the center of the page records her vision of the earth as God created it, as told in the story of Genesis: sea creatures, birds, and plants populate the world, which humans manage and cultivate.

her revelations. She also composed hymns, both the music and words. And when she could, she preached publicly in Trier and other cities in western Germany, converting her revelations into prophetic sermons.

By tradition only men could create liturgies or interpret the Bible. Hildegard, as she was the first to admit, had no formal education, and she suffered terribly throughout her life from physical pain and paralysis. She accepted her suffering as the direct work of God's hand, intended to prevent her from committing the sin of pride. Eventually, however, she found herself able to enter what had been largely male territory since the first generations of Christianity: "Heaven was opened and a fiery light of exceeding brilliance came and permeated my whole brain, and inflamed my whole heart and my whole breast, not like a burning but like a warming flame, as the sun warms anything its rays touch. And immediately I knew the meaning of the exposition of the Scriptures."

Hildegard corresponded with prelates and the Holy Roman emperor. As the extraordinary network of her contacts grew, so did the range of her speculations. By the end of her life, she had developed a coherent theory of the universe—one that was nourished by reading in her community's library and that followed the long-standing Neoplatonic tradition. She emphasized the connections between the higher realms of the angels and the stars and the lower one inhabited by humans. Adam, before he fell, had been able to hear "the voice of the living spirit," the cosmic harmony: "still innocent before his fault, he had no little kinship with the angels' praises." Music, now, might reach listeners and make them pious.

For five centuries, the form of music traditionally ascribed to Pope Gregory I (r. 590–604) and usually known as Gregorian chant—the chanting of psalms and other parts of the liturgy by male soloists and choirs—had spread through the Western Church, displacing older, local forms. No one expressed more vividly than Hildegard the power and beauty of the Latin Mass that had become the core of Catholic religious life. Her writings and compositions enable us to glimpse something of what the Cistercian nuns, who did not leave such rich testimonies behind, must have felt as they worshipped.

GOD'S ARCHITECTURE: CATHEDRALS The same passionate commitment to Christianity—and the same vision of an orderly, beautiful universe—that inspired Hildegard of Bingen also inspired the patrons and artists who began to transform the physical world of the Church. In late antiquity and after, as we have seen, great Christian churches took the standard form of Roman public

STAINED GLASS AT CHARTRES CATHEDRAL

As we have seen, Suger, the early-twelfth-century abbot of Saint Denis, wrote that the light inside his church, transformed by stained glass, "Should brighten the minds [of congregants], allowing them to travel through the lights / To the true light, where Christ is the true door." Suger proudly hired the most skillful artisans to create the church's windows.

By the mid-twelfth century, stained glass became a highly developed art form, exemplified by the windows at Chartres Cathedral. Of the 173 original windows completed in the early thirteenth century, 143 remain largely intact—the largest existing collection of medieval stained glass in the world. They provide a detailed visual archive of medieval culture and society.

The windows portray Christian figures such as Jesus Christ, the Virgin Mary, and the apostles. They also depict everyday life in the figures of bakers, butchers, furriers, masons, cobblers, and armorers. These workers are representatives of the guilds whose contributions helped build Chartres and other medieval churches.

In this detail from a window illustrating the story of Noah's Ark, a cooper nails hoops on a barrel. His labor in support of Noah's mission is a demonstration of artisanal skill and Christian faith.

QUESTIONS FOR ANALYSIS

1. How did the stained glass windows of medieval churches convey a sense of the sacred?
2. How did this art form reflect secular interests as well?
3. What does the depiction of a cooper in this great cathedral tell you about medieval society and its attitude toward work?

buildings: the basilica, a long hall flanked with columns. From the eleventh century on, in France and elsewhere, the clerics and builders who created cathedrals—the churches where bishops had their seats—began to aim for a different set of effects. A new form—the **Romanesque**—retained the design of the basilica but replaced its flat roof with an arched vault. Semicircular portals opened off the main church, but few windows pierced its thick walls.

In the twelfth century, another form—known as **Gothic**—developed. The nave—the long body of the church that led up to the high altar, lined with chapels—was now crossed by another, shorter segment: the transept. Sculptured reliefs, as varied and powerful as those of ancient Athens, surrounded the main entrance. New construction techniques made it possible to raise high, lightweight roofs supported by complex networks of rib vaults. Dramatic flying buttresses sprang from the walls to the ground, making it possible to raise spectacular towers and open up the walls for huge windows. Circular "rose" windows over the main entrance to the west, and sharply

Romanesque and Gothic Architecture In the eleventh century, churches such as Notre-Dame la Grande in Poitiers (left) were built in the Romanesque style, with its characteristic rounded arches, pointed roofs, and small number of doors and windows. In the twelfth century, Gothic constructions such as the Cathedral of Notre-Dame of Amiens (right) became popular. Built in the shape of a cross, Gothic buildings included high roofs, many pointed arches, and large stained-glass windows.

pointed ones along the nave—made of stained glass in deep, rich colors—told the stories of the Old and New Testaments and filled the interiors with multicolored light.

The first church to bring most of these features together was the basilica of Saint Denis, north of Paris, originally built in the Carolingian period. Suger, the early-twelfth-century abbot of Saint Denis, transformed the church's west facade. He turned it into a treble triumphal arch and pierced it with a massive rose window whose stained glass illuminated the church's nave—a feature that would soon be imitated in cathedrals in Chartres, Paris, and elsewhere. Clerestory windows pierced the upper sections of the walls, suffusing the church with light.

In his account of his time as abbot, Suger recalled with pride how he had spared no expense to bring the most skillful painters, sculptors, and bronze-casters to work on his church. Some of these skilled artisans proudly carved their names—and sometimes their self-portraits—into the stone panels and rich wooden pulpits of the cathedrals. Suger also noted the treasures he had lavished on the church, in the form of jewels and precious metals (Suger thought it a miracle, though a "humorous one," when monks from other abbeys turned up with gems for sale in the nick of time). Above all, though, he insisted that this material splendor served a higher spiritual purpose: "The noble work is bright, but, being nobly bright, the work / Should brighten the minds, allowing them to travel through the lights / To the true light, where Christ is the true door." Like the cosmic music that Hildegard of Bingen imagined,

the visible harmony and light of the church's symphonic set of spaces, hierarchically ordered in praise of the Creator and his saints, was meant to bring Christian minds to God.

NEW DIRECTIONS IN MEDIEVAL CULTURE

In the years from 1000 to 1200, Christian minds also turned to a new kind of learning, often centered in the great cathedrals. Europeans rediscovered classical and Christian texts that had been preserved in monastic libraries. They learned that in the Islamic world, the heritage of Greek philosophy, mathematics, astronomy, and medicine had not only been preserved but developed and expanded in powerful and creative ways. In monasteries and cathedrals, in the centers of busy Italian trading cities, and in the seclusion of hermitages, Europeans began to rethink everything from the structure of the universe to the practical problems of everyday life. They also created institutions for the pursuit of learning that still exist—the universities that have been a central feature of Western society for a thousand years.

CLERICS AND THE FOUNDING OF SCHOOLS

The Gregorian Reform movement made it clear that clerics needed learning—everything from literacy in Latin to a sophisticated understanding of theology, depending on their offices and ranks—to fulfill their new responsibilities. Yet this education was not easy to find in tenth- and eleventh-century Europe. Without the support that Charlemagne and his immediate successors had provided for scholarship, classical learning had declined.

BEC ABBEY Nonetheless, the clerics of the eleventh century began to collect and study ancient texts in a newly systematic way—turning back to the ancients for knowledge, just as the Gregorian reformers turned back to the ancients for a model of a true Christian life. Lanfranc (ca. 1005–1089), a cleric from Pavia in northern Italy, made a great name for himself as a teacher in France. The school he founded at Bec Abbey became one of the first of a set of new institutions that took shape for the study, copying, and use of texts, especially the Latin Bible. Lanfranc used his knowledge to defend the doctrine of transubstantiation, which held that the Eucharist truly became the body and blood of Jesus, even though the bread continued to look like bread and the wine like wine. His learning and piety won the respect of King William I of England, who appointed him archbishop of Canterbury.

GLOSSING THE TEXTS Informal schools grew up, usually in cathedrals. At first, individual masters offered instruction for small groups of pupils, who stayed until they felt satisfied with their level of knowledge. Gradually, teachers forged new tools, such as a basic commentary—a set of marginal and interlinear notes—on the Old and New Testaments. These notes were assembled by Anselm of Laon (in northern France; d. 1117) and other teachers into what came to be known as the Ordinary Gloss. The gloss drew much of its content from the church fathers and other earlier writers, but it made their views far more accessible than they had been. It spread through the commented Bibles used by scholars, and it provided baseline interpretations of passages central to Christian ritual and practice. Long commentaries by scholars at Chartres explored the work of Augustine, in particular his view that Plato's account of the universe was largely compatible with Christianity. Soon the effort to show that faith and reason were not in conflict became the central focus of what came to be called scholastic philosophy and theology. Propelled by a new method of teaching and learning—formal argument, or at least no-holds-barred debate—**scholasticism** spread through the Christian world.

PETER ABELARD AND THE NEW METHOD

Paris emerged as a center, first of the new formal way of argument and then of the scholastic system that rested on it. Combative teachers and their pupils argued both about the method a Christian should follow in study and about specific problems in theology. Peter Abelard (1079–1142), the son of a French noble family who brought his family's martial spirit into the classroom, became one of the most celebrated Paris masters. He laid out, under the title *Yes and No*, what seemed to be contradictory statements in the Bible and in the church fathers' commentaries on a vast range of theological questions. Some authoritative texts treated God as one, for example; others as three, or three in one. Abelard pointed out that the more Christian scholars learned, the more of these problems appeared.

Many readers found Abelard's collection of materials shocking: it seemed to them that he had traced fault lines in the solid body of Christian authority. But Abelard pointed out that church fathers such as Augustine and Jerome had already worried, centuries before his time, about what they saw as contradictions in scripture. He made clear that the right kind of analysis could remove many apparent contradictions. The interpreter must begin by assuming that what looked like mistakes or contradictions in the texts were probably the result of his or her own failure to understand, or that scribes might have made errors when copying the texts.

Above all, Abelard showed, the teacher had to master the tools of dialectic—the logic used in formal argument. For it was by making distinctions—for example, between the different senses of some words—that the scholar could hope to gain control over the apparent chaos of the Christian textual universe. Abelard himself became a great logician. He set out to determine whether universals, such as "man," actually existed, and concluded that they did not: there were only actual individuals, the unique people and concrete things that populated the universe. As he applied these tools to the texts, some of the contradictions resolved themselves without a struggle. Abelard's teaching of logic made him an intellectual star to whom students flocked. Older scholars who could not master his method, including his own teachers, found themselves relegated to obscurity.

THEOLOGY AND CHRISTIAN PRACTICE

By the middle of the twelfth century, Abelard and his rivals and successors had made Christian **theology** into a formal discipline. It had its own textbook: the *Four Books of Sentences* by Peter Lombard, an Italian who became bishop of Paris. This work provided students of theology with endless propositions to debate. Theology also had its own method: the logic of Aristotle, as reconfigured and developed to fit the needs of Christian scholars anxious to understand matters such as the nature of the Eucharist, which Aristotle could not have imagined.

Though medieval theology seems abstruse, it was tightly connected to vital Church practices. The Bible and the church fathers had not revealed for certain where the majority of Christians would spend the centuries after their deaths. In the first half of the twelfth century, theologians built on earlier discussions to establish a solution. The dead did not go directly to hell or heaven, for the most part. Instead, ordinary sinners inhabited purgatory, a realm of long-term punishment where cleansing fires could burn away the sins that they had committed in their lifetimes.

PURGATORY AND PENANCE This vision of punishment and correction supported one of the Church's fundamental practices, the sacrament of penance. Since the third and fourth centuries, Christians had confessed their sins to priests (at first in public) and received absolution for them. Manuals for confessors helped bring Christianity into daily life as Europe was evangelized in the seventh and eighth centuries. The theologians now explained that by doing penance in the proper way, Christians could shorten the time they would have to spend after death making up for their failures. Heaven and hell had long played dramatic roles in the Christian imagination. They were now joined by a third realm, purgatory, where even after death, change could still take place.

Over the centuries to come, religious visionaries, artists, and poets equipped purgatory with a precise landscape and imagined its inhabitants and their sufferings in vivid detail. Theology laid the foundations on which these complex and vital structures of religious life and artistic imagination were built. Formal argument—mastery of the cut and thrust of logic—offered the keys to this intellectual kingdom.

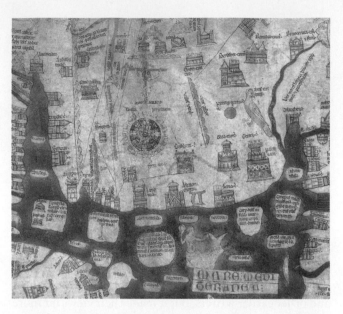

Mapping the World Medieval European cartographic efforts offered a view of the known universe embellished with rich symbolism. In this detail from a thirteenth-century English map of the world, Jerusalem is placed at the center (marked with a large cross and dark circle), and the Mediterranean Sea is imagined as a large body of water separating Europe (bottom left), Africa (bottom right), and Asia (top).

THE FORCE OF TRADITION

In one sense, the European intellectual world of the eleventh and twelfth centuries remained highly traditional. Scholars still imagined the heavens in terms that the ancients would have recognized. The earth remained the center of the universe—the theater where the cosmic drama of salvation and damnation of the human race was enacted. At its core, the devil raged and ruled over the damned. Outside its atmosphere, the seven planets (the moon, Mercury, Venus, the sun, Mars, Jupiter, and Saturn)—perfect globes quite different from the messy earth—moved ceaselessly on their crystalline spheres, as did the fixed stars on an even larger sphere. Beyond them, the orders of the angels, as perfectly ranked as the heavens, made their celestial music in praise of God. Human beings inhabited the intersection between the changeable world of matter and the perfect world of the heavens—the one place where salvation could be won or lost.

These structures were slow to change. Even as Latin Christians came into contact—and conflict—with Muslims, Jews, and Greek Christians, Persians and Seljuk Turks, many of whom knew Africa and Asia far better than they did, Latin mapmakers continued to divide the face of the earth into three continents, which they represented schematically. They placed Jerusalem at the center

of the world for theological reasons. They also knew only North Africa and depicted the Indian Ocean as enclosed by land, even though the Arab traders whose caravans crossed the Sahara and whose ships followed the trade winds across the Indian Ocean knew better. These mapmakers devoted huge effort to such symbolic, rather than empirical, enterprises as trying to fix the location of the Garden of Eden.

Pushing against the weight of tradition in the European intellectual world, the practical problems of an increasingly commercial society created new openings for innovation. Monarchs, merchants, and nobles all needed guidance as cities and their economies developed, and political conflict flared between states and with the Church. Laymen as well as clerics consulted the ancient books that covered everything from how to regulate commercial transactions to how to maintain the health of the human body.

INNOVATION IN THE LAW

One of these ancient works was the Roman *Corpus Iuris*. Although compiled under Emperor Justinian in Constantinople half a millennium before, it offered exactly the tools needed: powerful definitions of principles that could regulate relations, and clear statements about how they operated.

SECULAR LAW By the beginning of the twelfth century, scholars in Bologna, a large and prosperous commune with a thriving textile industry and a sophisticated city government, were offering lectures on Roman law. Like the theologians, the lawyers taught by lecturing on texts and holding debates; and like the Bible, the Roman law was soon barnacled with a thick coating of explanatory comments.

Rulers and their advisers, merchants, and nobles scoured the Roman law for insights and detailed legislation they could adapt to their own purposes. It could be used to support the pretensions of central power: "the king," it declared, "is emperor in his own realm." But it could also support the privileges and autonomies of particular groups or cities. The Roman law made clear that the Roman people had transferred their power to the emperors—a statement that could be cited for support as readily by republicans as by monarchists. The revival of secular law helped to regulate trade and other urban practices, but it also helped to spawn new debates about the foundations of politics.

THE CHURCH, LAW, AND MARRIAGE The Church, for its part, had substantial responsibilities in what would now be considered the realm of law. Marriage was a formal business in the Middle Ages—an opportunity for royal and noble families or established city merchants and craftsmen to form alliances with powerful counterparts. It was normally marked by an exchange of property, especially in the form of a dowry provided by the bride's family. The clergy, who were responsible for marriage, tried to convince ordinary Christians that marriage should be based on affection as well as political and economic strategy. They also gradually pushed people in northern Europe to give up the custom whereby a couple would become engaged and then have intercourse to seal their marriage, in favor of a marriage ceremony outside the church door, followed by a nuptial Mass inside the church presided over by a priest.

As the role of the clergy grew, priests became responsible for determining whether the prospective bride and groom could marry legally in the first place. With many noble families related by intermarriage, it was easy to mistakenly marry within the so-called prohibited degrees of kinship—especially when doing so might have the practical advantage of knitting together adjacent land holdings.

The rules for ending marriages were also complex. Jesus had forbidden his followers to divorce their partners. But if a king or a wealthy merchant could not impregnate his wife, for example, he might seek to have his marriage annulled by the Church on the grounds that she was infertile. This accusation was humiliating, and the exchanges of property that had to follow the dissolution of a marriage were intricate. Laws and tables were drawn up to give priests—and, when appeals to Rome took place, archbishops and cardinals—guidance on how to decide all of the questions that could provoke disputes.

In addition, the Church had its own vast properties and prerogatives to protect. Accordingly, clerics used the Roman model to create a second body of law—canon law, or the law of the Church—and built a system of courts to administer it. Canon law rested on a textbook, the *Decretum*, assembled by the Benedictine monk Gratian, who taught in Bologna in the mid twelfth century. Like the ancient Roman lawyers before them, the clerics compiled and taught these laws so effectively that by the end of the

Medieval Marriage An illustration from a twelfth-century Spanish manuscript displays the solemnity associated with marriage between nobles. The French viscount of Nimes (seated) formally sanctions the betrothal of his daughter Ermengarde—her hair uncovered to indicate that she is a virgin—to a Spanish count, while the viscountess looks on.

twelfth century the best way to rise to the highest positions in the Church was to study law. And like the Roman lawyers, the clerics provided arguments for partisans of radically opposed positions.

THE FIRST UNIVERSITIES

Alongside these changes in secular and canon law there came new institutions—institutions more formal, at first, than the Paris schools of Abelard's time—for pursuing practical studies. Bologna, as we have seen, became a center for legal studies early in the twelfth century. Salerno, in southwestern Italy, developed a medical school. As their numbers grew, the students in these cities emulated those engaged in other trades. They banded together and formed what they called a *universitas* (Latin for a corporation or guild) to regulate teaching and learning. Once organized and equipped with rules and privileges, they hired professors and insisted that they teach the full hour, until the bell rang to dismiss class. Students did not make all the rules. School faculties defined the texts that students must study to become qualified practitioners, laid out curricula, and set exercises to test mastery of particular subjects. By the end of the twelfth century, these Italian professional schools had crystallized as formal universities—one of the characteristic new institutions of medieval Europe.

The Early Universities, 1200

PARIS AND ITS STUDENTS
In Paris, meanwhile, the professors did what the students had done in the south. They formed a university in the mid-twelfth century, established faculties, and drew up a curriculum for formal study. In Paris, theology, not law or medicine, became the central course of study. Students in Paris—and at the other universities soon formed in its wake, such as Oxford—were clerics. They mastered the liberal arts and logic, and carried out the exercises that made them first bachelors and then masters of arts. Most finished at that point, but an elite few continued and took doctorates in theology.

Many students came—as Peter Abelard did—from the nobility. But able students from farms and city streets also gravitated to the schools in Paris and elsewhere. They survived at first by begging, but systems of scholarship support gradually took shape, which enabled poor students to concentrate on their work. These students acquired a new status. At a time when most young people were bound to the land they worked, to the shops where they served as apprentices, or to the knights or ladies whom they served as pages or maids, students enjoyed great freedom. They lived in cities, in inns and halls, with little supervision. Often they spent their free time in taverns and brothels. Students became known not only for their intellectual skills but also for their willingness to fight when challenged by citizens whom their behavior annoyed, or innkeepers whom they refused to pay.

NEW AVENUES TO POWER
For all their differences of emphasis and curriculum, these new universities had much in common. In the same years when poets created new forms of literature in the vernaculars, professors created new forms of lecture and treatise in Latin, devising technical terms that had not existed in the ancient world. In this case, as in others, a language with no native speakers proved so useful that it not only survived, it also developed in new and unexpected ways. The masters used their new technical language to teach students how to read and debate about authoritative texts. And they all recognized one another's degrees. Become a Master of Arts at Paris, and you could teach the liberal arts at any other university. A common culture of learning based in the new institutions spread across Europe, especially as it became clear that popes, kings, and city governments highly valued the graduates. For the first—but certainly not the last—time in European history, formal education offered access to political and economic power.

THE IMPACT OF ISLAMIC LEARNING

As the foundations of Western intellectual life were renewed, Latin culture also absorbed new information and new ways of thinking from the Islamic world. Specialized disciplines such as philosophy, astronomy, technology, and medicine flourished in the age of Saladin, as they had in Hellenistic and Roman Alexandria. Prosperous and sophisticated Islamic states created libraries, mosques, and formal institutions. Al-Azhar, the Muslim

MEDIEVAL PARIS, ca. 1200

66 I PREFERRED THE WEAPONS OF DIALECTIC TO ALL THE OTHER TEACHINGS OF PHILOSOPHY, AND ARMED WITH THESE I CHOSE THE CONFLICTS OF DISPUTATION INSTEAD OF THE TROPHIES OF WAR. 99

PETER ABELARD, *HISTORY OF MY CALAMITIES*

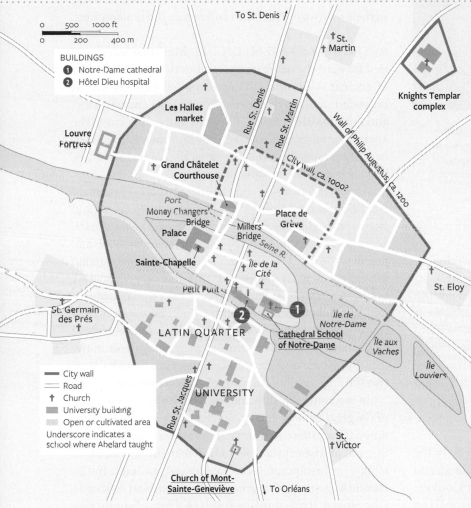

BUILDINGS
1 Notre-Dame cathedral
2 Hôtel Dieu hospital

To St. Denis

† St. Martin

Knights Templar complex

Les Halles market

Louvre Fortress

Rue St. Denis

Rue St. Martin

Wall of Philip Augustus ca. 1200

City wall, ca. 1000?

Grand Châtelet Courthouse

Port Money Changers' Bridge

Millers' Bridge

Palace

Place de Grève

Sainte-Chapelle

Seine R.

Île de la Cité

Petit Pont

St. Eloy

St. Germain des Prés

LATIN QUARTER

Île de Notre-Dame

Île aux Vaches

Île Louviers

Cathedral School of Notre-Dame

—— City wall
═══ Road
† Church
▪ University building
▪ Open or cultivated area
Underscore indicates a school where Abelard taught

Rue St. Jacques

UNIVERSITY

St. Victor

Church of Mont-Sainte-Geneviève

To Orléans

0   500   1000 ft
0   200   400 m

POPULATION
Early thirteenth century: ca. 50,000.

UNIVERSITY ATTENDANCE
2,000–3,000 students living and studying in the Latin Quarter.

STUDENT EXEMPTIONS
As clerics, all students were exempt from secular laws and the jurisdiction of city courts and lords, occasionally leading to friction with local residents.

A professor lectures on a theology text at a Parisian school in this fourteenth-century manuscript illustration. Professors used Latin in new ways to teach students how to read and debate their texts.

66 I, A WANDERING SCHOLAR LAD, / BORN FOR TOIL AND SADNESS, / OFTENTIMES AM DRIVEN BY / POVERTY TO MADNESS. / LITERATURE AND KNOWLEDGE I / FAIN WOULD STILL BE EARNING, / WERE IT NOT THAT WANT OF PELF / MAKES ME CEASE FROM LEARNING. 99

ANONYMOUS STUDENT POEM, FROM *CARMINA BURANA*

This fourteenth-century French manuscript shows Parisian students at prayer. From the cathedral school of Notre-Dame to the University of Paris, schools were intimately connected to the Church, and theology formed the core of their curricula.

66 SOME ARE GAMING, SOME ARE DRINKING, / SOME ARE LIVING WITHOUT THINKING; / AND OF THOSE WHO MAKE THE RACKET, / SOME ARE STRIPPED OF COAT AND JACKET; / SOME GET CLOTHES OF FINER FEATHER, / SOME ARE CLEANED OUT ALTOGETHER; / NO ONE THERE DREADS DEATH'S INVASION, / BUT ALL DRINK IN EMULATION. 99

STUDENT DRINKING SONG, FROM *CARMINA BURANA*

QUESTIONS FOR ANALYSIS

1. What made Peter Abelard's argumentative approach to teaching so exciting to students?

2. What can you say about student life in medieval Paris from the evidence here?

3. How did students in the medieval universities experience a new independence in their social and intellectual lives?

Mosque of Córdoba The Great Mosque of Córdoba (completed in 987), with its vaulted, striped archways, is not only a magnificent example of the architecture of the Islamic world but also inspired builders of Christian cathedrals throughout Europe.

and omnipotent God could have created a universe that included evil of so many kinds.

Both men ended up in exile: Averroës was banished by the emir of Córdoba in 1195, and when a new dynasty from North Africa seized Córdoba and exiled its Jews in 1148, Maimonides was forced to leave with them. Yet their works became classics, not only in their original Arabic but in the Latin translations that made both of them standard authorities for Western thinkers anxious to show, in their own ways, that faith and reason did not conflict.

ASTRONOMY AND MEDICINE

Muslim scholars carried forward the quantitative studies that had flourished in ancient Alexandria. They compiled new terrestrial maps and star charts, improved on the ancient astrolabe, and built massive clocks. They did more than study the ancient astronomer Ptolemy: they built mechanical replicas of his models for the motion of the planets and stars, and uncovered shortcomings in his work.

Astrology, as we have seen, had deep roots in the ancient Near East, and occupied a substantial place in Greek and Roman thought. Muslim astronomers, for the most part, accepted it as a profound discipline and used its symbols and practices to predict the future. They composed a vast stream of horoscopes to account for everything from the foundation of cities and empires to the careers and travels of individuals. Educated Latin Christians followed suit. From the twelfth century on, they incorporated astrology into the medical curriculum. Gradually it came to play a major role in the daily life of courts, churches, and cities, even though Christian theologians since Augustine had generally rejected it.

In medicine, Muslim and Jewish scholars studied two of the great ancient authorities, Aristotle and Galen, and noted their differences on vital points: whereas Aristotle insisted on the central role of the heart in human physiology, for instance, Galen emphasized the liver. In the eleventh century, the great Persian scholar Avicenna (Ibn Sina; d. 1037) confronted this problem of conflicting authorities and compiled a massive medical encyclopedia, *The Canon of Medicine*, which laid out the elements of Galen's system. Avicenna set out the basic causes of health and illness, described the constitution of the universe, and offered detailed discussions of anatomy, physiology, and therapy. Late in the twelfth century, the Italian scholar Gerard of Cremona (ca. 1114–1187) translated the *Canon* into Latin. It served as the basis of medical teaching in Christian universities for centuries.

university in Cairo, took shape in the tenth century, long before any Western one.

In many parts of the Islamic world, multiple religious and philosophical traditions flourished side by side. Córdoba had been the capital of Muslim Spain in the ninth and tenth centuries. It boasted an enormous, magnificent mosque—a building so splendid that, after Córdoba fell to Christian forces in 1236, architects of cathedrals in Spain and France did their best to copy it. The Christian population of Córdoba had their own bishop while under Muslim rule, and in the tenth century the caliph's personal physician was a learned and wealthy Jew.

CÓRDOBA: AVERROËS AND MAIMONIDES

In the twelfth century, Muslim Spain was no longer united, and Seville replaced Córdoba as its leading city. But Córdoba still gave birth to extraordinary thinkers. Averroës (Ibn Rushd; 1126–1198), who served for many years as a judge, drew up commentaries on almost the entire body of Aristotle's works. Averroës argued that Aristotle offered a consistent, powerful understanding of the universe, and that his thought did not conflict with the revelations of Islam. Where philosophy and religion appeared to disagree, they were actually offering different kinds of truth. Moses Maimonides (1138–1204) also came from Córdoba. The most influential Jewish thinker of the Middle Ages, he too became an expert on law—in his case, Jewish law—and a medical man as well. In a massive philosophical work, *The Guide for the Perplexed*, he asked how a benevolent

TRANSLATING THE ISLAMIC CANON

For Muslims as for Latins, knowledge mostly meant the contents of books. As the Crusades and travel brought the two cultures into closer contact, educated Westerners realized how great a wealth of material was accessible to scholars in the Muslim lands. Scholar-explorers from all over the Latin West made the difficult trip to Sicily and the Iberian Peninsula in the first half of the twelfth century. There some learned Arabic and all gained access to the Islamic canon of philosophical and scientific texts. Often collaborating with local helpers, they rendered many of the classic, systematic works of ancient philosophy and science from Arabic into Latin: Aristotle's works, Euclid's *Geometry*, Ptolemy's major works, and much more. The Greek originals of these works had been translated in literal fashion, word for word, by the scholars of Baghdad's House of Wisdom in the ninth century. Now Latin scholars followed suit, rendering the Arabic translations word for word into Latin. The results were not elegant, but these translations gave Western thinkers direct access, for the first time in several hundred years, to many of the central works of Greek thought.

THE TRANSFORMATION OF LATIN THOUGHT

A wealth of technical books from the Islamic world became accessible in the West for the first time in the twelfth century, and their impact was profound. Western scholars hungrily seized on them. Latin libraries expanded to include their astronomical tables and medical textbooks. Arabic numerals spread alongside the traditional Roman ones. In the lively, urban world of the universities, the newly available ancient texts and the works of more recent Muslim scholars found a natural audience. Latin thinkers developed new skills and, even more important, a newly critical attitude toward many of the ancient authorities and their assumptions.

BEYOND TRADITION: ABELARD AND HÉLOÏSE

The rise of new sources and methods for intellectual life was accompanied by striking changes in its style and temper. Learning and brilliance assumed a value that they had never previously possessed in the Latin tradition. In this strange new world, Peter Abelard, the deft practitioner of the new style of formal argument, became a cultural hero of a new kind. As Héloïse d'Argenteuil (d. 1164), the young woman who knew him more intimately than anyone else, described in a letter to him, his brilliance as a philosopher had made him a celebrity, one whose presence called crowds into the streets: "For who among

kings or philosophers could equal you in fame?" Héloïse described Abelard as a glamorous poet who could "captivate the heart of any woman" with the songs he composed and sang—an art form, she noted, that philosophers had rarely pursued.

Héloïse's testimony has a special value. For she was not only Abelard's friend but also his philosophical pupil, his secret lover, and his equal as a writer. She became pregnant with his son, whom she named Astrolabe—a testimony to the passion for knowledge she shared with Abelard. Her uncle and guardian, Fulbert, who became increasingly angry at his niece's relationship with Abelard, eventually arranged to have him castrated—and thus inflicted not only a monstrous physical wound but also a terrible psychic one, since the event immediately became public. Abelard found himself not only mutilated but humiliated.

REVEALING VOICES What makes this story most remarkable—and most characteristic of the extraordinary world in which it unfolded—is that both Abelard and Héloïse recorded their story and their responses to it: Abelard in his *History of My Calamities* as well as in letters to Héloïse and others, and Héloïse in complex, spectacular letters to Abelard. Abelard related, with unsparing precision, the details of his earlier career—the passion with which he had first sought out great teachers such as Anselm of Laon, and the demonic pride with which he had waged intellectual war against them. It was in the full heat of pride, Abelard insisted, that he—who had always preserved his virginity and hated casual sex and prostitution—taught and then fell in love with Héloïse, and in doing so betrayed his calling as a teacher. Like Augustine, Abelard set himself on what proved a twisting path to peace and salvation. Unlike Augustine, he set down in detail the machinations of the unworthy and the enemies that he encountered, even after God had so powerfully drawn his attention to his own faults.

HÉLOÏSE: A NEW CONSCIOUSNESS Though Héloïse had been Abelard's adoring pupil and might have been expected, as a woman who had borne a baby out of wedlock, to remain silent from shame, she now spoke for herself—and did so even more powerfully than he did. After she became pregnant, Abelard suggested that they marry secretly. Héloïse, in a magnificent tirade that Abelard summarized, insisted that it would be wrong for either of them to marry, since by doing so they would enter a state of misery and distraction. The true philosopher, she argued, must embrace solitude and contemplation: "What possible concord could there be between scholars and

Abelard and Héloïse In this fourteenth-century illustration, the two lovers—Abelard wearing a scholar's garment, and Héloïse dressed as a nun—converse together. Their hand gestures indicate their passion for argument.

domestics, between authors and cradles, between books or tablets and distaffs, between the stylus or the pen and the spindle?" She could not imagine herself, any more than Abelard, combining the pursuit of wisdom with the cares of married life.

In an extraordinary passage—one closer in spirit to the new poetry of courtly love than to the Latin and Christian classics that Héloïse had studied with Abelard, but even more defiant of conventions and tradition—she transformed the bond between man and woman from a practical connection to a communion of souls. Héloïse explained herself with a moral clarity next to which Abelard's severest efforts at self-flagellation look flat and insincere. With characteristic originality, she reclaimed the abusive terms for women who lived with men outside the social bonds of marriage. These were more appropriate to the philosophical life she wanted to share with Abelard—a relationship of equals—than the standard role and position of wife:

> The name of wife may seem more sacred or more binding, but sweeter for me will always be the word mistress, or, if you will permit me, that of concubine or whore.... God is my witness that if Augustus,

Emperor of the whole world, thought fit to honor me with marriage and conferred all the earth on me to possess for ever, it would be dearer and more honorable to me to be called not his Empress but your whore.

In Héloïse's brave words we hear the voice of a new consciousness—that of someone who is absolutely committed to scrutinizing her own conduct and judging it by the highest standards of morality, but who frames those standards for herself rather than accepting the norms of a society that expected women to be silent and decorous. Christian Europe was witnessing the birth not only of a culture of higher education, but one of individualism as well.

CONCLUSION

At the end of the twelfth century, Europe was still collectively poor—far poorer than China, at the other end of the great Silk Road trade route—even if some Europeans were enormously rich. Society was still organized into three basic orders: those who prayed (the clergy), those who fought (the military aristocracy), and the great majority who worked (primarily as serfs tied to the land). European monarchs had developed new systems for gathering revenue and administering justice, but even the most powerful rulers still depended on their aristocratic and clerical vassals for political counsel and military support. Struggles for authority between rulers and popes, and between rulers and cities that wished to be independent of their authority, consumed vast resources.

Still, Latin Europe was now on the move. Cities were growing again, and bound laborers who made their way to them and managed to remain for a time became legally free. The merchants and craftsmen who built the cities also created new forms of self-government of lasting consequence. Europeans were developing trade routes and mounting military expeditions into areas that had not been part of the Latin world since Roman times. They were mastering ancient texts, many of which had been lost to Latin culture and preserved in Arabic in the Islamic world, and composing new ones, in both Latin and new vernacular languages. The social and cultural changes of this period enabled some Europeans to begin to see themselves as unique individuals, who could imagine lives outside the normal categories that seemed to organize society. The individualism of the modern era may have begun in this deeply Christian world that remains almost wholly strange to us.

[CHAPTER REVIEW]

KEY TERMS

manorialism (p. 251)
serf (p. 251)
Peace of God (p. 252)
guild (p. 254)
commune (p. 255)

William the Conqueror (p. 258)
Domesday Book (p. 258)
chivalry (p. 263)
East-West Schism (p. 266)
Investiture Controversy (p. 267)

Gregorian Reform Movement (p. 267)
Concordat of Worms (p. 268)
Reconquista (p. 268)
Crusades (p. 270)
Cistercians (p. 273)

Romanesque (p. 275)
Gothic (p. 275)
scholasticism (p. 277)
theology (p. 277)

REVIEW QUESTIONS

1. What means of control did lords have over their serfs in the manorial system?

2. What innovations helped to spur the development of commerce in the cities?

3. What types of freedom did city life afford that were not available on the manor?

4. What steps were taken to create new, independent city governments?

5. How did King William I establish his authority over England?

6. What were the most important elements of the chivalric code?

7. What issues sparked conflict between the European monarchs and popes?

8. What were the initial motivations for Christian Europeans to undertake the Crusades?

9. What were the most important spiritual innovations of the medieval period?

10. What intellectual contributions did the Islamic world make to Latin scholarship?

CORE OBJECTIVES

After reading this chapter, you should have a solid understanding of the following core objectives. To strengthen your grasp of the core objectives, use the resources on the Student Site for The West.

- Analyze the social and economic changes in Europe that began in the eleventh century.
- Describe the new political institutions that arose in medieval society.
- Evaluate the evolution of the medieval church and its relationship to secular power.

- Identify the origins and outcomes of the Crusades.
- Assess the developments in medieval religious practices.
- Trace the development of medieval scholarship and institutions of learning.

 GO TO **inQuizitive** TO SEE WHAT YOU'VE LEARNED—AND LEARN WHAT YOU'VE MISSED—WITH PERSONALIZED FEEDBACK ALONG THE WAY.

CHRONOLOGY

Early 13th century
Dominican and
Franciscan
Orders develop

1214
Philip Augustus completes
reclamation of Norman
lands from England

1204
Crusaders sack
Constantinople

1215
Fourth Lateran Council;
King John of England
signs Magna Carta

1271–1295
Marco Polo journeys
throughout the East

1315–1322
Famine follows poor
harvests across Europe

1209–1229
Albigensian Crusade

1217–1229
Fifth and Sixth
Crusades

1238
Mongols invade Muscovy

1291
Last major Christian
stronghold in Palestine
falls to the Mamluks

1309–1377
Avignon papacy

1330s–1453
Hundred Years' War

1202–1204
Fourth Crusade

Consolidation and Crisis

THE HIGH MIDDLE AGES

1200–1400

1381
Wat Tyler leads Peasants' Revolt

1347–1350
Black Death strikes Europe

1358
Jacquerie rebellion

1382
Oligarchical republic takes control of Florence

The Florentine merchant and banker Giovanni Villani (d. 1348) spent his last years composing a history of his city. His ambitious book began with the fall of the Tower of Babel. He traced the origins of Florence back to ancient Rome, and those of Rome back to Troy. It was normal for medieval historians to frame the history of their city or their monastery in this grandiose way. Late in the work, though, Villani offered a striking innovation. He broke off from his narrative, pulled his camera back from the day-to-day details of politics and war, and surveyed his city.

It was, to begin with, a vast community: "Careful investigation has established that at that time there were in Florence approximately 25,000 men capable of bearing arms, ages fifteen to seventy, all citizens, of which 1,500 were noble and powerful citizens.... There were then around seventy-five fully-equipped knights." Graphic details made clear what it took to support this immense male population—as well as the population of women and children, and the members of religious orders. All goods that passed through the city gates had to be registered and a duty paid. Every year, the records showed, Florentines consumed 4,000 oxen and calves, 60,000 sheep, 20,000 goats, and 30,000 pigs, and drank at least 5.9 million gallons of wine. Any contemporary reader could imagine the noise

Commerce and Guilds The High Middle Ages saw rapid increases in commerce and wealth in European cities. In this bustling scene from a Bolognese manuscript (ca. 1300), members of a merchants' guild display wares ranging from wine to horses, count money, and weigh goods to determine their value. An angel casts a benevolent eye over the scene, granting divine sanction to the hive of economic activity.

FOCUS QUESTIONS

- How did economic growth transform parts of high medieval Europe?
- What major changes transformed European states in the High Middle Ages?
- What were the major new directions for the Church in the high medieval period?
- What developments brought medieval society to crisis in the fourteenth century?

these hordes of animals made as they entered the city, their screams as they were butchered, and the smell of their meat and carcasses. Here was clear evidence, inscribed in blood and offal, of the scale of urban living in the fourteenth century. The magnitude of the slaughter had a certain grandeur. So did the thought of the 4,000 loads of cool melons that came through the city's San Friano Gate every July, as temperatures rose.

Villani did his best to show that the city was more than a vast mouth that consumed nature's resources. Its citizens took a special pride in their handsome public and private buildings, from the churches and monasteries inside the walls to the "large and rich estates" and mansions outside them. The "sumptuous buildings and beautiful palaces," towers, and walled gardens in the suburbs were so dense and impressive that they fooled first-time visitors into thinking the city even bigger than it actually was. A single, unified world of city and country, palace and villa, Florence as Villani portrayed it was something new: not the city as refuge from a violent countryside; not the city as Babylon, the den of evil from which those who sought peace, quiet, and an environment free from sin had to flee; but a kind of urban paradise—a community that inspired, as a whole, a secular version of the rapture that Abbot Suger had felt as he saw light streaming through the new rose window of the Saint Denis basilica.

Historians in the Middle Ages, as in antiquity, commemorated the past and recorded the present to instruct the men and women of the future. In most chronicles, examples of heroic and saintly deeds provided Christians with models for imitation. What Villani looked for, by contrast, were readers who shared his interest in the quantitative details

that measured the city's health, and could learn from these details how to maintain greatness in the future. His readers would be, like him, experienced in trade, banking, and city planning, and passionate analysts of balance sheets: "the wise and worthy citizens who [will] rule in future times." We do not know how precisely Villani's statistics reflected Florentine realities. But in the data we can see something striking: the textures of city life from the eleventh and twelfth centuries onward. The power and independence of these cities were among the most distinctive features of the civilization of the High Middle Ages.

Between 1200 and about 1350, European cities grew to sizes not seen since Roman times. Their citizens pursued finance and industry, art and craft. And they continued to show immense ingenuity and energy in developing effective forms of government and administration. In the same years, European monarchies built new institutions and exercised new powers. The Church adapted in creative ways to these changing conditions: efforts were made to ensure that both clergy and ordinary Christians acted in accordance with religious teachings, and novel forms of religious life were invented.

This confident, cosmopolitan world Villani knew so well would soon be swept away by the Black Death, the great plague that struck Europe in 1347 and very probably killed Villani himself, along with thousands of others. Yet long before this, as we will see, the problems that come with growth and the stresses of life in a new and complex society were starting to be felt.

TRANSFORMING CITY AND COUNTRYSIDE

The new urban society that filled Villani with such pride rested on foundations laid in the late twelfth and thirteenth centuries. The rise of the great abbeys and cathedrals required the mobilization of far more than spiritual energy, vitally important though that was. Vast quantities of stone had to be quarried. To build Notre-Dame Cathedral and other great structures in Paris, stonecutters excavated more than 180 miles of tunnels under the city (the entire modern Paris subway system, the Métro, is only two-thirds as long). To connect the stones and provide structural stability, vast amounts of iron had to be forged. Ten percent of the expense of building a cathedral went on iron ore and the forges where it was processed. Water-powered hammers replaced some of the human labor and accelerated the production of bars and fasteners.

As the crafts became more complex and productive, rulers began to compete for the best practitioners. Skilled miners were favored by royal houses: when King John exempted English tin miners from ordinary taxation and military service in 1201, he unleashed the growth of what became a vast industry. German miners, famed for their expertise at extracting iron, were encouraged to migrate into the Balkans and beyond by rulers anxious to extract the commodities and precious metals hidden in their own hills. Soon new towns grew up, such as Kutna Hora in Bohemia—a center for silver mining that exploded in size in the thirteenth century and soon rivaled Prague, the capital, in wealth and splendor.

SPECIALIZATION: FROM WOOL TO CLOTH

At first, as we have seen, medieval cities were less like their modern counterparts than collections of villages. Their inhabitants usually came from nearby regions, and most of them continued to do at least some small-scale farming if they could. In a world of masons, blacksmiths, miners, and carpenters, however, the old way of life, which mixed urban and rural pursuits, made way for a new system: one of division of labor, in which the inhabitants of towns mostly worked for money. Whole regions specialized. In Flanders and northern France, the first part of Europe to become a center of commerce and trade fairs, and in central and northern Italy, connected by sea to markets around the Mediterranean, a massive cloth industry developed in Ghent and Bruges, Florence and Milan.

When considering the High Middle Ages, it is important not to let an apparently familiar word such as *industry* delude us into thinking in terms of the nineteenth and twentieth centuries. There were, as yet, no large factories like those that developed in the modern world; medieval industry had its own ways of working. Wool was turned into cloth in a series of stages, most of which were carried out by specialized workers in their own homes.

Entrepreneurs guided and organized the process. In Florence, for example, some 200 firms, whose principals belonged to the guild of Linaiuoli, manufactured woolen cloth. Two or more partners would contribute the necessary capital. They would also hire a factor, or agent, who would follow the cloth through the stages of

Medieval Industry Northern Italy was one center of the vast European cloth industry in the Middle Ages. An illustration from 1390s Italy shows merchants at a market stall measuring, cutting, and sewing silk garments.

its manufacture. The factor ordered wool from suppliers as far afield as Spain and England, and hired workers to prepare it in his shop under the supervision of a foreman. Then brokers began to move the wool, at first back out into the countryside around Florence, where women, working in their own cottages, spun it into thread. The finished thread went to weavers, who turned it into cloth on their looms. The brokers would then take the cloth to fullers, who trampled it into a mixture of fuller's earth (a kind of clay that absorbed and removed the wool's natural grease) and urine (which helped to clean and whiten it) until it took on a thick, smooth texture. Dyers added color, sometimes to the yarn, but sometimes to the finished cloth.

Once the cloth was sheared, smoothed, and pressed, the entrepreneurs exported most of it. Bales went to the big ports at Venice and Naples, and from there to stalls in markets around the Mediterranean and in the north. It seems remarkable that these many transactions could all be governed and tracked not by computers but in simple handwritten ledgers.

This dispersed production process soon reached an astonishingly large scale—large enough to transform the uses of agricultural land across the English Channel. In 1273, the farmers of England—from smallholders who kept a few sheep, to the great abbeys of Fountains and Rievaulx that had flocks of thousands on their vast landholdings—sheared 8 million sheep and sent some 7 million pounds of wool across to the clothiers of Flanders. Town after town grew to 10,000 or 20,000 inhabitants, as specialist industries in everything from glassmaking to armor and weapon smithing took shape. Yet the increasing scale of production also brought with it a new vulnerability to external economic and political events—as in the years 1270–74, when the English monarchy embargoed exports of wool to promote the domestic cloth industry, a decision that shocked the Flemish.

A NEW ECONOMY

The thirteenth century saw massive economic development across much of Europe, and populations rose. In England, according to one historian's estimate, the population more than doubled, rising from 3.4 million to 7.2 million. Even in sectors of the economy that had remained more or less bound to traditional ways, new methods and attitudes became visible. Instead of depending on the incomes set by their traditional agreements with their serfs and tenants, landowners now sought to exploit their own properties for everything they were worth. They hired expert managers to organize the work and ruthlessly exploited the labor of their serfs. Everywhere, or so it seemed, buying and selling, exchanging one specialized product for another, replaced the old self-sufficient economy of the manor.

MONEY AND EXCHANGE Perceptive observers realized that a new world was taking shape—one in which money played a vital role. Even in the countryside, whole regions came to depend not on the crops and animals they could raise but on the income their products brought in. As commodities became more accessible and more varied, demand and supply both grew. Great monastic communities founded to provide a refuge from the cities of the twelfth century were now sucked back into the economic orbits of the bigger and more sophisticated cities of the thirteenth century, as they transferred large portions of the acreage they had once devoted to crops to the

cultivation of grapevines (viticulture) and actively marketed their products.

In the middle of the thirteenth century, an Italian friar named Salimbene of Parma (1221–ca. 1290) traveled through northern Europe. A member of the new Franciscan religious order known for its strict pursuit of poverty, he was struck by the rise in consumption. Salimbene noted with interest that "the French delight in good wine." He showed understanding when he remarked that "we must forgive the English if they are glad to drink good wine when they can, for they have but little in their own country." What impressed this perceptive observer most, though, was the dramatic way in which, in some regions, viticulture had become a monoculture. In the Auvergne, a wine region in southern France, he noted that "these people sow nothing, reap nothing, and gather nothing into their barns. They only need to send their wine to Paris on the nearby river that goes straight there. The sale of wine in this city brings them in a good profit that pays entirely for their food and clothing."

BANKS AND INTEREST New financial systems and practices were needed to meet the needs of merchant capitalists and monarchs. As the trade networks that Salimbene described spread across Europe—with masses of raw material paid for in Britain and processed in Flanders by workers whose wine came from France—cash payments proved increasingly inadequate for the needs of the economy. Merchants needed to move money if they were to move goods. And, as we will see, kings and other rulers needed money if they were to muster their military forces, now made up of professional soldiers rather than vassals serving for the traditional—but often inadequate—term of forty days.

In theory, Christians were prohibited from lending money at interest. Philosophers and theologians argued that charging interest was, in essence, selling time, which belonged only to God. The Bible seemed to support their position. Hebrew prophets condemned usurers, and Christ drove the moneychangers out of the Temple in Jerusalem. In practice, however, Christians loaned and borrowed money. And during the course of the thirteenth century, Italians branched out from trade into banking, which became a specialty in Florence, Genoa, and elsewhere.

Early banks were small firms like any others: just a shop or market stall with a *banco* ("counter") where the proprietor met his customers. Money in the Middle Ages was local: in every city, artisans' private mints, licensed by the monarchs to use their official images, produced coins. Professional moneychangers were experts. They had to know

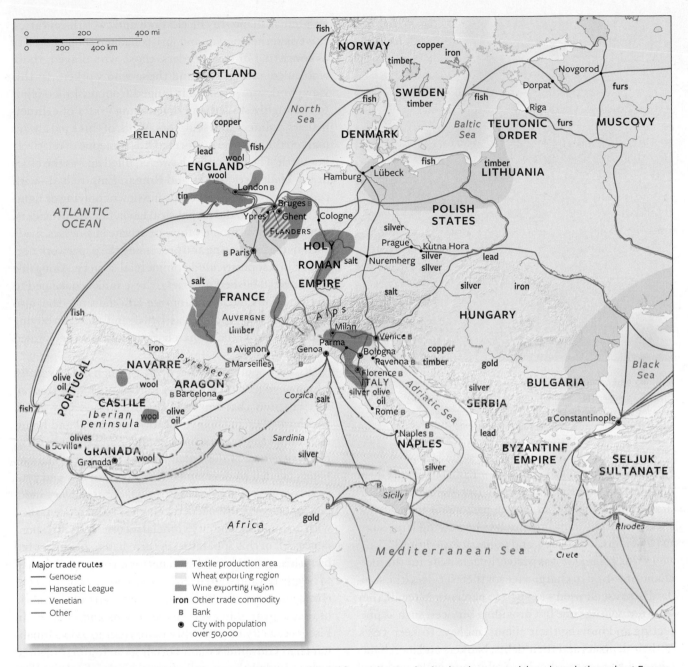

Economic Development in Europe, ca. 1300 Sophisticated trading and financial networks circulated raw materials and goods throughout Europe in the High Middle Ages. Ships plied trade routes across the Mediterranean and Baltic Seas, conveying precious metals, timber, silk, and wool. Luxury foodstuffs, such as wine, olives, olive oil, and salt, were transported to major cities and then exported. Branches of Italian banks opened in the larger cities, connecting merchants to an international financial system.

the value of every form of coinage and how to tell fake coins from genuine ones. They also had to keep abreast of monarchs' efforts to inflate their currencies and reduce their debts by cutting the amount of precious metal that their coins contained. Biting coins—the traditional test of genuineness—was only the beginning of the banker's work.

Gradually, merchant firms that could provide such services—most of them beginning as family partnerships, such as the Bardi and Peruzzi of Florence—spread across Europe. Family members or trusted friends opened branches in cities from London to Constantinople. These banks and the networks of messengers that they maintained gave vital support to the new economy of long-distance, large-scale trade. A cloth manufacturer

Banking and Moneylending The coat of arms of the Moneychangers' Guild of Perugia, Italy, from the guild's 1377 Statutes and Register, includes a gryphon—an emblem of the city—standing atop a money chest, suggesting the security that banks offered to their clients.

could deposit money in a Florentine bank branch in Ghent or Ypres, travel to England with a letter of credit, and withdraw cash from another branch in London to buy wool. Even monarchs found themselves borrowing large sums to pay for great banquets and military expeditions.

In this context it was perfectly legitimate for the merchants involved to charge a fee for their services (the standard interest allowed was up to 20 percent). After all, they were not selling time but providing services, such as protecting and moving their clients' money. To keep track of their deposits and their debts, bankers and merchants adopted the more efficient Arabic numerals, and used them for double-entry bookkeeping (probably invented in thirteenth-century Florence). This system required that every transaction be recorded as both a debit and a credit, so that a partner could establish a firm's exact financial position at any moment by balancing the accounts. Though errors crop up in many medieval balance sheets, this method made the firms that adopted it—and the governments that eventually emulated them—more efficient than ever before.

SERVICE PROVIDERS With the rise of banks and commerce, the world that city-dwellers knew took on an unfamiliar shape. In the eleventh and twelfth centuries, as we saw, theologians and jurists had envisioned society as consisting of three orders: those who prayed, those who ruled and fought, and those who worked. In this view, work was physical: it ranged from unskilled labor to the highly skilled and demanding crafts of cabinet-makers, painters, and sculptors. Work of this kind always marked the one who performed it as someone of relatively low birth. The new cities, however, filled up—as the cities of the Hellenistic states and Roman Empire had—with people who did not make a profession of praying or fighting, but who also did no physical labor. Service providers, working in government offices or private businesses, made their living by creating and processing the paperwork necessary in a sophisticated commercial society. Alongside the long-established notaries, whose ranks continued to swell, bankers and merchants not only multiplied but also flourished. Some became vastly rich and ended up buying noble titles from the monarchs for whom they performed their services.

Rising populations soon burst through old city walls, which were torn down across Europe. The new rings of fortifications that replaced them enclosed vast areas, which filled up in their turn. As commercial and financial enterprises became more complex and larger in scale, the very nature of the urban legal system had to change. Cities needed to develop codes of private law and provide commercial as well as criminal courts. Every independent city, finally, needed a chancery—an office tasked with maintaining the city's official records and correspondence. All of this apparatus, in turn, had to be supported by tariffs and taxes, and systems for collecting them had to be created and staffed. Notaries, who drew up the contracts and deeds for land that became part of the fabric of life, appeared in ever smaller towns and villages. In Florence, a city of somewhat more than 100,000 inhabitants, as Giovanni Villani noted, some 10,000 boys and girls attended the so-called abacus school, where they learned to read, write, and do calculations. High medieval society was, among its other qualities, highly literate and numerate.

CITIES AND CULTURE: THE NEW WRITERS

Giovanni Villani was in many ways a typical member of this new urban elite. Starting out in the last years of the thirteenth century as a wool merchant, he invested in the Peruzzi bank, for which he undertook commercial travels across Europe. In later life he served Florence as a diplomat and skillfully led his city's delicate negotiations with its Tuscan rivals—though he also underwent public humiliation and even spent time in jail when the Buonaccorsi bank, to which he had transferred his business, failed. A cosmopolitan man who knew many cities and languages, Villani made sense of his complicated world, as we have seen, by describing it in vivid detail in his chronicle of Florentine history, which he composed in Italian, the language of daily life.

BRUNETTO LATINI Medieval cities produced many people who combined active political lives with serious writing, and who transformed the languages they spoke into vehicles for great literature. Brunetto Latini (ca. 1210–1294) was a Florentine notary who held high government offices. He was also a versatile writer who brought the learning of a scholar into the vernacular. In *On the Government of Cities*, written in prose, he explained why he thought it possible for a commune like Florence to govern itself as a republic, laid out the principles of justice and fairness that needed to inform the making and enforcement of laws, and provided guidelines for the podesta, whose job it was to translate ideals and principles into the everyday work of fair government. Latini also wrote a long poem in which he surveyed the universe, from God down to the globe of earth and water that humans inhabit. This wide-ranging work covered planets, elements, physiology, plants and animals, as well as human virtues and the nature of love. Latini's readers had access to a wealth of ancient learning and modern experience, all crisply conveyed.

DANTE ALIGHIERI No one read Latini more eagerly than **Dante Alighieri** (1265–1321), another Florentine of good family who served in the highest public offices until he and his allies lost out to a rival faction. Condemned for corruption in 1302, he insisted on his innocence and refused to pay the fine assessed. His sentence of exile was extended from its original two years to eternity. Dante served the prince of Ravenna, but devoted himself above all to writing in vernacular Italian. His *Divine Comedy* (1308–21) was a spectacular poetic triptych in which he portrayed himself voyaging through Hell, Purgatory, and Heaven, convoyed first by the Roman poet Virgil and then by Beatrice Portinari, the daughter of a Florentine banker, whom he had long admired. As sweeping and powerful as Virgil's *Aeneid*, Dante's series of poems amounted to a magnificent revenge, in the realm of the spirit, for his defeat in the city: a passionate, powerful demonstration that the universe is governed by a divine order that would

Dante Alighieri The Florentine painter Sandro Botticelli created this portrait of Dante 175 years after the poet's death. The laurel wreath attests to Dante's artistic greatness as well as his connection to the classical tradition.

eventually put Dante's enemies, as it had put the murderers of Julius Caesar, in the underworld.

GEOFFREY CHAUCER The works of Latini and Dante—and their chivalric predecessors—were read by the cosmopolitan, polyglot inhabitants of cities across Europe. Geoffrey Chaucer (ca. 1340–1400), scion of a prosperous London family, explored France as a soldier and visited Italy to negotiate a commercial treaty with Genoese merchants who wanted to trade in England. Still later he served as controller of customs, a vital job in the heyday of the British wool trade. A master linguist, he was a prolific writer whose output included a treatise on how to use the astrolabe as well as his great poem of love, *Troilus and Criseyde*, which he adapted from the influential Italian poet Giovanni Boccaccio. But Chaucer's greatest work was

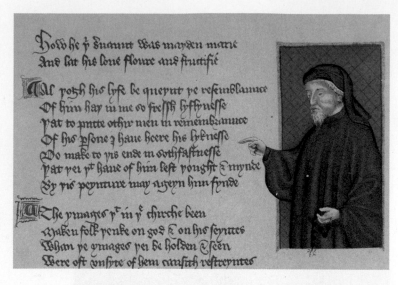

Geoffrey Chaucer Though posthumous and idealized, this portrait in an early-fifteenth-century manuscript is the best likeness we have of Chaucer. His extended arm points at a verse that praises him.

the extraordinary set of narratives known as *The Canterbury Tales*, with their vivid portraits of a group of people from every part of society who meet at the Tabard Inn in Southwark, south of London Bridge, and embark on a pilgrimage to Canterbury. The twenty-three stories that he completed bring to life characters such as the Wife of Bath, with her passionate disdain for the opposite sex and her strong conviction that women want and deserve to rule in love and marriage.

A NEW SOCIETY

It was no accident that writers like Boccaccio and Chaucer found the lives of ordinary men and women—including their sexuality—to be fascinating subjects. Family life was growing more complex in cities. According to the male clerics and patricians who wrote the traditional books of advice for men and women, the family was a simple hierarchy. Marriage joined unequal partners. The husband possessed wisdom and moderation as well as property and power. The wife, by contrast, was possessed by forces beyond her control: her senses, which ruled her mind and made her less capable of reasoning; and the legal authority, first of her father and then of her husband, which gave them control over her life and property. Believed incapable of taking part in the wider worlds of work and politics, women were to remain indoors and devote themselves to running clean, efficient households. As one theologian put it, "a husband is to his wife as a superior being is to an inferior, as perfect is to imperfect, as giver is to receiver."

These traditional attitudes were not completely disconnected from reality. Male bankers, merchants, and craftsmen normally waited to marry until they could maintain independent households. They chose wives who were young enough to produce multiple heirs and came from families that could equip them with adequate dowries. At a time when marriage was arranged by negotiation and designed to perpetuate the family as an economic and political enterprise, and regularly involved mature men marrying teenage girls, it was easy to imagine women as beings who existed only to support and give comfort to their male lords.

CITY WOMEN In fact, however, city women often participated as actively as men in the new urban economies. One-fifth of the *commenda* contracts issued in Genoa between 1200 and 1250 involved women, who invested almost 15 percent of the total capital involved. From Ghent and Cologne to Florence, women served as business partners to their husbands—especially their second husbands, since by the time they had outlived their first husbands, many women had accumulated property and experience. Some women managed the family firm during their husband's business trips, traded in commodities, and bought

City Women The frequency with which women participated in urban commerce is illustrated in a fourteenth-century medical tract, showing a woman fishmonger selling saltwater fish to a man.

LORENZETTI'S *EFFECTS OF GOOD GOVERNMENT IN THE CITY AND IN THE COUNTRY*

Ambrogio Lorenzetti painted the *Effects of Good Government in the City and in the Country* (1338) in Siena's town hall to celebrate the Italian city's prosperity under its commune. Lorenzetti's fresco adorns the walls of the Room of the Nine, the private meeting place of the rotating nine leaders of the commune.

Among the effects of good government seen in this detail is work, commerce, a family ritual, and a public celebration, all occurring in a prosperous, peaceful cityscape. To the left we see what might be a wedding procession. A woman wearing a crown rides a white horse, followed by what might be her male relatives. In the near background we see men playing a board game, perhaps in a tavern, with children nearby. At the center are nine dancers celebrating Siena's harmonious republicanism. To their right, cobblers sell shoes, a lecturer teaches students, and a merchant displays his wares. All of this activity is set within the brilliantly colored lines of Siena itself, its balconies and battlements towering over the people.

QUESTIONS FOR ANALYSIS

1. In what sense is good government the foundation of the scene depicted here?
2. How does the fresco represent the social and economic changes taking place in European cities in the fourteenth century?
3. Does the fresco strike you as a more realistic or a more idealistic portrayal of the city? Why?

and sold properties. They became guild masters in industries that were growing so rapidly that there were too few men to rule all of the shops—for example, the cloth industry in thirteenth-century Barcelona. In the shops of the many master artisans who worked without journeymen or apprentices, wives and daughters provided expert assistance and served as sales staff.

In Paris, women worked as butchers and fishmongers, made rosaries, ground glass, and tailored clothing. In England, women played an especially prominent role as brewers of beer, but also worked as barber-surgeons, bakers, and candle-makers. Around 1300 the German city of Nuremberg enacted a statute that forbade women from selling fish, except when their husbands were absent—evidence that women had been working regularly at the fish stalls in the market. Though some moralists insisted that women should not learn to read and write unless they planned to become nuns, city governments acknowledged that women needed to be literate. Many cities opened schools for girls (Paris had more than twenty of them) and paid female schoolmasters to teach.

The women of wealthy families dressed in the expensive fabrics and jewelry that fit their rank. Even a pious woman, such as the wife of Jacopo dei Benedetti, a successful young lawyer in thirteenth-century Italy, wore expensive robes. But she wore a hair shirt under them, as he discovered when she died in an accident. Another wealthy and pious wife, the saintly Florentine Umiliata dei Cerchi, trimmed the excess fabric off the hemlines of her skirts and gave it to the poor. Rich women balanced the claims of social status and religious ideals in many ways.

THE CITY POOR For the majority of the population, urban life was harsh. The semiskilled workers who spun thread and wove cloth, the men and women who worked as unskilled laborers, and those whom injury, illness, or age deprived of the ability to work, lived not in comfortable houses, but in ancient tenements or the crude shacks that spread, unplanned and without services, as the population grew. In the countryside, the poor had ways to supplement their income. They could invade the forests that belonged to their lords and keep pigs, gather nuts, or trap game animals, and they could cultivate even small plots of ground intensively and effectively. In the cities, these ways of supplementing income and diet were largely out of reach. The wages of the poorer workers were inadequate to support themselves and their families. And cities did not provide safety nets to catch those who did not flourish. Crowds of the poor, sick, and maimed gathered in public places—in market squares, at church doors, by city gates—to ask for

The Urban Poor Beggars, vagabonds, and the sick were always part of the fabric of medieval city life. In this illustration from a mid-fourteenth-century French manuscript, a bishop displays a relic to an injured man and a group of pilgrims. The injured man's bandaged leg and crutches imply he would have trouble finding work.

alms. Food riots were rare—partly because the well-off saw it as a Christian duty to give to the poor who confronted them. But much of the population was undernourished and vulnerable to illness and injury.

A NEW INDEPENDENCE IN THE CITIES

In the eleventh and twelfth centuries, as we have seen, cities in the more economically developed parts of Europe—Flanders, northern France, Italy—often achieved independence after massive struggles with the bishops and other local lords who had previously ruled them. These struggles continued through the thirteenth century, even after guilds and other new economic structures took shape. To put an end to the violence, cities—especially the wealthier merchants and artisans—declared the powerful nobles "magnates" and excluded them from holding government offices. In Florence and many other cities, their towers—centers of noble resistance to city government— were torn down.

CAPTAINS OF THE PEOPLE The established city rulers also excluded newly arriving merchants and craftsmen from participation in government. But as many of the new arrivals rose to prosperity, they formed pressure groups. In Italy the members of these groups were often known, a little misleadingly, as "the people." Gradually they took over certain government responsibilities and chose their own professional administrators, the "captains of the people." Now housed in massive buildings designed to overawe potential criminals and rebels—especially the older, noble elites who still resorted to violence when challenged—these complex city governments grew to include professional specialists in law, finance, and military and police affairs.

Though small by the standards of later periods, these administrations enabled cities in Flanders, Italy, and elsewhere to emulate the legal, political, and military independence that Venice and Genoa had established for themselves centuries before. And though these cities normally offered obedience to a great lord— the pope, the Holy Roman Emperor, or a more local magnate—in practice they effectively were self-governing cities, as independent (and in some cases as inventive in maintaining their independence) as the cities of ancient Greece. Their counterparts in the monarchies of northern Europe were more closely controlled and taxed by their rulers, but cities such as London and Paris also created civic institutions, from city halls to prisons.

A NEW CITYSCAPE Public buildings –along with the massive halls built by the stronger guilds for meetings and ceremonial feasts– dominated the thirteenth century cityscape. Larger than any conceivable private building, the Palazzo Vecchio, built at the end of the thirteenth century to house the city's government, still looms over

Florence A fifteenth-century fresco documents the impressive skyline of medieval Florence, including its major public buildings: the octagonal Baptistery (1), the tower of the Badia abbey (2), and the Palazzo Vecchio (3).

the city of Florence. Public buildings were strategically placed at points where they would make the strongest possible impression on rulers and diplomats who visited the city or on citizens who might harbor rebellious thoughts. Roads were deliberately sunk and curved so that these buildings would seem to heave up like immense icebergs as visitors or citizens came in sight of them. In times of confrontation or rebellion, the government could defend its authority. These structures were the embodiment of a new civic world—one in which men of substance, but not of noble birth or chivalric skills, appeared as the rulers of a new society, mercantile in its foundations and, in Italy, republican in its form of government.

THE HANSA CITIES Similar developments took place in northern Europe. In the later twelfth century, cities began to grow on the northern edge of the Holy Roman Empire. Hamburg, near the North Sea on the river Elbe, and Lübeck, on the river Trave near the Baltic Sea, developed trade with the eastern Baltic, a rich source of grain, amber, wax, and furs. German colonists moved into the area, led by a military order, the Teutonic Knights, and founded trading stations at Dorpat, Riga, and eventually at Novgorod, an old princely state on the Volkhov River that had become a republic in 1136. Traders also moved west. As early as 1157, merchants from Cologne won from Henry II the right to trade in England without paying tolls.

By 1241 Hamburg and Lübeck had formed an alliance, which won further privileges. As Cologne and other cities joined, it grew into the **Hanseatic League** (from *Hansa*, "convoy of ships"), a loose but powerful association of trading cities. As free imperial cities ruled directly by the weak Holy Roman emperors, the Hansa cities became centers of manufacture, making silk and linen cloth, armor, and religious art, and moving cloth from England to the east and salt fish and other products from the Baltic to the west. By 1356, when representatives of the cities assembled in their first formal meeting, or diet, in Lübeck, the league was a far-flung and powerful group of cities that made war and signed treaties with other powers.

LIFE ON THE LAND: THE PEASANTS' WORLD

Agrarian life in thirteenth- and early-fourteenth-century Europe was still immensely varied. It included everything from the country—flat, open lands that could be intensively tilled by heavy plows pulled by eight oxen—to the remaining forest with its small communities of peasants who produced charcoal. The constantly burning fires and black-smudged faces of these peasants reminded aristocratic hunters of the devils in hell. Yet, as urban economies grew, they also transformed the countryside.

Even in small villages, legal and financial arrangements became more complex. Landlords employed workers in two ways: as tenants bound to the land and legally required to do manual work, and as free workers who were paid wages. By the thirteenth century, many well-established peasants held some of their lands as serfs—some rich serfs even had serfs of their own—and worked others' land as free laborers, for pay. Two families that worked similar amounts of land might live in very different conditions, with one required by law to pay for permission to marry and to provide labor services for their lord, the other able to bargain for the highest price for its work and for its produce. Many serfs fought to escape, or at least to evade, legal restrictions. In England, many bought land and passed it on to their heirs, even though the law forbade them to do so. In France, as inflation bit into the incomes of landlords, many of them freed their serfs: these peasants escaped their degraded status, and the landlords could exploit their estates more efficiently than with forced, unwilling labor.

Village life was hard, and the work that went into sustaining it could be as complicated and demanding, in its own way, as artisanal work in the cities. Shepherds, cowherds, and swineherds all had to learn how to care for their animals, which were harder to replace, in normal circumstances, than human children. Shepherds had to master the long trails on which their flocks moved seasonally. Special knowledge was needed for beekeeping, which produced wax for candles and honey for use in food and drink—especially mead, made from fermented honey. Millers, carpenters, and leatherworkers had to master the tools of their trade and to bargain with clients.

In the countryside, most women married young, to somewhat older men. Before and after marrying, they took part in every form of rural work. Women goaded the animals that pulled the plows steered by men, sowed grain and pulled weeds, gathered crops and separated grain from chaff. They were normally responsible for poultry and dairy products—some of which, like cheese, also demanded specialized expertise. They also brewed ale. In at least one English village, a woman was even appointed to the honorable office of Taster of the Ale, though many more were indicted for trying to evade the regulations that governed brewing.

Peasant diets were varied. In addition to bread and vegetables, they ate rabbits and pigeons, large quantities of pork, and the fish and eels with which millponds and other bodies of fresh water were often stocked. The sophisticated, literate world of the cities was distant: few peasant men, and almost no women, received even the elementary education that was becoming more common there. But more and more they became part of a cash economy, selling what they produced to middlemen to feed the hungry cities, and if they lived close enough to them, spinning or doing other jobs for the urban manufacturers in addition to their work in the fields and tending livestock.

TRANSFORMING THE STATE

In diverse ways, the monarchs of the thirteenth and fourteenth centuries set their authority on new foundations. For the first time since the Roman Empire—but in forms that varied from place to place—the state once again became a major factor in the lives of people who had long lived without much interference from central authority.

FRANCE: ROYAL AUTHORITY AND ADMINISTRATION

The French monarchy flourished as never before in this expansive era. Energetic rulers innovated in multiple ways, extending their own powers and the state apparatus that supported them.

PHILIP AUGUSTUS During the reign of Philip Augustus (r. 1180–1223), it seemed that the French monarchy

Peasant Work Peasants perform farm labor in this illustration from an English manuscript (ca. 1300). One worker wields a sickle for cutting grain, while another—wearing a white cloth, perhaps for protection—shoos bees away from their hive.

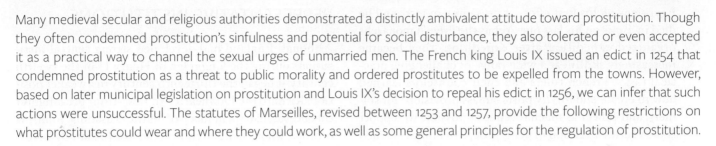

REGULATING PROSTITUTION IN MARSEILLES

Many medieval secular and religious authorities demonstrated a distinctly ambivalent attitude toward prostitution. Though they often condemned prostitution's sinfulness and potential for social disturbance, they also tolerated or even accepted it as a practical way to channel the sexual urges of unmarried men. The French king Louis IX issued an edict in 1254 that condemned prostitution as a threat to public morality and ordered prostitutes to be expelled from the towns. However, based on later municipal legislation on prostitution and Louis IX's decision to repeal his edict in 1256, we can infer that such actions were unsuccessful. The statutes of Marseilles, revised between 1253 and 1257, provide the following restrictions on what prostitutes could wear and where they could work, as well as some general principles for the regulation of prostitution.

With the present statute we ordain that no public prostitute shall dare or be able to wear any clothing dyed with grana,[1] or furs of vair,[2] either grey squirrel or ermine, nor any mantle except one made of striped cloth, or with bars of another cloth; however, she may wear a shoulder cape dyed with grana if she wishes. And if any prostitute should rashly dare to go against this statute in any way, then the court is held to take away from her 60 sous royaux coronats for every time that she crosses it. And if she cannot provide this, she should be publicly beaten through the city of Marseille; for we judge that infamous and notorious women ought to be separated from chaste ones. A public prostitute is understood to be a woman who has intercourse publicly in a brothel or whorehouse, or who offers herself publicly to make a profit, or to whose house two or more men come publicly as if to a public woman,

either by day or by night, with the intention or for the sake or reason of gratifying their lust or passion with her.

We decree accordingly that henceforth no prostitutes should dare or ought to make a house or residence, even a modest one, anywhere near the monastery of St. Sauveur of Marseille...nor around the church of Notre Dame des Accoules, from the hills of the mill-houses and the meat-market of the Towers, as far as it extends through the butchers' quarter up to the house of Bernard Bonaffossi. ...And within one month after the proclamation of this Chapter all the said prostitutes shall be completely removed and expelled from the said places by the judgment of the honest men of the neighbourhoods, with whom it ought to rest [to judge] whether the said women who will have been accused of this are prostitutes or not, or also whether they should be expelled.

Moreover, we decree that the Court of Marseille should be held to expel all prostitutes who linger among the honest and respectable men of Marseille at the request of those honest men who are henceforth aggrieved.

[1]grana: an insect-based red dye
[2]vair: bluish-gray fur used to trim garments

Source: Translation by Kirsten Schut

QUESTIONS FOR ANALYSIS

1. How would you characterize the basic attitude of civic authorities in Marseilles toward prostitution?
2. Why was prostitution prohibited in specific areas of the city?
3. What responsibilities does the statute assign to men and women in the regulation of prostitution?

would carry all before it. After losing the kingdom's official account books, which the court normally carried with it, on the field of battle, Philip Augustus decided that he needed a permanent base, and established Paris as the capital of his realm. He also defeated King John of England (r. 1199–1216) and won back the Norman lands that the kings of England had governed, by dynastic right, since the conquest of 1066. Working with the existing apparatus of officials, especially the regionally based judicial officers called bailiffs, he and his successors did much to unify the many powerful principalities of the French kingdom. The tradition of crusading, which Philip Augustus continued, also strengthened the position of France as the leading monarchy of Europe.

LOUIS IX Philip Augustus's successors—above all Louis IX (r. 1226–1270)—maintained the traditions Philip founded, and elaborated on them. They also went on crusade, even though the costs were enormous and the successes limited: Louis IX saw his army crushed by the Egyptians on his first effort at crusading in 1250, and he died in Tunis on his last one. Yet as the French monarchs organized expedition after expedition, they became increasingly skillful at a wide range of challenging practical tasks. French rulers and their counselors learned how to create and fortify ports, amass provisions for soldiers, and collect as much revenue as possible to support these ventures. Although many groups in France claimed exemption from taxation, the monarchy's jurists used the principles of Roman law to argue that "absolute necessity" and the common good could override these privileges.

ROYAL JUSTICE AND THE PARLEMENT In the realm of justice, in particular, Louis IX advanced beyond any of his predecessors or rivals. The bailiffs, originally jurists sent out to the provinces but now professional administrators appointed by the king, had strengthened the monarchy's ability to claim and defend its rights. In some cases, though, they proved as tenacious in defending the local privileges and customs of their fellow noblemen as in fighting for the prerogatives of the crown. Louis IX—a man so pious that he became a saint after his death—was determined to collect everything that was due the state and willingly entered into conflict with nobles or clerics to do so. But he also had a passion for providing justice to his subjects. He appointed men he could trust—often members of the new orders of mendicant friars, discussed later, who would not be tempted by personal ambition—to make formal inquiries into royal administration in the provinces. He also made himself available—sitting, as legend has it, outdoors, under a great oak at Vincennes, a few miles outside Paris—to hear the appeals of his subjects.

Over time, the French crown developed its own highly professional central law court comprised of jurists who laid down the theoretical basis of royal authority in treatises and imposed it in legal practice. The **Parlement**, as this sovereign court came to be called, became the apex of the French judicial system. It made clear to all that justice, everywhere in France, emanated from royal authority. Though Louis's successors differed from him in many important respects, they continued to assert, as he had, that royal authority was absolute. The king, as they and their jurists insisted, was emperor within his own kingdom: the leader of what French churchmen and writers

described as the most holy nation of France—a unique community, divinely chosen.

ENGLAND: ORIGINS OF REPRESENTATIVE INSTITUTIONS

Although England had developed strong central institutions during the long reign of Henry II in the twelfth century, it began the thirteenth century in a weaker position. Richard the Lionhearted (r. 1189–1199), great fighter that he was, had spent much of his life crusading. John, his brother, who remained in Europe, lost his family's Norman territories to the French.

THE KING AND THE BARONS Worse still, Richard and John had angered the barons of England by infringing on their privileges and by repeatedly imposing the tax known as scutage ("shield duty")—a tax paid by noble vassals in lieu of the forty days of military service that they owed their lord each year—only to spend this revenue on fruitless wars on the Continent. Inspired by rumors of threats to their rights and the precedent of an earlier charter issued by Henry I, the barons rose against John. Henry I had issued formal promises on his accession in 1100 that he would rule by ancient custom, which meant that he would cease charging his barons immense sums when they inherited their estates, and would stop collecting the revenues of churches between the death of a bishop or abbot and the installation of a successor. This charter was basically a dead letter, which Henry had no intention of following. But the barons took it as a model when in 1215, at Runnymede, an area of meadows and ponds by the river Thames twenty miles from London, they forced John to sign the document later known as **Magna Carta**.

MAGNA CARTA The new charter offered several guarantees. The king, in council with his barons, proclaimed that he would maintain the traditional liberties of the Church and the city of London. More important still, he promised to maintain justice throughout his realm, guaranteeing that no one would be deprived of land or goods except by a jury from his county of origin. Magna Carta also stated that "[n]o freeman shall be captured or imprisoned or disseised [unlawfully deprived of real property] or outlawed or exiled or in any way destroyed, nor will we go against him or send against him, except by the lawful judgment of his peers or by the law of the land," and that "[t]o no one will we sell, to no one will we deny or delay right or justice." The king thus bound himself to guarantee justice—not solely, or mainly, as a source of revenue for himself and the crown, but as a duty that he owed his subjects.

These guarantees were originally seen as applying to the nobility: to the barons, who held their estates from the king; and to the knights, who held their estates from the barons. But the English courts gradually applied them more and more widely. Magna Carta made no revolutionary claims. But it specified that if the king needed to ask for an "aid" (a subsidy) for his expenses, he would do so after obtaining "the common counsel of the realm" by summoning the great clerics and barons to meet him. This suggested a new view of the king's rule in England: not as an expression of the ruler's absolute will, but as carried on with the consent and in the interests of his subjects.

Henry III, whose long rule in England (r. 1216–1272) paralleled that of Louis IX in France, struggled endlessly for precedence with his barons. He provoked them into staging a (polite and very English) revolt: they did not depose him but attempted to limit his autonomy by imposing their own controls. Disputes continued, and efforts at mediation by the French king, to whom both sides appealed, failed to prevent civil war. Eventually, in 1265, the forces of Henry's eldest son, Edward, defeated the barons at Evesham in Worcestershire and killed their leader, Simon de Montfort, leaving the kings of England firmly in command.

PARLIAMENTS Yet during and after the decades of debate over privileges, new customs developed in England, some of them inspired by Magna Carta. These defined and strengthened the position of the monarchy by solidifying its connection to the rest of the English people. It became the custom, for example, for the king to make his laws and decisions in the presence of the barons, whom he summoned for that purpose, as he was supposed to do when asking for aids. As time passed, representatives of the knights of the shires (counties) and of the burgesses—free citizens of the boroughs (towns)—were also summoned to these meetings, which came to be called **parliaments** ("talkings together"). Gradually a principle was established: decisions made by this assembly represented the will of the realm as a whole. Whatever the Magna Carta authors had meant, they now seemed to state that when the king spoke in this council, he spoke for all of his subjects.

THE COMMON LAW A remarkable consensus developed also on English law. For all the struggles of the thirteenth century, by the end of it the English king could offer justice in all the counties of England. His justices

King's Council This miniature of a king sitting in council with his bishops and nobles comes from a fourteenth-century English manuscript that outlines the ideal form of parliamentary procedure.

traveled regular circuits to hold court in major towns, and followed the principles of England's distinctive law, which had been developed less by formal legislation than by the decisions of generations of judges. English jurists proudly proclaimed that the **common law** of England was not, and could not be, written down. Like the French, the English saw themselves, by the end of the thirteenth century, as members of a single community—one that stretched across the borders of individual counties, had its own distinctive laws and customs, and supported, served, and claimed justice from a single ruler. Even the sacred monarchy of France did not rest on more solid foundations than the realm of England.

SPAIN: CONSOLIDATING AUTHORITY

Monarchies elsewhere in Europe developed on similar lines. Alfonso IX (r. 1188–1230) of León and Galicia began his reign by summoning representatives of towns to formal meetings. Similar developments took place in

The Reconquista, ca. 1200–1400 In the thirteenth and fourteenth centuries, strong Spanish monarchs consolidated territory and conquered lands previously in Muslim hands. In the first half of the thirteenth century, Ferdinand III of the unified kingdoms of Castile and León led an army southward, winning major battles at Córdoba and Seville and reducing Muslim-controlled territory to a small portion of the southern coast.

Castile, in the north-central region of Spain, and on a larger scale. Ferdinand III (r. 1217–1252) unified the kingdoms of Castile and León and pushed hard against the Muslims, whose Almohad Caliphate was in political crisis. He took city after city, finally conquering Seville, the greatest city in Andalusia, in 1248. The Nazirid dynasty succeeded in founding a new Islamic state, the Emirate of Granada, in 1238. It became an important center of the arts and scholarship, and survived until 1492, but only at the price of accepting the Christian kings of Castile as overlords.

THE CORTES To pay for his military campaigns, Ferdinand needed regular financial help from his subjects. In the Spanish kingdoms, as in England, it became normal for the king to summon high-ranking clerics, noblemen, and representatives of the towns to meetings, known as *cortes* ("courts"), which took place every two to four years. The king would typically ask for a subsidy, and the members of the Cortes would reply by asking for

redress of their grievances (the Catalans refused to grant subsidies until the king had replied to their demands). Gradually, the Cortes developed a sense of responsibility not only for taxation, but also for the general welfare of their realm.

ALFONSO X The Castilian king Alfonso X (r. 1252–1284), long known as Alfonso the Wise, was a descendant of the German Hohenstaufen family that had fought for generations to enlarge and strengthen the Holy Roman Empire. Alfonso himself had aspired to become Holy Roman emperor, but at home he concentrated on Spanish matters. At first, Alfonso enlisted Jews and Muslims, as well as Christians, in his service; later he turned against the Jews. But he worked consistently to make the crown of Castile the center of a unified community. Like Louis IX and Henry III, he emphasized the importance of providing justice to his subjects. At his command, jurists compiled a massive legal code in Spanish, the Siete Partidas. Far earlier than in other parts of Europe, it became normal in Castile and elsewhere in Spain to formulate legal documents in Spanish rather than Latin. Alfonso also encouraged the formation of the Mesta, a large association of sheepherders who began to compete against producers of wool elsewhere. He also placed special importance—more than any of his royal rivals—on having up-to-date Islamic scientific work translated from Arabic into both Latin and Spanish.

Alfonso's Translators The Spanish king Alfonso X formally supported efforts to translate Arabic texts into Latin and Spanish, as conveyed by this illustration from a thirteenth-century manuscript showing the king flanked by his translators at court.

THE HOLY ROMAN EMPIRE: THE RULE OF FREDERICK II

In at least one case—that of the Holy Roman Empire—efforts to centralize authority proved less successful. Emperor Frederick II (r. 1220–1250), the last truly powerful member of the Hohenstaufen dynasty, proved to be a brilliant military leader. He regrouped the forces of the empire and asserted his power against the papacy and all other opponents. But his advances for the empire were not lasting.

A CAPABLE RULER Despite papal denunciations of his impiety and disobedience, Frederick II crusaded more successfully than most of his rivals, and in 1229 he managed to negotiate a return of Jerusalem to Christendom. (However, the city proved indefensible, so this restoration was temporary.) In the early part of Frederick's reign he also defeated a coalition of the most powerful northern Italian states, and sank the vessels of many of the church officials traveling to Rome to attend a council called against him. His court at Palermo became a center of poetry, classicizing art (his mint issued gold coins that represented him as a new Augustus), and intellectual inquiry: legend held that in order to find out if the soul really existed, Frederick ordered men to be nailed into barrels, which were opened after they died to see if they contained anything besides the corpses.

In fact, Frederick was not a freethinker but a deeply curious individual schooled in the philosophy of Aristotle. Documents show that he sent philosophical inquiries about the structure of the universe to Muslim thinkers around the Mediterranean as well as to his own court astrologer. He also showed an open mind—as well as an acute sense of his own advantage—in his response to an accusation that Jews in one imperial state had carried out the ritual murder of a Christian child. Frederick asked kings elsewhere in Christendom to send him Jewish converts who could explain whether the accusation was justified. He learned from two English converts that Jews not only did not practice but also abhorred human sacrifice. In 1236 he declared the accusations false, but also asserted the special status of the Jews as "serfs of our chamber." Frederick offered the Jews protection, but also insisted on his own rights as their exclusive lord—including the right to draw on them for financial help.

THE CONSTITUTIONS OF MELFI Frederick concentrated much of his effort on building a state in Sicily, outside the traditional territories of the empire, but even there much of what he did followed precedents established elsewhere. He insisted on his absolute right as monarch to frame the laws. Yet the legal code that he issued in 1231, the Constitutions of Melfi, included innovations. Frederick insisted, for example, that no judge should hold office in a territory in which he held estates—a new principle, and one that suggests Frederick hoped to rely on professional officials. In the end, though, his university in Palermo developed too slowly, and he had to rely on local nobles to fill positions in the state. When he promised his subjects rapid justice and prohibited Christians from moneylending, he followed the same paths as contemporaries such as King John of England.

EMPIRE IN DECLINE To retain the loyalty of as many of the German princes as possible, Frederick gave them so much freedom that they dominated the core imperial territories in Germany. His own successes terrified neighboring powers in Italy and strengthened the hand of the papacy. After he died, it did not take long for his enemies to overcome his family. With the death of Conradin of Hohenstaufen in 1268, the power of the Holy Roman emperors was decisively broken, as their long contest with the papacy ended in victory for the Church.

TRANSFORMING THE CHURCH

Paradoxically, the greatest monarchy of all—and the one that played a crucial role in inducing subjects to look to their secular rulers for justice—was the Church. By the end of the twelfth century, as we have seen, the papacy had established itself as the center of a vast web of institutions—cathedrals and monasteries, schools and local churches. Although the heads of these institutions were often appointed by monarchs or lords, in theory the vast realm of the Church was ruled from Rome by the popes, with the help of the College of Cardinals. The popes claimed the right to appoint bishops to govern the dioceses from their cathedrals, and to appoint the heads of the great monastic houses. The popes also asserted their rights to payments from the bishops' dioceses and from monasteries, in return for appointing new heads. By the beginning of the thirteenth century, the canon law of the Church had become so well established that it was taught together with Roman law in university faculties of law. Many students became "doctors of both laws" so that they could practice in state and clerical courts. Universal in reach, wealthy in influence as well as money, and with social strength based on a carefully woven web of legal principles, the Church saw itself as rivaling the monarchies of France and England in power.

POPE INNOCENT AND THE FOURTH LATERAN COUNCIL

In one crucial element of practice, the Church deliberately refused to rival those monarchies. The hierarchy was now staffed, in its upper ranks, with men who had studied theology and canon law, many of whom looked back to the enthusiastic years of the Gregorian Reform movement of the eleventh century. With the accession to the papacy in 1198 of Lothario Segni, who became **Pope Innocent III** (d. 1216), a great scholar and thinker inspired by the Gregorian reformers occupied the summit of the system.

An Italian nobleman who had studied theology in Paris, Innocent saw humankind as the children of Adam and Eve, conceived in sin and in desperate need of the salvation that only the Church could extend: "Man has been formed of dust, clay, ashes, and, a thing far more vile, of the filthy sperm. Man has been conceived in the desire of the flesh, in the heat of sensual lust, in the foul stench of wantonness. He was born to labor, to fear, to suffering, and, most miserable of all, to death." Only the Church could draw on its treasury of grace to save such vile creatures from themselves. Innocent fought to reform the Church so that it could reach these goals throughout his reign, which climaxed in the **Fourth Lateran Council** of 1215. The assembled clerics laid down strong principles

Pope Innocent III A striking fresco from a church in Italy, painted shortly after Innocent's death in 1216, gives some indication of the pope's authority. Innocent used his power to reform the Church, suppress heresy, and call for new crusades.

regarding the lives of the clergy, their relation to laypeople, and the Church's role in the world.

THE ORDEAL AND THE CHURCH Pope Innocent believed that to achieve its sacred task, the Church must assert its sovereign independence from the world. For centuries, European monarchs considered themselves, in terms that went back to antiquity, divinely anointed rulers. This meant not only that they often claimed the right to appoint Church officials but also that they saw their own function as givers of justice in divine terms. In the eleventh and twelfth centuries, royal judges often faced problems that they could not resolve: how to fix responsibility for crimes that had no reliable witnesses, or how to settle civil complaints in which each side claimed to be in the right. Like the Carolingians before them, the royal judges settled such problems by offering the accused, or both parties in a dispute, the chance to swear an oath to their veracity and undertake an ordeal to prove it. (The parties could also appoint champions to undertake ordeals in their place.) Trial by ordeal continued to be a widespread practice throughout the twelfth century, although in England the rise of the jury system in criminal and civil law had already challenged and, to some extent, replaced it.

Ordeals ran from "taking the cross" (holding one's arms out in the form of a cross until it became impossible to hold them up; the party who collapsed first would be seen to be in the wrong) to the more notorious ordeals by fire and water. In the first, the person accused or demanding rights, or the appointed champion, would reach into a cauldron of boiling water to extract a ring or another object, carry hot iron for several paces, or walk across red-hot iron plates. The singed hand or foot would be bandaged for three days. If there was no sign of infection when the limb was unwrapped, the accusation was refuted or the oath confirmed. In the other, those who sank when immersed in a pool of water were held to be telling the truth, since the water accepted them.

These ordeals belonged to secular government, but priests had always taken part, and were paid fees for doing so. Before the accused grasped the hot iron, for example, the priest addressed God, asking that he "bless and sanctify this fiery iron, which is used in the just examination of doubtful issues." In the twelfth century—that great age of distinctions and law codes—more than one thinker had raised doubts about ordeals. The French theologian Peter the Chanter, for example, worried that the ordeal by hot iron tested not guilt or innocence but the thickness of the calluses on the hand and the heat of the metal.

Trial by Ordeal This page from a mid-fourteenth-century German law book illustrates the concept of the ordeal. One man stirs a cauldron of boiling water for an ordeal by fire, while another looks on, either participating in the preparations or getting ready to plunge his hand into the water. At left a man bears a sword and shield, perhaps readying for a trial by combat.

Pope Innocent finally transformed these scattered criticisms into firm legislation—not because he, or anyone else, suddenly decided that God never intervened in everyday life, but because he thought it vital to distinguish clergy from laity, and Church authority from secular. Secular authorities shed blood. Clerics, the Fourth Lateran Council decreed, must not do so. They were forbidden not only to do violence to others themselves, or to be present when blood was shed, but also to take part in ordeals. The decree established as a principle that the Church should not involve itself in purely worldly matters. For all its wealth and influence, the Church now also stood for a powerful distinction: the firm dividing line between that which belonged to Caesar and that which belonged to God.

TORTURE AND PROOF

One consequence of the Fourth Lateran Council's decree was to reinforce—even more than royal action had already done—the power of the secular state. The withdrawal of clerical participation, accompanied by the creation of courts and the provision of judges, made it clear that justice, in this world, was a secular matter, and that subjects must look to the state for it.

Sadly, though, this did not make trials more humane. For centuries in Continental Europe it became standard, following the precedents in Roman law, to employ a formal system of "inquisition" (inquiry by torture) to determine the accused's guilt or innocence when a confession or eyewitness testimony was lacking. The wisest rulers, from Frederick II to Alfonso X, agreed that this was the best method. In England, however, only those suspected of treason could be legally tortured. Suspects who refused to plead and accept the judgment of a jury could be subjected to the application of weights until they died or confessed. Even now, centuries after torture was abolished, Continental jurisprudence does not make the same presumption of innocence that the Anglo-American tradition does, and, especially in France, it relies on formal inquiry led by officials—a long-term consequence of the decisions made in the thirteenth century by a powerful pope and his contemporaries.

REFORMING CHRISTIANITY

The ordeal was not the only practice that Pope Innocent set out to transform. The Fourth Lateran Council's decrees applied broadly to the organization of the Church and deeply to the intimate lives of clergy and laypeople. To ensure that the Church administered the true Christian message to its flock, the council held every bishop responsible for holding synods ("gatherings") of his clergy, visiting religious houses, and combating **heresy**. Bishops who could not preach effectively must appoint preachers who would regularly address their congregations. Monastic orders and provinces of the Church (groups of diocese) were instructed to hold regular meetings and follow orthodox doctrines and proper procedures.

In keeping with Innocent's beliefs about the sinfulness of the flesh, the council insisted that clerics must be celibate. This principle, rooted in decrees from councils of the Roman period, had fallen away after the collapse of the Carolingian Empire. The Gregorian reformers had tried to restore celibacy, demanding that married priests separate from their wives. They encountered widespread, fierce resistance. Those who refused to divest themselves of families were excommunicated. The council of 1215 condemned priests, monks, and nuns who broke their vows—who failed to wear their proper habits, engaged in gluttony or sexual intercourse, watched mimes and entertainers, or went to taverns (except when on long journeys). In 1239, the council's decree on celibacy was reconfirmed on papal authority—strong evidence that resistance continued.

Faced with individuals such as Abelard and Héloïse, who asserted their passions even when laws or rules condemned them, the council took aim at the full-scale transformation of every Christian's life through the relationship between ordinary priests and their congregations. As we have seen, the Church had developed the practice of private confession in the early Middle Ages, when the first manuals were written to guide confessors. Now the practice was made mandatory. Every adult Christian must

Life in the Church In three of the panels from a late-thirteenth-century French manuscript, a nun prays before an altar with an image of Christ or one of the saints. At top left, a nun kneels to make confession—a mandatory practice after the Fourth Lateran Council of 1215—to a Dominican friar, who makes the sign of the cross over her in absolution.

confess his or her sins at least once a year, and receive the Eucharist at least annually (at Easter), or face excommunication and denial of Christian burial. And every priest must be able to perform the Mass, administer the sacraments, and serve as a sensitive, sympathetic, and discreet spiritual adviser who could treat spiritual wounds just as a skilled doctor would treat physical ones. Priests could seek advice in difficult cases, but they must never reveal the identities of those they served. In theory, at least, the confessional had been sealed and made private, though it would take centuries to realize a high level of consistency in clerical practice.

REVIVING THE CRUSADES Pope Innocent passionately believed that Christians should hold and guard the places where Jesus had lived and suffered. In 1187, as we have seen, Saladin (Salah al-Din Yusuf ibn Ayyub) had defeated the Christians in the battle of Hattin, opening the

way for the Muslim reconquest of Palestine. Innocent was horrified. More dramatically—and more systematically—than any of his predecessors, he made crusading a central priority of the Church. And as he did so, he reinserted the Church into political and military life with a vengeance by insisting that the Church, as the superior entity, should direct the policies of secular states, wherever necessary. At the very start of his papacy in 1198, Innocent issued a public statement calling for a new crusade. He claimed that Christ himself called for war against the Muslims, whose capture of faithful Christians reenacted the injury that the Jews had inflicted on the Savior when they crucified him.

The early crusades had suffered from the disunity of the Christian powers and from a lack of funds. So Innocent mobilized the enormous wealth of the Church to support a holy war. Every cleric in Christendom, he pronounced, must contribute one-fortieth of his income to a special tax to support the new crusade. His example had long-lasting impact. The Fourth Lateran Council promulgated a new crusading tax in 1215. Soon a comprehensive system of clerical taxation was built into the structure of the Catholic Church. In 1274, Pope Gregory X would divide all of Christendom into twenty-six "collectorates," or tax districts. Though the Church had washed its hands of Christian blood, it had also become a state in a new sense. If it could not wage war on its own, it could declare war and finance it.

THE LATER CRUSADES (1202–1272) The first result of Pope Innocent's decision—the Fourth Crusade of 1202–4—was a debacle. To cross the Mediterranean, the crusaders made an arrangement with Venice, which promised to build, crew, and provision enough ships to carry 35,000 men, in return for a substantial payment and a half share in booty from any conquests that the crusade accomplished. Enrico Dandolo (ca. 1107–1205), the aged but sharp-witted Venetian doge, bargained with the crusaders to start by attacking Egypt as the more strategic target, rather than Palestine. The crusaders' envoys agreed.

But the necessary compromises went much further. The crusaders appeared in smaller numbers and with less cash than had been promised. Led by Dandolo, the Venetians conveyed them, in the first instance, to Zara, a Christian city on the Adriatic coast of what is now Croatia, which had recently rebelled against Venetian control, ironically placing itself under the lordship of the pope. Despite papal condemnations and protests from some of the crusaders themselves, the Christian army began its efforts in November 1202 by besieging and taking a

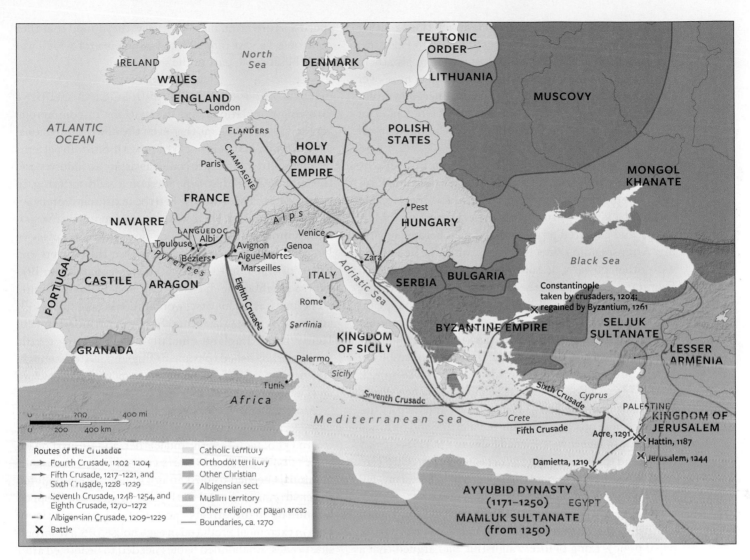

The Later Crusades, 1202–1272 Pope Innocent III renewed calls for holy war, though the ventures that followed were largely unsuccessful. The crusaders who crossed the Mediterranean and invaded Constantinople and Jerusalem did not make any lasting territorial gains, though they fought several battles in the eastern Mediterranean. Of greater consequence, however, was the crusade against the Albigensian Cathars in southern France, which established a precedent of war against heretics.

Christian city. Innocent denounced them, hurling all his metaphors into one basket: "Behold, your gold has turned into base metal and your silver has almost completely rusted since, departing from the purity of your plan and turning aside from the path onto the impassable road, you have, so to speak, withdrawn your hand from the plough."

But the pope's rhetoric had no immediate practical effect. In fact, the Venetians took the crusaders not to Egypt or Jerusalem but to Constantinople, capital of the Byzantine Empire and still the richest city in the Christian world. Amid riots by the Byzantine inhabitants, in 1204 the crusaders attacked the ancient city, managed to break through the walls, and pillaged Constantinople with terrible brutality. A quarter of the booty went to the treasury

of the great Venetian basilica of San Marco. No effort was made to invade Muslim lands or to recover Jerusalem.

Furious, but helpless to intervene, Pope Innocent eventually absolved the crusaders and accepted what they had done. Nonetheless, he continued to see holy war as a central purpose of the Church. At the end of his pontificate, the Fourth Lateran Council issued another call for a crusade. The opponent was the Ayyubid dynasty founded by Saladin, who had divided his territories among his sons after his death in 1193. This Fifth Crusade, chiefly made up of armies from the Holy Roman Empire, Flanders, and Hungary, took a Nile Delta port, Damietta, in 1219, but two years later the crusaders accepted a peace offer and left Egypt in Muslim hands.

In 1228 Holy Roman Emperor Frederick II led another crusade (the sixth), first to Cyprus and then to Palestine. He bargained with the Muslims, promising to give them freedom of worship, and regained Christian control over Jerusalem, Bethlehem, and Nazareth. Energetic diplomacy on the part of the crusader Theobald, Count of Champagne (1201–1253), reestablished the kingdom of Jerusalem after years of struggle.

After Muslim forces retook Jerusalem in 1244, the French monarch, Louis IX, mounted the Seventh Crusade. His preparations were systematic and effective. He gathered a massive army, built a special port near Marseilles, and gathered provisions and men before embarking. After spending time in Cyprus, where he negotiated with other powers, he sailed to Egypt and recaptured Damietta in 1249. But the Egyptians rallied to defeat Louis's main army, and a new sultan, Turanshah, captured Louis in 1250. His release cost an enormous ransom. Twenty years later, when Louis gathered a second massive force for the Eighth Crusade, he set out to establish a base in Tunis. But disease ravaged his army, and he himself died of "flux." The crusade was abandoned. When Prince Edward of England (son of Henry III) abandoned a campaign to shore up Christian rule in Palestine and returned to Europe in 1272 to be crowned Edward I (r. 1272–1307), it put an end to the crusading efforts of the thirteenth century. Acre, the last major Christian base in Palestine, fell to the Mamluk Sultan Kahlil (r. 1290–1293) in 1291.

During the course of the thirteenth and fourteenth centuries, the crusade would become a normal part of papal policy. Long before, Augustine had argued that a truly Christian ruler would use force to make heretics convert to Christianity. Now, orthodox doctrine became even harder. Christ, a great canon lawyer explained, had come into the world to bring sinners to repentance. The war against heretics—and any others whose resistance to the Church put the salvation of others at risk—was Christ's cause. Popes declared crusades against Frederick II; against a Roman noble family, the Colonna, that politically opposed the family of Pope Boniface VIII; and even against a company of German mercenaries, who were welcomed back to papal service as soon as conditions changed. Holy war had become a standard—if not a central—part of the Church's portfolio of activities.

THE CHURCH AND THE URBAN POOR

When Pope Innocent III and his successors trimmed the sails of the great ship of the papacy and tried to control its speed and direction more precisely, they found that they confronted a vast range of new problems for which war could be, at most, part of the solution.

ECONOMIC PROBLEMS AND SOCIAL UNREST Growing populations and fluctuations in commercial activity posed problems that even the newly professional city governments could not keep up with. Shifts in patterns of trade and manufacture could devastate an industry and the communities that depended on it, and suffering, in turn, led to civil violence. When the textile entrepreneurs of Flanders pressed their workers to accept lower wages, strikes broke out. The first one on record took place in Douai in 1245. A quarter century later, the weavers and fullers of Ghent left their city en masse, moving to Brabant, a neighboring duchy of the Holy Roman Empire. Sometimes, as in this case, workers could take their skills and move to cities that still offered opportunity. In 1271, Henry III of England officially welcomed any textile workers who wished to come to England. Often, though, violence broke out between the craftsmen who made cloth and cut stone and their masters.

More generally, too, living conditions in the biggest cities worsened. Coal fires, chemical waste from the treatment of metal, cloth, and leather, and the vast quantities of body parts and ordure created by the thousands of animals needed to feed an urban population polluted the environment. So did the layers of excrement dropped by animals on dirt streets—and the further quantities of human excrement produced in each house, often from outside privies. Abandoned babies needed to be looked after or face immediate death. Thousands of city dwellers were undernourished.

On the land, an ever-growing rural population divided farms until the small plots could no longer support a family. In parts of Italy in the later thirteenth and early fourteenth centuries, farmers pushed cultivation to altitudes where agriculture could not be sustained. Landlords, themselves squeezed by inflation, demanded more money and work from tenants who had paid to free themselves. Peasant revolts like that of the *pastoureaux* (shepherds), which broke out in 1253 in France, may not have threatened the existing order, but they resulted in the deaths of officials and in frightening if temporary disorder.

NEW RELIGIOUS ORDERS: DOMINICANS AND FRANCISCANS As hunger and diseases spread—especially leprosy, the disfiguring, disabling illness that became endemic in medieval Europe—the orderly sermons offered in the cathedrals provided little practical help. Nor

Saint Francis Francis's poverty and humility infuse these scenes from an Italian church fresco, probably painted soon after his death. At top, barefoot and clad in a simple robe, he washes the feet of the poor in imitation of Jesus. The bottom image shows him founding a monastery.

Both men sought a new model of the religious life. Dominic, worried by the spread of heresy, found the Church's efforts to combat it counterproductive. He insisted that clerics show true dedication and constant self-discipline. As he explained in a letter to a community of nuns in Madrid, "From now on I want silence to be kept in the forbidden places, the refectory, the dormitory, and the oratory, and your law to be observed in all other matters.... Avoid talking idly to one another. Let not your time be wasted in conversation." Francis, a gentle soul whose belief in the kinship of all creatures emerges clearly from his hymns to Brother Sun and Sister Moon, was horrified by the suffering of the poor in cities like his own Assisi, a center of cloth manufacture in central Italy.

Both men gathered followers. And despite papal reluctance to see new orders founded, both received permission to create what rapidly became the most successful religious orders of the time. Like the members of existing orders, Dominicans and Franciscans felt a profound vocation for the religious life, and after spending time as novices, took vows of poverty, chastity, and obedience. Unlike monks, however, the friars, as they were called, did not pursue their salvation in the remote and quiet places of the world. Instead, they confronted the worst problems head on. **Dominicans**, who specialized in preaching orthodox

did the prayers offered up for all Christian souls in the aristocratic monasteries do much to console the urban poor. As in the past, the Church proved capable of responding to these challenges. Individuals appeared with the insight and energy to create institutions and offer solutions.

The religious innovators of the early thirteenth century were a Spaniard and an Italian: Dominic de Guzmán (1170–1221), who became Saint Dominic, and Giovanni Francesco di Bernardone (ca. 1182–1226), who became Saint Francis. Both devoted themselves to the Church, Dominic from early youth and Francis after long, bitter struggles with his merchant father, who wanted him to pursue profit. Both were ascetics: as a student, Dominic sold his books and clothes to help the victims of a plague. Francis insisted that his followers accept Jesus's words literally and not prepare at all for the next day. When he found himself locked out in a storm with nothing to eat, Francis rejoiced.

Saint Dominic Illustrations from a fifteenth-century French history display Dominic's piety. Above, the poor receive charity; below, Dominic leads a group of people in the burning of heretical texts. Dominic's own book does not burn in the flames, proving that it alone is true.

Catholic doctrine, traveled the roads of Europe looking for people who needed instruction and heretics who had to be defeated in debate. Franciscans, hoping to care for those whom the rest of society rejected, preached and built hospitals in the cities. Turning away from the models of Christian life that had been most popular in recent times, Francis instructed his followers to imitate Christ and Mary—to be as poor as the first Christians depicted in the Gospels. Both orders grew, as the Cistercians had a century before, with startling speed. Saint Clare (1194–1253), an Italian noblewoman inspired by Francis's teaching, created a new order for women. She drew up their rule, the first composed by a woman, and they became the second **Franciscan Order**.

THE LEARNING OF THE FRIARS Originally, Francis had planned that he and his followers would live on whatever Christians happened to give them. One of the terms for the new friars, *mendicants*, literally means "those who beg." Over time, Franciscans as well as Dominicans found themselves in need of stable bases where they could carry out their tasks, train their novices, and receive gifts and legacies from grateful Christians. As preachers, moreover, members of both orders needed to devote years to the study of formal theology. Soon Dominican and Franciscan study houses came into being in Paris, Oxford, and other centers of theological study. They built up libraries of theological textbooks and collections of examples for use in preaching.

In their commitment to serving the practical needs of their fellow Christians, the mendicants adopted innovative positions: they saw that money was vital to the urban economy and allowed the charging of interest. They also developed their own highly practical style of book production, in which tables of contents and indexes allowed rapid consultation. These thirteenth-century friars invented the modern reference book.

HERETICS: ENEMIES OF THE CHURCH

European society—at least as viewed from the Roman citadel of the Church—seemed to be not only creating new wealth and perpetrating new injustices but also spawning new commercial values and new ideas even about basic Christian doctrines. Since the Schism of 1054, the formal opponents of Catholic teaching had been the theologians of Byzantium—or so the Catholic theologians held. Now, eloquent teachers within the walls of Latin Europe were devising new understandings of Christ's message, seducing the faithful away from orthodoxy, and leading them into religious error. Over the centuries, clerics and rulers had stumbled, repeatedly, on individuals and small groups who dissented from standard teachings. Often these dissenters claimed to follow Christ in rejecting the wealth and power of the institutional Church. Most of them were treated fairly gently, unless—like Arnold of Brescia (ca. 1090–1155), who led a rebellion against the popes at Rome in the middle of the twelfth century—they were clearly dangerous. But by the late twelfth and thirteenth centuries, heretics were becoming more numerous, more aggressive, and in some cases more powerful than ever before.

WALDENSIANS Heresy could begin inconspicuously, and even unintentionally. Around 1173 a merchant named Waldes in the French city of Lyon heard a minstrel sing about a saint who gave away his wealth and became a

Waldensians This anti-Waldensian tract (ca. 1460) depicts members of the group engaged in the alleged rite of kissing the rear of a goat during a meeting—a heretical act of idolatry. Demons and witches fly above the scene, cementing the Waldensians' link to Satan.

beggar. Stunned, he consulted a theologian, who told him what Jesus had said to a rich man in the Gospel of Matthew: "If you wish to be perfect, go and sell what you have, and give it to the poor . . . and follow me." Waldes decided to become a beggar himself, but he also paid priests to translate more of the Bible from Latin, and to preach. Soon he found followers, male and female, who begged their way through the world. The Waldensians' ostentatious poverty irritated traditional clerics, who denied them permission to teach. Like the ancient Donatists, the Waldensians came to feel contempt for ordinary priests, who, they thought, betrayed their own callings. Soon they challenged central Roman doctrines—for example, the existence of purgatory and the need for prayers for the dead. Waldensians held that women as well as men could serve as priests. And they developed their own hierarchy of priests and bishops.

The new church spread from southern France and the Piedmont region of Italy to Bohemia. Savage persecution wiped out Waldensians in most cities, though they survived in mountain valleys and isolated farming communities. As their case makes clear, even brief exposure to the raw text of the Gospels, with their vision of a religion that refused wealth and power, could start Christians on a path that led to radical dissidence. In the literate, mobile world of the late twelfth and thirteenth centuries, such exposure was common, and the results frightened the authorities.

CATHARS One group in particular, the **Cathars**, posed a danger that alarmed Church authorities, including Pope Innocent III. Unlike the Waldensians, they may have been inspired by missionaries from outside western Europe— from the Eastern Orthodox world, where dualist heretics had begun to develop their own theology and liturgy in the tenth century in Bulgaria, and carried their views to Constantinople and beyond. The numbers of Cathars never approached those of orthodox Catholics, and their theology was never so firmly and fully developed. Yet by the second half of the twelfth century, groups of Cathars were spreading in economically advanced areas such as Flanders, Champagne, and northern Italy, while others were moving into the Languedoc, an area in southern France where royal control was hard to exercise. Fiercely ascetic, they appealed to Christians from all levels of society, from nobles and wealthy merchants to peasants and poor laborers. The contrast between their poverty and purity and the wealth of the clerical establishment probably lay at the core of their appeal.

Cathar doctrines were not uniform, but they were

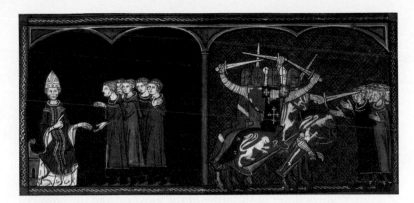

Albigensian Crusade This illustration from a French history (ca. 1335) depicts Pope Innocent III excommunicating the Albigensians, and crusading knights attacking them.

definitely unorthodox. Catholics who followed standard teachings believed in one omnipotent God and the Trinity. Cathars—who also saw themselves as Christians— embraced dualism. They envisioned the universe as a battlefield on which a good and an evil power, evenly matched, fought for supremacy. Whereas Catholics admitted that the material world was the domain of sin, Cathars denounced it as wholly evil, the creation of Satan. And whereas Catholics who decided to pursue holiness renounced marriage, Cathars renounced it entirely. They rejected the world of matter as evil and saw it as a sin to bring more souls into its contamination.

Pope Innocent III, the great defender of the Church, set out in the 1190s to attack the Cathars. But his efforts were largely unsuccessful, and his senior representative, who excommunicated the Cathar count of Toulouse in 1207, was murdered. In 1209, Innocent declared a crusade against the Cathars, also called Albigensians after their place of origin, the wealthy city of Albi in southern France. (See the map on page 307.) A massive army— with 500 knights from France alone—took the cross and marched south to besiege Cathar strongholds. At the small hilltop city of Béziers, crusaders asked the pope's representative how they could tell Cathars from Catholics. "Kill them all," he answered. "God will know his own." The crusaders massacred everyone they found, and those who had taken refuge in the cathedral died when it burned and collapsed on them. The war was waged with great cruelty, and even after it ended, continued inquisitions traced networks of Cathar believers and stamped out their safe houses and hiding places. Royal power and orthodox Catholic teaching were thus firmly established throughout southern France.

THOMAS AQUINAS: FRAMING ORTHODOXY

Confronted by heretics at home; by the Jews, who still inhabited most parts of Christian Europe; and by the Muslims, who threatened Christian pilgrims and traders throughout the Mediterranean, the mendicant orders raised intellectual bulwarks to protect the Church. **Thomas Aquinas** (1225–1274), an Italian Dominican who studied and taught theology at Paris, was a passionate believer in the order of the universe and the power of reason to master it. He used the best tools of the ancients—such as Aristotle's logic—to show that even they had been wrong on vital points where Christian teaching was right.

Thomas Aquinas A fourteenth-century fresco from an Italian church portrays Thomas, dressed in his Dominican habit, as a teacher of high stature. He holds open a book while the young monks sitting at his feet copy his teachings.

Aquinas's enterprise built on precedents set in previous centuries, but also went far beyond them. Whereas Abelard had collected opinions and raised questions, Aquinas developed a coherent structure of doctrines, argued point by point—and thus gave the definitive form to what has since been known as scholastic theology. In every case, he ensured that his arguments were free of errors and omissions by first assuming the negative of what he planned to prove and then disproving it. His proofs of the existence of God, for example, began with the statement that there is no God, followed by a cogent refutation of it. Only after Aquinas had stated and refuted the relevant errors did he set out to prove what he meant to prove. He worked with beautiful lucidity from assumptions that he and his pupils considered as solid as the structure of the Notre-Dame Cathedral. Many of these assumptions came from Aristotle and his commentators: for example, that all beings in the universe are ordered in a hierarchy, each at its own distinctive level, and that all things remain at rest unless they are set in motion by an outside cause. Yet Aquinas used these materials to support Christian arguments that Aristotle would have rejected: for example, the thesis that the universe had not existed forever.

Scholastic theology, which Aquinas and other university teachers developed to an extraordinary pitch of elegance and sophistication, became a specialty of the mendicants, and a natural candidate for their favorite style of book production. Not everyone in authority accepted Aquinas's conviction that reason, at its ancient best, could be relied on to support revelation: in 1277, the archbishop of Paris actually prohibited the study of Aristotle in the schools. Over time, however, formal argument based on Aristotelian logic—and on later elaborations of it, crafted by brilliant logicians—established itself as the core of Christian theology.

INQUISITIONS: ROOTING OUT HERESY

A coherent theology was necessary if the heretics were to be defeated, but it was certainly not sufficient. Dominicans and Franciscans did not confine themselves to formal debates in universities. Once trained, they went out into the field. They accompanied the crusaders into Languedoc to defeat the Cathars, and as their expertise in the detection and refutation of heresies won recognition, they moved into other areas as well. From the 1230s on, Gregory IX and later popes began to appoint Dominicans as inquisitors. They were not members of a single permanent office, for no permanent Inquisition existed in the

Middle Ages, but specialists given authority to hold an **inquisition**—that is, to inquire into the spread of heresy in a given diocese, acting independently of the local bishop if necessary.

There were never many Dominican inquisitors, and they did not cast the chilling shadow across high medieval society that later commentators have suggested. But they did become experts at finding, interrogating, and forcing confessions from those suspected of heresy. They even drew up handbooks for their colleagues. These works assumed that those interrogated were guilty, offered useful hints on how to confuse them and trip them up, and held—as those who persecute others so often do—that the imprisoned heretics were the true criminals.

Systematic, tireless interrogation broke many suspected Cathars. But in more difficult cases, torture—the standard tool of inquiry in the world of civil crime, once the ordeal was abolished—offered vital help. The inquisitors worked more carefully, and with more respect for procedure and the spiritual needs of those they investigated, than any secular court. But at times—as in Toulouse in 1247–48, when inquisitors interrogated almost 5,500 suspects—they tore to shreds the fabric of the societies that they meant to save. Most problematic of all was the vision of heresy that they created. Inquisitors treated heretics as if they were their fellow mendicants—methodical theologians who drew their ideas from authoritative texts—rather than a cross section of a complex society influenced by sermons and rumors, friends and lovers.

THE SPREAD OF PERSECUTION: ATTACKS ON THE JEWS

The drive against heretics and other enemies of Christian belief and society hardened attitudes against non-Christians as well. From the period of the First Crusade on, many Christians had come to view Jews with distaste, and sometimes charged them with the ritual murder of Christian children. In the late twelfth and thirteenth centuries, the pressures that Christians exerted on Jews grew heavier. Rulers sometimes protected Jews, partly or wholly to assess taxes on them, but such benevolence was not reliable. Philip Augustus expelled the Jews from France in 1182, and even though they were allowed to return somewhat later, the general expulsion was renewed in 1306 by Philip IV (r. 1285–1314). As Richard I prepared to join the Third Crusade in 1189, anti-Jewish riots broke out across England and Jews were massacred in London. Not long before Passover of the following year, the Jewish

Persecution of Jews An illumination from a mid-thirteenth-century French Bible shows lords or monarchs executing two Jews (kneeling at right). In the top left corner, Jesus looks down from heaven in approval.

community of York, alarmed by threats, took refuge in a tower of the royal castle. Besieged by crusaders, the Jews committed mass suicide. By 1218 England's remaining Jews were legally required to wear badges, and in 1290 King Edward I, who had made laws exacting special taxes from the Jews, expelled all of them from England.

FORCED SEPARATION Theologians—many of them Dominicans—urged Jews to convert, demanding that they defend their doctrines and practices in formal public disputations, the first of which took place in Paris in 1240. Copies of the Talmud, the massive code of Jewish law and belief, were confiscated and publicly burned there in 1242. In many communities, those who refused to convert were forcibly separated from the Christians among whom they had lived, in steady tension but also in productive coexistence, for centuries. Forbidden to own or farm land, Jews were required to wear yellow patches and other distinctive forms of dress, and to live in certain districts. The Jew was transformed, by force of law, preaching, and public pressure, into a greedy creature who lived by lending money—a vision that found expression in this period, for the first time in Western history, in caricatures of Jews portrayed with hooked noses and other features to identify them and express their evil characters. Lepers and prostitutes—though not representatives of a forbidden religion—were singled out as well for comparable treatment: a mixture of exploitation by rulers and cities, in the case of prostitutes, and confinement to houses specially built to keep them from spreading their contagion into the Christian world.

PERSECUTION AND SCHOLARSHIP From the heartless standpoint of the historian, persecution yields one unique benefit. Inquisitors and other specialists genuinely wanted to know as much they could about their enemies. As professional scholars and ordinary people grew increasingly hostile to their Jewish neighbors, they came to see Jews—reasonably, from their own theological standpoint—as caught in a web of superstition that had first trapped them when they refused to acknowledge Jesus. This refusal to convert when the Messiah came meant that Jews could not change, and those who claimed they had converted were suspect: their conduct was regularly scrutinized for signs of nostalgia for their birth religion. The French Dominican Bernard Gui explained that Jews resembled dogs and liked to return to their own vomit. Accordingly, Gui offered inquisitors substantive information about Jewish prayer books and rituals—notably those in which, as he saw it, they denounced Christians and other Gentiles.

Some of Gui's colleagues went much further. A fellow Dominican, Ramon Martí, became Europe's greatest expert, in his own time and for centuries to come, on the Jewish tradition. After scrutinizing Jewish biblical commentaries and the Talmud, Martí compiled a spectacularly learned book, *The Dagger of the Faith* (ca. 1280), in which he argued that the canonical Jewish texts, rightly interpreted, showed that Jesus was in fact the Messiah whom the Jews had expected. Only their obstinacy had led them to reject him and to falsify some of their own texts in order to pretend that he was not the Son of God.

THE CONFESSIONS OF BEATRICE DE PLANISSOLES

The same combination of fascination and fury that motivated Martí's feats of scholarship impelled another inquisitor—Jacques Fournier, who would become Pope Benedict XII (d. 1342)—to interrogate the last Cathars in the Pyrenees, early in the fourteenth century. As the manuals of inquisitors recommended, Fournier interrogated each suspect systematically, pressing for revelations of doctrine and fact. Their depositions reveal worlds that would otherwise have been wholly lost. The testimony shows that shepherd boys gossiped about God and the angels while tending their sheep in high mountain passes, and that ordinary peasant women might discuss theology in their little houses while delousing one another. One of the most extraordinary characters who come to life in these inquisition transcripts is the noblewoman Beatrice de Planissoles.

One man recalled her vividly, sitting by the fire with "two of her daughters of whom one must have been six or seven years old and the other 4 or 5, and several other persons," and musing critically about the Eucharist: "We began to speak of priests and the sacrament of the altar, which is the concern of the priests. Beatrice said . . . that she wondered how, if God was present in the sacrament of the altar, he could permit himself to be eaten by priests (or even by a single priest). Hearing this, I left that house very upset." Pressed by the inquisitor, a witness revealed the names of "the persons very intimate with this Beatrice, who would have known her secrets." After others testified, Beatrice finally confessed to heresy.

In her confession Beatrice claimed that Raimond Roussel, the bursar of her husband's estates and an adherent to Cathar belief, had urged her to leave her family and accompany him to the "good Christians." Only they, he explained, would be saved. Always a critical listener, Beatrice demanded that he explain "how can it be that God has created such a quantity of men and women if so many among them will not be saved?" Raimond told her of the charisma of the Cathar "perfect ones": "He said he himself had seen and met several of these good Christians. They were such people that when one had heard them speak, one could not ever leave them, and if I myself heard them just one time, I would be theirs forever." Fascinated, Beatrice rejected his approaches only when he hid under her bed and tried to seduce her.

Years later, however, Beatrice succumbed to another Cathar: the local priest, Pierre Clergue, who not only seduced her but "also knew me carnally one year on the night of Christmas and he nevertheless said mass the next day, even though there were other priests present." Clergue, she recalled, instructed her in the history of the cosmos and the souls within it, explaining as he did so why the Cathars ate no flesh. She laid out a full account of the Creation and the Fall, as Clergue had narrated them. He had told her that the spirits of the fallen angels inhabited animals as well as humans: "This is why it is a sin to kill such a brute beast or a man, because each one as well as the other has a spirit endowed with reason and understanding." After a period of imprisonment, she was condemned to wear crosses on her garments.

Beatrice's story—and those of the others condemned with her—come from sources that cannot reveal everything we would like to know. But they show that the lively world of religious speculation the Dominicans sought to fix in a single, absolutely valid set of arguments was not the sole province of professional theologians. Up and down the social scale, by the fires in village houses as well as in the faculties of theology, men and women actively debated the structures of doctrine that everyone recognized as one of the characteristic achievements of the day. They mingled intellectual speculation with personal lives of astonishing passion and complexity.

THE MEDIEVAL WORLD IN CRISIS (1238–1382)

The extraordinary society of the High Middle Ages—aggressive and argumentative, expansive and self-destructive—would soon meet the limits of its resources and energy. Encounters with a world outside Europe—from confrontations with nomadic warriors to invasion by plague bacilli—were only the most dramatic of the events that shattered many of the formative structures reared in the late twelfth and thirteenth centuries. Famine prepared the way for plague, and plague in turn for bitter new kinds of conflict.

MONGOL INVASION AND THE ROAD TO ASIA

The first clear sign of crisis appeared as early as the middle of the thirteenth century, when the **Mongols**, nomadic horsemen from Central Asia, streamed into the Christian world. Skilled archers, they used compound bows built up from layers of birch wood, horn, and bark, which could fire arrows through the strongest armor. Led by the brilliant tactician Genghis Khan (r. 1206–1227), the Mongols carved out an empire in the early thirteenth century that ran all the way from northern China in the east to the Caspian Sea in the west. In 1238, led by Genghis Khan's grandsons, the Mongols burst into Muscovy, a new Christian state that had taken shape in the thirteenth century. They conquered it in short order. The Mongols inflicted

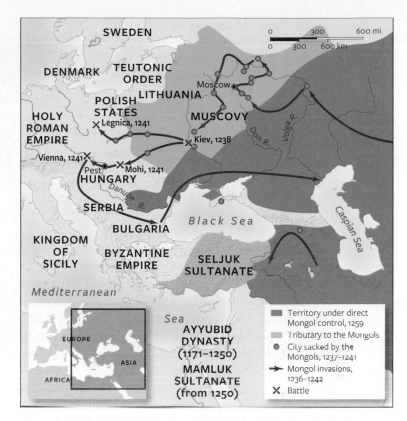

Mongol Incursions into Europe, 1206–1295 Genghis Khan's violent strategy of conquest quickly won the Mongols a vast empire, which within the span of only twenty years stretched from the Pacific in the east to the Caspian Sea. After Genghis's death in 1227, his successors pushed farther into Europe, conquering much of Muscovy and reaching as far as Vienna.

terrible damage on the Christian kingdoms of Hungary and Poland, and their forces reached as far as the gates of Vienna. No Christian army had been able to stop—much less defeat—them. Though the Mongols eventually turned back to Asia in the late 1240s, Europeans knew that they might have lost their autonomy almost overnight—as the Chinese actually did.

THE TRAVELS OF MARCO POLO The irruption of the Mongols opened Christian eyes to the vast, rich societies to the east, which they had never explored, much less tried to conquer, as they had tried to conquer the Islamic world. In 1271 Marco Polo (1254–1324), a young scion of a Venetian merchant family, set out with his father and uncle on a journey to the East—a journey that would take them along the Silk Road and, in the end, all the way to China. There, north of the Great Wall, they met the Mongol Kublai Khan (r. 1260–1294), emperor of China. Marco's father and uncle continued to trade, but Marco joined the khan's service. In the course of missions to southern China and Southeast Asia, he admired the greatness of Chinese cities and the calm and security of Chinese society under Mongol rule. Marco finally returned to Venice in 1295, after traveling some 15,000 miles by land and by sea.

While held prisoner by the Genoese, Marco Polo dictated an account of his travels to a Pisan friend, who in his turn produced a complex text, at once a granular, detailed travel account and a fantastic romance. *The Travels of Marco Polo* became immensely popular. Widely copied, illustrated, adapted, and read, this book and other travel accounts helped reveal to Europeans the true state of global economic and political affairs: that they occupied a relatively small spit at one end of the vast Eurasian landmass, the other end of which was inhabited by people far wealthier and more cultured than they were. The Dominicans and Franciscans responded to this enormous challenge by training missionaries and sending them along the merchant routes to try to convert the khan and his nation, a transformation that never took place. But they realized, for the first time that, as two Dominicans reflected during a five-year journey to the Arabian Sea and Ethiopia, "we who are the true Christians, are not the tenth, no not the twentieth of all men."

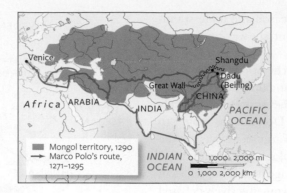

Marco Polo's Journeys, 1271–1295

SHAKING THE FOUNDATIONS OF CHURCH AND STATE

Yet even as the larger world opened up, some of the structures that had supported Europe's medieval revival and expansion crumbled. At the very end of the thirteenth century, Philip IV—the aggressive and brilliant French king who saw himself, in the old way, as a holy leader of a holy people—came into conflict with an equally aggressive and passionate pope, Boniface VIII (r. 1294–1303). Mobilizing for a crusade, Philip insisted on taxing his clergy aggressively. Eventually he arrested and tried a bishop, clearly violating the Church's canon law. The pope denounced Philip, and French jurists fought back. In April 1302, emboldened by a French defeat, Boniface revived and exceeded the most radical claims of his predecessors. In a bull—an official papal proclamation that took its name from the lead *bulla* ("seal") attached to it—Boniface declared the pope master of the entire world, lord over all kings. Philip refuted this claim in the most direct way: he sent an army to storm the papal palace at Anagni in central Italy and briefly imprisoned Boniface, who died soon after. Accusations flew against both sides.

Marco Polo This Spanish map from 1375 records the journey of Marco Polo and his caravan, including camels bearing supplies, shown here crossing a desert on their route through Asia.

Avignon Papacy A French chronicle from around 1370 illustrates the 1342 coronation of Pope Clement VI in Avignon. King Philip IV looks on at left, signaling the French crown's support.

TRAVELS OF MARCO POLO AND RABBAN BAR SAUMA

The networks of long-distance trade that developed in the thirteenth and fourteenth centuries brought Europeans new perspectives on their place in the world. The Venetian merchant Marco Polo (1254–1324) is probably the most famous traveler of the period. Though not everyone fully accepts the authenticity of the account of his travels (as dictated to Rustichello of Pisa, a popular writer of romances), the book is incontestably important because of its influence on European ideas of exploration and the East. Rabban Bar Sauma (ca. 1220–1294) was a Christian monk who traveled west from China to Europe at about the same time that Marco Polo was heading east. Bar Sauma's account of his journey, lost for hundreds of years and only rediscovered in the late nineteenth century, suggests how a Christian traveler from the East saw Europe in the thirteenth century.

From Marco Polo and Rustichello of Pisa, *The Travels of Marco Polo*

This excerpt from *The Travels of Marco Polo* (ca. 1298) describes lively commerce in the eastern Chinese city of Kinsay (modern Hangzhou).

[T]he city [Kinsay] is wholly on the water, and surrounded by it like Venice. It contains twelve arts or trades, and each trade has 12,000 stations or houses; and in each station there are of masters and labourers at least ten, in some fifteen, thirty and even forty, because this town supplies many others round it. The merchants are so numerous and so rich, that their wealth can neither be told nor believed....

There are within the city ten principal squares or market-places.... Each of these, on three days in every week, contains an assemblage of from 40,000 to 50,000 persons, who bring for sale every desirable article of provision. There appears abundance of all kinds of game, roebucks, stags, fallow-deer, hares, and rabbits, with partridges, pheasants ... quails, common fowls... ducks and geese almost innumerable; these last being so easily bred on the lake, that for a Venetian silver grosso you may buy a couple of geese and two pairs of ducks. In the same place are also the shambles, where cattle, as oxen, calves, kids, and lambs, are killed for the tables of the rich and of magistrates. These markets afford at all seasons a great variety of herbs and fruits; in particular, uncommonly large pears, weighing each ten pounds, white in the inside like paste, and very fragrant....

To give some idea of the quantity of meat, wine, spices, and other articles brought for the consumption of the people of [Kinsay], I shall instance the single article of pepper. Marco Polo was informed by an officer employed in the customs, that the daily amount was forty-three loads, each weighing 243 pounds.

From Rabban Bar Sauma, *The Monks of Kublai Khan, Emperor of China*

With the permission of Kublai Khan, the monk Rabban Bar Sauma (also known as Rabban Sawma) visited many cities in Asia and Europe, including Paris, where he met the French king Philip IV and viewed Christian relics.

Rabban Sawma and his companions remained for a month of days in this great city of Paris, and they saw everything that was in it. There were in it thirty thousand scholars [i.e. pupils] who were engaged in the study of ecclesiastical books of instruction, that is to say of commentaries and exegesis of all the Holy Scriptures, and also of profane learning,...and all these pupils received money for subsistence from the king. And they also saw one Great Church wherein were the funerary coffers of dead kings, and statues of them in gold and in silver were upon their tombs. And five hundred monks were engaged in performing commemoration services in the burial-place [i.e. mausoleum] of the kings, and they all ate and drank at the expense of the king.... In short Rabban Sawma and his companions saw everything which was splendid and renowned.

And after this the king sent and summoned them, and they went to him in the church, and they saw him standing by the side of the altar, and they saluted him. And he asked Rabban Sawma saying, "Have you seen what we have? And doth there not remain anything else for you to see?" Then Rabban Sawma thanked him [and said "There is not"]. Forthwith he went up with the king into an upper chamber of gold, which the king opened, and he brought forth from it a coffer of beryl wherein was laid the Crown of Thorns which the Jews placed upon the head of our Lord when they crucified Him. Now the Crown was visible in the coffer, which, thanks to the transparency of the beryl, remained unopened. And there was also in the coffer a piece of the wood of the Cross.

QUESTIONS FOR ANALYSIS

1. Which aspects of Kinsay's economy are most remarkable to Marco Polo?
2. What does Rabban Bar Sauma find most impressive about Paris?
3. How do these descriptions reflect the travelers' values as merchant (Polo) and monk (Bar Sauma)?

Sources: Hugh Murray, ed., *The Travels of Marco Polo* (New York: 1855), pp. 166, 169–71; E. A. Wallis Budge, trans., *The Monks of Kublai Khan, Emperor of China* (London: 1928), pp. 183–5.

THE AVIGNON PAPACY By 1309, the papacy itself had moved, under Philip's auspices, from Rome to the southern French city of Avignon. The **Avignon papacy** would remain there for almost seventy years, a period known as its Babylonian Captivity, during which it was constantly criticized for being overly wealthy, dominated by the French, and generally corrupt. Philip, for his part, also denounced another prominent Church institution, the Templars—one of the military orders that had formed to support the Crusades—as heretics and sodomites. Tortured, condemned, and expelled from France, the Templars also lost their property to expropriation by the French king. The immunity of the clerical estate would never seem absolutely safe again.

THE HUNDRED YEARS' WAR Neither, however, would royal authority. In the 1330s, after a long series of minor hostilities, England and France engaged in what would eventually come to be known as the **Hundred Years' War**. This exhausting conflict was rooted to some extent in the ancient claims of the king of England to the duchies of Aquitaine and Normandy and much other territory in France. But it had no single cause, and its nature and purpose changed from decade to decade. What is clear is that the war left both monarchies shattered and their countries devastated.

In the early years of the war, the English scored major successes. Edward III (r. 1327–1377) demolished French armies at Crécy in 1346 and Poitiers in 1356, and took the port of Calais in 1347. As always, war proved more expensive than anyone had expected. Edward had to renege on his debts, helping to send the Florentine banks that had backed him, the Bardi and the Peruzzi, into bankruptcy. In a second phase of the conflict, from 1360 to 1413, the British failed to repeat their early successes, and Charles V (r. 1364–1380), who modernized the French forces, sharply reduced the territory that the English held. Henry V of England (r. 1413–1422) started the third phase with a brilliant victory at Agincourt in 1415, where a smaller English force of dismounted men-at-arms and archers surprised the world by defeating a larger French army. Henry reconquered Normandy in 1415–20, but by the war's final battle, at Castillon in 1453, the French had permanently regained Aquitaine and Normandy from the English.

FAMINE AND PLAGUE

Even more devastating than the damage done by rebellious humans were the blows dealt by nature in the fourteenth century. In the spring of 1315 the seasonal rains went on far longer than usual. In 1316 rain fell steadily across northern Europe. Unusual extremes in summer weather—alternating between droughts and deluges—and terribly cold winters followed until 1322. Both dry and wet weather drastically hindered plowing. Crop yields fell sharply—so much so that in some regions peasants harvested less than they had originally sown. Fruit rotted on vines and trees. Sheep and cows died off, as the wet weather brought infestations. Droughts dried out the millponds and killed off vast numbers of fish. Horses and pigs survived better than other animals, but the horses were overworked and underfed, and pig herds fell in size as pork was substituted for other kinds of meat that were no longer available.

The poor weather made it difficult to transport food from more prosperous regions to those harder hit.

The Hundred Years' War, 1330–1453 Early in England's long war with France, it achieved several key victories, and by 1360 controlled more than half of present-day France. In later phases of the war, France regained control. Despite Henry V's famous victory at Agincourt in 1415, by the end of the war in 1453, England had lost almost all its territory on the Continent.

Famine In this illustration of the 1335 famine from a fourteenth-century manuscript, townspeople receive rations of grain in the street outside a church in Florence. The angel at the top declares, "I will make you ache with hunger and high prices," casting the famine as a divine judgment.

Warfare and piracy also hindered distribution. And efforts to impose price controls were more likely to encourage hoarding than to help the poor. The biggest cities—London, Paris, and the large textile-producing centers in Flanders and Italy—could import and distribute grain, and the wealthy could feed themselves. But the poor starved in large numbers. Accusations of cannibalism circulated, while collective prayers were offered across Europe until the seven terrible years of famine finally came to an end in 1322.

THE BLACK DEATH Then the plague struck. The travel and trade that was opening the Eurasian world also carried microorganisms to vulnerable populations. Rodents carrying fleas infected with plague were spreading the highly contagious disease in Asia in the 1330s, and by 1345–46 it had reached Muscovy. Borne, it seems, on the ships of Genoese merchants fleeing the Mongols, bubonic plague struck. This outbreak—known as the **Black Death**—was devastating. Bubonic plague caused painful swellings and hemorrhages. Europe's population dropped by 40 to 50 percent in the four years of the outbreak, from 1347 to 1350. Religious communities and other closed groups suffered even higher death rates than the general population. Historians once thought that contemporaries exaggerated the effects of the Black Death, but excavations have revealed urban graveyards with bodies piled five or more deep, as contemporary chroniclers claimed.

IMPACT OF THE PLAGUE The plague moved quickly enough that it could not be escaped, but slowly enough that most cities knew it was approaching them for weeks before it struck. Inhabitants could only wait, "frantic with terror," in the words of a contemporary. Nothing authorities or medical practitioners could do could cure or even alleviate the plague. Many thought that it signaled the beginning of the biblical Apocalypse. Fraternities of flagellants marched in public, whipping one another to demonstrate penitence. Across Europe, many blamed Jews for causing the disease by poisoning wells. Though Pope Clement VI (d. 1362) formally denied these accusations and the authorities tried to protect them, Jews in the Holy Roman Empire, Switzerland, and southern France were tortured until they confessed to their imaginary crimes, and entire Jewish communities were massacred.

The plague never seemed to end. Periodic recurrences,

Black Death A 1352 Flemish medical text shows townspeople burying scores of victims of the 1349 plague.

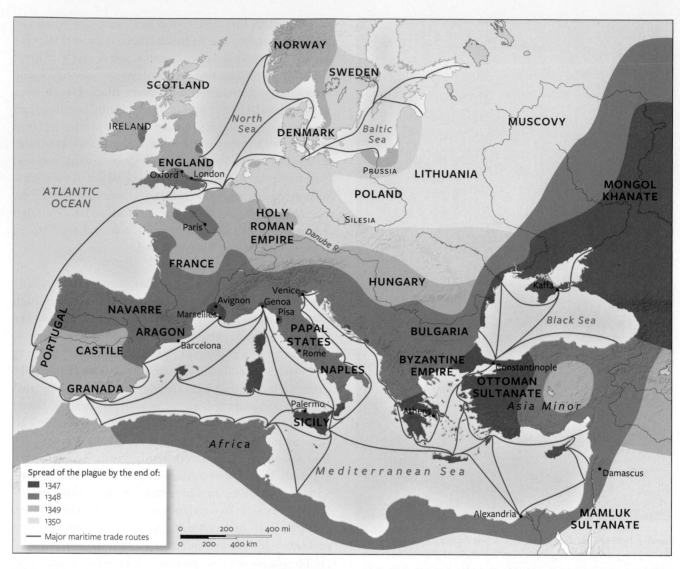

The Black Death, 1347–1350 The plague originated in Mongol-controlled Asia, but infected rats quickly spread it throughout the extensive network of maritime trade routes crisscrossing Europe. Within four years, the pandemic had spread from the eastern Mediterranean to areas as far north and west as Scotland and Scandinavia.

some of which caused very high mortality rates, continued through the fifteenth, sixteenth, and seventeenth centuries. Its last major outbreak in western Europe was the Great Plague of London, which struck in 1665–66 and killed an estimated 100,000 people.

SOCIAL UPHEAVAL

Massive outbreaks of human disease can, in some circumstances, benefit survivors, economically if not emotionally. Livestock, equipment, and capital generally remain, leaving some survivors better off. In the wake of the Black Death, however, the positive was difficult to

discern. Modern photography, archaeological surveys, and studies of the written record have made it possible to trace large networks of twelfth- and thirteenth-century farming settlements in the German lands and Britain that were abandoned forever after the plague devastated these communities.

ECONOMIC DISLOCATIONS The population collapse caused by the plague massively lowered demand for inexpensive products made on a large scale, such as the traditional products of the Florentine woolen cloth industry. Production in many other crafts fell as well, actually raising prices for goods even though fewer people remained to buy them. In the cities, masters responded to

The Jacquerie This chronicle (1475) illustrates a scene of mounted troops brutally suppressing the Jacquerie in the town of Meaux. The rebels' corpses are thrown into the river Marne below the town.

the dislocations of the mid-fourteenth century by making it much harder for journeymen to join their ranks, and by pushing wages lower. In the countryside, landlords fought to regain control of common areas and goods. In much of eastern Europe—especially Poland, Silesia, and Prussia—serfdom was reimposed on the rural laboring population that had so dramatically shrunk.

THE JACQUERIE

Violent responses followed in some areas. In 1358, shortly after the English defeated the French at Poitiers, the town's peasants, clerics, townsmen, and even some minor royal officials savagely attacked local nobles, furious at the defeat and the lack of protection from roving bands of soldiers and brigands. Called the Jacquerie, from "Jacques," the name that nobles applied indiscriminately to the poor, the movement was put down with brutal force.

WAT TYLER

In this same period, the English Parliament caused deep resentment by trying to use statutes to control the mobility of laborers and limit their wages. Then a series of three poll taxes enacted in Parliament between 1377 and 1380 to support the wars against France turned angry peasants into rebels. In 1381, enraged villagers in Essex, a relatively prosperous area northeast of London, attacked government officials sent to investigate tax evasion. Peasants in nearby Kent, just southeast of London, followed an able but otherwise unknown leader, Wat Tyler, to join their Essex comrades in a march on the city.

Another local leader, John Ball, a former Lollard priest, denounced the power and wealth of the Church. Sympathetic London artisans allowed the peasants to enter the city gates. When Tyler confronted King Richard II (r. 1377–1399) with demands for the abolition of serfdom and the redistribution of Church property, a scuffle broke out and Tyler was killed. Richard, only fourteen but thinking on his feet, told the peasants he would be their captain, and they followed him out of London. The king's professional soldiers then surrounded the rebels and sent them home, suppressing the Peasants' Revolt of 1381 with relatively little violence.

OLIGARCHY IN FLORENCE

In Florence, unskilled cloth workers had long resented their pay and working conditions. In 1345, shortly before the plague struck, a wool carder named Ciuto Brandini tried to organize them so that they could "more strongly resist" their masters. He was executed. After the disruptions caused by the plague, efforts to limit wages again brought crowds of laborers and poorer artisans into the streets. In June and July 1378, palaces were burned and city records destroyed. The brokers and subcontractors of the wool industry sided with the workers, and a new regime came into power. The laborers were allowed to form a guild of their own, but the cloth manufacturers closed their shops to put pressure on the workers. At the end of August, when the laborers again rose in revolt, the manufacturers and more established artisans joined to put them down in a short, sharp

Wat Tyler and the Peasants' Revolt In a French chronicle (ca. 1460–80), Wat Tyler, on horseback, leads a large army of armored men toward the king's forces. Both sides carry the royal standard and the English national flag.

outbreak of street fighting. By 1382, an oligarchical republic tightly controlled by rich bankers and wool merchants had taken power in Florence.

Short-lived though they were, these movements, like the heretical religious movements that sometimes intersected with and amplified them, spread fear and uncertainty, especially among those who ruled Europe's states and the Church, even as these elites put a stop to efforts by the urban and rural poor to improve their conditions by direct political action.

CONCLUSION

Fertile in innovations of every kind—from new ways of building and administering states to new ways of leading a Christian life, from new forms of economic activity to new kinds of literary creativity—the civilization of the High Middle Ages in many ways reached its own natural limits: its populations surpassed the ability of its agriculture to feed everyone; its cities surpassed the ability of its institutions to govern effectively; and even the Church encountered limits to its expansive authority. It collided repeatedly with those it considered heretics, and with the refusal of ordinary Christians to accept clerical leadership in all aspects of life. The great institutions of the High Middle Ages wore one another down in endless wars and confrontations, and their collapse might have taken place even if the plague had not arrived. Yet these institutions also laid foundations, as we will see, on which Europe would build again, as it began to move towards political and cultural expansion across the earth.

[CHAPTER REVIEW]

KEY TERMS

Dante Alighieri (p. 293)

Hanseatic League (p. 297)

Parlement (p. 300)

Magna Carta (p. 300)

parliament (p. 301)

common law (p. 301)

Pope Innocent III (p. 304)

Fourth Lateran Council (p. 304)

heresy (p. 305)

Dominican Order (p. 309)

Franciscan Order (p. 310)

Cathars (p. 311)

Thomas Aquinas (p. 312)

inquisition (p. 313)

Mongols (p. 315)

Avignon papacy (p. 318)

Hundred Years' War (p. 318)

Black Death (p. 319)

REVIEW QUESTIONS

1. How did the expansion of commerce help connect different regions in Europe, and link Europe and Asia?

2. How did the new urban economy change the way people worked?

3. What steps did cities take to break free from noble and clerical control?

4. How did European monarchies work to reestablish central authority in the High Middle Ages?

5. What were the most important legal and political principles set forth in Magna Carta?

6. What consequential reforms were made to Christian doctrine and practice by the Fourth Lateran Council?

7. In what ways did the papacy become more like a secular monarchy in the medieval period?

8. What were the most pressing problems facing urban residents in thirteenth-century Europe?

9. What methods did the Church employ to repress heresy and promote orthodoxy and uniformity?

10. How did famine and the Black Death affect European society?

CORE OBJECTIVES

After reading this chapter, you should have a solid understanding of the following core objectives. To strengthen your grasp of the core objectives, use the resources on the Student Site for The West.

- Analyze the growth of economic specialization and the cash economy of Europe in the High Middle Ages.

- Describe the culture and politics of urban life in the High Middle Ages.

- Describe the evolution of the medieval state in western Europe.

- Evaluate the institutional and doctrinal changes in the Church in the high medieval period.

- Assess the perceived threats to Church authority and the Church's response to them.

- Describe the crises that struck European society starting in the thirteenth century.

 GO TO **inQuizitive** TO SEE WHAT YOU'VE LEARNED—AND LEARN WHAT YOU'VE MISSED—WITH PERSONALIZED FEEDBACK ALONG THE WAY.

CHRONOLOGY

Renaissance Europe

A WORLD TRANSFORMED

1400–1500

I n June 1502, a Florentine civil servant named Niccolò Machiavelli (1469–1527) reached the military camp of Cesare Borgia (1475/6–1507); Cesare was the son of Rodrigo Borgia, now Pope Alexander VI. Cesare had been campaigning successfully in central Italy, where he was working, with his father's support, to build a state for himself. Having taken Bologna and massacred a group of mercenaries who had plotted against him, Cesare was now contemplating a campaign against Florence. The city seemed vulnerable in the wake of a political crisis brought on by invading French forces and the actions of a charismatic Dominican preacher, Girolamo Savonarola, whom the Florentines, acting under papal pressure, had arrested, tortured, and executed a few years earlier.

Machiavelli spent several months with Cesare, reporting back to the Florentine government on the twists and turns of Cesare's policies, doing his best to sniff out the military leader's secrets and to reveal none of his own. He saw that Cesare's rule, dependent on his father's support, was much more vulnerable than it seemed. On this basis Machiavelli correctly predicted that Cesare would not be able to attack, much less conquer, Florence.

1494–1517
Early Italian Wars
1494
Treaty of Tordesillas
1498
Savonarola is executed
Late 15th century
Leonardo da Vinci, Raphael, and Michelangelo begin their work

1508
Maximilian I becomes Holy Roman Emperor
1521
Cortés conquers the Aztecs
1492
Reconquista is achieved; Alhambra Decree
1492
Columbus's first voyage across the Atlantic

Renaissance: Art and War Around 1438–40, Paolo Uccello created this ten-foot-long painting of the battle of San Romano (1432) between Florence and Siena, a Florentine victory in the wars between Italian city-states that dominated the early fifteenth century. With Uccello's use of brilliant colors and linear perspective, the work is an early example of the characteristics that would later define the achievements of Italian Renaissance painting.

FOCUS QUESTIONS

- How were states changing the ways they organized themselves and competed?
- What were the dynamics of change in religious life?
- How did new technologies and skills enable Europeans to expand their reach?
- What were the major effects of first contact between Europe and the Americas?
- How did Renaissance humanism encourage new ambitions in European culture and society?

Machiavelli was playing a new game: professional diplomacy, as conducted by ambassadors sent abroad by their states to live with and report on foreign rulers. Both this position and the skills that Machiavelli brought to it were the products of a transformation in European politics.

The period in which Machiavelli lived, now known as the Renaissance, witnessed spectacular creativity in many areas of life. Europeans devised more effective ways of organizing and governing states, waging war, and making peace. They found their way by sea to Asia and the Americas, altering patterns of trade that had existed for hundreds or even thousands of years, and opening the Old and New Worlds to a transforming exchange of goods, ideas, beliefs, practices, and pathogens. They began to study the ancients in new ways that also reshaped their understanding of the world. They turned painting and sculpture into learned arts, and invented a way to print books instead of copying them by hand. Across Europe, borders and barriers fell as institutions and disciplines took on radically different forms.

Machiavelli himself helped to create both a new kind of state and a new way of writing and thinking about politics. His most famous and influential work, *The Prince*, rested on his own experience of states, including his own, undergoing revolutionary change, and on his study of the Greek and Roman classics. In this chapter, we will watch Machiavelli and his contemporaries begin to create what we can recognize as modern Europe.

RENAISSANCE STATES

In the fifteenth century, states of a new kind took shape across Europe. They developed permanent powers for raising revenue and waging war. They built civil services that could handle the large amounts of documentation, verbal and numerical, required to exercise these powers. Thinkers—many of them directly involved as civil servants—developed political theories that described, and made sense of, the changing political world.

ITALY: TERRITORIAL STATES (1454–1494)

In Italy, the centuries-long political decline of the empire and the papacy had left individual cities effectively independent. Through the late thirteenth and fourteenth centuries, trade rivalry and warfare had raged. Many Italian cities had been republics during the Middle Ages: independent communes inefficiently governed by local merchants and bankers, who appointed outside officials to preside over them. In the fourteenth and fifteenth centuries, most of these republican states came under princely rule. Noble families supported by mercenaries built their own tiny courts, which imitated the French and Burgundian ones. In some cases—as in Naples—these families claimed ancient dynastic rights. In others, they simply took power.

As city-states struggled against one another, weaker territories could not maintain their independence and consolidation followed. By the early fifteenth century, most of Italy belonged to one of five major powers: Venice, still rich and still a fiercely independent republic, ruled by a well-defined group of patricians; Milan, the center of a vast territory ruled by the Visconti family; the Papal States, ruled by the pope, who relied on them for his economic and military power; Naples, where a Spanish court dominated the large capital city and the vast agricultural estates around it; and Florence, which transformed itself gradually from a republic into a territorial state under the **Medici family**. Locked in competition for territory and power, all of them found their governments under pressure and developed new ways of coping with it.

FLORENCE In the late fourteenth and early fifteenth centuries, Florence was a republic in reality as well as in name—even if participation in government was limited to a small group of wealthy citizens. Day-to-day governance was handled by the Signoria, the group of nine officials chosen by lot for two-month terms, who moved into the government palace and made the vital decisions. Other citizens served rotating terms on committees that made the major political decisions, such as whether to go to war, and if so, whether to raise taxes. A small group of families that belonged to the city's most powerful guilds, dominated by the Albizzi, held enough of these offices to shape most decisions. Paid officials—especially the chancellors and their assistants—drafted the city's official correspondence with other powers, maintained the archives, and wrote histories and propaganda pamphlets.

Warfare tested this system to its limits. To pay its professional soldiers, the state had traditionally relied on taxes assessed on the basis of neighbors' testimony and informers' accounts—an inefficient system, to say the least. In the 1420s, Florence faced a vast public debt, the result of a war with Milan. To deal with it, the government created a wealth tax based on a systematic census of the city's entire population, carried out household by household. The records of the *catasto*, as this census was called, provided the Florentine government with a detailed understanding of the city's resources. Today, they offer historians a vivid record of family structures. They show, for example, that relatively few Florentines lived for very long in a patriarchal family dominated by an elderly male. Since men married late, they often died before their children were independent, leaving the children in families headed by mothers. In these circumstances, widows often steered their families' economic and political enterprises, achieving considerable authority.

Despite these reforms, Florence's republic proved unstable. Cosimo de' Medici (1389–1464), head of his family's bank, was a prominent member of the city's oligarchy. Exiled in 1433 for his part in a disastrous war against a neighboring city, he returned to take power a year later. Working largely behind the scenes as a power broker, Cosimo retained the committees that had traditionally ruled the city but manipulated the selection of their members in order to dominate them. During his twenty-year rule, it was still possible to believe that Florence was a republic in the traditional sense. Those who praised Cosimo in public wrote with deliberate vagueness that he had brought peace to the city, without discussing how. When Cosimo died, his son Piero (1416–1469) borrowed troops from his fellow ruler in Milan, lined the central square—the Piazza della Signoria—with them, and only then called in the citizens to hear a public announcement of his succession to power.

Cosimo de' Medici The Florentine painter Agnolo Bronzino created this portrait of Cosimo de' Medici, probably in the mid-fifteenth century.

Using the influence and resources of the Medici bank, as Cosimo had, Piero ruled the city effectively and defeated Venice in 1467—thanks to his alliance with Milan and the Papal States.

Cosimo's grandson Lorenzo (1449–1492) continued the Medici rule of Florence through surrogates who held the traditional offices. He behaved in some ways like a prince, holding tournaments and encouraging the prominent families of the city to build enormous palaces. When under his direction the Medici bank began to encounter serious difficulties, Lorenzo and his friends exploited state finances to maintain their incomes. Though officially still a republic, Florence looked more and more like such princely states as Milan, and Lorenzo himself like a ruler. Still, as he noted with pride, he and his predecessors had given a great deal to their city, spending 663,000 florins (a brand new palace might cost 11,000 florins) on taxes, charity, and building projects between 1434 and 1471.

One major enterprise continued uninterrupted

LORENZO GHIBERTI'S DECLARATION IN THE *CATASTO* OF 1427

The *catasto*, a census of the population and wealth of Florence, enabled the government to collect precise records of all households in the city, from the poor to the rich. The first survey was conducted in 1427 by ten officials and their staff, who interviewed the heads of almost 10,000 households. Each household's record lists property held, including land, payments received, and investments; other business interests; deductions for dependents; and debts owed, which reduced the taxable amount.

This record lists the possessions and debts of the sculptor Lorenzo Ghiberti as declared in the catasto of 1427, when he was forty-nine. His assets include balances owed to him for the sale of works, including one purchased by Cosimo de' Medici. His debts offer insight into the diverse trades in Florence's bustling economy. Ghiberti's taxable assets, valued at 999 florins[1]—worth about $42,000 today—assured his family a comfortable lifestyle, but his wealth was far from that of the top 1 percent of Florentines, who were assessed at upward of 10,000 florins.

[Assets]

A house located in the parish of S. Ambrogio in Florence in the Via Borgo Allegri…with household furnishings for the use of myself and my family…　0

A piece of land in the parish of S. Donato in Franzano…　100-0-0

In my shop are two pieces of bronze sculpture which I have made for a baptismal font in Siena.…I estimate that they are worth 400 florins or thereabouts, of which sum I have received 290 florins; so the balance is 110 florins.　110-0-0

Also in my shop is a bronze casket which I made for Cosimo de' Medici; I value it at approximately 200 florins, of which I have received 135 florins. The balance owed to me is 65 florins.　65-0-0

I have investments in the *Monte*[2] of 714 florins.　714-0-0

I am still owed 10 florins by the Friars of S. Maria Novella the tomb of the General [of the Dominican Order, Lionardo Dati].

Obligations

Personal exemptions:

Lorenzo di Bartolo, aged 46　200-0-0

Marsilia, my wife, aged 26　200-0-0

Tommaso, my son, aged 10 or thereabouts　200-0-0

Vettorio, my son, aged 7 or thereabouts　200-0-0

I owe money to the following persons:

Antonio di Piero del Vaglente and company, goldsmiths　33-0-0

Nicola di Vieri de' Medici　10-0-0

Domenico di Tano, cutler　9-0-0

Niccolò Carducci and company, retail cloth merchants　7-0-0

Papi d'Andrea, cabinet-maker　16-0-0

Mariano da Gambassi, mason　7-0-0

Papero di Mea of Settignano
Simone di Nanni of Fiesole
Cipriano di Bartolo of Pistoia }
(my apprentices in the shop)　48-0-0

Antonio, called El Maestro, tailor　15-0-0

Domenico di Lippi, culter　2-0-0

Alessandro Allesandri and company　4-0-0

Duccio Adimari and company, retail cloth merchants　8-0-0

Antonio di Giovanni, stationer　3-0-0

Isau d'Agnolo and company, bankers　50-0-0

Commissioners in charge of maintenance and rebuilding of the church of S. Croce　6-0-0

Lorenzo di Bruciane, kiln operator　3-0-0

Meo of S. Apollinare　45-0-0

Pippo, stocking maker　8-0-0

[Total of Lorenzo's taxable assets]　999-0-0

[Total obligations and exemptions]　1074-0-0

QUESTIONS FOR ANALYSIS

1. What does this declaration tell you about Ghiberti's personal life?
2. What do Ghiberti's debts and the balances owed to him suggest about the importance of banks and credit in Renaissance Florence?
3. What does the catasto suggest about Ghiberti's work as a sculptor and as a craftsman?

---

[1]**florin:** a skilled craftsman made slightly less than 1 florin for four days of work; a house in the upscale city center would rent for 20–50 florins per year
[2]**Monte:** a public fund

Source: Gene Brucker, ed., *The Society of Renaissance Florence: A Documentary Study* (Toronto: 1998), pp. 10–12.

throughout this period of institutional change: the city of Florence made itself the capital of a substantial state. Florentines proudly traced their city's origins back to republican Rome, and claimed that when they fought fiercely against the papacy in the late fourteenth century and against Milan and Naples in the early fifteenth, they were defending "Florentine liberty." Rather like the ancient Romans, the Florentines showed no reluctance to subject other states that had also been independent republics, such as Pisa, to their rule. Indeed, after the conquest of Pisa in 1406, the Florentines used it as a base for a state fleet of ten galleys. These ships made regular voyages between Florence and ports in the eastern Mediterranean, North Africa, and the North Sea, carrying Florentine wool and silk cloth to exchange for wool from England and spices from the East.

MILAN Although Florence offered the smaller states it conquered relatively little compensation, other Renaissance states offered their new subjects significant advantages. The Visconti, who ruled Milan in the late fourteenth and early fifteenth centuries, sponsored canal-building projects that eased travel and transport. They also subsidized the introduction of mulberry bushes and silkworms. By the later fifteenth century, rich merchants, mostly from Florence, created an independent silk industry. The Milanese government encouraged these foreign entrepreneurs to settle, and allowed them to import skilled artisans. In the middle of the sixteenth century, silk manufacturing was Milan's major industry, along with the production of other luxury goods such as tapestries.

VENICE Venice was also a self-governing republic ruled by an oligarchy: a small set of patrician families whose male members were eligible to sit in the representative assembly, or Great Council. Members of this body selected the doge, or chief of state, and elected the members of the smaller Senate and the Council of Ten, which did much of the work of governing the city. By the sixteenth century, more than 2,000 males had the right to take part in the meetings of the Great Council, ruling a city whose population was well over 100,000. Members of the Venetian oligarchy were expected to serve the city in multiple ways: representing Venice to foreign powers, governing cities that Venice had conquered on the mainland, or supervising communities of Venetians overseas. Few willingly left the city to serve. But those who did acquired knowledge about the world outside Venice, which they put to use in their commercial enterprises and in making laws and policies.

THE RISE OF DIPLOMACY: THE TREATY OF LODI
All of these Italian states, finally, developed a new way of conducting foreign affairs—one based on professional diplomacy, which would become a central institution in the rise of modern states. After a long series of wars and a transfer of power in Milan from the Visconti to the Sforza family had almost destroyed the Italian political system, Milan, Naples, and Florence made peace at Lodi, a city in Lombardy, in 1454. The Treaty of Lodi set permanent boundaries between Milanese and Venetian territory. Soon Venice and the Papal States also signed agreements with the other states. They pledged to maintain a balance of power, promising that they would all join in making war on any signatory that decided to attack another.

The Italian states devised a diplomatic system that they hoped could sustain this balance. They assigned resident **ambassadors** to one another's capitals: officials who

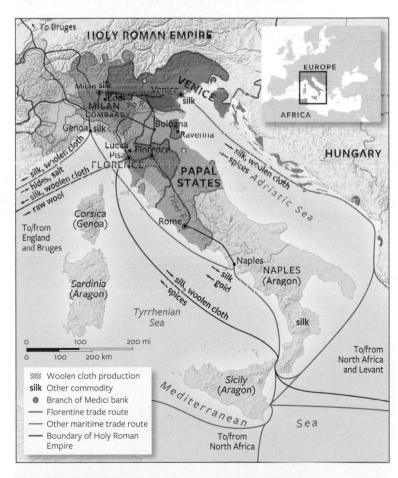

Italian States at the Treaty of Lodi, 1454 Despite their rivalries, the city-states that controlled the Italian Peninsula were tied together through mercantile relationships, with Florence at the center. The Medici bank had branches in Milan, Venice, Rome, and other cities, while Florentine trade routes conveyed luxury commodities such as silk from Milan, Venice, Genoa, and Naples to distant lands.

could represent their state's interests, gather information, and convey official communications. Governments developed systems for encoding dispatches to keep their communications safe and secret, and formulated rules for the treatment of ambassadors by hostile powers and during wartime. Diplomacy had existed for centuries, carried on by heralds and, often, through encounters between rulers. Now the Italian system of rapid interstate communication, run by political experts, gradually became a model for the rest of Europe.

Peace nevertheless remained precarious as limited wars broke out again and again. In 1478, when the Florentine Pazzi family conspired to assassinate Lorenzo de' Medici and his brother Giuliano and take over the state, the Pazzi had promises of help from the papacy and Naples. A mercenary captain in the papal service, Federigo da Montefeltro, was waiting outside Florence with his army, ready to move in and help the Pazzi consolidate their power. Though Giuliano was killed, Lorenzo survived the attempt and took brutal revenge on the Pazzi. The pope excommunicated Lorenzo, put Florence under the interdict, and went to war against the city with his ally, Naples. Offered little support by Milan, which was undergoing a political crisis of its own, Lorenzo eventually made his way to Naples, where, after a stay of months, he ultimately ended the crisis. In this case, as in many others, successful negotiations resulted as much from luck and determination as from skill. But in the sixteenth century, Lorenzo would be remembered—with some exaggeration—as the Magnificent, not only as a patron of the arts but also the master of balance-of-power politics. Italians had become—or so

many of them believed—the professional masters of politics, proud of the skill with which they manipulated powers both large and small to do their will.

MONARCHICAL STATES (1450–1494)

The Italians did not realize, however, that in the very decades in which they had been making politics into an art of feints and alliances, plots and proxy wars, the states of northern and western Europe had not only recovered from the crises of the fourteenth century but had developed stronger political and military resources. Improved military technology and large-scale forms of state organization gave them powers that dwarfed those available to the Italian states.

BURGUNDY During the wars that dominated the first half of the fifteenth century, as we have seen, the French royal house was challenged, for the last time, by the English, as well as by rivals of royal descent. These struggles left the French state weaker at times —and in control of less territory—than the rulers of some of its regions. The most important of these was Burgundy, a duchy in central and eastern France that was united by marriage, early in the fifteenth century, with Flanders and Brabant. These were the rich provinces of the **Low Countries**, the coastal region to the north and west whose cities, such as Bruges and Ghent, still ranked among Europe's most productive centers of industry and commerce. The Burgundians' French lands produced great wines. Their capital, Dijon, well located in eastern France, became a major trading center and the base of important commercial fairs.

For centuries, Burgundy had been ruled by branches of the same dynasties that ruled France—the Capetians and now the Valois. The last Valois dukes—especially Philip the Good (1396–1467) and Charles the Bold (1433–1477)— built Burgundy into a state that was, at its height, wealthier and more powerful than the kingdom of France itself, ruled by their Valois cousins. The Burgundian dukes pushed for independence, claiming prerogatives appropriate for a king. In 1423, for example, Philip the Good created a chivalric order—a small group of specially chosen noblemen, with their own meetings and rituals. Eventually Charles the Bold convinced the Holy Roman emperor to recognize him as the monarch of a separate kingdom, and had himself crowned. In 1465 he organized the League of the Public Weal—a group of powerful nobles, including the dukes of Brittany, Berry, and Lorraine, who demanded that the French king restore their ancient feudal prerogatives.

Federigo da Montefeltro In 1465, the artist Piero della Francesca painted this double portrait of Federigo and his wife, Battista Sforza.

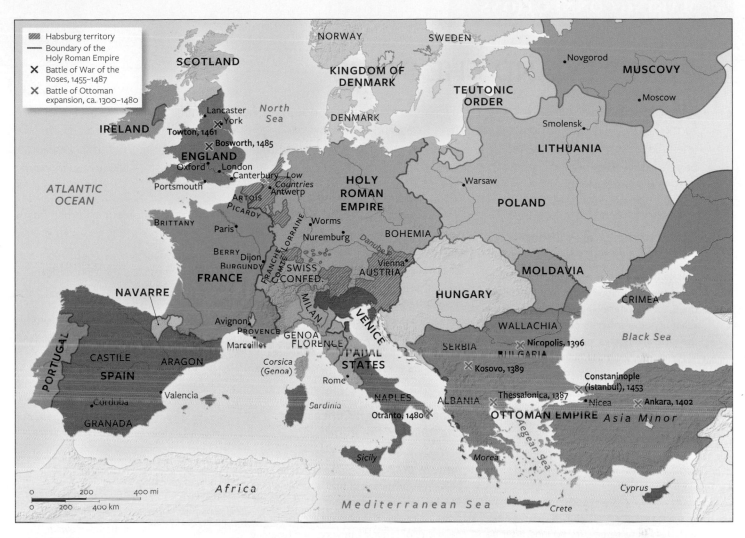

European Monarchies, 1492 By the end of the fifteenth century, European monarchs ruled powerful and stable states. Louis XI achieved sovereignty over most of modern-day France; in England, Henry VII unified the country after defeating his rival Richard III at Bosworth. Maximilian I expanded the territory of the Holy Roman Empire and established new Habsburg claims, while Ferdinand and Isabella unified the Spanish kingdoms in 1469 and completed the Reconquista in 1492. Meanwhile, the Ottoman Empire under Mehmed I and II expanded dramatically.

FRANCE Yet the French monarchy had great residual strengths. Through the hard years of the fifteenth century, as fragmentation threatened, meetings of the **Estates General**—representatives of the Church, the nobility, and the Third Estate of urban merchants and traders—helped to preserve and enlarge the sense that France was a single nation. Although this assembly sometimes resisted individual kings, it also offered the monarchy essential help. As early as 1439, the Estates General conferred on King Charles VII (r. 1422–1461) the right to collect a permanent tax, the **taille**, from all those who were neither clerics nor nobles, and use it to support a permanent military formation, the Company of Ordinance. The taille rarely brought in enough to support all of the crown's military needs, especially as mercenaries played an increasingly prominent role in warfare. The French kings supplemented their revenues with such problematic expedients as selling offices in the government, and the right to pass them on by inheritance. Still, the French monarchy had established its right to develop a standing army and to use the power of the royal purse to support it.

Louis XI (r. 1421–1483), known to his enemies as "the universal spider" for his skill at weaving webs of intrigue, managed to rebuild and extend the power of the monarchy. He made truces with most of his opponents, and when Charles the Bold, who unwisely invaded Switzerland, was defeated and killed, Louis dismembered much of Burgundy. In 1482, the Treaty of Arras gave him sovereignty over the historical duchy of Burgundy as well as Picardy, Artois, and Franche-Comté. An active ruler,

POVERTY AND THE STATE

Even as manufacturing and trade expanded in Renaissance Europe, poverty continued to afflict rural areas and cities alike. Farmers struggled against poor harvests, high taxes, and marauding bands of soldiers. In cities, abandoned children, the unemployed, and the sick begged on the streets. It had traditionally been the responsibility of the Church to ameliorate poverty, but as Renaissance states grew in scope and competence, people began to call on the state to harness its power to help the poor. The documents here address the problem of poverty in France and in Flanders.

Cahier of the Estates General, "The Plight of the French Poor"

This cahier, a catalog of grievances submitted to the king following the 1494 meeting of the Estates General, includes a plea for the relief of poor farmers from the demands of the taille and nobles' pensions.

When the poor labouring man has paid with great difficulty the quota he owes as tallage,' for the hire of the men of arms, and when he takes comfort in what is left to him, hoping it will be enough to live on for the year, or to sow, there suddenly come men of arms who eat up or waste this little reserve which the poor man has saved to live on....

While in the time of King Charles VII the quotas of the tallage imposed by the parish officials were counted only in the twenties, such as twenty, forty, sixty pounds, after his death they began to be levied by hundreds, and since, they have grown from hundreds to thousands....

Some have fled...others in great numbers have died of hunger, others in despair have killed their wives and children and themselves, seeing they had nothing left to live on. And many men, women, and children, having no animals, are forced to work yoked to the plough, and others labour at night out of fear that in daylight they will be seized and apprehended for the said tallage....

These things considered, it seems to the said estates that the king should take pity on his poor people, and relieve them of the said tallage and taxes.... And this they beg of him very humbly....

And may it please my lords who take pensions to content themselves with income from their own lords, without taking any extraordinary pensions or sums of money. Or at least if some receive them, let the pensions be reasonable, moderate, and bearable, out of regard for the afflictions and miseries of the poor people.... It is only the poor labourer who contributes to paying the said pensions.

Juan Luis Vives, "Concerning the Relief of the Poor"

In response to a request from the government of Bruges, longtime resident Juan Luis Vives proposed in 1526 a detailed plan for the state's improvement of living conditions in the city. This passage argues for the necessity of reducing poverty and teaching trades to the poor.

Surely it is a shame and disgrace to us Christians, to whom nothing has been more explicitly commanded than charity—and I am inclined to think that is the one injunction—that we meet everywhere in our cities so many poor men and beggars. Whithersoever you turn you encounter poverty and distress and those who are compelled to hold out their hands for alms. Why is it not true that, just as everything in the state is restored which is subject to the ravages of time and fortune—such as walls, ditches, ramparts, streams, institutions, customs, and the laws themselves—so it would be suitable to aid in meeting that primary obligation of giving, which has suffered damage in various ways?...

Some of the poor live in those institutions commonly called hospitals...; others beg publicly;...I call "hospitals" those places where the sick are fed and cared for, where a certain number of paupers is supported, where boys and girls are reared, where abandoned infants are nourished, where the insane are confined, and where the blind dwell. Let the governors of the state realize that all these institutions are a part of their responsibility....

Should the native poor be asked whether they have learned a trade? Yes; and those who have not, if they are of suitable age, should be taught the one to which they say they are most strongly inclined, provided it is feasible. If it is not feasible, let them be taught some similar trade....But if this trade is too difficult, or he is too slow in learning, let an easier one be assigned to him, all the way down to those which anyone can learn thoroughly in a few days: such as digging, drawing water, bearing loads, pushing a wheelbarrow, attending on magistrates, running errands, bearing letters or packets, driving horses.

QUESTIONS FOR ANALYSIS

1. What are some of the sources of poverty for French farmers?
2. How does Vives recommend reducing poverty in Bruges?
3. According to these sources, what responsibilities do governments have for the poor?

'**tallage:** the taille

Source: "The Plight of the French Poor," *Journal des états généraux de France tenus à Tours en 1484*, ed. A. Bernier (Paris: 1835), quoted in J. B. Ross and M. Martin, eds., *The Portable Renaissance Reader*, trans. J. B. Ross (New York: 1953), pp. 215–18; Juan-Luis Vivès, "Concerning the Relief of the Poor," trans. M. M. Sherwood, *Studies in Social Work* 11 (New York: 1917), pp. 10–11, 14–15.

Louis traveled constantly. He rebuilt the king's traditional council of advisers, adding professional jurists who extended the jurisdiction of the royal courts, and developed a system of post roads so that news and messages could be transmitted rapidly across his kingdom. He promoted trade fairs, supported the silk industry, and saw the potential of the Mediterranean port of Marseilles, which belonged to Provence and was united with France in 1481. Above all, Louis was good at outliving other nobles of royal blood and inheriting their lands. By the end of his reign, he ruled most of what is now France.

ENGLAND In the second half of the fifteenth century, England was divided by the **Wars of the Roses** (1455–87), a protracted local appendix to the Hundred Years' War named for the white and red roses that symbolized the two warring parties. England's ruling family, the Plantagenets, was divided into two separate houses, both descended from Edward III and thus both with a claim to the throne. The Lancastrians were led by the ruling king, Henry VI (r. 1422–1461, 1470–1471), who suffered from bouts of insanity; the Yorkists by Richard, Duke of York. After war broke out in 1455, control passed repeatedly from house to house. The Yorkist victory in the bloody battle of Towton in 1461 made Richard's first son king. Edward IV (r. 1461–1470, 1471–1483) suppressed Lancastrian resistance and captured Henry, but eventually lost the support of his chief adviser, the powerful and wealthy earl of Warwick. Known as "the Kingmaker," Warwick decided to replace Edward by restoring Henry to the throne, but Edward defeated his opponents, killed Warwick in 1471, and had Henry murdered in the Tower of London. In this period of warfare, Warwick the King maker was only one of many lords who hired retainers and built up their own military forces—sometimes, as in Warwick's case, to the point where they were able to challenge the crown itself.

When Edward IV died suddenly in 1483, his brother, Richard of Gloucester, seized the throne. As King Richard III (r. 1482–1485), he was an effective ruler with close ties to the city of London. He began to build new institutions—such as the Council of the North, an administrative body centered in the northern city of York—and to offer rapid and inexpensive justice through the Court of Requests. He also saw to it that the laws of England were translated, at long last, from Latin and French into English. But Richard was defeated and killed at the battle of Bosworth Field, in central England, by Henry Tudor, a Lancastrian claimant to the throne who founded the new dynasty of the Tudors.

Henry VII (r. 1485–1509), in his own way, introduced a

Wars of the Roses An illustration from the French historian Jean de Wavrin's 1471 chronicle of England shows a battle of the Wars of the Roses. Wavrin was from Burgundy, an ally of the House of York, which may explain the royal standards and white roses (representing York) that appear in the manuscript's margin.

model of kingship as novel as Louis XI's in France. Some of his policies were borrowed from the talented Richard III, whom he denounced as a usurper; others were created by his chief minister, John Morton, the archbishop of Canterbury. Henry relied heavily on the system of **justices of the peace**, unpaid local officials recruited from the ranks of local notables. They served for a year at a time, making them dependent on him for reappointment. Henry tasked them with overseeing the juries that decided cases, keeping public order, and ensuring that legislation was enforced. At the same time, he adopted new laws against "livery and maintenance"—the tradition by which powerful nobles had amassed armed retinues that amounted to private armies. These laws and the Court of Star Chamber, which Henry used to break the power of aristocrats suspected of plotting against him, established the monarchy as far more powerful than any potential rival.

In 1494 Henry engineered a boycott of the Flemish cloth industry that led, two years later, to an agreement favorable to British merchants trading in Antwerp—one of the industrial and financial centers of Europe. Over time, Henry became notorious for his demands for taxes and personal income. He went over financial records himself and annotated them in his own hand. And he used his gains not only to enrich the monarchy but also to begin the creation of a royal navy, with its own harbor, dockyard, and dry dock at Portsmouth. So in England, as in France, policies and institutions that would play essential roles in the creation of a modern state had their origins in the consolidation of monarchical power at the end of the fifteenth century.

HOLY ROMAN EMPIRE The Holy Roman Empire, which had undergone a sharp decline in power during the crises of the fourteenth and early fifteenth centuries, also began to recover. In 1440 Frederick of Habsburg, a member of the **Habsburg dynasty** that had long ruled Austria, was elected Holy Roman Emperor Frederick III, and in 1452 he was finally crowned by the pope. He married Eleanor of Portugal, establishing connections with other royal dynasties, and consolidated his power over the other members of the Habsburg family. Frederick's son and successor, **Maximilian I** (r. 1508–1519), was a true believer in the traditional codes of chivalry. He loved falconry and hunting, tournaments and chivalry—he famously took only 97 shots to bring down 100 birds—and nourished a special passion for splendidly decorated suits of armor.

Maximilian not only practiced the courtly arts of a medieval monarch; in some ways, he acted like one in politics as well. He saw himself not as creating a single, unified realm, but as pulling together multiple territories that he and his Habsburg successors could rule. Through advantageous marriages, both his own and that of his son

Maximilian's Power Artwork such as this 1526 woodcut by the printmaker Albrecht Dürer symbolizes Maximilian I's power and authority. The Holy Roman emperor and his wife, Mary, Duchess of Burgundy, ride a richly decorated chariot bearing a crest that represents the unification of their families. They are surrounded by admiring courtiers and mythological figures.

Philip, he established Habsburg claims over much of Burgundy, the kingdoms of Aragon and Castile, and Milan. Like the Italian rulers of his time, Maximilian believed in the powers of astrology and magic, and dispensed patronage to professors at Vienna whose predictions, he thought, could give him accurate information about the shifting fields of politics and war.

Yet Maximilian was also a modern prince. Lacking a single capital city and many of the other trappings of royalty found elsewhere, he wielded the powers of art and print—especially those of artists such as the brilliant Nuremberg painter and printmaker Albrecht Dürer (1471–1528)—to create images that emphasized the venerable antiquity of the Habsburg house and his own accomplishments. In an effort to create warmer support within the empire, Maximilian placed special emphasis on his German roots. In 1495, at a meeting of the Reichstag (the imperial general assembly) in Worms, he led an ambitious effort to reshape the empire, which was reorganized into a set of administrative districts and equipped, for the first time, with a supreme court. Imperial reform had only limited success, and Maximilian's early efforts to maintain authority over the Swiss and intervene in wars with the French elsewhere were unsuccessful. Nonetheless, he laid the foundations for what would remain, for centuries to come, the great power of the Habsburg family. The policy of creating alliances by marriage, at which he proved so successful, would continue to work well for his successors, and even gave rise to a famous proverb: "Let others wage war. You, happy Austria, need only marry."

SPAIN More dramatic still was the political transformation taking place on the Iberian Peninsula. In the fifteenth century, Spain had been divided into a number of states: chiefly the kingdoms of Castile, Aragon, and Portugal. From 1475 to 1479, Castile was torn by a war over succession, as France and England were. But the 1469 marriage of Isabella and Ferdinand, the so-called Catholic kings, connected Isabella's Castile, with its crusading traditions and military nobility, with Ferdinand's Aragon, the most economically advanced part of Spain. Valencia, a port city on the east coast of Aragon, had become wealthy in the fourteenth and fifteenth centuries as a center of banking, trade, and textile production. Politically, Aragon was oriented to the Mediterranean, and its rulers also claimed vast, productive agrarian lands in Sicily and southern Italy.

The energetic partnership of Aragon and Castile led to a renewal of the Reconquista, the effort, which began

Ferdinand and Isabella An anonymous fifteenth-century portrait depicts the Catholic monarchs of Castile and Aragon who united the Spanish kingdoms. They are dressed austerely, but wear jewelry that signifies their royal status.

as early as the eighth century, to restore all of the peninsula to Christian rule. The Reconquista culminated in 1492 when the last Muslim state—Granada, ruled from the magnificent eleventh-century Alhambra palace at the center of its splendid capital city—fell. The year 1492 also marked an end point for the Jews of Spain, who had long been pressured to convert to Christianity, and sometimes forced to do so. Now the **Alhambra Decree**, issued by Catholic monarchs Ferdinand and Isabella, gave Jews four months to convert or leave. Thousands fled, many of them to the rising empire of the Ottoman Turks. Tens of thousands of Jews converted to Christianity, but remained under suspicion of backsliding for decades to come.

Under Isabella and Ferdinand, each Spanish region retained its own name and individuality, and dealt with the crown through its own representatives, who met, as they had for centuries, in each region's Cortes. Still, a new system of government through royally appointed officers, the *corregidores* ("magistrates"), spread from Castile to the rest of the lands of the Catholic kings. Noble families cast their fate with the monarchy, serving—often for generations—as military officers and governors of settlements abroad.

The Spanish also developed their own formidable infantry, many of them professionals and veterans. They were organized in units called *tercios,* each with 1,500 to 3,000 soldiers armed with pikes, swords, and arquebuses, a new firearm. Their mastery of tactics and disciplined ability to dig in and repel attacks by formidable, numerically superior opponents enabled them to fight the Swiss and the German mercenaries on equal terms. Under the

leadership of Isabella's "Great Captain," the Castilian general Gonzalo Fernández de Córdoba (1453–1515), the Spanish became the most formidable army in Europe.

THE OTTOMAN EMPIRE

Even as the great monarchies of Europe were attaining new levels of political unity, a new empire in the eastern Mediterranean, that of the **Ottomans**, could muster even more resources than any of these Christian states. In 1261 the independent Greek state of Nicea, a remnant of the former Byzantine Empire, reconquered Constantinople from the so-called Latin empire established by the Fourth Crusade in 1204. The new Byzantine emperor, Michael VIII (r. 1261–1282), founded the Palaeologan dynasty and worked hard to repair the damage that had been done when the crusaders sacked the city. Michael also tried to restore parts of the ancient Byzantine Empire, but full restoration proved impossible.

Gradually, one of the small Muslim states near Constantinople, led by Osman I (1258–1326), began to expand. By the end of the fourteenth century, his Ottoman successors controlled most of Asia Minor. They had taken the ancient Greek city of Thessalonica from the Venetians in 1387, defeated the rival, rapidly growing Serbian empire, at the battle of Kosovo in 1389, and in 1396 routed a crusading army sent against them at the battle of Nicopolis in Bulgaria. They besieged Constantinople but were prevented from conquering the city itself when the Mongol leader Timur, who had already conquered vast amounts of territory in India, Persia, and Syria, invaded Asia Minor. Timur defeated the Ottoman sultan Bayezid I in 1402 at the battle of Ankara and imprisoned him. But Timur died only three years later, and his state collapsed.

Mehmed I (r. 1413–1421) restored the Ottoman lands and conquered new territory in Albania and the Crimea. Murad II (r. 1422–1451) and his son Mehmed II (r. 1451–1481) returned to the offense. The Byzantines appealed for help to the pope and the Latin powers. But the price of substantial aid was accepting papal primacy, and though the Byzantine emperor John VIII (r. 1425–1448) negotiated a union of the two churches, most of the Eastern Orthodox clergy rejected it. In 1453, Mehmed II conquered Constantinople. His soldiers killed the last Byzantine emperor, and after transforming the city into his capital, he went on to conquer the Morea peninsula (the Peloponnesus), Serbia, Albania, and Wallachia. In 1480, the Ottomans raided Italy itself. When Mehmed died in the next year,

Mehmed II This fifteenth-century Turkish portrait of the Ottoman sultan owes much to Italian artistic influence, particularly in the colors used and the subject's slightly turned pose. Yet his clothes and accoutrements—from the archer's ring on his right thumb to the scholar's turban—identify him as a Central Asian warrior and intellectual. The roses he holds in his right hand allude to his aesthetic and intellectual refinement.

still campaigning, the Ottoman Empire sprawled across much of Europe as well as Asia Minor.

Latin Europe knew that the Ottoman Empire was not only large but well administered. The sultans' special guard of Janissaries—boys taken from Christian families and trained to be professional soldiers—impressed observers with their loyalty to the ruler, their military skills, and their ferocity. The millet system—which allowed Christians and Jews to live in their own semiautonomous communities, with leaders approved by the state—kept the peace in the empire's massive European domains. Mehmed hired the best architects and artisans, Christian

as well as Muslim, to transform Christian Constantinople into the Muslim capital, which the Ottomans called Istanbul. Minarets were added to Justinian's church of Hagia Sophia, turning it into a spectacular mosque, and massive palaces and other public buildings went up rapidly. The Ottoman Empire was, in many ways, the most formidable of Europe's new states.

THE TRANSFORMATION OF WARFARE

Christian or Muslim, these new states acquired new kinds of military power. As early as the fourteenth century, the classic missile weapon of the Middle Ages, the British longbow, had proved its ability to decimate large armies of heavily armored knights. In the same period, European records begin to show the appearance of "fire-pots"—primitive metal cannon that used gunpowder to fire stone projectiles. The Chinese had invented gunpowder in the ninth century, and by the thirteenth they were using it in firearms. Knowledge of these devices reached Europe by unknown means—perhaps along the ancient routes of the Silk Road.

Between 1350 and 1450, guns developed in Europe with astonishing speed. Cannon—forged first of bronze, and then of iron—took multiple forms. Huge siege guns were made by expert iron founders such as Orban, the Hungarian Christian who built the cannon that Mehmed II used to breach Constantinople's legendarily impregnable walls. Smaller guns that could be pulled by horses or pivoted by their gunners also came into use, with devastating effect, on the battlefield and aboard ships. Projectiles themselves became more varied and effective, as metal balls replaced stones, and explosive shells came into use.

Poor regions—the cantons of Switzerland, the mountains of central Italy, some of the German states of the Holy Roman Empire—and areas torn by war such as England and France during the Hundred Years' War spawned professional soldiers, as landless young men left the homes that could not support them. Some mercenary units, such as the well-disciplined White Company led by the Englishman John Hawkwood (1320–1394), specialized in terrorizing civilian populations, burning villages, and destroying crops. Others—especially the Swiss—were skilled in fighting with long spears called pikes, with which they defeated the Burgundians in 1477.

Gunpowder gave these professional soldiers new possibilities. The arquebus—a muzzle-loading gun with a stock—became a standard infantry weapon. Aimed from

Arquebuses In an illustration from a 1517 German epic, opposing armies aim arquebuses at each other. In the foreground, a single soldier has wounded two enemy knights, indicating the new weapon's power.

the shoulder and fired with a new matchlock mechanism, the arquebus could penetrate the hardest armor at close range. Rulers soon realized that paid soldiers who could handle firearms could concentrate great force on their enemies. The king of Hungary built and trained a professional military force, the Black Army, from the 1450s on. Every fifth member of the force had an arquebus. Hungary and the German states became early centers of production, and during the course of the fifteenth century, the use of the arquebus spread from Portugal to Muscovy, a Russian monarchy that had taken shape in the late thirteenth century. Upholders of tradition hated these new weapons. Even more effectively than the longbow, they enabled men of low social position to kill their betters from a safe distance. Yet artisans such as Orban who built guns and cannon rose in stature—especially as illustrated texts about the new military devices began to circulate, and states competed for the services of the military engineers who wrote them.

The immediate impact of cannon, in particular, was dramatic. In Italy—where warfare was almost continuous in the fifteenth century—gunnery soon transformed the waging of war. The high stone walls that had traditionally protected cities and bastions against sieges proved too thin to withstand cannon fire. Within fifty years, Italian architects and their patrons had learned to replace the old style of fortification with a new one: low, thick walls of earth and stone designed to absorb the force of projectiles. These walls made it possible to resist a besieging army equipped with artillery. Projecting bastions served as gun platforms for defenders and enabled them to fire on attacks from the side. Ships equipped with cannon could engage in battle without having to draw alongside their opponents and engage in hand-to-hand combat. The European vessels that began to move outward into the Atlantic Ocean carried small crews, but they were far more formidably armed than any opposition they were likely to encounter, even in East Asia.

THE CAULDRON OF THE EARLY ITALIAN WARS (1494–1517)

The first to recognize how the political and military world had changed were the Italians—especially the Italian political classes—in the years around 1490. In 1492, Piero, the heir of Lorenzo de' Medici, succeeded his father as de facto ruler of Florence. Clumsier than the uniquely deft Lorenzo, Piero lost support in the city and failed to emulate his father in keeping a firm hand on foreign affairs. In 1494, Ludovico Sforza, Duke of Milan, worried that the Spanish forces in Naples threatened his rule, offered the French king Charles VIII (r. 1483–1498) free passage if he wished to take up the Valois family's ancient dynastic claim to the rule of Naples. Charles promptly invaded Italy. His massive army terrified the Italian rulers, who had honed their skills fighting on a far smaller scale and in less destructive and ruthless ways. Piero immediately surrendered Florence's fortresses to the French—only to find himself ejected from office and from the city. Girolamo Savonarola (1452–1498), a popular Dominican preacher, had reported visions in his recent sermons: he saw a sword over Italy, threatening divine vengeance, and Florence in triumph as the city of lilies—then as now the symbol of France. The invasion seemed to bear out his visions, and his prestige was enhanced when he helped to persuade Charles to move on from Florence without disturbing its inhabitants.

A believer in republican government, Savonarola used his influence to persuade the Florentines—split between wealthy patricians, many of whom still supported the Medici, and members of the craft guilds, who had been

Early Italian Wars, 1494–1517 The Italian Wars transformed the great powers of Europe and helped forge new, modern features of politics and war.

Christopher Columbus's sailors, broke out among them after they reached Naples. In 1498 the French invaded again, led by Charles VIII's successor Louis XII (r. 1498–1515). Though Sforza arrived with a Swiss army of his own, the French dispatched him easily. In 1501 Louis joined with the Spanish to conquer Naples. But they fell out, and the Spanish commander, "The Great Captain," Gonzalo Fernández de Córdoba, rapidly defeated the French. The Treaty of Lyon, signed in 1504, left the Spanish in Naples and the French in Milan. But the situation was highly unstable, and for more than five decades, the peninsula would be the site of what came to be called the Italian wars. This long series of conflicts established the modern form of warfare as a contest of professional soldiers armed with gunpowder weapons. Florence's republic, first put down in 1512, would revive for a last period of defiance from 1527 to 1530. In the end, the Spanish would control most of Italy, directly (in Milan, Naples, and Sicily) or indirectly.

The great powers transformed Italy, but they also were transformed by their experiences there. They learned to employ architects and build modern fortifications; to form and train a diplomatic corps and use it in the making of treaties and, even more important, the weaving of secret alliances; and to exploit propaganda of many kinds as a basic instrument of policy. By the 1530s, England, France, Spain, and the Holy Roman Empire all had chancellors and ambassadors who matched the Italians in craft and policy, but served their own, far more powerful states.

excluded from power and profit—to build a more open set of institutions than had been in place before the Medici took power. They preserved the traditional committee structure, but created a sovereign Great Council, in which more than 3,000 Florentines were eligible to serve—far more than had ever served actively in government before. Savonarola himself came into sharp conflict with Pope Alexander VI (r. 1492–1503). The threat of a papal interdict, which could have brought about the confiscation of Florentine goods everywhere, led to Savonarola's arrest and torture in 1498. He confessed that he had invented his visions, and was executed. But the republic he helped to bring into being survived him. Led by Piero Soderini, whom Machiavelli served as ambassador to Cesare Borgia, Rome, and France, the Republic lasted for another eighteen sharply contested years.

In 1494 French forces had moved down the Italian peninsula virtually unopposed—only to be driven back when syphilis, introduced by the Genoese mariner

Savonarola's Execution An unknown artist painted this picture of Girolamo Savonarola's 1498 execution by fire in the Piazza della Signoria in Florence. The cityscape includes the Palazzo Vecchio at right.

A new political and military world—one with distinctively modern features—was forged when Europe's revived territorial states were transmuted in the cauldron of the Italian Wars.

CHRISTIANITY: CRISIS AND REFORM

The papacy, once the most universal of European organizations, had lost power, resources, and spiritual authority during the thirteenth and fourteenth centuries. After seventy years of French domination in Avignon, the papacy returned to Rome in the 1370s. While in Avignon, the papacy had reorganized its central institutions, such as the supreme court of canon law, or Rota, and developed more efficient systems for collecting revenues. But its concentration on these practical matters had earned it a reputation for greed and corruption—one reinforced by its endless assertions of power over appointments to church offices (benefices), which were given out only in return for fees.

Antipope An illumination from a late-fourteenth-century French chronicle shows cardinals crowning the antipope Clement VII in Avignon.

THE GREAT SCHISM (1378–1417)

The return to Rome from Avignon was desired by many, from Italian members of the Curia itself to the influential writer Petrarch, who called Avignon "Babylon" and described the papal residence there as an exile like the Babylonian Captivity of the ancient Jews. Still, the return proved rough, even violent: the papacy waged war with Florence, traditionally a pro-papal city, over conflicting territorial claims in central Italy. And when the French pope Gregory XI (r. 1370–1378), who had brought the papacy back to Rome, died in 1378, the cardinals, pressed by the Roman populace, elected an Italian successor, Urban VI (r. 1378–1389). His conduct soon filled the cardinals with buyers' remorse. Urban insisted on the sole authority of the pope and demanded that the cardinals abandon their claims to a share of papal revenues. He called on them to live more simply and humbly, and continually abused them, exploding in fury at unpredictable intervals.

At the invitation of the French king Charles VI (r. 1380–1422), the French cardinals reconvened, deposed Urban, and elected Cardinal Robert of Geneva, who took the title of Pope Clement VII (r. 1378–1394) and set up his court in Avignon. Suddenly the universal church had two leaders, both apparently elected in the same way and by the same officials. Almost all of the Italian cardinals remained loyal to Urban. They declared Clement an antipope. Then the two popes excommunicated one another. For the next forty years, a period known as the **Great Schism**, Christians' allegiance was split, not between conflicting theologies but between two—and at one point among three—popes.

Much of Europe's business went on untroubled through this period. Bankers continued to transfer money and merchants to trade. Many Christians, having come to see the papacy as a purely administrative institution, paid little attention to which pope claimed ultimate authority over their sector of the Church, so long as masses were performed and the dead were buried. By the end of the 1380s, however, the Avignon church had increased its fiscal demands to even higher levels, while the Roman one campaigned to take control of Naples and southern Italy. The new Roman pope, Boniface IX (r. 1389–1404), became notorious for the financial pressures he exerted to maintain his political position. In 1390 alone, he excommunicated thirty bishops and sixty-five abbots for having fallen behind on the payments they owed the papacy for their offices. Savage attacks on the Roman papacy began to circulate, especially in northern Europe. More important, French clerics and theologians began to argue for other ways of defining the church. They identified it not with the pope but with the body of the faithful, represented by the bishops.

French kings and Burgundian dukes began to demand that both popes resign. A council held in Pisa from March through August 1409 declared both popes deposed for their grave sins. The popes struck back: they held councils of their own and eventually found successors. In 1417, at the **Council of Constance** (1414–18) in southern Germany, a Roman from the Colonna family, one of the noble clans that dominated the city of Rome, was elected Pope Martin V (r. 1417–1431). His international and financial positions were very weak. To gain the recognition of rulers and clerics across Europe, he had to give up many of his rights to bestow benefices and charge fees for doing so. His income amounted to a third of what his predecessors before the Great Schism had received. Accordingly, Martin used his local connections to begin the long process of reestablishing papal rule in Rome. From now on, there would be only one pope, and he would rule the Church from its ancient center, acting more and more like an Italian prince and drawing his chief power and revenues from Italy.

REFORM MOVEMENTS

Yet the Avignon Captivity and the subsequent Schism, together lasting from 1309 to 1417, had scratched and dented the aura of sanctity on which, in the end, papal authority rested. Signs of external resistance to papal authority accompanied these internal challenges. The English Parliament adopted the Statute of Provisors (1351), which prohibited papal interference in appointments to English benefices, and the Statute of Praemunire (1353), which forbade legal appeals outside the realm (i.e. to Rome). The latter also prohibited English subjects from obtaining bulls or other legal documents from the courts of the Roman Church, under penalty of expulsion from the king's protection and the forfeiture of property.

In England and Bohemia (now part of the Czech Republic), two vital centers of Christian culture, radical critics of the existing Church demanded that the Bible be translated from Latin and made available to all, and that religious services be held in the languages of ordinary men and women. Two theologians did much to form these movements. The Oxford theologian John Wycliffe (ca. 1330–1384) insisted on testing the institutions and practices of the Church against scripture. He found no support there for the idea that some Christians should lead a holier life than others as members of religious orders,

or for many of the Church's practices, which he insisted were superstitious. Jan Hus (ca. 1372–1415), trained in theology at Prague, was inspired by Wycliffe as well as by his own study of the Bible. He denounced the immorality of the clergy and the wrong doctrines they taught. Both men found followers.

LOLLARDS John Wycliffe's message spread rapidly, at first primarily in England. His followers, who came to be known as Lollards, included a few men and women of high birth and a much larger number of small merchants, artisans, and peasants. Lollard beliefs spread mostly through personal ties: spouses converted spouses, parents instructed children, masters and mistresses taught servants. Lollards believed that every Christian, women as well as men, should read and interpret scripture—and in many cases spent long hours teaching basic literacy to members of their families. On the basis of their reading of the Bible, they rejected the whole hierarchy of the Church, from the pope on down, and demanded radical changes in religious services. They held their own religious meetings.

An initial period during which Lollards found some support at the universities gave way by 1400 to intense persecution by the Church and the English state. When a rebellion in England led by the Lollard Sir John Oldcastle failed in 1414 and another effort was repressed in 1439, Wycliffe's followers ceased to be an active force for a time. Still, they made their own editions of the Bible in English, copying them in secret scriptoria, and around 1,500 groups of them began to emerge from the shadows.

HUSSITES Dissent traveled with surprising speed and found more fertile ground on the Continent than it had in Britain. The kingdom of Bohemia was the richest part of central Europe in the fourteenth century. Its ruler, Charles IV (r. 1346–1378), who would later become Holy Roman emperor, built Prague, its capital, into a metropolis with some 40,000 inhabitants. He spanned the Vltava River with a magnificent stone bridge, began a cathedral, and founded a university. The countryside was relatively rich, cultivated by free peasants. Under his patronage, the Church became extraordinarily wealthy, controlling a third of the Bohemian lands. Reformers began to denounce the clergy for their wealth and worldliness. Czech scholars who studied in England brought back Wycliffe's new message.

Jan Hus, a young theologian who copied Wycliffe's works, developed his own reforming program, which he expounded in eloquent sermons. He believed that all lay Christians should join clerics in partaking of the wine

Jan Hus's Heresy In this fifteenth century manuscript illustration, a priest looks on as men—some stern, others celebratory—stoke the flames burning Hus at the stake. Hus wears the robe of a dissident cleric, while the sign on his hat condemns him as a heretic.

and bread during Communion, and that the Church must reform itself by giving up most of its wealth and power. At first, he found support from every level of the population, from nobles to artisans and peasants. Although a relative moderate who hoped to persuade the authorities to carry out necessary changes, Hus was imprisoned and condemned by the Council of Constance. In 1415 he was burned at the stake for heresy.

Hus's death turned his movement into a revolution. Hussites in Prague, most of them craftsmen, threw German nobles from the windows of the city hall in the Czech part of the city, and destroyed religious images and relics. Artisans and peasants in southern Bohemia, frightened by outbreaks of the Black Death, saw this movement as the beginning of the end of the world. They took up residence in a fortress south of Prague, to which they gave the biblical name Mount Tabor. Traveling when necessary in wagon trains that could be chained together in fortified camps, they abandoned all distinctions of clothing between priests and laypeople, demanded the abolition of courts and oaths, and fought off the crusades that the papacy sent against them. In 1434 the Taborites were defeated by more moderate Hussites, who negotiated a compromise treaty with the Latin Church, which allowed them to read their scriptures and practice their rites so long as they formally acknowledged papal supremacy. The wealth and power of the Church in Bohemia remained

greatly diminished, and the Hussites were allowed to use their own liturgy and give Communion with both bread and wine: a powerful exception to the long-established unity of the Latin Church.

CONCILIARISTS (1409–1449) Through the first decades of the fifteenth century, reforming cardinals and theologians, concerned about these threats to the Church as well as the problems of papal governance, continued to call councils. As early as the thirteenth century, some theologians—worried by increasing papal power and the possibility that its holder might become a heretic—theorized that although the pope was the steward of God, those who had elected him on behalf of the Christian people could also depose him when necessary. During the Great Schism, advocates of the councils—in later years they came to be called Conciliarists—argued that a representative body composed of cardinals, bishops, and others should hold supreme authority in the Church. The Council of Constance decreed that the authority of the council, since it came directly from God, was binding on all Christians, even the pope. Further councils met in Basel, Switzerland; Florence; and Ferrara, Italy, in the 1430s. All of these efforts, though attended with much powerful rhetoric and supported by some sincere believers, ran into the sand. Pope Pius II (r. 1458–1464), an Italian scholar and onetime Conciliarist, gained firm control of the Church in 1458 after he turned back a conspiracy of cardinals who hatched a plot against him in the Vatican lavatory, where they had gathered in the hope of electing a weaker Frenchman. Yet the papacy had lost much ground.

ORTHODOXY IN OTTOMAN LANDS Long before Pius became pope, he insisted that the whole Christian church was really one, and that Catholics had a duty to help the Orthodox Christians of Byzantium defend themselves against the Ottomans. Serious efforts were made to reunite the Greek and Russian Orthodox Churches with the Roman Church. At the Council of Florence in 1439, prelates from both eastern churches signed an act of union with Rome. But Vasily II (r. 1425–1462), the Grand Prince of Moscow, rejected the agreement. And though the Byzantine emperor John VIII Palaeologus accepted the union, the clergy and monks of the Greek Orthodox Church never did.

After Constantinople fell to the Ottomans in 1453, Pius proclaimed a crusade to retake the city. A brilliant writer of Latin, he did his best to appeal to all of the mixed groups of Europeans who held power and might take part, from feudal lords in northern Europe to merchants in Italy.

But only a small crusading force arrived in the port of Ancona on the eastern coast of Italy, most of which dissipated when the promised transport was slow to arrive. Pius himself died of fever, but the crusading ideal lived on, revived again and again, especially as Christian propaganda against the Ottomans.

A measure of coexistence developed in the Ottoman lands, where the Orthodox Church adapted to surviving under Muslim rule. Granted authority over all its churches and their property, the patriarchate of Constantinople was reestablished by Mehmed II in 1454 and conferred on a reliably anti-Catholic cleric. For centuries to come, the Greek Orthodox Church survived within the larger Ottoman framework. The Orthodox clergy were left in charge of powerful institutions, such as their many wealthy and massive monasteries. Gradually the Church was charged with legal as well as religious power over all of the sultan's Christian subjects. The patriarch collected taxes from Christians for the sultan, and handled all legal cases connected with marriage, divorce, or commercial relations between Christians and Muslims in the Ottoman lands.

"APPETITE FOR THE DIVINE"

The vast majority of western Europeans continued to be faithful Catholics, as their ancestors had been. If anything, in fact, they were more faithful than the generations that immediately preceded them. Most Christians made their yearly confession, attended their church each week, and followed the rituals of the Christian year, relatively austere in summer and fall but crammed with feast days in winter and spring. They attended the Latin Mass that was sung for them by cathedral or parish clergy, and viewed the stories of the Old and New Testaments rendered in sculpture, tapestry, or stained glass.

People who were neither rich nor saintly still showed—as the great French historian Lucien Febvre once remarked—a "boundless appetite for the divine." Plays and rituals based on the Bible continued to be staged before broad audiences. **Confraternities** (lay religious organizations) promoted active pursuit of Christian virtue in many ways. Hundreds of them flourished across Europe, especially in cities. Counting women as well as men as members, their activities ran the gamut, from doing penance together by flagellation, to visiting the sick, accompanying the condemned to execution, and writing letters to Saint Peter recommending fellow members, with whom they were buried.

A few saints continued to walk the streets, their

Christian Confraternities Members of the Florentine Compagnia dei Buonomini confraternity distribute clothes to the poor in this late-fifteenth-century fresco by the artist Domenico Ghirlandaio.

sanctity recognized by all. In the mid-fifteenth century, Rome was still largely vacant, with no more than 40,000 inhabitants wandering its streets and squares. Courtesans and merchants selling pilgrims' badges and other mementoes from small shops and outdoor tables crowded around the great Roman churches. Mingling among them was Saint Francesca Romana (1384–1440), the mystic who followed the course charted by her medieval predecessors as she made the ascent to spiritual union with God. Francesca had vivid visions and revelations, and worked, with the efficiency that only mystics and other supremely single-minded individuals enjoy, to create a hospital and a confraternity. She enjoyed such prestige that her very presence on the dark, violent streets of Rome could bring an end to feuds and, supposedly, heal mortal wounds.

NEW DIRECTIONS IN RELIGIOUS LIFE

Impresarios of the sacred created new ways of living a Christian life as deftly as Francis and Dominic had in the thirteenth century, when they called the mendicant orders into being. The Dutch cleric Geert Groot (1340–1384) founded houses for men and women who called themselves the Brothers and Sisters of the Common Life. They lived together, not taking vows. All of them—aristocrats and artisans, rich women and poor—worked for their living with their hands, in order to pursue poverty in a simpler, more literal way than that practiced by the powerful religious orders. Some members of this movement worked at first as scribes, then became printers when the new technology reached their city, using it to provide prayers and meditations for readers who shared their desire for a simple piety.

BEGUINES Across Europe, women experimented with new ways of life, inspired by religion. In the thirteenth century, beguines appeared in French and Netherlandish cities: women who lived in their own houses or in communities without taking vows, dressed simply, and did not marry. In the fourteenth and fifteenth centuries, beguine residences in Bruges and other cities in the Low Countries grew as women from poorer families joined, expanding into large courtyards lined by tiny houses in which the women lived. In the same period, religious houses of women living communally, but without a rule or, in some cases, male supervision, appeared in every Italian city. A new literature took shape: lives of the sisters who had created the houses and treatises on contemplation, written by and for women.

DEPARTURES FROM SCHOLASTICISM The energies of the Church went in other directions as well. In the twelfth and thirteenth centuries, scholastic theology had been a specialty of the universities of northern and western Europe. From the middle of the fourteenth century on, however, the effort to arrive at fundamental truths about God and the universe by formal argument spread into new parts of Europe. From Spain to Bohemia to Scotland, new universities popped up. And theologians were beginning to challenge the beautiful, coherent structures of doctrine that scholastics such as Thomas Aquinas had reared.

The Franciscan Roger Bacon (ca. 1214–ca. 1292), originally trained at Oxford, became an influential teacher at Paris in the mid-thirteenth century. He revised the scholastic program in multiple ways. It was wrong, he argued, to content oneself with word-for-word Latin translations from Aristotle, often hard to understand and sometimes inaccurate. Theologians must study Greek and other languages in which important forms of knowledge were preserved, and learn to read texts critically and correct them—or declare them spurious—when necessary. A believer in astrology, which he thought explained the course of world history, Bacon was also an engaged empiricist who devised experiments with lenses and argued that the university scholar needed to study the practical men who had learned to steer ships using a magnetic compass. In some ways, Bacon called for a return to the world of Aristotle and the Alexandrian scholars who had combined the study of texts with practical investigation of nature,

or that of the earlier House of Wisdom. But he believed that even more could be done. Someday, he claimed, magnificent technologies unknown in his day would make it possible for men to fly and transmute metals.

More radical, in some ways, than Bacon—and more influential in their time—was another Franciscan, William of Occam (ca. 1287–1347). Thomas Aquinas had believed, in a tradition going back to Plato, that general terms such as *beauty* and *goodness* referred to ideal forms that actually existed somewhere in the universe. Occam denied the existence of such abstract entities, and insisted that human language and argument could never prove the existence and justice of God. Fifteenth-century theologians took up and continued the debate between Occam and Aquinas; some shared Bacon's interest in astrology. And as the weighty issues about the structure of the Church and the location of its authority became the subjects of long, impassioned debates in the era of schism and councils, the French Conciliarist Jean Gerson and others began to devise ways of treating theological questions in shorter, more accessible forms such as pamphlets, which could be read by anyone literate, even if he or she did not have formal training in theology.

WITCHCRAFT: THEORY AND PRACTICE The most fertile of all the late-medieval approaches to the scholastic form of argument, tragically, was taken by German Dominicans. Since antiquity, Christians had determined that the devil not only existed but also regularly intervened in everyday life, hoping to lure Christians to their damnation and drawing on the help of lower devils. They had also accepted that some humans were witches—magicians who invoked the help of the devil to cast spells. But the theologians of the fifteenth century applied their full methods—for the first time—to the scattered anecdotes and sometimes-contradictory laws about witchcraft. They developed a coherent theory, which they laid out in systematic, cogently presented treatises. Devils, they argued, really walked the earth. They were replicas of human beings, which could take either male or female form and could speak and act. In their male form, they seduced human women, whom they persuaded to join the legions of the evil and to conjure harm by killing babies, drawing down hailstorms to destroy crops, and rendering men impotent. Worst of all, they produced diabolic offspring by injecting women with corrupted sperm that, in their female form, they had drawn from men they seduced. Every time a wife failed to conceive, a baby died in childbirth, crops failed, or livestock died, a witch might be to blame—and the devil with her.

Dominican theologians believed that only subtle, trained interrogators—backed, as always, by the threat and application of torture—could wring the truth from these enemies of the human race, avert their efforts to seduce their accusers, and combat the terrifying threat they represented. By the end of the fifteenth century, the first large witch trials were being held in Germany, Switzerland, and Italy. True, the real rage for holding them did not catch on until after 1560 or so, when a series of trials began that would eventually take some 30,000 to 70,000 lives across Europe, the majority of them female. But the belief in a conspiracy to destroy mankind—as neat and logical in its own way as the universe that Aquinas had built—made sense in a precarious world where plague endlessly returned and death threatened humans and animals alike. Every Christian baby, after all, was exorcized to remove the corruption of the devil before being baptized—a practice not abandoned until a Church council ended it in the 1960s. It made sense—the specialty of the scholastic theologian—to take seriously the idea of diabolic intervention in the world, and to draw out all of the ramifications it might have, one by one.

PERSECUTION OF NON-CHRISTIANS If witches did not materialize immediately on cue, however, other enemies did. In Trent, on the border between Italy and the Holy Roman Empire, Jews were accused in 1475, as they had been for centuries, of murdering Christian boys to use their blood for ritual purposes; several were condemned and executed. Further ritual-murder trials spread across the German world, and Jews were ejected from cities such as Regensburg, where they had lived since Roman times. The Jews of Spain, as we have seen, were forced in 1492 to convert or leave the country. In Italy, Jews were forced, far more systematically than ever before, to wear yellow patches—and in the case of women, earrings—to set them apart from Christians. Gradually they were confined to small, closed neighborhoods known as ghettos. Small groups of Ashkenazi Jews from western Europe and much larger communities of Sephardic Jews expelled from Spain and Portugal settled in cities across the Ottoman Empire, from Istanbul and Salonika in northern Greece to Jerusalem and Safed in Palestine. Like Orthodox Christians, the Jews lived as a protected nation in the Ottoman Empire, and many flourished in trade and banking.

Meanwhile, officials in Spain became increasingly expert in working out which supposed Christians not only had Jewish ancestors but continued to observe certain Jewish rituals, and which Moriscos, as Muslim converts were called, did the same with their traditions.

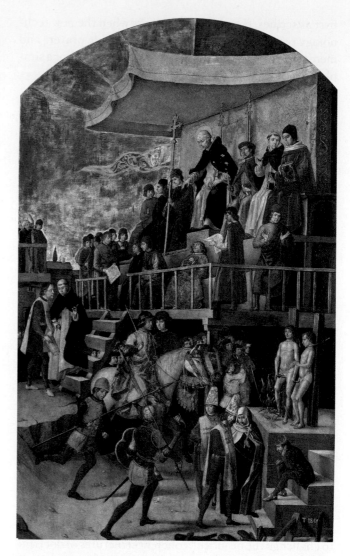

The Spanish Inquisition After ferreting out heretics, the Inquisition tribunal would pronounce judgment in a ceremony called the *auto da fé* (Portuguese for "act of faith") that would often include a procession, a mass, and a reading of the sentence in the town's piazza. Secular authorities would then carry out the sentence. In 1499, the tribunal asked painter Pedro Berruguete to depict Saint Dominic, the founder of the Dominican order, presiding over an *auto da fé*, as proof that the practice was a holy one.

From 1478, moreover, an official tribunal, the Spanish Inquisition, made the detection of crypto-Jews and, to a lesser extent, Moriscos its central business. Close inspection of genealogies and behavior, from eating to praying, enabled the inquisitors to detect the enemies of humanity. Modernity—as the history of the twentieth century shows—has brought with it both horrors and enlightenment. Both were amply present at the birth of the modern world, from the European settlements in the Iberian Peninsula to the heartlands of Catholic culture.

EUROPE EXPANDS: NEW TECHNOLOGIES AND THEIR CONSEQUENCES

Renaissance Europe was born under the signs of contraction and despair. The Black Death had devastated Europe in the mid-fourteenth century, and recurrences of the plague kept population levels low into the fifteenth century. And yet, beneath the turbulence, as we have seen in the areas of state formation and religion, Europeans were laying the foundations for recovery and transformation. The paired discoveries of a new world and an ancient past brought changes more startling than anything Europe—or the world—had previously experienced.

MARITIME ADVANCES

Even after 1453, when the Venetians lost the immense foothold in the eastern Mediterranean that Constantinople had provided, they and the Genoese continued to expand their mercantile empires. Venetian fleets, developed by state action, and Genoese ones, normally financed by private partnerships, ranged the Mediterranean. Venetians, Genoese, and other European mariners, moreover, continued to develop new techniques.

Although no one knows who invented the maps known as **portolan charts**, which came into widespread use in the fourteenth and fifteenth centuries, they were practical in a way that the scholars' schematic maps never had been. Portolan charts detailed the coastlines where European merchants mingled with the Asian and North African merchants with whom they could bargain for gold, spices, and silks. The new maps largely ignored the mainland interiors that Ptolemy and his Greek copyists had filled with rivers, mountains, and cities. Instead the maps traced, with ever-increasing precision, the primary routes that led from port to port. Equipped with portolans—and with magnetic compasses, the floating lodestones that also came into widespread use in the fourteenth and fifteenth centuries—European merchants could explore more widely than ever before.

The ships themselves, moreover, became capable of undertaking longer journeys. Alongside the low galleys, powered by oars and a single square sail, that had plied the Mediterranean since ancient times, new types of ships were developed with three or four masts. Equipped with complex rigging, they could both sail into the wind and tack before it, and could carry larger cargoes.

Portolan Charts New cartographic technology allowed navigators to follow the routes between ports. This fifteenth-century portolan chart of Italian trade routes includes illustrations of Venice and Genoa.

Caravels—small, slender, and maneuverable—navigated shallow coastal waters and explored rivers. Carracks—larger, with high, rounded sterns—were more stable and could carry more goods. The Europeans who sailed these ships mastered new navigation techniques. They learned, for example, that the Atlantic winds blew steadily back to the east. To return to Europe, ships entering the Atlantic from the Mediterranean or the western coastlines of Europe had to keep sailing west until they caught the wind, which brought them home.

EARLY ATLANTIC EXPEDITIONS

Support for these expeditions into the unknown came from more than one source. Henry the Navigator (1394–1460), fifth son of the king of Portugal, joined his father and brothers in 1415 in an attack on the Spanish city of Ceuta on the Moroccan coast, a convenient base for raids on Portugal across the narrow Strait of Gibraltar. Their success in taking the city encouraged Henry to organize

Henry the Navigator The Portuguese prince appears in a detail from a 1465 painting that shows the most important members of Portuguese society venerating Saint Vincent—hence Henry's pious posture and expression.

a series of further expeditions, which gradually pushed down the western coast of Africa and westward into the Atlantic. He was impelled by the hope of joining forces with a Christian ally in Africa, the king of Ethiopia, whose wealth and power were exaggerated by European reports. But possibilities of profit were also attractive.

The spice trade brought Europeans not only the sharp flavorings they demanded for their food but also a wider range of products, including such substances as opium, mummy (an aromatic exuded by embalmed bodies), and tutty (dried chimney scrapings), which were used in medicine. It yielded immense profits to the Muslim merchants who brought products to India and then across the Persian Gulf and Red Sea, where land routes continued to Europe. Venice had dominated the western end of these routes in the Mediterranean, but once Constantinople fell in 1453, the Ottomans controlled the trade and could raise taxes at will. Was it possible, the Portuguese and others now began to ask, to sail around Africa to reach the sources of spice directly?

By the beginning of the fifteenth century, the new techniques and vessels carried Spanish and Portuguese sailors and traders farther and farther from the known Mediterranean routes. Both groups found and settled massive island chains in the Atlantic: the Portuguese took the Azores, and the Spanish—after struggles with the Portuguese that ended only in 1479—the Canary Islands. These islands offered timber and land for cultivation. When the Madeira archipelago proved poor territory for grain production, Henry ordered the planting of sugarcane and sugar beets, both successful crops on the Mediterranean island of Cyprus. In the Mediterranean, Venice held a monopoly on the shipping of sugar. Genoese investors supported the building of sugar plantations on Madeira, which eventually surpassed Cyprus as a producer of sugar and brought great profits to Portugal.

TO THE INDIAN OCEAN

Gold, and ornaments made out of it, had always filtered north to Europe from Guinea, carried by Arab caravans across the Sahara to the ports of the North African region known as the Maghreb. But after the Portuguese established an African base in 1415, sailors made their way down Africa's west coast, where they came into direct contact with the kingdoms of Guinea. Their progress was often violent, combining trading with raiding. Slowly the Portuguese built forts, established trading posts, and staged a long series of expeditions that gradually charted the entire western coast of Africa.

Finally, the Portuguese navigator Vasco da Gama (ca. 1460–1524) rounded the Cape of Good Hope in an epic ocean journey that lasted from 1497 to 1499 and covered a greater distance than any previous European voyage. He touched down in eastern Africa, stunned by the quality and quantity of goods traded in the Indian Ocean. Da Gama was turned away, however, by the Muslim ruler of Mozambique, who found his gifts insultingly poor. With the help of an experienced Indian Ocean pilot, da Gama negotiated the monsoon winds and reached India in twenty-three days. He made land in Calicut, on the Malabar Coast, the center of the spice trade. Da Gama possessed only modest trading goods and found opposition at the hands of Muslim merchants, but he and his crew obtained some spices by bartering on the docks. Only a gift of meat and oranges from the ruler of Malindi enabled da Gama and his crew to make the voyage home, and fewer than a third of the crew survived. But when da Gama returned to Portugal in July 1499, it was clear that eastward voyages could yield extraordinary returns.

Further Portuguese voyages to Indian Ocean ports carried more extensive trading goods and were better prepared for the journey. The first was led by Pedro Álvares Cabral (1467/8–1520), who became the first European explorer to reach Brazil before he turned east to follow da Gama's route. But the Portuguese also came into sharp conflict with Muslim merchants, who killed fifty of Cabral's men. He retaliated by burning ten Muslim cargo vessels and killing almost 600 men, then moved on to establish a trading post at Cochin, also on the Malabar Coast. His return to Portugal, with seven of his original thirteen ships, showed that the old monopoly of Muslim traders on the spice trade was broken. Da Gama's next

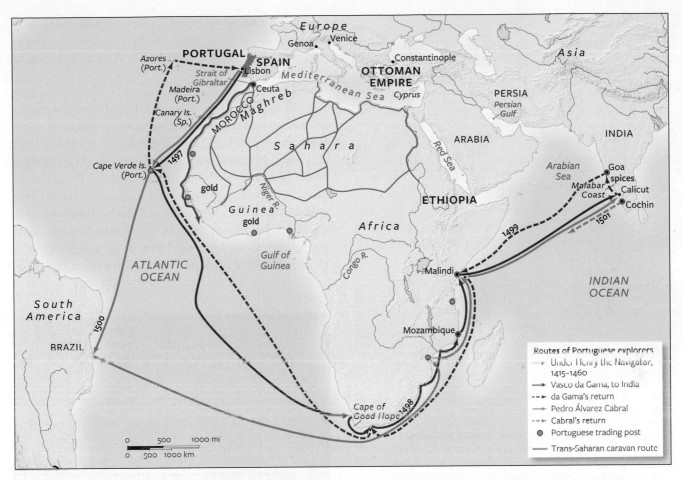

Portuguese Expeditions, 1415–1500 Following Henry the Navigator's voyage to western Africa in 1415, the Portuguese established trading posts along the coast and claimed the Azores and the Madeira archipelago. In 1497–99, Vasco da Gama's first voyage to western India opened up access to the spice trade, leading to expedition and Portuguese naval dominance in the Indian Ocean.

expedition amounted to a terror campaign against Muslim shipping, and he left a Portuguese naval force in Indian waters. Thanks to their superior military power, the Portuguese were soon able to establish a network of colonies that stretched from Mozambique to Goa, and to create a vastly profitable trade.

SLAVERY AND THE SLAVE TRADE

Europeans, Arabs, Africans, and others had traded for slaves for centuries. From the second half of the thirteenth century, Venetian and Genoese merchants bought slaves in markets around the Aegean and Black Seas. The high mortality induced by the Black Death helped to expand the market for this trade—most of whose victims were Mongols, Slavs, or Circassians, with a small number of Greeks and Christians from the Balkans. Practices differed according to local conditions. In Genoa, the number

of slaves doubled to 4,000 or 5,000—almost 10 percent of the population—during the fifteenth century. In Florence, by contrast, there were only 360 slaves in a population of 37,000 in 1427. These northern Italian slaves were mostly young women bought to serve as domestic workers. In the agricultural lands of southern Italy, by contrast, Muslim slaves were also sold, and men as well as women were bought to work in the fields.

Africa, like other parts of the world, had long been the scene of multiple forms of slavery: slaves included people captured in raids or in war, those who could not pay their debts, and people required for sacrifice in religious rituals. Slave women and children worked in the fields and households, men in the salt mines of the Sahara. Slaves were sold by Nubian, Ethiopian, and Funj masters, and brought by Arab merchants from the kingdoms of eastern and western Africa across the Sahara to markets in Algiers, Tripoli, and Cairo. The trans-Saharan slave trade supplied labor for the sugar plantations developed

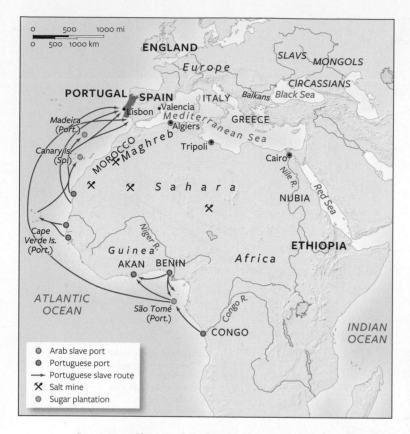

Portuguese Slave Trade, 1444–1500 Enslaved Africans had long worked in the salt mines of the Sahara and had been sold in the Arab ports of Algiers, Tripoli, and Cairo. But the Atlantic slave trade began in 1444 when Portuguese traders brought slaves from western Africa to work on the sugar plantations on Madeira, the Canary Islands, and the Cape Verde Islands.

bought a house for meetings, and interceded successfully, in at least a few cases, when Christian masters set out to imprison or send into distant slavery African women who displeased them.

Black men and women moved into the rest of Europe, from Britain to Italy and beyond. They labored in dozens of occupations, as domestic servants, musicians, printing workers, and Venetian gondoliers. As couples formed and marriages took place, people of mixed race further diversified the crowds in European streets. Exclusionary practices spread: many guild statutes, such as those of the goldsmiths of Lisbon, prohibited slaves from becoming members. But these practices were not universal: Lisbon pie-makers, though they too banned slaves, explicitly proclaimed that free Christian black people from Africa and

Africans in Europe A portrait from the late sixteenth century, attributed to Italian painter Annibale Carracci (1560–1609), depicts an African woman in European clothing holding a clock of European manufacture, evidence of the presence of Africans in European society.

by Moroccan entrepreneurs. In 1444, however, the Portuguese began to transport slaves by ship directly from western Africa to their homeland, eliminating the Arab middlemen of the Maghreb. Portuguese shipments of slave labor to the sugar plantations of Madeira, the Canary Islands, and the Cape Verde Islands formed the beginning of what would become the vast transatlantic slave trade, which the Portuguese extended to their colony in Brazil in the 1530s.

In Europe, more and more Africans, male and female, were brought to do every sort of work. Peoples and cultures mixed. Guinean artisans began to craft small sculptures of gold and ivory that included European objects (such as ships) and people, represented in styles that reflected European tastes. Enslaved and free black people entered Portugal—where, in some cities, they lived by the thousands, forming their own Christian congregations. In Valencia, a wealthy city on the Mediterranean coast of Spain, African slaves formed a religious confraternity, people of mixed European and African descent could be considered. The population on the streets of Europe was now, in part, nonwhite.

PRINTING: THE BOOK TRANSFORMED (1450–1517)

As transformative as the new ships and navigational techniques were, in some ways the most powerful—and potentially the most explosive—of all the new technologies that Europeans adopted in the fifteenth century was the printing press. For centuries, Asians had carved wood blocks and used them to print texts and illustrations. By the thirteenth century, Chinese printers were using wood blocks and moveable wooden type, which for the tens of thousands of Chinese characters were easier to produce and cheaper to replace than the cast metal type developed by the Koreans around the same time. Korea even developed a form of moveable type with a simplified alphabet rather than characters—though it was kept a royal monopoly and used only for official publications. Still, in the fifteenth and sixteenth centuries, bookshops in China and elsewhere in Asia brimmed with offerings of every kind, from official texts to pamphlets and gazetteers.

Europeans came later to the field, as the products needed for printing gradually reached the Continent. From the thirteenth century on, another Asian invention, paper made with cloth fibers from rags, came into wider use. It did not entirely replace parchment, made from the skin of calves and sheep, which had been the standard medium for centuries and continued to be used, especially for many types of legal documents. But paper sharply lowered the cost of writing materials and books. Through the first half of the fifteenth century, Europeans carried out experiments with printing single sheets from wood blocks and metal plates. These revolutionized the visual arts and yielded a fair number of illustrated books, printed page by page. They were narratives of biblical history and saints' lives, for the most part, reproduced in outline and then colored by hand, like graphic novels that combined a traditional faith in the old sacred narratives with an interest in new stories about the monsters that dwelled at the ends of the earth.

GUTENBERG In the 1450s, however, **Johannes Gutenberg** (1398–1468) created something that Europeans had not seen before. A craftsman—he seems to have been both a goldsmith and a blacksmith—Gutenberg came from a well-off merchant family in the German city of Mainz. His ancestors had worked in the mint of the local bishop, and Gutenberg may have learned about presses and molds from them. He spent the 1430s and 1440s tinkering with various projects, including a device for polishing metal mirrors. At least one of these efforts ended in bankruptcy. By the late 1440s he was borrowing money and working on something new. By bringing together old and new technologies, Gutenberg made it possible to produce books mechanically, rather than by hand.

Gutenberg himself may have devised one of the vital components: an oil-based ink that would stick to the metal type and then transfer neatly onto paper. He also crafted type for the Latin alphabet, molding the individual characters in sand. And he worked out how to set lines of type into a frame and lock them in place. This frame could be set into the existing technology of the hand press, long used for producing olive oil and metal badges. Simply

Gutenberg Bible Early printed books were often decorated with elaborate illustrations in the style of handwritten illuminated manuscripts, as on this page from a Gutenberg Bible. The large initial letter "P" surrounds a miniature portrait of King Solomon, and marks the beginning of the book of Proverbs.

by turning a large metal screw that pressed the frame down onto paper, Gutenberg's workers could print a whole series of pages at one time. Each sheet of paper would then be extracted from the press, dried, and folded so that its component pages appeared in the correct order.

In some ways, Gutenberg—like other early modern revolutionaries—was conservative. The first book that he printed—the enormous and beautiful book known as the Gutenberg Bible—faithfully reproduced, in larger format, what had been a standard form for manuscript Bibles since the early thirteenth century: a Latin Bible laid out in two columns of text per page. An observer who saw the book as it went through the press was struck by the neatness and legibility of its type, not by the novelty of its production. Manuscripts were not only written but illuminated (illustrated): decorated with very large initial letters, for example, that incorporated exquisite miniature paintings. Many copies of the Gutenberg Bible were also illustrated by hand, giving them the look of traditional manuscripts. Some were purchased for use in monasteries, probably for reading aloud, since their large, clear type would have been helpful for that purpose.

THE IMMEDIATE IMPACT OF BOOK PRINTING

Gutenberg's breakthrough did not so much revolutionize literacy in Europe as accelerate a revolution that was already under way. Medieval European society was already highly literate. Cities swarmed with notaries, accountants, and government clerks, all of them skilled in writing and computation. Religious dissidents copied their own Bibles, prayer books, and commentaries. More conservative Christians did the same. Many of the most popular books—the ones that printers immediately began to reproduce—were highly traditional: for example, the books of hours, which developed from the breviaries used by priests to recite the daily service in the mid-thirteenth century. Some of these, beautifully illuminated by such artists as Jan Van Eyck (ca. 1395–ca. 1441), were spectacular works of art reserved for the wealthiest patrons. But stationers in France and the Netherlands also mass-produced less-expensive versions without full-page illustrations. By 1500, a British female pauper was indicted for stealing a book of hours from a female servant—evidence that these functional books were available not only to the rich.

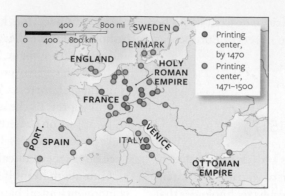

The Spread of Printing, 1455–1500

Printers rapidly transformed the existing networks of the book trade. Master printers found bankers to lend them capital so that they could obtain a house, type, a press, ink, and paper. Some printers formed partnerships with colleagues in other cities to exchange their products, so that each had a wider range of books to sell. Large and costly books, which required a great deal of paper, were produced by two or more printers working together in a syndicate. Universities, with their large student markets, proved especially welcoming. Two professors at the Sorbonne in Paris created a press in 1470, and then moved it to what became the center of the trade, the Rue Saint-Jacques. Other presses nested inside the colleges of the University of Paris, printing textbooks in small runs when the teaching staff needed them. Printing reached the University of Oxford by 1478.

Over time, printing proved to be, if anything, even more adaptable than the scribe's trade. Gutenberg printed not only his famous Bible, but also an almanac with instructions for bloodletting (a popular form of therapy) and a papal bull against the Turks in both German and Latin. Soon printers were turning out everything from editions of the Latin and Greek classics designed to please the educated elite, to theological and legal texts for the universities, to tiny pamphlets. Large books were designed to rest on wooden stands in university halls and scholars' studies. Books in the small octavo format—more or less the size of a modern mass-market paperback—could be carried in a bag or purse and dipped into at leisure. Broadsides—single sheets with vivid woodcut illustrations that described strange happenings and major battles—could be rapidly produced and peddled in city squares and village marketplaces. For the first time, people began to expect news to arrive regularly, in printed form.

Books multiplied faster than ever before, and as we well know, the speed with which messages travel can vastly increase their impact. By the end of the fifteenth century, some 27,000 distinct works had been printed—a flood of texts and images of every kind, ancient and medieval, Christian and Muslim, genuine and forged. One early media event makes clear their impact. At the beginning of the sixteenth century, almanac makers noticed that a conjunction of the planets would take place in 1524 in the zodiacal sign of Pisces, the Fish. They predicted that this

The Book Trade A French woodcut from around 1500 illustrates a Parisian street vendor hawking cheap books of hours and alphabet books for children, which the printing press made readily available to the public.

would cause a terrible flood, and the prediction went viral in almanacs and other small, inexpensive books. When 1524 came, the rains did not prove especially heavy. But thousands of Italians and Germans took to the hills, propelled by the rumors spread by the printing press. They and the astrologers became laughingstocks, mocked for years to come in another form of popular media, the comic plays performed in market squares.

It is difficult to assess the impact of printing in more general terms. It made books cheaper, though not cheap: prices for classical texts dropped by about half in Rome after a press was established there in 1470. The circulation of alphabet books, primers, and broadsides put literacy within the reach of more people across society than manuscript culture had. Print was provocative. Texts that had never been edited to ensure that they were factually accurate or theologically orthodox could now circulate in thousands of copies. Printing also gave publicity to figures whom the political and religious authorities would have liked to suppress. Thus small, elegant Italian editions of the works and doings of Savonarola, the rebellious

Dominican friar, helped to preserve his legacy and inspire his followers. Yet the traditional books of hours went through many more editions. Some of the first witnesses of presses in action praised the speed with which books could be produced. Others denounced printing as an invention of the devil. Even today, the effects of the first modern media revolution evade simple judgments.

DISCOVERY: A NEW WORLD

It was the products of the press—as well as the navigational skills and maritime technology that Europeans had amassed—that impelled the Spanish to undertake their extraordinary expansion to the New World and beyond. **Christopher Columbus** (1457–1506) was a skilled mariner from Genoa, who served in the 1470s and 1480s as a business representative for influential local families and helped to man armed convoys. By the late 1470s, he was sailing on a Portuguese ship and trading for Genoese backers at the Portuguese stations in western Africa. A passionate reader, he came across Latin texts by medieval and contemporary theologians that led him to believe that the world was approaching its end. All peoples, he thought, might soon be reunited as Christians. More important still, he read Ptolemy's *Geography*, the most detailed and technically precise ancient description of the surface of the earth, composed in second-century Alexandria. Ptolemy greatly overestimated the length of the continent of Asia and believed that only water separated it from Europe. Inspired by this ancient authority and filled with enthusiasm by his reading of theologians and prophets, Columbus became convinced that it must be possible to reach Asia relatively quickly by sailing due west.

COLUMBUS'S VOYAGES

Columbus persuaded the rulers of Spain, Ferdinand and Isabella, to support his enterprise by arguing—on the basis of Ptolemy—that the distance to Asia was far shorter than it actually is. On August 3, 1492, he set off with three ships. After stopping in the Canary Islands, he landed at a still unidentified island in the Bahamas. His mind stuffed with ancient reports of the strange races and gleaming treasures to be found in India, at the far eastern edge of the inhabited world, Columbus never worked out exactly what he had discovered. He described the natives he met as poor, naked, and generous, willing to swap treasures for

Columbus's Journeys This 1493 woodcut, from one of the earliest accounts of Columbus's first voyage to the Caribbean, shows King Ferdinand directing Columbus's ships to sail across the ocean. In the top half, the Spanish ships land in the New World, whose native inhabitants flee at the sight of them.

trinkets. But he also noted that some of them were "very fierce and eat human flesh," though he never explained how he had managed to learn this without knowing their languages.

This first trip took him to Cuba and Hispaniola, where one of his ships ran aground and had to be abandoned, and he left a small settlement behind. Using his mastery of the Atlantic winds, he sailed back to Europe, reaching Lisbon in March 1493 and Spain a week later. The news of his voyage spread rapidly, and the monarchs of Portugal and Spain both laid claim to the new discoveries. The dispute was eventually settled in 1494 by the **Treaty of Tordesillas**, which drew a boundary line 370 leagues (1,185 miles) west of the Cape Verde Islands, with Portugal controlling lands east of the line and Spain west.

Columbus set out again in September 1494, this time with seventeen ships and 1,200 men, planning to create settlements in the New World. Though his explorations were mostly confined to the Caribbean Islands—Guadeloupe, the Greater and Lesser Antilles and Hispaniola—on his third voyage in 1498 he reached the Orinoco delta at the northern edge of South America. Columbus correctly argued, from the vast amount of fresh water that the river sent out into the ocean, that he must have found an entire continent, but he believed then and for the rest of his life that the continent he had reached was Asia.

By the end of his third voyage, weakened by age and disease, Columbus found himself under attack by the colonists he had brought to the Americas. A fourth expedition launched in 1502 took him to Panama but ended with his ships beached in Jamaica, where he was stranded for a year. Beleaguered, criticized, and under heavy financial pressure, Columbus became convinced in the course of his later expeditions that he had actually discovered the Earthly Paradise, and believed that his discoveries were harbingers of the return of the Messiah. Bookishness could imprison as well as inspire readers.

EUROPEAN EXPLORATION AFTER COLUMBUS (1497–1522)

For all his illusions, however, Columbus was certain of one thing: the shores on which he landed offered resources of every kind for exploitation, from sheltered harbors to treasures of silver and gold to timber and spices. Expeditions set out from Europe in every direction. John Cabot (ca. 1450–ca. 1499), an Italian backed by King Henry VII of England, sailed straight west from Bristol in 1497 and made landfall in what was probably Newfoundland. By 1500 another Spanish fleet, led by the Florentine Amerigo Vespucci (ca. 1454–1512), had reached the mouth of the Amazon River. Portuguese expeditions, including a second one by Vespucci in 1501–2, found and explored the bulge of South America's eastern coast, and a French fleet landed in southern Brazil in 1504. In 1519, the Portuguese navigator Ferdinand Magellan (1480–1521) led a Spanish fleet of five ships on a voyage to circumnavigate the world. They sailed from Spain to South America and crossed through what is now called the Strait of Magellan into the Pacific Ocean, which they crossed on the way to the Spice Islands (now the Indonesian archipelago called the Moluccas). Though Magellan himself died in the Philippines, one ship returned to Seville in 1522.

Printing spread the news—often in the attractive if unreliable form of pamphlets, such as the short letters attributed to Vespucci that described both the Southern Cross and the cannibalism of American natives. Land expeditions began to fill in the vast blank spaces on the maps, as when Vasco Núñez de Balboa (1475–1519) crossed Panama in 1513 and became the first European to see the Pacific from the land side. Soldiers of fortune and missionary priests followed the first explorers. They spread

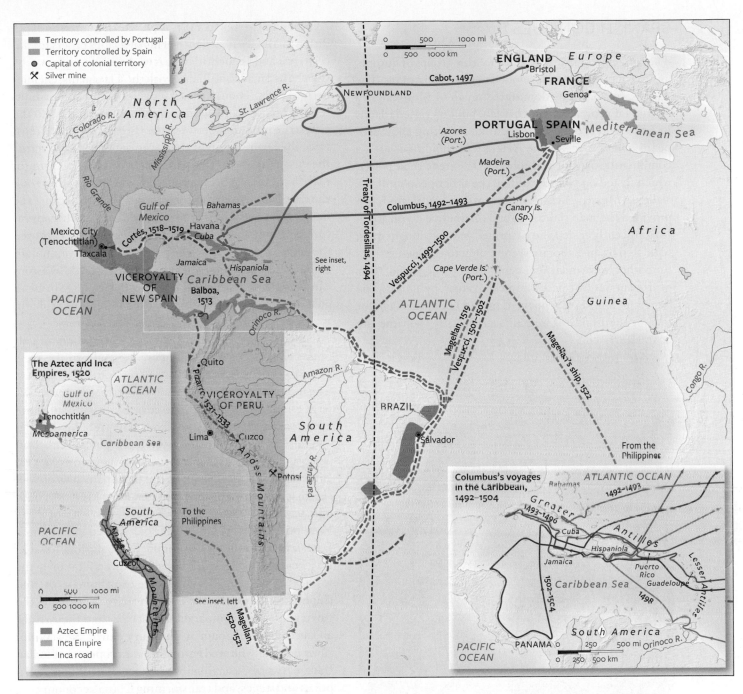

European Expeditions to the Western Hemisphere, 1492–1550 By the mid-sixteenth century, exploration and colonization linked Portugal and Spain to an expanse of new territory in the Americas and beyond. Christopher Columbus's voyages to the Caribbean first made Europeans aware of the resources of the Americas. Soon after, Amerigo Vespucci discovered the mouth of the Amazon River. Magellan crossed below the southern tip of South America into the Pacific, and one of his ships completed the first circumnavigation of the world. Later, Cortés travelled as far as central Mexico and conquered the Aztecs, and Pizarro pushed down into the Andes, where he overthrew the Inca. Once these ancient civilizations were defeated, the Spanish established control over much of the New World.

smallpox and other European diseases among the inhabitants of the New World, who had never been exposed to these pathogens and had no immunity. Millions died in the pandemics, radically weakening their states.

Exact statistics are impossible to provide, but many specialists believe that the population of the Americas fell from some 50 million in 1492 to as low as 6 million by 1650.

SPANISH CONQUEST

The pandemics made it possible for tiny groups of Europeans to conquer highly developed native civilizations. The Aztecs, for example, dominated much of Mesoamerica from their capital at Tenochtitlán, built on raised islands in Lake Texcoco—a setting unlike anything the Europeans had ever seen. The Aztecs and their allies used a combination of trade and conquest to extend their power, which rested on tribute paid by the other peoples of the Valley of Mexico. A caste of peasants who cultivated corn provided the material basis for a distinctive civilization. Magnificently armed and costumed warriors fought wars, regulated by an elaborate system of heroic values, to capture other brave men. War captives were sacrificed, their hearts cut out by priests atop the Aztecs' pyramids. The largest pyramid in Tenochtitlán had been the stage for tens of thousands of human sacrifices by the time the Spanish arrived.

Cortés and the Aztecs An illustration from a late-sixteenth-century Spanish history of the New World shows a tense meeting of Spanish and Aztec forces. The Aztec king Montezuma waves his finger angrily at Cortés and his soldiers, while an Aztec interpreter stands between the two parties.

Hernán Cortés (b. 1485–1547), who mounted an expedition to Mexico in defiance of his superior's orders to cancel it, reached Tenochtitlán by 1519. An adroit diplomat, by then he had made an alliance with the Tlaxcalans, enemies of the Aztecs. Though the Aztec ruler Montezuma admitted the Spanish and about a thousand Tlaxcalans to the city, strife broke out between the three parties. On July 1, 1520, the Spanish fought their way out of the city, across the raised causeways that gave access to it. In the spring of 1521 they returned to lay siege, and on August 13 they took the city, destroying it in the process. Cortés became the first governor of what was now New Spain. Another adventurous soldier, Francisco Pizarro (ca. 1475–1541), captured the emperor of the Incas, the people whose rich mountain empire stretched across the Andes, held together by astonishing roads and bridges. Though offered a huge bribe in gold, Pizarro found a pretext to execute the Inca ruler in 1533, making him master of another vast territory.

As the native kingdoms fell, great numbers of colonists emigrated from all regions of Spain to the New World—some 300,000 of them in the sixteenth century. The most successful of these migrants created *encomiendas*, large estates where they exercised near-absolute authority and used enserfed natives for labor. They rebuilt old cities and raised new ones on neat, systematic plans: Tenochtitlan, originally built on a grid, was reconfigured as Mexico City, capital of New Spain, one of two Spanish viceroyalties in sixteenth-century Latin America; Lima was built on a grid plan as the capital of the Viceroyalty of Peru. Vast lodes of silver in the sugarloaf-shaped mountain at Potosí, in modern Bolivia, founded as a mining town in 1545, became the site of the largest mining operation in the world. The treasure dug up at staggering human cost and shipped to Europe by the Spanish silver fleets made the rulers of Spain incomparably wealthier than their rivals, and strengthened Spain as a military power. New World silver gradually filtered through the European and Asian trade networks, exerting inflationary pressure on global prices and wages, and transforming China's economy.

Meanwhile, a historical struggle took shape in the Americas. Initially at Cortés's request, Franciscan and Dominican missionaries—many of them idealists—arrived in the New World nourishing high hopes for the American Indians, whom they saw as innocent and virtuous. They did their best to teach Christian doctrine and practice, and—as they became aware of the oppression many natives suffered as serfs of the colonists—tried to protect them against brutal exploitation. Bartolomé de Las Casas (1484–1566), a Dominican who became the first bishop of

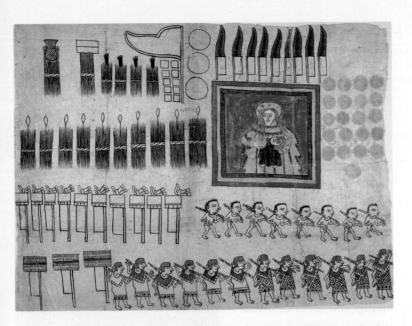

Christianity in the New World In a set of 1531 legal documents drawn up by the Huexotzinco people, from an area near Mexico City, a pictographic rendering lists the taxes the Spanish colonial authorities demanded of them. The inclusion of a banner of the Virgin Mary and Baby Jesus indicates the influence of Spanish religion on indigenous perceptions only ten years after conquest.

Chiapas, in southern Mexico, actually to live and work in his diocese, pleaded with the Spanish crown to end the system of forced labor. He argued that the Indians were highly intelligent, as the complexity of their preconquest societies proved, and should enjoy decent living conditions and a chance to become believing Christians. Largely due to Las Casas's efforts, in 1542 the Spanish king promulgated the New Laws, which forbade the *encomenderos* to force Indians to work for them or to bequeath their estates to their children. Although the encomiendas were made heritable again in 1545, and *encomenderos* resisted the New Laws, the number of serfs fell. But the population decline continued, indicating that the majority of American natives who survived the Spanish conquest suffered in many ways for having done so.

COLUMBIAN EXCHANGES

The encounter between European and New World peoples was one of the great dramas of human history—a drama that continued long after the initial, catastrophic population loss unleashed by conquest and disease. Europeans brought with them all the elements of their civilization, from their domesticated dogs and horses and their

technical devices to their Christian religion and romance literature, which helped to inspire the conquistadores as they rode out to battle. In Latin America a new society took shape—one whose elite was often created by intermarriage between the conquerors and the descendants of native princes. Intermarriage was common at all levels: by the eighteenth century, the majority of Mexicans and Central and South Americans were so-called mestizos, people of mixed blood. They were served by a distinctive form of Christianity. Church architecture and religious images blended traditional Christian stories and teachings with native imagery. Indians took part with special enthusiasm, as the best-informed missionaries realized, in those Christian rites and festivals that fell on significant days in their own ancient calendars. Meanwhile, the horse—unknown in the New World before the conquerors arrived—spread throughout the Americas, transforming the lives of the Plains Indians, who had relatively little direct contact with either the Spanish or the inhabitants of Latin America.

In return, the New World had far more to offer the Old. Transported east across the Atlantic, staple agricultural products found acceptance in Europe at differing rates. Tomatoes and potatoes had little impact in the sixteenth century, but eventually they transformed Old World agriculture and diet. By contrast, tobacco and chocolate—both far stronger than their modern versions, and both central to American Indian religious rituals that fascinated Western observers and taught them how to consume these powerful stimulants—reshaped European social customs. In 1500, Europeans did not use tobacco or anything like it. A hundred years later, Europeans of all social ranks smoked or inhaled it. Taverns and other gathering places reeked of tobacco, as they would for centuries to come. Meanwhile, hot chocolate became a beloved luxury of elites, served at festive meals and sipped elegantly from tiny cups.

European sailors and soldiers also returned home with an unwelcome import: syphilis, a sexually transmitted disease that seems not have existed in Europe before 1492. It spread across the European continent, where it soon became an epidemic, with results that horrified sufferers and observers. The standard treatment involved drinking or applying a medicine made from the bark of the guaiacum tree, which—like the disease—came from the New World. The Fuggers, a prominent German banking family, soon established a monopoly on the sale of this bark, as they did with mercury, another treatment that could be effective but caused horrific side effects.

At the same time, the feather headdresses, jewels, and

illuminated codices of New World rulers were exhibited in the court museums of Europe. The skill of their makers won the admiration of such great artists as Albrecht Dürer, who saw what he described as a sun of gold and a moon of silver, along with other treasures and weapons from Mexico, in Brussels in 1520. "All the days of my life," he reflected, "I have seen nothing that rejoiced my heart so much as these things, for I saw among them wonderful works of art, and I marveled at the subtle intellects of people in distant lands."

REDISCOVERY: RENAISSANCE CULTURE

Like Dürer, the Florentine philosopher Marsilio Ficino (1433–1499) marveled at the cultural splendors of a world in discovery, this one located not across the ocean but in the ancient past. Ficino had these rediscovered riches in mind when he declared, "This century, like a golden age, has restored to light the liberal arts, which were almost extinct: grammar, poetry, rhetoric, painting, sculpture, architecture, music." Explorers claimed to have found a new world, but European thinkers came to believe that they had brought about a rebirth—a renaissance—of ancient Greece and Rome. The Italian cities had always supported communities of notaries and lawyers—practical men who used ancient texts and medieval contract forms with equal dexterity to meet the practical needs of merchants and bankers. In the fourteenth century, some of them developed new cultural ambitions. They began to study the classics of Latin literature: the prose of Cicero and Seneca, the epic poetry of Virgil, and even the love poetry of Catullus.

PETRARCH

The fourteenth-century Florentine writer Francesco Petrarca, or **Petrarch** (1304–1374), pulled these threads together and wove a new intellectual program from them. Pushed by his father to study law, Petrarch found himself repelled by the way in which contemporary jurists read the ancient texts. To make Roman laws fit modern cases, they assumed that every reference to a pagan temple must apply to Christian churches as well. Petrarch, by contrast, was thrilled by what he described as the "history" concealed in the legal texts. He saw them not as a set of timeless codes but as the revelation of a lost world, at once unfamiliar and

more powerful and attractive than his own. Leaving the law, he pursued literature. Petrarch's Italian lyric poems—in which he described, at meticulous length, the sufferings of lovers and the beauty of the women who refused their pleas—made him famous. He created the language used by writers of sonnets down to the time of William Shakespeare and John Donne.

Petrarch's Latin scholarship and writing made him the standard-bearer of a new intellectual movement. Networking with learned men in the papal offices in France and Rome, he collected, and corrected, as many classical texts as he could. He annotated everything he read, both responding to the texts and entering personal remarks: for example, we know from a note in his

Petrarch In Andrea del Castagno's early-fifteenth-century rendering, the poet holds a book—the symbol of his craft—and extends his right hand in a delicate, artistic gesture.

massive copy of Virgil's works that Laura, the woman who inspired Petrarch's sonnets, died during the Black Death in 1348. And he carved out a career as the most expert and eloquent Latinist of his day.

As he discovered new texts—such as the highly political letters that Cicero addressed to his friend Atticus—Petrarch responded to them with verve and passion, showing just how serious a matter reading was for him. In the Middle Ages, clerical readers had thought of Cicero above all as the author of his late, Stoical works on philosophy. Now it became clear that he had been an active participant in the final drama of the Roman Republic. Horrified, Petrarch dashed off a letter to Cicero in which he denounced the Roman for betraying the ideals of philosophy—only to soften his judgment in a second, follow-up note.

A pious Christian who often criticized the Church but never questioned basic doctrines, Petrarch knew that his love of ancient literature might seem questionable or worse—as it had to Saint Jerome, whose work he knew intimately. At times he reproached himself for loving the beauty of the ancients' books too much. But challenged by friends, he devised a powerful justification for studying the literary classics—one partly based on the thought of Augustine, whose books he loved even more than those of the Romans. Contemporary philosophers and theologians, Petrarch argued, tried to learn the truth, a quest that often led them into blind alleys. They wasted their energy seeking goals no human could reach, and ended up fiercely debating questions of no relevance to the ordinary person. The ancients, by contrast, thanks to their mastery of rhetoric, had known how to make their readers want to change their lives, to be better men and women. And in the end, he argued, for Christians in his own day as for pagans in antiquity, "it is more important to will the good than to know the truth." The study of the classics had an eminently practical goal: it was the best way to make oneself a moral agent and to persuade others to do so as well.

SALUTATI'S BREAKTHROUGH

Petrarch's fame, and the power of his work, persuaded many younger scholars to follow him in the middle of the fourteenth century and after. His fellow Florentine, Giovanni Boccaccio (1313–1375), emulated him in many ways. Boccaccio developed a cultivated Italian prose, comparable in purity to Petrarch's verse, in which he composed his *Decameron*, a magnificent set of 100 tales in Italian about sex and love, marriage and deception. But he also searched for manuscripts of ancient books that had remained hidden in monasteries, and compiled a massive Latin book in which he sorted out the complex genealogies of the pagan gods. Even more influential was Coluccio Salutati (1331–1406), a younger notary who became chancellor of Florence in 1375. A systematic scholar in the new manner, Salutati also wrote about ancient myths, revealing a clear sense that the ancient world had been very different from his own. Confronting the many loves of Hercules, he explained both simply and radically that pagans, unlike Christians, had not been bound to monogamy.

Many younger men came under Salutati's influence—notably two deft Latinists, Leonardo Bruni (ca. 1370–1444) and Gian Francesco Poggio Bracciolini (1380–1459), both of whom would serve after him as chancellor of Florence. Poggio, who wrote in an open, highly legible script, worked with Salutati to define a layout for books more appropriate to the classics than the spiky, highly abbreviated books used in the universities. The model they chose—a clear minuscule script, written with few abbreviations

Poggio Bracciolini An illuminated initial letter "C" on the first page of one of Poggio's translations gives an indication of what the Latinist might have looked like as a young man.

and presented on its own, rather than immersed in a sea of minute commentary—was actually Carolingian, not ancient. Adopted by the efficient stationers of Florence, it became, first in manuscripts and then in print, the basic form of the modern book: a book designed not to serve as a source of information but to be read for its own sake, whether chained to a library table or carried on a journey.

Most important, in 1397 Salutati persuaded an eloquent and learned Byzantine, Manuel Chrysoloras, (d. 1415) to teach Greek in Florence. Bruni and others who studied with him began to read the Greek historians and philosophers, and to translate their works into Latin. For the first time in a thousand years, Latin intellectuals could read the works of Plato and his followers as well as Aristotle, whom they had known for centuries in the Latin translations used in universities. Chrysoloras—who, like many Byzantine scholars, took as strong an interest in the sciences as in literature—explicated Ptolemy's *Geography*, which was soon translated into Latin, and thus provided part of the inspiration that would send Columbus on his voyage west. The encounter with these alien works from another world could be shocking: the first Latin translation of Plato's *Symposium* discreetly eliminated the references to same-sex love. Soon, however, it became clear that, as Petrarch had already suspected, Plato offered a vision of the universe and a method of writing philosophy that seemed closer to Christianity in substance and better fitted to the needs of ordinary readers than the more technical books of Aristotle.

When Marsilio Ficino spoke of a great revival of the arts in his own day, he referred partly to his own project to translate and comment on the complete works of Plato—a project that came to fruition in 1484, when his work was printed in Florence. In the larger sense, what he saw himself as living through was nothing less than a revolution—one that looked not forward, as revolutions have in the nineteenth and twentieth centuries, but backward, and that sought to rebuild culture on a basis of ancient texts properly established and understood.

HUMANISM

The scholars who set out on this new road to the ancient past—from Petrarch to Ficino—took a special interest in the arts of language, grammar, and rhetoric; in poetry; and in the further studies that would help to inform and improve the characters of men and women who played important roles in society. These studies came to be known as "the studies of humanity," and those who pursued them as "humanists"—not in the modern secular sense, since almost all of them were faithful Christians, but in a larger one. All of them recognizably adopted the same general intellectual program, called **humanism**.

POLITICS Becoming a humanist did not imply a commitment to a particular view of society or the state. Petrarch, and many humanists after him, saw monarchy, when carried out by just and virtuous rulers, as a laudable form of government. Drawing on Seneca, who had offered an idealistic version of Roman imperial government as created by Augustus (until he was forced by Nero to commit suicide), Petrarch praised the rulers of Milan for their justice, their clemency, and their own commitment to urban planning, which had made their city cleaner and more beautiful than any other. Many later humanists would write similar "mirrors of princes." Bruni and his successors in the Florentine chancery took the opposite course. They learned from Thucydides, Aristotle, and Polybius how to analyze Florence as a classical republic, and effusively praised the city's balanced government, tradition of defending liberty, and splendid architecture.

Humanism also found a niche, and a large one, in the papal court. The fifteenth-century popes who rebuilt the Roman Curia (the papal administration) as a going

concern established that the papacy was as committed to classical learning as any secular monarchy, and surrounded themselves with bright young scholars of the sort Salutati had recruited. Humanists in papal employ translated many of the Greek classics, wrote new lives of the ancient saints in an up-to-date style, and made the liturgy classical. By the beginning of the sixteenth century, they drew up official documents for the popes that referred to God as Jupiter Optimus Maximus and avoided using the special vocabulary of Christian Latin. In 1475 the popes created a great library for these humanists to work in: not a religious collection, as is often wrongly thought, but a systematic assembly of Greek and Latin texts meant to be used by the members of the Curia when they too turned to the ancients for practical advice. The Vatican Library remains one of the world's great centers of scholarly research.

SOCIETY Studying the classics was eminently practical. The subjects that the humanists cultivated proved useful in the new states and societies that had taken shape in fifteenth-century Italy. Ambassadors, for example, needed to give speeches, write forceful memoranda, and use history to shed light on the difficult moments of the present—all humanist skills. The families that ruled the most powerful cities embraced them. Many appointed humanist teachers, opened schools that offered instruction to princes and aristocrats, and built libraries designed, as the Vatican's was, for quiet reflection.

Humanism also created new possibilities for women, even within the social traditions of Renaissance cities and courts. For the most part, marriage among members of the elite continued to be arranged by parents to promote family strategies, and women in the Renaissance married much younger than men in the expectation that they would produce as many children as possible. They and the dowries they brought with them in marriage were in their husband's power, and even when they were widowed, they were normally put under the guardianship of a male relative of their late husband. Yet as we saw in the catasto records of Florence, many widows achieved considerable authority as heads of families.

CHRISTINE DE PIZAN Christine de Pizan (1364–1430) was a humanist who, writing in French rather than Latin, posed new questions about women and their social position. Married at the age of fifteen and widowed with three children a decade later, Christine found support in the courts of Burgundy and France for her poetry. She created a circle of scribes and miniaturists who produced beautifully illuminated copies of her works; she took charge

GHIRLANDAIO'S *PORTRAIT OF A LADY*

In Renaissance Italy, portraits served as tokens of friendship, political alliance, and marital exchange between courts or powerful families. Domenico Ghirlandaio (1449–1494) was a successful painter who operated a workshop in Florence with his family; Michelangelo apprenticed in the workshop. Ghirlandaio most likely created his *Portrait of a Lady* (ca. 1490) to commemorate the sitter's marriage.

Italian portraits of the second half of the fifteenth century, especially those featuring women, expressed both the subjects' personal characteristics and the broad cultural values of the time. In this portrait, the young woman's golden hair, fair skin, and formal posture conform to a standard of female beauty present in many other portraits of the period, inspired by the medieval poetry of Dante Alighieri (1265–1321) and Petrarch (1304–1374). The orange blossom in the woman's hand, representing chastity, and the pearls on her necklace, symbolizing purity and associated with the Virgin Mary, also convey the subject's moral integrity. Her pearls and elegant dress communicate the wealth of the woman's family, always of importance in marriage negotiations. Ghirlandaio combined these elements to create an image of femininity that aligned closely with Florentine values.

QUESTIONS FOR ANALYSIS

1. What does this portrait suggest about the woman's social status?
2. How would you describe the image of femininity conveyed in the portrait?
3. Why would Ghirlandaio include Florence and the surrounding countryside in this portrait?

Christine de Pizan The frontispiece of a 1411 manuscript of her writings shows Christine de Pizan hard at work at her desk. She closely supervised the creation of this manuscript, which she presented to the queen of France in 1414.

of every detail, including the scripts that her scribes employed.

In her allegorical history of women, *The Book of the City of Ladies* (1405), Christine conjured up Lady Reason, who gave her a powerful lesson. Christine had believed, in a traditional way, in the evil character of women, which male authors such as Boccaccio had repeatedly confirmed. Lady Reason urged her to forget the slanders that had been heaped on women, and carry them away like "hods of earth" on her shoulders—a brilliant image of the woman writer as workmanlike scholar. "If it were customary to send little girls to school," Christine now argued, "and teach them the same subjects as are taught to boys, they would learn just as fully and would understand the subtleties of all arts and sciences." Marriage, she wrote, when unaccompanied by a spiritual connection, was no better than slavery.

UNDERSTANDING THE PAST Like the scholastics, the humanists developed a new and powerful set of technical skills—one based less on formal argument (though some did cultivate that) than on the knowledge that language, forms of writing, laws, customs, art, and religion all changed over time. Whereas scholastics enjoyed finding contradictions in arguments, humanists hunted anachronisms—errors and inconsistencies that showed that a given work could not have been written or painted by its supposed author or in its supposed period. The last thousand years, during which ancient books survived only when fallible individuals copied them in full, had left the canon in some confusion—a state rendered worse by the habit of many medieval writers and librarians of ascribing works they admired, whatever their origins, to particular ancient authors.

The most dramatic exposure of a medieval forgery involved the so-called Donation of Constantine. Old documents, produced by the papal chancery in the age of Charlemagne, purported to show that Pope Sylvester I (r. 314–335) had cured Constantine, the first Christian emperor of Rome, of leprosy, and that the emperor had given the popes the western empire in gratitude. Lawyers and theologians debated for centuries about whether this grant was legitimate. In 1440, Lorenzo Valla (1407–1457) a humanist who worked for the king of Naples, used the new scholarly tools to show that the documents in question were fakes that could not have been written at the time claimed. It did not matter whether Constantine's gift had been just or unjust—it had never taken place.

Humanists even created a new kind of history—one based on the material remains of the ancient world. Cyriac, a merchant from the Italian port of Ancona, revealed the ancient world vividly to his contemporaries. He traveled the Mediterranean for decades in the fifteenth century, sketchbook in hand, hopping from one Venetian or Genoese ship to another. Cyriac brought western Europeans their first news—and their first images—of the ancient temples of Greece, including the Parthenon, and of the obelisks and sphinxes of Egypt.

During the fifteenth century, humanists also revived every form of philosophy that the ancient world had known. Not only Aristotelianism and Platonism but Stoicism, Skepticism, and Epicureanism were reconstructed by scholars and exhaustively debated in Latin. New and varied syntheses took shape. Ficino, the translator of Plato, found connections between the works of Plato, a wide range of later Neoplatonic texts, and the learned tradition of natural magic and astrology that had taken shape in the medieval Islamic world. Ficino's younger friend Giovanni Pico della Mirandola, by contrast, believed that all serious schools of thought—Islamic as well as Christian, modern as well as ancient, scholastic as well as humanist—possessed distinctive elements of the truth. Humanism, which began as the discovery of the otherness of ancient Rome, gradually opened eyes and minds to the richness of a wide range of ancient traditions.

INNOVATIONS IN THE ARTS

Marsilio Ficino celebrated the revival of the visual arts as well as classical learning. Painting, sculpture, and architecture had flourished in the late thirteenth and fourteenth centuries in the most economically advanced parts of Europe—Italy and the Low Countries. But they had been seen as crafts. Those who practiced them learned their techniques as apprentices in masters' workshops and became journeymen once fully trained. They did not even have guilds of their own in most cities: sculptors joined and were regulated by the masons' guild, and painters by that of physicians and apothecaries. In the later fourteenth and

fifteenth centuries, however, what we now call the fine arts began to pull away from other crafts. Architects insisted that their work required knowledge not only of traditional building crafts, but also of mathematics and physical science. They found support in the ancient Roman handbook on architecture by Vitruvius (d. after 15 CE), who made the case that an architect needed to have encyclopedic knowledge of nature as well as building techniques in order to build healthy houses and cities.

FLORENCE In 1418 Filippo Brunelleschi (1377–1446), a stunningly innovative Florentine sculptor and architect, told the committee responsible for finishing the city's Cathedral of Santa Maria del Fiore that he could build its enormous dome without any pillars to support it—as if deliberately mocking his predecessors, who had relied upon small forests of buttresses to support their cathedrals. The committee members treated him as insane at first, but eventually he convinced them. Brunelleschi worked with highly skilled craftsmen, but emphasized that he was responsible for their innovations. He designed the lifts, hoists, and scaffolds that enabled his crew to complete the dome in 1436—the biggest one built since the creation of the church of Hagia Sophia some

Brunelleschi and the Cathedral of Santa Maria del Fiore A 1427 fresco depicts Filippo Brunelleschi (right) alongside several contemporaries, including the painter Masaccio (left) and the writer and architect Leon Battista Alberti (center). Brunelleschi designed and built the magnificent dome of Florence's Cathedral of Santa Maria del Fiore using numerous architectural innovations, such as the rib-like support structure and an inner and outer dome.

Giotto's Frescoes In a vivid panel from Giotto di Bondone's frescoes narrating the Passion of Christ (1303–5), Jesus kisses Judas, who has betrayed him. The artist draws out the anger and tension of the scene through the facial expressions and gestures of the guards, disciples, and bystanders.

900 years earlier by the Roman emperor Justinian. As brilliant an engineer as he was an artist, Brunelleschi also devised war machines and transportation devices for the Florentines. He took out what amounted to the first modern patent to protect a piece of his intellectual property. He also created a new style of building that seemed classical, although, like the style of Renaissance books, it was medieval—in this case derived from churches of the twelfth century. He used it for the hospital built by the Florentines to accommodate foundlings.

Painters and sculptors also began to innovate. Giotto di Bondone (d. 1337), the most famous painter of the fourteenth century, used the large frescoes and mosaics that he was commissioned to create to find new ways of representing people, vividly and powerfully, as dominated by their emotions. Brunelleschi carried out experiments in linear perspective from the steps of the Florentine cathedral. He showed that by using a geometrical system of one-point perspective, he could produce an image of the octagonal Baptistery (the twelfth-century building across from the cathedral) that seemed genuinely three-dimensional.

Soon Florence became a center of artistic experiment. Brunelleschi's rival, the sculptor Lorenzo Ghiberti (ca.

1378–1455), experimented with foreshortening and perspective as he cast biblical scenes for the bronze doors of the Baptistery. Artists of the next generation—men such as Masaccio and Paolo Uccello, born around the year 1400—covered the walls of Florentine churches with vivid paintings: from a shrine, painted flat on the wall, that seemed to recede from the onlooker as if it were in three dimensions, to crowds and buildings that looked startlingly like their real-life counterparts. Uccello and other painters began to make systematic sketches, starting with nude figures and only later imagining them clothed. They depicted graceful men and women standing with their bodies curved symmetrically around vertical lines—figures as idealized, but also as apparently real, as the exquisite works of ancient Greeks like Phidias, whose sculptures filled the Parthenon.

NORTHERN EUROPE Innovation was just as rapid in the Low Countries, which produced a flood of illuminated manuscripts and tapestries as well as sculptures and paintings. Since the twelfth century, northern European artists had occasionally used oil as a painting medium, rather than the tempera (a mixture of pigment and a water-soluble binder such as egg yolk) that southern artists used when creating panels. In the fifteenth century, northern painters such as Jan van Eyck, who served his Burgundian master, Philip the Good, as diplomat as well as painter, learned how to apply oil paint in multiple thin layers. This technique enabled them to create rich, glowing colors and to produce microscopically faithful renditions of every sort of surface material, from stone to cloth, fur, and skin. They created many devotional pictures, but also specialized in painting portraits from life of prominent men and women. Works of art and techniques crossed the Alps and the Pyrenees. By the middle of the fifteenth century, Italian painters such as the Venetian Giovanni Bellini (ca. 1430–1516) were using oil as a medium, and the portrait was becoming a standard feature of Italian art.

PATRONAGE Support for the arts came from many sources. Committees of local notables oversaw the building and decoration of churches, such as the Florentine cathedral. Guilds also took part. The Florentine church of Orsanmichele, originally a grain market, was converted between 1380 and 1404 into the chapel of the Florentine craft and merchant guilds. Popes, princes, and patricians did their best to transform the built world. Merchant families and cardinals constructed huge palaces, drawing features from ancient structures like the Colosseum, in

❝ WHO COULD EVER BE HARD OR ENVIOUS ENOUGH TO FAIL TO PRAISE PIPPO THE ARCHITECT ON SEEING HERE SUCH A LARGE STRUCTURE, RISING ABOVE THE SKIES, AMPLE TO COVER WITH ITS SHADOW ALL THE TUSCAN PEOPLE? ❞

LEON BATTISTA ALBERTI, *DE PICTURA*, ON FILIPPO BRUNELLESCHI'S DOME OF THE CATHEDRAL OF SANTA MARIA DEL FIORE

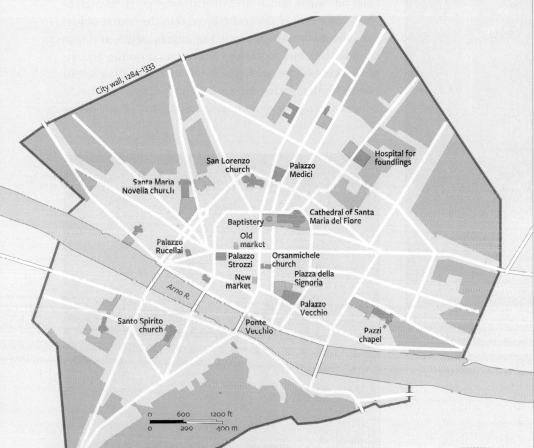

Through much of the fifteenth century, a painting's materials, selected by its patron, determined its value. In this work (ca. 1483) by Florentine painter Filippino Lippi, the ultramarine pigment of the Virgin Mary's mantle would have been many times more expensive than gold. But by the end of the century, many patrons valued artists' skills more than the materials they used.

❝ THIS CENTURY, LIKE A GOLDEN AGE, HAS RESTORED TO LIGHT THE LIBERAL ARTS, WHICH WERE ALMOST EXTINCT: GRAMMAR, POETRY, RHETORIC, PAINTING, SCULPTURE, ARCHITECTURE, MUSIC... AND ALL THIS IN FLORENCE. ❞

MARSILIO FICINO, "THE GOLDEN AGE IN FLORENCE"

This bronze relief panel (1425–1452) from the doors of the Baptistery, depicting a Biblical scene, displays Lorenzo Ghiberti's ingenious use of perspective. He took great pride in his ability to set himself demanding technical problems and solve them with virtuosity.

WORKSHOPS, 1472

54 marble workers and stonecutters
44 master gold- and silversmiths
at least 30 master painters

NOTABLE PATRONS & WORKS THEY COMMISSIONED

MEDICI FAMILY
Brunelleschi's church of San Lorenzo and various works by Michelangelo

FILIPPO STROZZI (BANKER)
Benedetto da Maiano's Palazzo Strozzi and Lippi's frescoes in the Strozzi Chapel at Santa Maria Novella

GIOVANNI RUCELLAI (MERCHANT)
Alberti's façade of Santa Maria Novella and his design of the Palazzo Rucellai

QUESTIONS FOR ANALYSIS

1. What innovations in the arts and learning appeared in Renaissance Florence?
2. In what ways did artists and their patrons embellish the city?
3. How did the city's artists resemble and also distinguish themselves from craftsmen?

Map labels: City wall, 1284–1333; San Lorenzo church; Palazzo Medici; Hospital for foundlings; Santa Maria Novella church; Baptistery; Cathedral of Santa Maria del Fiore; Old market; Palazzo Rucellai; Palazzo Strozzi; Orsanmichele church; New market; Piazza della Signoria; Arno R.; Palazzo Vecchio; Santo Spirito church; Ponte Vecchio; Pazzi chapel; 0 600 1200 ft; 0 200 400 m work of the best masters. Some 16,000 letters record her requests to the greatest artists of the time.

ALBERTI: A NEW VISION As artists' practices changed, so did their position in society. In the 1430s, a Florentine exile named **Leon Battista Alberti** (1404–1472), a humanist who worked in the service of the papacy, returned to his native city. What he saw astonished him. Cast off by his family and illegitimate, given to melancholy, Alberti had always believed that the course of history was downward, a process of degeneration, and that he and his contemporaries could never rival the accomplishments of the ancients. Now, he told Brunelleschi in a passionate letter, he realized he had been wrong: "I believe the power of acquiring wide fame in any art or

Jan van Eyck One of van Eyck's notable portraits of prominent members of society is this 1434 painting of a newly married Italian merchant and his wife. The picture showcases in realistic detail the luxurious interior of the couple's house, while a mirror in the background allows the viewer to glimpse the scene from another perspective.

which they walled themselves off from the turmoil of the streets and created private worlds of great splendor, decorated according to their owners' distinctive tastes.

Wealthy individuals also presented paintings and chapels to the churches they favored, and bought painted chests, tapestries, and other expensive items for their homes. These consumers of luxury goods became more discriminating in the fifteenth and sixteenth centuries: not only in choosing beautiful things but also in selecting the artists they employed. A few women forged careers that would have only been possible in this new world. At the highest social levels, noble and royal women became as expert as any man in the new skills of connoisseurship and collection. Isabella d'Este (1474–1539), Marchesa of Mantua, spent her large income on art objects and became renowned for her determination to pay for only the best

Isabella d'Este The Venetian painter Titian created this 1534–36 portrait of the influential art connoisseur and collector Isabella d'Este. She was in her early sixties at the time, but Titian portrayed her as she might have appeared in her youth.

Alberti's Emblem This mid-fifteenth-century medallion bears Leon Battista Alberti's emblem, a winged eye, an allusion, perhaps, to the eye of the artist, as well as the precision to which new forms of art and learning aspired. The motto below the eye, "Quid tum," is more mysterious, possibly meaning "What then?" or "So what?"—a hopeful anticipation of future developments in human knowledge.

science lies in our industry and diligence more than in the times or in the gifts of nature." Brunelleschi's dome ("ample to cover with its shadow all the Tuscan people, and constructed without the aid of centering or great quantity of wood"), Ghiberti's bronze doors for the Baptistery, and other achievements of Florentine art showed that progress was still possible.

Recognizing these dramatic changes when they had only just begun, Alberti set out to give painting—and by extension the other arts—a new theoretical foundation. He argued that painters really resembled scholars. As the humanist wrote in order to move readers, the painter depicted dramatic scenes—such as the Annunciation and the Crucifixion—in order to achieve the same end. And as the humanist's mastery of a classical vocabulary proved his worthiness to take part in public discussion, so the painter's mastery of techniques—anatomy, perspective, foreshortening—proved his worthiness to tell great stories in visual form. Traditionally, the painter had needed to know where to find the best pigments. Now he needed to master the geometry of the picture plane and the bony and muscular structures of the body, especially if he wanted to challenge the great ancient artists, whose feats of creating illusion Alberti described at length.

Most painters continued to work as guild members (though Brunelleschi refused to do so, even when he was imprisoned for refusing to pay his dues). But the new vision of the painter that Alberti described—someone who crossed what had previously been rugged intellectual borders, combining skilled hands with the sort of knowledge that had once been the province of scholars—proved infectious to painters and convincing to patrons. Even at lower levels, contracts for paintings now specified that the master must execute all hands and faces. Some of what we now call the fine arts were being identified as different from other crafts, and their products were coming to be seen not as the collaborative work of many craftsmen but as that of especially brilliant individuals.

LEONARDO, MICHELANGELO, RAPHAEL Three of these individuals have seemed—in their own time and since—to epitomize the new intellectual and cultural standing of the artist: Leonardo da Vinci (1452–1519), Raphael Santi (1483–1530), and Michelangelo Buonarotti (1475–1564). Leonardo and Michelangelo both came from Tuscany, near the centers of artistic innovation; Raphael came from the hilltop court town of Urbino, where his father was a painter. All three learned their arts in the traditional way, as apprentices. All three established their fame by creating ambitious and spectacular paintings: Leonardo's *Last Supper*, his *Mona Lisa*, and *The Virgin of the Rocks*; Raphael's frescoes in the papal palace that depicted the School of Athens (a panorama

Michelangelo's Sistine Chapel Ceiling The famous frescoes Michelangelo painted on the Sistine Chapel's ceiling in 1508–12 illustrate scenes from the Old Testament, including Adam and Eve eating the forbidden fruit and being banished from Eden (top) and God's creation of Eve (center) and Adam (bottom).

The School of Athens This fresco by Raphael Santi in the Vatican palace conveys the Renaissance's reverence for the famous figures of classical philosophy and science: Plato and Aristotle converse (center), Pythagoras reads (bottom left), and Euclid points at a writing slate (bottom right). The seemingly receding arches in the background demonstrate Raphael's command of one-point perspective.

These men embodied—and still embody—a distinctive vision of the artist. Far grander figures than the humanists, the great artists of the years around 1500 fought for their independence even as they were fought over by the patrons whose tastes were most refined. Michelangelo waged endless battles with his chief patron, Pope Julius II (r. 1503–1513), even as he decorated the ceiling of the Sistine Chapel. Their quarrels became legendary, as did the bill the painter presented, in which he asked thousands of ducats for his work but only a small amount for pigments.

Traditionally, in European society, people trained for specialized occupations: craftsmen did the work that they had mastered as apprentices, and scholars wrote about the

of the great classical philosophers in disputation) and the Parnassus; Michelangelo's Sistine Chapel ceiling, with its panorama of the Old Testament, and his *Last Judgment* on the altar wall of the same chapel. And all three knew and responded to one another—especially in 1500 and just after, when Leonardo and Michelangelo were both creating masterpieces in the council chamber of Florence's town hall, the Palazzo Vecchio.

Yet they were much more than brilliant practitioners of a single art form. Leonardo and Michelangelo were as much sculptors as painters. Although Leonardo's enormous equestrian monument for Milan was never cast in bronze (and the clay original was destroyed when the city fell to the French), Michelangelo's figure of David dominated the Piazza della Signoria, Florence's central square. Both were also military engineers: Leonardo in the service of the Sforza family in Milan and then of Cesare Borgia; Michelangelo in that of the Florentine Republic. And all three were architects: Both Raphael and Michelangelo served as the official architect for St. Peter's Basilica in Rome, which was begun by Donato Bramante (1444–1514). Michelangelo finished the design for the church's dome, though he died before it was completed. Leonardo pursued the study of nature, reading and drawing with fantastic energy and compiling his results in enormous, fascinating notebooks. Michelangelo wrote brilliant Italian poetry.

The Virgin of the Rocks Leonardo da Vinci included this painting as part of an altarpiece for the church of San Francesco Grande in Milan in 1506–8. The Virgin Mary sits with the infant John the Baptist and Jesus, while an angel wearing a red cape watches over them.

subjects they had studied at universities. In the Renaissance, as Alberti noted, such barriers began to come down. These powerful artists seemed able to cross the boundaries between the worlds of craft and high learning, and between the crafts themselves. Leonardo challenged the learned physicians of his time in his notebooks. He argued that his knowledge of anatomy and his accurate drawings, with their minutely skillful perspective and foreshortening, enabled him to observe and describe the human body more precisely than they could. He and his two rivals came to be seen as geniuses—unique talents not subject to the rules or limitations that restricted others.

MACHIAVELLI: THE NEW POLITICS

And yet, even as Italian society seemed to reach its zenith of development during the Renaissance, and even as the monarchs and noblemen of France and Germany whose armies ravaged the Italian Peninsula were captivated by the new classical culture of scholarship and art—it seemed that all might be a dream. One of the most loyal servants of the Florentine Republic in the years from 1498 to 1512 was **Niccolò Machiavelli**, whom we met at the beginning of this chapter. Trained in the classics, he worked in the city's chancery and eventually became the right-hand man of Pietro Soderini, chief executive of the republic. Machiavelli went on diplomatic missions and wrote detailed reports about Florence's allies and enemies. He came to see, through the eyes of the other states he visited, just how weak the Italian ones were. Always a believer in the exemplary character of Rome, he organized a civic militia, with uniforms and systematic drill sessions, in the hope that it might provide Florence more protection than mercenary armies. After the republic fell once again to the Medici in 1512, Machiavelli came under suspicion of treason. He was tortured and then exiled from Florence. Settled on his farm outside the city, he pursued an understanding of the events he had been forced to witness: the easy destruction of the Italian states, including his own, by the powerful armies from the north.

Like a good humanist, Machiavelli went back to the ancients—above all to the historians—in the hope of understanding the crisis of his state. In a letter to a trusted member of the Medici regime that had replaced the republic, he described his life—one in which casual reading mingled with lower pursuits such as gambling. But after passing the day in trivialities, Machiavelli explained, he returned home and engaged in reading of a different kind: "I enter

Machiavelli The Florentine artist Rosso Fiorentino painted this early sixteenth-century portrait of the politician and diplomat Niccolò Machiavelli writing in a book.

the ancient courts of ancient men. . . . I am not ashamed to speak with them and to ask them the reason for their actions, and they in their kindness answer me."

The book Machiavelli was writing as he spoke with the ancients was *The Prince*—perhaps the most famous book written during the Renaissance. It represented a radical departure from convention. Earlier humanists from Petrarch on, following ancient precedent, had advised princes to practice virtue at all times and to show mercy and generosity whenever possible. But Machiavelli had watched real princes and other powerful men behave, and he had seen, with fury and contempt, how the princes of Italy and their humanist counselors collapsed before the foreign onslaught. Now he recorded what he saw as the savage truth: safety, for a prince like Ludovico Sforza of Milan, had to come not from his subjects' love, but from their fear; violence, rationally and economically dealt out, was the monarch's chief tool for dealing with both his subjects and his enemies. Machiavelli insisted that "how one lives is so far distant from how one ought to live, that he who neglects what is done for what ought to be done, sooner effects his ruin than his preservation.... Hence it is necessary for a prince wishing to hold his own to know how to do wrong, and to make use of it or not according to necessity." Seneca had warned monarchs to be human, not to imitate the cruel lion or the vicious fox. Machiavelli advised the monarch to imitate both, as circumstances demanded.

Machiavelli went even further. He demanded, more eloquently than any previous writer, that people shake themselves free of the comforting belief that God might help them, and create the only order they could. Unlike many other humanists, Machiavelli clearly saw that the ancient Romans had not been pious in the Christian way. He even praised their warlike religion, which he considered better than Christianity for the health of the state. Yet even Machiavelli, clear-eyed radical that he was, did not foresee the greater tensions and contradictions that would soon tear the fabric, not only of Italy, but of Europe as a whole.

CONCLUSION

The Renaissance was a transformative period. The balance of power in society began to tip away from the powerful noblemen who still played such important roles in later medieval society, and toward central governments, with their new revenue systems, fortifications, and professional soldiers. Merchants and navigators, soldiers and sailors began to turn outward, to explore and conquer parts of the world that had been unfathomably remote or entirely unknown. Scholars discovered in the ancient world new models for understanding the cosmos and human society. Christians experimented with new ways of gaining contact with the divine and some assurance of salvation. And artists devised brilliant and unexpected forms of painting, sculpture, and architecture, transforming the public spaces in cities across Europe. Machiavelli was more pessimistic than the other innovators who were his contemporaries, but he shared with many of them the capacity for seeing the world as it is, and the belief that central governments must prevail.

[CHAPTER REVIEW]

KEY TERMS

Medici family (p. 326)
ambassador (p. 329)
Low Countries (p. 330)
Estates General (p. 331)
taille (p. 331)
Wars of the Roses (p. 333)
justices of the peace
 (p. 333)

Habsburg dynasty (p. 334)
Maximilian I (p. 334)
Alhambra Decree (p. 335)
Ottomans (p. 335)
Mehmed I (p. 335)
Great Schism (p. 339)
Council of Constance
 (p. 340)

confraternity (p. 342)
portolan chart (p. 345)
Johannes Gutenberg
 (p. 349)
Christopher Columbus
 (p. 351)
Treaty of Tordesillas
 (p. 352)

Hernán Cortés (p. 354)
Petrarch (p. 356)
humanism (p. 358)
Leon Battista Alberti
 (p. 364)
Niccolò Machiavelli
 (p. 367)

REVIEW QUESTIONS

1. What were the primary models or structures of government in the city-states of Renaissance Italy?

2. How did the French, Spanish, and English monarchs of the fifteenth century consolidate their power and authority?

3. What were the most important innovations in warfare during the Renaissance?

4. Who were the leading religious reformers of the fourteenth and fifteenth centuries, and what changes did they champion?

5. Why did the European states intensify their efforts in maritime exploration?

6. How did the slave trade change Europe both economically and demographically?

7. How did the arrival of the printing press transform European society?

8. What are the some of the most significant elements of the Columbian Exchange?

9. In what ways was the humanism of the Renaissance revolutionary for its time?

10. What are some of the most important innovations of Renaissance art and architecture?

CORE OBJECTIVES

After reading this chapter, you should have a solid understanding of the following core objectives. To strengthen your grasp of the core objectives, use the resources on the Student Site for The West.

- Describe the political changes that took place in Renaissance Europe.
- Evaluate the crises and reforms that transformed the Church during the Renaissance.
- Trace the emergence of new technologies and areas of knowledge in the fourteenth and fifteenth centuries.

- Analyze the encounter between the Old and New Worlds that began with Columbus's voyages.
- Assess the intellectual and artistic breakthroughs of the Renaissance.

 GO TO inQuizitive TO SEE WHAT YOU'VE LEARNED—AND LEARN WHAT YOU'VE MISSED—WITH PERSONALIZED FEEDBACK ALONG THE WAY.

CHRONOLOGY

1511
Erasmus publishes
In Praise of Folly

October 31, 1517
Luther presents his
Ninety-Five Theses
for formal debate

1524–1525
Peasants' War

October 1529
Luther and Zwingli
divide over Eucharist

1536
Calvin publishes *Institutes
of the Christian Religion*

1543
Copernicus argues
universe is heliocentric

1516
More publishes
Utopia

April 1521
Diet of Worms

1527
Holy Roman Emperor
Charles V's troops
sack Rome

1534
Henry VIII declares
himself head of
independent
Church of England

1540
Pope permits
Loyola to found
Jesuit order

1545–1563
Council of Trent

1555
Peace of Augsburg

Reformations

PROTESTANT AND CATHOLIC

1500–1600

1562–1598
French religious wars
1566–1648
Dutch Revolt
August 24, 1572
Saint Bartholomew's
Day Massacre

1580
Montaigne publishes
his *Essays*

1598
Edict of Nantes

On October 31, 1517, an obscure professor of biblical theology at Wittenberg, the capital of Saxony, changed the world. Martin Luther (1483–1546) published a series of ninety-five theses about indulgences (remissions of penalties for sins, granted by the Catholic Church) and presented them to his superior, the bishop of Brandenburg, and to the archbishop of Mainz. Luther intended to preside over a formal debate of the theses among theologians, a type of public discussion that had been a normal part of academic life for centuries.

But Luther's theses were more radical than most. He denied that Christians should confess to priests, that the pope could remit guilt, and that indulgences could help a dead sinner or a living one who was not repentant. Luther's first concern—confession—was one of the standard practices of the medieval church. To cleanse themselves of sin, Christians had to confess their actions to a priest, feel genuine contrition, and make satisfaction for what they had done by, for example, saying particular prayers or going on pilgrimage to a shrine. Indulgences—certificates that drew on the Treasury of Merit that Christ's sacrifice and the virtues of the saints had created for the church—could remit the actual penalties that the priest imposed. They worked, in theory, only if the sinner had confessed and was repentant. In practice, however, as Luther objected, pardoners sold indulgences not

---

Reformed Worship In 1564, in a Calvinist church in Lyon, France, attendees practice a new style of worship. Sitting on benches that line the round room, they listen as a preacher delivers a sermon, the central feature of services in many of the reformist movements that spread across Europe in the sixteenth century.

FOCUS QUESTIONS

- Why were Luther's criticisms of the Church so influential?
- How did the Reformation movement spread and then splinter?
- How did political and religious allegiance become entangled?
- In what ways did Catholicism renew itself in the sixteenth century?
- What new understandings of the natural world were emerging at this time?
- Why were the religious wars so devastating?
- How did observers make sense of the disruptions of this period?

only to those who wanted to benefit from them after death but also to those who wanted to shorten the time that a dead relative might have to spend in the fires of purgatory to be cleansed of their sin. Some pardoners promised that "so soon as the penny jingles into the money-box, the soul flies out [of purgatory]." But Luther insisted that no human cleric could legitimately make such a promise: "It is certain that when the penny jingles into the money-box, gain and avarice can be increased, but the result of the intercession of the Church is in the power of God alone."

The particular indulgence to which Luther objected was intended to raise money for the construction of the greatest of Renaissance churches, Saint Peter's Basilica in Rome. Pope Leo X (r. 1513–1521) commissioned a Dominican, Johann Tetzel, to sell indulgences in the Holy Roman Empire. Student reports of Tetzel's abuses of the system aroused Luther to action. But it was not only the pardoners' excessive zeal and absurd promises that bothered Luther. The whole enterprise seemed wrong to him. It had made many laypeople worry about the pope and his concern for ordinary Christians. "Why does not the pope empty purgatory," so Luther paraphrased them, "for the sake of holy love and of the dire need of the souls that are there, if he redeems an infinite number of souls for the sake of miserable money with which to build a Church? The former reasons would be most just; the latter is most trivial."

In the end, what mattered most to Luther was not the purpose for which the indulgence was offered but the very idea of it. Christian repentance took place inside the soul. Anyone who preached that Christians could ease their consciences and reconcile themselves with God by paying money failed to understand that all Christians were called to suffer. Their optimistic message, which Luther summed up as "Peace, peace," could not simply be corrected; it must be replaced with the true teaching that Christians must follow Christ, "their Head, through penalties, deaths, and hell."

By early 1518, Luther's theses were being printed in Latin and translated into German so that ordinary people could understand them. Copies flew through the Holy Roman Empire and beyond. Luther himself became a celebrity, a bold German hero who had stood up for his fellow countrymen against the greedy Church of Rome. More important, he became the leader of a movement, one that put an end to the unified Catholic Church that had survived all challenges to its authority in the West for more than a thousand years, and did so not only in the Holy Roman Empire but also across the European world. The movement took its name—Protestantism—from the protest in 1529 of German princes against the Imperial Diet (assembly) in Speyer, which prohibited further religious reforms in the Holy Roman Empire. How did Luther's small act of defiance in a corner of northern Germany have such seismic consequences?

MARTIN LUTHER AND THE CULTURE OF CHURCH REFORM

Part of the explanation of Luther's influence lies in his character. The son of a hard man, a mining entrepreneur, **Martin Luther** joined a religious order at age twenty-two in gratitude to Saint Anne, who, he thought, had saved him from a lightning bolt that struck near him during a thunderstorm. He observed the rule of his order with absolute, almost fanatical devotion. He fasted, prayed, and made himself an expert on the Bible. Luther learned Greek and Hebrew so that he would be able to read the Old and New Testaments in their original languages. He printed special editions of the Psalms for his students, stripping them of commentaries to force the students to confront the original texts, but leaving wide margins so that they could enter their own reflections as they read.

Martin Luther The German artist Lucas Cranach the Elder, a friend of Luther's, painted his portrait in 1529, when Luther was forty-five.

LUTHER'S BREAKTHROUGH

From 1513 to 1517 Luther taught courses on the Psalms, on the apostle Paul, and on the works of Augustine. Meanwhile, he himself suffered from fear and at times paralysis. He worried that God's law, as stated in the Old Testament, was too harsh and demanding for anyone to follow. He continually reproached himself for failing to accomplish one religious duty or another, or for having done it only incompletely or halfheartedly. And then suddenly, one day, he found all his questions answered, all of his problems solved. By reading the Bible in a new way, he discovered, he could absolve himself of the need to follow a massive, arbitrary code of conduct without abandoning his search for grace.

Luther realized that Paul, the author of many of the New Testament epistles, had the answer to his problem. In Romans 1:17, Paul had written: "For therein is the righteousness of God revealed from faith to faith: as it is written, 'The just shall live by faith.'" Here, Luther thought, Paul's message was that the righteousness of God was not something that Christians had to seek endlessly, in a futile effort to curb their own bodies and cure their own vices, but something that Christ had earned for them by his sacrifice. They could share his righteousness if they wanted to: not by buying **indulgences**, not by endless pursuit of perfect obedience to a monastic rule, but simply by having faith in him. Because the New Testament verse contained an internal quotation from an Old Testament prophet, Luther argued, it encapsulated the meaning of the Bible as a whole. The Old Testament taught righteousness, the evil nature of mankind after the Fall, and the demands of God's law. But the New Testament taught faith: that Jesus, by sacrificing himself, had made it possible for all who believed in him to become just as well.

Luther's mastery of theology and his command of the Bible enabled him to view the basic problems of sin and damnation from a new perspective. As we will see, his

Sale of Indulgences A 1539 cartoon from Nuremberg mocks the proliferation of indulgences. The man is dressed in a costume made from letters of indulgences, and the caption explains that the letters are so ridiculous that the man had no choice but to join in the festivities of the Nuremberg carnival.

determination and abilities as a speaker and writer enabled him to bring his message to multiple audiences. Yet it was by no means obvious in 1517 and 1518 that Luther would create anything permanent, much less the first of many new versions of the Christian Church.

CHRISTIANITY IN 1517

In the first place, the world in which Luther lived—the world of late-medieval Christianity—seemed extremely solid. Serious, principled opposition to papal power in the Church had mostly come to an end with the conciliar movement by the middle of the fifteenth century. Girolamo Savonarola's defiance of papal authority in the 1490s had ended with his disgrace and death. The heretical movements of the decades around 1400 were fading slowly away by 1500. Even the once-defiant Hussites of Bohemia saw their movement as coming to an end. One compared it to a dying candle.

Wittenberg itself, where Luther taught, was a center of some of the traditions that he objected to most fiercely. Frederick the Wise (r. 1486–1525), Elector (ruler) of Saxony, believed in the Church's Treasury of Merit. He gained access to it by collecting relics—fragments of the True Cross and the Holy Spear that wounded Jesus on the cross, bones and garments that had belonged to saints, and many more, all encased in splendid vessels that displayed them discreetly through small windows. Frederick's subjects crowded into the local church every year on All Saint's Eve when the collection was put on display. In 1520, his secretary computed that the collection as a whole had earned Frederick and his subjects 1,902,202 years' and 270 days' indulgence from the time they would otherwise have had to spend in purgatory.

The popular response to Frederick's collection of relics showed that the Catholic Church still attracted affection and engagement from most believers, many of whom warmly valued the traditions that Luther challenged. Ordinary Christians crowded parish churches, finding deep rewards in hearing their priests perform the Mass. They embraced the rituals that celebrated the seasons of the agricultural year, such as the Harvest Home festival in the fall, and the yearly reliving of Christ's Passion in the Easter season. In cities, laypeople banded together in confraternities, religious organizations that among other benefits guaranteed their members proper burial.

Christians had always prayed. But the later Middle Ages saw the development of new, engaged forms of prayer. The

Thomas More's Family This 1593 copy of a painting originally by Hans Holbein shows Thomas More (far left) surrounded by his family, all holding books of hours.

rosary, for example—a devotion to the Virgin Mary that consisted of repetitions of the Lord's Prayer and ten Hail Marys—had been created in the thirteenth century. During the fifteenth century, it became normal to repeat the sequence fifteen times, with meditations on the mysteries of the Virgin added. Christians still saw the society of heaven as a hierarchical mirror of society on earth, and sought the help of the members of God's family and the larger community of saints. At the same time, though, worship became more intense and individual, as is clear from the spread of printed books of hours. A famous portrait of the family of Thomas More—English scholar, lawyer, and statesman— shows parents and children with their books of hours in hand, making their household a place of regular and intense devotion. Prayer seemed so precious that wealthy men and women endowed chantries—altars or chapels where masses would be said in perpetuity for their souls.

Serious efforts at reform continued to be made in the monastic and mendicant orders, some of which had become aristocratic preserves. The German Benedictine houses of the Bursfeld congregation, for example, came together for meetings at which the brilliant scholar Johannes Trithemius (1462–1516) called for a revival of the early monastic spirit. He laid out sensible rules for restoring discipline in houses for monks and nuns, and brought the rich spiritual writings of Hildegard of Bingen back into circulation. Franciscans and Dominicans, similarly, made serious efforts to restore their orders to the form that their founders had envisioned.

HUMANIST CRITICS OF THE CHURCH

Others found the Church, and the textures of Christian life, seriously problematic, and they helped to give Luther both the intellectual tools with which he set to work and a receptive audience. Some critics of the Church were rooted in the culture of humanism, which spread through northern Europe in the fifteenth century. As Italian humanists such as Aeneas Silvius Piccolomini (who became Pope Pius II) visited northern lands, and northern scholars such as the Englishman John Free visited Italy, the new methods of Italian humanism provoked increasing interest in the north. The scholarship of the humanists took on new forms, and showed new potentials, in the very different societies of England, France, and the Holy Roman Empire.

DESIDERIUS ERASMUS No one championed the humanism of the north more exuberantly or developed it more effectively than **Desiderius Erasmus** (1466–1536), and no one had a deeper impact on Luther. Born the

Erasmus Albrecht Dürer's 1526 engraving of Erasmus depicts the humanist priest in his element, surrounded by books and with pen in hand.

illegitimate son of a priest in the Netherlandish port city of Rotterdam, Erasmus studied in a school of the Brothers of the Common Life, whose members did not take vows but lived in community houses and earned their living as teachers, scribes, and early adopters of the new technology of printing. After joining a religious order, the Augustinian Canons, Erasmus became a priest. He found monastic life stifling, but never lost the taste he developed there for the meditative, gentle piety of the Brothers' and Canons' movement for religious reform known as Modern Devotion. Soon it became clear, to him and others, that he had unusual talents, especially for writing Latin. A French bishop employed him as a secretary and then gave him a stipend to study in Paris. Erasmus loathed the terrible food and squalid conditions of the Paris colleges, as well as what he considered the sterile pedantry of scholastic theology.

Gradually, however, he made the contacts that would determine the course of his intellectual life. Always a passionate classicist who hated what he called the "barbarians" of the university faculties with their inelegant Latin jargon, he turned out to have a wonderful knack for drawing up textbooks that could help aspiring Latinists become fluent and eventually find careers, as Erasmus had, in the employment of high-ranking clerics and government officials. In London in 1499, he met and was deeply impressed by John Colet (1467–1519), an austere senior scholar who loved the Platonist philosophy of Marsilio Ficino but insisted, at the same time, that Christians must study the New Testament directly. It was in the life, teachings, and death of Jesus, Colet insisted, not in formal theology and philosophy, that Christians would find the central principles of their faith. In 1504, Erasmus discovered a copy of the Italian humanist Lorenzo Valla's commentary on the New Testament. Valla taught him that just as the classics should be read in their original languages, so should the Christian scriptures. Erasmus, who had mastered Greek to support his secular scholarship, was delighted to apply his skills to the Bible.

From 1506 to 1509 Erasmus lived in Italy, where he earned a doctorate in theology from Turin. In Venice he found a home for several months in the printing shop of Aldus Manutius (1449–1515), whose handsome typefaces he admired. Manutius and the Byzantine exiles who corrected Greek texts for him made a wealth of Greek books available to this brilliant visitor. Even as Erasmus established himself as the first northern scholar who knew Greek and wrote Latin as well as any Italian, he continued to look for ways to connect his pursuit of learning with Christian piety.

As Erasmus steeped himself in the New Testament—especially the Gospels, with their vivid depiction of the life and teachings of Jesus—he found himself more and more at odds with society and the Church. The policies of the popes, with their pursuit of worldly power, seemed to contradict the message of Jesus, who had preached poverty and charity. So did the policies of most secular rulers. City burghers pursued wealth as passionately as kings, and nobles pursued power and glory. Their lives did not exemplify Christian principles in action—especially when they refused aid to the many poor people who lived in the streets outside their palaces.

Returning from Italy, Erasmus spent the years 1511 to 1514 in England, where he was professor of theology at the University of Cambridge and worked on the text of the New Testament. But he found other ways to try to reach and change public opinion. Imitating one of his favorite ancient writers, the second-century Greek satirist Lucian, Erasmus wrote a mock oration, *In Praise of Folly*, in which he ridiculed every order of Christian society—but reserved especially sharp mockery for the powerful. He couched criticisms of central features of Church practice in humorous form. Instead of denouncing the scholastic treatises on witches, for example, he made fun of a scholastic who defended them. He heaped ridicule on what he portrayed as the lifeless abstraction of scholastic theology. His book, which first appeared in Strasbourg in 1511, became a bestseller. It provoked furious protests from more traditional theologians.

THOMAS MORE'S *UTOPIA* Erasmus's wit made him friends, as well as enemies, across Europe. A brilliant young English lawyer named **Thomas More** (1478–1535), for example, learned from both Colet and Erasmus and applied their principles in his own highly original way. The Church of the first Christians, as the Gospels portrayed it, had been very different from its contemporary counterpart: not a wealthy, established institution with stiff hierarchies of officials, monks, and mendicants competing for recruits and bequests, but a frail, countercultural movement that had stood against war and tried to help the poor. A gifted student of Greek, More took inspiration from Plato's *Republic* and from contemporary reports of newly discovered lands. In his own book, More imagined a society that he called Utopia (Greek for "no place") and a brilliant, worldly traveler, Raphael Hythloday, who described it to More and other friends. On this pagan island, far from Europe, everyone worked, no one went hungry, and a rigorous system of

More's *Utopia* An illustration from the original 1516 edition of Thomas More's book shows a ship sailing to the island of Utopia.

discipline ensured that no one desired money, the root of all evil.

More's book did not confine itself to portraying an ideal society. In its opening sections More has Hythloday apply the lessons of Utopia and the other imaginary countries he has visited to contemporary England. More, who served in the Parliament and was an expert in international trade, made clear that he thought the society of his day deeply unchristian in Erasmus's sense. It was unfair to the soldiers who were cast off after being injured in its service, and to the peasants whom landlords were allowed to evict so their land could be used more profitably for raising sheep. The sheep, More's narrator complained, were eating the people of England. He was equally critical of Christian kings who wasted their subjects' money on wars meant to pursue their own narrow dynastic aims.

More's *Utopia* was published in 1516 and soon reprinted with approving prefaces by European scholars and enthusiastic marginal notes by Erasmus himself. Although More's narrator claims that work in a royal council would corrupt him rather than improve matters, More himself agreed to serve as a counselor to his young, dynamic king, Henry VIII. In the meantime, though, many readers saw *Utopia* and the *Praise of Folly* as the works not of isolated thinkers but of a more or less united European avant-garde, who were finding sharp new ways to show that classical scholarship and authentic Christian piety complemented one another.

REFORMING THE BIBLE Erasmus did more than remind European readers that Christ had told his followers to give all they had to the poor and turn the other cheek when violence was done to them. As a boy he had learned that true piety was not a matter of observances, of relics collected and indulgences bought, but of repentance and faith. Reading the New Testament in Greek, he found this central message in the words of Jesus and John the Baptist. In the Vulgate, the Latin translation of the Bible carried out in the late fourth century and used in all Catholic churches, Jesus tells Christians that they should "do penance." His command provided the foundation on which the complex system of confession, absolution, and remission of sin rested. In the Greek, however, Jesus instructs his hearers to "repent," meaning to come back to their right minds. Here and in many other passages, Erasmus held, the Latin Bible of the Church was clearly wrong.

Erasmus set out, accordingly, to reform the Vulgate itself. He prepared a revised Latin translation of the New Testament that made his new interpretations clear, and printed it with the Greek text to support it. Erasmus urged readers to refound theology, substituting direct study of the Bible for the logical arguments about doctrine that had traditionally formed the core of the field. His bold undertaking was flanked by even grander enterprises: an edition of the Psalms in Hebrew, Greek, and Arabic, as well as Latin; and a vast edition of the entire Bible, with the Old Testament in Hebrew, Greek, Aramaic, and Latin, and the New Testament in Greek and Latin. This polyglot Bible was sponsored by the Spanish cardinal and statesman Francisco Jiménez de Cisneros. A conservative, he compared the Vulgate text of the Old Testament, which his scholars printed between the Hebrew and the Greek, to Christ crucified between two thieves. But he still supported the study and publication of the originals. A massive controversy flared up in Germany over whether it was legitimate for Christians to learn from Jews and draw on their traditions of scholarship. The very identity of the Bible seemed debatable—just when Erasmus had placed its study at the center of theological inquiry.

LUTHER AND ERASMUS Luther came to maturity in the years when Erasmus and his friends attained the peak of their prestige. He followed Erasmus's teachings and example in making the New Testament the source for all Christian truths, and he used Erasmus's New Testament edition. His critique of indulgences began from the same point that Erasmus had made: that Jesus commanded not the doing of penance but repentance. Many of those who read Luther's theses and sent them on to colleagues and printers were clerics and officials who had read Erasmus's textbooks in their youth and shared his belief that Christians needed to return to their original principles. Like Erasmus himself, they saw Luther at first as an ally—as someone who continued the Christian humanist critique of the Church and offered the Bible as a template for its reform.

LUTHER'S MESSAGE

In fact, however, as Luther's message began to spread—and to encounter challenges—it became clear that his vision differed sharply from that of Erasmus: Luther represented not a movement to reform the existing Church but a challenge to its very existence. Between 1517 and 1521, he definitively stated most of his central doctrines in short, accessible books in Latin and German. Only scripture, Luther argued, contained the truths a Christian needed. Only divine grace made it possible to read scripture properly. And only faith in Jesus could win salvation. Everything else the Church did and believed, Luther now argued, was superfluous, and much of it harmful. The Church must be rebuilt on a solid foundation of scripture, correctly interpreted.

Traditional Catholic doctrine held that priests occupied a special spiritual as well as social position: they could intervene for other Christians, releasing them from the consequences of their sins. Luther argued that all Christians were priests who could pray for one another. Whereas Catholic priests offered seven distinct sacraments, Luther recognized only two: infant baptism and the Eucharist. And whereas the Catholic Church presented itself as a spiritual body that transcended mere political and linguistic borders and owed obedience only to the pope, Luther demanded that Christian rulers emulate Constantine, the emperor who had established Christianity as the religion of the Roman Empire and convoked the Council of Nicea to settle disputed points of doctrine. Secular rulers, Luther insisted, must take responsibility for the local churches that were under their political jurisdiction.

THE DIET OF WORMS AND ITS AFTERMATH (1521)

Luther's ideas now circulated in high official circles, especially after Albert of Brandenburg, Cardinal and Elector of Mainz, forwarded the **Ninety-Five Theses** to Rome. In July 1519, the eminent Catholic theologian Johann Eck (1486–1543) engaged Luther in a debate at Leipzig. Eck forced Luther to admit that he believed popes and even Church councils could err: only scripture was infallible. Eck pushed for a response from the Church, and in June 1520 Pope Leo X issued a bull condemning Luther.

Called to the **Diet of Worms**, a formal meeting of the Imperial Estates in April 1521, Luther accepted the invitation and stood before Holy Roman Emperor Charles V (r. 1519–1556) himself. Eck showed Luther a display of his writings and asked if he acknowledged them as his own. Luther requested time to reflect, but the next day he gave his opponents a sharp answer that expressed his conviction that he was acting as grace dictated:

> Unless I am convinced by the testimony of the Scriptures or by clear reason (for I do not trust either in the pope or in councils alone, since it is well known that they have often erred and contradicted themselves), I am bound by the Scriptures I have quoted and my conscience is captive to the Word of God. I cannot and will not recant anything, since it is neither safe nor right to go against conscience. May God help me. Amen.

Of Luther's extraordinary courage there can be no doubt. But his unflinching stance did not impress the emperor, who soon afterward delivered an impressive reply. He insisted on his duty, inherited from his ancestors, to defend the Catholic faith. On May 25, 1521, the emperor made Luther an outlaw. He forbade all subjects of the empire to give Luther food or water and permitted anyone to kill him without fear of consequences.

When Luther left the Diet, he was arrested by servants of Frederick the Wise, Elector of Saxony. They took him to the Wartburg castle in Eisenach, almost in the center of Germany, where he remained for several months under a loose form of house arrest. He used the time to translate the New Testament into German, realizing Erasmus's program to make the Bible available to all Christians. He poured out a series of pamphlets and treatises in which he began to draw the full consequences of his new theology. He argued, for example, that monks and nuns need not follow their vows of chastity, since marriage was a holy state, or of obedience, since obeying a superior would not bring them farther along the path to salvation.

By the end of 1521, Luther was hearing worrying messages from Wittenberg. Another minister who wished to reform the Church, Andreas Karlstadt (1486–1541), had taken over Luther's pulpit there. A radical by temperament, Karlstadt was inspired not only by Luther but also by miners from a nearby city, uneducated men who had visions and prophesied. Together they set out to transform the Church in Wittenberg beyond recognition. Whereas Luther argued that Christians should be able to understand the Bible for themselves, Karlstadt replaced the Latin Mass with a German-language service. And whereas Luther argued that Christians should not set too much store on images of saints, Karlstadt gained consent from the city council in 1522 to remove them from Wittenberg's churches.

Allowed to return to Wittenberg in March 1522, Luther appeared on his pulpit in the robes of his Augustinian Canons order. In a brilliant series of sermons, he convinced his fellow inhabitants of Wittenberg that it was wrong to move too quickly or to change things too radically, since by doing so they threatened the consciences of Christians who were not yet certain of the truth. Taking command of the situation, Luther began to create a new Church order. Soon cities across the Holy Roman Empire and beyond,

Diet of Worms A sixteenth-century history of Germany illustrates the dramatic scene of Luther's defense of his ideas to Holy Roman Emperor Charles V. The Catholic theologian Johann Eck (holding a book at center left) interrogates Luther as courtiers look on.

especially in Switzerland, were publicly joining the cause of reform. Luther himself was certain of what made his views—some of them highly abstract and difficult—take wing as they did. He and his dear friend and helper Philip Melanchthon simply sat in Wittenberg, he told his students much later, and drank the local dark beer. The Holy Spirit did the rest.

THE REFORMATION MOVEMENT

Between 1521 and 1529, Luther's challenge to the authority of the Church became a movement—the movement that became known, after the Diet of Speyer in 1529, as the **Protestant Reformation**. Princes and cities across the Holy Roman Empire and Switzerland, and individuals across a far wider area, found inspiration in Luther's writings to transform local churches. But they also encountered resistance—sometimes from Catholics faithful to the established order of things, sometimes from fellow Protestants who disagreed with them on basic questions of theology or Church discipline. By 1529, it was clear that the Protestant challenge would not soon disappear. But it was also clear that Protestantism would not take a single form or remain a unified movement. Luther's success was extraordinary—and partial.

THE MOVEMENT'S APPEAL

Many clearly identifiable features of Luther's world, beyond Wittenberg's dark beer, made his success possible. The power of print and the structures of authority in cities and states played vital roles in transforming a message into a movement.

THE ROLE OF PRINT Most important, the printing press gave Luther a megaphone that previous critics of the established Church lacked until the late fifteenth century, when the followers of Savonarola in Florence printed multiple editions of the Dominican's sermons. Luther used it with determination and brilliance. He became the master of the theological pamphlet, in both Latin and German. As a writer and translator, he developed a flexible German idiom that he could use both to render the word of God and to make his own arguments. He printed much of what he wrote—so much that, by the end of 1521, more than 100 editions of his works had already appeared. If each edition was produced in the period's standard quantity of 500 to 1,000 copies, then tens of thousands of copies of Luther's

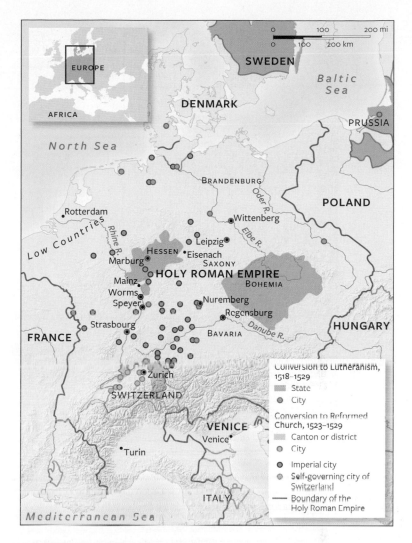

The Reformation Movement, 1521–1529 By 1529, Lutheranism had spread from the central German cities where Luther's message first took hold to large states like Bohemia, Hessen, Prussia, and Sweden. In the area around Zurich, meanwhile, Zwingli's Reformed movement gained converts.

texts must have been in circulation four years after the outbreak of his movement. Luther and his printers developed a uniform format that became closely associated with him—some historians call this the first media brand.

Luther and his followers used illustrations as well as texts to appeal to their fellow Christians. Even before printing with moveable type was introduced in the West, collections of woodcut illustrations with some text, known as block books, brought graphic versions of the biblical narratives to readers of modest means and education. When printers learned to reproduce substantial texts with moveable type, they continued to adorn them with woodcut illustrations. Illustrated texts were far more accessible than unbroken blocks of type. A single

Printing Bibles A 1465 "pauper's Bible" demonstrates how printing technology could make the stories and ideas of the Bible accessible to all. Short excerpts from the text of the Latin Vulgate are set alongside woodcut illustrations of key stories, such as the birth of Jesus (center).

literate person could read them aloud to a circle of illiterate hearers, who could still appreciate the illustrations. And illustrations lent themselves to polemic. They could be used to contrast the poverty and humility of the Jesus of the New Testament to the arrogant, overstuffed clerics in Rome. They could also be used to spread news of portents, such as the fall of meteors or the birth of strangely deformed animals, which suggested that God was warning his people of important changes soon to occur. The artists who followed Luther—above all Lucas Cranach the Elder (1472–1553), the Wittenberg court artist—became expert at composing religious comic books and illustrating the Bible with polemical woodcuts that presented a bold challenge to the established Church.

SOCIAL BASES OF REFORM Luther's message would never have found the reception it did if he had not been speaking to the passions and interests of Christians, powerful and not, across the social spectrum. When Luther appealed to secular authorities to take control over the churches in their domains, he addressed princes and kings eager to enlarge their power and revenues, and city magistrates who believed that they were more qualified than any outsiders to see to the moral and spiritual health of their fellow citizens. When he addressed social and economic questions—such as bankers' practice of charging excess interest, which he denounced, or landlords' exploitation of their tenants—he seemed to offer hope to many that the message of the Gospel, as he defined it, would also change their position in life for the better. And when he told Christians that in so far as any of them were priests, all of them were, and all of them could intercede for one another, he seemed to offer women a religious position and role very different from anything that traditional Christianity in the West had provided. Support for Luther also came from master artisans and journeymen, printers and (in Saxony) miners—practitioners of new and expanding crafts.

REFORM IN THE CITIES Luther's message held special appeal in the imperial cities of the Holy Roman Empire—some sixty-nine cities such as Nuremberg, most in southern Germany, that acknowledged no authority below the Holy Roman emperor himself—and in the self-governing cities of Switzerland. City magistrates had long taken responsibility for settling disputes between such Catholic institutions as religious orders in their territory. Many cities had traditional shrines to which pilgrims came, bringing income; but many resented the need to pay ecclesiastical dues to the Roman Church every time a new bishop or abbot was inaugurated. Each city played out its own complex drama, following its own pace; in many, members of established elites—wealthy merchants, for example, and university professors—acted as a brake on both popular pressure and government action.

The case of Regensburg, an imperial city in Bavaria, illustrates the complexity of these processes. In 1519, the city expelled its Jewish community, which had been there since Roman times, and destroyed their synagogue. During the destruction a workman fell from a roof or was struck by a beam (accounts vary), but escaped harm. He claimed that the Virgin Mary had held his hand. Others ascribed his salvation to a medieval image of the Virgin in Regensburg. A wooden chapel was built on the site to hold it, with a statue of the Virgin outside. Crowds began to visit it. "'All sorts of people came,' one witness noted: 'some with musical instruments, some with pitchforks and rakes; women came with their milk cans, spindles, and cooking pots. Artisans came with their tools: a weaver with his shuttle, a carpenter with his square, a cooper with his measuring tape.'" More than 100,000 pilgrims visited within a year, buying

The Virgin of Regensburg Printed at the height of enthusiasm for the Virgin at Regensburg, this woodcut image shows the statue in front of the wooden chapel, which is decorated with the arms of the city. Pilgrims line up to view the statue, with the most fervent collapsing in adoration.

badges to stick in their caps to show that they had done so. But by 1524, enthusiasm for the miracle-working image had ebbed. The city council busied itself trying to reform the local church while expelling Lutherans—clear evidence that Luther's message was being preached. By 1542, however, the council officially made the city Lutheran. A stone structure begun in 1525 to replace the wooden chapel was completed in 1542 and became the city's first Protestant church. Many cities experienced religious changes as rapid and unexpected as these in the 1520s.

LUTHER'S CRITICS

Yet Luther's success was anything but complete. In the first place, the radicalism of his challenge to the Church posed the question of authority in a new way. If the pope and his theologians had no right to determine the correct interpretation of the Bible or the theological doctrines that rested on it, then who did? Luther claimed that this power rested with the individual Christian. But even many of the humanists who had agreed that traditional Church structures and doctrines needed reform were shocked by the clean sweep that Luther proposed to make. Thomas More, for example, persisted in believing that the prayers of the living were needed by the souls who suffered in purgatory—a place whose very existence Luther denied. More lampooned Luther as an "infallible donkey" who proposed to replace the infallible pope of tradition with his own equally unquestionable authority.

ERASMUS'S HUMANIST CRITIQUE Erasmus, on the whole, agreed. As the contours of Luther's doctrines became clearer, Erasmus realized that the reformer really saw human nature as devoid of any value or virtue except what came to it through faith. By definition, men and women could play no active part in their own salvation. Ever the humanist, Erasmus believed that the best of the pagans had lived and thought in a virtuous way—so virtuous that they were almost Christians. And he could not accept the idea that God simply reached down and saved certain individuals. In a treatise against Luther published in 1524, Erasmus attacked him for claiming certainty on issues too difficult for human understanding. True Christians, he explained, preferred to avoid the sort of furious debates with colleagues that Luther's brand of theology required.

More important, Erasmus claimed, Luther was simply wrong about the relationship between humankind and God. A little child, Erasmus explained, cannot walk without the help of an adult—or be made to walk by that adult if he or she refuses to cooperate. This was also the situation of the Christian soul: too weak to save itself, but a vital participant in the drama of its own salvation. Luther—a far more rigorous theologian than Erasmus—devastated the humanist in his reply, but by the same token he made clear that he was now going down a road where some of those who had supported him would not follow.

ULRICH ZWINGLI Even those who dedicated themselves to reform in Luther's sense, moreover, did not always agree with him on vital details. What was the sacrament of the Eucharist, for example? Catholics believed that though the bread and wine of the Mass still looked like the original substances, the priest's words transformed them into the body and blood of Christ (the doctrine of transubstantiation). Luther argued that the Eucharist contained both sets of substances at once: bread and body,

Ulrich Zwingli An uncompromising reformer, Zwingli founded the Reformed church and transformed public conduct in Zurich and beyond.

wine and blood (a doctrine called consubstantiation). But **Ulrich Zwingli** (1484–1531), a former priest who led the transformation of the church in the Swiss city of Zurich, took a different view. Zwingli and others argued that the bread and wine remained themselves, rather than changing into a new substance, and represented the body and blood of Christ only as symbols. Luther denounced these views. After some polemical exchanges, the disagreeing parties met at Marburg Castle, in Hessen, in October 1529. When Luther chalked "This is my body" on a table, laid a cloth over the words, and defended his views forcefully, Zwingli insisted that "is," in this context, meant "stands for," as it did when Jesus said "I am the true vine" or "I am the road." Discussion soon broke down as the theologians traded insults. What had started out as a single movement began to fragment into multiple reformations.

FISSURES IN THE MOVEMENT: ZURICH AND THE REFORMED TRADITION

In Zurich, Ulrich Zwingli built a distinctive church. He was inspired not only by Luther, who taught him to insist that all believers were priests and to eliminate the old clerical estate, but also by Erasmus and other Christian humanists who had hoped to see Christianity transform society. Uncompromising in his reforms, Zwingli found support in the radical journeymen and women who, in Zurich, wielded a measure of political influence and power. Through two public disputations and a long series of sermons, he and his colleagues won over the Zurich population and their magistrates, who accepted the Reformation in 1523.

Zwingli's church—the first of the Protestant churches, based in Switzerland, that came to be called Reformed rather than Lutheran—differed from Luther's in both style and substance. Whereas Luther refused to eliminate all Catholic observances at once, Zwingli fought to reduce Christian ritual as soon as possible to the minimum clearly prescribed by the New Testament. Whereas Luther retained, and reformed, church music, Zwingli banned both instrumental music and singing. When Zwingli denounced religious images as a violation of divine law, the authorities had the great triptychs in Zurich's main churches closed. But their action inspired Zwingli's followers to tear down other shrines and images. In June 1524 the local authorities made Zwingli's position official, ordering that all churches be "cleansed" of their religious images and stained glass. Zwingli was delighted by the "white" and "luminous" look of the undecorated churches.

Zwingli also set out to impose Christian discipline on the citizens of Zurich. Here too differing from Luther, who held that what mattered to Christians was the condition of their souls, Zwingli argued that the Christian magistrate must reform public behavior as well as worship. Zurich adopted laws that regulated Sabbath observance and other forms of public conduct, while a new Marriage Court oversaw the making of marriages and the conduct of married life. By the mid-1520s, the church of Reformed Zurich looked very different from the one that Luther had built in Wittenberg.

TRANSFORMING SOCIETY: THE PEASANTS' WAR (1524–1525)

In the same decade, moreover, the messages of Luther and his rivals rippled through German society, sometimes joined to social and political grievances held by people across the social order. Early in the 1520s, for example, the German knights—a group of minor aristocrats who, like the governments of the imperial cities, recognized only

MARTIN LUTHER AND THE PEASANTS' WAR

The rebels who took part in the Peasants' War of 1524–25 were influenced by radical religious ideas as well as long-standing social grievances. Their demands are well stated in their manifesto, the Twelve Articles of the Peasants (1525), largely the work of the preacher Christoph Schappeler and a journeyman furrier, Sebastian Lotzer. Several Reformation theologians published responses to the Twelve Articles, notably Martin Luther, who in his *Admonition to Peace Concerning the Twelve Articles of the Peasants* (1525) urged lords and peasants to reach an understanding. Luther's position hardened into strong opposition to the peasants, however, as the uprising intensified.

Twelve Articles of the Peasants

The First Article. First, it is our humble petition and desire, indeed our will and resolution, that in the future we shall have power and authority so that the entire community should choose and appoint a minister, and that we should have the right to depose him should he conduct himself improperly. The minister thus chosen should teach us the holy gospel pure and simple, without any human addition, doctrine or ordinance....

The Second Article. Since the right tithe is established in the Old Testament and fulfilled in the New, we are ready and willing to pay the fair tithe of grain. Nonetheless, it should be done properly. The Word of God plainly provides that it should be given to God and passed on to his own. If it is to be given to a minister, we will in the future collect the tithe through our church elders, appointed by the congregation, according to the judgment of the whole congregation. The remainder shall be given to the poor of the place, as the circumstances and the general opinion demand....

The Third Article. It has been the custom hitherto for men to hold us as their own property, which is pitiable enough considering that Christ has redeemed and purchased us without exception, by the shedding of his precious blood, the lowly as well as the great. Accordingly, it is consistent with Scripture that we should be free and we wish to be so. Not that we want to be absolutely free and under no authority. God does not teach us that we should lead a disorderly life according to the lusts of the flesh, but that we should live by the commandments, love the Lord our God and our neighbor....

Conclusion...If any one or more of these articles should not be in agreement with the Word of God, which we do not think, we will willingly recede from such article when it is proved to be against the Word of God by a clear explanation of the Scripture.

Martin Luther, *Admonition to Peace Concerning the Twelve Articles of the Peasants*

To the Princes and Lords

We have no one on earth to thank for this disastrous rebellion, except you princes and lords, and especially you blind bishops and mad priests and monks, whose hearts are hardened, even to the present day.... You do nothing but cheat and rob the people so that you may lead a life of luxury and extravagance. The poor common people cannot bear it any longer.... If it is still possible to give you advice, my lords, give way a little to the will and wrath of God. Try kindness first, for you do not know what God will do to prevent the spark that will kindle all Germany and start a fire that no one can extinguish....

To the Peasants

In the first place, dear brethren, you bear the name of God and call yourselves a "Christian association" or union, and you allege that you want to live and act according to divine law. Now you know that the name, word, and cities of God are not to be assumed idly or in vain....

I say this, dear friends, as a faithful warning. In this case you should stop calling yourselves Christians and stop claiming that you have the Christian law on your side.... So again I say, however good and just your cause may be, nevertheless, because you would defend yourselves and are unwilling to suffer either violence or injustice, you may do anything that God does not prevent. However, leave the name Christian out of it....

It...you will...keep the name of Christian, then I must accept the fact that I am also involved in this struggle and consider you as enemies who, under the name of the gospel, act contrary to it, and want to do more to suppress my gospel than anything the pope and emperor have done to suppress it....

Admonition to Both Rulers and Peasants

Now, dear sirs, there is nothing Christian on either side and nothing Christian is at issue between you; both lords and peasants are discussing questions of justice and injustice in heathen, or worldly, terms.... For God's sake, then, take my advice! Take a hold of these matters properly, with justice and not with force or violence and do not start endless bloodshed in Germany....

QUESTIONS FOR ANALYSIS

1. How do the Twelve Articles interpret grievances according to religious principles?
2. What are Luther's greatest objections to the Twelve Articles?
3. Compare the ideals of the peasants and Martin Luther as articulated in these sources.

Sources: From "The Twelve Articles of the Peasants," in *Christianity and Revolution*, ed. Lowell Zuck (Philadelphia: 1975), pp. 14–16; from *Admonition to Peace Concerning the Twelve Articles of the Peasants*, in *Luther's Works*, vol. 46, eds. Robert C. Schultz and Helmut T. Lehmann (Philadelphia: 1967), pp. 19, 23–24, 32, 40.

the emperor as their superior—rebelled, claiming among other things that they meant to restore the true Church. They were soon put down. But during the **Peasants' War** of 1524–25, hundreds of thousands of peasants and craftsmen rebelled against their lords across central and southern Germany. This was not the first time, by any means, that peasants in these areas had risen. In 1476, thousands of them had converged on a town in southern Germany to hear the dramatic speeches of a former drummer turned prophet, Hans Böhm, who denounced the corruption of the clergy and demanded that all forests and waters be held in common. Others had followed a banner in the form of a peasant's rough shoe to denounce unjust taxes. In these earlier uprisings, peasants aimed generally for the restoration of traditional rights that had been taken from them.

The peasants who rose in 1524–25 also denounced

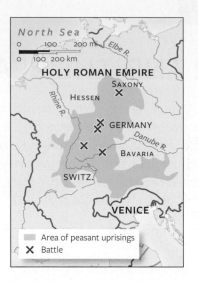

The Peasants' War, 1524–1525
Peasants' rebellions spread throughout a wide area of central and southern Germany, drawing thousands into pitched battles with royal forces from Bavaria, Hessen, and Saxony.

their landlords for depriving them of such traditional rights as gathering fallen firewood in the forests. Many of them were aggrieved by governments' and landlords' increasing use of written law and legal documents. But in the collections of articles drafted for them, they demanded much more. For the first time, peasants appealed to a fixed, printed text—that of the Gospels—to define their rights. As Christians, they claimed, they should be allowed to hear the true Gospel preached. As believers, moreover, they were free men and women, as Luther himself had written in a tract of 1521. Therefore, their lords had no right to make them serfs and bind them to the land.

The wave of peasant unrest and demands began in the countryside outside Zurich. Inspired by the transformation of the city, peasants and others called for a transformation of German society. The preacher Christoph Schappeler imagined that they might form a peasant republic, directly subject, as the imperial cities were, to the Holy Roman emperor. Schappeler defended their right, founded on the need to create a society of "brotherly love," to depose tyrants who opposed them. For a time, the princes and prelates seemed paralyzed as bands of peasants sacked castles and monasteries unopposed.

From Luther's standpoint, the peasant rebels were remaking his message of spiritual liberty into a charter for fundamental social change. Horrified by what he saw as a diabolic perversion of his enterprise, Luther called on the authorities to massacre the peasants. In May 1525, the princes of Bavaria, Hessen, and Saxony destroyed armed peasant bands in a series of pitched battles: in one encounter, 5,000 of the 6,000 peasants who took part were massacred in a single day.

The defeat of the peasants seemed total. Yet lords in much of the Holy Roman Empire came away from the uprising determined never to provoke another movement of the same kind. They changed the legal status of peasants to give them freedom of movement and of marriage, and peasants were accorded the clear right to long-term possession of their dwellings. Especially in the western parts of the Holy Roman Empire and in Switzerland, the successors of the massacred peasants enjoyed, from the sixteenth to the eighteenth centuries, many of the rights that they had demanded. By contrast, in eastern Germany,

Peasant Preaching Inspired by the writings of Martin Luther, peasants began to frame their sufferings and demands within the context of the Gospels. In this 1525 woodcut, a peasant preacher and follower of Luther gives a sermon to an attentive crowd.

Poland, and Russia during the same period, landlords succeeded in enserfing their peasants, building large estates, and tying their workforces to the land.

RADICAL REFORMATION: THE ANABAPTISTS

Even as the heaped corpses of the peasants were being buried, small groups, mostly in cities, were moving in what ultimately became an even more frightening direction for Luther, Zwingli, and other founders of reform. This movement began, like the Peasants' War, in Zurich, where Conrad Grebel (ca. 1498–1526) and other radical reformers were both inspired and infuriated by Zwingli. They agreed with him that the reform of religion meant the reform of society, and that scripture should serve as the rule for all changes. But they rejected Zwingli's defense of the tradition of infant baptism even though the New Testament always depicted baptism as for adults. When their ideas met resistance in Zurich, the radicals moved into the countryside. Peasants who found the city's rule oppressive were impressed by the denunciation of the tithes that they had to pay and the heavy hand of the city's government on areas outside the city walls. Others who heard these radicals preach, including merchants, craftsmen, and women, turned back to their own Bibles and found there a literal pattern for Christian life. They came to be known as **Anabaptists** ("re-baptizers"), because they believed that one could not properly join a church until one was an adult, like the adult converts of John the Baptist and Jesus.

Luther, in the tradition of Augustine, envisioned the Church as a universal community of the saved and the damned in this world. By contrast, the Anabaptists—like Augustine's ancient opponents, the Donatists—saw the Church as a small community of the saved, who had committed themselves to lead a Christian life. Luther accepted the need for private property, law, warfare, and all the other appurtenances of civil life in the world. The first Anabaptists refused to take oaths or fight, and they tried to live a literal version of the precepts of Jesus in the Gospels.

Luther was slow to turn against fellow reformers. Though he had helped to expel Andreas Karlstadt from the pulpit in Wittenberg and viewed him as a dangerous radical, he sheltered Karlstadt in his own house during the Peasants' War. But in the course of that conflict, as we saw, Luther had sided with the German princes—even Catholic princes—against the rebels. He and the secular

Persecution of Anabaptists A sixteenth-century engraving shows a crowd surrounding the cage containing the body of the Anabaptist leader John of Leiden, who was tortured and executed in Münster.

authorities responded to what they saw as the subversive program of the Anabaptists with special savagery. They made practicing or praising adult baptism and pacifism capital offenses. A number of the Anabaptists were executed for their beliefs. The ex-Benedictine monk Michael Sattler, who wrote the Anabaptist articles of faith known as the Schleitheim Confession and served as a roving missionary for his causes, was tortured and executed in 1527 while on a mission in southern Germany.

Many Anabaptists began to believe—as Luther himself did—that they were living through the last days of the world and that they were the holy martyrs whose lives and suffering were the central drama of the biblical book of Revelation. Divisions began to appear among them, and some of their leading figures, such as the one-time furrier-turned-preacher Melchior Hoffmann, predicted that the new era was about to start. Hoffmann was imprisoned in Strasbourg, the city where he had expected the

New Jerusalem to rise, and died in captivity in 1543. In Münster, in western Germany, groups of Anabaptists took up arms in 1534, expelled the bishop who ruled the city, and created a polygamous commune loosely modeled on the Israel of the Old Testament. After months of fierce resistance, they were crushed in June 1535, and their prophet, John of Leiden, was brutally executed some months later.

Surviving Anabaptists responded to this disaster in different ways. Pilgram Marpeck, a successful businessman from the Tirol, became an Anabaptist in 1527 and settled in Strasbourg in 1528. He became city engineer, first there and then in Augsburg, and his usefulness to governments protected him from violence. Weaving networks to bring his coreligionists together, he urged them to take oaths and pay taxes when the law required. Other Anabaptists, above all the Dutch ex-priest Menno Simons, insisted on the central importance of maintaining a communal life and the authority of the church. His followers, called Mennonites, became known for their commitment to pacifism. Thousands of Anabaptists took refuge in Moravia, now part of the Czech Republic, where they were eagerly sought as tenants by lords looking for reliable farmers. Some of the Moravian Anabaptists accepted the need of states to use force to defend themselves, while others rejected the use of arms on principle. The members of this latter group, which came to be known as Hutterites after their leader, Jacob Hutter (d. 1536), also decided to share all their property. Though the Anabaptists soon ceased to pose a serious challenge to the larger churches, they continued to be seen as a threat and were regularly persecuted. Their presence did much to make Luther and other reformers emphasize the need for central authority in church and state.

Lutheran Schools A 1516 painting illustrates the access to literacy that Lutheran Sunday schools provided. A schoolmaster directs a student in writing the alphabet, while other students read bound books.

RELIGIOUS EDUCATION

Luther and his allies saw education in the true principles of Christianity as one way to prevent further divisions, and did their best to ensure that all Lutherans knew the fundamentals of their faith. This view brought Philip Melanchthon, Luther's friend and a brilliant Greek scholar, to Wittenberg, where he created the curricula for what became Protestant secondary schools and universities. Luther's followers also established Sunday schools, where children learned the elements of literacy and the fundamentals of doctrine, which they memorized from catechisms. Bishops undertook regular visitations to ensure that ministers preached true doctrine and to oversee the quality of the schools. Luther loved music, and he and others wrote hymns that would become a cornerstone of Protestant religious practice. This was not complex music performed by professionals, as in the Catholic Church, but participatory singing in which the congregation could take part. In some Lutheran countries—especially in Denmark—male and female literacy seems to have become almost universal, and knowledge of religious doctrines with it. In Luther's own Germany, however, efforts at Protestant education met with varied levels of success. Some visitations reported orderly classes and knowledgeable parishioners; others described drunken mockers who scorned the Lord's Day. Building a new church was not easy.

WOMEN AND THE REFORMATION

Luther followed Paul in arguing that all Christians—women as well as men—were priests and could pray for one another. He himself married a former nun to show his rejection of celibacy as a human tradition. But he may have been surprised when he saw that some women were not only listening to and reading him but also imitating him. When a young man was imprisoned for Protestant heresy at Ingolstadt, a stronghold of traditional Catholicism, a Bavarian noblewoman, **Argula von Grumbach** (1492–ca. 1554), denounced what she considered to be the effort of Church authorities to attack the true Gospel.

A pious woman who had learned in her youth to pray to the Virgin Mary and to imagine herself conversing with angels, von Grumbach had also read the Bible—especially the Prophets and the New Testament. When she read the pamphlets that the Wittenberg presses were shipping in barrels across the Bavarian border, she was immediately convinced of the truth of Luther's message. She set out to defend the young man under accusation with all her strength. In a long letter to the theologians at Ingolstadt, she cited verse after verse from the Bible in support of Luther's new theology: "What do Luther and Melanchthon teach you but the word of God?" She used both the powerful language of the prophets and her own sharp idioms to tell the theologians that they were in the wrong: "The pot burns: and truly you and your university will never extinguish it."

Von Grumbach's letter to the Ingolstadt theologians circulated first in manuscript and then as a pamphlet, which was reprinted fourteen times. By the time she stopped writing, as many as 29,000 copies of that and other pamphlets by her may have been in circulation. She became a Protestant celebrity, who had the chance to share a meal with the legendarily busy Luther. She even gave him advice, for his wife, on how to wean her children. Von Grumbach and others—such as the former abbess Marie Dentière—rejected Paul's principle that women should not teach, arguing that Jesus had commanded all to preach his message. The British Protestant Anne Askew, who courted arrest by preaching, was tortured and then executed by burning at Smithfield in June 1546. She became one of the most famous Protestant martyrs; contemporary Protestant historians compared her to the early Christians who had died for their faith. Yet most of the women who set out to preach and write in public were silenced without winning fame.

Queens and noblewomen commanded the respectful attention of reformers—and were sometimes rewarded in special ways for doing so. Anna von Stolberg, abbess of Quedlinburg in the Black Forest, governed nine churches and two male monasteries. In the 1540s, when she converted to Protestantism, she ordered her priests to swear loyalty to Luther and turned her Franciscan monastery into an elementary school for boys and girls. Under her rule, Quedlinburg remained a convent even as it turned Protestant—as did many others.

Protestant women could leave convents and marry—as Katharina von Bora (1499–1552) did: after leaving her Cistercian monastery, she married Luther. Like earlier women we have encountered, von Bora participated actively in economic life even after finding a husband. The elector of Saxony gave her and Luther the property of the Augustinian cloister in Wittenberg. Teaching, preaching, and writing kept Martin busy. Accordingly, von Bora managed the estate, rising every day at 4:00 a.m. In addition to bearing Luther six children, she bred and sold cattle, brewed beer, and operated a hospital when epidemics struck. Yet von Bora always recognized Luther's supremacy in their

Katharina von Bora In 1528, Lucas Cranach the Elder painted this portrait of Katharina von Bora, the former nun who married Martin Luther.

marriage, calling him "Sir Doctor" and insisting that his calling was higher than hers.

As this case suggests, the larger position of women was not clearly transformed by the Reformation. The guildsmen who dominated cities that reformed their churches, such as Nuremberg, believed in the central importance of the patriarchal family. New legislation limited the roles that women could play—especially when, as happened in most Protestant cities, the convents were abolished and women could no longer live celibate lives as nuns. Sexual crimes were redefined: rape, for example, came to be treated less as a violent crime perpetrated by men than as evidence of licentious behavior by women. Male supremacy was reinforced in many ways: even Argula von Grumbach wrote with sorrow of the violence that she had suffered at the hands of her husband. Equality in the realm of the spirit did not bring with it the leveling of gender hierarchies.

THE MESSAGE SPREADS

By the later 1520s, Luther's period as the most influential spokesman of reform was coming to an end. But the messages of reform were spreading farther across Europe through efficient networks of exchange. Merchants and artisans—especially journeymen printers—carried the call for reform south to the Mediterranean and west and north to France, Britain, and Scandinavia. Hans Tauler, a former monk, preached the Reformation in Denmark and Norway. Though the king of Denmark and Norway, Frederick I (r. 1523–1533), claimed to oppose the Protestants, he protected Tauler and encouraged others to translate the Bible into the vernacular. Frederick was succeeded by Christian III (r. 1534–1559), who formally abolished the Mass, removed Catholic bishops, and installed Lutheran ones. Even in Spain, followers of Erasmus challenged and criticized traditional practices and beliefs. Some Italians—such as Bernardino Ochino, general of the Capuchin order, a branch of the Franciscans—realized that they agreed with the Protestants, and fled into exile in the north. Others continued to attend Catholic services but worshipped a Protestant God in secret. Germans in London made the Steelyard—the residence of merchants from the northern German trading cities that belonged to the Hanseatic League—a center of Protestant propaganda, to the fury of the British government. Even in France, traditionally "the most Christian nation" and loyal to the papacy, radical teachings spread. In 1534, in the Affair of the Placards, posters denouncing the Mass appeared all over Paris and other important cities—one of them on the king's bedroom door. These developments unleashed a vigorous effort to extirpate the new religion.

CALVINISM: THE CHURCH OF GENEVA

Many of the French Protestants who fled the campaign against them headed for Geneva, a small city in French-speaking Switzerland known chiefly for manufacturing kettles. One of the refugees, **John Calvin** (1509–1564), became the leading minister of Geneva and the second great intellectual leader of the Protestant movement. Trained as a humanist and Roman lawyer, Calvin initially encountered resistance in Geneva but overcame it by a combination of brilliant tactics and absolute commitment to his mission. By the early 1540s, Calvin and his allies dominated the city.

What Calvin devised there was, in the first place, the most rigorous version of Protestant theology, which he

John Calvin In this anonymous sixteenth-century portrait, Calvin appears as a determined young man, dressed somberly in black.

laid out in systematic form in his *Institutes of the Christian Religion*, a formal textbook of theology first published in 1536. In it he argued, more forcefully and consequentially than Luther, for the doctrine of predestination. Salvation was only God's affair, not man's. Human nature, Calvin explained, was vile, "a teeming horde of infamies." Only God could save humanity, and he did so by his own absolutely free choice, determining the fate of all—the damned as well as the saved. Evil as they were, human beings could not presume to question God's decision: "man falls by God's decree, but by his own fault." The rigor of this doctrine, which clarified points that Luther had not made clear, attracted many highly educated followers.

But Calvin did more than create a citadel of ideas. In Geneva, he also built up a church of a new kind—a Reformed church that went even further than Zwingli's in the imposition of discipline on all areas of life. He opened an academy to train ministers in Hebrew and Greek so that they could master the Bible in the original languages and learn its true doctrines as he had. Regular meetings and synods (formal meetings of all the clerics in a large district) oversaw the clergy once they were in the field, ensuring that they remained on message doctrinally

CHRISTMAS IN ST. ANDREWS

Kirk ("church") sessions were church courts in Scotland that, like the consistory in John Calvin's Geneva, enforced social discipline. They began to be established in Scottish towns during the Reformation, led in Scotland by John Knox, and within a generation had spread throughout much of the country. Ministers moderated weekly meetings of the courts, which focused largely on the morality of parishioners. Common charges ranged from fornication and adultery to popular but illegal Christmas customs such as singing carols. This excerpt is from the kirk session of St. Andrews in the winter of 1573/74.

The which day…upon Sunday the 24 day of January…Waltir Ramsay lorimer,[1] Waltir Lathangye cutler,[2] and Johne Smyth blacksmith in Ergail, being accused and convicted before for observing of superstitious days and especially of Yule Day,[3] became penitent and made open satisfaction therefore in the presence of the whole congregation then being present. And therefore the minister, at command of the assembly, publicly [an]nounced that all persons, within this parish, that observe superstitiously the said Yule Day or any other days, should be punished in like manner; and such like should be punished in like manner if they abstain from their work and labour that day more than any other day except Sunday, which only should be kept holiday. And hereupon the session interposed their decision.

The said day, James Clwny cutler and Waltir Zownger being accused for violating the Sabbath day by superstitious keeping of Yule Day holiday, and abstaining from their work and labour that day, James Clwny promised to desist and cease from keeping of Yule Day in time coming, under pain contained in the act immediately preceding. And Waltir Zownger…being accused…that [he] made his neighbors disobedient to the kirk, saying, in the Gallowlaik[4] that it does not become honest men to sit upon the penitent stool[5] which words he confessed: and also said that he is a young man and saw Yule Day kept as a holiday, and that the time may come that he may see the like yet; and therefore would not become obliged or restricted in time coming to abstain from work that day, but at his own pleasure. In respect of the aforesaid, the session decides and orders that him to be admonished by public admonition to make satisfaction upon the penitent stool under pain of excommunication, and also [because] he being required would give no other answer nor yet submit himself to the voice of the kirk.

QUESTIONS FOR ANALYSIS

1. What were the people in this record accused and convicted of having done?
2. What evidence does this record provide about how people marked Christmas in sixteenth-century Scotland?
3. These cases came before the kirk session more than ten years after the Reformation was accomplished in Scotland. Is their appearance evidence of the success or failure of the reformers' agenda?

[1]**lorimer:** maker of bits, spurs, and other small metal objects
[2]**cutler:** maker or seller of knives and other utensils
[3]**Yule Day:** Christmas Day
[4]**Gallowlaik:** a meeting place for craftsmen
[5]**penitent stool:** a seat used for public shaming rituals

Source: *Register of the Minister, Elders, and Deacons of the Christian Congregation of St. Andrews*, pt. 1, ed. David Hay Fleming (Edinburgh: 1889), pp. 387–89; text modernized by Mairi Cowan.

and that they dealt vigorously and honorably with their parishioners. Every Calvinist cleric had to take his turn presenting a sermon in French and then waiting for comments from his hearers on both style and content. The consistory—an institution, based on the model of the Zurich marriage court, which brought together elders and ministers—oversaw the behavior of Genevans. It summoned and punished individuals for everything from quarreling with spouses and failing to attend or listen to the sermons given by Geneva's ministers to adultery and gluttony. Some patricians resisted, but Calvin defeated them in 1555, after a long struggle, thanks to the support of French immigrants who became Genevan citizens and elected a city council that supported him.

By the time Calvin died in 1564, Geneva had become a startlingly disciplined town, where heads of households presided over family prayers. The city became a symbol of independent Protestantism, and many of the young intellectuals who went there emerged as effective clergymen, brilliant missionaries for the cause of reform. In France and the Low Countries, and to a considerable extent in England and the Holy Roman Empire, Protestantism was Calvinism—even if the Zwinglian citizens of Zurich would not have agreed.

CHURCHES AND MONARCHS: A CHANGING BALANCE

Rulers watched as city councils accepted the Reformation movement, abolished the Mass, and set their clergy to preaching the Gospel in the vernacular. Some rulers, such as the brilliant soldier Philip of Hesse (1504–1567), took action themselves. There were, after all, many advantages to be had. On becoming a Protestant, Philip abolished the rich monasteries in his territory, which no longer had any function. He used 41 percent of their wealth to found schools and the University of Marburg, and to provide dowries for the noble nuns whose world he had shattered. But he kept 59 percent of it for his own use.

HENRY VIII AND THE CHURCH OF ENGLAND

Henry VIII of England (r. 1509–1547), the king whom Thomas More served as a counselor, also broke with the Catholic Church. Henry, who feared and hated disorder, at first saw no reason to transform the practice of Christianity in England. For years, he and his ministers—above all Thomas More, who became his lord chancellor from 1529 to 1532—hunted British Protestants such as William Tyndale, who translated the Bible into English and was strangled and burned by Catholic authorities in Flanders. Henry himself published a treatise that defended the sacraments against Luther. Thomas More engaged in literary duels with heretics. He defended the souls in purgatory against Protestants who claimed that purgatory did not exist and that prayers for the dead were wasted.

But Henry wanted desperately to have his marriage to his brother's widow, Catherine of Aragon, annulled on religious grounds, and marry Anne Boleyn, a noble at

Henry VIII This painting shows Henry flanked by his only legitimate son to survive him, the future Edward VI, and his third wife, Jane Seymour.

court. Though Henry failed to convince the papacy that his cause was just, he married Boleyn in 1533. He then declared himself head of an independent national church in 1534. More and the others who retained a passionate commitment to the universal church, and who refused to acknowledge Henry's supremacy, found themselves in danger. In 1535 More was executed, as were the members of the London Charterhouse, the most rigorous of the old monastic orders. Boleyn herself was executed for adultery, incest, and treason in 1536.

Henry, like most other kings, was always in need of money. He also showed sympathy, as a young man, for humanists like Erasmus and their criticisms of the wealth of the Church. His chief minister, Thomas Cromwell (ca. 1485–1540), convinced him to disestablish the monastic orders and confiscate their property. Cromwell made serious efforts to ensure that the monasteries could never be reestablished. His men used explosives to demolish them, and looted the sites of everything of value. Efforts to restore the old religion—such as the 1536 Pilgrimage of Grace, a rebellious movement based in Yorkshire and sparked in part by high grain prices—were put down with remorseless violence. Protestant doctrines spread in the universities, and the tutors who brought up Henry's son Edward, a superbly educated young man, saw to it that he was grounded in what they took as the true doctrines.

Despite the passive resistance of parishioners and priests who loved their ancient rituals, England slowly became a Protestant land. In 1539 Myles Coverdale, a

Protestant trained originally in the Augustinian order, produced the Great Bible, which was for the most part a revision of Tyndale's translation of the Bible into English, and was approved for use in church services. Thomas Cranmer, the archbishop of Canterbury, changed Communion so that the laity as well as the priest received both wine and bread. And he oversaw the translation of one element after another of the liturgy until, in 1549, the entire service was in English. Clerics with reformed sympathies complained that too much of the tradition had been retained. John Hooper, a Calvinist, refused to be made a bishop if he had to wear the traditional vestments, which, he thought, derived from the practice of Jewish priests. Through the 1540s, the English church was taking shape as a great compromise between tradition and innovation.

FRANCIS I AND CHARLES V (1521–1546)

Religious reform spread through Europe at a time when states were rapidly developing their powers. The brilliant young monarchs who controlled England (Henry VIII), France (Francis I), and the Holy Roman Empire (Charles V) benefited from vast personal resources; so did the princes of smaller territories, such as the Wittelsbachs, who ruled Bavaria. The French monarchy, which had revived during the course of the fifteenth century, worked effectively with its Estates General. The French state also devised increasingly efficient systems of tax collection and continually looked for other forms of revenue. One of these—the sale of offices in the state administration ultimately proved counterproductive, since state officers held their positions by right, as private property, and could resist royal orders. Nonetheless, French state revenues were large enough to enable Francis I (r. 1515–1547) to wage a long and exhausting series of wars in Italy, where he tried to make good on the French claim to rule over Naples and Milan.

Charles, son of the Habsburg king of Spain Philip I, became Holy Roman Emperor **Charles V** and the lord of a vast series of domains before he was twenty. Born in Flanders in 1500, at age six he inherited his paternal grandfather Maximilian's Burgundian territories in the Low Countries. His aunt, Margaret of Austria, acted as regent until Charles was fifteen, and went to war with France to establish that Flanders was not a French fief. At sixteen, when his maternal grandfather, Ferdinand II, died, he became King Charles I of Spain, though he had

little knowledge of it. Three years later, when Maximilian died, he inherited the Habsburg monarchy and became the natural candidate to become Holy Roman emperor. The vast expense of bribing the German electors to make him emperor and maintaining his costly Flemish court placed him under financial pressure.

FOUNDATIONS OF STATE POWER State power was sustained not only by taxation and conquest. In the decades around 1500, European economic life entered a new phase. Entrepreneurs, such as the banker **Jacob Fugger** of Augsburg, worked with the Habsburgs and other monarchs to which they lent money. For each loan he issued, Fugger extracted something more important in return—for example, the right to exploit minerals that belonged to the sovereign. At a time when mining technology was rapidly improving, Fugger secured permission to dig for silver in the Tirol, copper in Hungary, mercury in Spain, and even gold and silver in the New World. The metals he extracted were vital for everything from making bronze cannon to coining money, and Fugger made money from each use, which he then employed to seek out new business opportunities, such as the trade in pepper from Asia.

Charles V borrowed enormous amounts from Fugger, which he tried to repay by raising taxes. The Spanish kingdoms of Castile and Aragon were already in financial difficulties, having spent vast amounts on the destruction of the last Islamic emirate, in Granada, in 1492, and on maintaining their armies. Agitation against Charles began in Toledo and Segovia in 1520, and soon other cities joined. The *comuneros*, an unstable coalition of lesser nobles, urban artisans, and others who saw Charles as an outsider, rebelled against him. They formed a new government, recognizing Charles's mother as queen, and raised armies. But Charles's representative in Spain raised more effective armies of his own, in alliance with much of the landed aristocracy, and defeated the comuneros.

HABSBURG CONTROL OF ITALY Even as the Spanish authorities crushed the comuneros, the old war between France and the Habsburgs in Italy was revived by Charles V and Francis I. Charles mustered an enormous force, including German mercenaries as well as his Spanish armies. Employing superior tactics, Charles's forces pulled the French army apart at Pavia in 1525, and Francis himself was taken prisoner. Frightened by Charles's power, Pope Clement VII, a member of the Medici family, formed a coalition against the emperor, the League

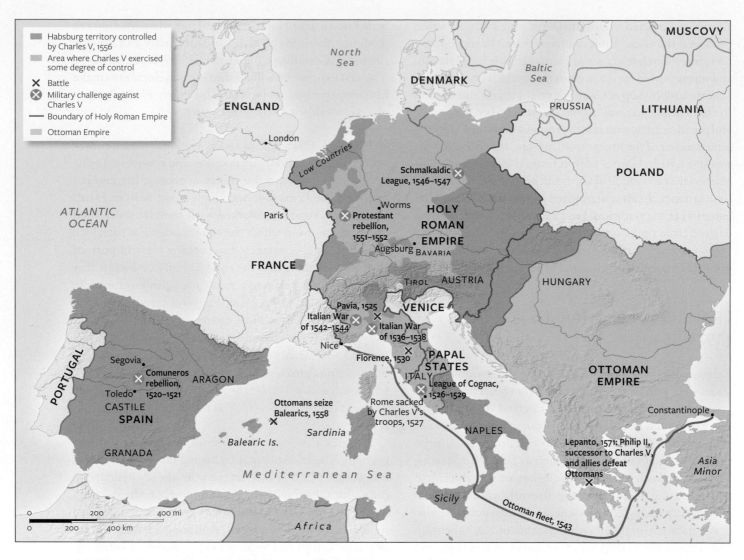

Habsburg Lands, ca. 1556 At the height of his power, Charles V controlled much of Europe, including inherited kingdoms in the Low Countries and Spain, the Holy Roman Empire, and conquests in Italy. He sustained his power with military might, putting down rebellions in Spain and defeating the Protestant Schmalkaldic League and several Italian uprisings. But rebellions in Protestant central Europe and pressure from the French and the Ottomans at the borders limited Charles's total control of the continent.

of Cognac, allying himself with Venice, Florence, and other powers. But the Venetians refused to take an active part, and Charles, after defeating Florence, found himself unable to pay his troops. In 1527 his soldiers shocked the world by sacking Rome, including the Vatican. The pope was imprisoned, and Charles now commanded the Italian Peninsula.

The Florentines rose up in one last attempt to defend their republican tradition—a magnificent, doomed effort that won the warm support of Michelangelo. But after furious resistance, they were defeated in 1530. Though Venice remained independent—and though Francis would launch more Italian wars—Italy would remain under the

control of the Habsburgs for centuries, as the Spanish transformed the south and Sicily into the agrarian province of the Iberian kingdom.

STALEMATE: PEACE OF AUGSBURG

Charles V never managed to win the one decisive victory that would have enabled him to pacify all of his territories and defeat the Protestant princes of the empire definitively—a goal that he thought it his religious duty to pursue as Holy Roman emperor. The French challenged him again in 1536 and 1542—both times in league with the Ottomans, whose empire, under Sultan Suleiman the Magnificent (r. 1520–1566), reached from North Africa to Asia Minor and deep into Hungary—but both wars ended in stalemates. In 1547 Charles did manage to defeat the Schmalkaldic League of Protestant powers, created in 1531 by Philip of Hesse and John Frederick I, Elector of Saxony, and gradually enlarged to include other German states and imperial cities. Charles imprisoned Philip, the league's most formidable commander. But the overwhelming power Charles thus achieved terrified many, and in 1552 a Protestant rebellion, supported by the new French king, Henry II (r. 1547–1559), drove Charles out of the German

lands. Dogged by ill health, he gave his Spanish crown to his son Philip in 1555, while his brother Ferdinand succeeded him as Holy Roman emperor in 1556.

In 1555 the **Peace of Augsburg**, a formal treaty agreed by Charles and the members of the Schmalkaldic League, officially recognized that the empire no longer followed one religion. The principle *cuius regio, eius religio* ("his realm, his religion") acknowledged that each prince could decide which religion, Catholic or Protestant, to establish in his domain. Those who refused to go along had the right to leave—itself a major innovation. At the Diet of Worms long before, Charles had stated that he had an inherited

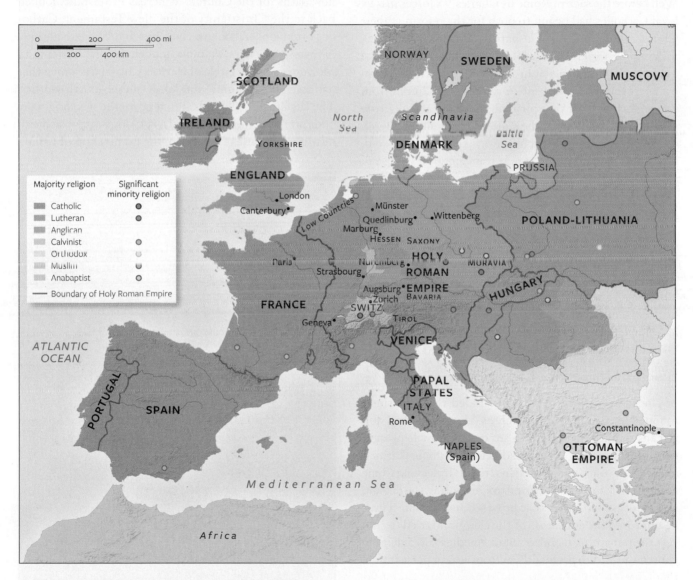

Europe after the Peace of Augsburg A complicated religious and political landscape followed the treaty: for the most part, northern Germany, Scandinavia, and Prussia were Lutheran, Scotland and Switzerland were Calvinist, England had its own state church, Muscovy and the European portion of the Ottoman Empire were Orthodox, and the rest of Europe remained Catholic. But religious minorities now had a foothold in many regions as well, from Catholics in northern Germany to Calvinists in France and Poland and Anabaptists in Germany and Hungary.

duty to defend the Catholic Church against innovators and rebels. Now it was clear that he had failed. Yet this religious and political settlement was highly provisional. The Anabaptists and vigorous Calvinists did not win acceptance from the rulers of Protestant and Catholic states, and they resented their precarious position. Meanwhile, the Catholic Church was beginning to regroup and even to go on the offensive against its critics and enemies.

RENEWING CATHOLICISM

Well before the sack of Rome by Charles V's forces in 1527, loyal Catholics had begun to push for the reform of their Church. The Venetian Gasparo Contarini (1483–1542), for example, experienced a spiritual awakening not unlike Luther's, but he pursued it in a different direction. He and others formed a movement to reform the Church from within, insisting on the spiritual, internal nature of true religion and denouncing the simony (payment for church offices) and courtly, hierarchical ways that, they believed, had corrupted the papal Curia. After Contarini's long and successful career as a diplomat in the Venetian service, Pope Paul III (r. 1534–1549), who wanted to harness the spiritual movement to the Church, made him a cardinal in 1535.

SOURCES OF RENEWAL

There were many others like him. The diplomat and bishop Gian Matteo Giberti, and Gian Pietro Carafa—later Pope Paul IV (r. 1555–1559)—founded the Oratory of Divine Love, a free association of clerics and laymen, in Rome in 1517. Its members practiced an intensive discipline of prayer and confession, visiting hospitals as a work of charity. Other new orders included the Theatines, founded in 1524, and the Capuchins, a branch of the Franciscans founded in 1525; both set out to provide preaching of high quality. Jacopo Sadoleto, a brilliant Latinist and elegant courtier, shocked his friends by leaving Rome after the sack in 1527. He moved to Carpentras, the distant, rural diocese in France that provided his income. There he improved the education of the clergy and tried to convert the remaining members of the medieval Waldensian church—in part to protect them from violent persecution.

HOLY WOMEN Women played a central role in the renewal of Catholicism. Many women did so through highly practical religious activities: Catherine of Genoa, for example, who later became a saint, moved with her husband into a hospital, where she dedicated herself to the care of incurable victims of syphilis. Other women became known—as Hildegard of Bingen had in the Middle Ages—as living exemplars of holiness. Known for their deep penitence for their sins and their pursuit of mystical union with God, some also developed renown as prophetesses and reformers. Holy women inspired and mentored the founders of the new Theatine order.

THE URSULINES Other new orders—such as the Ursulines, founded by Angela Merici in 1535—forged new paths for the Church. Whereas Protestants looked back to the Christianity of the New Testament, Catholics often looked back to the Church of the late antique Fathers: Merici, for example, modeled a new community for women on the circle of learned Christian women that had assembled around Saint Jerome in the fourth century. The Ursulines taught girls and cared for the sick, originally without taking formal vows. In 1572, long after the death of Merici, Charles Borromeo, the archbishop of Milan,

Angela Merici An anonymous 1550 painting depicts an elderly Angela Merici, the founder of the Ursuline order.

insisted that the Ursulines become a religious order and live an "enclosed" life. Their houses spread through the New World as well as the Old.

TERESA OF ÁVILA As in the Middle Ages, mystics of the sixteenth century showed that their union with God gave them an energy and efficiency that others lacked. Teresa of Ávila (1515–1582), who came from a Spanish family partly made up of Jewish converts, wrote dazzlingly of her religious experiences, vividly evoking the pains and torments she suffered, as well as the ecstasy of her final union with God. She created a new model of female monasticism for the Carmelite order, to which she belonged, eliminating outside visits and insisting that members remain strictly confined and pursue sanctity. John of the Cross, another mystic who, like Teresa, later became a saint, collaborated with her to found new houses. In the later sixteenth century, the Catholic religious authorities would turn a more critical eye on many holy women, looking for possible cases of diabolic possession that mimicked true sanctity, and cutting down the areas of free action that religious women had found in the early period of Catholic renewal. But the movement for renewal itself was shaped in considerable part by female hands.

The Society of Jesus In a 1540 French engraving, Ignatius Loyola and a group of his fellow Jesuits kneel before Pope Paul III to offer him a copy of their rule. The pope raises his right hand in a gesture of benediction.

THE SOCIETY OF JESUS

Though different in many respects, all of these Catholics believed that their church was the true one, and remained ardently faithful to it. One of them in particular—Ignatius Loyola (1491–1556), a Spanish nobleman who was badly wounded in the Italian wars—showed as vividly as Luther how an individual with a spiritual vocation could change the world, especially a world divided over questions of belief. After a long period of preparation, which included years of meditation as a hermit and intensive study in Paris, Loyola went to Rome in 1535 with a few ragged followers, and gained papal permission to create a new order, the Society of Jesus, in 1540.

What made the **Jesuits** special was not their numbers, for there were never many of them, but the training on which Loyola insisted and the intense commitment that it both demanded and generated. To join the order, one had to go through a long preparation of studying, doing humble tasks as a novice, and—most important—making the Spiritual Exercises (a set of meditative exercises that Loyola designed) under the supervision of a Jesuit spiritual director. By undergoing these rigors, Loyola argued,

Jesuits would establish for certain that they possessed a religious vocation, a question that earlier orders had too often ignored. Equally important, they and their superiors would learn exactly which tasks they were best equipped to carry out for the order: teaching in schools, working in cities with the poor, or going on missions to Asia and other lands.

Although the rigorous Jesuit training resembled that of Calvinist ministers in some ways, its texture and content were completely different. Full members of the Jesuit order not only swore the traditional vows of poverty, chastity, and obedience but also pledged to go at once to the Holy Land if ordered to do so and preach the word of God. The Jesuits saw themselves as committed to everything that Calvin hated. They would obey the pope absolutely, "like a stick in the hand." They would defend the church fathers and the scholastic theologians of the Middle Ages against Protestant insistence that only scripture mattered. They would serve wherever the order or the pope sent them.

Many Jesuits went on missions to preach and find converts. Some missions took them into perils of every kind, especially in lands that had turned Protestant. In other cases, they followed the Catholic empires of Spain, Portugal, and France into the New World and Asia. As teachers, they founded schools across the globe and often induced the children of Protestant nobles, sent to them solely for an education, to convert back to their ancestral faith. As priests, they built shrines—including countless replicas of the house of the Virgin Mary at Loreto, which had supposedly been brought there from the Holy Land by angels. As spiritual directors, they counseled rulers and nobles, scholars and merchants through spiritual crises. And as historians, they documented every step they took, from recruiting novices to dying as martyrs in Japan. By the 1540s and 1550s, Jesuits were crossing Europe, ready to engage Protestants in a war for Christian souls.

THE COUNCIL OF TRENT

The reformers were never wholly isolated within the Church, and soon they found powerful allies. From 1545 to 1563, a broad, ecumenical council of the Church met at Trent, on the border between the Holy Roman Empire and northern Italy. After long deliberations, the **Council of Trent** settled disputed questions of doctrine: for example, it decreed that the true text of the Bible was "the old and Vulgate edition," by which it meant the Latin text on which the Catholic Church had long relied. It affirmed such traditional practices as the sacraments and the veneration of saints. It laid out a set of tasks for the popes, including revision of the Mass and new editions of the Bible. And it filled participants with a new energy.

As clerics left the council to return to their dioceses, they felt a new responsibility to the Christian laity and

Council of Trent A Dutch watercolor from 1560 illustrates a meeting of the Council of Trent. Cardinals, monks, priests, ambassadors, generals, and other laymen pack the galleries of a church in Trent, while speakers from these groups discuss matters of doctrine.

devised new ways to raise the standard of the clergy and improve the religious lives of laypeople. In Italy, determined archbishops imposed order on religious services and created seminaries to ensure that clerics were literate and able to do their jobs. They also reformed monastic orders and adopted new ways of instilling Catholicism with the vitality that Luther and so many others had missed. The archbishop of Milan, for example, devised the confessional: an enclosed, private space in which the Christian would confess to a priest and receive instructions for amendment. Confession, long a public, external ritual, as Erasmus and other Christian reformers had complained, became a private, internal matter: a frightening leap into the spiritual darkness, made safe only by the presence of the confessor.

Meanwhile, the papacy restructured its administrative apparatus, the Roman Curia. Cardinals remained courtiers, as they had long been: aristocratic clerics who lived in palaces. But they also found themselves assigned to committees tasked to oversee particular areas of Church life. One of these committees took charge of the censorship of the printing press, which—if it had been institutionalized more effectively in earlier years—might have made it possible to suppress the Reformation entirely. By the 1550s, the Church was issuing indexes of forbidden books: detailed lists of books that Catholics could not read at all, or that they could read only after designated passages had been removed.

A system of censorship took shape. Catholic authors had to submit their works before publication to Church censors, whose approbations must be included in the published books. Protestant librarians soon found these indices useful instruments for creating libraries of past heretical works, the products of movements that they saw as ancestors of their own. Catholic thinkers, however, found themselves subject to a partial but serious effort at thought control. In Spain, the Inquisition was repurposed as a mechanism for examining and punishing suspected critics of Church doctrine.

RETHINKING THE NATURAL WORLD

The bite of censorship was all the more painful to thoughtful Catholics because, in the middle decades of the sixteenth century, Europe experienced widespread intellectual ferment. For centuries, the universities, with their canonical texts and elaborate curricula, had dominated the study of the natural world and much more. Humanists and reformers challenged them. But so, even more, did the simple facts that now came to light. The existence of a sea route to Asia and the New World proved that ancient maps of the earth and the sky were erroneous and incomplete. Not until the seventeenth century would Europeans carry out something like intellectual iconoclasm, arguing that moderns knew far more than the ancients had. But the roots of that development lie in the Reformation period.

OBSERVATION AND COLLABORATION

One intellectual who embraced the new knowledge was the brilliant, irascible German doctor Theophrastus Bombastus Paracelsus (1493–1541). By the late 1520s, he had decided that the traditional medical textbooks were useless. Like Luther, who burned the bull of excommunication against him, Paracelsus publicly burned the standard textbook, *The Canon of Medicine* by Avicenna (Ibn Sina; d. 1037). Paracelsus told his readers that they should rely instead on the empirical knowledge of ordinary men and women, which was worth far more than the nonsense of "the high colleges," and he elaborated his own alchemical version of medical theory and practice.

Nicolaus Copernicus (1473–1543), a cathedral canon whose career unfolded in Poland, devised an even more radical theory. Though he observed the heavens himself and used observations made by others, he was looking not for greater accuracy but for greater simplicity. The universe, he argued in 1543, was not geocentric (centered on the earth), as practically every thinker since Aristotle had believed, but heliocentric (centered on the sun). The earth, moreover, was not at rest: it rotated on its axis once a day and revolved around the sun once a year. Copernicus's theory revolutionized the understanding not only of the cosmos but also of the earth, since it could no longer be assumed that when objects fell they were seeking the center of the universe. By accepting these views, Copernicus argued, astronomers could simplify their models for the motion of the planets—but to do so they had to imagine a universe much larger than they had traditionally believed.

Andreas Vesalius (1514–1564), who studied and taught medicine at the university in Padua, took a lesson from artists such as Leonardo da Vinci. Vesalius argued that the study of the human organism must rest on actual

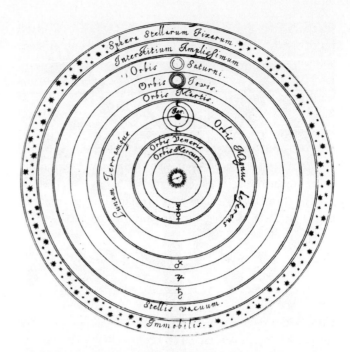

The Copernican Universe A 1647 scientific text includes this diagram of Copernicus's heliocentric theory of the cosmos. It shows the planets and Earth's moon orbiting the sun, surrounded by an immobile sphere of stars.

dissection of human bodies, as he thought it had in the ancient days of Greek physician and writer Galen, and the results recorded not only in writing but in detailed drawings. As Vesalius dissected the bodies of criminals, he discovered that Galen had committed many errors, some of them serious, because he had actually dissected apes rather than humans. In 1543, Vesalius brought out a magnificent study of the human body, illustrated by a Venetian artist. His work transformed medical study and laid the foundations for the further series of discoveries that would culminate, with William Harvey in 1628, in the demonstration that human blood circulated through the body, like the earth in the heavens.

Another sign of the radicalism of much—though not all—of the innovative thinking done in the sixteenth century is its collaborative character. Like Vesalius, many intellectuals found themselves changing the established body of knowledge by working with colleagues who were not learned at all. When the German botanist Leonhart Fuchs printed his illustrated guide to plants and their uses in 1542, he included portraits of the artists who had drawn the images and made and colored the printed woodcuts. It was a clear indication that knowledge was no longer, if it had ever been, the property of an elite trained to read canonical texts, but something to be discovered and

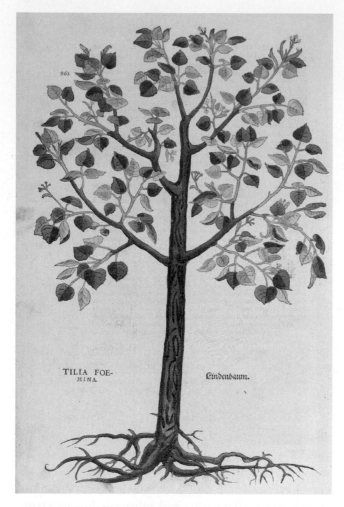

Fuchs's Botany One of the many painted woodcuts from Leonhart Fuchs's *De Historia Stirpium* (1542), this lime tree is labeled in Latin and German.

recorded by teams whose members crossed the boundaries of social orders and occupations to work together. In another example, Europeans learned from dozens of Native American informants, male and female, about the properties of New World plants and the products derived from them. Some of these products, such as chocolate and tobacco, were powerful stimulants whose use would transform Western society.

THE PERILS OF NEW THINKING

In a time of fear and censorship, ideas as radical as these could lead those who framed them into grave danger. Sometimes compromises were made: Andreas Osiander (1498–1552), the Lutheran cleric who oversaw the printing of Copernicus's work as the author was dying, added an anonymous preface in which he declared—contradicting the text that followed—that the author had meant only to advance a hypothesis, not to tell the truth about the universe. Though Copernicus's work was placed on the Church's indexes of forbidden books, this preface helped it survive, and annotated copies in libraries across Europe show that many were able to read it.

Not every book or author was so lucky. Michael Servetus (ca. 1511–1553), a Spanish theologian and medical specialist who speculated about the circulation of the blood, denied the doctrine of the Trinity. He managed to escape both Catholic and Protestant authorities for a time by using pseudonyms and moving frequently. In 1553, however, he made the fatal mistake of traveling to Geneva, even though Calvin was one of his harshest critics. Arrested and condemned, he was burned to death outside the city—a rare fate even for a heretic in the Protestant world—by Calvinists determined to show that they were no more lenient, when deadly heresies were concerned, than the Catholics.

WAR ACROSS THE CONTINENT

The peace established in the Holy Roman Empire by the Treaty of Augsburg (1555) did not extend to the rest of Europe. In England, Queen Mary I (r. 1553–1558), daughter of Henry VIII and his first wife, Catherine of Aragon, succeeded her half brother, Edward VI. A committed Catholic, Mary did her best to reestablish the Church. Hundreds of Protestants were forced to flee England; many sought refuge in Swiss cities. Almost 300 were burned, including the archbishop of Canterbury, Thomas Cranmer. In Italy, war had flared again in 1551, when a new French king, Henry II, declared war on Holy Roman Emperor Charles V, seeking to supplant Spanish control over the Italian Peninsula. After Charles abdicated, his son became King Philip II of Spain (r. 1556–1598) and opposed Henry.

Warfare was now completely professional, and both France and Spain had to borrow massive amounts to pay their troops. The capital came from banks and monarchs across Europe and beyond, including officials of the Ottoman Empire. Much of the capital flowed through Antwerp, the trading center of Europe. Its bourse, or financial exchange, founded in 1531, could broker enormous financial transactions. By late in the 1550s, neither country could maintain interest payments on the loans. First Spain and then France reneged on these debts, bankrupting thousands of investors. Forced to negotiate an end to the conflict, Henry and Philip signed the Peace of Cateau-Cambrésis in 1559. Henry II died after a joust held to celebrate the treaty, when a splinter of the lance belonging to one of his guards penetrated his eye.

GOVERNMENT AND WAR IN A NEW KEY: PHILIP II OF SPAIN

Bankruptcy did not deter Philip II from his systematic effort to make Spain the dominant European power. Neither did the death of Queen Mary I of England, whom he had married, and whose efforts to bring England back into the Catholic fold he had encouraged. In 1559 Philip took the reins of power in Spain, assuming direct charge of the councils that dealt with finance, war, and the colonies. In his search for information about all his domains, he read and annotated thousands of documents every year. His habit of bringing memoranda to every meeting with his counselors won him the title "the paper king." Though he had to deal with separate assemblies, or estates, in Castile, Aragon, and Navarre, he established himself as a uniquely powerful monarch. He compensated for the debts that his father had left him with the immense wealth generated by the trade and industry of the Habsburg-controlled Low Countries, and the gold, silver, spices, tobacco, and sugar carried by Spanish convoys from its empire in the New World. These convoys, connecting Spain to its colonies in the Philippines, Mexico, Cuba, and elsewhere, began in 1565 and soon reached fifty or more ships at a time.

A passionate believer, Philip devoted himself to what he saw as the cause of Christendom—the defeat of the Ottoman Empire in the Mediterranean, the defeat of Protestantism in western Europe, and the final purification of Spain. No expense seemed to him too great, no effort too arduous, where this cause was concerned. When his efforts to suppress the Islamic customs still observed by some Moriscos (former Muslims) provoked a revolt in Granada in 1569, he had them expelled from the city and scattered throughout Spain. And when an Ottoman fleet took the Balearic Islands off Spain's eastern coast, he organized a Holy League of the Popes, the Venetians, the grand dukes of Tuscany, and others to oppose Sultan Selim II (r. 1566–1574). They eventually demolished the Ottoman navy at Lepanto, off the western coast of Greece,

in 1571. And when Mary's sister, Elizabeth, rejected his proposal of marriage, and Protestant leaders flocked back to England as it became clear that the new queen was one of them, Philip planned a gradual, massive campaign to defeat Protestantism, first in the Low Countries and then in England.

RELIGIOUS WAR, POLITICAL UPHEAVAL

In France and the Low Countries, the conflict between the Catholic Church and the Calvinists—known in French as **Huguenots**—soon blazed up in a new way. Reformed preachers and their congregations gathered at night, often in the fields outside towns and cities, with women and children protected by armed aristocrats. Calvinism had little appeal for peasants, but in the cities, workers, merchants, and members of the nobility all found its starkly clear message compelling. Catholic preachers, including many Jesuits, did their best to combat what they saw as this frightening development. After Henry II's death in 1559, his widow, Catherine de' Medici, served as regent, but she lacked the authority to impose order as violence broke out between Protestants—to whom, at first, she made concessions—and Catholics. Protestants destroyed religious images and interrupted Catholic processions, while Catholics preferred to massacre Protestants when they found them praying in groups. War erupted in France in 1562—followed, a few years later, by war in the Netherlands.

THE DUTCH REVOLT (1566–1648) Philip II's first representative as governor of the Netherlands was Margaret of Parma, the politically savvy and experienced illegitimate daughter of Philip's father, Charles V. She had tried to find some compromise that could preserve order, and when a group of noblemen formally requested that persecution of Protestantism come to an end, she agreed. But oppressive taxes, attempts to introduce the Inquisition, and a famine caused by poor harvests and rising wheat prices in 1565 led to increasing anger against the Spanish. Influential Dutch nobles withdrew from the government, and in 1566 religious statues, pictures, and stained glass windows were smashed across the Netherlands.

Philip's response in 1567 was to send his extremely effective general, the duke of Alba, with an army to quell the spreading revolt. But Alba's stern policies made matters worse—especially when two local noblemen who had remained loyal to Spain but opposed the introduction

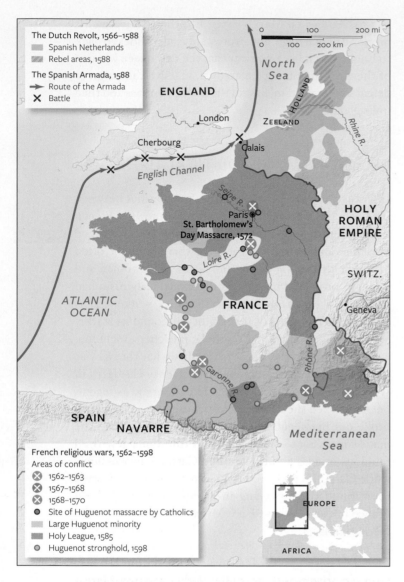

The Dutch Revolt and the French Religious Wars, 1562–1598
Violence between Protestants and Catholics flared throughout France in the 1560s and 1570s—particularly in southern areas with large Huguenot minorities—culminating in the St. Bartholomew's Day Massacre in Paris in 1572. In the Netherlands, Calvinists in the north rebelled against Catholic Spanish rule. Religious divisions also spurred Spain's naval conflict with England in 1588, ending with the English defeat of the Spanish Armada.

for more than eighty years, as we will see, and religious war spread across Europe.

ENGLAND: ANGLICANS AND PURITANS Even in England, where Queen Elizabeth I (r. 1558–1603) refused "to make windows into men's souls," conflict spread. On the one hand, the archbishops and bishops of the Church of England set out to create an Anglican church that combined stern Protestant doctrine with a rich and appealing liturgy. Against them were arrayed the Puritans—reformed believers who wanted to rid the church of all traditions not supported explicitly by the Bible. Anglicans and Puritans clashed over proper priestly vestments and central theological doctrines. Thanks to the political astuteness of Elizabeth and her closest friends, the dispute between these two sides, though often bitter, never broke out in actual civil or religious war.

THE FRENCH WARS OF RELIGION (1562–1589) On the Continent, however, savage wars erupted in 1562–63, 1567–68, and 1568–70. They were conflicts of a new kind, spawned by churches of a new kind. Both sides saw themselves as fighting for God against the devil. Violence became ritualized and almost normal as Catholics strove to cleanse the world of Protestant heretics, and Protestants sought to purify churches of the images, vessels, and incense that turned them into something like pagan temples.

The most famous atrocity of the French religious wars was the **Massacre of Saint Bartholomew's Day** in Paris on August 24, 1572. Catherine de' Medici, mother and regent of the young French king, Charles IX (r. 1560–1574), arranged a marriage between the Protestant Henry of Navarre and her daughter, the Catholic princess Margaret of Valois, and invited the Huguenot nobility to attend. This was provocative enough in a city that strongly favored the Catholic side. But on August 22, an assassin wounded the Protestant admiral Gaspard II de Coligny. Fearing reprisals from the Huguenots, the next day Charles ordered his own Swiss guards and other loyal troops to murder some 100 Protestant noblemen. The task was carried out, but instead of damping down violence, it ignited far more. Parisian civilians killed hundreds more Protestants—perhaps 2,000 in all. They mutilated the bodies of Coligny and others. Some were "tried" or "baptized" by being thrown into the Seine or soaked in the blood of their loved ones. These ritual parodies of the operations of courts and churches made clear that the Catholics saw themselves as carrying out an official act

of the Inquisition were arrested and executed. Another local nobleman, William the Silent (1533–1584), Prince of Orange, who had also served the Spanish state as a member of Margaret's council, fled and raised an army against Spain. Many of the Dutch—especially the Calvinists among them—renounced their loyalty to Philip II, whom they denounced as a tyrant. The **Dutch Revolt** continued of cleansing. Similar scenes took place in the provinces, where 3,000 more victims died—some of them, at Orléans, to the sound of serenades from musicians playing lutes and guitars.

The massacre put a stop to the expansion of the Huguenot church. Protestant numbers in northern and central French cities shrank. But in southern France, their stronghold, Protestants were, if anything, even more determined to resist what they saw as Catholic tyranny. Before the massacre, Protestant writers on politics had argued (following up a hint given by Calvin) that rebellion against a tyrannical monarchy might be legitimate if led by a lower official—since lower officials were appointed by God, just as higher ones were. Now they made open appeals for revolution, evoking a democratic French constitution. Soon the French Protestants had created their own, essentially independent kingdom in the south, close to Geneva, the capital city of Calvinism, and to Henry of Navarre's stronghold. The radical new temper of political thought—and politics—proved contagious. When Henry of Valois came to the French throne as Henry III (r. 1574–1589) and made concessions to the Protestants, a Catholic Holy League formed against him. Catholic political writers also claimed a right of resistance against tyranny, and in 1588 Henry fled Paris when the leader of the league, the duke of Guise, entered the city. Even political assassination became a tool of government. First, William the Silent, leader of the Dutch Revolt, was assassinated. Then Henry III, who had had the duke of Guise and his brother, a cardinal, murdered at the end of 1588, was himself killed in 1589 by a fanatical Dominican friar.

POLITICAL SETTLEMENTS

The Catholic forces of Spain, concentrated on the rebellious Netherlands, scored more successes at first. But for all their military superiority to the Dutch on land, the Spanish proved unable to suppress the Dutch Revolt, especially when many of its supporters took to the sea. Though Elizabeth infuriated some of her warlike subjects by her refusal to commit herself to a land war on the Continent in defense of European Protestantism, her privateers harried Spanish fleets and colonies. She gave modest but crucial assistance to the Dutch, and in 1588 the English fleet scattered and defeated the **Spanish Armada** that Philip II sent against her. Slowly it became clear on the larger European scale, as it had on the smaller German scale

Saint Bartholomew's Day Massacre The Huguenot painter François Dubois began this gory work shortly after the massacre took place in August 1572. Blood and corpses are strewn everywhere. Standing in front of the Louvre palace (in background at center) and dressed in black, Catherine de' Medici looks at a pile of bodies.

fifty years before, that neither party was strong enough to defeat the other definitively.

After witnessing the destruction caused by religious war, some influential French Catholics, including powerful lawyers and royal counselors, decided that it mattered more to have a unified state than a single religion. Known as *politiques*, these moderates often had valued Protestant as well as Catholic friends. They helped forge the brief alliance between Henry of Navarre—a Protestant but also a direct descendant of Louis IX—and the Catholic Henry III to fight the Spanish. After Henry III's assassination, Henry of Navarre renounced his Protestant faith (according to legend, he declared that "Paris is worth a mass"). Though his change of faith angered many Protestants, he was soon able to put an end to the resistance of the Holy League. In 1594 he was crowned King Henry IV, and in 1598, working from the principles of the politiques, he promulgated the **Edict of Nantes**, which gave Protestants limited religious freedom. Henry took up the tasks of restoring prosperity in France and rebuilding Paris, activities at which he proved very successful.

Though it took until 1609 for the Dutch to make a truce with the Spanish, the defeat of the Spanish Armada, repeated mutinies by Spanish troops, and the assumption of command by General Maurice of Nassau meant that the Dutch were able to conquer a number of major cities in the 1590s. Their independence secure, the counties of Holland and Zeeland, and the other states of Holland, reconfigured themselves as a Dutch republic, ruled by

DE WITTE'S *THE INTERIOR OF THE OUDE KERK*

John Calvin was even more rigorous than Martin Luther in his vision of reform. Whereas Luther expressed ambivalence toward religious images, which were sometimes retained in Lutheran churches, Calvin, like Zwingli, inspired Protestant reformers to shatter, burn, melt, or whitewash such images and decorations in their churches.

When Amsterdam's Oude Kerk (Old Church), built in the early fourteenth century, was transformed from a Roman Catholic to a Calvinist church in the late sixteenth century, Protestants destroyed its religious images. In this painting, *The Interior of the Oude Kerk* (ca.

1660), Emanuel de Witte portrays its clean columns, whitewashed walls, elegant arches, semicircular nave, and most important of all, its pulpit, where the word of God was preached.

The church was not only the community's religious center but also a popular meeting place where merchants conversed and sailors and their families prayed for the safe and successful conclusion of sea voyages. De Witte portrays scenes of everyday life in this unadorned setting: merchants discuss business (right), a mother nurses her child (far right), and a dog even urinates on a column (left). In the foreground, a burial is being prepared.

QUESTIONS FOR ANALYSIS

1. What does this depiction of a church's interior tell us about the influence of Calvinist theology in the Netherlands?
2. As indicated by this painting, what role did Reformed churches play in everyday life in the Netherlands?
3. How would you compare this scene to life in Calvin's Geneva as described earlier in the chapter?

their representative assemblies, or estates, and protected, but not ruled, by the House of Orange.

RUSSIA AND EASTERN EUROPE

More slowly than in the West, monarchs in Eastern Europe began to build up their states on modern lines. The power of Russian grand princes had been limited by the rival power of the boyars, or great noble families, and by their relatively old-fashioned armies, largely made up of mounted archers who offered their service in return for small grants of land. Ivan IV, known in Russian tradition as Ivan Grozny ("Ivan the Awesome"), was grand prince from 1533 to 1547, when he was crowned the first "Tsar of all the Russias," a title he held until he died in 1584. He thus claimed the status of an imperial ruler, like the early kings of Kiev and the emperors of Byzantium, and highlighted the existing claim that, after the fall of Constantinople, Moscow had become the third Rome.

Articulate and charismatic, Ivan rebuilt many Russian institutions. He established a council of advisers, forced the boyars to accept the duty of serving the tsar, regularized the system of taxation, and established a unified currency. He also gradually added well-trained musketeers and artillerymen to his armies. By conquering the Muslim Khanates of Kazan (1552) and Astrakhan (1556), he created a buffer against the Mongols and made Russia itself a multi-ethnic empire. Ivan celebrated these accomplishments by building a vast cathedral, St Basil's, in Moscow. In this and other ways he emulated the Renaissance rulers of Western Europe. Ivan built new fortresses, brought in foreign artists and craftsmen to improve Moscow, and engaged in elaborate diplomatic relations, especially with England. Though a formal alliance with Mary or Elizabeth eluded him, the Muscovy Company granted a monopoly, imported luxury goods and exported timber, tar, and other products needed to build English ships.

Like the western monarchies, Russia experienced crisis when Ivan's conduct became unpredictable. In 1564 he blackmailed his boyars into granting him absolute power, and used it to divide Russia. He established absolute control over a northern area, called the Oprichnina, in the former territory of Novgorod. A black-clad private army terrorized the inhabitants. On Ivan's orders they sacked Novgorod, already stricken by plague, in 1570. In 1572 he abolished the Oprichnina: his intentions in creating it remain unclear, though some historians believe he may have seen himself as creating a holy kingdom for the end of time. The Grand Duchy of Lithuania and the Kingdom of Poland, both also expanding in resources and power, were joined in 1569 by the Union of Lublin, and in 1576 they joined the Ottomans in attacking Ivan's Empire. In 1581 he killed his son Ivan Ivanovich, apparently by accident. Expansion did not end. Toward the end of Ivan's reign, Cossacks —Slavic-speaking steppe dwellers, skilled in cavalry warfare, who served many lords— conquered Siberia and recognized him as Tsar. Famine, plague and war had exhausted Russia, which would fall into a crisis soon after Ivan's death. Yet he had established his country as the empire it would remain until the 20th century.

A TIME OF DARKNESS

The second half of the sixteenth century was—so many Europeans thought—a terrible age, perhaps uniquely terrible. The flow of silver and gold from the New World caused a slow but steady inflation of prices across the Continent. In a society that believed it possible to set fair prices and wages by statute, even a 2 percent rate of inflation was deeply unsettling. Harvest failures caused local spikes in the price of bread, which led to famines and often set off the most violent outbursts of religious rioting.

WITCH TRIALS

The famines also help to explain the outburst of witch trials across Europe during the period. The causes of

Burning Witches This woodcut illustration from a 1555 leaflet depicts witches being executed. Men stoke the flames, while a demon clings to one of the burning women. The women are shown again at right, descending into hell.

these trials varied, though they were always rooted in everyday events. Sometimes a woman who had difficulty giving birth, or whose baby was injured or died in the process, denounced her midwife; sometimes poor, older women who would have been objects of charity in traditional Catholic society provoked rage and denunciation from Protestants. In either case, the use of torture to interrogate those accused of witchcraft often led to further accusations. The largest witch hunts, sparked by famines, stopped only when members of the elite were accused.

The theory that witches conspired to attack Christian society took shape, as we have seen, in the fifteenth century. But it was in the age of religious war that the theory was applied in massive witch trials. By the time they came to an end in the late seventeenth century, some 30,000 to 70,000 people, 80 percent of them female, had been executed as witches. Thousands more were tried. The late sixteenth century genuinely was a time of darkness, and the fires that illuminated it too often consumed human beings.

TWO RESPONSES TO POLITICAL AND RELIGIOUS CRISIS: JEAN BODIN AND MICHEL DE MONTAIGNE

Jean Bodin (1530–1596) and Michel de Montaigne (1533–1592) both lived through the long series of religious wars unleashed in France by the Reformation; both were in their prime when the Massacre of Saint Bartholomew's Day took place. And both eagerly followed the intellectual revolutions of the mid-sixteenth century. Both realized that their world had changed, though they expressed their perceptions in different ways. Both were versed in the classics, trained in Roman law, and cosmopolitan in their interests and their reading. Bodin insisted that the only way to find the best constitution for one's country was to collect and compare laws from all over the world. He drew up one of the first guides to the study of history, which instructed the reader to pay as much attention to the East as to the West and as much to modern history as to ancient. Montaigne, who read Bodin's book, followed his instructions on how to read historians critically and fruitfully.

Both men took a deep interest in civilizations and religions other than their own, and regarded them with clear respect. Bodin wrote a provocative dialogue in which representatives of seven religions debate peacefully before parting from one another on terms of respect and affection. This work, with its suggestion that no religion could claim a monopoly on truth, could have endangered its author. It was not published, though manuscripts of it circulated widely. Montaigne, attending the circumcision of a Jewish baby in Rome, noted that Jewish babies cried "just as our babies do when they are baptized." Both Bodin and Montaigne, finally, were involved in trying to restore peace and stability to France.

BODIN But the solutions they arrived at differed radically. Bodin originally believed that constitutions could and should be mixed, as he thought the ancient Roman one, with its monarchical, aristocratic, and democratic elements, had been. He at first supported efforts by the French Estates General to limit the powers of the king, but in the late 1560s and 1570s he changed his mind. Only a ruler of absolute authority, he now insisted, could possibly maintain peace and order. Sovereignty—formal command over a state—could not be divided among contending parties but must rest with one of them: preferably the king, who should have the power of life and death over his subjects that the Roman head of household had held over his children. Bodin's doctrine, which came to be known as absolutism, proved highly attractive to monarchs and their ministers in the decades to come.

In the end, Bodin sided with the Catholic Holy League against the Huguenots and politiques, who included many of his former friends. More surprising still, he came to believe that witches, as well as heretics, threatened France. His treatise, *Of the Demonomania of Sorcerers*, made a powerful case for the prosecution of witches of both sexes. Its festering anecdotes of diabolic action in the world made it a reference book for two generations of witch-hunters.

MONTAIGNE Montaigne, by contrast, retired from public life as a lawyer in middle age to an estate outside Bordeaux. Reading and contemplating in his study, its rafters inscribed with classical proverbs, he tested the precepts of the ancients against his own experience. Although the Stoics, who had insisted that the wise must ignore pain and other distractions, had many followers in Montaigne's time, he found their precepts too demanding to be realistic. The ancient Skeptics, with their refusal to make dogmatic pronouncements, appealed to him more. Perhaps they offered a way out of the labyrinths of religious war. Gradually, Montaigne evolved a new literary form, the essay—literally, a trial or experiment. Whereas Bodin wrote formal treatises in Latin that propounded a single, absolute truth, Montaigne wrote short pieces in French that began from some supposed truth and subjected it to examination.

Dogmas of all kinds, Montaigne confessed, repelled and depressed him. He found it implausible that witches deserved to be burned for conspiring against humanity or that European culture, in its authoritarianism and violence, could claim ethical superiority to the so-called cannibals of the New World. Montaigne argued in a famous essay that New World natives practiced the arts with grace and subtlety, and had created an egalitarian society that put the supposed Christians of hierarchical, bloodthirsty Europe to shame. He expressed his horror at the Stoical hard men, Catholic and Protestant, who did not realize that knowing when to yield was a basic part of the moral life.

Montaigne's *Essays* (1580) spared few of the follies of his time. But Montaigne saw himself as a human brother, as much the prey of emotions and illusions as everyone else, and he made fun of his own tendency to draw radical conclusions. At the end of his essay on cannibals, for example, he told the story of how Brazilian natives brought to Europe to take part in royal ceremonies had exposed the un-Christian nature of Christian society to France's King Charles IX when he questioned them. Montaigne learned that they found two things odd: that grown men—strong, bearded, and armed—would obey a king who was still a child, and that the European poor did not kill the rich and take their goods. Montaigne's Indians sound like Thomas More's Raphael Hythloday denouncing the immorality of Europe. Unlike More, however, Montaigne immediately struck a comic note, conceding that he could not have understood everything he was told about the alien society he had tried to describe. He admitted that he had found it almost impossible to communicate with an Indian, even using an interpreter. And he summed up his elaborate, critical comparison of societies with rueful simplicity: "What's the use? They don't wear pants."

The first two books of the *Essays*, published in 1580, became best sellers. Now a celebrity, Montaigne traveled to Rome, examining the cities he passed through, their antiquities and customs. On his return to France, he continued writing essays, composing a third book in which he made himself, in all his own weaknesses and inconsistencies, his principal subject. But Montaigne also served as mayor of Bordeaux, political adviser to Henry of Navarre, and an intermediary in the negotiations between Catholics and Protestants that brought the French religious wars

Montaigne This portrait of a richly dressed Michel de Montaigne was painted during the writer's life by an anonymous artist.

to a close. The man who hated violence and intolerance did more than most to find a way to end what was, to that point, Europe's most violent and intolerant age. Neither Bodin nor Montaigne was an ordinary writer, typical of his time. But both shared their views with the thousands of readers who made their works so popular. And both, in their radically different ways, expressed the contradictions of a Europe torn by contending beliefs—and soon to be torn, in different ways, by new political, religious, and intellectual movements.

CONCLUSION

The Europeans of the sixteenth century lived through some of the most wracking changes in history. They became print professionals and skilled users of verbal and visual media, which could reproduce their ideas in hundreds, rather than dozens, of copies. They profited from the geographical discoveries of the late fifteenth century, and thought hard about what these discoveries implied about their traditional sense of Europe's central place in the universe. And they saw the unified Catholic Church, already more than one thousand years old, challenged by rivals that it could not defeat, even as its own powers revived.

Most Christians continued to believe that their own form of religion was the only true one. They saw it as reasonable—even virtuous—to persecute those who insisted on worshipping differently, or to rebel against political authorities that persecuted them. Only a few, such as Montaigne, shared the qualified belief in tolerance that had made Erasmus leery of persecuting heretics when the Reformation broke out. Eventually, however, the sheer human cost of religious conflict clearly outweighed any benefits, even in the eyes of many staunchly orthodox Catholics and Protestants. By the end of the sixteenth century, foundations had been laid for a development no one could have foreseen a century earlier: the creation not only of separate Catholic and Protestant churches but also of distinct Catholic and Protestant societies.

[CHAPTER REVIEW]

KEY TERMS

Martin Luther (p. 372)

indulgence (p. 373)

Desiderius Erasmus (p. 375)

Thomas More (p. 376)

Ninety-Five Theses (p. 378)

Diet of Worms (p. 378)

Protestant Reformation (p. 379)

Ulrich Zwingli (p. 382)

Peasants' War (p. 384)

Anabaptists (p. 385)

Argula von Grumbach (p. 386)

John Calvin (p. 388)

Henry VIII (p. 390)

Charles V (p. 391)

Jacob Fugger (p. 391)

Peace of Augsburg (p. 393)

Jesuits (p. 395)

Council of Trent (p. 396)

Nicolaus Copernicus (p. 397)

Huguenots (p. 399)

Dutch Revolt (p. 400)

Massacre of Saint Bartholomew's Day (p. 400)

Spanish Armada (p. 401)

Edict of Nantes (p. 401)

REVIEW QUESTIONS

1. What were Martin Luther's primary criticisms of the Catholic Church?

2. What factors spurred the expansion of the Reformation movement?

3. What were the most important differences in the thinking of Luther, Ulrich Zwingli, and John Calvin?

4. How did the Reformation inspire the Peasants' War in Germany?

5. How did the Reformation affect the lives of women?

6. What actions did Holy Roman Emperor Charles V take to expand and solidify his territories?

7. What were the most important outcomes of the Council of Trent?

8. What advances in scientific thinking took place during the Reformation?

9. Why did Europe's religious divisions lead to war in the sixteenth century?

10. What developments in the sixteenth century allowed for greater religious toleration?

CORE OBJECTIVES

After reading this chapter, you should have a solid understanding of the following core objectives. To strengthen your grasp of the core objectives, use the resources on the Student Site for The West.

- Analyze the intellectual and cultural context that influenced Martin Luther's ideas.

- Describe the major events of the Protestant Reformation.

- Compare the different Protestant movements inspired by Luther's message.

- Describe the social and political conditions that led to conflict between Protestants and Catholics.

- Explain the Catholic Reformation that arose in response to Protestantism.

- Identify the intellectual innovations and political conflicts that coincided with the Reformation.

 GO TO inQuizitive TO SEE WHAT YOU'VE LEARNED—AND LEARN WHAT YOU'VE MISSED—WITH PERSONALIZED FEEDBACK ALONG THE WAY.

FURTHER READING

CHAPTER 1 Origins (12,000–600 BCE)

Assmann, Jan, *The Mind of Egypt: History and Meaning in the Time of the Pharaohs*. New York, 2002.

Cline, Eric, *1176 B.C.: The Year Ancient Civilization Collapsed*. Princeton, 2014.

Damrosch, David, *The Buried Book: The Loss and Rediscovery of the Great Epic of Gilgamesh*. New York, 2007.

Foster, Benjamin, and Karen Pollinger Foster, *Civilizations of Ancient Iraq*. Princeton, 2009.

Liverani, Mario, *The Ancient Near East: History, Society and Economy*. New York, 2014.

Podany, Amanda, *The Ancient Near East: A Very Short Introduction*. Oxford, 2013.

Romer, John, *A History of Ancient Egypt: From the First Farmers to the Great Pyramid*. London and New York, 2012.

Shapiro, H. A., ed., *The Cambridge Companion to Archaic Greece*. Cambridge, 2009.

CHAPTER 2 "The School of Greece" (600–400 BCE)

Beard, Mary, *The Parthenon*, rev. ed. Cambridge, Mass., 2010.

Lloyd, Geoffrey, *Early Greek Science: Thales to Aristotle*. New York, 1970.

Missiou, Anna, *Literacy and Democracy in Fifth-Century Athens*. Cambridge, 2011.

Ober, Josiah, *Democracy and Knowledge: Innovation and Learning in Classical Athens*. Princeton, 2008.

Ober, Josiah, *Mass and Elite in Democratic Athens: Rhetoric, Ideology, and the Power of the People*. Princeton, 1989.

Ober, Josiah, *The Rise and Fall of Classical Greece*. Princeton, 2015.

Pomeroy, Sarah, *Goddesses, Whores, Wives, and Slaves: Women in Classical Antiquity*. New York, 1975.

Pomeroy, Sarah, et al., *Ancient Greece: A Political, Social, and Cultural History*, 3rd ed. New York, 2012.

Samons, Loren J., II, ed., *The Cambridge Companion to the Age of Pericles*. Cambridge, 2007.

Waterfield, Robin, *Why Socrates Died: Dispelling the Myths*. New York, 2009.

CHAPTER 3 From Classical Greece to the Hellenistic World (400–30 BCE)

Barnes, Jonathan, ed., *The Cambridge Companion to Aristotle*. Cambridge, 1995.

Bartlett, John, and Ronald Williamson, *Jews in the Hellenistic World*, 2 vols. Cambridge, 1985–89.

Bugh, Glenn R., ed., *The Cambridge Companion to the Hellenistic World*. Cambridge, 2006.

Casson, Lionel, *Libraries in the Ancient World*. New Haven, 2001.

Kraut, Richard, ed., *The Cambridge Companion to Plato*. Cambridge, 2006.

Lloyd, Geoffrey, *Greek Science after Aristotle*. New York, 1973.

Parsons, Peter, *City of the Sharp-Nosed Fish: Greek Lives in Roman Egypt*. London, 2007.

Pomeroy, Sarah, *Women in Hellenistic Egypt: From Alexander to Cleopatra*. New York, 1984.

Rice, E. E., *The Grand Procession of Ptolemy Philadelphus*. London, 1983.

Shipley, Graham, *The Greek World after Alexander*. London, 2000.

CHAPTER 4 Rome (1000 BCE–14 CE)

Beard, Mary, *SPQR: A History of Ancient Rome*. New York, 2015.

Cornell, Tim, *The Beginnings of Rome: Italy and Rome from the Bronze Age to the Punic Wars (c. 1000–264 B.C.)*. London and New York, 1995.

Erdkamp, Paul, ed., *The Cambridge Companion to Ancient Rome*. Cambridge, 2013.

Flower, Harriet, *Roman Republics*. Princeton, 2010.

Flower, Harriet, ed., *The Cambridge Companion to the Roman Republic*. Cambridge, 2014.

Galinsky, Karl, ed., *The Cambridge Companion to the Age of Augustus*. Cambridge, 2007.

Stevenson, Tom, *Julius Caesar and the Transformation of the Roman Republic*. London and New York, 2015.

CHAPTER 5 The Roman Empire and the Rise of Christianity (14–312 CE)

Beard, Mary, *SPQR: A History of Ancient Rome*. New York, 2015.

Burkett, Delbert, *An Introduction to the New Testament and the Origins of Christianity*. Cambridge, 2002.

Erdkamp, Paul, ed., *The Cambridge Companion to Ancient Rome*. Cambridge, 2013.

Fredriksen, Paula, *Jesus of Nazareth, King of the Jews: A Jewish Life and the Emergence of Christianity*. New York, 1999.

Heffernan, Thomas, *The Passion of Perpetua and Felicity*. New York, 2012.

Kulikowski, Michael, *The Triumph of Empire: The Roman World from Hadrian to Constantine*. Cambridge, MA, 2016.

Mitchell, Margaret, and Frances Young, eds., *The Cambridge History of Christianity*. Vol. 1, *Origins to Constantine*. Cambridge, 2006.

CHAPTER 6 The Late Roman Empire and the Consolidation of the Church (312–476)

Beard, Mary, *SPQR: A History of Ancient Rome*. New York, 2015.

Brown, Peter, *The Rise of Western Christendom: Triumph and Diversity, A.D. 200–1000*. Chichester and Malden, 2013.

Canaday, Augustine, and Frederick Norris, eds., *The Cambridge History of Christianity*. Vol. 2, *Constantine to 600*. Cambridge, 2007.

Herrin, Judith, *Byzantium: The Surprising Life of a Medieval Empire*. Princeton, 2007.

Herrin, Judith, *Unrivalled Influence: Women and Empire in Byzantium*. Princeton, 2013.

Lenski, Noel, ed., *The Cambridge Companion to the Age of Constantine*. Cambridge, 2012.

O'Donnell, James, *Pagans: The End of Traditional Religion and the Rise of Christianity*. New York, 2015.

O'Donnell, James, *The Ruin of the Roman Empire*. New York, 2007.

Ward-Perkins, Bryan, *The Fall of Rome and the End of Civilization*. Oxford, 2005.

CHAPTER 7 Between Worlds (476–900)

Berkey, Jonathan, *The Formation of Islam: Religion and Society in the Near East, 600–1800*. Cambridge, 2003.

Brown, Peter, *The Rise of Western Christendom: Triumph and Diversity, A.D. 200–1000*. Chichester and Malden, 2013.

Geary, Patrick, *Before France and Germany: The Creation and Transformation of the Merovingian World*. New York, 1988.

Herrin, Judith, *Byzantium: The Surprising Life of a Medieval Empire*. Princeton, 2007.

Herrin, Judith, *The Formation of Christendom*. Princeton, 1988.

McKitterick, Rosamund, *Charlemagne: The Formation of a European Identity*. Cambridge, 2008.

Noble, Thomas, and Julia Smith, eds., *The Cambridge History of Christianity*. Vol. 3, *Early Medieval Christianities, c. 600–c. 1100*. Cambridge, 2008.

Wickham, Chris, *Medieval Europe*. New Haven and London, 2016.

CHAPTER 8 Europe Revived (900–1200)

Colish, Marcia, *Medieval Foundations of the Western Intellectual Tradition, 400–1400*. New Haven, 1997.

Epstein, Stephen, *An Economic and Social History of Medieval Europe*. Cambridge, 2009.

Herrin, Judith, *Byzantium: The Surprising Life of a Medieval Empire*. Princeton, 2007.

Jordan, William, *Europe in the High Middle Ages*. London, 2001.

Noble, Thomas, and Julia Smith, eds., *The Cambridge History of Christianity*. Vol. 3, *Early Medieval Christianities, c. 600–c. 1100*. Cambridge, 2008.

Partner, Peter, *God of Battles: Holy Wars of Christianity and Islam*. London, 1997.

Rubin, Miri, and Walter Simons, eds., *The Cambridge History of Christianity*. Vol. 4, *Christianity in Western Europe, c. 1100–c. 1500*. Cambridge, 2009.

Thompson, John, *The Western Church in the Middle Ages*. London and New York, 1998.

Tierney, Brian, *The Crisis of Church & State, 1050–1300*. Englewood Cliffs, NJ, 1964.

Wickham, Chris, *Medieval Europe*. New Haven and London, 2016.

CHAPTER 9 Consolidation and Crisis (1200–1400)

Baldwin, John, *Paris, 1200*. Stanford, 2010.

Colish, Marcia, *Medieval Foundations of the Western Intellectual Tradition, 400–1400*. New Haven, 1997.

Epstein, Stephen, *An Economic and Social History of Medieval Europe*. Cambridge, 2009.

Gimpel, Jean, *The Medieval Machine: The Industrial Revolution of the Middle Ages*. New York, 1976.

Herrin, Judith, *Byzantium: The Surprising Life of a Medieval Empire*. Princeton, 2007.

Jordan, William, *Europe in the High Middle Ages*. London, 2001.

Rubin, Miri, and Walter Simons, eds., *The Cambridge History of Christianity*. Vol. 4, *Christianity in Western Europe, c. 1100–c. 1500*. Cambridge, 2009.

Tierney, Brian, *The Crisis of Church & State, 1050–1300*. Englewood Cliffs, NJ, 1964.

Wickham, Chris, *Medieval Europe*. New Haven and London, 2016.

CHAPTER 10 Renaissance Europe (1400–1500)

Andrade, Tonio, *The Gunpowder Age: China, Military Innovation, and the Rise of the West in World History*. Princeton, 2016.

Baxandall, Michael, *Painting and Experience in Fifteenth-Century Italy*, 2nd ed. Oxford, 1988.

Fernández-Armesto, Felipe, *1492: The Year the World Began*. New York, 2009.

Fletcher, Catherine, *Diplomacy in Renaissance Rome: The Rise of the Resident Ambassador*. Cambridge, 2015.

King, Margaret, *The Renaissance in Europe*. London, 2003.

Kraye, Jill, ed., *The Cambridge Companion to Renaissance Humanism*. Cambridge, 2006.

Pettegree, Andrew, *The Book in the Renaissance*. New Haven, 2011.

Rubin, Miri, and Walter Simons, eds., *The Cambridge History of Christianity*. Vol. 4, *Christianity in Western Europe, c. 1100–c. 1500*. Cambridge, 2009.

Skinner, Quentin, *Foundations of Modern Political Thought*. Vol. 1, *The Renaissance*. Cambridge and New York, 1978.

CHAPTER 11 Reformations (1500–1600)

Benedict, Philip, *Christ's Churches Purely Reformed: A Social History of Calvinism*. New Haven, 2002.

Eire, Carlos, *Reformations: The Early Modern World, 1450–1650*. New Haven, 2016.

Greengrass, Mark, *Christendom Destroyed: Europe 1517–1648*. London, 2015.

Holt, Mack, *The French Wars of Religion*. Cambridge, 2005.

Hsia, R. Po-chia, ed., *The Cambridge History of Christianity*. Vol. 6, *Reform and Expansion, 1500–1600*. Cambridge, 2007.

Kaplan, Benjamin, *Divided by Faith: Religious Tolerance and the Practice of Toleration in Early Modern Europe*. Cambridge, MA, 2007.

Kraye, Jill, ed., *The Cambridge Companion to Renaissance Humanism*. Cambridge, 2006.

Pettegree, Andrew, *Brand Luther*. London, 2016.

Richardson, Glenn, *Renaissance Monarchy: The Reigns of Henry VIII, Francis I and Charles V*. London, 2002.

Skinner, Quentin, *Foundations of Modern Political Thought*. Vol. 2, *The Reformation*. Cambridge and New York, 1978.

Acropolis: The steep hill dominating the center of Athens that is home to many famous structures, most notably the Parthenon. More generally, an acropolis is the uppermost part of a city, usually where a fortress or citadel is positioned.

Adrianople: The site in Thrace of a 378 CE battle in which the eastern Roman emperor Valens suffered a devastating defeat to the Goths.

agricultural: Relating to the cultivation of plants and animals. On a large scale, agriculture produces food surpluses, which enable people to settle in one place and develop a level of culture not found in nomadic societies.

Alberti, Leon Battista (1404–1472): A renowned Italian humanist with a wide range of talents and interests, mainly in the arts. He is best known as the author of important and influential fifteenth-century treatises on painting, sculpture, and architecture.

Alexander (356–323 BCE): The son of Philip II of Macedon, and a brilliant general who conquered an area spanning from Greece and Egypt in the west to India in the east. He is known to history as Alexander the Great, and his empire promoted the diffusion of Greek culture throughout the eastern Mediterranean and Middle East.

Alhambra Decree (1492). A decree issued by Ferdinand and Isabella that gave Jews four months to convert to Christianity or leave Spain.

Alighieri, Dante (1265–1321): Usually referred to simply as Dante, an Italian poet and writer. His most famous work is *The Divine Comedy*, an epic poem describing his allegorical journey through Hell, Purgatory, and Heaven.

ambassadors: Beginning in Italy in the mid-fifteenth century, diplomats sent to capitals to represent their state's interests, gather information, and convey official communications.

Anabaptists: A radical Protestant denomination found primarily in Switzerland and Germany starting in the sixteenth century. Anabaptists constituted an apocalyptic sect that rejected infant baptism in favor of adult baptism and that argued the Bible was a blueprint for creating the perfect society. Members of this faith were often persecuted by both Catholics and more mainstream Protestant groups.

Aquinas, Thomas (1225–1274): A Dominican friar and Catholic priest who was one of the leading philosophers and theologians of the Middle Ages. His *Summa Theologica* is considered the high point of scholastic theology, a philosophical and theological movement that aimed to apply Aristotelian logic to the study of faith.

Arianism: Defined as the teachings attributed to the Egyptian Christian priest Arius in the third and fourth centuries CE. Arianism's main departure from standard Christian dogma is on the matter of the Trinity. Arius argued in his concept of Christ that the Son did not always exist and was therefore distinct from the Father. This went against the orthodox teaching established at the Council of Nicaea, which marked Arianism as heretical.

Aristotle (382–322 BCE): A student of Plato and a key figure of classical Greek philosophy. Breaking with Plato over the idea of the forms, he instead argued that the essence of an object can be found in the object itself.

Athena: The Greek goddess of wisdom and the patron goddess of Athens.

Augustine (354–430): Arguably the most important of the early church fathers, Augustine lived in North Africa. He was highly influential on Christian theology, especially on the matters of God's grace and original sin. His writings, including *The City of God* and *Confessions*, are cornerstones of the Christian worldview.

Augustus (63 BCE–14 CE): The great-nephew and adopted son of Julius Caesar, Augustus defeated the enemies of Caesar, and his former allies in the Second Triumvirate, to become the unquestioned leader of Rome following the battle of Actium in 31 BCE. Born Octavian, he was renamed Augustus, or "the revered one." Augustus brought stability to Rome and ushered in the beginning of the Roman Empire.

Avignon papacy (1309–1377): Also known as the Avignon Captivity, the period during which popes resided in Avignon instead of Rome. During this time, the papacy was widely criticized for being corrupt and being dominated by the French.

barbarians: A term originally used by the Greeks to describe people who did not speak Greek and were therefore considered "uncivilized," the word was also used by the Romans to describe the various Germanic tribes that lived along their northern border.

Benedict (480–545): Benedict of Nursia, later canonized by the Catholic Church as Saint Benedict, lived in Italy. He is famous for writing the *Rule of Saint Benedict*, which became the foundation for most religious communities in Europe during the Middle Ages. Because of this, he is often referred to as the founder of Western monasticism.

bishop: An ordained member of the Christian clergy who holds a position of leadership within their community. Bishops claim a direct historical lineage back to the original twelve apostles, thus justifying their authority within the religion. Bishops have several main responsibilities, including preaching, performing religious instruction, raising and controlling funds, carrying out administrative duties within their district, and representing their communities within the Christian world.

Black Death: An outbreak of bubonic and pneumonic plague that migrated from China along the Silk Road, eventually reaching the port city of Genoa in 1347 CE. The disease killed approximately half the population of Europe in the first four years of the pandemic.

Caesar, Julius (100–44 BCE): A brilliant general, politician, and author, Julius Caesar used his victories on the battlefield to propel himself to the height of power at the end of the Roman Republic. Caesar was a *populare* who assumed the title "Dictator in Perpetuity" before he was assassinated on the Ides of March by the senators Brutus and Cassius.

caliph: The title used by the spiritual and political leader of the Muslim community. The term means "successor," indicating that the caliph had taken on the authority of the original leader of the followers of Islam, the prophet Muhammad. The split between Sunnis and Shiites originated in a dispute over who was the rightful successor as caliph following the death of Muhammad.

Calvin, John (1509–1564): An important figure in the Protestant Reformation, Calvin created a branch of the church that came to bear his name. His most important theological contributions were ideas about predestination. Calvin became the de facto ruler of the city of Geneva for twenty years in the mid-sixteenth century.

Carolingian Renaissance: A cultural and intellectual flowering that took place around the court of Charlemagne in the late eighth and early ninth centuries.

Carolingians: Named after the king Charles Martel, the Carolingian family replaced the Merovingians as leaders of the Franks. This royal house ruled from 750 to 987 CE.

Carthage: A Phoenician settlement on the coast of North Africa in the area of modern-day Tunisia. The Carthaginians controlled vast areas of the western Mediterranean in the middle of the first millennium BCE and ultimately became a major rival of Rome. Carthage lost its empire in a series of clashes with Rome known as the "Punic Wars" (264–246 BCE).

Cathars: Members of a Christian religious sect in northern Italy and southern France that rejected important elements of Catholic doctrine. Deemed heretics by the papacy, the Cathars were subject to a crusade and multiple inquisitions and were essentially destroyed by the mid-thirteenth century CE.

Charlemagne (r. 768–814): The second of the Carolingian kings, Charles the Great is known to history as Charlemagne. Crowned Holy Roman emperor in the year 800 by Pope Leo, Charlemagne was instrumental in reviving the classical liberal arts education, modernizing the Latin language, spreading Christianity throughout the Germanic lands, and unifying western Europe for the first time since the fall of Rome.

Charles V (r. 1519–1556): Heir to three of Europe's largest royal houses, Charles V was also Holy Roman emperor in the first half of the sixteenth century. Charles saw it as his duty to defend the Catholic faith against the Protestant reform movement. Because of his vast empire, he was in nearly constant warfare with the other major states of Europe.

chivalry: An ethic forged during the twelfth century, chivalry was a code that set forth the qualities found in the ideal knight. These included courage, honor, piety, learning, and the willingness to protect women and others seen as weak.

Cistercians: Members of a religious order founded in 1098 at Cîteaux in France and based on a return to strict observance of Benedict's teachings. Leaders such as Bernard of Clairvaux emphasized humility and the power of the Virgin Mary.

city-state: A political entity based on an urban center and surrounding territories. Ancient city-states were sovereign and were connected internally through politics, economics, culture, and infrastructure.

civilization: Society characterized by a social hierarchy, written communication, domestication of plants and animals, political and economic centralization, and advanced forms of culture, such as religion and monumental architecture.

Code of Hammurabi: A written collection of statements that describe 282 laws covering criminal, civil, and commercial activities. Recorded around 1700 BCE, the code portrays Hammurabi as the protector of divine justice.

coloni: The plural term for a *colonus*, a tenant farmer in late antiquity and the early Middle Ages. The *coloni* paid landowners a portion of the crops in exchange for the use of their farmlands. The growing numbers of *coloni* signified the decline of the independent farmer in the Roman Empire; they were comparable to medieval serfs.

Columbus, Christopher (1457–1506): The Genoese mariner Columbus received a commission from the monarchs of Spain to chart a new route to the East Indies in 1492. Over the course of a decade and four voyages across the Atlantic, Columbus established settlements throughout the Caribbean Sea and ushered in the era of Spanish colonization in the New World.

common law: The body of English law that is derived from custom and judicial precedent, unlike statutory law, which is created through the legislative process.

communes: Groups of noblemen in eleventh-century Italian cities who formed new governments independent of their bishops or local lords.

Concordat of Worms (1125): The agreement between Henry V and Pope Calixtus II that formally ended the Investiture Controversy, though the struggle between church and state continued.

confraternities: Lay Christian associations founded beginning in the Middle Ages as charitable organizations or as groups to conduct rituals and worship.

Constantine (r. 306–337 CE): The leader who emerged from the last tetrarchy to become sole ruler of the Roman Empire in 312 CE until his death. He was the first Christian emperor of Rome, and his conversion was the first step toward Rome becoming a Christian state.

Constantinople: The capital city of the Roman Empire and subsequent Byzantine Empire built by the emperor Constantine I in the fourth century CE. Constantinople was the political, religious, and economic hub of these empires and remained so until it was captured by the Ottomans in the fifteenth century. Constantinople lies at the meeting point of Europe and Asia and is now the modern-day Turkish city of Istanbul.

Copernicus, Nicolaus (1473–1543): The Polish astronomer who advanced the idea that the earth revolves around the sun.

Corpus Iuris: A new law code for the Roman world that was produced by a ten-man commission established by Justinian. This "Body of Civil Law" contained the existing statutes of the emperors, the legal opinions of leading Roman jurists, and new laws added by Justinian. The code provided a systematic approach to law with a focus on justice as its underlying principle.

Cortés, Hernán (1485–1547): The Spanish *conquistador* who defeated the great Aztec Empire of mainland Mexico in the early sixteenth century. His victory enabled the Spanish to claim lands throughout Central America, Mexico, and the area known today as the United States. Cortés was the first governor of the colony known as New Spain.

Council of Constance (1414–1418): A council of the Catholic Church called to end the dispute between French and Italian claimants to the papacy. The result of the Council was the removal of the two rival popes and the ascension of Pope Martin V to the papal throne.

Council of Nicea (325): Assembled by Constantine, the first general council of the Catholic Church. The bishops at the council ruled against Arianism and in favor of Jesus's divinity, a decision that shaped the core beliefs of the Catholic religion.

Council of Trent (1545–1563): An ecumenical council of the Catholic Church held in the Italian city of Trent. The Council sought to clarify Catholic doctrine and answer criticisms of the Church brought forth by the Protestant movement.

Crusades (1095–1291): Military campaigns called for by the Catholic Church against Muslim "infidels." The main goal of the Crusades was to conquer and claim the Holy Land for the Christian west.

cuneiform: A writing system that developed in Mesopotamia (specifically, Sumer) during the third millennium BCE and that was characterized by wedge-like symbols pressed into clay tablets.

Delian League: An alliance created by the Athenians in 478 BCE to evict the Persian fleet from the Aegean Sea. Named after the island of Delos, where the member city-states conferred, the league eventually became the basis for the growing Athenian naval empire.

deme: A local unit or ward of ancient Athens.

democracy: A form of government in which citizens participate in the creation of the laws and institutions of their society. Fifth-century BCE Athens is typically cited as the world's first democracy. From the Greek words *demos* ("people") and *kratos* ("rule").

Diet of Worms (1521): A meeting of the imperial parliament called by the Holy Roman emperor Charles V to address the growing Protestant movement. Luther refused to renounce his views and was arrested afterward.

Diocletian (r. 284–305 CE): A decorated soldier from a lower class family who ascended to the rank of Roman emperor. Rising to power after a century of chaos and instability in Rome, Diocletian pushed through important political, economic, and military reforms that stabilized the Empire.

divination: The practice of attempting to predict the future by looking for messages imprinted in the natural world.

Domesday Book: The extensive survey of English landowners' property conducted by William I.

domesticated: In terms of wild plants or animals, the condition of having been brought under human control.

Dominican Order: Founded by the Spanish priest Dominic de Guzmán in 1216 CE, an order consisting of friars and nuns with a special focus on preaching, education, conversion, and combating heresy. The Dominicans are considered a mendicant order: they wander through cities and countryside as opposed to staying cloistered.

Donatists: North African Christians who in the fourth century denounced bishops who survived persecution by compromising their faith. The Donatist church demanded adherence to a strict set of principles.

Dutch Revolt (1566): The largely Calvinist population of the Dutch provinces of the Spanish Empire began a revolt against what they saw as the increasing repression of Philip II's rule. The Dutch broke free and formed the United Provinces in 1581, finally achieving officially recognized independence in 1648.

East-West Schism: Also known as the Schism of 1054, the divide between the Roman and Orthodox churches that was driven in part by disagreements about the nature of the Holy Spirit.

Edict of Milan (313): The decree passed by the emperor Constantine I that allowed for religious tolerance in the Roman Empire. It was specifically geared toward the growing Christian community, which had suffered great persecution under many previous emperors. The Edict was the first step toward Rome accepting Christianity as its official religion.

Edict of Nantes (1598): Signed by the French king Henry IV, the Edict granted the Huguenots substantial rights within the state and allowed for a greater degree of toleration after the French Wars of Religion of the sixteenth century.

empirical: A method of study favored by Aristotle in which evidence is attained through the observation of nature. Focusing on experimentation, empirical study later became the foundation of the modern scientific method.

epic: A form of literature that was a foundational part of the unified Greek culture that developed during the archaic age. Homer's great epic poems, the *Iliad* and the *Odyssey*, recorded around 800 BCE, are set in the Mycenaean period and deal with events surrounding the Trojan War.

Epic of Gilgamesh: An Akkadian poem from Mesopotamia about the hero Gilgamesh and his encounters with various gods and goddesses as he tries to discover the path to eternal life. It was compiled in the eighteenth century BCE from earlier Sumerian stories.

Epicureans: Followers of the Hellenistic philosopher Epicurus (314–270 BCE), who broke from the classical Greek model of an ordered and rational universe and argued for something more chaotic and random. Epicureans tried to gain peace of mind through the rational pursuit of pleasure.

Erasmus, Desiderius (1466–1536): A Dutch teacher, scholar, theologian, and humanist. Erasmus is considered one of the most important forerunners of the Reformation owing to his criticisms of the Catholic Church, although he himself did not leave the faith.

Estates General: The representative body of the three estates in France. In 1789, King Louis XVI summoned the Estates General to meet for the first time since 1614 because it seemed to be the only solution to France's worsening economic crisis and financial chaos.

Etruscans: A people of unknown origin who settled the Po River valley of north-central Italy and were the dominant power in the area for approximately three centuries, from around 800 to 500 BCE. The Etruscans strongly influenced the culture of ancient Rome, specifically in architecture, art, and dress.

Eusebius (ca. 260–ca. 339): A Caesarean Christian cleric who compiled complex histories of the world and the Church.

excommunication: A decree from a high-ranking church official, usually a bishop or even the pope himself, that prohibits a parishioner from participating in the sacraments of the Church. The excommunicated were also subject to isolation from the social community.

fealty: Beginning in the early Middle Ages, the practice of vassals swearing loyalty to a lord, who in turn granted protection.

Five Pillars of Islam: These are the basic duties of every observant Muslim. They include: acknowledging the oneness of God, praying five times a day, fasting during the holy month of Ramadan, providing alms to the poor, and making a pilgrimage to Mecca at least once in one's lifetime.

forms: The Platonic term for eternal, unchanging absolutes that exist separately from matter. Plato argued that forms constitute ultimate reality and are accessible through meticulous and careful reflection and study.

Fourth Lateran Council (1215): The Church council convened by Innocent III that created rules firmly separating secular and church authority and required all Christians to confess once per year.

Franciscan Order: Founded by the Italian clergyman Francis of Assisi in 1209 CE, this order had a strict vow of poverty and, like the Dominicans, was a wandering order. The Franciscans were effective preachers of the Crusades, agents of conversion, and missionaries on the borders of the Catholic world.

Franks: A group of Germanic tribes originating in the lower Rhine region in the third century CE. Eventually, the Franks became rulers of northern Gaul and reached the peak of their territorial gains under Charlemagne in the ninth century. They are credited with halting the Muslim advance into continental Europe as well as becoming the successors of the emperors of the western Roman Empire. Modern-day France derives its name from this group.

Fugger, Jacob (1459–1525): A wealthy German banker who lent money to the Habsburgs and other monarchs in exchange for mining and trading rights.

Gnostics: Taking their name from the Greek word for "knowledge," *gnosis*, Gnostics were identified by their rejection of the material world and their connection to Platonic thinking. There were many gnostic Christian groups in the first centuries of the religion, often at odds with orthodox thinking around the nature of God, the resurrection, and the interpretation of scripture. Gnostics emphasized the importance of hidden truth.

gospels: Deriving from the Old English word *god-spell*, meaning "good news," the four Gospels are narratives of the life, teachings, death, and resurrection of Jesus Christ. There were many different gospels written in the late first to early second centuries BCE, but only those attributed to Matthew, Mark, Luke, and John are considered canonical and form part of the Christian Bible.

Gothic: The architectural style that came to supplant Romanesque as the most popular style in Europe and lasted until the fifteenth century. Gothic architecture is characterized by pointed arches, ribbed vaults, and thin walls with large expanses of stained glass.

Goths: An east Germanic people whose two main branches, Visigoths and Ostrogoths, were instrumental in the downfall of the western Roman Empire in the fifth century CE. The Goths and other Germanic tribes had an uneasy peace with the Romans for centuries, but it was shattered with the introduction of the Huns, a nomadic group from Central Asia who moved into central Europe in the fourth century, displacing the Goths.

Gracchi: Two brothers from the Gracchus family, Tiberius and Gaius, who rose to power in the second century BCE with a reform agenda appealing to the mass of Roman citizens, specifically involving land reform. Both men were assassinated by rival factions in the Senate, who felt the brothers' policies were too radical.

Great Persecution (303): The Christian persecution ordered by Diocletian, destroying churches and attacking Christians throughout the Roman Empire.

Great Schism (1378–1417): A divide in the Roman Catholic Church caused by two—and at one point three—simultaneous claims to the papacy. The division between Italian and French claimants was largely driven by politics as opposed to theology

and did great damage to the reputation and power of the Church.

Gregorian Reform Movement: Late eleventh-century efforts of Pope Gregory VII and his associates to codify the preeminence of the pope, ordained by God, above all others both within and outside of the Church. Imperial theologians responded by arguing the absolute authority of secular rulers.

Gregory (r. 590–604 CE): Commonly referred to as Saint Gregory the Great. A prolific writer, Gregory was known as the "Father of Christian Worship" for his work on the liturgy and rites of the Catholic Church. He was also instrumental in spreading Christianity to the British Isles.

Grumbach, Argula von (1492–ca. 1554): A Bavarian noblewoman whose pamphlets in defense of Luther and Protestantism were printed as many as 29,000 times.

guild: A professional organization in commercial towns that regulated business and safeguarded the privileges of those practicing a particular craft.

Gutenberg, Johannes (1398–1468): A German metalsmith and printer, Gutenberg is credited with introducing the printing press to Europe in the 1450s. The printing press allowed for the rapid and inexpensive production of books and made them accessible to people at all levels of society.

Habsburg dynasty: One of the most influential royal houses in Europe, the Habsburgs ruled over Austria, Spain, and various other European states from the eleventh to the twentieth century. They also controlled the title of Holy Roman emperor for most of the early modern era.

Hanseatic League: Beginning in the twelfth century, a loose but powerful network of trading cities in northern Europe that were centers of manufacture, including silk and linen cloth, armor, and religious art.

Hellenistic: The term used to describe the Greek-based culture that developed in the wake of Alexander's conquests. Hellenistic means "Greek-like" and refers to the fusion of existing cultures with Greek language and culture.

helot: A member of a Greek-speaking Messenian culture of the southwestern Peloponnesus enslaved by the Spartans in the eighth century BCE. Helots were tied to the land and forced to produce food so their Spartan masters could focus their efforts on military training and conquest.

Henry VIII (r. 1509–1547): The second monarch of the Tudor dynasty, Henry ruled England from 1509 until his death in 1547. Although he was famous for his marriages, his most consequential policy was to break

with the Catholic Church in the 1530s and establish the independent Church of England.

heresy: A teaching of belief not considered to be orthodox, usually referring to violations of important church teaching. Someone who challenges orthodox teaching is called a "heretic."

hetairai: Professional female companions who entertained elite men during the classical and Hellenic periods in Greek culture. Hetairai were educated, sophisticated, relatively independent women who were welcomed out in public and in the social circles of prominent men.

hieroglyphs: A system of writing from ancient Egypt in which pictographs represent both sounds and objects.

Holy Roman Empire: The name used for the old eastern Frankish Empire starting in the twelfth century, a multi-ethnic federation of states in central Europe nominally under the control of the Holy Roman emperor. The empire lasted until the nineteenth century, when it was dissolved by Napoleon I.

hoplite: A citizen-soldier of a Greek city-state of the seventh to fourth centuries BCE. Hoplites were armed with helmet, spear, and large wooden shield, and they fought in a tightly packed infantry formation called a "phalanx."

Huguenots: French Calvinists. The Edict of Nantes led to increased toleration of the Huguenots, but Louis XIV reversed it in 1685 when he abolished all legal recognition of Protestantism in France.

humanism: The intellectual worldview held by leading figures of the Renaissance, who were attempting to revitalize classical culture. Humanists celebrated reason and rationality, the liberal arts, and civic engagement. Humanism emphasized the value and potential of mankind.

Hundred Years' War (1337–1453): A long series of battles between the English and French. The conflict was in part about succession to the French throne as well as control over various territories such as the duchies of Aquitaine and Normandy.

Huns: A nomadic people who originated in Central Asia, the Huns were skilled horsemen and fearsome warriors. The arrival of the Huns into the heart of Europe displaced many Gothic tribes and helped hasten the fall of the western Roman Empire.

iconoclasm: The rejection or destruction of religious images as heretical. The concern of iconoclasts is that worshipers venerate the object rather than God. The emperor Leo III initiated a policy of iconoclasm in the Byzantine Empire starting in 731 CE, furthering the schism between eastern and western branches of the Christian church.

indulgence: A donation made to the Catholic Church for the remission and forgiveness of sins. Abuse of the sale of these indulgences, as well as the question of their validity, was the subject of Luther's Ninety-Five Theses.

Innocent III (1198–1216): A pope who held a deep belief in human sin and sought to reform the Church, most notably through the Fourth Lateran Council, to set stricter bounds on the behavior of clergy. He also revived the Crusades, beginning with the Fourth Crusade of 1202–4.

inquisition: An ecclesiastical court established by the pope in the thirteenth century to combat heresy. Mainly from the Dominican order, clerical inquisitors targeted Cathars, Jews, Muslims, and eventually Protestants.

Investiture Controversy: The name given to a series of debates over the limitations of spiritual and secular power in Europe during the eleventh and early twelfth centuries, it came to a head when Pope Gregory VII and Emperor Henry IV of Germany both claimed the right to appoint and invest bishops with the regalia of office. After years of diplomatic and military hostility, the controversy was partially settled by the Concordat of Worms in 1122.

Jerome (ca. 345–ca. 420): One of the most important of the early church fathers who became a "Doctor of the Church," Jerome was a theologian and priest. Jerome was a prodigious writer who became most famous for his translation of the Bible into Latin.

Jesuits: Officially known as the Society of Jesus, the Jesuit religious order was founded by Ignatius Loyola and recognized by the pope in 1540. The Jesuits were particularly active in education and missionary activity and were leaders of the Catholic Reformation.

Jesus (ca. 4 BCE–33 CE): A Jewish religious leader, Jesus was the founder of the Christian religion. A wandering teacher and prophet who was believed to be the Son of God by his followers, Jesus was executed by the Romans by the method of crucifixion. Jesus is called the "Christ," which means the "anointed one," and Christians believe his death and resurrection make possible the cleansing of sin and entrance to the afterlife.

justices of the peace: Beginning in the fourteenth century in England, justices of the peace were unpaid local officials, serving terms of one year, that oversaw juries, kept public order, and enforced legislation.

Justinian (527–565 CE): Justinian is considered one of the most consequential leaders of the Byzantine Empire. His many accomplishments include reclaiming lost territory in the west, instituting major building programs, and creating a comprehensive law code.

Kaaba: Located in the holy city of Mecca in modern-day Saudi Arabia, the Kaaba is the most important shrine for the Muslim community. During their pilgrimage to Mecca, observant Muslims circle the Kaaba seven times. Islamic tradition states that the shrine was originally built by Abraham in the city of Muhammad's birth.

latifundia: From the Latin word meaning "widespread estates," *latifundia* were extensive parcels of land privately owned by wealthy Roman patricians. The produce on these massive farms was grown with slave labor and was typically used for export.

Latin right. After 330 BCE, the right of Latins to marry and trade with Romans and gain citizenship if they settled in Rome.

Law of the Twelve Tables (450 BCE): The set of laws that defined the legal rights and procedures of the Roman Republic.

legions: Disciplined detachments of around 5,000 soldiers in the Roman army. Legions also built camps, roads, and bridges throughout the empire.

Low Countries: The coastal region of northwest Europe, including the area of the modern-day Netherlands and Belgium, which was a center of trade and manufacturing in the fifteenth century.

Luther, Martin (1483–1546): A monk and professor with a doctorate in theology who was the primary figure in the early Protestant Reformation. Luther's criticisms of the Catholic Church ended that institution's dominance over the religious culture of western Christianity.

Lyceum: The school founded by Aristotle around 335 BCE on the outskirts of Athens. Dedicated to the god Apollo, the school focused on both debate and the study of textual sources.

ma'at: A complex concept from ancient Egypt describing the fundamental cosmic order established by the gods, and also encompassing justice, truth, and balance.

Maccabees: The leaders of a Jewish rebel army who overthrew the Seleucids in 166 BCE. The Maccabees established the Hasmonean dynasty, which ruled over Judea for the next century.

Machiavelli, Niccolò (1469–1527): An Italian Renaissance diplomat, historian, and political theorist most famous for his work *The Prince.* Machiavelli is considered one of the most influential political thinkers of the early modern era due to his essays concerning the nature of power and leadership.

Magna Carta: Latin for "The Great Charter," the Magna Carta is considered the foundational document of the English constitutional tradition. In 1215, members of the English nobility forced King John to sign the charter, which pledged the king's respect for the traditional privileges of the nobility, free cities, and the clergy.

Mani (216–276): A Persian Christian mystic whose dualist belief system argued that the evil realm of matter had invaded the good realm of spirit, dooming humans to sin. His followers, known as "Manicheans," continued to challenge conventional Christianity after his death.

manorialism: The dominant socioeconomic system of medieval Europe. Centered on the manor, a parcel of land controlled by a lord, the manorial system placed legal and economic power with a lord who had control over, and responsibility for, the local peasantry.

Maximillian I (r. 1508–1519): The Holy Roman emperor who established Habsburg claims over much of Burgundy, Aragon and Castile, and Milan, while leading an ambitious effort to reform the empire.

Medici family: An Italian banking family and political dynasty that dominated Renaissance Florence. The Medici were also important patrons of the arts and proponents of civic humanism, which made them instrumental to the Renaissance.

Mehmed I (r. 1413–1421): The Ottoman ruler who expanded the empire's territory throughout Europe and Asia Minor, conquering Constantinople in 1453.

metics: Resident aliens of a Greek city-state who lived there legally but were not considered citizens. Many were invited to settle in Athens if they were skilled in trade, arts, crafts, or teaching.

monastic: A term describing communities that were created throughout the Christian world as places where men and women could pursue a life of spirituality. The monastic life was built around work, prayer, and an ascetic lifestyle.

Mongols: A nomadic people from the steppes of Central Asia who were united under the ruler Genghis Khan. His conquest of China was continued by his grandsons, whose armies also seized Muscovy and then moved through Hungary and Poland, reaching as far as the gates of Vienna.

monotheistic: A term describing a religious system that espouses a belief in only one god, or the oneness of God. The three major Western faiths—Judaism, Christianity, and Islam—are all monotheistic religions.

More, Thomas (1478–1535): An English scholar, lawyer, politician, and humanist. More wrote *Utopia* and was the lord chancellor of England before being executed for refusing to recognize Henry VIII's Church of England. He was also one of the most vocal and harshest critics of Luther.

mosques: Islamic houses of worship, often serving as centers of communities.

Muhammad (570–632 CE): The founder of the Islamic religion. It is said that he was approached by the archangel Gabriel with the word of God that formed the holy book of Islam, the Qur'an. Muslims believe that Muhammad was the last in a line of prophets dating back to Abraham and that the message he received was the culmination of God's word to mankind.

Neoplatonism: A school of philosophy heavily influenced by the Platonic tradition and developed largely by Plotinus in the third century. Neoplatonists conceived of a universe in which all matter is closely linked to the gods. Unlike Platonism, Neoplatonism held that philosophers were holy men who spoke directly to the gods, and instead of expressing their arguments in dialogues, they wrote treatises.

New Testament: The collection of texts, taken together with the Hebrew Bible, or Old Testament, that form the Christian Bible. The New Testament took shape over the first two centuries CE and contains the four Gospels, the Letters of Saint Paul, and other early Christian documents. All of the original books of the New Testament were written in Greek.

Ninety-Five Theses: Penned by Luther in 1517, the theses were a stinging criticism of the Church's practice of selling indulgences and are considered the first event in the Protestant Reformation.

oligarchy: As first established in ancient Greece, particularly in Sparta, rule of the state by the few rather than by a monarch or all citizens.

oracle: A place or a person the ancient Greeks considered a vessel through which the words of the gods and goddesses could reach the public. Oracles were often asked for counsel and predictions of the future.

ostracism: A procedure in Athenian politics that gave the members of the Assembly an opportunity each year to vote to expel a citizen they deemed a danger to the state. From the Greek word *ostrakon*, a piece of pottery used as a ballot in the ostracism proceedings.

Ottomans: The Ottomans, first led by Osman I, were a nomadic, warrior people who originated in the area of modern Turkmenistan. By the end of the fourteenth century, they controlled most of Turkey; led by Mehmed II, they sacked Constantinople in 1453. Their empire lasted until their defeat in World War I and the emergence of the modern Turkish state.

papyrus: An ancient Egyptian writing material made from reeds.

parlement: Beginning in the thirteenth century, the French court that established in theory and enforced in practice royal authority.

parliament: From the French verb *parler*, "to speak," parliaments are legislative bodies with enumerated rights in a system of representative government. During the High Middle Ages, especially in England, Parliament came to be seen as representing the will of the realm as a whole.

paterfamilias: Derived from the Latin term for "father of the family," the *paterfamilias* was the oldest living male in a household and held complete control over all other family members.

patricians: According to the Roman historian Livy, the patricians were the noble families of Rome that descended from the original 100 senators appointed by Romulus. Constituting the legally defined upper class of the Roman world, the patricians dominated the economy and political institutions of the state.

Paul: An educated Jew and Roman citizen, Saul of Tarsus, who changed his name to Paul, became one of the most important apostles of the Christian religion. Paul was instrumental in spreading Christianity throughout the eastern Mediterranean and is usually credited with writing fourteen of the twenty-seven books of the New Testament.

Pax Romana: Latin for "Roman Peace," the Pax Romana refers to the era of relative peace that began with the reign of Augustus and lasted until the end of the second century CE.

Peace of Augsburg (1555): The settlement between Charles V and the Schmalkaldic League (an alliance of Protestant German states), that created the policy of *Cuius regio, eius religio*: the rulers of the German states could decide the official religion of their territory.

Peace of God: A tenth- and eleventh-century movement that condemned violence against the innocent. The movement proclaimed the Truce of God, which forbade warfare during the days Thursday through Sunday.

Peasants' War (1523–1525): A widespread popular revolt of the German peasantry. The war was fueled by several factors, primarily centered on issues of class, economics, and the Reformation. The revolt was put down in particularly brutal fashion following Luther's denunciation of the peasants.

Pericles (r. 460–430 BCE): As a leading statesman and general, Pericles began many of the major building projects of classical Greece and was central in further democratizing the city-state.

Petrarch (1304–1374): Often referred to as the "Father of Humanism," Petrarch was an Italian scholar, linguist, and poet who was an important figure in the beginning of the Renaissance. He rediscovered many lost texts, which inspired him to work at revitalizing the study of classical Latin.

Pharisees: An influential group within the Jewish community of Palestine during the Second Temple period, the Pharisees consisted largely of "common" Jews as opposed to the more elite Sadducees. The Pharisees argued that law was the center of Jewish life, and their interpretation of the Torah and Hebrew legacy became the foundation of modern Judaism.

Philip II (r. 359–336 BCE): The leader of the northern Greek-speaking state of Macedon. Philip led Macedon to the peak of its power through his tactical military innovations, including a new, more lethal version of the phalanx.

Phoenicians: A seafaring Semitic people based on the eastern coast of the Mediterranean Sea whose culture was particularly vibrant from the Bronze Age through the classical Greek era.

Plato (ca. 425–347 BCE): A student of Socrates, the teacher of Aristotle, and a central figure in Western philosophy who lived in Athens. Plato taught that absolute concepts and virtues existed on a higher level of reality compared with the everyday world.

plebeians: The general body of free Roman citizens who were not part of the patrician class. Plebeians made up the majority of the Roman citizenry.

polis: Singular form of *poleis*: independent cities in ancient Greece that developed formal constitutions between the eighth and sixth centuries BCE.

polytheistic: A term describing a religious system that involves the worship of multiple gods and goddesses. The religions of ancient Mesopotamia, Egypt, Greece, and Rome were polytheistic.

pope: The head of the Roman Catholic Church.

populares: Roman political leaders in the late Republican period, usually from the upper classes, who garnered support among the common folk with their calls for land reform, public works projects, and government subsidies for the masses. The Gracchi brothers and Julius Caesar are examples of *populares*, which is Latin for "favoring the people."

portolan chart: A detailed rendering of the coastlines, ports, and trade routes of Europe, Africa, and Asia created by fourteenth- and fifteenth-century European cartographers using compasses. These maps were incredibly accurate and helpful for establishing trading posts.

princeps: A Latin term usually translated as "first citizen," this title was first given to Octavian in the year 30 BCE. The term served to imply his position as a first among equals and to pay homage to the Republican past, but the new system, known as the "principate," put control of the Roman state ultimately into the hands of one man.

prophet: An individual who claims to have contact with the divine and acts as an intermediary between humans and God. Within the context of Judaism, prophets were religious reformers who argued that the Hebrew people were breaking their covenant with Yahweh and therefore needed to transform society in order to be more religiously pure.

Protestant Reformation: The movement, starting in 1521 and inspired by Martin Luther, that called into question the theology and practices of the Catholic Church. Due to the decentralized nature of reform, many different Christian denominations emerged under the umbrella of Protestant churches.

Ptolemies: The dynasty established by Ptolemy that ruled a Hellenistic kingdom in Egypt for nearly three centuries (305–30 BCE) as a successor to Alexander's empire. The Ptolemies epitomized the features of Hellenistic rule, as their society fused Greek and Egyptian customs, language, and institutions.

Punic Wars (264–146 BCE): A series of three wars fought between the Roman Republic and Carthage. These clashes were mainly over control of the western Mediterranean, with Rome eventually emerging victorious over its chief rival in the area. "Punic" comes from the Latin word for Phoenician, as Carthage was originally founded by the Phoenicians.

Puritans: A group of English Protestant reformers who felt that the reforms of the Church of England under the Tudor and Stuart monarchs did not go far enough to "purify" the English church of all vestiges of Roman Catholicism. Many Puritans left England for the North American colonies starting in the 1630s.

Qur'an: Literally meaning "the recitation," the Qur'an is the central holy text of the Islamic faith. Muslims believe it to be the final revelation of God to the prophet Muhammad in the seventh century CE. To be considered truly authentic, the Qur'an must be in its original Arabic.

Reconquista (711–1492 CE): Spanish for "reconquest"; the term refers to the period of approximately eight centuries when Muslim and Christian princes battled for control of the Iberian Peninsula.

Romanesque: An architectural style that spread throughout western Europe beginning in the late tenth century and ended approximately 200 years later. Romanesque buildings are characterized by rounded arches, barrel vaults, massive stone pillars, and thick walls.

Saint Bartholomew's Day Massacre: The mass murder of French Protestants (Huguenots) instigated by Queen Catherine de' Medici of France and carried out by Catholics in Paris on August 24, 1572 (Saint Bartholomew's day).

satrap: A provincial governor of the Persian Empire and its successor states. Upon conquering Persia in 330 BCE, Alexander installed his own governors but kept this traditional Persian title.

scholasticism: Beginning in the eleventh century, an approach to Christianity that centered on teaching, learning, the study of scripture and commentaries, and debate.

Second Temple: The center of Jewish life and worship during the Hellenistic and early Roman periods. The Second Temple (the first having been destroyed by the Babylonians in 586 BCE) was built on the Temple Mount in Jerusalem, remaining until its destruction by the Romans in 70 CE.

Senate: An essential Roman political institution established soon after the city's founding in the eighth century BCE that survived throughout the Republican and imperial periods. Primarily an advisory body, the Senate was dominated by the Roman nobility.

Septuagint: The Greek translation of the Hebrew Bible made in the third century BCE. From the Latin word *septuaginta* ("seventy"), which refers to the legendary seventy Jewish scholars who worked on the project.

serf: In medieval Europe, a dependent agricultural worker who performed labor on a manor in exchange for the security and rudimentary government provided by the local lord.

Silk Road: A network of trade routes spanning the Asian continent from the Mediterranean in the west to China in the east. The Silk Road extends over 4,000 miles and was essential for creating economic, political, and cultural connections among the various peoples of Asia. It was named after the lucrative silk trade centered in China that lured merchants from around the region.

Social War: A revolt of Rome's allies on the Italian peninsula whose demands for full citizenship were denied by the Senate in the early first century BCE. The rebels succeeding in briefly forming their own state outside of the confines of Rome, but after a year of conflict they were haltingly re-assimilated back into the Roman state.

Socrates (ca. 470–399 BCE): An Athenian teacher and one of the founding figures in Western philosophy, whose ideas come to us chiefly through his pupil Plato. Socrates was a passionate promoter of critical thinking, and his willingness to challenge conventional wisdom landed him in trouble with the Athenian authorities, who sentenced him to death for allegedly corrupting the city's youth.

Solon: The ruler of Athens appointed in 594 BCE and charged with ending the social and economic unrest plaguing the city. Solon brought major reforms to the Athenian system and was an important transitional figure on the road from aristocracy to democracy.

sophist: An itinerant teacher of philosophy and rhetoric during the archaic and classical periods. Sophists focused on the skills of argument and debate rather than the search for absolute truths. From the Greek word *sophia* ("wisdom" or "wise").

Spanish Armada: The fleet of warships sent against England by Philip II of Spain in 1588 but vanquished by the English fleet and bad weather in the English Channel.

Stoics: Followers of the Hellenistic philosopher Zeno (ca. 335–263 BCE), who argued that people must accept that their life is determined by fate, and that upon this acceptance they can devote themselves to duty. Stoicism later heavily influenced Roman society.

Struggle of the Orders: The conflict between patrician and plebeian orders beginning in the early years of the Roman Republic. The plebeians gradually won a greater share of political power as a result of these efforts, and the struggle greatly affected the development of the Roman constitution.

symposium: An important Hellenic social institution that provided a forum for upper-class men to discuss important issues of the day, including philosophy and politics.

taille: Established as early as 1439 in France, a permanent tax used to support the military, collected from all those who were neither clerics nor nobles.

tetrarchy: One of the most important reforms of the emperor Diocletian was the creation of the tetrarchy in 293 BCE. Meaning "the rule of four," the tetrarchic system included two senior emperors, each called an *Augustus*, and two junior emperors, each called a *Caesar*. Each pair of emperors ruled over one half of the Roman Empire, split between east and west. This system was created to help end the battles for succession that plagued third-century Rome as well as to make administration of the empire more efficient.

Theodora (ca. 500–548): Wife of the emperor Justinian, Theodora was arguably the most powerful woman in the history of the Byzantine Empire. She was Justinian's most trusted adviser and helped to shape religious and social policy from her position as empress.

Theodoric (r. 475–526): Leader of the Ostrogoths who established a Gothic realm that stretched from the area of modern France to the Balkans. Though officially a representative of the emperor in Constantinople, Theodoric ruled essentially independently.

theology: The study of religious faith, practice, and experience, especially the nature of God and God's relation to the world.

Thucydides: An Athenian historian and general who wrote the definitive history of the Peloponnesian War before his death around 400 BCE.

tragedy: A form of Greek theater that reached its peak in fifth-century BCE Athens with the playwrights Aeschylus, Sophocles, and Euripides. Tragedies highlighted the suffering that underlies human society and provided lessons for the audience through the tribulations of their main characters.

Treaty of Tordesillas (1494): A treaty dividing the newly explored, non-Christian lands of the New World between the Spanish and the Portuguese in the wake of Columbus's first voyage.

Trinity: An essential element of Christian theology, the Holy Trinity consists of God the Father, the Son, and the Holy Spirit. According to accepted Christian orthodoxy, all three members of the Trinity are equal, eternal, and of the same substance.

trireme: A military vessel used by the Athenians and later by the Romans. Its name derived from the three rows of oars on either side of the ship.

Twelve Tables: Representing an important victory for the plebeians in the Struggle of the Orders, the Twelve Tables helped standardize basic legal proceedings in the Republic and formed one of the centerpieces of the Roman constitutional system. Completed around 450 BCE, the Twelve Tables, according to the Roman historian Livy, were based largely on Greek law.

Umayyads: Members of the seventh- and eighth-century Islamic caliphate that ruled an empire stretching from the Middle East to Spain. The Umayyad Caliphate saw the development of the Qur'an and other fundamental aspects of Muslim culture.

vassals: Typically, low-ranking knights or noblemen who swore an oath of fealty to bring both financial and military aid to their lord, usually in return for lands to support themselves. The lord–vassal relationship was the foundation of the medieval feudal system.

Vulgate: A Latin translation of the Bible from the late fourth century CE written by Jerome. This was the most widely used Bible in the Latin-speaking west and became the official Bible of the Catholic Church during the Council of Trent in the sixteenth century.

Wars of the Roses (1455–1487): A series of wars waged between the Houses of Lancaster and York for control of the English crown. The Lancastrian Henry Tudor emerged victorious and established his family's dynasty for the next century.

William the Conquerer (r. 1035–1087): Duke of Normandy and later King William I of England following his conquest of England in 1066. The first Norman king of England, he reigned until his death.

ziggurat: A monumental tiered or terraced temple found in ancient Mesopotamia beginning in the early third millennium BCE. Most ziggurats were built of mud brick, with ornamental facades and stairways and ramps for access to the shrines.

Zwingli, Ulrich (1484–1531): The leader of the Reformed church in Zurich, Zwingli broke from Luther over differing interpretations of the Eucharist. He argued that public behavior should be regulated by the Christian magistrate.

CHAPTER 1

Making Connections, p. 21 Excerpts from "I Will Praise the Lord of Wisdom" from *The Ancient Near East, Vol. II*, pp. 151–154, edited by James B. Pritchard, translated by Robert D. Briggs. © 1975 by Princeton University Press. Reprinted by permission of Princeton University Press.

Documenting Everyday Life, p. 27 "Pap. Kahun I, 1 (ca. 1900 BC)," http://www.stoa.org/diotima/anthology/wardtexts.shtml#I, translated by William Ward. Reprinted by permission of the Estate of William Ward.

CHAPTER 2

Documenting Everyday Life, p. 64 "77: Funeral Law. Ioulis on Keos, Late 5th Cent. BC" from Mary R. Lefkowitz and Maureen B. Fant, eds., *Women's Life in Greece and Rome: A Source Book in Translation, 2nd Edition*, pp. 58–59. © 1982, 1992 M.B. Fant & M.R. Lefkowitz. Reprinted with permission of Johns Hopkins University Press and Bloomsbury Academic, an imprint of Bloomsbury Publishing Plc.

Making Connections, p. 66 From *Xenophon, Vol. VII*, pp. 479–481, translated by E.C. Marchant and G.W. Bowersock, Loeb Classical Library Volume 183, Cambridge, Mass.,: Harvard University Press, Copyright © 1968 by the President and Fellows of Harvard College. Loeb Classical Library ® is a registered trademark of the President and Fellows of Harvard College.

"The Berezan Lead Letter" from Michael Trapp, ed., John Chadwick, trans., *Greek and Latin Letters: An Anthology with Translation* (Cambridge: Cambridge University Press, 2003), p. 51. © 2003 Cambridge University Press.

CHAPTER 3

Making Connections, p. 86 Excerpts from *The Campaigns of Alexander*, by Arrian, edited by James Romm, translated by Pamela Mensch (New York: Pantheon Books, 2010), pp. 168–9. Originally published in *Alexander the Great: Selections from Arrian, Diodorus, Plutarch, and Quintus Curtius* (Indianapolis: Hackett Publishing Company, 2005), pp. 106–7. © 2005 Hackett Publishing Company. Reprinted with permission from the publisher, Hackett Publishing Company, Inc. All rights reserved.

Documenting Everyday Life, p. 93 "Woman scalded by bath-attendant" from Jane Rowlandson, ed., *Women and Society in Greek and Roman Egypt: A Sourcebook* (Cambridge: Cambridge University Press, 1998), pp. 172, 174. © 1998 Cambridge University Press.

CHAPTER 4

Documenting Everyday Life, p. 130 "The Humble Townspeople: From the Walls of Pompeii" from Naphtali Lewis & Meyer Reinhold, eds., *Roman Civilization, Selected Readings, Vol. II: The Empire, 3rd Ed.* Copyright © 1990 Columbia University Press. Reprinted with permission of the publisher.

CHAPTER 5

Documenting Everyday Life, p. 176 Excerpt from Allan Chester Johnson, Paul Robinson Coleman-Norton, and Frank Card Bourne, *Ancient Roman Statutes* (Austin, TX: University of Texas Press, 1961), p. 232. © 1961 by University of Texas Press. Reprinted by permission of the publisher.

CHAPTER 6

Making Connections, p. 194 "Goals and Laws of Marriage" from "Stromateis, Book Two" in *The Fathers of the Church, A New Translation: Clement of Alexandria, Books 1–3*, edited by Thomas P. Halton, translated by John Ferguson. Copyright © 1991 The Catholic University of America Press. Reprinted with permission.

CHAPTER 7

Making Connections, p. 239 "The Titles of the Patus Legis Salicae," from Katherine Fischer Drew, trans. and ed., *The Laws of the Salian Franks* (Philadelphia: University of Pennsylvania Press, 1991), pp. 59–63. © 1991 by the University of Pennsylvania Press. Reprinted with permission of the University of Pennsylvania Press.

Documenting Everyday Life, p. 243 Excerpts from Marcelle Thiébaux, trans. and ed., *Dhuoda, Handbook for her Warrior Son: Liber Manualis* (Cambridge: Cambridge University Press, 1998), pp. 101, 103, 105. © 1998 Cambridge University Press. Reprinted with the permission of Cambridge University Press.

CHAPTER 8

Documenting Everyday Life, p. 259 Excerpt from "The Survey of Huntingdonshire in Domesday Book," *English Historical Documents 1042–1189 2nd Ed*, edited by David C. Douglas & George W. Greenaway. Copyright © Eyre Methuen Ltd. 1953, 1981. Reproduced with permission of Taylor and Francis Books UK.

Making Connections, p. 265 "Quan vei la lauzeta mover" by Bernart de Ventadorn, translated by Keith Anderson in *Music of the Troubadors* by Ensemble Unicorn, 1996. Reprinted courtesy of Naxos Music Group.

Translation of "L'autrer jost' una sebissa," in *Marcabru: A Critical Edition*, edited by Simon Gaunt, Ruth Harvey, Linda Paterson with John Marshall (Cambridge: D.S. Brewer, 2000), pp. 379, 381. Reprinted by permission of Boydell & Brewer Ltd.

CHAPTER 9

Documenting Everyday Life, p. 299 "Regulating Prostitution in Marseilles," translated by Kirsten Schut. Based on *La prostitution à Marseille* (Paris: Libraire du la Societe des gens de lettres, 1882), pp. 365–366. Printed here by permission of Kirsten Schut.

Making Connections, p. 317 "Rabban Sâwmâ in Fransâ" from *The Monks of Kublai Khan, Emperor of China: Medieval Travels from China through Central Asia to Persia and Beyond*, by Rabban Sawma, translated by Sir E.A. Wallis Budge. Originally published by Harrison & Sons, Ltd. in 1928 for the Religious Tract Society. Reprinted by permission of Lutterworth Press.

CHAPTER 10

Documenting Everyday Life, p. 328 "The Declaration of Lorenzo Ghiberti, sculptor" from *The Society of Renaissance Florence: A Documentary Study*, edited by Gene A. Brucker (Toronto: University of Toronto Press, 1998). Reprinted by permission of Gene A. Brucker.

PHOTO CREDITS

public domain; p. 189: Album/Art Resource, NY; p. 190: akg-images/Rabatti – Domingie; p. 191: Museo Archeologico Nazionale, Naples/Bridgeman Art Library; p. 195: Bibliothèque nationale de France; p. 196: Alfredo Dagli Orti/The Art Archive at Art Resource, NY; p. 197: akg-images/ Andrea Lemolo; p. 198: Werner Forman/Art Resource, NY; p. 199: akg-images/Interfoto; p. 200 (left): Ancient Art and Architecture Collection Ltd./Bridgeman Art Library; (right): Scala/ Art Resource, NY; p. 201: De Agostini Picture Library/Getty Images; p. 202: Archiv Gerstenberg/ullstein bild via Getty Images; p. 203: DeAgostini/Getty Images.

Chapter 7: Pages 210–211: DeAgostini/Getty Images; p. 213: De Agostini/Getty Images; p. 214: Album/Art Resource, NY; p. 216: Scala/Art Resource, NY; p. 217: Artur Bogacki/Alamy Stock Photo; p. 218 (left): Erich Lessing/Art Resource, NY; (right): Ancient Art and Architecture Collection Ltd/Bridgeman Images; p. 219: Image copyright © The Metropolitan Museum of Art. Image source: Art Resource, NY; p. 223: Image copyright (c) The Metropolitan Museum of Art. Images source: Art Resource, NY; p. 224: halil ibrahim kurucan/Alamy Stock Photo; p. 228: Pictures from History/Bridgeman Images; p. 229: akg-images/De Agostini Picture Lib./G. Dagli Orti; p. 230 (top): Bildarchiv Steffens/Bridgeman Images; (bottom): SSPL/Science Museum/ Art Resource, NY; p. 231: Gianni Dagli Orti/The Art Archive at Art Resource, NY; p. 232: Private Collection/Bridgeman Images; p. 234: Bibliotheque Municipale, Rouen, France/Bridgeman Images; p. 235 (left): DeAgostini/Getty Images; (right): akg-images/De Agostini Picture Lib./G. Nimatallah; p. 236: De Agostini Picture Library/G. Dagli Orti/Bridgeman Images; p. 237: © The Board of Trinity College, Dublin, Ireland/ Bridgeman Images; p. 241: RMN-Grand Palais/ Art Resource, NY; p. 242: Gianni Dagli Orti/The Art Archive at Art Resource, NY; p. 244: Kunsthistorisches Museum, Vienna, Austria/Bridgeman Images; p. 245: © BnF, Dist. RMN-Grand Palais/Art Resource, NY.

Chapter 8: Pages 248–249 (from left to right): Kunsthistorisches Museum Wien, Kunstkammer (KK 5118); Landesmuseum Württemberg, Stuttgart (KK grau 53); Kunsthistorisches Museum Wien, Kunstkammer (KK 5088); p. 251: British Library, London, UK/© British Library Board. All Rights Reserved/Bridgeman Images; p. 255: Gianni Dagli Orti/The Art Archive at Art Resource, NY; p. 256 (left): Kharbine-Tapabor/ The Art Archive at Art Resource, NY; (right): British Library Board/Robana/Art Resource, NY; p. 258: Universal History Archive/UIG/Bridgeman Images; p. 261: DeA Picture Library/Art Resource, NY; p. 263: Granger Collection; p. 264: akg-images/World History Archive; p. 266 (top):

akg images; (bottom): Interfoto/Alamy Stock Photo; p. 267: Pictures from History/Bridgeman Images; p. 268: akg-images/André Held; p. 270: akg-images/De Agostini Picture Library; p. 272: © British Library Board/Robana/Art Resource, NY; p. 273: Pictures from History/Bridgeman Images; p. 274: Gianni Dagli Orti/The Art Archive at Art Resource, NY; p. 275: Stuart Whatling http://www.medievalart.org; p. 276 (left): Shutterstock; (right): Peter Willi/Bridgeman Images; p. 278: Hereford Cathedral, Herefordshire, UK/ Bridgeman Images; p. 279: Archivo de la Corona de Aragon, Barcelona/Bridgeman Images; p. 281 (top): Gianni Dagli Orti/The Art Archive at Art Resource, NY; (bottom): Kharbine - Tapabor/ The Art Archive at Art Resource, NY; p. 282: Ken Welsh/Bridgeman Images; p. 284: Photo12/UIG/ Getty Images.

Chapter 9: Pages 286–287: Biblioteca Nazionale, Turin/Bridgeman Images; p. 289: Bibliotheque Nationale, Paris; p. 292: akg-images/ De Agostini/A. Dagli Orti; p. 293: Private Collection/Bridgeman Images; p. 294 (top): Universal History Archive/UIG/Bridgeman Images; (bottom): Album/Art Resource, NY; p. 295: De Agostini Picture Library/G. Nimatallah/Bridgeman Images; p. 296: akg-images/British Library; p. 297: Universal History Archive/UIG via Getty Images; p. 298: © Bodleian Libraries/Douce 88 folio 111V/The Art Archive at Art Resource; p. 301: British Library, London/Bridgeman Images; p. 302: Album/Art Resource, NY; p. 304: Alfredo Dagli Orti/The Art Archive at Art Resource, NY; p. 305: Herzog August Bibliothek; http:// creativecommons.org/licenses/by-sa/3.0/de/; p. 306: akg-images/British Library; p. 309 (top): DEA/G. DAGLI ORTI/Getty Images; (bottom): DEA/M. Seemuller/Getty Images; p. 310: akg-images; p. 311: akg-images/British Library; p. 312: akg-images/Tristan Lafranchis; p. 313: Granger Collection; p. 316 (left): akg-images/ullstein bild; (right): bpk, Berlin/Vatican Museum/Alfredo Dagli Orti/Art Resource, NY; p. 319 (top): Scala/ Art Resource, NY; (bottom): akg-images/VISIOARS; p. 321 (top): HIP/Art Resource, NY; (bottom): British Library/The Art Archive at Art Resource, NY.

Chapter 10: Pages 324–325: National Gallery, London, Bridgeman Images; p. 327: Scala/Art Resource, NY; p. 330: Alinari/Art Resource, NY; p. 333: Jean of Wavrin (1398–1474), manuscript/ British Library, London, UK/De Agostini Picture Library/Bridgeman Images; p. 334: Bridgeman Images; p. 335: Album/Art Resource, NY; p. 336: Topkapi Palace Museum, Istanbul/Bridgeman Images; p. 337: Erich Lessing/Art Resource, NY; p. 338: World History Archive/Alamy Stock Photo; p. 339: akg-images/British Library; p. 341: bpk, Berlin/Art Resource; p. 342: Photo © AISA/ Bridgeman Images; p. 344: Copyright of the

image Museo Nacional del Prado/Art Resource, NY; p. 345: Gianni Dagli Orti/The Art Archive at Art Resource, NY; p. 346: Museu Nacional de Arte Antiga, Lisbon, Portugal/Bridgeman Images; p. 348: Tomasso Brothers Fine Art, UK; p. 349: bpk, Berlin/Staatsbibliothek zu Berlin, Stiftung Preussicher Kulturbesitz/Art Resource, NY; p. 351: PHOTOAISA/BEBA/Interfoto; p. 352: Granger Collection; p. 354: Biblioteca Medicea-Laurenziana, Florence/Bridgeman Images; p. 355: Library of Congress; p. 356: Scala/Art Resource, NY; p. 357: Biblioteca Medicea Laurenziana, Florence, Ms. Strozzi 50, 1 recto. By permission of the Ministero per i Beni e le Attivita Culturali with all rights reserved; p. 359: Sterling and Francine Clark Art Institute, Williamstown, Massachusetts/Bridgeman Images; p. 360: British Library, London/© British Library Board. All Rights Reserved/Bridgeman Images; p. 361 (left): Brancacci Chapel, Santa Maria del Carmine, Florence/Bridgeman Images; (right): Alinari/Art Resource, NY; p. 362: De Agostini Picture Library/A. Dagli Orti/ Bridgeman Images; p. 363 (left): Baptistery, Florence/Bridgeman Images; (right): Image copyright © The Metropolitan Museum of Art. Image source: Art Resource, NY; p. 364 (left): National Gallery, London/Bridgeman Images; (right): Kunsthistorisches Museum, Vienna/Ali Meyer/Bridgeman Images; p. 365 (left): Scala/ Art Resource, NY; (right): Vatican Museums and Galleries, Vatican City/Bridgeman Images; p. 366 (left): Vatican Museums and Galleries, Vatican City/Bridgeman Images; (right): Louvre, Paris/Bridgeman Images; p. 367: Scala/Art Resource, NY.

Chapter 11: Pages 370–371: akg-images/World History Archive; p. 373: (left): Erich Lessing/ Art Resource, NY; (right): SZ Photo/Scherl/ Bridgeman Images; p. 374: The Art Archive at Art Resource, NY; p. 375: Foto Marburg/Art Resource, NY; p. 376: British Library Board/ Bridgeman Images; p. 378: Bibliotheque Nationale, Paris/Bridgeman Images; p. 380: Library of Congress; p. 381: © The Trustees of the British Museum; p. 382: akg/De Agostini Picture Library; p. 384: akg-images; p. 385: Roger-Viollet, Paris/ Bridgeman Images; p. 386: SEF/Art Resource, NY; p. 387: Lutherhalle, Wittenberg, Germany/ Bridgeman Images; p. 388: Erich Lessing/Art Resource, NY; p. 390: DeAgostini/Getty Images; p. 394: Gianni Dagli Orti/The Art Archive at Art Resource, NY; p. 395: Bibliotheque Nationale, Paris/Bridgeman Images; p. 396: akg-images/ Imagno; p. 397: Universal History Archive/UIG/ Bridgeman Images; p. 398: The Art Archive at Art Resource, NY; p. 401: De Agostini Picture Library/G. Dagli Orti/Bridgeman Images; p. 402: akg-images/Quint & Lox; p. 403: akg-images; p. 405 Musee Conde, Chantilly/Bridgeman Images.

Page numbers in italics refer to illustrations, maps, and tables.

Babylonian Captivity of Avignon papacy, 318, 339, 340

Babylonian Captivity of Jews, 31, 339

Babylonian Talmud, 221

Bacon, Roger (ca. 1214–ca. 1292), 343

Bactria, Alexander the Great invading, 84, *84*

Bahamas, Columbus landing in, 351–52

Bahrain, 17

Balboa, Vasco Núñez de (1475–1519), 352

Baldwin II (r. 1118–1131), 271

Baldwin III, 271

Ball, John, 321

banks

    European warfare costs financed by, 398–99

    interest charges of, 290–92, 399

    in Middle Ages, 255

    in Middle Ages, High, 290–92, *292*

baptism

    of adults, 385

    Anabaptists on, 385

    of infants, 377

Baptistery of Florence, bronze doors of, 362, 365

barbarians

    in Greece, 72

    in Roman Empire, *152*, 152–53, 154, 189

Barberini diptych, 218, *218*

Bar Sauma, Rabban (ca. 1220–1294), 317

Barsine, marriage to Alexander the Great, 85

Basil I, the Macedonian (r. 867–886), 228

baths

    in Hellenistic period, 93

    in Roman Empire, 155, 158

Battle of the Trench (627), 225

Bavaria, miracle-working image in, 380–81, *381*

Bayeux Tapestry, *258*

Bayezid I, Ottoman sultan, 335

Beatrice de Planissoles, 314–15

Bec Abbey, 276–77

Becket, Thomas (ca. 1120–1170), 268, *268*

Bede, Venerable (d. 735), 237–38

Bedouins, 223

beguines, 343

Belisarius, commander under Justinian, 214, 220, 221

Bellini, Giovanni (ca. 1430–1516), 362

Benedetti, Jacopo dei, 296

Benedict (ca. 480–ca. 547), 235, *235*

    at Monte Cassino, 235, *235*

    Rule, 235, 273

Benedictines, 235, 273, 374

Benedict VIII, Pope (r. 1012–1024), 266

Benedict XII, Pope (d. 1342), 314

Berenice II, 94

Bernard of Clairvaux (1090–1153), 272, 273, *273*

Bernard of Cluny, 273

Bernart de Ventadorn, 265

Berruguete, Pedro, *344*

Bible

    Abelard analysis of, 277

    Books of Moses in, 30, 31, 102, 103, 162

in codex form, 163, *163*, 200, *201*

English translation of, 391

Erasmus study of, 375–76, 377

Eusebius study of, 196

Genesis in, 20, 103, 162

Greek translation of, 77–78, 103, 104

Gutenberg, *349*, 350

Hebrew, 30, 31, 77, 102–3, 158, 159, 164, 193

in Latin, 205, 276, 311, 340, 350, 377, *380*, 396

Luther studies of, 372, 373

Marcion on, 172

New Testament of, 160, 167–71. *See also* New Testament

Origen assembly of, 193

plays based on, 342

Porphyry study of, 192

printing of, 380, *380*

Septuagint of, 103, 193

Vulgate, 205, 377, *380*, 396

women in, 103–4

bishops, as leaders in early Christianity, 173, *173*, 183, 202

Black Army of Hungary, 337

Black Death, 290, 319, *319*, 320, 341, 345, 347. *See also* plague

Boccaccio, Giovanni (1313–1375), 293, 294, 357

Bodin, Jean (1530–1596), 404

Boethius (ca. 480–524), 232, 233–34, *234*, 235

Bohemia

    Hussites in, 340–41, 374

    medieval power and prosperity of, 262

Böhm, Hans, 384

Boleslaw, duke of Poland, 262

Boleyn, Anne, 390

Bolivia, silver mining in, 354

Boniface, Saint (d. 754), 241

Boniface VIII, Pope (r. 1294–1303), 308, 316

Boniface IX, Pope (r. 1389–1404), 339

Book of Durrow, 237

The Book of the City of Ladies (Christine de Pizan), 360

books

    Catholic censorship of, 396, 398

    in High Middle Ages, 310, 312

    printing of, 343, 349–51

    Renaissance innovations in, 343, 349–51, 357

books of hours, early printing of, 350, 351

Bora, Katharina von (1499–1552), 387, *387*

Borgia, Cesare (1475/6–1507), 325

Borgia, Rodrigo (Pope Alexander VI), 325

Borromeo, Charles, archbishop of Milan, 394–95

botany, Fuchs study of, 397, *398*

Botticelli, Sandro, *293*

Bracciolini, Gian Francesco Poggio (1380–1459), 357, *357*

Bramante, Donato (1444–1514), 366

Brandini, Ciuto, 321

Brazil, European exploration of, 346, 348, 352

Britain

    Christianity in, 238

    Germanic tribes in, 231–32, *233*

    Romans in, 207

bronze, 4

    in Greek warrior statue, 54

    in Near East, ancient, 14, 17

    in weaponry, 14, 17, 33, 35, 54

Bronze Age, 14

    Crisis during (12th century BCE), 18, 20, 38

    Greece during (2700–1200 BCE), 32–34

Brothers, as fellow believers of Paul, 163–64, 166

Brothers and Sisters of the Common Life, 342–43, 375

Brunelleschi, Filippo (1377–1446), *361*, 361–62, 364–65

Bruni, Leonardo (ca. 1370–1444), 357, 358

Brutus, Lucius Junius, 113

Brutus, Marcus Junius, 136, *136*

Burgundy

    in Middle Ages, 260

    in Renaissance, 330, 331

burial practices

    in ancient Egypt, 23, 24, 25

    in Athens, 55, 64

    in early Christianity, 165, 173–74

    of Etruscans, *111*

    in Iron Age Greece, 34–35

    of Jews, 104

    of Mycenaeans, 33

Burrus, 150

Byzantium, 212–22

    in Fourth Crusades, 307, 335

    under Heraclius, 221–22, 228

    and Islam, 227, 228–31

    under Justinian, 212–21. *See also* Justinian, Byzantine emperor

    religious icons in, *218*, 218–19, 228

    in Renaissance, 335

    territories controlled by, 220

    war with Sasanian Persia, 221, 222, *222*

    women in, 213, 214, 219, 219–20

Cabot, John (ca. 1450–ca. 1499), 352, *353*

Cabral, Pedro Álvares (1467/8–1520), 346

Caesar, Julius (100–44 BCE), 110, 134–36, 139, 164

    bust of, *135*

    death of, 136, *136*, 140

    territory conquered by, *135*

Caesarea, 192, *193*

cahier of Estates General, 332

calendars

    of Constantine, 183–84

    Julian, 136

    Roman, 113, 136, *190*

Caligula, Roman emperor, 149, 153

caliphs, Islamic, 226–27

Calixtus II, Pope (r. 1119–1124), 268

Callimachus (ca. 305–ca. 240 BCE), 91, 94

Calvin, John (1509–1564), *388*, 388–90, 402